UNCERTAIN VICTORY

Uncertain Victory
Social Democracy and Progressivism in European and American Thought, 1870–1920

James T. Kloppenberg
| | |

Oxford University Press

New York   Oxford

Oxford University Press

Oxford   New York   Toronto
Delhi   Bombay   Calcutta   Madras   Karachi
Petaling Jaya   Singapore   Hong Kong   Tokyo
Nairobi   Dar es Salaam   Cape Town
Melbourne   Auckland

and associated companies in
Beirut   Berlin   Ibadan   Nicosia

Copyright © 1986 by James T. Kloppenberg

First published in 1986 by Oxford University Press, Inc.,
200 Madison Avenue, New York, New York 10016

First issued as an Oxford University Press paperback, 1988

Oxford is a registered trademark of Oxford University Press

Library of Congress Cataloging in Publication Data
Kloppenberg, James T.
Uncertain victory.
Bibliography: p. Includes index.
1. Political science—Europe—History. 2. Political science—
United States—History. 3. Socialism—Europe—History.
4. Socialism—United States—History. 5. Democracy—History. I. Title.
JA84.E9K57   1986   320.5′315′094   85-21636
ISBN 0-19-503749-9
ISBN 0-19-505304-4   pbk.

2 4 6 8 10 9 7 5 3
Printed in the United States of America

65, 103

FOR MY PARENTS

Preface

"Dare to know!" Kant's challenge to the eighteenth century expressed the Enlightenment's audacious faith in reason. We now judge that confidence a delusion, at least in part because philosophers such as William James and Wilhelm Dilthey dared admit they could not know. They could only dare to think. Their conception of critical inquiry as the endless process of testing hypotheses in practice informs this study of their ideas. Uncertainty imposed the burden of creating new cultural standards. This book examines that quest for new understandings of knowledge, ethics, and politics, a quest that for democratic cultures must always be renewed.

These intellectuals' commitment to "the strenuous mood," to use James's phrase, was not only to a way of thinking but also to a way of life. I am grateful to my parents, George A. Kloppenberg and Zona B. Kloppenberg, for showing me that way of life long before I discovered that way of thinking. They taught me to work and then encouraged me to decide what work needed doing. I thank them for their unwavering support. My brothers, George F. Kloppenberg and Joseph R. Kloppenberg, have been reliable sources of good sense and good will; my debts to them are deep.

Many people contributed to the completion of this book. Carl N. Degler, who was my adviser at Stanford, has continued to be a model of scholarship, teaching, and friendship. He challenged me to think big, and his enthusiasm has kept up my spirits. David M. Kennedy helped me understand the joys and perils of comparative history during the wonderful spring in Florence when I first conceived this study. He has since helped me understand much more. Paul A. Robinson worked to nudge my prose toward clarity with his special combination of high spirits and high standards. Kurt Mueller-Vollmer and the Graduate Program in Humanities saw to it that my graduate education was a liberal education.

I would like to thank those who read various versions of this manuscript: Thomas Bender, Michael Ermarth, Thomas Haskell, Bruce Kuklick, Julie Reuben, Richard Rorty, and Jerome Schneewind. Their comments have improved its quality, and their commitment to the life of the mind has convinced me that the community of scholars is more than an empty phrase. I am doubly indebted to David A. Hollinger, who read two different versions of this study, and whose criticism and support have been invaluable. At Brandeis, David Hackett Fischer, Morton Keller, Rudolph Binion, and Frank E. Manuel have been friendly critics, inspiring me to aim for the high ground even though we all have different ideas about where it is located. After reading an early draft of this book, Mark Hulliung challenged me to convince him I was not trying to mix oil and water. Since then our conversations have sharpened my sense of how to study ideas historically, and I have continued to stir. This book will not satisfy all of these people, since they had contradictory ideas about what it should be. They are implicated in the strengths of the book; its weaknesses would be more serious were it not for their help.

For assistance of a different sort, I would like to acknowledge the American Council of Learned Societies, the Bernstein Faculty Fellowship Committee at Brandeis, the Danforth Foundation, the Mazer Fund for Faculty Research at Brandeis, the National Endowment for the Humanities, the Stanford Center for Research in International Studies, and the Whiting Foundation.

Working with the staff of Oxford University Press has been a pleasure. I am happy to join the ranks of historians indebted to Sheldon Meyer, whose enthusiasm for this project, and whose efforts to accommodate my wishes for it, have been gratifying. My copy editor, Melissa Spielman, has been intelligent, thorough, and considerate. Readers of this book should be as grateful to her as I am.

Without Ann Marie Kloppenberg and James Anthony Kloppenberg, this book would have been completed with more speed but less joy. Without Mary Cairns Kloppenberg, it would not have been completed at all. She has taken an active part in every stage of this project. I have been inspired by her dedication to her own teaching, and I have been able to depend on her judgment even though it is corrupted by kindness. Through endless readings of a seemingly endless manuscript, she has tempered criticism with love, and vice versa, managing to be at once my most demanding critic and my best friend. After sixteen years of trying I still cannot find the words to say what I owe to her, but I think she understands. That is enough.

Wellesley, Massachusetts   J. T. K.
May 1985

Contents

UNCERTAIN VICTORY

Introduction

Between 1870 and 1920, two generations of American and European thinkers created a transatlantic community of discourse in philosophy and political theory. Discarding accepted distinctions between idealism and empiricism in epistemology, between intuitionism and utilitarianism in ethics, and between revolutionary socialism and laissez-faire liberalism in politics, they converged toward a *via media* in philosophy and toward the political theories of social democracy and progressivism. This is a history of their ideas.

While the chains linking Marxism to idealism and liberalism to empiricism have been carefully reconstructed, the philosophical origins of social democratic and progressive theory remain obscure; as a result these ideas, which diverged from the socialist and liberal traditions toward the end of the nineteenth century, appear to be simply unstable accommodations to the new realities of organized capitalism in an urban-industrial environment. Like most simple explanations, however, that is misleading. Not merely ideological expressions pressed into service to rationalize politically attractive positions, the theories of social democracy and progressivism instead elaborated, extended, and applied ideas about knowledge and responsibility articulated by a generation of renegade philosophers. In this study I focus on those two successive processes of convergence in ideas about how we know and what we are to do, explore the connections between them, and suggest that the best of these ideas continue to be both philosophically and politically vital.

The search for alternatives to the idealist and naturalist philosophies dominant in the mid-nineteenth century began in the 1870s and reached fruition during the next three decades. The thinkers who made the most important contributions to this quest for a *via media* were Wilhelm Dilthey,

3

Thomas Hill Green, Henry Sidgwick, Alfred Fouillée, William James, and John Dewey, who despite their differences shared several fundamental ideas that distinguished them from their predecessors and from most of their contemporaries. They denied both mind-body and subject-object dualisms inherited from Descartes, and they considered both passive sensation and active decision essential and inseparable aspects of experience. Knowledge, from their perspective, can neither be abstracted from nor entirely reduced to the historical circumstances of individual lives. Truth must be cut free from notions of eternity and necessity and grounded instead in human experience, never definite and subject always to revision. These mavericks insisted that ideas emerge from, and must be validated in, neither language nor logic but life. Theirs was a profoundly historical sensibility, imbued with the belief that meaning is woven into the fiber of experience, that becoming rather than being is the mode of human life, and that people make rather than find their values. I will call this cluster of ideas the radical theory of knowledge, radical because it cut to the core of attempts to find an Archimedean point for epistemology and substituted an acceptance of contingency for the standard quest for certainty.

From this unconventional perspective, these thinkers envisioned an ethics that modified both Kantian and utilitarian models by recognizing rules and results as complementary in moral reasoning. They faced the unsettling possibility that an irreconcilable conflict separates prudence from justice in ethical decisions, and their interpretations of the consequences of that dilemma struck chords ranging from heroic to tragic that reverberated through their own political writings to the theories of social democracy and progressivism. Following Sidgwick, whose *Methods of Ethics* provided the most penetrating and influential elaboration of these ideas, I will label these philosophers' moral theory the ethics of rational benevolence. Sidgwick coined that term to fuse Kant's notion of rationally intuited duty with the utilitarian principle of maximizing happiness, and it conveys his synthetic intent while suggesting the uneasy and paradoxical relation between self-interest and social obligation. If our ethical ideas, like the rest of our knowledge as these philosophers understood it, cannot conform to prescribed standards but derive instead from reason reflecting imperfectly on experience, then right and good, like truth, must be unhitched from certainty and made historical.

The political writings of these genial eclectics lacked the acuity of their other work. Pioneers in epistemology and ethics, they were left behind intellectually when Germany, France, England, and the United States reconstituted themselves as urbanized and mechanized nation states. This generation matured prior to the second industrial revolution, and a certain poignancy pervades their reflections on the sociopolitical world that dawned near the end of the nineteenth century. Aware that new circumstances made nonsense of prevailing political ideas, the philosophers of the *via media* groped toward unorthodox positions on reform strategy and toward altered ideals of liberty, equality, and justice consistent with their theories of knowledge and responsibility. Victorian anxieties about the rise of science and the fate of religion afflicted them despite the unsettling implications of their own ideas; they were uncertain whether science could exert sufficient power to serve as culture's compass. Moreover, as emphasis on individual moral responsibility seemed to shrink as the state expanded, political action tended to replace personal conscience as the locus of reform, and the relation of state to society became increasingly problematical. The technical knowledge prized by the urban-industrial world and wielded with increasing confidence by the state challenged traditional cultural values, and this generation of philosophers worried about the future of a world whose religious meaning was dissolving under the corrosive influence of the secular society's mania for consumption. They feared that political, social, and economic progress might bring prosperity only by transforming life into a meaningless scramble for the shallowest of satisfactions. James expressed this discontent when he lamented the "irremediable flatness" threatening to smother "the higher heroisms and the rare old flavors of life," and he was not alone in wondering whether the promise of modernity was worth its cultural price.[1]

James's generation considered existing liberal and socialist ideas unsuited to the landscape of the late nineteenth century, but they failed to articulate a satisfactory alternative. That task fell to the generation that followed them by roughly twenty years, a generation of social democrats and progressives who helped provide blueprints for the welfare state during the 1890–1920 period. Modified repeatedly by committees and constructed of shoddy materials by unskilled hands over more than a century, the welfare state in its various national forms has become so ramshackle that it requires major renovation. It is maligned by the left as paternalist, by the right as inept, and by everyone as less than completely successful. Unfortunately, this avalanche of criticism threatens to bury its original purpose and distort the intentions of those who contributed to its creation. I want to examine the theorists of social democracy and progressivism in part to disconnect their ideas from certain developments they could neither anticipate nor prevent. The German, French, English, and American welfare states have been shaped by conflicting political, economic, and social forces, and by countless individuals who used or misused, willfully or inadvertently, the ideas discussed in this study. Much of the criticism leveled against social democratic and progressive theorists, born of a coupling between the slick condescension accompanying hindsight and the easy imputation of unstated motives, reveals a failure of historical imagination masquerading as tough-minded savvy.

The theory of social democracy emerged in the 1890s when new ideas about knowledge and responsibility combined with new political circumstances to transform socialist doctrine. A number of thinkers met at that junction of abstraction and reality, including those to be considered in this study: English Fabians Beatrice and Sidney Webb, German revisionist Eduard Bernstein, French socialist Jean Jaurès, and the two most prominent radicals of the American social gospel movement, Richard Ely and Walter Rauschenbusch. Ideas filtered into the theory of social democracy primarily from

Marxist and utopian socialism and from the tradition of Christian social criticism, but also from German and English economic theory, classical liberalism, positivism, and Darwinian evolutionary theory. While theorists blended these elements in varying proportions according to personal preferences, national political traditions, and socioeconomic conditions, they created an identifiable body of ideas with certain distinguishing characteristics. First, like the philosophers of the *via media*, they located the foundation of knowledge in experience and maintained that history provides a source of judgment more reliable, despite its uncertainties, than metaphysical or ideological doctrine. Second, they shared a commitment to extend the democratic principle of equality from the civil and political spheres to the entire society and the economy. Third, they championed gradual, constitutional reform instead of revolution. Finally, although they embraced socialism as an ideal, they emphasized the connection between their goal and the means necessary for its realization, and for that reason they concentrated more on proximate reforms than on ultimate ends.

The political meaning of social democracy has been problematical since the term first appeared in Germany during the mid-nineteenth century. From the time Marx scorned collaborators with states that masked co-optation beneath democratic disguises until the recent embourgeoisement of European social democratic parties, commentators have questioned whether social democracy could be as reactionary as its critics have charged or as radical as its partisans have claimed. The fact that social democrats have played different roles in different nations at different times has not prevented the storm of controversy surrounding their historical significance from descending into a fog of polemics. I will not presume to settle so vexing a question in this study, but I do hope to recover the ideas that animated the discourse of social democracy as it rose to prominence with the transformation of European and American politics from 1890 to 1920. Its chameleonic quality reflected not only changing conditions but a genetic proclivity to adaptation. Lacking certainty about what we know and what we are to do, these wayward socialists claimed that such limited knowledge makes politics less a science than a perpetual search for ideals of justice constituted historically rather than intuited a priori, a goal to be approached neither by individuals seeking private visions of the good, nor by classes fulfilling their revolutionary potential, but by communities struggling to order themselves democratically. A persistent tension regarding the implications of scientific knowledge further complicated assessments of the social democratic prospect. While science as the method of an enlarged empiricism offered an alternative to traditional authoritarian solutions of political problems, the relation between expertise and democracy was murky. For the anodyne to subservience promised by the scientific temper might prove simply a newer version of the snake oil that despots peddled to cure religious oppression, and experts dispensing knowledge in the name of science could become an equally formidable source of social control.

As social democrats tugged socialist theory away from its preoccupation with revolution, they found themselves backing into a group of intellectuals pulling the theory of liberal individualism in the opposite direction. Accustomed to seeing one another from a distance, the heirs to socialist and liberal orthodoxy recognized only slowly that they were standing on common ground. While this realization delighted some of them, others quickly built fences to protect their turf from intellectual interlopers. The convergence of political thinkers from the traditions of socialism and liberalism paralleled the convergence in philosophy between idealism and empiricism, and in both cases the differences in background and rhetoric have obscured important similarities. Without minimizing the very real and revealing differences separating social democrats from progressives, I will examine the convergence between those who sought to extend the democratic principle of equality and those who renounced possessive individualism and embraced an ideal of solidarity to supplement the customary liberal commitment to personal freedom. Building upon a more radical empiricism and a revised utilitarianism, progressives scrapped the rickety notions of a hedonistic psychology and a self-guiding market and replaced their liberal ancestors' model of an atomistic society with an ideal incorporating positive as well as negative liberty, duties as well as rights. Those who translated liberal theory into an idiom appropriate to the twentieth century often called themselves progressives, in Europe as well as in the United States, and that is the term I will adopt in this study. Of the many thinkers who contributed to this reorientation, I will concentrate on English sociologist Leonard Trelawny Hobhouse, French radical politician Léon Bourgeois, American publicists Herbert Croly and Walter Lippmann and philosopher John Dewey, and German sociologist Max Weber.

Loaded with mental equipment obtained from diverse sources and suited to widely different purposes, those who searched for new ways of thinking about philosophy and politics from 1870 to 1920 were less an organized expedition than a number of independent-minded explorers who ended up neighbors in a territory of new ideas. They got along with each other in different ways, sometimes borrowing freely and acknowledging mutual debts, sometimes feuding, sometimes picking up stakes and moving on. The more generous among them, notably William James and Jean Jaurès, welcomed almost anyone and expected that tolerance would breed understanding and eventual cooperation. Others such as Max Weber found the new intellectual vistas no more inspiring, and perhaps less comforting, than those left behind. Some, including Richard Ely and Léon Bourgeois, for example, finally judged themselves unsuited to pioneering and returned to more comfortable surroundings. I realize that my conception of such an intellectual community is unconventional, and some readers may rub their eyes after seeing Fouillée placed next to Sidgwick or Rauschenbusch beside Bernstein. There is admittedly something jarring about labeling Ely an American social democrat and Weber a German progressive, since the absence of socialism is a distinctive fact of American history just as surely as the absence of liberalism is the tragic fact of German history. Yet I want to emphasize precisely such apparent incongruities, because the tendency to pigeonhole thinkers according to national or assumed ideological categories blurs our vision of the inchoate world of ideas in which creative minds operate.

Some of my groupings will occasion little surprise, because they conform so clearly to Marc Bloch's familiar adage that comparative study should seek to unearth significant differences obscured by surface similarities.[2] Yet comparison can yield equally valuable insights if phenomena assumed to be dissimilar can be shown to exhibit similar features when viewed from a new perspective. For example my comparison of Weber and Dewey, arguably the most important European and American thinkers of the twentieth century, will seem particularly heretical, for I contend that their images as antidemocratic *Machtpolitiker* and hardheaded scientific naturalist need revision in light of their contributions to the progressives' community of discourse. Both were drawn to positions between liberalism and socialism. Weber lamented the polarization of German politics and longed for a viable alternative to revolution and reaction; Dewey regretted the hegemonic consensus preventing American radicals from shifting political debate off dead center. From their opposite vantage points they posed the questions of leadership and community participation, bureaucracy and democracy, science and value, more clearly than did any other social democrats or progressives, and their conflicting answers set the terms for continuing political debate.

I understand that ideas are no more identical than snowflakes unless they are melted, and I do not intend to run these ideas through an analytical furnace to make them equivalent but vapid. I want to examine with equal care their differences and their similarities. Although the parallels will never be exact because of individual idiosyncrasies, distinctive cultural traditions, and the inevitable complications arising from problems of translation, comparative analysis can kindle new insights from ideas grown stale in conventional classifications.

As historians join philosophers, literary critics, and social scientists in awakening from idealist and positivist slumbers in which ideas were imagined to exist somehow apart from social reality, they see that thought and behavior are two sides of the coin of human experience, whose value derives from the meanings culture stamps on it. But this realization, integral to the radical theory of knowledge a century ago, itself threatens to become a simplification purchased at the cost of accuracy. The restraints imposed on creativity by prevailing ways of thinking can be exaggerated, for while ideas change slowly, they do change. William James explained the process with characteristic insight: "The individual has a stock of old opinions already," James wrote, "but he meets a new experience that puts them to a strain." Instead of collapsing from the "inward trouble to which the mind till then has been a stranger," he "seeks to escape by modifying his previous mass of opinions." At last he latches on to a new idea "that mediates between the stock and the new experience and runs them into one another most felicitously," and he stretches the older beliefs just enough to "make them admit the novelty."[3] What James understood, perhaps more clearly than recent students of the coercive power of mental structures, is the individual's creative role in cultural change. Existing patterns of thought limit possibilities without eliminating new ideas. The restless challengers discussed in this study jolted philosophical and political discourse from standard categories and made possible new ways of thinking that were neither idealist nor empiricist, socialist nor liberal.

My approach to this process of intellectual change, which might briefly be called hermeneutical and contextualist, owes more to the thinkers I analyze here than to any other source. I would rather exercise this method to examine its origins in the writings of Dilthey, Fouillée, James, Dewey, and Weber than provide a rationale for it by way of introduction. Perched between documentary and presentist purposes, my perspective is hermeneutical in the restricted Diltheyan sense of an ongoing interpretation of meanings rather than in the more expansive ontological sense used by Heidegger and Gadamer. Resistant to Marxist and Freudian techniques even more problematical than its objects of analysis, this approach takes into account the various contexts provided by socioeconomic and political conditions and by other thinkers, both contemporaries and predecessors, without over-looking the contributions of dynamic minds in altering patterns of discourse.

Part One deals with the imaginative construction of a *via media* in epistemology and ethics and its creators' tentative gropings toward new political ideas. Part Two concerns the second generation's completion of this project by extending ideas about knowledge and obligation and elaborating theories of social democracy and progressivism. My procedure in examining each group is similar: after explaining why prevailing alternatives failed to satisfy them, I discuss their efforts to escape, as James put it, the inward trouble occasioned by new experiences straining old ideas. Much of the analysis, particularly in Chapters Two through Four, has an intramural quality that reflects the mutual engagement of thinkers trying to resolve shared difficulties. Ideas composed of tightly wrapped bundles of arguments sometimes change shape or even unravel as they bounce back and forth between lively minds, and it is impossible to chart their course accurately and understand their final form without attending closely to what happened along the way. As my organization implies, the convergences in philosophy and politics were to a certain degree distinct from one another. Two different generations with rather different preoccupations were involved, and the strength of the connection between the philosophical and political ideas varies among the individual thinkers. Certain members of the first generation, notably Green and Fouillée, fashioned fairly sturdy political ideas, while others such as James and Dilthey sketched their political positions in tones more suggestive than definitive. Likewise some social democrats and progressives, such as Jaurès and Hobhouse, contributed substantially to philosophical as well as political debates, while others such as Bernstein and Bourgeois skimmed terminology from bubbling philosophical controversies without dipping fully into them. Only Dewey played an equally decisive part in both stages of the progression from philosophy to politics. For that reason he alone figures

prominently in both parts of this study; he illustrates most clearly the continuities among the radical theory of knowledge, the ethics of rational
benevolence, and the politics of progressivism.

Among the dangers of intellectual history is the tendency to generalize
beyond the limits of the evidence. Although I scan the larger contours of
politics and ideas during this period, I am not trying to erect such overarching
analytical constructs as the "Social Democratic Mind," the "Progressive
Temper," or anything of the sort. As political theories and political movements, the American and European varieties of social democracy and progressivism were too multifaceted and dynamic to be contained neatly within
generalizations drawn from twenty or even several hundred individuals. Nor
do I claim that these thinkers were representative of the "American mind" or
the "European mind," which I consider similarly seductive but misleading
fantasies. I will try to suggest how these ideas emerged from and reflected
different traditions, but to go beyond suggestions would be to ignore the
contestational quality of ideas deliberately conceived to challenge inherited
ways of thinking, ideas shaped within a transatlantic community of discourse
rather than a parochial national frame of reference.

I have chosen to concentrate on the individuals who figured most
prominently in two processes of intellectual convergence. It would be
tendentious to deny that others participated as well, and a broader survey
might include among philosophers Royce and Peirce in the United States,
Rickert and Windelband in Germany, Renouvier and Boutroux in France,
and Bradley and Schiller in England; among social democrats such figures as
Walling, Vollmar, Millerand, and Wallas; and among progressives at least
Brandeis, Naumann, Bouglé, and Hobson. While my focus may expose me to
charges of myopia, the exchange of depth for breadth may not be a good
bargain in examining difficult ideas. I have consciously resisted the temptation to provide thumbnail sketches of more individuals and ideas than I could
portray with adequate respect to their complexities. This analysis is not an
overview and has no pretensions to comprehensiveness. It promises not an
intellectual grand tour but visits to a sufficiently limited number of thinkers to
enable readers to understand how their minds worked. Merely to mention
Veblen or Henry Adams, Nietzsche or Freud, Sorel or Bergson, McDougall
or Shaw, of course suggests currents of cultural criticism running contrary to
the tendencies examined here. Although I do not deny the shattering impact
of these thinkers on the generation that came of age in Europe in 1914 and
later became fatally attracted to varieties of fascism and communism, part of
my purpose in writing this book is to call attention to those who acknowledged the importance of subjectivity and the limits of rationality without
turning to philosophies of force or succumbing to despair.[4]

In a celebrated passage, John Dewey once suggested that "intellectual
progress usually occurs through sheer abandonment of questions together
with both of the alternatives they assume—an abandonment that results from
their decreasing vitality and a change of urgent interest. We do not solve
them: we get over them."[5] Just as prewar generations "got over" idealism and

empiricism, socialism and liberalism, so those who came after them abandoned their alternatives and turned instead to phenomenology and logical empiricism, scientific naturalism and existentialism. The unsteady synthesis created by Dewey's generation proved too fragile to survive war and revolution, and new ideas prevailed in a world whose urgent interests were Lenin and Hitler. Now in turn, as thinkers from diverse backgrounds again suggest that we discard questions whose vitality has been drained during the years since World War I, the ideas examined in this study are attracting increasing attention. The philosophers of the *via media* suggested a genuinely new approach to the problems of knowledge and responsibility, an approach whose limited claims to certainty make it an attractive alternative to philosophical programs that seem unable to fulfill their grander ambitions. By contrast, the rhetoric, if not the ideas, of social democracy and progressivism has moved so successfully from the periphery to the center of the political stage that the significance of these programs has been consigned by familiarity to contempt. Yet this political progress has been marked by irony more than triumph, for the genuinely radical impulses of social democratic and progressive theory have filtered into the political process in a way that has enabled systems of welfare capitalism premised on very different principles to perpetuate themselves. That outcome may testify merely to the enduring pathos of politics, but it may be instead the particular problem of twentieth-century democracy. Although things have not turned out as these generations hoped, they accepted the unpredictability of the democratic project as an integral part of its value in a world where truth and justice are to be carved from culture rather than found already etched in reason. They understood that such indeterminacy leaves open the possibilities of liberation or control, community participation or domination by elites, and they did not take for granted the outcome of such struggles. If the failures of the welfare state have mocked their confidence and provided melancholy confirmation of their doubts, the last sixty years have also failed to provide better answers to many of their questions. In philosophy and in politics these thinkers proclaimed the fruitfulness of uncertainty; in both spheres their victory has itself proved uncertain. While I would not suggest that we ignore the gulf of time separating our world from theirs, it may be time to build bridges back to their ideas.

PART ONE

1

The Philosophy
of the *Via Media*

1. Beyond Kant:
Religion and Science in Nineteenth-Century Thought

The critical philosophy of Kant cast a shadow over nineteenth-century thought. Kant began by trying to fuse Continental rationalism with British empiricism, but he ended by exploding both traditions when his efforts at consolidation led him to separate judgment from sense experience. That distinction precluded even the possibility of unifying metaphysics with science, or man with nature, by sharply delimiting the scope of empirical investigation and positing categories that inevitably condition our knowledge of the phenomenal world. While the noumenal world of things-in-themselves remained a necessary presupposition for Kant, he denied that either traditional rationalism or experimental science could penetrate that sphere. Empiricism, although accorded sovereignty in the realm of causally determined phenomena, was barred from the territory of faith and morals. In Kant's words, he "had to limit knowledge in order to make room for belief."

Thus the age of reason culminated in the ironic diminution of reason's reach, and successive attempts to reunite the pieces left scattered by Kant's dichotomies undercut one another throughout the nineteenth century. Partisans of various forms of realism, idealism, and positivism tried to recover the unity of experience after Kant, and it is possible to view their efforts schematically as a series of competing rescue attempts staged by skirmishers who proclaimed allegiance to different aspects of his philosophy.[1] Evading Kant's dilemmas by subsuming either the real into the rational or the noumenal into the phenomenal saved intellectuals from despair, but as the century wore on much of their confidence dissolved into pathos. After 1870, a generation of philosophers who accepted Kant's separation of knowledge from belief abandoned the fruitless search for unity to chart a new course between idealism and empiricism. Before presenting portraits of these renegades, however, I want to sketch their intellectual background and outline briefly the struggles between science and faith involving champions of common sense realism, idealism, and positivism, struggles that ended in an unsettling but fertile uncertainty.

During the early decades of the nineteenth century, British and American philosophers resisted the challenge posed by Kant and embraced instead the common sense realism of his contemporary Thomas Reid. According to Reid, only "the enchantment of words" prevented philosophers from recognizing the correspondence of ideas with reality, and only by freeing themselves from the tangled web stretching from Locke through Hume to Berkeley could they return to common sense as the legitimate foundation of philosophy. Reid shared both Kant's desire to refute Hume and his emphasis on the active role of the mind in perception, but whereas Kant placed religious questions beyond the grasp of human knowledge, Reid claimed that theism derived undeniably from common sense. This combination of reason and faith exerted a broad and powerful appeal: it justified the scientific research of the Enlightenment while shielding faith from skepticism.

Among Reid's numerous followers, the most influential in Britain and America was William Hamilton, who amalgamated Kantian arguments about the structural conditions of knowledge with Reid's common sense epistemology. Hamilton elaborated a system of logic and metaphysics resting on his Law of the Conditioned that seemed to suggest, although he was ambiguous on this crucial issue, that our faith in the existence of the unconditioned, including God, might be less unsteady than Kant believed. Hamilton's prestige, enormous during his lifetime, did not survive the associationist critique John Stuart Mill leveled in his *Examination of Sir William Hamilton's Philosophy* (1865), and those who sprang to Hamilton's defense—notably his student James McCosh—proved unable to restore his reputation or infuse new vitality into the realist tradition.

While McCosh aimed to praise Hamilton in *An Examination of Mr. J. S. Mill's Philosophy* (1866), he probably did as much to bury common sense as Mill did. Mill's polemic, although unfair to the subtleties of Hamilton's system, presented a strong case for Mill's own developing sensationalism. In his defense of Scottish realism, McCosh raised pertinent questions about the problems of memory and the nature of a mind capable of associating discrete sense impressions, questions that cut to the core of Mill's epistemology. Yet McCosh directed his criticism almost as forcefully against Hamilton's use of Kant. He perceived that the idea of an impenetrable noumenal realm threatened the defense of faith by reason more profoundly, albeit less directly, than did Mill's materialism, and for that reason he retreated from Hamilton's position to defend the direct intuition of God as a basic truth of realism. That move shifted the emphasis of common sense, which had left room for faith but also encouraged hardheaded scientific observation, from the reconciliation of German and Scottish philosophy to the reconciliation of common sense and evangelical Presbyterianism. In order to restore theism McCosh tried to purge realism of all Kantian impurities. He sapped the critical spirit from Hamilton's writings in his defense of them, and he further stamped the entire common sense tradition with his own evangelical hallmark by virtue of his influential history *The Scottish Philosophy* (1875). McCosh's career, like the career of the ideas he championed, was doubly ironic. When he left Britain in 1868 to assume the presidency of Princeton, he intended to shore up a sagging American Presbyterianism and restore the university to national prominence. His academic reforms, however, eventually undercut his evangelism by contributing to the secularization and professionalization that eventually transformed Princeton from a denominational college into a modern university. Moreover, McCosh's philosophical contributions backed common sense into a theological corner; when thus trapped in apologetics, it shrank rapidly into obscurity.[2]

The rise and fall of Scottish common sense realism during the century separating the deaths of Reid and McCosh had a curious parallel in France, due largely to the efforts of Victor Cousin. The Scottish school rode to prominence in Britain and America in part because it uniquely suited the needs of universities and rapidly proliferating American denominational colleges trying to fulfill occasionally contradictory religious and educational commitments. A version of common sense realism served a similar function in French education after 1840, when Cousin became minister of public education and director of the Ecole Normale Supérieure. As a lecturer in philosophy at the University of Paris, Cousin had produced editions of Descartes, translations of Plato, and a report on the Prussian system of education that catapulted him to national prominence in 1833. Cousin's own philosophy, which he appropriately termed eclecticism, purported to be a synthesis of numerous systems but drew its inspiration primarily from Reid. Like the Scottish realists, Cousin tried to ward off threats to religion stemming from sensationalism, espoused in France by the heirs of Condillac, while claiming to base his ideas on experience rather than dogmatism. Cousin's philosophy, articulated most fully in *Du Vrai, du beau et du bien* (1853), became the centerpiece of mid-nineteenth-century French thought, in part because it proclaimed the comforting message that reason was faith's ally, and in part because Cousin successfully parlayed his formidable intellect and eloquence and his even more formidable arrogance into a kind of philosophical *imperium in imperio*. Given the centrality of philosophy in final examinations for the *baccalauréat* and Cousin's personal control of teacher training, placement, and curriculum throughout the July Monarchy and the Second Empire, his eclecticism was nearly as ubiquitous in France as was the Scottish realism from which it derived in Britain and America. But his ideas failed to exert the force he was able to wield personally, and his version of common sense, a thin verbal wallpaper covering the cracks between science and religion, faded quickly after his death.[3]

Common sense never caught on in Germany. Instead Kant's successors, dissatisfied with the limitations imposed by his categories, tried to recover the unity of experience by exploring the airy heights of *Geist*. In mind or spirit they believed they could find what Kant had lost, the wholeness of life and the reconciliation of man with himself, nature, and God. J. G. Fichte extended Kant's insight regarding the active role played by consciousness in structuring experience. The subject's role is decisive, Fichte reasoned, because at the heart of experience is the activity of volition. "Willing is the real essential character of reason," he proclaimed, and only through the exercise of freedom in ethical action does the individual find fulfillment and the divine manifest itself on earth. For Fichte, the self-affirmation of the ego should culminate in a great process of national development assuring freedom to act in accordance with duty for all members of the community, an ethical ideal that ought to be pursued although it can never be fully realized. Fichte thus obliterated the walls Kant built around the noumenal. The unconditioned absolute was not beyond the mind's reach; it was to be found instead within the mind's fundamental activity and expressed in the creative and free ethical development of the self and the community.[4]

Fichte adumbrated the preoccupations of romanticism. Although springing from different sources and differing in emphasis and mood, romantic philosophers and poets shared a desire to resurrect dimensions of human experience they thought buried in the Enlightenment's obsession with science, empiricism, and reason. The romantics endorsed Fichte's attempts to reunite subject and object, reason and emotion, man and nature, and man and God, although they substituted for transcendental reflection the intuition of artistic genius. Overcoming the first gulf, between the knower and the known, was the goal of Friedrich Schiller, who found in the creative play of aesthetic impulses a way to escape Kant's dichotomies. Schiller's dictum *"immer wird, nie ist"*—always becomes, never is—became a popular slogan among British and American as well as German romantics after Thomas Carlyle endorsed it in his essay "Characteristics" (1831), and the ideal of the poet as dynamic spirit refocused the vision of self-development taken from Fichte away from ethical activity toward artistic exploration. Romantics adopted a radically different aesthetic from that of their eighteenth-century predecessors: scrapping the mirror that might reflect the world, to use the image of Samuel Taylor Coleridge, in preference for a lamp that might illuminate their own experience, they cultivated feelings, intuitions, and unconscious urges ignored during the age of reason. The distinction Friedrich von Schlegel drew between the classic and romantic sensibilities in lectures delivered between 1801 and 1804 gave shape to a number of inchoate impulses, and as these ideas were disseminated in France by Madame de Staël and in America through the writings of Coleridge and Carlyle, numerous thinkers began to express their belief that intuition, a higher faculty than intellect, yields insights into the ultimate nature of reality.

Accompanying the romantics' elevated estimate of the artist's importance and their revolutionary aesthetic were equally unconventional and intricately intertwined ideas about nature and God. Friedrich Schelling's *Naturphilosophie* epitomized the romantic mood in philosophy in its insistence on the original unity of man with nature, a unity that dissolves in the abstractions of conceptual thinking and can be recovered solely through artistic creation. Only imagination, Schelling announced in his *System des transzendentalen Idealismus* (1800), enables man to reconcile contradictions between subject and object, reason and emotion, and man and nature. Underlying this conception of man's fundamental but interrupted oneness with nature was a neo-Platonic understanding of God emerging over time through his creation, a pantheistic notion that filtered into America through the transcendentalism of Ralph Waldo Emerson, into France via Gérard de Nerval and—in watered down form—Cousin's later writings, and into Britian through the work of Coleridge, Carlyle, and William Wordsworth.

A longing for the infinite occupied a central place in the romantic world view. In conscious reaction against the perceived irreligion of the Enlightenment, romantics wanted to rekindle religious sensibilities although they generally scorned institutionalized religion. For that reason they were attracted to the ideas of Friedrich Schleiermacher, who defined religion as "neither thought nor action but intuition and feeling." Schleiermacher deprecated the metaphysics and ethics of Kant and Fichte, which he considered distorting abstractions of the ultimate reality in which spirit and nature are unified in God. The primary fact of self-consciousness, according to Schleiermacher, is the unconditioned and unreflective feeling of dependence on the absolute. In this immediacy of intuition the differentiations that shatter the universe's organic wholeness are not yet present. Philosophy must proceed from—although it cannot finally account for—this basic religious feeling.

Roman Catholicism, anathematized by the *philosophes* as the archetypal foe of reason, received a similar infusion of romantic feeling from the Vicomte de Chateaubriand. In *Le Génie du christianisme* (1802), Chateaubriand bypassed standard doctine and grounded faith on emotion. The God of the romantics was immanent in man and nature, and the feelings of alienation at the heart of Judeo-Christian religious thinking were challenged by their conviction that they could approach unity with God not after death but in life. Through the cultivation of religious feelings and their expression in artistic creation, man could intuit the spiritual essence of reality and thereby recover the primal unity of the universe. For Carlyle that meant not sinking the supernatural into the natural, as the materialistic *philosophes* had mistakenly tried to do, but rather "raising the natural to the supernatural."

In America such a project required an assault on the rationalistic character of Unitarianism, which had elevated reason to a level higher than revelation as a basis for faith. The transcendentalists who launched that attack replaced reason with feeling, scientific knowledge with spiritual intuition. Emerson believed the gap separating the creator from his creation could be bridged. In *Nature* (1836) he wrote, "The world proceeds from the same spirit as the body of man. It is a remoter and inferior incarnation of God, a projection of God in the unconscious." By allowing himself to become a "transparent eyeball," the individual enables "the currents of the Universal being" to circulate through him, and becomes "a channel through which the spirit works." Transcendentalism, in short, like other versions of romanticism, offered a route to the reunion of man and God through an emotionally charged and spiritualized nature.

Yet romanticism had two sides, and Emerson's optimism had its obverse in the dark forebodings of Herman Melville and Heinrich von Kleist, who doubted the possibility of such reconciliations. A tension persisted in the romantic soul between the impulses toward freedom on the one hand and unity on the other. While romantics emphasized the unique richness of the individual artistic sensibility, they also strove to merge that sensibility into a larger whole, whether it was the community, the natural world, or the ultimate spiritual realm of God or the universe. Oscillations between these poles gave their writing a certain unsteadiness, because beneath the longing for fulfillment crept an inexplicable regret, a nagging fear that the loss of unity was permanent. The pervasiveness of romantic *Sehnsucht*, that irresistible yearning for a mysterious something, lured romantics away from the geometric order of the *philosophes'* mental garden into shadowy forest worlds containing the possibilities of rapture or death, or occasionally both, which prompted Goethe to declare romanticism finally unhealthy. Carlyle and his allies in Europe and America tried to elevate the natural to the supernatural, but the inevitable disparity between that aspiration and its achievement hovered over romanticism largely due to the incommensurability of its twin aims of independence and unity.[5]

The most ambitious attempt to reconcile the romantic goals of radical freedom and expressive wholeness was the idealism of G. W. F. Hegel. Although he sharply repudiated the romantics' emphasis on intuitive insight and stressed the systematic character of reason, Hegel shared their vision of the infinite Absolute finding expression in the finite world. Romantics tended to think of the Absolute as an all-pervasive unity, a mystical oneness that Hegel found distressingly murky. He ridiculed the contention of his erstwhile ally Schelling that "in the Absolute all is one," for example, as the night in which all cows are black. Hegel's search for a more illuminating conceptualization of the relation between the pieces of existence and their totality led him to the dialectic, which enabled him to resolve problems in logic, philosophy of mind, and ontology in terms of the progressive overcoming of dichotomies. Whereas the romantics envisioned the Absolute as a transcendental ideal revealing itself in its earthly manifestations, Hegel countered that *Geist* cannot be separated from its determinate existence. "Without the world," as he put it, reversing the romantics' perception, "God is not God."

This formula was not merely a harmonious variation on the romantics' theme of natural supernaturalism. Hegel believed that all of reality exists as a process, a progressive unfolding of the Ideal through a teleological dynamic that gives the Absolute its character. Spirit does not simply reveal itself in the world, it develops itself through history. Existence, Hegel argued, cannot be pure undifferentiated subjectivity for *Geist* any more than for any individual. In both cases disembodied awareness and objective embodiment must be transcended—canceled in their former particularity and preserved in what emerges—and reconciled in the ceaseless progression that is the essence of being conceived as becoming. Whereas Schelling employed the dialectic merely as a method, Hegel thought it expressed the nature of things. The dialectic offered an escape from the dead ends confronting those romantics who celebrated the independence of the endlessly creative artist alone in the universe and those who found unity by surrendering their autonomy entirely to a God immanent in nature. In individuals' free exercise of reason Hegel perceived the emergence of *Geist*. Thus history was the locus of reconciliation between man and God; the impulse toward radical freedom and the longing for expressive unity joined in the historicization of Spirit.

Hegel's scheme of historical development was only one of many that bubbled up from the romantic imagination. Romantics believed that the *philosophes* had exaggerated reason's power and underestimated history's weight. Because the French Revolution annulled ties to fertile traditions, its marriage of politics and principles proved sterile. Romantics drew widely different conclusions from their studies of the past, as the distance separating Hegel from Burke or Michelet or Bancroft might suggest. But they shared a common concern for historical continuity and the importance of the *Volksgeist*, and the continuing vogue of idealist philosophy after the more emotional forms of romanticism faded reflected the heightened interest in questions of national development. Following Hegel's death in 1831, the endless controversies swirling around his intellectual legacy provided an ironic epitaph for his claim that he had restored clarity to philosophy after the fuzzy speculations of the romantics. Indeed, perhaps the dominant characteristic of mid- and late nineteenth-century idealism was its eclecticism: the battles fought between left-Hegelians and right-Hegelians in Germany were duplicated, in form if not in fury, in America and Britain, where versions of Hegelian idealism dominated philosophical discourse for brief periods in the latter half of the century. Hegel emphasized the difficulty Minerva's owl encounters when turning its gaze from the past to the present; the disagreements among his self-proclaimed heirs testified to the diversity of the images the dialectical vision can yield when focused on different scenes.[6]

As romantics and idealists worked to merge natural and spiritual, positivists offered a competing solution to the problem posed by Kant's disjunctive categories. Positivists endorsed versions of historical development as all-embracing as Hegel's, but they denied that anything spiritual holds the key to change. Instead their universe progressed according to an internally driven and altogether naturalistic dynamic, a curiously inverted Hegelianism that embraced teleology while banishing *Geist*. Claude-Henri de Saint-Simon, Auguste Comte, and Herbert Spencer shared Hegel's vision of history as a continuous and necessary progression, but they looked to Condorcet instead of Fichte for clues to the substance of reality and preferred the scientific method to transcendental reflection. Whereas Hegel believed that history culminated in his idealism, positivists thought it time for man to leave behind the primitive theological mode and the intermediate metaphysical mode and to bring to maturity the positive mode of thought, action, and emotion: science. Unswayed by the impulses driving romantics and idealists, positivists expressed the desire to discover laws governing human thought and behavior as durable as the laws of Newtonian physics. At the pinnacle of their overarching synthesis stood sociology, the ultimate science, systematically constructed to yield positive knowledge concerning social organization. Unlike Saint-Simon, who derived from his study of man a utopian vision of socialism, Comte and Spencer concluded that existing political institutions indicate at any given time the historical stage attained by civilization. Their political ideas thus resembled Hegel's more than Marx's. The oddly religious quality of Comte's and Spencer's doctrines also distinguished their positivism from that of Saint-Simon, who was one of the nineteenth century's few outright materialists, and linked them paradoxically with the otherwise quite contrary sensibilities of romanticism. Comte anointed himself the high priest of humanity and conjured up new rituals to substitute for those rendered obsolete in the progression from theology to science. Spencer claimed in his autobiography that as science matures it approaches increasingly abstract conceptions until it "merges into the inconceivable or unthinkable," at which point science delivers to man beliefs "intrinsically more religious" than those of standard but unscientific theology. He also admitted to a fatal weakness for discovering "cardinal truths," an inclination that left him vulnerable to Huxley's familiar jibe that Spencer's idea of a tragedy was a deduction killed by a fact.[7]

The giddy iconoclasm of the Enlightenment ended in Kant's severe demarcation of what man could know from what remained inaccessible to him. Positivists no less than common sense realists and idealists strained to free the mind from those boundaries through different blends of faith, art, and science. Familiar characterizations of the nineteenth century in terms of an assault on faith by science thus mistake effects for causes by misunderstanding the pervasive anxiety of thinkers who did not court unbelief but feared it. Yet even intellectuals who intended to fortify their faltering confidence in man's ability to attain certainty undermined the stability of prevailing ideas by launching a series of challenges which, although designed to redirect and purify knowledge, served ironically to erode its foundations. First came questions from philology, anthropology, and sociology that rocked Biblical authority: David Friedrich Strauss in 1835 and Ernest Renan in 1863 examined the life of Jesus and discounted the miracles of the Gospels as illusions. In *The Essence of Christianity* (1842), Ludwig Feuerbach explained faith as a projection of human inclinations, and his perspective was deepened by Max Stirner and further radicalized by Marx's criticism. E. B. Tylor in *Primitive Culture* (1871) traced religious beliefs to the animism of "primitive" cultures, and Sir James Frazer in *The Golden Bough* (1890) located the source of religion in the failure of magic to account for the supernatural and the consequent need to invent gods. Such efforts undercut the position taken by Protestant theologians who claimed to base their faith on the evidence of miracles, a position they considered consistent with the empiricism of Scottish common sense. Thinkers such as Strauss and Feuerbach thus added momentum to the shift in religious thinking from theology to emotion: although they challenged Biblical authority, they did not invalidate and perhaps even reinforced the romantics' emphasis on the importance of feelings in faith.[8]

But if the romantics' recourse to intuitions of a God immanent in nature survived challenges of that sort, evolutionary naturalism staggered their belief that the universe manifests divine beneficence. Not only did the geology of Lyell and the biology of Lamarck challenge literal readings of the Bible, Darwin's theory of natural selection indicated that the world was neither well ordered nor harmonious. Instead of conforming to the Great Chain of Being or Newton's vision of regularity, the only law of nature was the struggle to survive. If evolution proceeded by means of random variations and competition for scarce resources, then Darwin's ideas made nonsense of theological arguments from design and romantic visions of a peaceful world. Theodicy's prospects seemed to vanish in the face of a process that was not only haphazard but wasteful and even cruel. As the new Biblical criticism, the anthropological interpretation of religion, and new findings in geology had challenged revelation, so Darwinism challenged the arguments from design that sustained natural theology. Only if natural selection could be interpreted as a progressive process developing higher from lower forms of life could Darwinism be assimilated into a religious cosmology. The Great Chain of Being might have been unfastened from eternity, but the comforting thought of progress offered some escape from the otherwise bleak prospects of defending faith without relying on the Bible or nature's harmonious order as evidence of divine purpose. Some partisans of religion such as John Fiske consequently fell into peculiar alliance with Spencer and his disciples, who argued that the theory of natural selection validated their notions of cosmic progress. Less sympathetic to spiritual interpretations but equally enthusiastic concerning the idea of evolution, positivists such as Ernst Haeckel broadened Darwin's insights by adding vaguely Comtean visions of development to the concepts of fortuitous variation and selective pressure to form an all-inclusive system. Thus reinvigorated by Darwinian ideas, positivism exerted a powerful influence in late nineteenth-century European thought, and although the United States never produced a systematic positivist like Comte or Haeckel, the prestige of Spencer in America—where, due to the efforts of Fiske and others, his ideas were not considered inconsistent with religion—was unequalled by that of any contemporary.[9]

The confidence of systematic positivism, dramatically enhanced by extrapolations from geology and biology, was itself undercut as a result of developments within the physical sciences and mathematics. While the most decisive steps along this path were taken in Europe, *The Education of Henry Adams* provides the *locus classicus* for understanding their significance. In contrast to the exuberance of scientists who believed Darwinian theory held the key to knowledge about nature, certain philosophers of science during the final two decades of the nineteenth century questioned not only specific findings but the fundamental legitimacy of claims to certainty based on science. Uneasy about the grand post-Darwinian syntheses and equally troubled by challenges striking at the heart of scientific knowledge, Adams recounted, in terms of a fanciful but instructive conceit, his search for a solution to his conundrum. His intellectual voyage, he explained, began in England, but there he found in Karl Pearson's *Grammar of Science* (1892) only chaos. Concepts of order, routine, and necessity, Pearson argued, do not reflect the nature of things but provide merely a "conceptual shorthand" that helps man make sense of experience without answering metaphysical questions about reality. Dissatisfied, Adams turned from such disorder, which he dismissed as characteristic of the untidy English mind, and looked confidently to Germany. There he found not the expected systematic rigor but rather, in the writings of Ernst Mach, the source of some of Pearson's most unsettling ideas. Even more disorienting was the experimental evidence contained in Mach's *Science of Mechanics* (1883), indicating that absolute space and motion, two of the mainstays of Newtonian mechanics, are, in Mach's words, no more than pure mental concepts, which "cannot be produced in experience." Adams, fearing the imminent collapse of classical physics, sought refuge in France, where he hoped the Cartesian passion for order would rescue him from such anarchy. Instead of comfort he received confirmation of his fears in Henri Poincaré's counsel that scientific hypotheses do not conform to nature but derive from fertile human minds. Scientific theories are thus neither true nor false but simply convenient. Poincaré maintained that even geometry is the creation not of a divine mind whose order Euclid discerned but merely a convention enabling man to think productively about space. Critical positivists such as Pearson, Mach, and Poincaré, following in the wake of Lyell and Darwin, effectively dismantled the Newtonian system; moreover, they made clear that science could offer no clues to a cosmology capable of taking its place. Two centuries after Newton had called the universe to order, it lay in complete disarray around reflective thinkers like Henry Adams.[10]

Throughout the nineteenth century, religion and science proved themselves the oil and water of modern culture. No sooner had romantics and idealists tried to infuse nature with divinity than Darwinians demonstrated that the ways of such a God operating through "nature red in tooth and claw" were mysterious indeed. Before positivists could topple faith and establish an empire of science, however, their own tools were shown to be inadequate to the task. Scientists demolished arguments religion brought into the nineteenth century, ruling out literal interpretations of the Bible and upsetting natural theology, but by 1900 their own presuppositions appeared equally unsteady. Ironically, by locating the source of religion in emotion and its object in nature—even a nature that was developing constantly and painfully—religion found its scope broadened over the course of a century that witnessed unprecedentedly powerful attacks launched against theology. Lodged in the heart and pointed toward the world as God's manifestation, faith proclaimed itself impervious to science. When critical positivists like Pearson, Mach, and Poincaré pointed out that science had no metaphysical clothes, the gaudy claims of Comte, Spencer, and Haeckel began to unravel. According to Chauncey Wright, the American thinker perhaps closest in spirit to the critical positivists and bitterly scornful of systematic positivists like Spencer, science could neither disprove nor contradict religion even in principle. "Progress in science is really a progress in religious truth," Wright reasoned, "because advancement in knowledge frees us from the errors both of ignorance and superstition." By abandoning theology, faith secured its borders from a science chastened by the awareness of its limitations. Matthew Arnold at midcentury expressed the anxiety of Victorians who were "wandering between two worlds, one dead, the other powerless to be born," and the next fifty years only confirmed his fears. One world, a world of revelation and dogma, had indeed expired. Its self-proclaimed successor, a world to be governed by science instead of religion, had proved unable to banish noncognitive claims and had acknowledged its presuppositions as conventional rather than grounded in the nature of things. In the wake of critical positivism, that world seemed chimerical. Common sense realists, romantics, idealists, and positivists had launched successive campaigns to make faith and science consistent with or subservient to each other. But their efforts culminated in the proclamation of a truce on terms offered by scientists, who confessed that they could not account for religious feelings, and accepted by religious thinkers, who admitted that theology could no longer dictate its beliefs to science. When both religion and science recognized each other's sovereignty in their enlarged spheres and no longer represented immediate threats to one another, an unsteady intellectual peace seemed possible. What failed to survive was certainty.[11]

Uncertainty can animate or disable. When certainty inhibits exploration, its loss can be liberating, but when conviction fortifies resolution, doubt can end in paralysis. Thinkers in the late nineteenth century experienced uncertainty in both forms. Some, like Nietzsche, rejoiced that an "open sea" lay before a culture cut free from its ties to faith in religion and science. Nietzsche stared into the abyss and called it good: if only modern man could irrevocably discard the "overestimation of truth" that propped up both science and Christianity's "ascetic ideal," he could embrace the freedom that should be his. Nietzsche turned his perspectivalism into a game he could not lose because he could always—and often did—simply call for another mask, a gambit enabling him to shield his cherished freedom behind a series of disguises. Others, however, saw in the demise of certainty only disaster. The kind of nihilism Nietzsche celebrated repelled various antimodernists in Europe and America. Some sought sanctuary with Henry Adams in the medieval mysteries of the Virgin at Chartres, some despaired of the pervasive world-weariness that descended when science and religion no longer seemed able to provide answers, and some simply buried their heads and reveled in *fin-de-siècle* decadence.[12]

Others tried to start over by rethinking the hubris of certainty and the challenge of doubt. Scottish realists had expressed confidence in common sense, romantics in intuition, idealists in *Geist*, and positivists in science. All aspired to an Archimedean point beyond Kant's demarcations of noumenal and phenomenal, a position from which they could penetrate the world's opacity and disclose the "really real." From the perspective of a number of critical thinkers in the late nineteenth century, all had failed. The separation of religion and science, although not consciously sought, was nevertheless effected by a quite unexpected cunning of reason that divided decisively what Hegel believed modern history would fuse. Kant's categories, as well as the failed efforts to transcend them and Nietzsche's and Adams's disparate attempts to escape them, assumed a new meaning in light of the cultural disjunction between the religious and scientific spheres, and a wave of neo-Kantianism surged across Europe and America as idealism and positivism ebbed. But independent of such Kantians as Heinrich Rickert, Wilhelm Windelband, Charles Renouvier, and Josiah Royce—although allied with them in spirit—was a group of radicals who aimed to be more Kantian than Kant, who sought to find the conditions of the conditions of experience. Kant's revolution consisted of his discovery that experience cannot be pure because it assumes a certain structure in consciousness, but he failed to subject the categories of time and space themselves to transcendental critique. An equally important revolution occurred when a number of rene-gade philosophers discovered that the conditions of experience are also dynamic rather than static, dependent rather than fundamental. This aware-ness suggested that the elusive epistemological bedrock simply does not exist. As that suspicion became stronger, the possibility of attaining certainty vanished. Not only had neither idealists nor positivists found the Archi-medean point; such a point could never be found because knowledge does not in any uncomplicated way correspond with what is "out there," nor does it directly reflect the conditions imposed by an unchanging internal structure of consciousness. Assimilating insights from Fichte and Hegel, Hamilton and Mill, mavericks who began by going "back to Kant," to use the neo-Kantians' rallying cry, ended by going beyond Kant and behind his categories to raw experience: contingent, open-ended, and unavoidably uncertain.

2. Portraits: A Generation of Radical Philosophers

When William James died in 1910, John Dewey tried to assess James's impact on modern thought. Reaching intellectual maturity in the 1870s, James's generation faced the uninspiring prospect of choosing between the rival traditions of idealism and positivism. Confronting such mutually exclu-sive world views, James set out to find what Dewey called "a *via media* between natural science and the ideal interests of morals and religion." At first, Dewey explained, "James stood practically alone—a voice crying in the wilderness." Gradually "the temper of imagination changed," and as the twentieth century dawned, James found himself riding the crest of the

Zeitgeist. James recognized as clearly as Dewey that a process of intellectual convergence was transforming the transatlantic world of ideas. In a letter he wrote in 1903 to the English philosopher F. C. S. Schiller about Dewey and his associates at the University of Chicago, James expressed his conviction "that from such opposite poles minds are moving toward a common centre, that old compartments and divisions are breaking down, and that a very inclusive new school may be formed." By that time James was no longer alone in his search for a *via media*. He had been joined by several of the most creative thinkers in Europe and America, all trying in their different ways to redirect philosophy away from tiresome quarrels between religion and science. They advanced interconnected arguments about epistemology and ethics, and those arguments pointed toward new and equally heterodox political ideas.

Because these thinkers drew from both the idealist and empiricist traditions, I will follow Dewey's suggestion and designate them the philosophers of the *via media*. It is important to specify, though, that they did not seek synthesis by simply blending incommensurable ideas. Mediators of that sort, as Nietzsche wisely warned, "lack eyes to see the unparalleled." The philosophers of the *via media* carefully avoided fruitless attempts to reconcile the irreconcilable; they tried instead to jostle philosophy into a productive confrontation with doubt. Nietzsche further counseled that "seeing things as similar and making them the same is the mark of weak eyes," and my grouping of those who contributed the most important ideas to the construction of a *via media* should not be misunderstood as an argument that their positions were identical. Because they came from different traditions they inherited different intellectual inclinations; for the same reason they had different devils to exorcise. Nevertheless, differences of style and substance notwithstanding, they shared a dissatisfaction with Kant and neo-Kantianism, and with the common sense, idealist, and positivist paradigms. While their community of discourse was lively and not always harmonious, from it emerged an important body of ideas about philosophy and politics.[13]

The six philosophers most important in this process were, with a single exception, members of the same generation, born within a decade of one another. Wilhelm Dilthey (1833–1911), Thomas Hill Green (1836–1882), Henry Sidgwick (1838–1900), Alfred Fouillée (1838–1912), and William James (1842–1910) all began to produce important work in the 1870s, in a world obsessed with conflicts between religious faith and scientific naturalism. Although he was considerably younger than the others, John Dewey (1859–1952) made contributions to epistemology, ethics, and political theory that helped to draw together a number of ideas articulated by the other philosophers of the *via media*. Moreover, his writings and his career demonstrate the continuity between these thinkers' ideas and those of the generation that followed them. This later generation developed and extended the ideas of social democracy and progressivism from their predecessors' analyses of knowledge and responsibility, and the connection between these two generations thus comes most sharply into focus in Dewey's work. These six philosophers stood uncomfortably between two different worlds. Their careers marked the transition between the vocation of the philosopher as preacher and the profession of the philosopher as academic, and their writings provided the epistemological and ethical pivot on which political theory turned from socialism and liberalism to social democracy and progressivism. While all of them came from religious families, all became professors of philosophy instead of clergymen. Furthermore, all agreed that in an age looking toward science to replace religion as a source of cultural values, philosophy needed to rethink its role and reexamine its premises. Before examining their ideas in detail, I want to present brief biographical portraits suggesting the shape of their lives and the questions addressed in their work.

In Germany, Wilhelm Dilthey best exemplified this spirit of radical reorientation in philosophy. Both Dilthey's grandfather and father were Calvinist ministers, and when he began his university studies in Heidelberg in 1852, he too intended to become a pastor in the Reformed faith. His father's unorthodox pietism and his exposure to the writings of Schleiermacher convinced Dilthey that theology should focus more properly on personal religious feelings than rationalist metaphysics, and when he felt his own faith slipping away he turned his attention increasingly toward philosophy and history. He completed his studies at the University of Berlin with F. A. Trendlenburg, who was developing from his criticism of Hegel a philosophy of *Idealrealismus* that moved away from the conflict between idealism and positivism in the direction of a new species of critical realism. Dilthey's creative blending of these influences became apparent in his first major writings, his dissertation on Schleiermacher's ethics (1864) and the first volume of his biography of Schleiermacher, which appeared in installments between 1867 and 1870. Schleiermacher appealed to Dilthey because he had the vision and courage to declare himself neutral in the war between idealism and realism that raged during his lifetime, and because he acknowledged the interdependence of thought and action, mind and body, without succumbing to the formalism of Kant, the voluntarism of Fichte, or the dialectical monism of Hegel.

In his work on Schleiermacher, Dilthey refocused the emphasis on religious experience toward epistemology, and the result illuminated a new philosophical perspective: "Christianity directs us back to ourselves and . . . our inner life," he wrote. That insight reveals that "man is the one true beginning of knowledge, whether it is of the self or of the concepts in which we think. The certainty of our knowledge rests in us ourselves, and as we move away from ourselves, our knowledge becomes gradually less certain."[14] Philosophy so conceived must begin with experience as it is lived rather than as it is conceived formally or explained dialectically, and that orientation was to be central in the philosophy of the *via media*. His study of Schleiermacher also prompted Dilthey to reflect on the problem of interpretive understanding and the historical method of examining ideas by tracing their origin, transmission, and transformation, a process through which the interpreter gradually comes to know the whole on the basis of the parts even as he knows the parts only on the basis of a preliminary although partial knowledge of the whole. This hermeneutical circle, the heart of Dilthey's historical method, requires exhaustive knowledge of details of individual lives as well as various socioeconomic, political, and intellectual contexts, and it is perhaps an index of its comprehensiveness—as well as a reflection of Dilthey's own Faustian character—that he labored on the Schleiermacher biography throughout his life without ever bringing it to completion.

The other theme adumbrated in Dilthey's early writings which pre-occupied him throughout his career was the question of grounding values in a secular era. In the absence of religious traditions expressive of the genuine and profound human impulses that give depth to the melody of life, modern culture appeared flat and unsatisfying. Reconstituting values on a new and solid foundation presented the central challenge Dilthey designed his philosophy to meet.

One of the most striking characterizations of Dilthey's personality appears in a typically delightful letter William James wrote to his sister Alice while he was studying in Berlin in 1867. James and Dilthey met at the home of art historian Hermann Grimm, whom James knew through his father's friend Emerson. Dilthey "was overflowing with information with regard to everything knowable and unknowable," James wrote. "He is the first man I have ever met of a class, which must be common here, of men to whom learning has become as natural as breathing." After a spirited and wide-ranging discussion of the anthropology of religion, Dilthey's speech grew languid, his head began to droop, and he awakened to accept Grimm's gracious if somewhat tardy offer of a quick nap, after which he "rose, refreshed like a giant, and proceeded to fight with Grimm" about Homer's identity and Hamlet's madness. As James's account suggests, the breadth and depth of Dilthey's knowledge was extraordinary, and his habit of working twelve to fourteen hours at a time, coupled with the insomnia and nervous disorders from which he suffered, may account for his unsteady grip on social proprieties. It was the brilliance of Dilthey's writings that earned him recognition, and in 1882 he was called to the center of the German academic world, the chair in philosophy at the University of Berlin, in which Hegel had felt himself well situated to chart the course of the World Spirit. But even from that intellectually prestigious and financially comfortable perch, Dilthey remained uncomfortable in society and uninterested in conversations of the sort James relished. "I wish I could turn my back on the world entirely," he wrote to his friend Graf Yorck in 1884. "For my old age, if I should reach it, I have no other thought except complete withdrawal from the world."[15]

Given Dilthey's reclusiveness, James was to be disappointed in his hope of becoming better acquainted with the German philosopher. Despite remarkable resonances between the ideas they developed from 1890 to 1910, and despite the respect that each expressed for the other's work, they never saw one another again after the evening at Grimm's. Finally, James was on the mark when he likened Dilthey's learning to breathing; the ceaselessness of his intellectual activity was at once a sign of his genius and an affliction. He read and wrote steadily, inhaling and exhaling ideas at a rate that, while it may not have exhausted him, leaves students of his work breathless. His voracious mind never rested at one place long enough to produce a comprehensive statement of his ideas, and as a result trying to present a definitive statement of his philosophy is rather like tapping a balloon that drifts slowly but maddeningly out of reach.

Dilthey's thought remains elusive for several reasons. First, although a certain continuity exists in the progression of his ideas, his interests shifted during his career from the theory and practice of the human sciences (*Geisteswissenschaften*) to a search for an adequate "descriptive and analytical psychology," and finally, after 1895, to the challenge of examining and exercising the method of interpretive understanding (*Verstehen*) of human expression and developing a hermeneutics capable of serving as a starting point for philosophy as well as history. Second, aspects of Dilthey's prodigious output remain generally unknown: seventy years after his death, six of the projected twenty-two volumes of his *Gesammelte Schriften* have not yet been published. Third, the thickets of interpretive controversy tangled around Dilthey's ideas further complicate their exploration, and as varieties of philosophical hermeneutics proliferate in contemporary scholarship, the problem threatens to become more rather than less difficult.[16] From the underbrush of obscurity and special pleading, however, it is possible to extract several particularly important contributions to the philosophy of the *via media*, notably Dilthey's analysis of the centrality of lived experience (*Erlebnis*) and his understanding of history as a source of immanent critique in the human sciences. I will pay special attention to those ideas.

T. H. Green played a pivotal role in English intellectual life, redirecting patterns of thought in philosophy, education, and political theory. Born in 1836, three years later than Dilthey, Green too was a clergyman's son who decided against entering the ministry in order to pursue a career in philosophy. Educated at home, in an atmosphere of fervent if unorthodox Evangelicalism, until he entered Rugby at age fourteen, Green manifested as a schoolboy what his friend Henry Sidgwick later called "a certain grave rebelliousness."[17] Upon completing his studies at Oxford in 1859, Green wavered between the ministry, journalism, and philosophy. His hunger for intellectual rigor ruled out Evangelical preaching, and his distate for privilege made the life of a clergyman in the Church of England unpalatable to him. He was offered the editorship of the Bombay-based *Times of India*, which appealed to his sense of adventure and his growing interest in social and political questions, but his mentor Benjamin Jowett advised against it. Instead Green accepted a teaching position as a Fellow of Balliol College, embarking on a career that would lead him to redefine the scope and purpose of university teaching and thereby enable him to satisfy his intellectual ambitions while fulfilling his religious and political impulses as well.

In 1862, Green and Sidgwick traveled with two other friends to Germany and Switzerland. Green became intrigued by the contrast between the mixture of romanticism and idealism still prominent in German philosophy and the positivism pervading British thought in an era dominated by Mill, Spencer, and Darwin. As he later expressed it in the lectures published post-humously as *Prolegomena to Ethics*, he felt the age required some form of philosophy that "does not profess to be a branch either of dogmatic theology or of natural science."[18] Such a philosophy, he believed, must take into account both the naturalistic world view derived from the Enlightenment that invalidated much religious doctrine—the scientific perspective of Mill's utilitarianism and Spencer's positivism—and also the quite opposite inclinations of idealism. Green pointed out that the entire effluence of romanticism stood between his generation and Hume's. If science had forced faith to reexamine its enthusiasm, the romantics had also shown the insufficiency of naturalism.[19]

Green's encounter with German thought in the 1860s shaped his ideas in much the same way Schleiermacher influenced Dilthey. Green found in Germany an avenue toward faith that bypassed dogma and depended on reason's reflections on experience. After 1867, when he became the first non-clerical tutor in Balliol College history, Green brought the ideas of Kant, Fichte, and Hegel to Oxford. Through his efforts and those of Bernard Bosanquet and F. H. Bradley, strong currents of idealism entered British philosophy. Green followed German theologians in emphasizing religious feelings over theology, but he spurned the cultivation of "personal sanctity" through mystical reflection and insisted that religion should lead instead to altruistic social service.[20] Green's zealous advocacy of that ideal, which struck a chord in British life as the pain occasioned by unrestrained capitalist expansion became increasingly acute, transformed him into an influential partisan of reform and—perhaps less an achievement then than now—even something of a hero. He served as the model for the inspirational Professor Grey in Mrs. Humphry Ward's widely read novel *Robert Elsmere* (1888), which contemporaries likened to *Uncle Tom's Cabin* as a spark igniting public sentiment toward reform. The novel's protagonist, after listening to Grey lecture at Oxford (in words drawn directly from Green's own lay sermons on the importance of self-sacrifice), takes up a country parish only to find his faith shaken by a local skeptic. He returns to Oxford to consult with Grey, then sets off, fired by the belief that his salvation lies in service to others, to work among the impoverished in London's East End.[21] Green exerted an equally significant if less dramatic influence on a number of the Oxford men who passed into British public life in the late nineteenth century, and it is no exaggeration to say that he helped to alter educated opinion regarding the nature of a good personal life and the proper role of government.

Green's prestige was at its peak in 1878 when he was named Whyte Professor of Moral Philosophy at Oxford; four years later, at forty-six years of age, he died from blood poisoning. Because he died young and unexpectedly, leaving much of his work in unfinished form, and because Bradley and Bosanquet took British idealism down roads quite different from those

Green traveled, Green's impact on the reorientation of philosophy in the late nineteenth century may be misunderstood in the ritualistic references to him as the father of Anglo-Hegelianism. Green did introduce idealism into British thought, but his writings had rather different kinds of significance in different areas of philosophy. I will not examine Green's vaporous metaphysics, the most thoroughly Hegelian aspect of his work, which is of little interest today and was less important in the convergence of ideas toward the *via media* than were other aspects of his thought.

Green's most influential and enduring philosophical contribution was his critique of empiricism. In his introduction to a new edition of Hume's *Works* (1874), Green argued that sensations cannot themselves account for knowledge because a mind is necessary to relate discrete impressions to one another. This notion of a continuous and developing subject also informed Green's moral philosophy. He replaced the psychological hedonism at the root of utilitarianism with a Fichtean voluntarism, and he substituted an Aristotelian concept of self-realization for the maximization of pleasure as the aim of ethics. Conceiving of the self as a subject that finds fulfillment in ethical action within a community that recognizes his rights, Green also posed a challenge to the atomistic individualism of British laissez-faire liberalism. His lecture "Liberal Legislation and Freedom of Contract" (1881) helped provide a rationale for increased state intervention into economic and social affairs. Although Green contended that the Lockean concept of negative freedom—freedom from interference—was no longer an adequate guarantee of liberty in the wake of the industrial revolution, his arguments in support of positive freedom—effective freedom to exercise rights—did not spring from any enthusiasm for Hegel's glorification of the state as the vehicle of the *Weltgeist*. Green remained within the British tradition in his focus on individual rights as the primary concern of politics, but he punctured the self-righteousness of liberals who masked the perpetuation of privilege beneath the rhetoric of freedom. From his youth Green detested what he called the pervasive "flunkeyism" of English society, which he recognized as "incompatible with any healthy political life," and he was actively involved in local and national reform movements to democratize politics and education.[22] Later generations, chastened by mass hysteria, have dismissed as naive Green's faith that democracy can resolve the problems of politics, and it is his faith in history as a teleological process that most clearly betrays Green's debt to Hegel. Green conceived of history as Hegel did, as the realization of God on earth, a heroic struggle that the forces of light cannot but win. His world had little room for tragedy. One of the major fault lines cutting across the philosophy of the *via media* divided thinkers who resigned themselves to a tragic view of life as perpetual conflict from those who saw history as epic, and Green clearly believed that the triumph of democracy would signal the beginning of the end of injustice.

World War I is frequently considered the terminus of an era of optimism in Western thought. Although its carnage and futility doubtless sobered countless observors—and participants—from delusions of steady progress, a sense of tragedy was scarcely alien to the prewar period. Thinkers like Green, it is true, expressed confidence regarding the course of change, but others, like his lifelong friend and philosophical adversary Henry Sidgwick, were less sanguine about the possibility of resolving the dilemmas of philosophy and politics and the cultural conflicts between religion and science. The pairing of Sidgwick and Green beneath the rubric of the *via media* is admittedly unconventional. They were the most prominent partisans of competing philosophical traditions in late Victorian England. Yet their divergence from those traditions, while it did not carry them as far as philosophical alliance, nevertheless suggests the paradoxical process of convergence in late nineteenth-century ideas. In epistemology, in ethics, and in politics, they imaginatively blended elements taken from the traditions of British empiricism, Scottish common sense, and German idealism. The disagreements between Sidgwick and Green, while important, should not overshadow the congruent differences separating them from earlier theorists whose ideas they modified. Just as Green altered Aristotle, Fichte, and Hegel by filtering them through the British tradition, so Sidgwick acknowledged that he was forced to "fall away from" and finally to "part company with" Mill and utilitarianism because Kant and realists such as Thomas Reid convinced him that "intuitions turn the scale."[23]

The personalities and careers of Sidgwick and Green present a similarly subtle pattern of contrasts and harmonies. Sidgwick's father was also a clergyman. It was Green, two years Sidgwick's senior, who persuaded Sidgwick while they were at Rugby to study philosophy. But whereas Green found in reason reassurance for his faith and a warrant for activism, the diary Sidgwick kept while a student at Trinity College, Cambridge, reveals the anguish he endured as a result of the conflicts he perceived between theology and philosophy. He prayed fervently for the strength to combat selfishness and pride of intellect, which he deemed his greatest weaknesses. A decade later, as a tutor at Trinity College, he was still trying to reconcile his scholarly interests with the desire to contribute something more tangible to the welfare of others.[24] In 1869, tormented by fears of hypocrisy, he resigned his fellowship rather than submit to the law requiring fellows to subscribe to the thirty-nine articles of the Church of England. Sidgwick's intransigence was less a show of defiance than an expression of his intellectual honesty and moral courage; Green, more outspokenly critical of English society and ecclesiastical hierarchy, did not find his misgivings about Church doctrine sufficiently important to take such a step. The law was changed and Sidgwick was reappointed to his fellowship, but the controversy symbolizes the strength of character, the "flawlessness in quality," to use William James's phrase for Sidgwick, that endeared him to perhaps as many as revered Green.[25] Although Sidgwick was not the inspirational speaker Green was—G. E. Moore recalled his lectures as rather dull—an irresistible warmth, charm, and compassion radiated from Sidgwick, whereas Green transferred the Evangelical fervor of his heritage into a relentless austerity that commanded more respect than affection. As much as Sidgwick admired Green, his former schoolmate was an equal rather than an idol in his eyes. The letter he wrote to Green's widow in 1882, although full of praise, deflates the devotional tone typical of such ritualized memoirs with a delightfully irreverent tale of Green's bluffing his way through a term of composition at Rugby with an absentminded tutor who thought him already at Oxford.[26]

Sidgwick participated in perhaps an even wider variety of reform activities than did Green. They were both among the founders of the Free Christian Union, established in 1870 for those disenchanted with the Church of England but not with Christianity. They also shared a commitment to educational reform, and Sidgwick was instrumental in the establishment of Newnham College, the first women's college at Cambridge, in which he and his wife lived after its founding in 1880. In recognition of their political activity, both Sidgwick and Green were asked to stand for Parliament near the ends of their lives; for similar reasons having to do with the desire to complete their scholarly work, both declined. From 1882 until his death in 1900, Sidgwick devoted considerable attention to the Society for Psychical Research, even serving for several years as its president. The prestige of counting among its members the Knightsbridge Professor of Moral Philosophy at Cambridge did much to lend legitimacy to the organization. Whether Sidgwick's interest in parapsychology testifies to his broadmindedness or to simple intellectual eccentricity, such activities intrigued a number of philosophers and psychologists at the time, including William James, who shared Sidgwick's fascination with loony clairvoyants and was as frequently disappointed by their antics.[27]

Sidgwick's philosophical writings covered a wide range of topics. His most celebrated book was his first, *The Methods of Ethics*, a classic of moral philosophy that appeared first in 1874 and went through six editions before Sidgwick's death. In it Sidgwick challenged the moral psychology of egoism at the center of utilitarianism. He argued that the contradictions between utilitarians and intuitionists could be resolved through the principle of benevolence he fashioned from a careful analysis of what competing ethical theories had in common. Although still often treated as a "classical" exponent of utilitarian ethics, Sidgwick severely altered the arguments advanced by earlier utilitarians such as Bentham and the Mills. His political writings evince a similar desire to harmonize discordant ideas, but their troubled tone distinguishes them from Green's more confident estimates of the efficacy of political reform. Sidgwick feared that intractable problems prevent the final resolution of political conflicts, problems related to, but not identical with, the conflict between the demands of prudence and justice in ethical decisions. That sensitivity to the pathos of ethics and politics, as much as any other feature of his character and thought, distinguished Sidgwick's outlook from Green's. It sprang from his inability to answer conclusively the question that gnawed at his generation, the question whether science and reason were compatible with religion and belief. Sidgwick felt compelled to acknowledge "the provisional character of the structure of thought" to which faith belonged, and he refused to cover his doubts with a veneer of confidence unwarranted by experience.[28] He regretted that reason could not carry him, as it carried Green, to faith, although he did not deny the existence of the personal feelings that he identified as the source of religious beliefs. His perspective left room for hope but excluded confidence that reason could solve the most difficult problems man faces. As he put it in the concluding passage of the first edition of *The Methods of Ethics*, "The prolonged effort of the human intellect to frame a perfect ideal of rational conduct is seen to have been foredoomed to inevitable failure."[29] We must proceed, Sidgwick advised, without knowing—or pretending to know—that our answers are correct, relying on experience and hoping it will shave the edge of despair from our uncertainty.

Unconventional ideas are more easily assimilated in cultures accustomed to intellectual diversity. The marriage of Hegel and Darwin could be performed more easily in Germany, England, or even the United States than in France, where the role of the Roman Catholic church offers a less obvious but possibly more instructive explanation than the fact of priests' celibacy for the failure of clergymen's "sons"—even in a figurative sense—to contribute to the philosophy of the *via media*. Whereas reflective young men like Dilthey, Green, and Sidgwick could think seriously about finding intellectual and spiritual fulfillment in the ministry, the polarization of French intellectual life in the nineteenth century linked dissent with anticlericalism and religiosity with orthodox Catholicism. Unlike many Protestant denominations that recovered from attacks on theology with fresh conceptualizations of faith, the Catholic church met new challenges with increasingly rigid assertions of its authority that culminated in the Syllabus of Errors (1864) and the Proclamation of Papal Infallibility (1870). Faced with a world of socioeconomic, political, and intellectual revolution, Catholic thinking ossified in France.

But if such orthodoxy repelled inquiring minds, other veins of French thought provided a richer source for nineteenth-century philosophers who turned from Catholicism but confronted the ubiquitous problem of reconciling naturalism and faith. The thinker who expressed ideas most clearly embodying the heretical spirit of the *via media* in France was Alfred Fouillée, an imaginative and extraordinarily prolific writer who was born in the same year as Sidgwick, 1838. Fouillée bridged the gap in French philosophy between the neocriticism of Renouvier, twenty-three years his senior, and the intuitionism of Bergson, twenty-one years younger than Fouillée. In the eleventh edition of his *Histoire générale de la philosophie* (1910), among the more popular of his thirty-six books, Fouillée added a chapter on contemporary philosophy in which he reflected on his lifelong desire to meet what he termed "the principal need of the age: the reconciliation of science and morality."[30] In France, he acknowledged, that project required the "extremely slow dissolution" of "positive religion" as science transformed religious feelings into a properly philosophical sensibility.[31] Unlike Comte or Spencer, both of whom he criticized repeatedly, Fouillée did not believe that science could serve as religion's successor. To "dechristianize without humanizing or moralizing" would be catastrophic. The goal instead should be to establish philosophy as the fusion of what is true in science, accompanied by an awareness of its limits, and what is true in religion, the experience of something beyond.[32] This emphasis on an ineffable religious feeling, reminiscent of German romantic theologians such as Schleiermacher but derived in Fouillée's case from Maine de Biran, ruled out the dogmatic claims of French Catholicism while resisting the positivists' siren song.

Fouillée burst upon the French intellectual scene in 1872 with a dramatic triumph that could have happened only in Paris, where the spark of new ideas can be fanned by oratorical flair into political controversy. Fouillée's impassioned eloquence transformed the ordinarily sedate ritual of a thesis defense into an ideological brawl. So spirited was his presentation that the philosophical dimensions of his argument in *La Liberté et le déterminisme* became lost in the furor surrounding its radical political implications. Gambetta, who knew good rhetoric when he heard it, may not have followed the ideas Fouillée expressed, but he was sufficiently impressed by their defense to offer Fouillée the prospect of a seat in the Chamber of Deputies and to predict for him a distinguished political career. Fouillée instead accepted a teaching position at the Ecole Normale, and he appeared to be on his way to exercising the sort of influence wielded previously by Cousin. Unfortunately for the fate of his ideas, however, Fouillée's fragile health forced him to leave the rue d'Ulm and settle in the south of France. Although he elaborated his ideas tirelessly until his death in 1912, the intellectual suzerainty of Paris allowed him only modest success in maintaining the prestige he earned during his brief stay at the summit of French education.

Fouillée's life in the south was tranquil and productive. He worked closely with his stepson and only real disciple, the philosopher Jean–Marie Guyau, whose widely discussed ethical theory centered on an altruistic impulse to creation that Guyau considered the source of the feelings of obligation analyzed by Kant in purely formal terms. When Guyau died unexpectedly in 1888 at the age of thirty-four, Fouillée lost his closest friend and collaborator as well as the gifted student who would have perpetuated his legacy. Although Fouillée worked feverishly to expound the ideas they developed together, the vacuum left in his personal life by the tragedy of his stepson's early death was never filled.[33]

Fouillée built his philosophy upon the concept of *idées-forces*, which he employed to resolve the apparent contradiction between the experience of freedom fundamental to human consciousness and the determinism assumed by scientific naturalism. Ideas, which in Fouillée's usage resemble intentions, are forces, in the sense of causes, when we act upon them and thus affect the order of things. There are no uncaused effects, and to that extent the logic of naturalism holds true. But our ideas—including religious beliefs—can themselves be causes, or *idées-forces*, when we translate them into action. Critics have accused Fouillée of juggling with words to divert attention from Hume's challenge or the dilemma posed by Kant's categories, and there is admittedly something elusive about Fouillée's idealist metaphysics, like Green's, that seems to warrant such charges. Leaving his metaphysics aside, however, and concentrating on his theory of knowledge, his ethics, and his political ideas, it is clear that Fouillée departed radically from Kant by searching for the solution to the noumenal-phenomenal problem in the richness and immediacy of experience. There he found thought and action interpenetrating in a way that muddied the neat explanations of idealism and naturalism and suggested a new conceptualization of man and his world.

Although Fouillée's knowledge was encyclopedic, his prodigious production finally outstripped even his considerable intellectual resources, and in the end he produced more books and articles than new ideas. Yet his philosophy was not simply a hyphen inserted by sleight of hand between idealism and positivism. It was an imaginative rethinking of experience and volition carefully articulated in widely read books, whose importance the other apostates of his generation recognized. He explored the various dimensions of his philosophy in an impressive series of studies concerning psychology, sociology, economics, education, law, and evolutionary theory. He also produced detailed analyses of the writings of other philosophers, indicting in particular Nietzsche and Bergson for celebrating will and intuition while overlooking the limits imposed by the real constraints encountered in experience. The doctrine of *idées-forces*, by contrast, focused on the crossroads of thought, will, action, and external reality in individual lives pursued within concretely bounded social and historical circumstances.[34]

No one understood more clearly the hazards of that intersection between consciousness and activity than William James, who was tortured by the feelings of uncertainty that strangled his will when neither religion nor naturalism could satisfy his philosophical and psychological longings. In a prolonged spiritual crisis that stretched his life to the boundary of suicide, James experienced the nineteenth century's cultural conflict between faith and science, and its philosophical friction between idealism and positivism, as an acutely personal affliction. His career in philosophy was a therapeutic as well as intellectual endeavor, and for him the *via media* offered not merely an attractive philosophical option but an escape from emotional paralysis. James was born in 1842, four years later than Sidgwick and Fouillée, and the various threads of nineteenth-century culture were wound together in his early life. His father, Henry James, Sr., was a minister without a church, a mystical philosopher who found in Swedenborgianism the kind of natural supernaturalism that romantics of his generation prized and his children's generation could neither fully understand nor endorse. William James as a child was more intrigued by science and art than spiritualism. Equipped with such paraphernalia as a microscope and a Bunsen burner, he delighted in experiments that baffled, bored, and occasionally unnerved his less adventuresome and more reflective brother Henry. William also studied painting seriously, attracted, suitably enough, more to the restless dynamism of romantics like Delacroix than to the well-ordered grace of neoclassicism. His father, whose sizeable inheritance and even more sizeable impulsiveness kept the family on the move between Europe and America, alternately encouraged and discouraged these scientific and artistic inclinations in his firstborn. As James approached his twentieth birthday, he embodied the tension between the experimental naturalism and the romantic aestheticism of the era.

He studied with the American artist William Morris Hunt in Newport and flirted seriously with a career in painting before he decided against it, regretfully, and enrolled at Harvard. There he studied first chemistry, then comparative anatomy, and finally medicine, all without enthusiasm or distinction. After a harrowing research trip to South America accompanying the naturalist Louis Agassiz, James returned to Boston in 1866 to begin his internship at Massachusetts General Hospital. The primitive state of nineteenth-century medical science alarmed him, however, and he was demoralized by the prospect of administering its quirky remedies for the rest of his life. His enthusiasm for practicing medicine could scarcely have been bolstered by the gruesome "cures" James himself endured in an effort to find relief from the various combinations of back pain, insomnia, eye trouble, and intestinal problems that plagued him during these years. In search of better therapy and hoping to study the physiological psychology stirring in the laboratories of Hermann von Helmholtz and Wilhelm Wundt, he sailed to Germany in 1867, where his encounter with Dilthey was a pleasant distraction from his desultory visits to spas and lectures. While in Germany, James sank into the malaise that continued for five years and carried him from near-suicidal depression to the affirmation of ideas that would serve as the armature for his psychology and philosophy.[35]

Whatever the hidden psychological dimensions of his despondency, at the conscious level James was distressed by the deterministic implications of the positivism championed by Helmholtz, Wundt, Spencer, and his own friend Chauncey Wright. When he returned to Cambridge to complete his medical training after eighteen months in Germany, his depression intensified until in February, 1870, something inside him shattered and he "became a mass of quivering fear." Peering inside to survey the ruins of his sanity, he recalled the "absolutely non-human" madness of an epileptic patient he had encountered, and he contemplated the awful prospect of meeting a similar fate. From the depths of that "collapse," as he called it, James ascended very slowly. By his own account, the decisive infusions of hope came from reading Wordsworth, whose poetry had earlier lifted the sagging spirits of J. S. Mill and T. H. Green, and Renouvier, whose defense of free will persuaded James that determinism is logically untenable and inconsistent with our experience of choice.[36] Yet the sustenance James drew from Wordsworth's romanticism and Renouvier's neo-Fichtean voluntarism was inadequate, by itself, to steel him against scientific argument. He was, after all, himself a scientist, although of admittedly idiosyncratic inclinations, and the science of his day pointed in the direction of an all-embracing determinism. Feeling himself restrained by science from wholeheartedly accepting the concept of free will that rescued him from despair, James found an escape from that impasse in Darwin's theory of natural selection. Human consciousness, James reasoned, including the ability to select and attend to specific features of experience, could not have evolved without selective pressure. If the human mind serves an evolutionary function, then the freedom to choose, far from contradicting scientific naturalism, instead finds in Darwinian theory its explanation as a useful adaptation that has helped man survive. The divergence of this interpretation from Darwin's own remained unknown during Darwin's lifetime, and James derived from it a confident belief that the lessons of science and the lessons of idealism are congruent. Man is not "the fatal automaton which a *merely* instinctive animal would be," James concluded, because his reason chooses freely among the various impulses, the spontaneous variations of the evolutionary process, that appear simultaneously in consciousness.[37] This fusion of naturalism and voluntarism redeemed James from his crisis, but his experience of personal fragmentation left a lingering taste of life's fragility. His brush with madness convinced him, as he explained in a letter to his future wife, "that the deepest meaning of things may be revealed in the Tragical."[38] James understood that the consequences of freedom could be defeat as well as victory, and that sensitivity to the precariousness of life was a distinguishing feature of his thought.

As James's reading of Wordsworth, Renouvier, and Darwin was decisive in helping him resolve the philosophical aspect of his personal crisis, so his appointment to a teaching position in anatomy and physiology at Harvard in 1872 helped resolve his vocational dilemma. His courtship of Alice Howe Gibbons, which culminated in their marriage in 1878, eased the anxieties stemming from his unsteady personal relationships. Thus relatively stabilized philosophically, professionally, and socially, James embarked on the research that eventuated in his epochal *Principles of Psychology* (1890). James's analysis, which rocked back and forth between the positivism of physiological psychology and the voluntarism of neo-Kantianism, evinced the persistent tension pulling him from the experimental naturalism of the laboratory to the mysterious depths of conscious experience. James's refusal to ignore the uncategorizable quality of mental life led him to sympathize with Sidgwick's activities in the Society for Psychical Research, and his trips to Europe during the 1880s and 1890s were as likely to involve excursions into strange psychic phenomena as they were to involve discussions of brain physiology. While neither James nor Sidgwick was credulous, neither were they cynical about parapsychology. Their suspensions of disbelief—which may seem silly now—represented to them merely the logical extensions of their conviction that because neither orthodox religion, nor positivistic science, nor philosophy in its idealist or empiricist forms, had succeeded in making sense of how we know, an extended empiricism must be sensitive to all forms of experience.[39]

That sensitivity manifested itself in James's *The Will to Believe* (1897) and *The Varieties of Religious Experience* (1902), in which he introduced radically new criteria to the discussion of faith's justification. He argued that belief, whether religious or otherwise, can have genuine experiential consequences whose importance cannot be excluded from philosophical consideration. James shifted the focus of religious investigations away from metaphysical inquiry into the nature of religious objects and toward internal examination of the nature of religious experience. Although he denied that the questions of traditional theology can ever be answered, he denied with equal vehemence that such knowledge moots the question of religion. He believed, as did Sidgwick, that faith can be no more than provisional, yet he emphasized, as did Fouillée, that faith can nevertheless play a decisive part in shaping our attitudes and, consequently, our actions.[40]

James's critics have long lamented his failure to express his ideas in systematic form or to present an overall synthesis of his philosophy. Despite the chronic ailments he suffered and the melancholy that hovered around the fringes of his inner life, he was a dynamic teacher whose vitality made him something of a celebrity as a public lecturer. He was unable to contain his energy in his study; like his rambling summer house in New Hampshire, all the doors of his mind seemed to open outward. Yet because he expressed many of his most important ideas in short essays and public lectures, the arresting formulations he adopted made his arguments attractive but rather elliptical. Like Dilthey, to whom he is frequently compared, James was a polymath whose range and protean quality have been reflected in the fate his ideas have suffered at the hands of his disciples. The differences between his personality and Dilthey's, however, are mirrored in the different shapes of their work. The reclusive Dilthey churned out thousands of pages of drafts, burrowing deeper and deeper into ideas and leaving false trails that have puzzled his critics and contributed to the misunderstanding of his thought. By contrast, it was James's popularity as a lecturer that prevented him from concentrating sufficiently on a single subject to provide more than sketches of the comprehensive philosophical treatises he never found time to write. James's thought may form a coherent mosaic, but the sparkle of the individual pieces tends to obscure the larger pattern of ideas.[41]

James tried consciously in his writings to stifle the impulse to systematize, which he considered an obstacle preventing philosophers from seeing the fullness of experience. The habit of conceptual thinking chops life into awkwardly shaped pieces, which crumble under analysis of that sort and thus cannot be accurately fitted back together. The great attraction of Bergson for James was precisely his insistence that reality itself is both continuous and open-ended, that it does not conform to the conceptual distinctions philosophers since Plato had invoked to make sense of it systematically. James was enthusiastic about Pearson, Mach, and Poincaré for similar reasons: the disappearance of eternal verities in mathematics and the physical sciences made it impossible to see in the universe anything more than "a kind of aimless weather." As human experience "boiled over" the limits of Ptolemaic astronomy, Euclidean space, Aristotelian logic, scholastic metaphysics, and finally the elegant systems of Kepler and Newton, it became apparent that scientific laws "are only approximations" and that "human arbitrariness has driven divine necessity from scientific logic."[42]

Yet the spirit of the *via media* was the spirit of Tennyson, whom James and Sidgwick in particular were fond of quoting, rather than the spirit of Henry Adams or Nietzsche, resolute rather than hopeless or nihilistic. The loss of certainty opened the way to a new understanding of experience and a new conception of truth, which James articulated most fully in *Pragmatism* (1907). Unlike Nietzsche, who concluded that because experience and truth are inevitably perspectival we can jettison our useless past and set sail beyond good and evil, James argued that while loosening the grip of religious and scientific dogma frees man to make the values to steer his culture, he must inevitably return from the "speculative voyage," to use James's term, and be "washed ashore on the *terra firma* of concrete life again."[43] Experience, in short, not simply desire, must be the source and test of our ideas, and we must consequently acknowledge their tentativeness even as we resist the despair and solipsism such awareness can engender.

During the last few years before his death in 1910, James worked intermittently on what he called "a systematic work on philosophy," but it is doubtful he would ever have completed it for a variety of temperamental and philosophical reasons. Among the notes he prepared for such a work, James scribbled on an envelope "philosophers paint pictures," and those words, at once descriptive and prescriptive, capture James's self-image.[44] Unlike Kant or Hegel, James did not consider himself an architect of an enduring structure of ideas but a painter of experience in all its manifold dimensions. His own life was a colorful and continually changing kaleidoscope, and he expressed, perhaps more effectively than any other thinker, the vibrant tones and darker shadings that are juxtaposed in consciousness. By capturing in his writings an image of experience more vivid and vital than the lifeless abstractions of idealism and more richly textured than the mechanistic physiology of positivism, he fulfilled as a philosopher the ambitions he seemed to abandon when he gave up painting to pursue a career in science.

To leave the world of William James and enter the world of John Dewey is to experience a peculiar sense of dislocation: the landscape seems familiar, yet the atmosphere is strangely different. Dewey's instrumentalism, first elaborated in his contributions to *Studies in Logical Theory* (1903), so forcefully impressed James, who was in the midst of formulating his pragmatic theory of truth, that James publicly embraced Dewey as a philosophical ally and privately proclaimed him a hero.[45] Dewey likewise acknowledged the striking resemblances between their ideas and identified *The Principles of Psychology* as his inspiration. Yet the surviving correspondence between James and Dewey suggests that their mutual admiration came as something of a surprise to both of them, following as it did upon their differences in the 1880s, when James was probing the physiology of knowledge and Dewey was proclaiming a neo-Hegelian idealism.[46] Indeed, it would be difficult to find two thinkers originally more different in orientation and character than James and Dewey. The common position they occupied from 1900 to 1910 testifies as strikingly as the resemblances between Green and Sidgwick to the convergence of thinkers from different backgrounds to the philosophy of the *via media*.

In contrast to James, who as the quintessential insider hobnobbed with elites wherever he went on either side of the Atlantic, Dewey was raised in modest surroundings as the son of a Burlington, Vermont, grocer. James's haphazard secondary education did not block his admission to Harvard. His self-confessed ignorance of basic medicine did not block his completion of his M.D. degree—he was personally shepherded through his examinations by Dr. Oliver Wendell Holmes, Sr., an old family friend. Dewey, on the other hand, after successfully completing his courses at the University of Vermont and languishing in two unsatisfying high school teaching jobs, applied for a fellowship to study philosophy at the newly opened Johns Hopkins University in 1882, and was turned down. Undaunted, he wrote back seeking a less generous grant, and his letter, characteristically simple, earnest, and awkward, reveals the gulf dividing his circumstances, his personality, and his prose, from James's: "Of course I should not make the request if I were not so situated pecunarily as to make it almost impossible to go on without aid and I feel confident that if I were to secure that aid, I could render a good account of it, and of myself."[47] When that homely appeal too was rejected, Dewey borrowed money to finance his studies and proceeded, from that unpromising beginning, to carve out a remarkably distinguished career ranging from philosophy and psychology to education and political theory.

While at Johns Hopkins, Dewey encountered a wide variety of gifted minds. Unimpressed by the "very mathematical" logic of Charles S. Peirce and the "purely physiological" psychology of G. Stanley Hall, he was drawn instead to George Sylvester Morris's combination of idealist metaphysics and realist epistemology, a brand of neo-Hegelianism that left what Dewey later termed a "permanent deposit" in his thinking. Like Dilthey, Morris was a student of Trendlenburg, whose philosophy of *Idealrealismus*, together with the idealism of T. H. Green and other British neo-Hegelians, provided the fountainhead of Morris's ideas. Idealism captivated the young Dewey for several reasons. It harmonized with the liberal evangelicalism he had imbibed from his mother, a strict Congregationalist who exerted the principal influence on Dewey in his childhood. The new Congregationalist theology Dewey encountered at the University of Vermont, reflecting the impact of Darwin on common sense realism, stressed the origins of faith in experience and, by extension, the religious component in all of life. The antidualist thrust of this theology found philosophical expression in Morris's modified Hegelianism, which concentrated less on the abstractions of pure being and pure consciousness than on the dynamic, organic connections between mind and body, self and other, man and God. In such an idealism Dewey perceived a way to reconcile the faith instilled by his mother, the pervasive common sense realism of American philosophy (it is revealing that Dewey later characterized even his first mentor at Vermont, the Kantian H. A. P. Torrey, as a realist), the romantic yearning for unity with nature, and the scientific spirit of the post-Darwinian era. Voicing a common refrain of nineteenth-century thought, Dewey explained the "liberation" he found in idealism from the "isolation of self from the world, of soul from body, of nature from God," which he had previously experienced as a "painful oppression" or an "inward laceration." From that affliction Hegel provided an "immense release," dissolving anxieties and antagonisms that Dewey's earlier philosophical studies—by comparison a mere "intellectual gymnastic"—had been unable to soothe. At this time Dewey was strongly attracted also to the poetry of Wordsworth, whose vision of organic wholeness promised relief from the dualisms that disquieted Dewey's mind and his emotions, thus fulfilling "a demand for unification," in his words, "that was doubtless an intense emotional craving, and yet was a hunger that only an intellectualized subject-matter could satisfy."[48]

When Dewey left Johns Hopkins in 1884 to teach philosophy at the University of Michigan, he intended fully to preach the gospel of idealism he· elaborated in his dissertation, a critique of Kant's psychology from a Hegelian viewpoint. After publishing several articles challenging the adequacy of materialistic psychology, he pieced together the arguments developed against Kant on the one hand and against empiricism on the other in his first book, *Psychology* (1887). Because Dewey's essay had stirred up some controversy, his book attracted considerable attention. While Morris not surprisingly praised it, James confessed his disappointment in a letter to the editor of *Mind*, Croom Robertson. As long as Dewey remained bewitched by the notion of a "bare miraculous self," James lamented, he would succeed only in taking "all the edge and definiteness away from the particulars" of life, thus blurring precisely the quality of experience James was to emphasize in his own *Principles of Psychology*.[49] The strength of Dewey's affiliation with idealism in those years is apparent from his appreciative essay of 1889, "The Philosophy of Thomas Hill Green." Particularly significant was his emphasis on Green's social and political ideas, which had a profound impact on Dewey's thought that persisted long after his interest in Green's metaphysics faded.[50]

Dewey's growing concern with social issues also manifested itself in the lectures he delivered before the Students' Christian Association during his years in Michigan. Customarily ignored or dismissed as quaint relics left over from Dewey's evangelical heritage, these lectures provide decisive evidence concerning the origins of his mature philosophical position, and without them the distinctive confidence in democracy and science evident in his later work is incomprehensible. In "Christianity and Democracy," an address he delivered on March 27, 1892, Dewey argued that democracy, understood not merely in political but also social and economic terms, is "the means by which the revelation of truth is carried on." Truth, Dewey insisted, is not revealed once and for all but created in time by individuals participating in a community dedicated to and fired by religious ideas. Truth is created on earth by man's thought, reason, and activity. "Man's action is found in his social relationships," according to Dewey, "the way in which he connects with his fellows." Democracy is uniquely suited to facilitate the "revelation of truth," because only democracy "enables us to get truths in a natural everyday and practical sense." This is not something mystical but a concrete challenge: "to fuse into one the social and religious motive." Thus for Dewey democracy becomes God's vehicle; faith is to manifest itself in social action. Religious values are incorporated into a form of social organization through which the individual can find the truth that can set him free, "free negatively, free from sin, free positively, free to live his own life, free to express himself." The idea of a God realizing himself on earth through human agency, as well as the idea of freedom as both negative and positive, can be traced through Green to Hegel. But the highlighting of democracy as the only means to accomplish this end, and the conception of the entire enterprise as a strictly human project, are distinctively Deweyan shadings that signal the decisive change in his thought from idealism to naturalism.[51]

Dewey was in the process of redirecting his search for radical freedom and expressive unity away from the world of spirit to the world of experience when James's *Principles of Psychology* appeared, and it provided, as Dewey wrote to James, "a great stimulus to mental freedom."[52] In an important but overlooked account of his intellectual development written in 1911, Dewey located the "point of transition" in 1891, precisely when he first encountered James's psychology. He contended that James's "biological conception" of experience was "perhaps the fundamental thing" prompting his reorientation. Dewey's enthusiasm for science, as his own testimony together with the evidence of his writings demonstrate conclusively, was inspired by the luminous portrait of experience James provided. Empiricism as James understood it was compatible with Dewey's deepest religious feelings. Just as importantly, it was compatible with the opposition to atomism and hedonism, and the commitment to the ideal of organic unity, which Dewey derived from Morris, Green, and Hegel, and never relinquished throughout his long career. James's provocative arguments pushed Dewey into a fresh confrontation with several problems, including the need to adapt Kant's and Hegel's logic to "the conditions of actual scientific inquiry"; the need to relate "reflection and reason to conduct" in order to develop a "theory of more organic connection between thought and action" in ethics; and the need to reconstruct educational theory in light of this radically altered conception of experience.[53]

To meet these objectives Dewey invented a new set of intellectual tools. His seminal essay "The Reflex Arc Concept in Psychology" (1896) and *The Study of Ethics: A Syllabus* (1894) both demonstrated not only his assimilation of James's ideas but his ability to apply them in fresh and productive ways. Dewey thus wove together in his "experimental idealism" the romantic philosophy of Hegel, embroidered with a democratic design by Green, and the naturalistic conception of experience, made durable by Darwinian biology and cleansed of positivism by James's psychology. Like all the philosophers of the *via media*, he believed that in such a fabric of ideas the richness of religious impulses could be blended with the toughness of the scientific temper.

When Dewey accepted a position as chairman of the Department of Philosophy, Psychology, and Education at the University of Chicago, he was heralded as a distinguished psychologist and ethicist with wide ranging interests. When he left Chicago for Columbia in 1904, with his reputation as a philosopher still rising, he was equally renowned as a theorist and reformer of education. Dewey had been associated with a group of reform-minded intellectuals at the University of Michigan, and during his decade at Chicago his interests shifted increasingly from speculation to social reform. He had visited Jane Addams's Hull House in 1892, and when he and his family moved to Chicago he became actively involved in its activities. Simultaneously his participation in formal religious activities dropped off. Projecting his religious feelings onto democratic social action, he lost interest in church-going and concentrated his energies on institutions such as Hull House and the laboratory school he established at the University of Chicago to test his ideas about education. Dewey attracted increasing national attention in Chicago, yet he remained personally modest, gentle, and reserved. He was admired for his sincerity more than his charm, and for his honesty more than his wit. Like his writing, Dewey's personality was never to sparkle as James's did. Given his reticence, Dewey's resignation from the University of Chicago because of bureaucratic wrangling over the administration of the university-affiliated schools surprised many observers, who considered it out of character. But this step merely signaled the beginning of a new and more self-assertive phase in a career distinguished at every stage by quiet, principled decisions.[54]

From the time of his arrival in New York in 1904 until his death in 1952, Dewey stood as a beacon not only in philosophical but also political controversies. His contributions to political theory grew directly from his ideas about epistemology and ethics, but they reflect concerns different from those of the older philosophers of the *via media*, all of whom were dead well before the outbreak of World War I. For that reason, rather than discussing his politics with theirs, in Chapter Five, I will examine Dewey's political philosophy in Chapters Nine and Ten, placing his ideas in the context of debates that raged in America and Europe between 1900 and 1920 about social democracy and progressivism. In his career and in his writings, Dewey embodied the transition between a generation raised in the mid-nineteenth century and preoccupied with the relation of religion and science, a problem they sought to solve by rethinking the focus of philosophy and the role of the philosopher, and a later generation that sought solutions to social and economic problems by rethinking political activity according to the radical conceptions of knowledge and responsibility they derived from their predecessors. Dewey understood politics as a form of problem solving, as part of a general cultural project involving democratic participation to achieve ideals generated from collective experience rather than revealed by theology or ideology. Politics, like all knowledge as the philosophers of the *via media* saw it, is uncertain because it is a human enterprise. Although our knowledge can only be provisional, we can skirt despair if we use the compass of accumulated cultural experience to help us choose among the options open to us. In the historical sensibility of these thinkers, the weight of the past and the potential of the future are held in delicate balance, for individuals collectively must determine their own values and decide their course, recognizing as boundaries human experience rather than God's or nature's law. Philosophy is freed from religion and science but constrained to explore the dimensions of possibility implicit in experience and to suggest reasons why some courses of action should be pursued and others avoided or even obstructed.

The philosophers of the *via media* shouldered an enormous burden by conceiving of their task in this way. When they cut the moorings to certainty, they simultaneously liberated the imagination and imposed an awkward responsibility on the thinkers who would presume to provide guidance in such an uncertain universe of ideas. Given the shattering effects of war and revolution, the uneasiness that accompanies doubt, and the persistent yearning for authority, it is perhaps not surprising that the "very inclusive" new philosophical school of James's dreams never materialized. Yet he and Dewey, along with Dilthey, Green, Sidgwick, and Fouillée, did suggest in different ways by the extent of their convergence that philosophy might continue to develop in the direction of a *via media* leading toward radically new conceptions of how we know and what we are to do. The moment vanished, of course, and philosophy followed a different course toward professionalization, in part to advance and protect personal careers by authorizing certain sorts of inquiry, and in part, perhaps, precisely to evade problems that could no longer be solved by appealing to authority and to evade questions that could no longer be answered with any certainty. To the generation of philosophers who embraced the kind of uncertainty that has unsettled many of their successors, however, doubt opened doors of possibility and suggested avenues of change. Some of them, including Dilthey, Sidgwick, and James, remained skeptical whether their intellectual explorations, and the sorts of political and social reforms their ideas implied, could remove the shadow of tragedy trailing man's efforts to manage his fate. Others, notably Green, Fouillée, and Dewey, found strength in their confidence that man was moving forward—albeit slowly and painfully—instead of whirling steadily and sadly in circles. Despite harboring different hopes for their own ideas, however, they shared the conviction that the answers of eighteenth- and nineteenth-century thinkers to the questions of philosophy were unsatisfactory. Before discussing the radical theory of knowledge they sought to erect, I will examine their criticism of the competing epistemological traditions they rejected.

3. Clearing the Field:
Critiques of Associationism and Idealism

The philosophers of the *via media* wanted to rethink the entire enterprise of epistemology. They saw that standard distinctions between mind and matter in experience, and between what is in and what is outside consciousness, perpetuated a set of misleading dichotomies inherited from the seventeenth century. They challenged prevailing paradigms of knowledge in order to set philosophy on a new course. They understood that Descartes had taken a fateful step. In the wake of his attempt to ground knowledge on experience by sweeping aside appeals to authority, philosophers turned their attention away from deductive logic and metaphysics and set out to find certainty through perception and reflection. Descartes established his epistemology on the undeniable fact of self-awareness. His admitted failure to solve the mind-body problem, however, slowly eroded the foundation of his philosophy.[55] From Descartes's unsteady interactionist position, his successors diverged into the empiricist and rationalist camps. Locke insisted that organisms react to sensory stimuli; Leibniz countered that consciousness actively organizes perceptions. Although Kant tried to transcend these distinctions, as I have noted, his antinomies sparked a series of struggles between idealists and empiricists that in turn led to the neo-Kantian revival of the late nineteenth century. Dilthey, Green, Sidgwick, Fouillée, James, and Dewey shared a desire to end this persistent squabbling and free philosophy from the tangle of misconceptions originating in Descartes's initial attempt to establish certainty. Important differences of background must be kept in mind while examining the arguments these thinkers advanced, because although they converged toward a similar position, the different emphases of their critiques reflect different preoccupations. Strong bonds tied James, Sidgwick, and Dilthey to the empiricist tradition. Despite their real and acknowledged debts to Kant, they directed their sharpest attacks against idealists such as Hegel. By contrast, Green, Fouillée, and Dewey, although scarcely uncritical followers of Hegel, drew important insights from idealism, and they concentrated their assaults on empiricists like John Stuart Mill. Their different affiliations notwithstanding, as a group they produced a strikingly congruent series of arguments that together cleared the way for their own radical theory of knowledge.

From its origins in Hobbes and Locke, British empiricism had developed by the late nineteenth century into a compound of several elements. Empiricist psychology modeled itself on empirical science, and it shared the mechanistic determinism characteristic of prevailing scientific theory. According to the associationist analysis, discrete components of sense data provide the foundation for knowledge. The brain associates individual impressions to form ideas, to which the organism responds according to inner physiological drives calibrated to a strict calculus of pleasures and pains. Meaning emerges from the history of past associations, and all ideas can be reduced, in principle at least, to the simple sensations of which they are compounded. Mind figures simply as a passive host in the process of understanding, because it does not effectively control either knowledge or action. After 1870, empiricist psychology came under heavy fire, not only from heretical idealists like Green and Fouillée, but also from philosophers who considered themselves more empirical than the British empiricists. These critics challenged empiricist positions ranging from the basic conceptualization of knower and known to the possibility of positive scientific knowledge, rejecting along the way most of the specific arguments advanced by generations of British psychologists.

Fundamentally, renegade empiricists like James, Dilthey, and Sidgwick denied the adequacy of associationism's mechanistic model of causality as a basis for understanding how we know. They shared Sidgwick's conviction that "no attempt to give a physical explanation of Cognition, or even to analyse it completely into more elementary psychical facts, has succeeded, or in my opinion is likely to succeed." The root of the difficulty lay in the rigid separation of subject from object posited by associationists, a separation that violated James's and Dilthey's more fluid conception of experience. "The world of our experience," James wrote, "consists at all times of two parts, an objective and a subjective part, of which the former may be incalculably more extensive than the latter, and yet the latter can never be omitted or suppressed." If the experiencing self stands at the intersection of external matter and internal reflection, then a lively interplay between subject and object, not merely a chain of sequential associations, accounts for knowledge. In short, empiricists were guilty of fragmenting what Dilthey called the "coherence of mental life."[56] Green and Dewey, by contrast, sought to escape the dualism of British empiricism by turning to the dialectic. Echoing Green in an early essay, Dewey maintained that Hegel provided "the completed Method of Philosophy" because he successfully bridged the gap separating subject from object by establishing a dialectical relation between the knower and the known.[57] Dewey later adopted a more critical attitude toward Hegel's theory of knowledge, but he never retreated from his antidualist stance; indeed, as he developed his instrumentalism, he became critical of Green too on precisely this score. By lifting the veil imposed by dualism, Dewey, James, and Dilthey uncovered richly textured contours of experience that eluded British empiricism.

According to these radicals, the materialism underlying empiricism presented even greater difficulties than its dualism, because materialism saddled associationist psychology with a clumsy scientistic method incapable of penetrating the recesses of human understanding. Positivists and empiricists used a mechanical model of knowledge "based upon a truncated experience," in Dilthey's words, a model that was "from the outset perverted by an atomistic theoretical conception of psychic life." Whereas epistemology ought to be grounded on "whole, full, unmutilated experience,"[58] positivist psychology locked itself in a materialistic cage. James described the materialist world view as "a monstrous abridgement of life," and he argued that the real world is "more intricately built than physical science allows."[59] There are more things in philosophy, James cautioned contemporary Horatios, than are dreamt of by their science.

Scientific psychology could not establish its validity because it stumbled over a basic inconsistency. Materialists, from the Greek atomists to the logical positivists, have found it difficult to justify intuited principles according to empirical procedures. Sidgwick pointed out that empiricists since Locke had relied on the mind's ability to establish relations among discrete sensations, yet they had discovered no empirical foundation for that claim. Similarly, the principles of inference underlying the central process of association and guiding the construction of knowledge out of sense data rested on no satisfactory empirical grounds. These elements of empirical psychology, Sidgwick concluded, had no firmer basis than the claims of metaphysical intuitionists, and although he did not mention Green explicitly, the reference to Green's idealism nevertheless seems clear. While Sidgwick considered himself an empiricist, he demanded that empiricism divest itself of materialism and admit the inadequacy of scientific naturalism as a model for understanding human knowledge. In an unpublished essay probably written about 1870, he put this crucial point succinctly: "We are impelled to science by a desire to get knowledge, to philosophy by dissatisfaction with the knowledge we have got."[60]

Not surprisingly, dissident idealists emphasized the materialism of empiricist psychology in dissecting its explanation of knowledge. As Fouillée wrote, "None but the incompetent can accept the materialistic dogma, and believe that brute atoms put together in a certain way, like the parts of a machine, eventually form something that thinks." He dismissed association-ism and positivism abruptly, concluding that "there are no materialists among philosophers worthy of the name."[61] Green agreed, calling for epistemology to return to its study of "the conditions of knowledge, which forms the basis of all Critical Philosophy, whether called by the name of Kant or no." Science as an epistemological tool must "presuppose a prin-ciple which is not itself any one or number of such matters of fact," and that inconsistency, Green concluded, invalidated associationism's claims to an empirical foundation.[62] In his first published essay, "The Metaphysical Assumptions of Materialism" (1882), Dewey focused on this decisive argu-ment, and although he later discarded the underlying idealist metaphysics, he never altered his belief that the reduction of mind to phenomena "is absurd." In order to "transcend phenomena," he contended, "there must be something besides a phenomenon." He extended the argument to draw out its inconsistency: "To prove that mind is a phenomenon of matter, it is obliged to assume the possibility of ontological knowledge—i.e., real knowl-edge of real being; but that real knowledge is necessarily involved with a subject that knows." In short, associationists faced a dilemma. Either mind constitutes merely another material phenomenon, in which case it can have no real knowledge, or empiricists must assume that it is a "substance." In either case, Dewey concluded, the arguments ultimately proved to be self-destructive, and philosophers seeking an adequate understanding of knowl-edge found themselves forced to reject British empiricism.[63] The weakness of Dewey's critique, as he later recognized, lay in its reliance on a Hegelian version of what "knowledge" means. Yet even after he freed himself from dialectical logic, the concept of "intelligence" he adopted was a far cry from associationism.

Beyond the dualism and materialism of empiricist epistemology, these critics focused on its atomistic conception of experience. Such arguments relied heavily on Green's analysis of Hume, perhaps Green's single most important contribution to the radical theory of knowledge. If Mill's *Examination of Sir William Hamilton's Philosophy* brought down the curtain on Scottish realism, Green's introduction to Hume's *Works* marked the opening of British philosophy to idealist criticisms of associationism. Empiricists had reasoned, following Locke, that the mind puts together complex ideas from simple sensations. Green reversed the sequence and insisted that relations, rather than being built up from the raw data of sense experience, are instead given in original experience.[64] We do not construct relations from discrete sense data; sensations exist for us within the context of an immediately experienced pattern of relations. Whereas Hume denied the reality of experienced relations, Green maintained that epistemology could escape the quicksand of skepticism that enveloped Hume only by abandoning atomism.

Green's emphasis on the relatedness of experience profoundly influenced James and Dewey, as well as a whole generation of British philosophers. James first approached British empiricism through Green's edition of Hume, and James's lifelong aversion to atomism derived, at least in part, from Green's treatment of Hume's failure to provide for relations in experience.[65] According to James, Hume illustrated the inadequacy of empirical psychology's empiricism: for the real experience of "felt relations," associationists substituted a false atomism. In an important early essay, "On Some Omissions of Introspective Psychology" (1884), James lamented "the mangling of thought's stream" in British psychology. He argued that empiricists perverted experience "from the continuously flowing thing it is" and "changed it into a 'manifold,' broken into bits, called discrete." In that false atomistic form, experience became the subject of "one of the most tedious and interminable quarrels that philosophy has to show," a quarrel that James, following Green, sought to settle by recovering the reality of relations and insisting that we experience life as "sensibly continuous," rather than as a "bundle of separate ideas." As he insisted in *The Principles of Psychology*, "*There is no manifold of coexisting ideas*; the notion of such a thing is a chimera." Although James's philosophy of radical empiricism differed in important respects from Green's unconventional idealism, Green's insistence on the relatedness of experience provided one of the sources of James's celebrated image of consciousness as a continuously flowing stream.[66]

While neither Fouillée nor Dilthey was preoccupied with the legacy of empiricism that dominated the Anglo-American philosophical tradition, both of them criticized the atomism of associationist psychology. In *L'Evolutionisme des idées-forces* (1890; cited hereafter as *The Evolution of idées-forces*), Fouillée frequently cited James's essay "On Some Omissions of Introspective Psychology" to establish the connectedness of experience and to demonstrate the problems involved in assuming that "perceptions are originally *isolated*." Experience is not a simple sequence of discrete sensations, according to Fouillée, but is at the most fundamental level a continuity.[67] Dilthey likewise rejected the atomistic assumptions of empiricist epistemology as false to the fullness of life. Atomism is a "psychological castle in the air," he wrote, because "all perceptions are in consciousness as a relation of part to whole. A simple percept is an abstraction."[68] Dilthey used his critique of associationism as a basis for his hermeneutics. His language and emphases thus distinguished his use of the idea of relation from that of Green, James, and Fouillée, yet his critique of empiricism's disconnected model of experience resembled theirs.

These theorists also rejected earlier empiricists' characterization of mind as a passive recipient of sense data. John Stuart Mill, the most prominent target of this campaign, offered physiological explanations for activity even where such explanations were transparently hypothetical. Dilthey protested that the "fundamental power of mental life" lay beyond the scope of such a reductionist psychology. Instead of studying the active functioning of the mind, Mill focused his attention on mental chemistry in a vain search for chain reactions that could unlock the puzzle of understanding.[69] The positivism that Mill imbibed from Comte filtered into his associationism to produce an even less satisfactory epistemology than Hume's, because Mill limited the role of the subject still further and reduced mind to the status of an epiphenomenon. Although the empiricists' passive model of the mind became obvious in Mill's epistemology, the source of this idea lay in Locke's psychology. In a comparison of Locke with Leibniz, Dewey enumerated Locke's "marks of sensation" and adopted Leibniz's critique. "Pure passivity of any kind is a myth," Dewey argued. Sensation is instead "an activity of the mind"; it is "the activity of reality made manifest to itself."[70] Although buried beneath a layer of Hegelian jargon, the seeds of Dewey's mature instrumentalism are perceptible in that early assessment of knowledge as active.

An element in the critique of empiricist epistemology, which only occasionally surfaced, lay beneath the attacks these theorists launched against the notion of passive knowledge. This argument figured more prominently in the evaluation of utilitarianism, because it centered on the hedonistic psychology at the core of British ethical theory, yet it entered epistemological discussions as well because it concerned the basic question of motivation. Empiricism, these rebels charged, rested on a faulty concept of desire. Empiricists assumed that the desire for pleasure could satisfactorily explain human action. That assumption, however, begged a troubling question that psychological hedonists overlook: how can we account for the desire for pleasure? The hedonistic model of motivation does not penetrate beyond the pleasure-pain calculus, and thus even to raise the question seems akin to remarking on the emperor's lack of clothes. Yet this issue lay at the heart of the radical theory of knowledge. Green in his *Prolegomena to Ethics*, Fouillée in *La Psychologie des idées-forces* (cited hereafter as *The Psychology of idées-forces*), Dewey in his and Tufts's *Ethics*, and James in *The Principles of Psychology* all posed the same question: why do we consider some experiences pleasant and others painful, and why do individual preferences vary so much?[71] How do we account for what James called "man's inner or subjective being, his psychic faculties or dispositions?"

James answered by emphasizing the "active element in all conscious-ness," and in a crucial passage in *The Principles of Psychology* he elaborated his argument: "It is the home of interest,—not the pleasant or the painful as such, but that within us to which pleasure and pain, the pleasant and the pain-ful, speak. It is the source of effort and attention, and the place from which appear to emanate the fiats of the will." James claimed to understand only imperfectly this "*self of all other selves*," as he called it, but he refused to ignore it merely because its adequate explanation eluded him.[72] The mysterious core of human motivation fascinated and puzzled all of the philo-sophers of the *via media*. Although they offered different explanations of its character, they agreed that there is more to experience than the passive reception of sense data and the straightforward calculation of pleasure and pain that associationist psychology took for granted.

Associationism substituted investigation into the origins of ideas for the philosophical consideration of their meaning, a mistake traceable to the empiricists' failure to recognize the active, evaluative capacity of the mind. The search for antecedents and concomitants does not exhaust the questions of knowledge, because all knowledge contains a qualitative dimension. A similar concern with meaning and value in experience distinguished Dilthey's hermeneutics, Dewey's instrumentalism, and James's pragmatism from the tradition of British empiricism. As James wrote in an early essay, "Rational-ity, Activity, and Faith" (1882), we must strive to understand "the real *meaning*" of our impulses, not merely to account for their physiological progress from the nerve endings to the brain.[73] Associationist psychology aimed at description and explanation, both of which were legitimate aspects of epistemology. But the partisans of an enlarged empiricism agreed that philosophy must set its sights beyond these more proximate goals on the ultimate achievement of understanding.

Understanding involves recognition of the sociocultural dimensions of human experience, still another aspect of knowledge that British empiricists overlooked. When psychologists such as Mill took the individual as the unit of investigation, they falsified experience by ripping man from his social environment. The radical theorists of knowledge decisively rejected that individualistic theory of man, insisting against the Hobbesian model that individuals are social beings and that epistemology must examine social experience to understand how we know and why we act. Scientific psychology excluded the contents of experience, in which meaning, and thus sociocultural context, is inherently involved.[74] Such empiricism, restricted to a formalistic analysis, only skimmed the surface of human experience.

Finally, the static quality of empiricist epistemology came under the cross fire of restless critics like James and Dilthey, who drew ammunition from Darwinian theory and the new science of the late nineteenth century, and straying idealists like Green and Fouillée, who were equipped with neo-Platonic and Hegelian theories of change as emanation and dialectical progression. All these thinkers contended that the historical quality of experience and knowledge placed the epistemology of theorists from Locke to Mill on very unsteady ground, and they linked the ahistorical quality of associationist psychology with the associationists' failure to recognize the sociocultural and value-laden quality of experience. Together with their analysis of the empiricists' dualistic, mechanistic, and atomistic model of subject-object interaction, and their critique of the conception of mind as a passive receptor, these arguments provided the philosophers of the *via media* with a powerful arsenal for their campaign against the British epistemological tradition.

They were equally critical of Hegelian idealism, which relied on a dialectical method incapable of bridging the gulf that yawned between life as experienced and the notion of pure, unmediated subjectivity. Although Green seems to have followed Hegel's philosophy quite closely in formulating his own ideas, his *Works* contain only two explicit references to Hegel. The first, which concerns politics, will be considered later; the second, in which he discussed Hegel's idealism in a review of John Caird's *Introduction to the Philosophy of Religion*, reveals an important difference between Green's British version of idealism and the more transcendental philosophy of Hegel. Green chided Caird for having been "too much overpowered by Hegel," not so much because of his conclusions, but rather because he followed Hegel's version of the dialectical method. Hegel, Green argued, proceeded "not by interrogating the world, but by interrogating his own thoughts." Thus Green ironically restated Marx's critique of Hegel: instead of beginning with the world of experience, Hegel remained a prisoner of the Cartesian *cogito* and tried to establish his dialectic on an unacceptable notion of pure subjectivity. "A well-grounded conviction," Green wrote, "has made men refuse to believe that any dialectic of the discursive intelligence would instruct them in the reality of the world."[75] Reality is not thought swallowed up in consciousness, it is instead the object thought comprehends. Consciousness cannot provide a sufficient foundation for knowledge, because knowledge derives only from experience, from "interrogating the world." While Green himself was lured into some metaphysical conclusions whose ties to the reality of the world were at best tenuous, he did resist the seductive pull of the dialectic.

Fouillée likewise dismissed Hegel's notion of a pure subject as a "metaphysical hypothesis and not a fact of psychological experience." Hegel argued in *The Phenomenology of Mind* that the subject encounters external reality through a dialectical process in which the pure subjectivity of the self confronts the pure objectivity of matter and transcends both stages to achieve self-consciousness. For his part, Fouillée insisted that thought is originally and at the same time unmediated consciousness and the representation of objects; their initial separation in Hegel's *Phenomenology* violated the facts of experience. Fouillée intended through his doctrine of *idées-forces* to eliminate that false dichotomy and to emphasize "the intimate union of being, thought, and action."[76] As Green, echoing Marx, challenged Hegel's dialectic because it was insufficiently grounded in experience, so Fouillée repeated Marx's objection to Hegel's neglect of praxis.

Green and Fouillée tried to redirect idealist epistemology toward the world of experience instead of reflection, yet they never considered themselves empiricists. The same cannot be said of Dewey. In two autobiographical accounts Dewey chronicled his progression from affiliation with Hegel and Green to his mature philosophy of instrumentalism. He recounted his struggle between "a native inclination toward the schematic and formally logical," which was nurtured by Morris at Johns Hopkins and drew him toward dialectical logic and the idea of organic development, and "those incidents of personal experience that compelled me to take account of actual material."[77] Dewey's writings confirm the accuracy of his perception of that conflict. His first published essay invoked idealist principles to criticize the metaphysical assumptions of materialism. In his essay "Kant and Philosophic Method," published two years later in 1884, he offered Hegel's dialectic as a talisman enabling philosophers to avoid the difficulties of Cartesian rationalism and British empiricism without accepting Kant's antinomies.[78]

While still at Johns Hopkins, though, Dewey was also becoming aware of the "new psychology" through his exposure to G. Stanley Hall. Although Dewey himself never developed a feel for experimental psychology, two essays published in 1886 suggest that he was beginning to be pulled in opposite directions. In "The Psychological Standpoint," he adopted a position with obvious affinities to Hegel and Green, arguing that "the individual consciousness is but the process of realization of the universal consciousness through itself." In "Psychology as Philosophic Method," on the other hand, hints of his dissatisfaction with idealism filtered through the expressions of "reverential gratitude" to Green. In essence, Dewey was subjecting Green to the critique Green had used on Hegel: with a "purely logical method," he wrote, "the *is* vanishes because it has been abstracted from," whereas "the psychological method starts from the *is*, and thereby gives the basis *and* the ideal for the *ought* and the *must be*."[79] Beneath the lingering shadow of idealism, Dewey's empiricist inclinations were beginning to reveal themselves.

His *Psychology* (1887) evidenced the tension between idealism and empiricism in his thinking, and experimental psychologists did not review the book favorably.[80] Dewey continued to rely on the idea of a universal consciousness to make sense of individuals' knowledge. That legacy of Green's epistemology, however, was becoming increasingly difficult for him to sustain. His final homage to idealism, the almost entirely uncritical essay "The Philosophy of Thomas Hill Green," concluded the first phase of his career, and a review essay that appeared in 1890 on Edward Caird's *The Critical Philosophy of Immanuel Kant* inaugurated a new era. Reversing Green's assessment of Caird's thought, Dewey suggested that Caird surpassed Green's achievement by recognizing that the "notion of a spirit, for which indeed reality exists, but of which nothing may be said," does not constitute an adequate basis for epistemology.[81]

Although he still considered himself an idealist as late as 1894, the label "experimental idealism" that Dewey applied to his philosophy suggests its transitional status. His fondness for the ideas of self-realization and organic wholeness testified to his continuing debt to Green, but he was gradually beginning to draw away from idealism. In his introduction to *Essays in Experimental Logic* (1916), Dewey presented his mature criticism of Hegel and his followers. Idealists "ignored the temporally intermediate and instrumental place of reflection." Instead they "set up as the goal of knowledge (and hence as the definition of true reality) a complete, exhaustive, comprehensive and eternal system in which the plural and immediate data are forever woven into a fabric and pattern of self-luminous meaning." Knowledge, Dewey argued, derives from the application of intelligence to experienced problems. It aims to control "the environment in behalf of human progress and well-being."[82] Dewey's progress from absolutism to experimentalism did not follow a trajectory running directly from idealism to empiricism. Instead his instrumentalism drew elements from various sources to form a new compound. Yet the high road of Hegelianism that he took to intellectual maturity differed dramatically from the path James traveled toward his radical empiricism, and even as he acknowledged their arrival at a similar destination, James pointed out to Dewey that "much depends on the place one starts from." Dewey came from Hegel and his terminology showed the effects of it, James noted, whereas he came from empiricism, and "though we reach much the same goal it superficially looks different from the opposite sides."[83]

The philosophical alliance of James and Dewey was all the more remarkable because James never had any use for Hegel. In the essay "On Some Hegelianisms," which he wrote around 1880, he insisted that the world of experience precedes the world of abstract reasoning. Moreover, he argued that Hegel's attempts to unify the rational and the real, pure subjectivity and pure objectivity, were senseless, because they established logical unities in place of the real differences we encounter in experience.[84] Dilthey raised a similar complaint in his study of Hegel and German idealism. While Hegel performed a useful service by denying the rigidity of static categories through his use of the dialectic, which made "thought fluid and concepts concrete," in the end he dissolved the real separations and tensions of life into the purity of abstract reasoning.[85] The progressive unfolding of the *Weltgeist* at the center of Hegel's vision continued to enchant Green, Fouillée, and Dewey, who read history as a long march forward despite their repudiation of Hegel's account of logic and his theory of knowledge. For James and Dilthey, however, who were more impressed by the persistence of problems than by the prospects for their transcendence, Hegel's philosophy of history represented merely an extension of his delusive abstractions to a grander scale.

The question of these philosophers' relation to Kant is considerably more complicated than their relation to either Mill's empiricism or Hegel's idealism. All were, in a certain restricted sense, neo-Kantians, yet the distance they kept from the neo-Kantian revival of the late nineteenth century must be recognized if the thrust of their radical theory of knowledge is to be properly understood. They were, like Kant, trying to move beyond the conflict between empirical and idealist philosophy. But while some of their contemporaries, such as Rickert, Windelband, Renouvier, and Royce, were crying "back to Kant," they agreed with Dilthey's counsel that philosophy should instead turn "back to reality." "*There* lies the path to a new philosophy," Dilthey insisted, and the other radical theorists of knowledge shared his perspective.[86]

What passed for neo-Kantianism after 1860 owed less to Kant than to the post-Kantian bifurcation of philosophy, and the "back to Kant" movement, centered in Germany but with lively counterparts elsewhere, passed through two stages that together only confirm the failure of Kant's successors to unify the elements of his thought. During the first phase, which began in the 1860s, philosopher-psychologists like Gustav Fechner and Hermann von Helmholtz sacrificed Kant's noumenal realm at the altar of "psycho-physics," the quest for exact measurement of psychological responses to physical stimuli which Dilthey dismissed as "a psychology without mind."[87] The movement entered its second phase after 1875 with the repudiation of this naturalistic orientation and the development, along several diverse paths, of a more idealistic and romantic philosophical style. Members of the Marburg School such as Hermann Cohen, Dilthey argued, were guilty of creating "an artificial logical web, spun from within, floating unsupported in the pure and empty air."[88] The Baden School, on the other hand, under the leadership of Wilhelm Windelband and Heinrich Rickert, sought to establish philosophy on a foundation of absolute transcendental values, and Dilthey likewise repudiated their effort as an uncritical exercise in metaphysical speculation.[89] Dilthey was sensitive to the tensions within Kant's philosophy that led to the elaboration and ultimately the exaggeration of either the phenomenal or the noumenal realms by those invoking his name. But he contended that neither Fichte, Hegel, Helmholtz, nor Rickert had succeeded in resolving problems that necessitated a radical rethinking of experience. To make progress, philosophers would have to conceptualize knowledge in an altogether different way—they would have to turn "back to reality."

Green, as I have already suggested, used Kant's dictum that "the understanding makes nature" to substantiate his rejection of the claims of pure empiricism. Whereas Kant located the pure forms of time and space within individual sensibility, Green insisted that the structuring of experience corresponds to the nature of external reality. Consciousness does not merely place sense data, or phenomena, within a comprehensible context of time and space; it links our experience with an external reality that contains temporal-spatial dimensions. Green thus explicitly rejected the division Kant established between the noumenal and the phenomenal realms. Our experience, Green held, reflects reality directly instead of giving us only a limited image of it.[90] Green accepted Kant's contention that knowledge is active, and he agreed that consciousness brings to experience an element that "is necessary to constitute a world, as the condition under which alone phenomena, i.e., appearances to consciousness, can be related to each other in a single universe."[91] It does not follow, however, that relations are in the structure of consciousness rather than in the world we experience. Fouillée dismissed Kant's pretense of transcendental perception by linking it with Descartes's *cogito*, "an *extract* and an *abstraction*" from the "empirical perception" that provides the basis for knowledge. Like Green, Fouillée judged Kant's conception of time illusory and incoherent. We cannot have an intuition of empty time, he concluded, because the basic idea of time derives from experience rather than intuition. Fouillée's larger critique of Kant simply extended this analysis: Kant's antinomies, and his separation of the noumenal and phenomenal realms, betrayed the facts of experience, in which the internal and external, subject and object, intersect.[92] This junction, Fouillée argued, could best be conceptualized in the doctrine of *idées-forces*. For the empty, rational forms of Kant's transcendental aesthetic, Fouillée considered it necessary to substitute "the most radical and the most complete experience," experience not bounded by speculative distinctions between noumenal and phenomenal but open to the "most profound experience of the real."[93] Fouillée charged Renouvier, the most influential figure in the French Kantian revival known as neocriticism, with failing to take this step toward a new appreciation of experience. As a result Renouvier's philosophy remained excessively formalist, merely another attempt to find refuge for abstract speculation in an "act of mystical faith," hardly the new approach to experience and reality Fouillée sought.[94]

It is difficult to untangle James's relation to Kant and neo-Kantianism.[95] He could be bitterly critical of those he judged too much under Kant's spell. In a letter to Royce in 1882, he referred to the "poor, feeble, dismal, serious Green," and in a letter to Renouvier in the following year he despaired of Fouillée, whom he considered lost in the "intuition of the Absolute Unity."[96] Yet those remarks notwithstanding, the very fact of James's close connections with Royce and Renouvier, and the very real similarities of several of his most important insights to those of Green and especially Fouillée (which will be discussed in Chapter Two), suggest that James's ideas themselves were peculiarly implicated with those of his supposed adversaries in the Kantian camp. Until the late 1890s, for example, despite the uneasiness it caused him, he felt himself unable to break away from the absolutism of Royce's idealist philosophy, and even in 1900 he wrote to Royce, "You are still the centre of my gaze, the pole of my mental magnet." "Different as our minds are," he continued, "yours has nourished mine, as no other social influence ever has, and in converse with you I have always felt that my life was being lived importantly." Yet James did envision himself as Royce's "conqueror," not his ally, and I consider it a mistake to interpret their personal closeness as philosophical agreement. James may indeed have fashioned his philosophy around the magnetic pole of Royce's idealism, but there was at least as much tension as attraction between their ideas.[97]

James's critique of idealist epistemology and his analysis of empiricism's inadequacies formed a congruent whole. He dismissed the simple materialism of associationists and positivists, and in *The Principles of Psychology* he conversely ridiculed idealists' "substantialist view of the soul" as "mind-dust" that "explains nothing and guarantees nothing." The empiricists' dualism found its counterpart in the writings of Kant, James pointed out, and he concluded, in contrast to both, that "*thought may, but need not, in knowing, discriminate between its object and itself.*" The empiricists' "bundle theory" of separate ideas seemed to James a distortion of experience. But he could not understand why "egoists," to use the epithet he applied to Kantians, "make the same mistake as the associationists and sensationalists whom they oppose." We need not invoke the ego to relate the separate parts of experience, he insisted, because "whatever things are thought in relation are thought at the outset in a unity, in a single pulse of subjectivity."[98] Siding with Green and Fouillée on this decisive issue, James claimed that relations are part of experience rather than something we add to experience as we attain knowledge. In a passage that reveals his radical stance, he elaborated his analysis of the inadequacy of both epistemological traditions: "The only service that transcendental egoism has done to psychology has been its protests against Hume's 'bundle' theory of mind. But this service has been ill-performed," because the egoists themselves "believe in the bundle," and in their own systems merely tie it up by invoking the ego as a transcendental string. Neo-Kantians thus ignored the "far more important duty of choosing some of the things the ego ties and appropriating them." The active, selecting role of the self, James argued, eluded idealists as well as empiricists, and for that reason psychology could learn nothing from Kant. James added to this battery of arguments the standard analysis of Kant's synthetic a priori categories of time and space as abstractions from experience, but he extended the point by denying any interest in the basic question of analytic versus synthetic propositions.[99] In sharp contrast to the generation of philosophers who followed him, James believed that philosophy should hunt bigger game than logic.

The Principles of Psychology, in which James clearly distinguished his ideas from the empiricist, idealist, and Kantian traditions, represented his final attempt to discover in psychology a science of the mind. His subsequent ventures into epistemology show greater sensitivity to the suppleness of experience and its resistance to the schematizations of positivist and functionalist psychology, and they testify to James's loss of faith in the possibility of capturing the sparkle of life with a set of categories or causal laws. Two years after the publication of *The Principles of Psychology*, in *Psychology. The Briefer Course*, he wrote emphatically, "This is no science. It is only the hope of a science."[100]

The draft of an unpublished article in the James papers, which Ralph Barton Perry dated between 1890 and 1896, further illuminates his judgment of Kant's strengths and weaknesses. In this article James hoped to "make clear my own position between *pure* empiricism (tabula rasa, w/impressions adding themselves by ass[n]. [association] and no [illegible] mental structure at all) and Kant's." James acknowledged that there is some sort of mental structure. As he put it in the *Principles of Psychology*, part of our intellectual life seems "to have entered the house by the back stairs," or rather "got surreptitiously born in the house."[101] Yet he contended that the congruence of nature with this mental structure is "a painfully attained compromise in which much mental structure has to be thrown away." Moreover, "the most *essential* features of our mental structure, viz. grammar and logic, *violate* the order of nature." Thus, James continued, if we take seriously Kant's "vindication of *some* active part played by the higher mind in the construction of experience, then of course he has refuted Hume." But on the other hand, since his description of the active part of the mind is "entirely false, you can ascribe to him very little merit, and must admit that the truth can be built up much better simply by extending Locke's and Hume's lines."[102]

After teaching a year-long graduate seminar on Kant's three *Critiques* in 1896–1897, James reached the conclusions he presented in "The Pragmatic Method," written in 1898 and revised in 1904. This essay, his strongest rebuke of Kant, indicates that he remained critical of Kant in his later years. Consistent with his earlier judgment, he argued that "Hume can be corrected and built out, and his beliefs enriched, by using Humean principles exclusively, and without making any use of the circuitous and ponderous artificialities of Kant." He then dismissed Kant's philosophy, with uncharacteristic condescension, as "the rarest and most intricate of all possible bric-a-brac museums." Despite his "perfectly delectable" temper, James wrote, Kant was "a mere curio, a 'specimen,'" and he concluded that the "true line of philosophic progress" could be found "not so much *through* Kant as *round* him." Rather than returning to Kant, philosophy should "outflank him, and build herself up into adequate fulness by prolonging more directly the older English lines."[103] Although aspects of James's philosophy, particularly his emphasis on the relatedness of experience and the activity of the knowing subject, derived indirectly from Kant, that debt hardly closed the substantial gap separating his radical empiricism from Kant's critical philosophy.

For the rest of his life, although James became increasingly impatient with mechanistic psychologies and more attuned to the fiduciary aspects of knowledge, he steadfastly maintained his distance from the German epistemological tradition. In both *The Varieties of Religious Experience* (1902) and *A Pluralistic Universe* (1909), he denigrated the relatively superficial knowledge available to idealists who looked to logic rather than experience for clues to the puzzle of subconscious life. James admitted that Bergson's case for the *élan vital* persuaded him to give up logic "fairly, squarely, and irrevocably," and to turn instead toward the immediacy and concreteness of life, which "exceeds our logic, overflows and surrounds it."[104] The key to epistemology's puzzles could be found neither in a science of experimental psychology, nor in the technical apparatus of Hegelian dialectics, nor in the artificial categories of Kant. It lay instead in a new empiricism sensitive to the flux of real experience.

As with James and Dewey, the attempt to understand Dilthey's epistemology in terms of a continuum running from empiricism to idealism can result only in confusion. Dilthey, like James rather than Dewey, began from a position outside either of the dominant epistemological traditions, and as his ideas developed he introduced elements that fit only awkwardly into any existing theory of knowledge. His critique of idealism illustrates the inadequacy of classifying him simply as a neo-Kantian. The German idealists believed that only logic and reflection could penetrate the realm of *Geist*, and they denied that psychology, a scientific pretender to the philosophical throne, could illuminate how we know. Although Dilthey, as I have suggested, shared many of the idealists' objections to empiricism and refuted categorizations of his own thought as a species of psychologism, he advocated consideration of "the critical possibility of psychology" in order to free it from its mechanistic shackles.[105] Epistemology should broaden its horizons, he argued, by turning on the one hand to experimental psychology and on the other to the history of culture. A radical theory of knowledge would recognize that epistemological investigation must not only include "reflection on life and consciousness," which had provided the focus for epistemology since Kant, but must widen its scope to encompass lived experience.

Dilthey resisted the tendency toward abstraction characteristic of much late nineteenth-century neo-Kantian epistemology. In place of the neo-Kantians' fascination with the transcendental self and the metaphysical subject floating in a timeless world of absolute meanings and rational principles, he emphasized the real, living, historical human being, who could be neither torn from his context nor placed in dualistic opposition to a world that entered his experience at every moment. Particularly after 1895, influenced first by critics who derided his search for a descriptive psychology and then by his reading of Husserl's early excursions into phenomenology, he turned increasingly toward hermeneutics and the investigation of culturally mediated experience, "the reflected experience of life," as he called it. Not only did he reject the neo-Kantians' attempts to construct a transcendental epistemology from logic and introspection, he insisted that even lived experience contains inherent cultural, historical dimensions that make the quest for pure knowledge futile.[106]

In revising a study of the Enlightenment, Dilthey argued against contemporary neo-Kantians that their obsession with the conditions rather than the contents of experience derived not from Kant but from Fichte. Kant, he maintained, never claimed to deduce an adequate epistemology from an examination of the form of consciousness. Fichte bore responsibility for directing German epistemology away from experience; Kant's role, Dilthey argued, was more complex. In a review of the burgeoning literature on Kant and *Kritizismus*, Dilthey praised the *Critique of Pure Reason* as "the greatest philosophical work ever produced by the German mind." By isolating the question of how consciousness structures experience, Kant raised the most universal problem of inquiry, and Dilthey's own theory of knowledge relied on Kant's recognition of the mind's activity in shaping the data it receives. Kant, however, failed to carry his criticism far enough, and Dilthey wanted to venture beyond Kant's limits and examine what Kant had overlooked: the historical dimension of experience.[107] Kant uncovered the core of consciousness in experience, but he abstracted his insight and failed to see that knowledge, although shaped by the mind's activity, does not result from the deduction of transcendental forms but from actual experience, from history. Kant, Dilthey concluded, was not sufficiently critical because he was not historical.

Dilthey thus drew elements of his critique of Kant from the empiricism of British psychology and from the dynamic quality of Hegel's phenomenology of mind. His incorporation of ideas from these sources as well as from Husserl and James testifies to the breadth of Dilthey's vision. As with James, if any one characteristic may be said to define his perspective, it was his opposition to systematizing. "We despise construction and love concrete investigation," he wrote, "remaining skeptical toward the machinery of a system. These forms of systematics and dialectics appear to us like a powerful machine operating in the void. At the end of a long life we are content to have multiple paths of scientific investigation leading into the depths of things. We are content to die underway."[108] Given the strength of that commitment to heterodoxy as a desirable, indeed fundamental, intellectual attitude, the difficulty Dilthey's interpreters face in trying to freeze an "essential Dilthey" should come as no surprise.

The philosophers of the *via media* were eclectics both on principle and by temperament. Dilthey's dissatisfaction with systematizing and his preference for "multiple paths" resemble James's criticism of closed systems and his pleas for recognition of the "multiverse" of experience. Sidgwick too resisted efforts to account for knowledge by either a "physical explanation" or an idealistic flight from experience into metaphysics. In his essay "Criteria of Truth and Error" (1900), Sidgwick argued that neither rationalist nor empiricist methods taken in isolation could provide "the ultimately valid basis" for epistemology. He suggested the consideration of two complementary approaches, intuitive verification and discursive verification, which relied on the emergence of consensus to resolve nagging questions that could not be answered by the other methods of testing knowledge. Although Sidgwick emphasized the "special and preeminent importance" of discursive verification, which derived from empiricist epistemology, he claimed that "the special characteristic of *my* philosophy is to keep the importance of the others in view." The dead ends encountered by each epistemological tradition could be avoided only by creatively selecting various approaches to the different kinds of knowledge we seek.[109]

Fouillée likewise criticized empiricists for holding too low an estimate of the role of consciousness in knowledge and idealists for exaggerating its importance. "Consciousness," he wrote, "is not a power independent of the natural mechanism, but neither is it a simple accidental and superficial effect of this mechanism. It is the interior," he concluded, "of which the mechanism is the exterior."[110] Dewey argued that philosophers had to free themselves from the antagonism separating empiricist from idealist theories of knowledge, because the strengths of each system were the weaknesses of the other. Although alone each tradition was sterile, together they could lead to the fruitful resolution of epistemological problems.[111] Dewey later extended this analysis. He argued that the distinctions between empiricism and rationalism, particularism and universalism, etc., culminated in a fatal disjunction "between knowing and doing, theory and practice, between mind as the end and spirit of action and the body as its organ and means." Since physiology, psychology, and philosophy no longer supported those disjunctions, Dewey advocated, as did the other philosophers of the *via media*, a theory of knowledge unrestricted by such misleading distinctions.[112]

These mavericks did not aim at systematic synthesis. They tried instead to create a genuine alternative to the systems they criticized. Their radical theory of knowledge incorporated ideas from both empiricists and idealists but differed on fundamental issues from both traditions. James and Dilthey explicitly drew that distinction in their analyses of different temperaments or world views in the history of philosophy. In "The Present Dilemma in Philosophy," the first of the lectures he delivered in 1906 that were later published as *Pragmatism*, James drew his familiar distinction between "tender minded" rationalism and "tough minded" empiricism. Rationalists navigate by principles, he contended, while empiricists navigate by facts. To the idealism, monism, and dogmatism of the rationalist mentality, he contrasted the empiricists' sensationalism, pluralism, and skepticism. Judging both of these temperaments one-sided, he counseled selecting elements from both categories with an eye toward their contributions to our need to live rather than our fondness for logically coherent philosophical systems. James denied that his philosophy could be fitted into either the rationalist or the empiricist category, and his claim reflected his desire to depart from both systems. His radical empiricism, like his pragmatism, cannot be treated as a species of any philosophical genus that preceded it.[113]

In "The Types of World View and Their Development in the Metaphysical Systems" (1911), Dilthey's categories of objective idealism and naturalism roughly paralleled James's rationalist and empiricist groupings. Like James, Dilthey recognized that volition and feeling, as well as cognitive thinking, figured in an individual's selection of a world view. Objective idealists, Dilthey wrote, attempted to dissolve the discord of life into a universal harmony. According to their world view, the "tragic sense of the contradictions of existence" and the acknowledgment of life's limits served only as stages leading toward the attainment of "a universal context of existence and value." Proponents of objective idealism, according to Dilthey, included the stoics, Giordano Bruno, Leibniz, Hegel, and Schleiermacher. He listed as naturalists such thinkers as Democritus, Epicurus, Hume, and Comte, whose world view consisted of "sensualism as its theory of knowledge, materialism as its metaphysics, and a double-sided practical attitude— the will toward enjoyment and the reconciliation with the overpowering and alien course of the world by submitting oneself to it through reflection." To these two categories, which mesh nicely with James's scheme, Dilthey added a third, which he called the idealism of freedom. He considered the experience of free will and moral obligation as "independent from nature and related to a spiritual order" fundamental to this world view, and he included Plato, Aristotle, most Christian thinkers, Kant, and Bergson as idealists of freedom.[114]

Dilthey also placed James in this third category, and his decision seems reasonable at first glance. Indeed, if the ideas of freedom and obligation are the essential elements of the idealism of freedom, all of the philosophers of the *via media* might be enlisted into this company, because those considerations run through all of their ideas like two intertwined threads. But these thinkers' search for a radical theory of knowledge carried them beyond the transcendental subjectivism of Kant and away from Bergson's intuitionism. Moreover, the empiricist elements in their epistemology fade out of focus when they are made to stand beside Plato and Augustine. Dilthey reasoned that he could not be placed within any of the world views he described because he adopted a critical stance toward all of them, and the same must be said of James, Dewey, Sidgwick, Green, and Fouillée. Thus far my treatment of these philosophers' analysis of empiricism and idealism has revealed only a silhouette of their constructive ideas. In the next chapter, by shifting the light from their critique to their positive contributions, I will examine in detail the radical theory of knowledge they created.

2

The Radical Theory
of Knowledge

1. The Immediacy of Lived Experience

In the soggy late winter of 1869, while ostensibly preparing for the examination that would end his tedious medical training, William James felt distracted from science by philosophy. He was swamped in the naturalism of Chauncey Wright, a frequent visitor to the James household in Cambridge. Although James felt drawn toward determinism by an irresistible yet unsettling logic rooted in empiricism, something in him struggled against the conclusion that "not a wiggle of our will happens save as a result of physical laws." In a letter to his friend Thomas W. Ward, James revealed his predicament, and he further suggested the path that he and others of his generation would take in search of its resolution. "It is not that we are all nature *but* some point which is reason," he wrote, "but that all is nature *and* all is reason too. We shall see, damn it, we shall see."[1]

To James and the other radical philosophers of the *via media*, the conventional dualisms separating life into mind and body, soul and matter, seemed to collapse as the associationist and idealist theories of knowledge tumbled down around them. Yet razing an intellectual edifice requires less ingenuity than constructing the ideas to replace it, and the challenge remained of building something more durable from the scattered debris of epistemology. While Green and Sidgwick contributed little to this project, James, Dilthey, Fouillée, and Dewey went beyond their critiques of empiricism and idealism to develop a radical theory of knowledge, a set of ideas that challenged the fundamental conception of knowledge as a reflection of external reality.[2] They repudiated the idea shared since Descartes by Locke and Leibniz, Hume and Kant, Russell and Husserl, that philosophy, however it is conceived, should be understood as the quest for certain knowledge. Instead these radicals concentrated on the contingent quality of our most basic categories of thought, and instead of envisioning epistemology as foundational they judged it imperfect and open-ended. That does not mean they could avoid having a theory of knowledge themselves any more than those who reflect seriously on the limits of language can avoid expressing their misgivings about language in language: epistemology by whatever name is as much a condition of philosophy as language is. As diligently as the philosophers of the *via media* strained against the inadequacies of all previous accounts of how we know, they nevertheless did have a theory of knowledge, even though it was a theory conceived in radical opposition to the associationist and idealist models.[3] They understood more fully than did their predecessors, and many of their successors, that modern philosophy's search for apodicticity is fruitless. Instead they articulated a new conception of immediate lived experience, which shattered the links binding philosophy to Cartesian mind–body dualism and acknowledged the continuity of consciousness, the experience of freedom, and the provisional quality of truth itself. They conceived of knowledge as an unending experiment whose results can be validated only in activity rather than reflection, and whose conclusions are at best provisional and subject always to further testing in practice.

The philosophers of the *via media* argued that the perennial questions of epistemology were simply misconceived. They denied that an ontological gap distinguishes subject from object or mind from body. Those dualisms were rooted in the difference between consciousness, or what Dilthey called "lived experience" (*Erlebnis*) and James called "pure experience," on the one hand, and the world outside consciousness, everything that we do not experience from the inside, on the other. Philosophers had assumed that that difference corresponds to a real difference in the nature of mind and body, and they went through elaborate intellectual contortions to make sense of that supposed difference in order to explain how knowledge inside the mind could mirror, or correspond to, the world outside. By the late nineteenth century, however, the supposedly eternal and orderly Great Chain of Being had been shaken by Darwinian biology and then revealed as a conventional fiction by advances in mathematics and the physical sciences. The simultaneous challenges to associationist and idealist epistemology flowed with these currents to erode the confidence of philosophers in Cartesian dualism. Against centuries of epistemological argument, James, Dewey, Dilthey, and Fouillée maintained that reality is not broken into two parts. Instead it merely yields different answers to questions posed from different perspectives. The world of our immediate experience appears to us different from everything else merely because we are inside it, not because it is metaphysically or ontologically distinct from the rest of existence. As James wrote, "There is no thought-stuff different from thing-stuff." There is only "the same identical piece of pure experience" that "can stand alternately for a 'fact of consciousness'" when we view it from the inside "or for a physical reality, according as it is taken in one context or another."[4] James admitted no separation between the physical and psychical as components of reality; they differ only in terms of our perspective on the world of experience.

Dilthey likewise distinguished between the "scientific approach," which starts with the physical world and "proceeds from the external to the internal, from material to mental changes," and the perspective of "inner experience," from which the active role of consciousness in constituting the external world becomes apparent. Although his position is frequently misinterpreted, Dilthey, like James, insisted that the two perspectives must be combined: "My starting-point is the scientific approach," he wrote, and as long as we remain conscious of its limitations, the results of scientific investigation are incontestable. "But their value as knowledge," he concluded, "is more precisely defined from the point of view of inner experience," and therefore knowledge derived from the natural sciences (*Naturwissenschaften*) must be supplemented with knowledge derived from the human sciences (*Geisteswissenschaften*).[5] Dilthey never posited an ontological distinction between the objects studied by the natural and the human sciences. After Wundt first accused him of "logical dualism" in his monumental *Logik* (1906–1908), Dilthey denied emphatically that the realms of nature and man are independent and pointed out that "cognitions of both classes commingle everywhere." The difference between the physical and mental worlds is a difference in the nature of our perspective; that does not, however, imply the existence of an unbridgeable metaphysical chasm between matter and mind. Indeed, Dilthey frequently employed the term "psycho-physical unity" precisely to avoid falling into the trap of mind–body dualism. In a manuscript he wrote after 1908 he made a final attempt to rescue his argument from the distortion of his critics, a distortion that has unfortunately not disappeared. The language he used resonates with James's 1869 letter to Ward. "What one usually tries to separate as the physical and the psychical is really inseparable," Dilthey insisted, because man "contains the vital coherence of both the physical and the psychical." Despite the distinctive immediacy of lived experience, Dilthey concluded, "we ourselves are nature and nature works in us."[6] Both the study of nature and the study of man, James and Dilthey agreed, are empirical. Although the data taken from lived experience and from scientific investigation differ, they must be considered equally legitimate and equally provisional sorts of knowledge that are simply gathered in different ways. We have a more intimate understanding of lived experience than of the rest of the natural world, because science can only represent for us what Dilthey termed "an externality," whereas culture, values, and emotions are known to us from within as "an inner reality" that "we experience sympathetically" with "the power of our entire being."[7]

Fouillée subscribed to both parts of this decisive argument concerning the tentativeness of our ideas about how we know and how they relate to the rest of our knowledge of the natural world. Epistemology must be "the most experimental of studies," he argued, because it probes the conditions underlying experience—the conditions beneath Kant's categories. Yet our knowledge of immediate experience should not be subsumed under, or rejected on account of, the knowledge of objective facts we derive from scientific investigation, because while science can yield only hypotheses about a world we cannot know from within, our knowledge of subjective facts is "real and certain."[8] Philosophy, like science, must be experimental and subject to revision, because its subject matter is part of the same natural world. We only come to know lived experience in a different way from our knowledge of the rest of the world.

By denying subject–object dualism and proclaiming instead the integrity of two complementary paths to knowledge, James, Dilthey, and Fouillée suggested the rudiments of a radical theory of knowledge. During the 1870s and 1880s, they focused primarily on the inadequacies of standard accounts of epistemology. In the next decade, they began groping toward a new set of ideas that integrated their insights into the unity of subject and object in experience with their argument that valid knowledge could be derived from nature and from lived experience. In *The Principles of Psychology*, James took the first, faltering steps in that direction.[9] His *Psychology* reflected his uncertainty about the paradox of objective determinism and the subjective experience of freedom. In an effort to remain faithful to science and to lived experience, James pieced together an analysis that threatened to split apart at the seams connecting its positivistic account of physical processes with its vivid descriptions of the protean character of life. Both behaviorists and gestalt psychologists have laid claim to James's legacy, and both can find support in the split personality of his *Psychology*. James abruptly dismissed "'rational psychology,' which treated the soul as a detached existant, sufficient unto itself," yet when he turned to "the innermost SELF which is most vividly felt," he admitted that "an obscure feeling of something more" hovered beyond biological explanations. He concluded that its source "must at present remain an open question." In fact, James suggested, our answers to psychology's puzzles vary according to our point of view: "We may fairly write the Universe in either way, thus: ATOMS-producing-consciousness; or CONSCIOUSNESS-produced-by-atoms. Atoms alone, or consciousness alone, are precisely equal mutilations of the truth." James insisted on holding physiology and philosophy in tension throughout the *Psychology*, and his strategy masked neither confusion nor indecision. Just as he refused to take refuge in the standard positivist or idealist pseudo-solutions which he dismissed as "spiritual chloroform," he refused to claim a premature victory in the battle to understand how the brain relates to the conscious mind. Those psychologists who boasted that physiology would eventually explain what they still found baffling he scorned "for making a luxury of intellectual defeat." For his part, James preferred to display the ragged edges of his ignorance than disguise them.[10]

James consciously opted for a position that could not be characterized as wholly positivist, associationist, idealist, or Kantian, because he believed that psychology needed an altogether different model. A passage near the conclusion of the *Psychology* reveals his aim:

I now proceed to urge the vital point of my whole theory, which is this: If we fancy some strong emotion, and then try to abstract from our consciousness of it all the feelings of its bodily symptoms, we find we have nothing left behind, no "mind-stuff" out of which the emotion can be constituted.

Yet James cautioned that his impatience with "platonizers" should not be misinterpreted. "Let not this view be called materialistic," he warned. Even though the processes involved are at root "sensational," our emotions "must always be inwardly what they are, whatever be the physiological source of their apparition." In short, our feelings "carry their own inner measure of worth with them."[11] Our conception of lived experience must be rooted in the firm ground of physiology, and mind must not be abstracted from sensation, but the element of subjectivity remains. James wanted to do justice to inner experience, to life as it is lived subjectively, and he also wanted his account to jibe with our scientific understanding of how the human body functions. If the spectroscopic view of James's *Psychology* resulted from his refusal to offer simple solutions to difficult problems, it also indicated the limits of his vision in 1890. He had awakened from the nightmare of naturalism and the fantasies of empiricist and idealist epistemology, but his own thinking remained unfocused.

Fouillée recognized the positive contributions of James's *Psychology*. He cited James favorably several times in his *Psychology of idées-forces* (1893), although he misunderstood aspects of James's work.[12] In his chapter on volition, James had discussed an essay by Fouillée, "Le Sentiment de l'effort, et la conscience de l'action," and despite the resemblance between Fouillée's doctrine of *idées-forces* and James's own thoughts on the subject, he had criticized Fouillée for exaggerating the active role of the subject in thinking.[13] Fouillée, in turn, accused James of eliminating the role of consciousness in *The Principles of Psychology*, a misinterpretation of James's ideas at least as substantial as James's own misreading of Fouillée. Moreover, the position Fouillée offered as a corrective differed only slightly from James's own analysis, and in his subsequent work James moved even closer to that position.

In light of their mutual misunderstandings, it is not surprising that the similarities between them have been overlooked. Fouillée classified James with the "psycho-physiologists" and contended that James underestimated the role of consciousness. Yet as Fouillée explained his own concept of consciousness in his introduction to *The Psychology of idées-forces*, the proximity of his ideas to James's became apparent, Fouillée's comments to the contrary notwithstanding. "One can very well assert," Fouillée admitted, "that consciousness does not exist, if one means by that something different from the internal functions that we have enumerated: sensations, pleasures and pains, impulses and aversions, which are alone the positive and original (*primitif*) facts." That description all but paraphrased James's analysis of consciousness as a function rather than an entity, which may have been the key argument of the *Psychology*. Fouillée further emphasized the similarity, albeit unwittingly, by concluding that consciousness is "the psychic junction considered in its character of irreducible subjectivity."

The extensive markings in his own copy of Fouillée's *Psychology of idées-forces* make clear how carefully James followed Fouillée's argument.[14] A passage that James noted as particularly important in his copy of Fouillée's *Evolution of idées-forces*, published in the same year as the *Principles of Psychology*, further illustrates the convergence of their ideas. "Psychology is the only science of initial and immediate experience," Fouillée maintained, "which begins with what is given without postulates. It is the most direct, the most immediate, the most certain, and finally the most purely experimental of all the sciences of experience."[15] James's functional psychology, Fouillée's psychology of *idées-forces*, and Dilthey's analysis of *Erlebnis* all pointed toward a common idea of experience as the intersection of subjectivity and objectivity, a continuity that precedes the separation of self from other. Straining against the conceptual boundaries of dualism, these philosophers stood at the threshold of the radical theory of knowledge, and after 1895 they began to elaborate the ideas implicit in their early psychology.

After the appearance of *The Principles of Psychology*, James experimented with new words to express concepts that were inadequately served by standard psychological and philosophical discourse. During the 1895–1896 academic year, he struggled with his description of consciousness as a function and searched for a more adequate expression of its complexity. He settled on the word "field" because it transcended dualism and skirted the equally misleading notions of consciousness as either pure ego or material substance. Although he admitted that the idea of consciousness as a field in which subject and object meet "results in an almost maddening restlessness," he believed that it represented a positive step toward "concreteness." By examining what "we *mean* by knowing," he was turning away from traditional accounts to insist that "nothing is postulated whose nature is not fully given in experience terms." James's ideas of consciousness as a field, beyond containing the seeds from which his own radical empiricism later developed, continues to be a fruitful way of conceptualizing the perennially puzzling relation between the brain and perception.[16]

While James was exploring the concept of consciousness as a field, Dewey published his pathbreaking essay "The Reflex Arc Concept in Psychology" (1896). Extending a line of analysis suggested in James's *Psychology*, Dewey acknowledged that functional psychology's concept of a reflex arc joining stimulus and response represented a step forward from the "dualism of body and soul." Unfortunately, as Dewey pointed out, "the older dualism between sensation and idea is repeated in the current dualism of peripheral and central structures and functions." Instead of viewing sensory stimulus, central connections, and motor responses as separate and complete entities in themselves, psychologists should recognize them as parts of a single, complex whole. Conceiving of the process in terms of stimulus and response, Dewey argued, "leaves us with a disjointed psychology," an explanation of knowledge and action no less dualistic, and more mechanistic, than the older rationalist psychology it was intended to supplant.[17]

Dewey suggested an alternative conceptualization of experience similar to James's idea of a field. He argued that experience is "a circuit, not an arc or broken segment of a circle." As a circuit, it "is more truly termed organic than reflex, because the motor response determines the stimulus, just as truly as sensory stimulus determines movement." Indeed, Dewey continued, "the movement is only for the sake of determining the stimulus, of fixing what kind of stimulus it is, of interpreting it." In his characteristically oblique prose, Dewey introduced an important idea: stimulus and response are misconceived as separate processes. Instead they are indissolubly linked in experience. The idea of experience as a circuit, he concluded, provides "the co-ordination which unifies that which the reflex arc concept gives us only in disjointed fragments." Experience is a unity, a complex whole of which stimulus and response are merely different aspects. As Dewey concluded, in a phrase revealing the residue of Hegelianism apparent even in his mature writing, "it is the circuit within which fall distinctions of stimulus and response as functional phases of its own mediation or completion."[18] Dewey grounded his psychology in physiology, in the adaptation of the organism to its natural environment. He emphasized that the experiencing subject has responsibility for "interpreting" sensory stimuli and aims not merely for physical survival but for "completion." As James's tentative steps toward conceptualizing experience as a field prefigured his radical empiricism, so the roots of Dewey's instrumentalism lay in his revision of the reflex arc concept and his suggestion that experience is an "organic" circuit joining subjectivity and objectivity through the unity of stimulus and response.

James's and Dewey's ideas thus moved during the decade of the 1890s in the direction of Dilthey's concept of *Erlebnis*. In his "Ideas about a Descriptive and Analytical Psychology" (1894), Dilthey applauded James for "the astonishing, realistic power of his capacity for inner perception." Moreover, in direct contrast to Fouillée's treatment of James's *Psychology*, Dilthey praised James for buttressing, by the use of empirical analysis, arguments for the free and creative aspects of consciousness.[19] Dilthey's essay contains an early formulation of his mature epistemology. "In contrast to external perception," Dilthey wrote, "inner perception rests upon an awareness, a lived experience, it is immediately given. Here, in sensation or in the feeling of pleasure accompanying it, something simple and indivisible is given to us." This fundamental fact of experience lay beneath the attempts of constructive psychology to understand knowledge and action. Before psychology could *explain* behavior, Dilthey argued, it must put aside the artificial constructs that serve as analytical tools and return to the more basic task of *describing* lived experience. By attempting to dissect the thinking process in order to lay bare its physiology, psychology ignored the most elementary fact of experience. Psychology, Dilthey wrote, "must start with developed psychic life, not derive it from elementary processes."[20] We must concentrate on examining immediate experience as we encounter it rather than as it is reconstructed after physiologists have torn it apart.

Understandably, given the importance of Schleiermacher's concept of inner awareness in Dilthey's intellectual development, critics misinterpreted Dilthey as advocating romantic introspection or a return to the spiritual conception of the self. He explicitly rejected that option: "Certainly, analysis and synthesis and, subordinate to them, induction and deduction, cannot be entirely separated in psychology. They condition each other in the living process of knowledge like inhaling and exhaling, to use Goethe's beautiful phrase."[21] Abstractions from the concrete immediacy of experience distort it in the effort to explain it, and philosophers must resist such psychologistic efforts. Lived experience is "a reality immediately appearing as such, of which we are aware without abstraction." Because of its immediacy, it possesses an integrity that physiological psychology cannot challenge. Whereas in external perception we try to pass beyond the perceived qualities to the object behind them, "in lived experience there is only this qualitatively determined reality, and nothing is for us behind it."[22] Our most basic, "originary" experience precedes the separation of self from world, or subject from object. That division occurs only when we try to render experience in terms analyzable by the techniques of natural science. As Dilthey wrote in a crucial passage in "The Types of World-View and Their Development in the Metaphysical Systems" (1911), we are never given in experience only the inner life or the external world; they are intertwined. Their union dissolves only in the conceptualization or articulation of lived experience.[23] The self cannot without distortion be torn from the outside world. Neither can it be reduced to a set of analytical laws that presume to explain its reactions to external stimuli. In order to find a *via media* between reification and reductionism, epistemology must leave psychologism and turn toward the immediacy of experience.

James reached a similar conclusion. In *The Will to Believe* (1897), he discarded the positivistic trappings lingering in *The Principles of Psychology* and concentrated on sketching the outlines of his radical empiricism, which he defined in these words:

> I say "empiricism," because it is contented to regard its most assured conclusions concerning matters of fact as hypotheses liable to modification in the course of future experience; and I say "radical," because it treats the doctrine of monism itself as an hypothesis, and unlike so much of the half-way empiricism that is current under the name of positivism or agnosticism or scientific naturalism, it does not dogmatically affirm monism as something with which all experience has got to square.

As a "complete empiricist," he argued, he could no longer entertain the dogmas of positivism, agnosticism, or scientific naturalism, because the "one indefectibly certain truth," the truth even "pyrrhonistic scepticism itself leaves standing," is that "the present phenomenon of consciousness exists."[24] If by consciousness James did not mean a substance or an entity, he nevertheless insisted that a mysterious something we call a consciousness functions at the heart of our experience. His entry under the heading "Experience" in James Mark Baldwin's *Dictionary of Philosophy and Psychology* (1902) documents the radicalism of James's approach, and it also illustrates the congruence between his ideas and Dilthey's. Experience, James wrote, includes "the entire process of phenomena, of present data considered in their raw immediacy, before reflective thought has analysed them into subjective and objective aspects or ingredients."[25] Experience is prior to the divorce of self from other, James claimed, and philosophy should acknowledge that fundamental continuity of internal and external in experience. As he put it in "A World of Pure Experience" (1904), students of epistemology had staggered under the weight of an artificial conception of the relations between knower and known as "discontinuous entities." Viewing the problem from the perspective of radical empiricism, however, reveals that "in the very bosom of the finite experience every conjunction required to make the relation intelligible is given in full."[26]

When critics accused James of advocating a new species of subjectivism under the banner of radical empiricism, he replied that his concept of pure experience antedated the subject–object split prerequisite to subjectivism, and he offered pure experience as the "ambiguous reality" from which philosophical dualists could draw their two sets of data. James asked, "If you take the world as 'experience' in the 'subjective' sense, what is that experience *of*? What is its 'content'? Nothing but real things, 'objective' both in the epistemological and in the physical sense."[27] James's radical empiricism rested on the continuity between internal and external rather than the elevation of subjectivity. His was an empiricism with a new sensitivity to the subject, if not to pure subjectivity. The elaboration of both aspects of experience prior to the division of subject and object distinguished James's philosophy in precisely the manner indicated by his designation: it was truly a radical empiricism.

Dewey too denied that states of consciousness could be examined as something separate from concrete experience, which provides the basis of both psychological and philosophical investigation. In "'Consciousness' and Experience" (1899), Dewey extended his earlier analysis in "The Reflex Arc." He cautioned that psychology threatened to duplicate the unfortunate division of epistemology into warring camps of rationalists and empiricists by splitting into groups of intellectualists and sensationalists. Experience suggests no such separations, Dewey argued, because internal and external elements are bound together.[28] "To eyes not looking through ancient spectacles," experience appears "as an affair of the intercourse of a living being with its physical and social environment."[29]

In place of Cartesian dualism, these renegades substituted a model of knowledge in which subject and object intersect. They conceived of knowledge not as a mechanical operation in which discrete pieces and functions can be isolated and diagrammed, but instead as an ongoing organic process, like inhaling and exhaling, to use Dilthey's image. Epistemology pursued within the constraints of dualism was restricted to dissecting a corpse of knowledge and then trying to infer how it worked when it was alive. By refuting the deadening separation of mind and body, this generation sought to understand knowledge as the individual's continuous breathing in and out of the environment on which he depends for life, a steady, rhythmic process of interaction instead of a mirroring by mind of a world outside it. Having dissolved misleading dualisms in their concept of immediate experience, the philosophers of the *via media* turned their attention to the question of how the various objects of experience are related to each other, a seemingly abstract issue with veiled but important implications for social and political theory, which I will examine in the next section.

2. The Consciousness of Continuity and the Continuity of Consciousness

Green's analysis of Hume discredited the atomistic conception of experience on which associationists relied. Yet the denial of atomism raised another question: If we experience relations rather than discrete bits of data that the mind joins together after they are received by the senses, are the elements of experience combined originally and immediately in and by consciousness, or are relations instead outside of us and an integral feature of the reality we experience? James was not satisfied by Green's answer to that question. Dewey, Fouillée, and Dilthey tried to combine Green's and James's ideas to take into account both the role of consciousness in relating the various aspects of experience, which Green emphasized, and also the relatedness of experience itself, which James designated the "stream of consciousness." Although the distinction may seem too subtle to merit consideration, it illuminates important differences between James and Dilthey on the one hand, and Green, Dewey, and Fouillée on the other, which manifested themselves in these philosophers' ideas about practical activity and political organization.

Green denied that knowledge could be attained through the mechanistic association of sense data. Knowledge involves instead the system of relations that connects sense data, and in order to know, therefore, it is necessary for consciousness to intervene and to locate discrete impressions within a larger framework. Green argued that consciousness orders relations in experience, and thus he followed Kant's proposition that "the understanding makes nature." From this argument, which served as the principal weapon in his attack against Hume, Green drew a rather vaporous conclusion regarding the nature of an "eternal consciousness," which he claimed as the source of the "system of relations" and the guarantor that finite beings could achieve true knowledge.[30] Yet Green's arguments for the role of an individual consciousness apprehending an independently existing reality provided an escape from the mechanistic atomism of associationism. Every object we perceive, Green wrote in his *Prolegomena to Ethics*, "is a congeries of related facts," and he concluded that consciousness plays an active part in even the most rudimentary experience, "in the simplest perception of sensible things or of the appearance of objects, which is incompatible with the definition of consciousness as any sort of succesion of phenomena."[31] That much of Green's epistemology, a revision of Kant's transcendental aesthetic, contributed important insights to the radical theory of knowledge, including the independence and activity of consciousness in knowledge and the relatedness of the components of experience. Sense data do not merely appear to us, Green insisted, they are placed within a pattern, and he located that pattern in thought.

James accepted much of Green's Kantian critique of Hume. He agreed that sensations come to us as part of a larger pattern. He dissented, however, from Green's contention that we experience relations because of the intervention of consciousness. Whereas Green emphasized the "unity" and "completeness" of experience as it is put together in consciousness, James described experience itself as a "continuously flowing thing" that does not need to be unified by consciousness because it is "sensibly continuous" in the form in which it is given to us. In two important essays written in 1884, "The Function of Cognition" and "On Some Omissions of Introspective Psychology," James sharply criticized both the associationists' misguided attempts to analyze discrete bits of experience and Green's opposite error of assuming that the experience of relations implies the existence of an immaterial consciousness. Two seminal ideas, both of which James developed more fully in his later writings, enabled him to break away from the empiricist and idealist explanations of relations. First, he was groping toward the concept of immediate experience that denied any disjunction between subject and object and thereby obviated the need for a consciousness such as Green posited as the source of relations. Second, he was on the brink of discovering the stream of consciousness.[32]

In *The Principles of Psychology*, James combined these two insights to offer a refreshingly new perspective on the tired old problem of relations. "No one ever had a simple sensation in itself," he wrote. "Consciousness, from our natal day, is of a teeming multiplicity of objects and relations, and what we call simple sensations are results of discriminative attention, pushed often to a very high degree." Blending a fluid, antidualist empiricism with the idea of consciousness as a stream, James offered an account of experience in which relations do not need to be explained because they are recognized as an integral part of experience. Experience itself cannot be frozen and analyzed in pieces without distorting its essential quality of continuity. James explained that consciousness "does not appear to itself chopped up in bits." The images of chains and trains that philosophers customarily used could not adequately describe consciousness as we experience it. "It is nothing jointed," James maintained. Instead it flows; a "'river' or 'stream' are the metaphors by which it is most naturally described. In talking of it hereafter," he concluded, "let us call it the stream of thought, of consciousness, or of subjective life."[33] That understanding of experience freed James from the empiricists' bundle theory and from Green's notion of consciousness uniting the separate elements of experience. "Whatever things are thought in relation," James countered, "are thought at the outset in a unity, in a single pulse of subjectivity."[34] He thus resolved with one deft stroke the empiricists' problem of how discrete sensations can be joined and avoided the idealists' recourse to an immaterial consciousness. He rescued the fluidity and continuity of the experienced world from the contrivances of atomism without resorting to Green's or Kant's transcendental thread to perform the operation.

In James's later writings, he exhibited even greater confidence that his radical empiricism explained relations without recourse to either "mind dust" or a mechanistic model. In his preface to *The Meaning of Truth*, he offered as a statement of fact that "the relations between things, conjunctive as well as disjunctive, are just as much matters of direct particular experience, neither more so nor less so, than the things themselves." From that basis, he concluded that the relations holding together the pieces of experience are themselves parts of experience. James admitted in another essay that although in earlier years he was much troubled by Green's arguments against empiricism, the Kantian notion of a spectral consciousness accounting for the experience of relations no longer haunted him.[35] In his essay "A World of Pure Experience," James elaborated the concept that enabled him to "do full justice to conjunctive relations, without, however, treating them, as rationalism always tends to treat them, as being true in some supernal way, as if the unity of things and their variety belonged to different orders of truth and vitality altogether." The key, James argued, was his idea of pure experience, the name he gave to "the immediate flux of life which furnishes the material to our later reflection with its conceptual categories." Prior to conceptualization, then, we encounter in experience a "primal stuff" of which everything is composed, in which different things are joined and separated. "The great continua of time, space, and self," James wrote, "envelop everything." If within those continua some things remain distinct and others coalesce, all of them necessarily appear inside an encompassing context. In the world of pure experience, James insisted, "conjunctions are as primordial elements of 'fact' as are the distinctions and disjunctions." Just as the present fades into the past and yet lingers in the new pulse of life that replaces it, so the relations of self to other, and the relations among the pieces of experience, "flower out of the stream of pure experience."[36]

James presented his final statement on the question of relations in the Hibbert Lectures he delivered at Oxford in 1908 and published the following year as *A Pluralistic Universe*. Although critics alleged that he was escaping into a fanciful world of irrationality when he endorsed Bergson's idea of an *élan vital*, he invoked Bergson only to supplement his earlier contention that conceptual thought and logic tend to pervert experience by draining life of its fullness and substituting for it a tasteless distillate of abstractions.[37] The rationalist critique of empiricism missed the point entirely, he argued, because partisans of both traditions shattered the wholeness of reality into concepts from which it could never be reconstructed. Neither atomism, which assumed the association of elements that are not separated in experience, nor idealism, which swooped down on the supposedly isolated fragments of experience and gathered them into gossamer categories, recognized "the inextricable interfusion" of the contents of pure experience. By focusing on the expanding center of a human character, "the *élan vital* of a man," philosophy could eliminate false distinctions between subject and object, and among the pieces of experience, and recognize the existence of relations as part of the world of pure experience.[38]

Although Dewey eventually adopted this revision of Green's analysis and located relations in the world of immediate experience, initially he maintained the Kantian emphasis on the role of consciousness. In his early writings, Dewey subscribed to Green's entire argument, including the case for the existence of an "eternal consciousness." With his essay "The Reflex Arc," though, he began to emphasize the "organic coordination" of stimulus and response in the circuit image he used to illustrate the process by which we know and act. By 1903 Dewey had discarded Green's notion that thought must intervene to unify the elements of experience. He criticized the atomistic analysis of experience and adopted a Jamesian view of the relatedness of things. Connections, Dewey argued, are as much a part of experiential situations as the things related in them.[39]

Dewey finally completed his journey, apparently, by explicitly repudiating Green's theory of knowledge in *Reconstruction in Philosophy* (1920). "When experience is aligned with the life-process and sensations are seen to be points of readjustment," he wrote, "the alleged atomism of sensations totally disappears." With its disappearance, philosophy no longer required "a synthetic faculty of super-empirical reason to connect them." Liberated from British empiricism's misconception that "isolated and simple existences" constitute experience, philosophers no longer needed "the elaborate Kantian and post-Kantian machinery of a priori concepts and categories to synthesize the alleged stuff of experience." Despite Dewey's seemingly unqualified rejection of idealism, his conclusion revealed the indelible mark of his early idealism: experiential situations, which he designated "the true stuff of experience," could emerge in their true form only as "adaptive courses of action." In a phrase echoing Green and Hegel, Dewey concluded that experience "carries principles of connection and organization within itself." Unlike James, who took experience as it was given to him and built from it the entire structure of his radical empiricism, Dewey perceived in experiential situations certain patterns—"principles of connection and organization"—that carried the knowing subject beyond each experience toward the transformation of indeterminate situations into unified wholes. The idea of experiential situations, which served as the keystone of Dewey's philosophy, differed from James's radical empiricism in its greater emphasis on the progressive, integrative, unifying, and purposive nature of inquiry. That difference reflected the greater impact of Green's ideas, and of idealism in general, on Dewey's philosophy.[40]

Fouillée, like Dewey, tried to account for the experience of connections without recourse to the idealist notion of an independent consciousness unifying the elements of experience. He too located relations in the flux of experience. Fouillée's argument that experience flows steadily—and can be frozen for purposes of analysis only at the cost of distortion—clearly paralleled James's idea of consciousness as a stream. Consciousness, Fouillée wrote in *The Evolution of idées-forces*, "envelops simultaneous and successive impressions and reactions in continuity, not in a simple juxtaposition."[41] Instead of contrasting this conception of relations with the idea that consciousness unites the elements of experience, in the way that James distinguished his radical empiricism from Green's theory of knowledge, Fouillée tried to combine the two insights. His discussion of the continuity of consciousness in *The Evolution of idées-forces* prompted James to note in the margin of his copy simply, and accurately, "WJ."

In *The Psychology of idées-forces*, however, Fouillée altered his stance and maintained that consciousness contains a "principle of 'synthetic connection' among multiple and heterogeneous sensations." In a manner similar to Dewey's, Fouillée argued that consciousness apprehends relations immediately and also strives for wholeness. "The living being," Fouillée wrote, "longs for unity, because it strains eagerly to combine things." There is something in consciousness that responds to the unity of the sensations it apprehends, he argued, and his treatment of that aspect of consciousness resembled Dewey's analysis of inquiry as the substitution of determinate and unified wholes for indeterminate situations. "The living being, after having willed to be and to live, wishes to be and live with intensity." To that end it strives for order, harmony, and unity. "Thought, therefore, will continue the progression toward unity" that begins in sensation. "To survive and to develop," Fouillée concluded, consciousness works steadily to unify experience more completely, because only by fulfilling that "hunger and thirst of a superior level" can it nourish itself.[42] While Fouillée's rhetorical flourishes have no counterparts in Dewey's writings, both thinkers expressed a similar idea: beyond the relations we encounter in the wholeness of experience, consciousness strives for unity and integration; it is progressive and purposive. Neither Dewey nor Fouillée followed Green into an idealist metaphysics, but their conception of individual consciousness was distinctly teleological.

The tension between these ideas was resolved in Dilthey's conception of lived experience. Because experience is given to us from the outset *in* consciousness, and relations are part of that immediate experience, it is a moot question whether such relations occur because of the intervention of consciousness or in directly apprehended experience. We cannot step outside consciousness to answer it. We have only the fundamental fact of lived experience, of which the awareness of relations is an integral part. All of knowledge, Dilthey wrote, is empirical, "but all experience is originally connected, and given validity, by our consciousness (within which it occurs), indeed by our whole nature." It is impossible, he claimed, "to go beyond consciousness, to see, as it were, without eyes or to direct a cognitive gaze behind the eye itself."[43] Thus consciousness, conceived as the junction of subject and object, provides the baseline for the radical theory of knowledge.

We cannot determine whether consciousness or experience provides for the awareness of continuity because we have no justification for separating consciousness from experience in the first place. They are simply different aspects of the "overall coherence of life" (*Lebenszusammenhang*). "Mental connections" are a "directly experienced reality," according to Dilthey, and beyond that our explanation cannot, and need not, go. Because we experience relations and continuity immediately, we do not need to glue separate pieces together. The process of mental life in all its forms, Dilthey wrote, "is from the beginning a unified whole. Mental life does not arise from parts growing together," as both the empiricists and idealists mistakenly assumed; "it is not compounded of elementary units." Instead, it is "always an encompassing unity."[44]

Like James, Dilthey understood consciousness as a flowing stream in which experiences are given to us. Dilthey added to the dynamic quality of life as James described it an explicitly historical dimension: life not only flows, it is an onward movement both within an individual's life and across the broader sweep of historical change. Dilthey's philosophy of history developed out of an insight into "the continuity of mental life in time." Life is not merely a sequence of individual moments, he argued, it is "a unity constituted by relationships which link all the parts. From the present we run through a series of memories back to the point where our small, malleable, and unformed self is lost in the twilight, and we press forward from the present to possibilities, which are grounded in it, but, at the same time, assume vague and vast dimensions."[45] Over time as in each successive present, consciousness connects the parts with the whole of experience. Dilthey first formulated his conception of how consciousness alters over the course of one's life in an essay of 1887 on poetics, in which he wrote that the same representation "can no more return than the same leaf can grow back on a tree the following spring." The dynamism of life causes perceptions to change. As a result, all knowledge emerges within the context of a developing subject whose experiences provide a filter through which the stuff of lived experience must pass. Time never pauses, and in a sense there is never even a present, Dilthey wrote, "because what we experience as present always contains a memory of what has just been present. In other cases the past has a direct effect on, and meaning for, the present, and this gives to memories a peculiar character of being present through which they become included in the present." That conception of time, which Dilthey shared with James and Bergson, has of course proved to be one of the most distinctive and fertile ideas nourishing the modernist imagination.[46]

Dilthey recognized the resemblance. He praised James's treatment of the stream of consciousness and noted that his own leaf image had been grounded by James "with his amazingly realistic power to perceive inner experience."[47] Yet Dilthey's conception of time differed from that of James and Bergson in that he understood, certainly more fully than Bergson and perhaps also more fully than James, that time is not simply a flux in which all present moments disappear into new pasts. Time advances; it embodies a concrete progression, a pattern whose coherence can be recognized even if its explanation remains shadowy. Fouillée criticized Bergson's account of the inchoate intuition of *durée* because, as he put it, we are able to distinguish successive notes in the melody of life preserved in memory, whether voluntary or involuntary. Even James, who often swerved into hyperbole in assessing Bergson's work, resisted the notion of an "unconscious or subconscious permanence of memories" because it presupposed a faculty of intuition that was "the equivalent of a soul in another shape."[48] We experience time neither as mere restlessness nor as a shapeless morass of memories but as an onward movement. "Concrete time consists," Dilthey wrote, "in the indefatigable progression of the present in which what is present immediately becomes past and what is future becomes present. The present is a moment of time being filled with reality. It is a lived experience in contrast to the memory of it."[49] Despite the traces of the past in the present, our present experience nevertheless differs from our experience of the past. Dilthey's conception of time contains a concrete, progressive quality missing in Bergson's celebrated idea of *durée*. That understanding of time, rooted in these theorists' perception of how spatial as well as temporal relations flower from the pure spring of immediate experience, informed their interpretation of history as a source of values and a basis of immanent critique. Before considering that issue in Chapter Three, however, I want to examine the connection between their conception of experience, with its emphasis on the continuity and immediacy of consciousness, and their theories of voluntary action and pragmatism.

3. Voluntary Action and Pragmatic Truth

The nature of the will was among the most vexing problems confronting late nineteenth-century thinkers. Against positivists who dismissed religious arguments for free will as wishful thinking, and against neo-Kantians who insisted that the pure ego preserves its undetermined status despite the claims of science, the philosophers of the *via media* carved out a new theory of voluntary action, grounded on and validated in individual and collective experience. Their position differed not only from traditional empiricist and idealist solutions to the problem of freedom and determinism, but also from those of Schopenhauer, Kierkegaard, Nietzsche, and Bergson, who proposed radically individualist philosophies of self-actualization. By contrast James, Dewey, Dilthey, and Fouillée advanced a new theory of social activity based on a new theory of the will, ideas that they insisted must be tested in practice according to a new theory of verification.[50] Viewed from the perspective of immediate experience, idealist justifications of free will and naturalist arguments for determinism appeared insufficiently empirical because both attempted to resolve the issue by appealing to logic and metaphysics rather than experience.

The partisans of an extended empiricism argued that science and theology assume equally strict rules of causality. Within the realm of the physical sciences, uncaused or "free" events cannot occur; within the Judeo-Christian tradition, there is likewise room for only one first cause or "unmoved mover." Lived experience, however, in its prereflective immediacy, does not conform to either of these models. We are conscious of the ability to select, to choose among options, and we are further aware that by acting on our decisions we effect change. We experience, in short, the distinct feeling of freedom. In contrast to defenders of free will who conventionally tried to establish their arguments on metaphysical or theological foundations, these theorists argued from experience. Not surprisingly, given that completely different starting point, they reached a completely different conclusion concerning both the nature of choice and action and the meaning of truth.

Their ideas about freedom and activity, which I will designate the theory of voluntary action, were wrought in the crucible of personal anxiety. Although the perceptions of cultural crisis that preoccupied philosophers in late nineteenth-century Europe and America do not explain away the ideas they expressed, their uneasiness about the fate of a culture no longer fed by springs of religious belief played a significant part in their thinking about the question of values and the nature of the will. Dilthey believed that the problem of the will in a secular age was "the greatest and most difficult problem confronting modern man."[51] Fouillée became obsessed with this question while still in his twenties, and he devoted his entire career to demonstrating how his concept of *idées-forces* could reconcile natural determinism with the freedom of the will that he believed must lie at the heart of ethical philosophy.[52] Of the numerous intrusions of personal anxiety into philosophical argument, however, few examples were more dramatic than James's escape from the paralysis that gripped him as a young man.

James's experience illustrates, in microcosm, the importance of immediately felt freedom in the theory of voluntary action. On April 13, 1868, having just attended a performance of *Hamlet* in Dresden, James expressed in his diary and in a letter to his brother Henry the concerns that were slowly gathering their incapacitating power inside him. Unconsciously foreshadowing his own fate, James wondered whether the "fullness of emotion" so characteristic of the romantic sensibility manifested in Hamlet, an intensity "so superior to any possible words that the attempt to express it adequately is abandoned," might find its psychological counterpart in the disabling of the will. Hamlet "groans and aches so with the mystery of things" that in the end he despairs of understanding and allows "crazy conceits and countersenses" to "slip and whirl around the vastness of the subject, as if the tongue were mocking itself." So too might the sensitive individual (James as Hamlet, perhaps) judge "action of any sort" to be "inadequate and irrelevant to his feeling" and slide into idle melancholy or wild impulsiveness.[53]

During the next two years, as he tried to resolve the logical contradiction between determinism and freedom and tried to settle on a career for himself, the various threads of nineteenth-century culture that were wound together in his youth began to unravel along with his sense of identity. In February of 1870, a year after his letter to Thomas Ward and nearly two years after his prescient reflections on Hamlet's despair, he sank into the despondency that led to serious consideration of suicide and brief confinement to a mental institution. James's diary reveals that he began to climb out of this morass of psychological incapacitation and philosophical confusion by fastening himself firmly to the idea of freedom.

Reading the essays of Renouvier prompted a crisis in his life, James wrote on April 30, 1870, because he decided to accept Renouvier's definition of free will: "the sustaining of a thought *because I choose to* when I might have other thoughts." Although still years away from formulating his radical empiricism, James discovered in the immediacy of lived experience—in the primal fact of selective choice in consciousness—a justification for deciding, "My first act of free will shall be to believe in free will." Despite his professed intention to sustain that belief provisionally, "for the remainder of the year," he clung to it for the remainder of his life. From his early acceptance of his "individual reality and creative power" and his simultaneous recognition of "the self-governing resistance of the ego to the world," James constructed his mature philosophy.[54] His decisive encounter with Renouvier's writings, therefore, has a triple significance, revealing the experiential roots of his philosophy, indicating the turn to immediate experience instead of logic as the source of his voluntarism, and suggesting, finally, the connection between volition and activity in James's thought.

That connection first became explicit in the 1880s, when James emphasized the role of volition in the act of selecting a thought and sustaining it. In his essay "The Feeling of Effort" (1880), he focused on the associationists' contention that mechanical laws of association explain human choices. He insisted that conscious volition couples with intention to shape our decisions. Choice therefore constitutes "a psychic or moral fact pure and simple," a kind of "knife edge moment" in which will and attention reach a conclusion that the individual then translates into physical action.[55] The choice is rooted in experience, according to James, and it should not be viewed as a mere act of internal will because it must be completed in activity. James insisted that volition, like consciousness, cannot be wholly reduced to automatic physical processes; moreover, he maintained that choice, as part of pure experience, cannot be disproved on the basis of any conceptual scheme. For James, as for all the philosophers of the *via media*, the phenomenon of the will and the activity of the knowing subject formed interlocking pieces of a single puzzle. "The world's contents are given to us in an order so foreign to our subjective interest," James wrote in "Reflex Action and Theism" (1881), "that we can hardly by an effort of the imagination picture to ourselves what it is like." Only by deliberately choosing among the myriad elements of experience, "by picking out from it the items which concern us, and connecting them with others far away," can we "make out definite threads of sequence and tendency" and "enjoy simplicity and harmony in place of what was chaos."[56] Knowing involves selection, selection in turn involves will, and will is then translated into activity. Their intimate connection in James's philosophy mirrored his own psychological liberation through the voluntary decision to affirm his ability to sustain a thought and to act on the basis of that decision. In "Rationality, Activity, and Faith" (1882), he emphasized that cognition remains "incomplete until discharged in act."[57]

Prior to his elaboration of the doctrine of radical empiricism in the 1890s, James did not feel altogether secure in his voluntarism. *The Principles of Psychology* illustrates that uncertainty. In a passage that reflected his own experience, he wrote, "Freedom's first deed should be to affirm itself," yet he disclaimed any psychological basis for that contention. He suggested instead that because his position was grounded in ethics, he preferred not to discuss it in his *Psychology*. He did argue, however, that "effort of attention is thus the essential phenomenon of will," and he offered several variations of that theme in the book.[58] By emphasizing the significance of being able to sustain a thought "*because I choose to*," he established the importance of attending to an idea, which challenged the associationists' concept of a passive knower and hinted at the crucial interlocking of experience, voluntarism, and activity. James referred readers of his *Psychology* interested in the basis for his voluntarism to his essay "The Dilemma of Determinism" (1884), where he emphasized the experience of freedom and explicitly disclaimed any attempt to provide a sustained logical demonstration of free will. He admitted the force of the logic of strict causal determinism, but he protested that shutting out individual responsibility was inconsistent with his own experience of choice and offensive to his moral sensibilities. The other alternative, romantic subjectivism, satisfied his personal fancies but crashed headlong into the objective evidence of the physical world.

Without presuming to resolve the dilemma in its metaphysical dimensions, then, James hoped only to persuade his listeners that believing in freedom was consistent with the feelings of responsibility for their actions that they could not evade. To generations of critics who have challenged the consistency of his argument, James seemed to plead guilty in advance. "The indeterminism I defend, the free-will theory of popular sense based on the judgment of regret," is a theory, he admitted, "devoid either of transparency or of stability. It gives us a pluralistic, restless universe, in which no single point of view can ever take in the whole scene." Its only saving grace, he concluded defiantly, was its clear superiority to the other available alternatives when brought before the bar of experience.[59]

Denying that the juice had been pressed from the free-will controversy, James referred not only to Renouvier, but also to Green and Fouillée, whose writings "completely changed and refreshed the dispute" by placing it in the new frame of experience instead of metaphysics. Sorting out James's attitude toward Fouillée's arguments for voluntarism is no easy task. Despite James's claim in the *Psychology* that he considered Fouillée's discussion of thought as activity "more interesting and suggestive than coherent or conclusive," his own subsequent attempt to refine Fouillée's argument amounted, puzzlingly enough, to a rough paraphrase of the doctrine of *idées-forces*. In his copy of Fouillée's *Evolution of idées-forces*, moreover, James acknowledged that

Fouillée's treatment of the relation of the will to activity "seems to be perfectly in accord with WJ." Two letters James wrote in 1892 further complicate this issue, because in one he professed to be unimpressed by Fouillée's philosophy while in the other he described Fouillée's analysis of the connection between emotion and action as "pretty conclusive." While one can only speculate on the resolution of that paradox in James's mind, he did note in a review of Fouillée's *Psychology of idées forces* in 1893 that "nothing can surpass the vivacity with which M. Fouillée reprehends those who would reduce the entire science of life to animal mechanics, and explain man's intercourse with his environment by successive complications of reflex action." Fouillée's analysis appealed to James because of its challenge to the arguments of physiologically oriented psychologists who denied the efficaciousness of choice, and because Fouillée emphasized that experience consists not merely of sensations but also of psychic life, of voluntarily sustained thoughts that affect the disposition of the will and effect change outside the self through activity.[60] Paralleling the radical empiricism of James's later writings, Fouillée maintained in *La Morale des idées-forces* (1907; cited hereafter as *The Ethics of idées-forces*) that the most stable basis for the idea of freedom is our immediate experience. Shifting the question from experience to discussions of causality, he declared, requires an unjustified retreat from life to metaphysics.[61]

Oddly, just as James distinguished his outlook from Fouillée's despite their considerable similarities, so Fouillée responded to *The Principles of Psychology* by criticizing an argument that differed only marginally from his own. In his *Psychology of idées-forces*, Fouillée accurately traced to Renouvier James's treatment of the will as the simple sustaining of a thought, an argument he dismissed as simplistic and evasive. Voluntarism, Fouillée countered, must be conceived within all the bounds of experience, which include external constraints as well as the undeniable phenomenon of freedom, and he distanced himself from James, Renouvier, and also Bergson, because of his greater sensitivity to the limits of the will's freedom. When James later moved away from Renouvier and Bergson for precisely this reason, he at least tacitly acknowledged the legitimacy of Fouillée's critique.[62]

Dewey first addressed the question of the will in "The New Psychology" (1884), in which he contended that no conflict could separate reason from faith and implied that no contradiction, therefore, could exist between rational principles of causality and the belief in free will. This unsuccessful attempt to finesse a difficult issue by defining it away suggests Dewey's characteristic unwillingness to confront the problem of volition in his philosophy. As he wrote in this early essay, he envisioned the will as "a living bond connecting and conditioning all mental activity" rather than as "an abstract power of unmotivated choice." Dewey concluded that the "New Psychology" merely "attempts to comprehend life." That simple statement, which appears at first to be evasive, sums up the attitude toward voluntarism that Dewey maintained throughout his life. He believed that when we encounter difficulty, we decide to act to remove the obstruction, and he did not feel compelled to posit any faculty of will, or even to examine the issue further, because he simply assumed that choice is an integral part of our natural experience.

Dewey stated his position in "The Ego as Cause" (1894), in which he discussed James's treatment of the will in *The Principles of Psychology*. He professed surprise that James, "who recognizes so far as knowledge is concerned the entire uselessness of an ego outside and behind," and who expressly rejected such a notion in his *Psychology*, "should feel bound to set up its correlate when he comes to deal with will. If the stream of thought can run itself in one case," Dewey judged, "the stream of conduct may administer itself in the other."[63] In *The Study of Ethics*, published the same year, Dewey extended this analysis by arguing that "there is no more a dualism between non-volitional data on one side, and will, on the other, than there is in the process of intellectual judgment." Just as in knowing, Dewey continued, so in willing we do not have "two separate faculties, one that of gathering data, weighing, rejecting and accepting evidence, the other, an outside power, reason, to draw the inference." Both the form and the content of the process are rational, Dewey emphasized. "The drawing of the inference is the con-clusion arrived at when the data assume coherence and completeness."[64] Although it may beg the question of how one determines the "coherency and completeness" of the data necessary to make decisions, that statement indi-cates Dewey's confidence that the entire controversy surrounding volition dissolves under the light of empirical investigation. The mind simultaneously chooses and knows, as part of a continuous process in which sensory input and psychic activity interpenetrate. Without suggesting the independence of the will, Dewey assumed its involvement in the natural functioning of the human organism.

Both Dewey and James considered their accounts of the will consistent with the lessons of Darwinian biology. Evolutionary naturalism, in Dewey's words, proves that "every distinct organ, structure, or formation" serves as "an instrument of adjustment or adaptation to a particular environing situation."[65] Thus thinking and willing play contributory roles in the evolu-tion of the human species. Volition, rather than appearing as an atavistic remnant of dogma, survives through the process of selective pressure. If thought and will exist, as immediate experience indicates, then they must serve a purpose, and the interests that awaken them, the interests to which thought and will respond positively, are, in James's words, "the real a priori element in cognition." Beneath the responses to pleasure and pain lies the seat of thought and volition, interest, which James termed an "all-essential factor" in "mental evolution."[66] Dewey described the antecedent condition of reflective knowledge as "one of discrepancy, struggle, 'collision,'" a situation in which "certain elements stand out as obstacles, as interferences, as deficiencies."[67] That conception of the thinking process rests on the ability of the organism to recognize obstacles, an ability that assumes as fundamental a set of interests. The proponents of the radical theory of knowledge, as I will argue in Chapter Three, conceived of those interests not as static, given appetites, but instead as shifting preferences that emerge from experience and develop historically.

Dilthey argued along similar lines that philosophy must begin with a new conception of man that recognizes and integrates the full diversity of his powers as a "willing, feeling, and imagining being."[68] According to Dilthey, most psychologists and epistemologists ignored the totality of man's experience in favor of narrow empiricist or a priorist renderings of life. He identified James as an exception to this tendency because James's functionalism coupled empiricist methods with recognition of the creative aspects of consciousness.[69] Yet unlike James, who offered ethical rather than psychological reasons for his tentative affirmation of volition in *The Principles of Psychology*, Dilthey believed that the freedom of the will could be discerned in the source of all positive knowledge: experience. For we encounter the world not only through our senses, he argued, but also as thinking and willing beings.[70] Dilthey struggled to forge a theory of volition free from the vaporous abstraction of Fichte's notion of the will as the unconditioned pure act and from the empiricists' subsumption of volition within the logic of physical causality. While Dilthey proclaimed the freedom of the will, he carefully limited its scope within the boundaries of concrete situations. The individual cannot dictate his surrounding conditions, yet he does decide among a given group of options filtered through culture and presented to consciousness. He is thus not free from conditions, but neither is he wholly determined, because he can select his response to the conditions he encounters in experience.[71]

In sum, the theory of voluntary action comprised five interlocking ideas. First, freedom is part of immediate experience. The logic of causality cannot destroy our awareness of choice, to use James's example, at the fundamental level of choosing to sustain a thought, and thus we do not need to invoke idealist metaphysics to establish the fact of freedom. Second, the subject does not passively receive sense data and respond according to a preestablished calculus of pleasures and pains. Instead, activity is part of the fundamental process of attending to certain parts of the mass of data we receive, and consciousness actively sifts and selects from the elements of experience those that excite its interest. Third, experience consists of volition, thought, and feelings taken together. None of these can be ignored, and none is wholly dependent on, or independent of, the others. Fourth, the will is freely exercised only within given objective conditions that limit its options. Fifth, and finally, because the content of the will is a function of both personal and historical development, the interests that lie at the heart of volition are relative rather than absolute.

These renegades emphasized the continuity between this new conception of voluntarism and practical activity. Feeling, thinking, and willing together constitute only the first stage of a process that is completed in action. The idea that rational choices are not merely a matter of reflection but must issue in purposive action is most closely identified with Dewey's philosophy, and it is true that it was the cornerstone of his instrumentalism. Yet he was not alone in trying to fuse the processes of reflection and activity, which Western philosophers had tended to keep separate since the Greeks first distinguished *theoria* from *praxis*. An epigrammatic entry in Sidgwick's journal of 1867 expressed his opposition to the conventional spectator theory of knowledge in words that could have served as the manifesto of the philosophers of the *via media*. "Theory ∞ Practice. Let every effort be used to form this chain. Practise [sic] alone can correct theory. Theory alone can inform practice." If everyone, all at once, were to act upon what they claimed to think and believe, Sidgwick continued, "to what great grief we should come in details! but how rapidly we should improve not only in Practice but in Theory."[72] This emphasis on the interdependence of contemplation and action, on the completion of *theoria* in *praxis*, signaled a dramatic departure from the image of the mind as mirror prevalent in Western thought since Descartes, and it was tied to these radicals' conception of lived experience. When the subject and object are perceived as related immediately rather than as two distinct substances, the gap separating external reality from the thinking process disappears. It is then only a short step to the conclusion that man must act upon his environment, not simply think about it.

Dewey consistently argued that activity is necessary for completing the processes of thinking and willing. In his *Outlines of a Critical Theory of Ethics* (1891), he declared that "the real object of desire is activity,"[73] and he never wavered from that conviction. He argued that continuity characterizes the relation of thought and action just as it characterizes the relation of subject to object and psychical to physical. He conceived of the distinction between reflection and activity as just one more of the dualisms blinding philosophers to the wholeness of lived experience. His early essays in psychology illustrate his belief in the necessary unity of thinking and doing. In "The Significance of the Problem of Knowledge" (1897), for example, he declared that the theory of knowledge becomes "a social nuisance and disturber" when it neglects its principal function of "solving the problem out of which it had arisen." In *Studies in Logical Theory* (1903), he argued that thought does not arise in response to abstract problems of logic, but in specific situations in which we encounter real difficulties. Not merely reflection but action is required to solve such problems; we formulate plans of purposive activity in order to change the condition of the world around us.[74]

This notion of the instrumental purpose of thought underlay Dewey's philosophy of education as well as his epistemology. In his pathbreaking and widely read study *The School and Society* (1899), Dewey counseled that children should be induced to view education as problem solving. To that end he recommended freeing students from the passive listening and mechanical recitation of traditional schooling and encouraging them to work actively on the problems they would encounter in life. Dewey argued that education should prepare children for "normal thinking" before trying to guide them through the maze of more sophisticated mental operations. Discussing the aims and methods of education in a passage near the conclusion of his book, he encapsulated his ideas on the thinking process.

Thought "arises from the need of meeting some difficulty, in reflecting upon the best way of overcoming it, and thus leads to planning, to projecting mentally the result to be reached, and deciding upon the steps necessary and their serial order." Teachers should acquaint students with this way of thinking about thinking, in which the different stages flow into one another as part of a dynamic, ongoing process, because "this concrete logic of action long precedes the logic of pure speculation or abstract investigation, and through the mental habits that it forms is the best preparation for the latter." Dewey's later presentations of these ideas only elaborated and refined this position.[75]

Dilthey joined Dewey in affirming the continuity between thought and action. In an early statement of the position he maintained consistently, Dilthey wrote, "Man is not on earth simply to be but to act." The human sciences, according to Dilthey, should thus be considered the "sciences of acting man and the practical world," and he emphasized that philosophy must not only focus on man as an active being; it must also seek to "have an effect" itself.[76] Dilthey's ideas regarding praxis flowed from his analysis of lived experience. Like Dewey, he believed that knowledge is practical rather than speculative: We think in order to act; we use the mind as an instrument to effect change. A passage from his unpublished writings reveals similarities between this position and Dewey's. Imagine that we face a decision, Dilthey suggested. "In this situation we ponder existing conditions and those which might arise in the future: with all our vitality and experience we project ourselves testingly into these conditions."[77] Our knowledge is rooted in our situation, and thinking points toward altering what Dewey called "felt difficulties." Both because knowing is grounded in lived experience and because it must be translated into action, Dilthey argued, epistemology can have no a priori assumptions. It must begin and end in life rather than logic.

James likewise consistently affirmed that thought must issue in action. In "Rationality, Activity, and Faith," an article published in 1882 and included in *The Principles of Psychology*, he wrote: "It is far too little recognized how entirely the intellect is built up of practical interests." We respond to situations not simply by posing the theoretical query "What is that?" but by asking the practical "What is to be done?"[78] The difference between the two questions, between inactivity and abstraction on the one hand and activity and concreteness on the other, suggests the leitmotif of practice that runs through James's writings. James also grounded his idea of practical activity in his understanding of the continuity of experience. "Thinking," he wrote, "is only a place of transit, the bottom of a loop, both of whose ends have their point of application in the outer world."[79] Thought and volition are rooted in sensation and end in action, and philosophy falsifies experience when it severs that vital connection. The knowing subject, according to James, is not simply "a mirror floating with no foot-hold anywhere and passively reflecting a completed external reality." In a crucial passage expressing the essence of his ideas about practice and pointing toward his pragmatism, he proclaimed:

> The knower is an actor, and co-efficient of the truth on one side, whilst on the other he registers the truth which he helps to create. Mental interests, hypotheses, postulates, so far as they are bases for human action—action which to a great extent transforms the world—help to *make* the truth which they declare.

In other words, James concluded, unifying his voluntarism with his emphasis on activity, "there belongs to mind, from its birth upward, a spontaneity, a vote."[80] While that passage seems to echo Kant's dictum that the understanding makes nature, James carried the Kantian insight further. He emphasized that experience is shaped not merely by the conditions of knowledge, the transcendental forms of apperception, but just as decisively by the activity of the knowing subject interacting with his surroundings instead of reflecting on them. James conceived of that process as dynamic, continuous, voluntary, and ultimately self-correcting through the pragmatic theory of truth.

The unity of volition and activity was equally central to Fouillée's philosophy; he initially coined the phrase *idée-force* to express his conviction that ideas must not be considered idle abstractions isolated from action. Ideas become *idées-forces*, after all, only through praxis. Attempting unsuccessfully to put to rest a misunderstanding that dogged his philosophy from the beginning, Fouillée explicitly denied any ontological status to *idées-forces*. He used the phrase only as a convenient formula to emphasize the active side of consciousness and the human capacity to produce changes by acting to effect ideas. Ideas themselves, he pointed out, are impotent. They can have an impact only when human beings translate them into activity: i.e., ideas can become *idées-forces* only when action ensues from them. Despite the emphasis Fouillée placed on *idées-forces* in his philosophy, he did not grant ideas primacy in experience. To the contrary, he emphatically endorsed Faust's dictum, "In the beginning was the act."[81] Fouillée considered the *idée-force* the synthesis of thought, will, and activity. In both his *Evolution of idées-forces* and his *Psychology of idées-forces*, he cited James's arguments on the activity of the subject in knowledge and affirmed James's analysis of the necessary connection between volition and activity. Following James, he argued that in all mental activity, sensation, emotion, and appetite must be considered three aspects of a unity. To these we must add ideas, not conceived as abstractions, "but as active forces of preservation and progress, having their origin in desire, their ultimate effect in motion" and serving as "conditions of change" that qualify them as "real factors" in life. By thus joining thought, will, and activity, Fouillée concluded, we avoid the mysticism of Plato, the formalism of Kant, and the passivity of empiricism, and we substitute, with the concept of *idées-forces*, "reality and life."[82]

Explicit as were his endorsements of James's analysis of the connection among thinking, willing, and action, Fouillée's concept of *idées-forces* even more closely resembled Dewey's instrumentalism. I have discovered no direct references in Fouillée's or Dewey's writings to the others' ideas, yet the similarities, particularly on this subject, provide striking confirmation of their convergence. A composite of Fouillée's ideas on the thinking process, pieced together from several different discussions, conforms closely to Dewey's analysis. First, Fouillée wrote, we discern a change in our environment, a realization that enters through the senses and initiates the thinking process. Second, we become aware of either harmony or discord between the new situation and "the general direction of life." This vague awareness provokes either a positive or a negative reaction to the altered conditions, depending on whether we experience a sense of well-being or malaise. Our response, "which is the germ of preference and choice," derives from a combination of sensation, emotion, appetite, and reflection, and out of it emerges gradually a "sketch of our action toward things and the action of things toward us." This sketch is not merely an abstract design, but a plan of action, which we then translate into motion to effect change. Finally, the series of psychic changes culminates in reflection on the entire process.[83] Thus reconstructed, Fouillée's account corresponds almost exactly to Dewey's discussion of how we encounter and resolve difficulties instrumentally.[84]

Fouillée usually spoke in terms of realizing an idea in action, of bringing reality into harmony with an ideal situation, and that emphasis on acting toward a goal of greater integration and unity also resembled Dewey's. Indeed, their treatment of harmony, or completeness, as the aim of activity distinguished Dewey's and Fouillée's ideas from James's and Dilthey's rather more circumspect treatment of the end toward which we act, a difference whose significance for their ethical theories will be discussed in Chapter Four. At this stage I want only to point out the similarity between the manner in which Dewey and Fouillée treated the relation of thought, volition, and action, and Green's discussion of this question, because it reveals the distinction between the more idealist and the more empiricist interpretations of volition and activity advanced by the philosophers of the *via media*.

In his *Prolegomena to Ethics*, Green wrote that "the world of practice" is one in which "the determining causes are motives; a motive again being an idea of an end, which a self-conscious subject presents to itself, and which it strives and tends to realize." The desire to act, Green asserted, is rooted in "a consciousness that the conditions of the real world are at present not in harmony with it, the subject of the desire." This recognition of discrepancy between the self and the situation elicits an effort to adjust the conditions of the real world to produce satisfaction. Such an effort, Green concluded, derives "equally and indistinguishably" from the interaction of will, desire, and thought.[85] Clearly, this line of reasoning underlay the analysis of thinking and acting in Dewey's instrumentalism. Moreover, as James noted in his copy of Green's *Prolegomena*, Fouillée's ideas closely paralleled Green's and Dewey's on this matter.[86]

By contrast, James and Dilthey referred only to the fact of individual interest, rooted in experience, as the seat of volition. Although Dewey and Fouillée rejected Green's idealist metaphysics, their tendency to invoke concepts of wholeness, harmony, and completeness testified to the idealist teleology integral to their ideas. The exchange of letters between Dewey and James in 1903, occasioned by James's discovery of the *"new school of truth"* at the University of Chicago and the desire of Dewey and his associates at Chicago to dedicate *Studies in Logical Theory* to James, illuminates the similarities between their ideas on the issue of thinking, willing, and acting, even as it testifies to the differences that remained between them. "It may be the continued working of the Hegelian bacillus of reconciliation of contradictories in me," Dewey confessed in response to James's acknowledgment of their different origins in idealism and empiricism, "that makes me feel as if the conception of process gives a basis for uniting the truth of pluralism and monism, and also of necessity and spontaneity." An adequate analysis of activity, Dewey continued, "would exhibit the world of fact and the world of ideas as two correspondent objective statements of the active process itself,— correspondent because each has a work to do, in the doing of which it needs to be helped out by the other." So far that account paralleled James's, but Dewey then exhibited the distinctive verbal symptoms that showed the persistence of Hegel and Green in his thinking. "The active process itself transcends any possible objective statement (whether in terms of fact or of ideas)," he continued, "simply for the reason that these objective statements are ultimately incidental to its own ongoing—are for the sake of it. It is this transcendence of any objectified form, whether perceptual or conceptual, that seems to me to give the clue to freedom, spontaneity, etc."[87] While James shared Dewey's emphasis on the dynamism of experience, he rejected the notion that the flux of life conforms to the zigzagging upward path of the dialectic.

A corollary to the association of sensation, volition, thought, and activity in the radical theory of knowledge was the pragmatic theory of truth. Seven years after the appearance of Charles Peirce's seminal "How We Make Our Ideas Clear," James first presented his own version of pragmatism in "The Function of Cognition" (1885).[88] He later referred to this early essay as "the *fons et origo* of all my pragmatism," and when he had it reprinted in *The Meaning of Truth* (1909), he specified in a note appended to the essay those elements of his early account of cognition and truth that survived in his later work. He maintained that thought yields the "cognitive relation" by leading, or pointing, through the experienced environment, toward the resemblance between those pointings and the reality or meaning of objects. When he described this process as continuous and inescapably inexact, he broke radically from prior epistemological claims that we do have access to certain knowledge. We can never know *that* we know, James pointed out, and that uncertainty rules out any hope of apodicticity. Because all knowledge "falls within the continuities of concrete experience," the epistemological gulf separating knower from known disappears.[89] Epistemology, which presumed to survey truth calmly from an Archimedean point, would henceforth have to ride the roller coaster of experience.

Certain passages in James's *Principles of Psychology* and *The Will to Believe* also suggested a pragmatic theory of truth,[90] but he made his ideas explicit in the series of lectures published in 1907 as *Pragmatism*. The scope of pragmatism, he wrote, is twofold: "first, a method; and second, a generic theory of what is meant by truth." As a method, pragmatism is primarily a means of settling otherwise interminable metaphysical disputes by asking, "What difference would it practically make to anyone if this notion rather than that notion were true?" Countless philosophical problems simply dissolve when put to the pragmatic test, James maintained. Those that remain can best be settled through experience rather than abstract reasoning. Philosophy is not a solution. It is "a program for more work," and more specifically "an indication of the ways in which existing realities may be changed."[91] Pragmatism evaluates situations and responses according to experience; it assumes the efficacy of volition completed in praxis.

As a theory of truth, James emphasized, pragmatism "has in fact no prejudices whatever, no obstructive dogmas, no rigid canons of what shall count as proof." Pragmatism accepts any evidence, whether it comes from the senses or from logic or from the most personal experiences. Although James disclaimed any necessary connection between his pragmatism and his radical empiricism, his willingness to weigh all hypotheses derived from his appeal to immediate experience as the highest court for judging knowledge claims. According to James, truth is not an inherent property of an idea. Instead, "truth *happens* to an idea. It becomes true, is made true by events." In another of James's deliberately provocative formulations, he asserted boldly that "the true, to put it very briefly, is only the expedient in the way of our thinking, just as the right is only the expedient in the way of our behaving." His qualification that he meant "expedient in the long run and on the whole, of course,"[92] hardly mollified his critics. Individual interpretations of expediency vary widely, and some philosophers feared that James had escaped the block universe of monistic idealism only to seek asylum in solipsism. In a letter to his son William, James admitted that he considered *Pragmatism* the most important thing he had written, and he confessed his expectation that it would "stir up a lot of attention."[93] Given the epochal status of *The Principles of Psychology*, the first claim may be questionable, but the prediction proved accurate: the book provoked a furor.

One of the most frequently cited difficulties in *Pragmatism* had to do with the uncertain correspondence of pragmatic truth with objective reality. By emphasizing expediency, James seemed to confuse the effects of belief with the objects of belief, and to value the former while discounting the latter. Thus, critics charged, James elevated personal satisfaction derived from accepting a certain claim above the fundamental question of whether the claim corresponded to the facts. Fouillée concentrated on that problem in his discussion of James's pragmatism. For forty years, from his introduction of the concept of *idées-forces* in *La Liberté et le déterminisme* (1872; *Freedom and Determinism*) to his final book, *La Pensée et les nouvelles écoles anti-intellectualistes* (1911; *Thought and the New Schools of Anti-Intellectualism*), Fouillée held that the strength of ideas depends not only on the beliefs, choices, and actions of individuals, but also on the coercive force of "objective possibility" in which ideas prove either true or false. The *idée-force* itself was thus essentially pragmatic in conception, as James emphasized in his marginal notations to Fouillée's *Evolution of idées-forces*, because it required testing every belief in experience to measure its validity. Fouillée directed some of his sharpest remarks against abstract theories that admitted no possibility of empirical verification, and he intended his philosophy to serve as a corrective to such speculation. Fouillée consistently maintained that believing makes a substantial difference in choosing and acting, that "will and belief engender each other," yet he contended that James underestimated the constraints imposed on belief by external reality. Only when beliefs, or ideas, correspond with the facts, Fouillée proclaimed, can they be considered true. Their satisfactoriness for any individual, which Fouillée believed to be the ultimate test for James, provides insufficient grounds for asserting their truth.[94]

In an essay on *Pragmatism*, Dewey likewise concentrated on this issue, which he considered decisive in separating his ideas from James's. Dewey deemed it "unpragmatic for pragmatism to content itself with finding out the value of a conception whose own inherent significance pragmatism has not first determined." Instead of searching for truths, Dewey counseled, we should think in terms of working hypotheses that we test in experience. Dewey admitted that James sometimes seemed to adopt such a position "unequivocally," but at other times "any good which flows from acceptance of a belief is treated as if it were evidence [to that extent], of the truth of the idea." Dewey believed that to be a mistake. From the perspective of the Chicago School, Dewey wrote tersely, "the personal is not ultimate." He concluded, though, that James's excesses could be traced to his polemical insistence, contrary to rationalist pretensions, that truths are *made.* They are not "a priori, or eternally in existence," and "their value or importance is not static, but dynamic and practical."[95] While Dewey affirmed the legitimacy of that understanding of truth, he, like Fouillée, criticized James for underestimating the coercive force of objective conditions on personal belief.

James had to defend *Pragmatism* almost from the moment of its publication, and he intended *The Meaning of Truth* (1909) to serve as his final clarification of the pragmatic method. Suffering from angina and weary of the seemingly endless debate surrounding his theory of truth, he wished to put the subject to rest so he could concentrate on elaborating his doctrine of radical empiricism. As early as 1907, the year in which *Pragmatism* appeared, James had grudgingly conceded the legitimacy of the critique that Fouillée, Dewey, and others ranging from realists to absolute idealists advanced against his version of the pragmatic theory of truth.[96] He admitted that truth necessarily involves "agreement with reality." In *The Meaning of Truth* he elaborated his position, and he attempted, with only limited success,[97] to indicate that correspondence of belief with reality is *presupposed* rather than ignored in his conception of the pragmatic test of truth. Although he insisted that the personal satisfaction which his critics had assailed was an indispensable part of truth, it was insufficient by itself as a test of truth "unless reality is incidentally led to." James emphasized that "there can be no truth if there is nothing to be true about," and he claimed that he had always remained an epistemological realist who built his philosophy upon a firm empirical foundation.

In *The Meaning of Truth*, James attempted to answer the criticism directed against *Pragmatism* by suggesting three different conditions necessary for establishing that a statement is pragmatically true. First, it must be cognitively true; i.e., it must correspond to objective reality. James expressed astonishment that his critics could ever suppose he "let go" of this most basic requirement. He never stressed this point only because, as an empiricist, he took it for granted and did not consider its discussion philosophically interesting or important.[98] Second, the statement must fit the existing system of beliefs. The necessity of assimilating new truths with old serves as a brake built into the verification process, and the requirement that new claims establish themselves with reference to an entire body of well-established and generally accepted beliefs obviates the possibility of solipsism.[99] Finally, a statement is true if it fulfills the first two conditions *and* yields satisfaction. Critics had pounced on James's "will to believe" as a defense of irrational belief in the face of empirical evidence. James responded by pointing out that a belief can work in the long run only if the first two conditions are fulfilled, or at least if the idea cannot be proved false and does not contradict the accepted stock of beliefs. These three conditions taken together, not merely the third in isolation, constitute the pragmatic theory of truth.[100] In *The Meaning of Truth*, then, the final formulation of his pragmatism, James seemed to concede the force of the criticism advanced by such analysts as Fouillée and Dewey regarding the coercive force of objective reality. He grounded the "fiduciary element" in knowledge firmly upon an enlarged conception of experience.

Dilthey linked his analysis of lived experience directly to a pragmatic version of truth. As finite beings, we must be satisfied with "relative certainty" that begins in faith and ends in provisional acceptance pending disproof in future experience. While Dilthey thus identified the fiduciary aspect in all knowledge that James elaborated in his pragmatism, the source of Dilthey's theory of truth cannot be traced to America but to the *Idealrealismus* of the nineteenth-century German philosophers Schleiermacher, Trendlenburg, and Kuno Fischer. As Fischer wrote, "Only the effectual is the truly real, knowledge of which is the aim of philosophy."[101] Dilthey criticized the pretensions of Kantian and Hegelian logic to establish knowledge on a foundation of absolute certainty, and he denied that we are able to go behind or above our experience in the manner of neo-Kantian critique. In contrast to such formal cognitional theory, he developed a concept of self-reflection emphasizing man's active as well as his contemplative nature and relating knowledge to the validation of beliefs in experience: "In the interconnections of the facts of consciousness," he wrote, "self reflection equally finds the foundations of action as well as thought."[102] Despite the different sources of their ideas, Dilthey and James endorsed a similar theory of truth, and the echoes of Trendlenburg perceptible in Dilthey's writings resonate also in Dewey's instrumentalism.

These heretics all shared an aversion to dogma and a fondness for experimentation that sprang from their radical conceptions of immediate experience, voluntarism, and activity, and culminated in their pragmatic theory of truth. "Whether a knife is sharp," Dilthey argued in good pragmatic fashion, "can be discovered best when one cuts with it. The fruitfulness of a method," he concluded, "can finally be determined only by whether one makes discoveries through it."[103] The philosophers of the *via media* abandoned the search for certainty as fruitless when they found it inconsistent with the fundamental facts of experience. Through their new conceptualization of thinking, they were able to discover that all knowledge, in the human sciences as well as the natural sciences, can never be true in any final or ultimate sense. That realization, while extending Kant's strictures about phenomenal knowledge, nevertheless rescued these thinkers from the cynicism that captured many of their contemporaries, and it disclosed new vistas for understanding human culture and history.[104]

3

Culture, Understanding, and History

1. The Social and Meaningful Quality of Experience

The philosophers of the *via media* exchanged epistemology for history. They dismissed abstract questions about the nature of man and the nature of truth as unanswerable, because unless such questions are asked in the context of real historical situations they are meaningless. In contrast to those of their generation who were incapacitated by uncertainty, they found a new method of sounding the depths of social experience. They believed that with an understanding of the human sciences derived from hermeneutics, modern culture might be able to navigate without stars on the basis of its own accumulated experience. Although their denial of final truths and their reliance on a continuing process of interpretation seemed to promise only relativism, their historical sensibility shielded their doubt from despair.

Just as these thinkers maintained that immediate experience precedes the distinction of subject from object, so they considered the existence of others a primary datum of life, and they reasoned that attempts to isolate individuals from their cultural matrix for analytical purposes made as little sense as the effort to separate the subject from the object of knowledge. In experience we encounter other people immediately, and only by abstracting from life can the isolated individual as "natural man" be considered an object of study. Because this generation preferred empirical analysis to such hypostatizing, they disallowed all conceptions of individual life outside explicit sociocultural contexts. As Dilthey argued in his *Einleitung in die Geisteswissenschaften* (1883; cited hereafter as *Introduction to the Human Sciences*), we experience life from the beginning in a set of "common lived relations with others." Philosophers' attempts to analyze a pure ego foundered on the falsity of the concept itself. "The foremost trait of the individual," Dilthey protested, "is that it lives in something which is not itself," and it cannot be examined outside that context. The attempt to uncover a human essence, whether Descartes's *cogito*, Hobbes's solitary brute, Rousseau's *bon sauvage*, or Adam Smith's economic man, could not succeed, because the idea of man as a fact prior to society and history is a "fiction of genetic explanation." The "connection of the individual with humanity," Dilthey concluded, "is a reality," and the empirical study of man must therefore begin with recognition of man's rootedness in a specific context.[1] Several years later, he suggested that the "outer world is first given in other persons," and that formulation linked his view of the social dimension of experience even more closely with his analysis of *Erlebnis* as the foundation of knowledge.[2]

Fouillée likewise stressed the social dimension of individual experience. In his early study *La Science sociale contemporaine* (1880; cited hereafter as *Contemporary Social Science*), he asserted that all philosophical, ethical, and psychological questions must be conceived in social terms because the individual cannot be separated from society.[3] Fouillée argued that inasmuch as the human individual has any essence at all, it must be considered social, because an awareness of our social context enters at the very root of our conception of ourselves. He considered this awareness of others the basis of all human relations, and he believed that personal "realization" requires the integration of the individual self with the social self. He tried to establish this claim, in large part, by referring to recognition of others in immediate experience. In his later writings, Fouillée echoed Dilthey's challenge to the Cartesian concept of the ego by proclaiming the principle "*cogito ergo sumus*." This new formulation, Fouillée wrote in *Ethics of idées-forces*, expresses the fact of consciousness as encountered in "primordial experience." Fundamental to all experience, he contended, is individual consciousness, which, as part of its self-awareness, recognizes that the affirmation of one's life entails the affirmation of others' lives as well. This realization is based on "a pre-metaphysical and pre-critical viewpoint" grounded in "immediate and positive experience." Against Kant and Fichte, Fouillée claimed that consciousness cannot be examined in its pure form, because in experience it always has content. That content, he insisted, includes the recognition of others. As a result, one cannot obtain from a concept of pure individuality a knowledge of real life as it is embedded in social relations.[4]

The recognition of the social dimension of experience did not originate with these theorists, of course. The notion of society as an organism, whether derived from Hegelian, Comtean, or Darwinian insights, dominated late nineteenth-century thought. Because they based their analysis on the strictly empirical concept of lived experience, however, the partisans of the radical theory of knowledge differed from others who proclaimed varieties of social organicism. Instead of using the prisms of idealism, positivism, or scientific naturalism, Dilthey, Fouillée, Dewey, and James proceeded from their interpretation of individual consciousness to establish the inherently social character of life and thus of knowledge. This difference is apparent even in Dewey's early writings, where the influence of Hegel and Green is most evident. In *The Ethics of Democracy* (1888), Dewey wrote that "the ideal of all social organization" would be one in which "the individual and society are organic to each other," a social ideal with a clear idealistic lineage. But the argument Dewey developed from that premise indicates that he was already moving toward a more empirical perspective. "The nonsocial individual," he wrote, "is an abstraction arrived at by imagining what man would be if all his human qualities were taken away. Society, as a real whole, is the normal order, and the mass as an aggregate of isolated units is the fiction."[5] By rejecting that conception of individuals and society, which had been a standard notion of Anglo-American philosophers since Hobbes and Locke, he registered his preference for the organicism of Hegel and Green.

Dewey's claim that the nonsocial individual is an abstraction suggested the direction in which his ideas were moving. In "Psychology as Philosophic Method" (1899), he made his position explicit: "Psychology is a political science." The individual whom psychology studies is, "after all, a social individual," and thus "any setting off and apart of a sphere of consciousness as, even for scientific purposes, self-sufficient, is condemned in advance."[6] Dewey cut himself loose both from Fichtean notions of the pure, abstract ego and from empirical psychologies that did not admit the importance of social factors in the formation of the individual personality. Neither idealists nor traditional empiricists could establish satisfactorily what we know immediately from lived experience: all of our knowledge is entangled in a web of social life.

James's *Principles of Psychology* evidences a similar contextualist approach, although the standard interpretation of James emphasizes the supposedly individualistic orientation of his thought. There is a certain amount of truth to this familiar argument, particularly when it is advanced to support the contrast between James and Dewey.[7] Yet James, like Dewey, recognized that social relations lay at the heart of lived experience. Characteristically, he never speculated whether man is social or egoistic by nature, both because he consistently opposed dualism and because the search for an "essence of man" was alien to his style of thinking. He was more attuned to the nuances of human existence, and categorizations of human nature seemed only to drain the subtlety from life. Instead James turned to empirical study, where he discovered various appetites and preferences that shifted within and among different individuals in different situations. This led him to emphasize "man's Social Self," which he defined in terms of "the recognition he gets from his mates." Human beings are "not only gregarious animals," he wrote in his *Psychology*, "but we have an innate propensity to get ourselves noticed, and noticed favorably, by our kind." In a startling passage, he continued, "No more fiendish punishment could be devised, were such a thing physically possible, than that one should be turned loose in society and remain absolutely unnoticed by all the members thereof."[8] Fouillée advanced a similar argument. "In experience," he wrote, "the 'me' must oppose against itself not merely a 'not-me,'" as Kant and Fichte had argued; one also needs an "'other me,' another subject, and even a number of 'other me's'" forming a society. That system of social relations, Fouillée argued, in which individual consciousness is accompanied by consciousness of others not merely *not* himself but *like* himself, is given in immediate experience.[9]

Given their conception of experience, these radical empiricists applied the pragmatic theory of truth in a decidedly social rather than individualistic manner. This was as true of James as it was of Dewey, although commentators have tended to distinguish their philosophies on this point. Dewey focused his attention explicitly on the individual-in-context and on the social verification of truth. He advocated instrumentalism as a means by which the individual could validate his knowledge in activity as part of an entire community engaged in the process of inquiry. James distrusted Dewey's organic conception of society because he considered it an unfortunate legacy of Dewey's early Hegelianism, and he tended instead to emphasize the individual validation of truth in his pragmatism. Yet the difference was emphatic rather than absolute. James, like Dewey, considered experience itself to be fundamentally social. For that reason, his pragmatic standard necessarily involved a social test, because it would be impossible for an idea to work pragmatically "in the long run" should it prove inconsistent with the experience of others. If other people are an integral part of individual experience, their approbation cannot be separated from the satisfaction of the individual attempting to determine the validity of his beliefs. James did place greater emphasis on the personal than the social dimension of the pragmatic test of truth, and to that extent his pragmatism should be distinguished from Dewey's instrumentalism. I want only to insist that James recognized the necessity of social validation as well as personal validation of truth. In *Pragmatism*, he maintained that "truth lives, in fact, for the most part on a credit system. Our thoughts and beliefs 'pass,' so long as nothing challenges them." Ultimately, although some individual or individuals must verify each truth, many, and perhaps even most, of the things we accept as true we accept on trust. "You accept my verification of one thing, I yours of another. We trade on each other's truth." James cautioned that "beliefs verified by *somebody* are the posts of the superstructure." But he did not intend by emphasizing personal verification to suggest that it alone could establish the truths necessary for us to live. Indeed, he explicitly pointed out that "indirectly or only potentially verifying processes may thus be true as well as full verification-processes."[10] James accepted the legitimacy and even the inevitability of the social test of truth as an indirect process of verification.

James demanded that all truth must ultimately be confirmed in personal experience. Yet because social relations are part of personal experience, the contradiction between individual and social tests of truth can be exaggerated. As I have noted, James denied that his pragmatism necessarily related to his doctrine of radical empiricism. He did link the two ideas, however, and in conjunction they clarify the congruence between personal and social verification in his thought. Thus, by recognizing (1) the primacy of lived experience for James; (2) the social dimension of experience as he conceived it; and (3) his understanding that satisfaction ultimately depends largely on the recognition we receive from others, it is possible to discern beneath their discordant emphases the harmony of James's pragmatism and Dewey's instrumentalism.

Fouillée and Dilthey also tied their analysis of the social side of individual consciousness to the verification of truth by the community. Fouillée referred to the "indissoluble link between self and other" as the foundation of his concept of *idées-forces*. Ideas can only be validated, he argued, as they manifest themselves "in the living reciprocity of activity and passion" in the context of society. Because of the role others play in personal experience, we can only determine the strength (*force*) or truth of ideas by testing them in communal activity. Without social verification, an idea cannot become an *idée-force*.[11] The social verification of truth also served as the basis of Dilthey's hermeneutics. After 1900, in order to combat the charges of psychologism leveled against him, Dilthey shifted his focus increasingly to the manifestations of human knowledge in cultural production. In his earlier writings, Dilthey, like James, Dewey, and Fouillée, concentrated on the structure and contents of individual lived experience. In his later writings, he emphasized instead experience as mediated by culture. He introduced two concepts to fill out his doctrine of *Erlebnis*: "reflected experience of life" (*Lebenserfahrung*) and "life values" (*Lebenswerte*). By reflected experience of life, Dilthey meant expressions of lived experience objectified in a language that embodies the shared experience of a culture as it develops historically. *Lebenserfahrung* is personal experience raised "through the communal to the universal," thereby attaining a kind of generality, and validity, not available at the purely subjective level, and thus capable of disclosing objective knowledge. Expressions of this "reflected experience of life" possess an inherently social quality because they "constitute themselves in a collective circle of persons. They are statements about the nature and course of life, judgments about what has proved to be of value, rules of living, and determination of goals and goods. Their hallmark is that they are creations of a community."[12] This contextualist principle connects Dilthey's idea of lived experience with his hermeneutics much as James's concept of the "social self" connects his radical empiricism with his pragmatism. Both ideas close the gap between personal and community experience by acknowledging that individual selves are situated in layers of social and cultural context.

A passage from Dilthey's unpublished papers written in 1904 expresses his insight into the connections between the subjectivity of personal knowledge and the objectivity of cultural expression, a connection we know as part of individual lived experience. We must begin, Dilthey wrote, "with a type of thinking which directs itself to consciousness and the phenomena which are contained in that consciousness." We cannot proceed simply by making inferences from a single individual consciousness, for that would lead us, with Hume, toward skepticism. "Rather, the starting point lies in my consciousness insofar as it contains a coherence of knowledge which is in agreement with *other consciousnesses* perceived by me—a coherence therefore which extends beyond my own consciousness." Nothing transcendental needs to be invoked to accomplish this task, because such knowledge is given immediately in consciousness. Other persons, who are part of our experience, thus provide us with various perspectives on truth, and these perspectives validate our beliefs. Two crucial sentences encapsulate Dilthey's argument and belie accusations that he indulged in romantic subjectivism: "There is no perspective without an objective order. This is the fact which is finally the guarantee for the objective and real validity for our knowledge."[13]

Yet truth, even intersubjective truth in the sense of socially validated knowledge, remains imperfect for two reasons. First, as I have noted, truth "happens to an idea," in James's words, and we are thus able to attain at any time only what Dilthey termed "relative certainty." Second, our knowledge cannot be more than provisional because, inasmuch as our object is the reflected experience of life, we can only interpret rather than know positively. Because human cultural expressions are meaningful, our goal must be understanding rather than precise, absolute knowledge, and our approach must therefore be hermeneutic.

2. Interpretation as a Means of Knowing

The idea that human life is meaningful formed an integral part of the radical theory of knowledge. Both idealist metaphysics and empirical science envisioned the world as an essentially static collection of objects to be known, but experience gives us a world governed by neither logic nor clarity but frayed at the edges by ambiguity. Knowledge must be sought in meaning, Fouillée pointed out, because precise images of reality do not correspond to the fuzziness of life.[14] With characteristic opacity, Dewey presented a variant of this argument in "The Experimental Theory of Knowledge" (1906). Truth and falsity are significant concepts only "in situations in which specific meanings and their already experienced fulfillments and non-fulfillments" can be "intentionally compared and contrasted with reference to the question of the worth, as to reliability of meaning, of the given meaning or class of meanings." Knowing has to do with human purposes, with the meanings we impart to situations, and truth, like knowledge, Dewey concluded, "is an experienced relation of things, and it has no meaning outside of such relation."[15] Everything given to us in experience is meaningful, and we cannot determine truth or falsity in any sphere of knowledge ranging from physics to poetry outside the inevitably social context of human purposes.

James and Dilthey tied the meaningfulness of human experience to their concepts of consciousness. The significance of the objects of experience, according to James, derives from the "free water of consciousness" that surrounds every image entering our minds, water that imbues each impression with meaning. Although traditional psychologists, in their quest to discover a science of the mind, had ignored the meaningful quality of existence, no radically empirical analysis could overlook it.[16] Dilthey invoked a somewhat different image to describe the pervasiveness of meaning, likening it to our experience of color and tone. He denied that it could be further defined because he considered it "descriptively final."[17] Meaning, along with willing and causal relations, constitutes one of the fundamental categories by which we know reality, and Dilthey considered the relationship of these three in the mind to be "one of the ultimate facts" that consciousness could reach.[18] He further declared that we must evaluate the meaning of experience without recourse to anything transcendental, because there is nothing in life that "points to a meaning beyond itself."[19] According to the philosophers of the *via media*, meaning must be interpreted on the basis of lived experience and informed with an understanding of the reflected experience of life. That perspective of contextualism, as I will suggest, entailed a particular historical sensibility from which these theorists advanced their ethical and political arguments.

I believe that the radical theory of knowledge, focused as it was on immediate experience conceived as social and meaningful, logically culminates in a hermeneutics such as Dilthey developed in his later writings. While Fouillée, James, and Dewey did not write explicitly about hermeneutics, their understanding of the contingency of knowledge, the social verification of truth, the scope of philosophical inquiry, and their sensitivity to problems of interpretation stemming from their contextualism all point in that direction. This argument admittedly rests on muted harmonies rather than definite correspondences, and I do not want to cast James and Dewey in the role of proto- or quasi-hermeneuticists, but certain passages in their writings do suggest intriguing if scarcely conclusive similarities between some of their ideas and Dilthey's. First, they dismissed as misguided the attempt to transform philosophy into an exact science that would concentrate on logic and rule out all empirically unverifiable statements as meaningless. James advised Bertrand Russell to "say good-bye to mathematical logic if you wish to preserve your relations with concrete realities!" Elsewhere, James bemoaned the tendency of positivistic empiricists to "try to build the philosophy up out of the single phrases, taking first one and then another and seeking to make them fit," a strategy he considered doomed to failure. In a veiled reference to Russell, James criticized philosophers who "crawl over the thing like a myopic ant over a building, tumbling into every microscopic crack or fissure, finding nothing but inconsistencies, and never suspecting that a center exists."[20] James devoted his entire career to the attempt to rescue from positivists the utterly uncategorizable, unpredictable, and meaning-laden quality of human life. He was saddened by the prospect that the delightful serendipity distinguishing our experience of life from our experience of logic might be banished from the world of philosophical discourse by analytic philosophers. For his part, Dewey dismissed Russell's and Moore's analytic realism as an "affront to the common-sense world of action, appreciation, and affection," a movement that threatened to "land philosophy in a formalism like unto scholasticism."[21] Dilthey similarly denigrated philosophy's concentration on logic rather than life: "We must get away from looking at the kind of formal logic that takes thought in itself separated from its accomplishment. Such formal logic is an unfruitful abstraction; all thought consists only in relation to reality."[22] Like James and Dewey, Dilthey aimed to redirect philosophy away from abstract formulas and toward experience, and experience as these theorists conceived it contained at its center exactly the perplexing questions of meaning and value that analytic philosophy judged beyond its scope.

Second, James and Dewey were sensitive to the ubiquitous problem of relating the part to the whole in order to penetrate the meaning of experience, whether examined at the level of a culture developing over time, members of a community interacting at a specific moment, or an individual trying to express ideas in language. This awareness of the inevitable link between language, meaning, and interpretive understanding surfaced periodically in Dewey's writings. "Consciousness in a being with language denotes awareness of perception of meanings," he pointed out. "It is the perception of actual events, whether past, contemporary, or future, *in* their meanings."[23] Interpretation, requiring recognition of the relation between text (or individual, or culture) and context, is integral to the study of human knowledge and action, because people think, express themselves, and act within a universe of meanings which exist outside them and which they nevertheless help to shape. In his chapter "Meaning" in *How We Think* (1909), Dewey expressed an insight remarkably similar to that informing Dilthey's hermeneutics: "All knowledge, all science, thus aims to grasp the meaning of objects and events," Dewey wrote. "This process always consists in taking them out of their apparent brute isolation as events, and finding them to be part of some larger whole *suggested by them*, which, in turn, *accounts for, explains, interprets* them; i.e., renders them significant."[24]

This emphasis on the centrality of interpretation, on the search for meaning lodged in the relation of all objects or events to their contexts, reveals an intriguing aspect of Dewey's thinking. Dewey considered himself a naturalist by the time he wrote these passages, and they show the extent to which the distinction customarily drawn between his naturalism and Dilthey's hermeneutics may rest on a misunderstanding of both thinkers. Dewey did not intend by offering science as the paradigm for inquiry to minimize the importance of interpretation as a means of knowing. Quite to the contrary, he emphasized that science, like all other forms of knowledge, aims at the meaning of the phenomena toward which it is directed. He rejected the positivists' claim that science reveals information about the world that is privileged in some way. Instead he stressed the continuity between philosophical inquiry and physical science, both of which are experimental enterprises aiming to provide useful knowledge by inquiring of the world and finding answers that enable us to cope with reality. Dewey's naturalism and Dilthey's hermeneutics manifest a sensitivity to the sociology of scientific knowledge now familiar from the work of Thomas Kuhn, an awareness that science reflects human purposes as much as it reflects the nature of the world. We cannot attain knowledge of any object or event, whether it is the characteristics of a quark or a quatrain, the formation of DNA or democratic communities, without inquiring about its meaning for us, without interpreting its significance in terms of the multiple contexts of which it is a part.

Another revealing example of this contextualist attitude, which exhibits with equal clarity a sensitivity to the hermeneutic principle of relating the parts to the whole in order to achieve understanding, is a provocative passage in James's *Principles of Psychology*. If we remove a single word from a page and repeat it long enough, James suggested, "it ends by assuming an entirely unnatural aspect," because we have lifted it from its nest—we have severed the part from the whole. Isolated from its context, James wrote, the single word stares at the reader

> like a glass eye, with no speculation in it. Its body is indeed there, but its soul is fled. It is reduced, by this new way of attending to it, to its sensational nudity. We never attended to it in this way, but habitually got it clad with its meaning the moment we caught sight of it, and rapidly passed from it to the other words of the phrase. We apprehended it, in short, with a cloud of associates, and thus perceiving it, we felt it quite otherwise than as we feel it now divested and alone.[25]

Like the artist he nearly became, James understood that the richness of experience emerges from its gestalt: from its clarity, arrangement, and emotional coloring. Whether we are trying to make sense of a culture, a person, a text, or, as in James's example, a single word, meaning flows from composition and tone as well as from manifest content. In James's as in Dewey's work, the importance of context for understanding never received extended analysis as a separate theme, but it was very much a part of the atmosphere of their writings.

The necessity, and the problematic quality, of relating the part to the whole, the text to the context, became increasingly central in Dilthey's writings, especially in the years following publication of his "Ideas about a Descriptive and Analytical Psychology" (1894). While I consider Dilthey's later work a natural flowering of seeds planted in his earlier writings, it is true that he showed greater sensitivity after 1900 to the connection between lived experience (*Erlebnis*) and expression (*Ausdruck*) in the achievement of understanding (*Verstehen*).[26] Indeed, he considered the understanding of meaning-laden expression to be the culmination of his prior investigations. "The solution of the epistemological problem," as he put it, "leads on to the logical problem of hermeneutics."[27] Experience, expression, and understanding, Dilthey reasoned, are mutually dependent; an adequate account of how we know must incorporate all three of them.[28] Thus, in his view: (1) we *experience* life as meaningful; (2) we *express* that meaning in language; and (3) we *understand* such expressions of human experience hermeneutically.

Dilthey's analysis of understanding, the tool wielded by practitioners of the human sciences, has attracted considerable criticism, much of which has focused on the alleged psychologism of the concept.[29] That charge stems from Dilthey's own designation of *Verstehen* in Humboldt's terms as "the re-discovery of the I in the Thou," which seems to suggest that we know by the mystical or intuited reexperiencing of another's *Erlebnis*.[30] But he insisted that the lived experience of others is never directly accessible to us; instead, we understand *expressions* of experience rather than experience itself.

That focus on expression as the object of understanding enabled Dilthey to avoid the psychologistic trap that James discovered. "The antinomy of psychology," Dilthey wrote, "has been pointed out by James: that one can never grasp a feeling as such in self-observation." Because "such a feeling is always something very complex and compacted," he continued, "it can be partially reduced to its parts but not taken whole." It is possible to overcome psychologism only "through the relation of expression and understanding."[31] Dilthey introduced the explicit consideration of expression to supplement his analysis of experience, and he offered hermeneutics as the method providing access to the meaning of expression. Only by understanding mediated experience manifested in expression, he argued, can we escape psychologistic fallacies and penetrate the core of meaning in human life. Man understands himself "only through the circuitous route" of understanding others.[32]

Dilthey used the word *Verstehen* to designate the process whereby "mental life comes to be known through expressions of it given to the senses."[33] Expressions necessarily leave the purely subjective realm because they are embedded in language, a quintessentially sociocultural product that objectifies individual experience in terms held in common. This process of objectification and mediation, which prevents understanding from sliding into either psychologism or intuitionism, rests on the analysis of meaning as rooted in the social dimension of experience. Dilthey linked his concept of *Verstehen* with the objective social manifestations of experience in language, where the subjective thought-world and the objective world of culturally shaped meanings meet and interpenetrate. *Verstehen* is thus not an irrational and unverifiable process incapable of giving access to knowledge, even though the knowledge it yields must remain imperfect and open to revision pending further disclosures. The assumptions that underlie Dilthey's treatment of *Verstehen* do not belong to the realm of mystification or idealism, but derive instead from the analysis of lived experience as social and meaningful. Our shared human nature, he wrote, "makes common speech and understanding among men possible."[34] His insistence on the possibility of understanding rests on nothing more mysterious—and nothing more precise or less problematical—than the existence of sufficient commonality among individuals to enable them to create a mutually comprehensible system of communication. Beyond the confining boundaries of linguistic structures, which to a degree engender our view of the world, we cannot go, either in our expressions or in our understanding of others.

Dilthey defined hermeneutics as "the methodology of the understanding of recorded expressions." Hermeneutics involves unifying the two features of expression: the internal, or psychological, side of the author's subjective experience; and the external, or social, side of that experience objectified in language. Understanding emerges only from the integration of both aspects of expression, a difficult process further complicated by the necessity of recognizing that the researcher brings to his studies his own personal experience and his own historical context. Thus, understanding is a doubly perspectival process: both the author and examiner of the expression being examined must be seen in terms of the internal and external aspects of their experience. In all expression, experience manifests itself objectively, yet we cannot know either the pure subjectivity of another's experience or the pure universality of another's expression. We must relinquish claims to knowledge that is precise and final; the best we can do is to understand hermeneutically. We come to knowledge in the human sciences much as we come to knowledge of a friend, and even after we peel away layers of misconception and ambiguity, something impenetrable remains because no experience other than our own is finally accessible to us from within.[35]

Paradoxically, however, Dilthey maintained that "one has to understand an author better than he understands himself."[36] He grounded that bold assertion not only on his awareness of the perils of psychologism but on the hermeneutic principle of relating the part to the whole. Dilthey's hermeneutics emerged from the intertwined ideas discussed in the preceding chapter: the consciousness of continuity and the continuity of consciousness. In his "Ideas about a Descriptive and Analytical Psychology," Dilthey argued that "we explain by means of purely intellectual processes, but we understand by means of the cooperation of all the powers of the mind in apprehension." Thus the unity of sensation, volition, and cognition figures in understanding. "In understanding," he continued, "we start from the system of the whole, which is given to us as a living reality" as part of the unity of experience, and then proceed "to make the particular intelligible to ourselves in terms of it." From this analysis of *Erlebnis*, Dilthey advanced the fundamental idea of hermeneutics: "The fact that we live in the consciousness of the system of the whole is what enables us to understand a particular statement, a particular gesture, or a particular action. All psychological thinking retains this fundamental trait, that the apprehension of the whole makes possible and determines the interpretation of the particular part."[37] Understanding as the relation of part to whole involves at least four different hermeneutic circles. First, as Dilthey wrote in "The Origin of Hermeneutics," "The whole of a work must be understood from individual words and their combination, but full understanding of an individual part presupposes understanding of the whole." The same reciprocal process applies to the relation of an individual work with: (1) its author's mentality; (2) its literary genre; and (3) the historical context in which it appeared. Understanding each of these parts requires understanding the whole, and vice versa. Encircling all of these is the analyst's awareness of the relation between his own experience and understanding, a prism that inevitably colors his interpretation of others' expressions.[38]

Hermeneutics is an imperfect method of achieving understanding. Dilthey admitted its limitations when he pointed out that because understanding is connected with experience, "it contains something irrational because life is irrational." Rather than countenancing the indulgence of fanciful intuitions, however, Dilthey intended by that admission only to deny the possibility of attaining understanding in the human sciences by purely logical formulas. Recapturing the whole mental reality embedded in expression, Dilthey wrote, yields only "subjective certainty," yet beyond that we cannot penetrate due to the "limits set to the logical treatment of understanding by its own nature."[39] Although the process is imperfect, various interpretations do not simply cancel one another. Dilthey subscribed to neither an anarchy nor a democracy of interpretation. If "all understanding remains always relative and can never be completed," the process is nevertheless progressive and aims toward the "disciplined elevation of understanding to general validity." Hermeneutics has as its goal, "beyond its use in the business of interpretation, a second task which is indeed its main one: it is to counteract the constant irruption of romantic whim and sceptical subjectivity" by establishing "the foundations of valid interpretation."[40]

By their very nature the *Geisteswissenschaften* can never yield final and complete understanding any more than the *Naturwissenschaften* can, but the careful application of hermeneutic methods can refine our understanding of human expression to the point of "general validity." To reiterate the point made earlier, the distinction Dilthey drew between the *Geistes-* and *Naturwissenschaften* was emphatic, not ontic, and it reflected the portrait Dilthey drew of the distinctiveness of lived experience. "Mind can only understand what it has created," he wrote, echoing Vico. "Nature, the subject-matter of the physical sciences, embraces the reality which has arisen independently of the activity of mind."[41] That is not to say that knowledge derived from the natural sciences is more certain, or in any way more privileged, than the understanding we derive from the human sciences. It is merely to acknowledge that we ask different questions of proteins than we ask of politicians, and they provide different sorts of answers. Dilthey repeatedly stressed that "knowledge of both the natural sciences and the human sciences mingles" at the countless points of transition between the two sorts of inquiry. He offered as two obvious examples language and music, which we cannot understand without studying the natural laws of sound formation as well as the cultural contexts in which they operate. That clarification dissolves the notion of two independent spheres of knowledge in a manner congruent with Dewey's comments on the interpretive quality of all science. Another of Dilthey's formulations of this position further suggests its similarities with Dewey's instrumentalism. "All purposes lie with man's mental sphere," Dilthey wrote, "for only there is anything real for him." Yet consciousness is not independent, and the mental sphere cannot be studied independently from its physical context, because "the purpose seeks its means in nature."[42] Without trying to transform instrumentalism into hermeneutics or vice versa, I want to emphasize that Dilthey's supposed dualism was a heuristic construct rather than a set of ontological categories. Dilthey was as closely attuned to the interpenetration of mind and matter, the relation of thought and experimentation, as was Dewey, whose celebrated naturalism itself rested on a conception of science as interpretive rather than positivistic.

Dilthey's hermeneutics emerged from his analysis of experience. He insisted that because life is meaningful, values enter into immediate experience. Understanding, therefore, cannot be separated from the question of value; in other words, the human sciences can never be value-free. Meaning and value are the marrow of life, and both the researcher and the author whose expressions are being examined hold values that figure in the process of expression and interpretation. These values cannot be factored out as part of a quest for science, because any conception of human experience from which value considerations have been extracted possesses only a spurious neutrality. Dilthey denied the possibility of achieving a Rankean objectivity in the practice of the human sciences. We must study life as imbued with meaning, because that is how we experience it. Dilthey recognized the role of subjective values in the expression and interpretation of human experience. Instead of despair or irrationalism, however, he found in that realization an anchor for understanding. Having denied the legitimacy of traditional empiricist and idealist attempts to place knowledge on the high ground of certainty, he found implicit in the radical empiricism he shared with James, Dewey, and Fouillée a view of history as a source of immanent critique. This historical sensibility would provide the philosophers of the *via media* with a foundation for judgment.

3. The Historical Sensibility

Since the Renaissance, Western theorists have become increasingly sensitive to the importance of historical change. As ascriptions of the scope of change gradually expanded, the portion of reality considered immutable correspondingly shrank. Dilthey, Fouillée, James, and Dewey in a sense only contributed to that longer process, yet their writings reveal a distinctly radical sense of history which may represent the logical culmination of the trend. For they treated all ideas as historical, including their own. Rather than concluding that relativism signaled the final dissolution of judgment, they uncovered in the historical sensibility a source of ethical and political values. History, they proclaimed, offered an empirical foundation for judgment, a vital source of immanent critique.

The radical theorists of knowledge rejected the static models of reality and knowledge that empiricists and idealists advanced. James, for example, delighted in the persistence of novelty and possibility "forever leaking in" to spoil "neat schematisms with permanent and absolute distinctions."[43] Historical theories with built-in trajectories of change, whether progressive or catastrophic, seemed equally illusory. Responding only half in jest to Henry Adams's projection of civilization's inevitable ruin, James protested in a letter to Adams that "unless the future contains genuine novelties, unless the present is really creative of them, I don't see the use of time at all."[44] From the perspective of radical empiricism, truth appeared to have come unstuck from eternity and history from purpose, and theorists presuming to chart the course of the past or the future were doomed to hell's eighth circle for falsifying historical experience.

Both idealist and positivist philosophies of history distorted the historical process by circumscribing it within a preconceived form that could not contain it. As Fouillée pointed out, both the Hegelian and Comtean models represented extensions of theology and metaphysics whose roots could be traced to Augustine. Instead of indulging in such speculation, he suggested, philosophers should recognize that human beings make history, and they should base their investigations on facts rather than positing a priori stages of historical development.[45] Like Fouillée, Dilthey dismissed both Hegel's philosophy of history and Comte's positivist sociology as variations on an identical mistake: the attempt to find behind diverse historical facts a single principle to explain them all. Dilthey considered history to be a complex system of interactions involving myriad factors, and he could see only confusion issuing from attempts to simplify it.[46] Even Dewey, whose residual Hegelianism led him to exaggerate certain historical tendencies, denied the assumption of inevitability in history: "Progress is not automatic." Dewey further expressed his distaste for the "belief that each of us, as individuals and classes, might safely and completely devote ourselves to increasing our own possessions, material, intellectual, and artistic, because progress is inevitable anyhow."[47] History, according to these critical empiricists, does not unfold according to a preconceived pattern.

Even the theory of natural selection, according to this analysis, does not disclose the secret of historical change. Darwin, Dewey argued, demonstrated only that the phenomena of life change over time. When Darwin said of species what Gallileo said of the earth, "*e pur se muove*, he emancipated, once for all, genetic and experimental ideas as an organon of asking questions and looking for explanations."[48] Unfortunately, both Darwin's champions and his critics misunderstood his revolution. Theorists such as Spencer claimed to find in the principle of natural selection an adequate explanation for the course of human history as well as the origin of species. That extension of Darwinian biology, Dewey and James argued, had no foundation in science. James labeled such an evolutionary view of history "an utterly vague and unscientific conception," representing a lapse "into the most ancient oriental fatalism."[49] While these mavericks drew sustenance from Darwin's discovery that change ruled biology as well as physics, they tempered their enthusiasm with the recognition that scientific knowledge provides at best only an approximation of reality. They perceived in science, whether Darwinian biology or the "new physics," only a kind of "conceptual shorthand," not a magical key capable of unlocking the puzzle of human history.[50]

The historical sensibility of Dilthey, Fouillée, James, and Dewey rested on their idea of lived experience. All philosophies of history, whether idealist, positivist, or quasi-biological, they branded metaphysical illusions. Only the reality of experience, both personal and as understood in the lives of others, could provide a solid foundation for historical knowledge. Their conception of the continuity of consciousness informed their view of history. They understood immediate experience as sensibly continuous across both the dimensions of space and time. Implicit in that conception was the idea of life as the unfolding of present moments in which the past, although lost, is nevertheless enveloped. That insight, similar to Bergson's *durée* yet more sensitive to the progressive quality of individual life, implied that historical moments, if examined and understood critically rather than conceived as part of a grand scheme, similarly contain accumulated experience rather than simply the contents of each consecutive present. Although history does not unfold according to a transhistorical pattern, it can yield knowledge that is progressive.

The historical sensibility was an extension of the analysis of consciousness as a stream and experience as continuous in individual life. In *The Principles of Psychology*, James expressed his preference for studying psychic states "by way of history" instead of by static analysis, because "it is obvious and palpable that our state of mind is never precisely the same." Even when the identical experience recurs, James pointed out, "we *must* think of it in a fresh manner, see it under a somewhat different angle, apprehend it in different relations from those in which it last appeared." Our thought is "suffused with that dim context" lingering from the past, and thus we cannot but think historically.[51] Dilthey expressed a similar point even more boldly: "There is never a present," Dilthey suggested, because at every moment "experience is a temporal flow."[52] If there is an essence of lived experience, its essence is its mutability. That realization gave birth to a particular kind of historical sensibility, because when the conception of life as changing is coupled with the emphasis on praxis and the pragmatic theory of truth, history emerges as the empirical basis for knowledge about man.

Given the voluntarism and the conception of the active subject central to the radical theory of knowledge, historical development appeared to result from choices made by individuals whose decisions were conditioned but not wholly determined by a social matrix. History shaped, and was shaped by, individuals. The pragmatic theory of truth harmonized with this view of history. James argued in *Pragmatism* that truth "*happens* to an idea. It becomes true, is made true by events." While James was hardly a philosopher of history, his concept of truth was inherently historical. According to the rationalist conception of truth, he proclaimed, "reality is ready-made and complete from all eternity, while for pragmatism it is still in the making, and awaits part of its complexion from the future."[53] Essays James and Dewey wrote about each other reveal that this conception of truth as historical figured as prominently in Dewey's thought as in James's. In assessing Dewey's contributions to *Studies in Logical Theory*, James singled out for praise Dewey's recognition that "what is fact for one epoch, or for one inquirer, is theory for another epoch or another inquirer," because facts are ideas that work, whereas theories are untested hypotheses. James credited Dewey with recognizing that situations change through history, and that truth, as a result, "creates itself" differently in different times and places.[54] In his review of James's *Pragmatism*, in which Dewey noted points of difference between his ideas and James's, he offered as his "final impression" the judgment that they shared "two conclusions about the character of truths as *faits accomplis*: namely that they are made, not a priori, or eternally in existence, and that their value or importance is not static, but dynamic and practical."[55] Only as ideas are verified in practice, Dewey and James believed, can they be evaluated. The pragmatic theory of truth, based on the recognition of the relation between changing values and changing situations, pointed toward a critical historicism.

In the radical theory of knowledge, the categories of Kant's transcendental aesthetic were set in motion, and when time and space came to be perceived as dynamic rather than static, the idea of a permanent nature of man could not longer be sustained. For James, Dilthey, Fouillée, and Dewey, the evanescent quality of immediate experience, not Kant's universal categories, provided the foundation of knowledge, and their conception of life as flux and truth as pragmatic excluded the possibility of any non-historical existence or idea.[56] Human beings, conceived as knowing subjects and historical actors, have no timeless, unalterable nature. In Dilthey's words, "It is the essence of man that he is historical."[57] The human mode of life is thus one of becoming rather than being, and the study of man is inseparable from the study of history. While human purposes cannot be entirely reduced to historical circumstances, no human essence can be extracted from history and analyzed. Because man makes himself through his choices and his actions, the accumulated evidence of history offers the only avenue for understanding man.

Such a historical sensibility seems necessarily to end in relativism. When all ideas and activities must be placed within a shifting context that alters their significance, how is it possible to attain a stable critical perspective from which to assess knowledge or value? In *The Will to Believe*, James declared that "there is indeed nothing which someone has not thought absolutely true, while his neighbor deemed it absolutely false."[58] Conversely, Dilthey argued that "the development of historical consciousness destroys faith in the universal validity of any philosophy which attempts to express world order cogently through a system of concepts."[59] Both contemporaries and later analysts have interpreted such remarks as emblems of intellectual exhaustion, and it is true that similar sentiments prompted some late nineteenth-century intellectuals to embrace irrationalism as an alternative to relativism.[60]

Dewey and Fouillée never confronted the challenge of relativism in the historical sensibility. Because their conceptions of individual development differed somewhat from those of James and Dilthey, they maintained that the individual tends naturally to seek "unity" and that the broader sweep of history reflects the progressive character of individuals. Although in Fouillée's case the Hegelian influence is less clear, Dewey did subscribe to a watered-down version of the idealist philosophy of history expressed in

Hegel's and Green's writings. Neither Fouillée nor Dewey was willing to follow James and Dilthey toward the apparently relativistic conclusion implied in the historical sensibility. As I have pointed out, Fouillée and Dewey perceived in human activity a natural movement toward integration and wholeness. They stripped the metaphysical shell from idealism, but their conception of both individual and historical development revealed a kernel of teleology that seemed to distinguish their ideas from the more radical historicism of James and Dilthey.

Yet James and Dilthey ultimately tried to reconcile relativism with knowledge in a manner that muted this apparent difference. The obverse of relativism, they argued, is freedom. By recognizing the historicity of all ideas and values, they claimed to discover not the sterility of relativism but the vitality of human freedom. Dilthey and James tied their historical sensibility to their voluntarism and viewed history as a project rather than a pattern. History does exhibit, to quote Dilthey, an "immanent teleological character," not because of any transhistorical human nature or historical design such as idealists posited, but precisely because, in his words, "historical life is creative. It is constantly active in the production of goods and values."[61] Human life contains awareness of the past and the future; their fusion in the present shapes our decisions. Because we can both remember and anticipate, we have an empirical basis for our choices in collective experience, i.e., history.

According to these thinkers, humans as knowing subjects are critical in the sense that we discriminate and select, and we perceive and respond to meanings as part of immediate experience. From that position, it is but a short step to the conclusion that we are free to select those meanings and values that offer the greatest likelihood of working in the pragmatic sense. History reflects the consequences of choices, both successful and unsuccessful, and it thus illuminates the various options available in the present. The historical sensibility opens the door for the critical exercise of freedom. "The historical consciousness," Dilthey wrote, "of the finitude of every historical phenomenon, every human or social state, of the relativity of every sort of belief, is the last step towards the liberation of man." The historical perspective reveals the multifaceted nature of life. Beauty and ugliness, nobility and evil, all are disclosed in history. When freed from the constraints of dogma and aware of the relativity of life, "man attains the sovereign power to wring from every experience its content, to surrender wholly to it, without prepossession, as if there were no system of philosophy and no faith which could bind men." While the historical sensibility begins with skepticism, born of relativism, it thus ends in the acceptance of responsibility, because history provides a concrete record that "cannot be conjured away." In contrast to "relativity, the continuity of the creative force [of man in history] makes itself felt as the central historical fact."[62] Lodged firmly between the subjectivism of later existentialism and the objectivism of idealist philosophy, the historical sensibility confirms the freedom, within limits, of human choice.[63] Although conditioned by history, individuals either succeed or fail as their choices are tested in praxis and rejected or accepted in the working out of history. They cannot navigate according to compass points established a priori from metaphysics. Aspiring only to relative certainty, the radical theorists of knowledge looked to history to provide an alternative to the illusion of absolute certainty and the surrender of despair.

Dilthey considered history and philosophy to be mutually corrective. The historical sensibility, as Dilthey pointed out, is not seduced by relativism. It reaches for "the generally valid in the relative,"[64] a vision attainable only in the recognition of the concrete historical process as the context and also the standard for assessing various claims. "The historical consciousness is itself creative"; it approaches the past reflectively and interprets the meaning of past experience critically. Thus, Dilthey concluded, "it raises the capacity of man in society above the limits of time and place."[65] In short, the historical sensibility provides an empirical standard of judgment, a source of immanent critique. In his lecture "Present Day Culture and Philosophy," Dilthey wrote: "If human nature is to achieve its full reality and power and the full richness of human existence, it can only do so in historical consciousness; it must become conscious of, and understand, the greatest manifestations of mankind and derive concrete ideals of a more beautiful and free future from them." Succinctly expressing the essence of the historical sensibility, he concluded, "The totality of human nature is only to be found in history"; the individual "can only become conscious of it and enjoy it when he assembles the mind of the past in himself."[66]

This viewpoint, which takes history as the basis for understanding the scope of human achievement and potential, has been appropriately designated "transcendental historicism."[67] Consistent with Kant's transcendental perspective, transcendental historicism holds that philosophy should analyze the conditions and structure of experience itself, yet unlike Kant it treats those conditions and that structure historically. From the viewpoint of transcendental historicism, it is possible to discern the creative potential in man and to evaluate his achievements not according to an abstract ideal but according to standards derived from reflecting critically on historical situations.[68] Historical understanding, Dilthey believed, rescues knowledge from relativism by disclosing the emergence of a more universal standpoint. Although history is not progressive, the knowledge we gain from it can be. Moreover, such a historical sensibility leads man toward the realization of his full capacity, and it provides the ultimate source of judgment on which the radical theory of knowledge relies.

Dilthey's own historical writing best shows his conception of the historian's task. While an extended analysis of that subject is beyond the scope of this discussion, a sense of his intentions can be gleaned from the preface to his biography of Schleiermacher. Eschewing the Rankean attempt to recount the past as it actually happened, Dilthey proclaimed his desire to do more than simply tell a story. He wanted instead to leave the reader with a "coherence of lasting ideas, rigorously founded and penetrating deeply into the scientific work and active life of the present." Description, Dilthey believed, is not enough, because finally we must act. If history is to prove valuable, it must help clarify the questions that persist into the present. Life, as he put it, requires guidance by thought, and if history neglects to meet the challenge of critically confronting difficult issues of knowledge, action, and values, it becomes trivial.[69]

The historical sensibility remains a winding path that never leads to certainty. If it is thus not everything one might desire as a source of judgment, it is not nothing, and finally it is all we have if we take seriously the radical challenge to ultimate answers this generation posed. The possibility of certainty vanished when the focus of inquiry shifted from the epistemological search for representations of reality to the hermeneutical search for pragmatic and provisional understanding, but the responsibility of choice and action remains. The conversation of modern thought dissolves into cacophony if we treat all that has happened and all that has been written as a fictional text to be taken apart at our leisure. Even if we relinquish once and for all the hope of absolute answers, we can escape the temptation of Nietzschean subjectivism in the tentative and imperfect basis for judgment available through the historical sensibility.

A brief recapitulation of my argument should indicate how the various components of the radical theory of knowledge culminated in the historical sensibility. First, these thinkers erased the distinction between subject and object and isolated immediate experience, the intersection of knower and known, as the locus of knowledge. According to this analysis, the subject is embedded in an external world from which he cannot be abstracted. He becomes, in a word, historical, wrapped in a bundle of socioeconomic and political contexts. Second, these philosophers' conception of consciousness as a stream implied that the past lingers and the future intrudes on the present; they viewed experience as inherently dynamic and all knowledge as historical. Third, they denied that man is a passive receiver of sensations or a conscious automaton following the decrees of fate. His choices and his actions make history, and the truth of his beliefs and the correctness of his decisions are validated in the concrete historical process. Fourth, the radical theorists of knowledge conceived of experience as intrinsically meaningful, but they denied that its meaning is predetermined or deducible from any source other than experience. Instead, meaning emerges over time as societies develop and gradually modify their values by testing them in practice. A hermeneutical approach to expressions of past experience provides access to these meanings, and from such understanding we obtain a perspective for assessing them critically.

Finally, James, Dewey, Fouillée, and Dilthey insisted that immediate experience contains a social dimension and that the verification of truth is a social rather than strictly personal project. Although it received varying degrees of emphasis in these theorists' writings, a vague standard of social integration was implicit in their concept of experience. Even James, by reputation the hardy individualist of the group, emphasized the necessity of winning approbation from the community as part of attaining satisfaction.

Moreover, all four referred, either obliquely or directly, to the progressive quality of human activity. Even the historical sensibility of James and Dilthey contained, in the idea of a progressively refined understanding, an immanent teleological quality. The conception of man as social derived from their analysis of immediate experience, which revealed that a pure, isolated, pre-social individual is a figment of philosophers' imaginations. A vision of community played a central part in the radical theory of knowledge, both in the analysis of experience and in the conception of history as a source of imma-nent critique. Dilthey and James as much as Dewey and Fouillée relied on a certain set of standards as the basis for critical judgment, but in the end they examined the method of constructing those standards more carefully than they considered their content. The radical theory of knowledge culminated in the historical sensibility because an empirical basis for critical judgment could be established only on the carefully delimited claims of transcendental historicism. The good, as these thinkers conceived of it, came to be identified with a method, an approach, which was itself conceived as progressive, but whose meaning in terms of a concrete set of ideals remained elusive.

4

The Ethics
of Rational Benevolence

1. Beyond Utilitarianism and Intuitionism

The same spirit of uncertainty and experimentation that characterized the radical theory of knowledge flowed through the ethical writings of the philosophers of the *via media*. Dewey reflected in 1907 on the most incisive examination of moral philosophy in the late nineteenth century, Sidgwick's *Methods of Ethics*. The fundamental postulate of Sidgwick's ethics, Dewey wrote, "was the basic identity of happiness and duty," but when Sidgwick found these values "discrepant" in the world of experience, he conceded his doubts about the possibility of reconciling the contradictory demands of the good and the right. Fouillée concluded his study of Kant's ethics with a similar cautionary note. The aim of moral philosophy, he maintained, must be a synthesis of Kant's concentration on the purity of the will and the utilitarians' focus on an act's consequences, because both deontological and teleological systems severed the two essential components of ethics. Yet a shadow falls between conceptualizing that goal and achieving it. Philosophers must proceed carefully, in Fouillée's words, "without calling certain what is uncertain or only probable, and without calling categorical what remains subject to some circumstance." Disclosing the inadequacy of Kantian and utilitarian ethics, like disclosing the inadequacy of idealist and empiricist epistemology, did not reveal a more attractive alternative but instead showed the impossibility of establishing a final system of substantive ethical principles.[1]

Just as they revealed the continuities between subject and object, thought and action, and the individual and society, so these radicals challenged hypostatized distinctions that had distracted moral philosophers from the continuities between motive and intention, between duty and happiness. The theory of voluntary action fused together reflection, feeling, and volition, and it emphasized the necessity of verifying truths pragmatically in experience. In their moral philosophy, Dilthey, James, Sidgwick, Dewey, Fouillée, and Green stressed the social and historical dimensions inherent in experience, and they analyzed moral principles sensitive to the subtle interplay between individual desire and social responsibility. Finally, as they offered varying answers to the question of history's trajectory and its implications for understanding human activity, so they drew different conclusions for ethics from the realization that moral principles are derived from, and embedded in, our understanding of history.

Their contrasting theories of history were manifested in two different modes of ethical analysis that in turn shaped their conceptions of political rights and responsibilities. On the one hand, consistent with their tragic view of history as an open-ended process revealing no unambiguous answers to questions of value, Dilthey, James, and Sidgwick believed that we must sacrifice some convictions to satisfy others. Moral action, they maintained, involves painful but inescapable choices between competing conceptions of the good. As James put it in the most important exposition of his ethical ideas, "The Moral Philosopher and the Moral Life" (1891), in every moral decision "some part of the ideal is butchered."[2] Dewey, Fouillée, and Green, on the other hand, based their ethics on a more linear view of history, and they conceived of morality in terms of self-development and self-realization. Their moral philosophy thus extended their conception of history as epic. They rejected the tragic view of Dilthey, James, and Sidgwick in favor of a classical ideal whose roots lay ultimately in Aristotle. By defining ethics as self-realization, they tried to minimize the possibility of genuine conflict between opposite values. They argued that individual moral action necessarily harmonizes with the good of the community; by definition, according to this view, ethics involves the integration of personal desire with social needs. That difference, however, should not obscure these thinkers' common rejection of attempts to prescribe an unchanging system of ethics. They insisted on the open-ended nature of value judgments and the necessity of adopting a pragmatic and provisional method of distinguishing moral from immoral behavior. The contradictions they were unable to resolve ultimately bedeviled their attempts to construct a political theory including principles of substantive as well as procedural justice.

The philosophers of the *via media* judged utilitarian ethics inadequate because they considered it insufficiently empirical: it neglected the qualitative and social dimensions of experience in assessing the good. Utilitarianism received its classic formulation in the writings of Jeremy Bentham and James Mill, who premised utilitarian ethics on the psychological maxim that human beings act to maximize pleasure and minimize pain. Bentham offered a strictly quantitative felicific calculus as a means of deciding among competing courses of action. John Stuart Mill modified two important features of utilitarian ethics. First, he disputed Bentham's assertion that "quantity of pleasure being equal, pushpin is as good as poetry." Better Socrates dissatisfied, Mill maintained, than a pig satisfied. To this qualitative measure he appended a standard of social welfare as the measure of ethical behavior, a broadening of the scope of utilitarian calculations beyond the individualism of Bentham and James Mill.[3]

In their assessments of utilitarianism, James, Dilthey, and Fouillée concentrated on the inadequacy of ethical hedonism. Sidgwick, Green, and Dewey expanded that analysis, and they also drew out the inconsistencies between John Stuart Mill's utilitarianism and Benthamite principles. Their critique of English utilitarianism laid the groundwork for their dissent from the political theory of possessive individualism, which was linked logically and historically with utilitarian ethics. It is important for understanding the development of twentieth-century political theory to appreciate the inadequacies they perceived in the ethical doctrines of Bentham and the Mills. James expressed his dissent from utilitarianism most clearly in "The Moral Philosopher and the Moral Life." He admitted that the utilitarians had contributed to the clarity of ethical thinking by "taking so many of our human ideals and showing how they must have arisen from the association with acts of simple bodily pleasures and reliefs from pain." Significant as those considerations are, however, he declared that "it is surely impossible to explain all our sentiments and preferences in this simple way." Building upon the careful analysis of interest advanced in *The Principles of Psychology*, he maintained that motivation eludes straightforward hedonistic explanation. Our interests "deal with directly felt fitnesses between things, and often fly in the teeth of all the prepossessions of habit and presumptions of utility." The mysterious seat of interest, which James conceptualized in terms of his radically empiricist reading of experience, lay beneath calculations of pleasure and pain, and it escaped utilitarian ethical theorists entirely.[4] James identified utilitarianism with what he called the "don't care temper" or the genial mood, both of which he contrasted with the strenuous mood. This higher ethical attitude was "quite indifferent to present ill, if only the greater ideal be attained." The quest for this greater ideal provided the moral standard for James, and it distinguished his ethical theory clearly from the utilitarianism with which it is often mistakenly identified.[5]

A strong current of ethical concerns flows through all of Dilthey's writing, because he refused to allow a rigid distinction between fact and value. Lived experience is meaningful; we interpret all of our perceptions and activities through the gestalt of the value-imbued psyche. While Dilthey focused less explicitly on ethics than on the analysis of experience, because he believed that the preliminary spadework necessary for value theory had not yet been done, the lectures he delivered on ethics in 1890 expressed his dissatisfaction with prevailing ethical systems. He contended that Bentham's hedonism squeezed the richness of meaning from life and retained only a flat, quantitative representation, whose very simplicity belied the utilitarians' claim to provide an adequate ethical standard. Dilthey contended that value cannot be examined except in relation to an individual's entire life and his sociocultural milieu. Ethical theory thus cannot dispense with hermeneutics and substitute for genuine, historically sensitive empirical analysis an abstract set of rules.

Utilitarianism embodied a "rentier-philosophy" purporting to justify the values of Britain's capitalist ruling class by identifying their preferences with the greatest good of the greatest number. Dilthey scorned Bentham's attempt to finesse the conflict between individual and general welfare, and he asked rhetorically how the proletariat might respond to such transparent attempts to define the maximization of pleasure for the community in terms of the pleasure of the bourgeoisie.[6]

Fouillée's treatment of hedonism in *The Psychology of idées-forces* ran parallel to those of James and Dilthey. Although pleasure and pain "constitute the dominant quality of original sensations," he wrote, that dimension does not exhaust the content of consciousness. Experience is also qualitative; it is by virtue of precisely that "primordial element" of experience that we distinguish one pleasant or painful sensation from another. Only the capacity to differentiate among experiences can account for value, and utilitarianism, by overlooking that capacity, provides an inadequate account of ethical action. In his *Ethics of idées-forces*, Fouillée tied his analysis of hedonism to his radical empiricism. Bentham's felicific calculus falsified experience, he argued, because it abstracted sensations from their context and portrayed them as fundamental components of experience. To the contrary, Fouillée insisted, all pleasures and pains come to us embedded in a cultural code which affects our native determinations of value and to which we in turn actively respond. We react not only to sensation but to abstract ideals such as perfection, and our actions manifest those choices. Fouillée's entire philosophy rested on the notion that ideas play an active role in human life and history because we respond to them positively and negatively; it is not surprising that he found the utilitarians' attempts to reduce all qualitative states of consciousness to pleasure and pain singularly unpersuasive.[7]

Green pointed out a further problem with utilitarianism in his *Prolegomena to Ethics*, in which he argued that psychological egoism and the pleasure-pain calculus together transformed morality from problem to tautology. For if action must follow the strongest desire, which necessarily means maximizing pleasure, then the total of pleasures obtaining at any time must be the maximum, because all individuals cannot but choose to maximize their pleasures and minimize their pain. Since everyone thus acts precisely as he should act, questions about ethical or unethical behavior are moot. Utilitarianism blithely ignores the question of duty because its conception of behavior is circular: "The whole phraseology of obligation, in short, upon Hedonistic principles can best be explained by a theory which is essentially the same as that of Hobbes, and which in Plato's time was represented by the dictum of certain Sophists that 'Justice is the interest of the Stronger.'"[8] Not only did utilitarianism rest on a faulty conception of reasoning that overlooked the problematic nature of interest and the qualititative dimension of experience, its reliance on psychological hedonism rendered ethics tautological.

Sidgwick was careful to distinguish his universalistic utilitarianism from the egoistic utilitarianism of Bentham. Reflecting the distance separating Sidgwick from his predecessors, Dewey classified him with Green and James

Martineau under the rubric of "Intuitionism," and Sidgwick's treatment of utilitarianism in *The Methods of Ethics* substantiates Dewey's argument.[9] Sidgwick repeatedly criticized the reduction of ethics to simple calculations of pleasure and pain, and he insisted that "it is manifestly possible that our prospect of pleasure resulting from any course of action may largely depend on our conception of it as right or otherwise." It was over this central question of the desire for pleasure as the root of motivation that Sidgwick parted company with Bentham's psychological egoism:

> Our conscious active impulses are so far from being always directed toward the attainment of pleasure or avoidance of pain for ourselves, that we can find everywhere in consciousness extra-regarding impulses, directed towards something that is not pleasure, nor relief from pain; and, indeed, a most important part of our pleasure depends upon the existence of such impulses.

Moreover, the desire for personal pleasure tends occasionally to conflict with the desire to satisfy our extra-regarding impulses, and this incompatibility "is no doubt specially prominent in the case of the impulse toward the end which most markedly competes in ethical controversy with pleasure; the love of virtue for its own sake, or desire to do what is right as such."[10] Three features of this argument are noteworthy. First, it reveals Sidgwick's reliance on a Kantian conception of ethical action as motivated by a sense of obligation, a position he adopted after consulting Kant's ethical writings in his search for an escape from the selfishness of Bentham's and Mill's utilitarianism.[11] Second, Sidgwick isolated the extra-regarding impulses as a prominent element in pleasure and in ethical behavior. Finally, he relied on experience to establish his argument.[12] This use of Kant to supplement Bentham, the awareness of the social dimension of activity, and the reliance on empirical evidence characterized not only Sidgwick's ethics but also the ethics of the other philosophers of the *via media*.

Dewey's ethical writings illustrate this convergence of ideas regarding the inadequacy of utilitarianism. In *Outlines of a Critical Theory of Ethics* (1891), Dewey challenged hedonism on the grounds that it substituted individual pleasure for the "fulfillment of human powers and functions." Hedonists reduced the sense of satisfaction from social action to "mere having, to bare feelings or affections eliminating the element of doing." Dewey derived that much of his analysis from Aristotle's treatment of praxis, but he supplemented it with references to the critiques of utilitarianism advanced by James and Green.[13] In his sections of the *Ethics* (1908) that he coauthored with James Tufts, Dewey repeatedly cited Sidgwick's *Methods of Ethics*, and he compiled the various arguments leveled against utilitarianism into a comprehensive list of its difficulties. He first used James on the social self and the desire for approval as a source of motivation, then referred to Green on the confusion of the desire for goodness and the desire for pleasure, and finally invoked Sidgwick on the absence of any empirical foundation for the definition of happiness as the ultimate good. Dewey further argued that ethical theory should consider the agent's motive as well as his intention, his act, and the consequences of the act, and he criticized utilitarianism for mirroring the tendency of associationist psychology to split experience into discrete sensations by focusing on consequences and ignoring motives. In ethics as in epistemology, volition, activity, and results must all be viewed as pieces of a single puzzle.[14]

These radicals criticized both of John Stuart Mill's revisions of utilitarianism as inconsistent with the fundamental tenets of the philosophy. Although they considered the introduction of a qualitative standard to be a necessary revision of Bentham's scheme, they pointed out that such a standard rested on an a priori judgment incompatible with psychological hedonism. As Sidgwick wrote, "In order to work out consistently the method that takes pleasure as the sole ultimate end of rational conduct [i.e., ethical hedonism], Bentham's proposition [that "pushpin is as good as poetry"] and all *qualitative* comparison of pleasures must really resolve itself into quantitative." To be consistent, one must accept psychological hedonism as well as ethical hedonism. When other qualifications are introduced, which experience compels us to do, "then we are clearly introducing a non-hedonistic ground of preference: and if this is done, the method adopted is a perplexing mixture of Intuitionism and Hedonism."[15] Sidgwick in fact opted for a similar, albeit more straightforward, mixture in his own ethical theory, but he forthrightly acknowledged its reliance on principles that departed from hedonism. Second, Mill's critics denied his claim to have established the desirability of the general good on hedonistic grounds. Mill argued that each individual ought to desire the general good rather than individual pleasure. Yet as Sidgwick pointed out:

> This proposition is not established by Mill's reasoning, even if we grant that what is actually desired may be legitimately inferred to be in this sense desirable. For an aggregate of actual desires, each directed toward a different part of the general happiness, does not constitute an actual desire for the general happiness, existing in any individual; and Mill would certainly not contend that a desire which does not exist in any individual can possibly exist in an aggregate of individuals.

Although Sidgwick endorsed the principle that the individual ought to desire the general welfare, he asserted that there was a gap in Mill's argument that could be filled only by "some such proposition as that which I have tried to exhibit as the intuition of Rational Benevolence."[16] In short, as Dewey maintained, there is "no *direct road* from individualistic hedonism" or "private pleasure" to "universalistic" hedonism or "general pleasure." Like Sidgwick, Dewey adopted a universalistic utilitarian standard. He conceded that a similar, "thoroughly socialized ideal of happiness is the most characteristic feature of Mill's ethics. It is noble," he concluded, "but it is not hedonism."[17]

The search of the philosophers of the *via media* for the necessary ideas to complete utilitarian theory carried them back to Kant, but they considered his ethics incomplete for a different set of reasons. While Kant admitted that we follow our passions in order to satisfy our sensual nature, he denied that we are entirely slaves to our senses. There exists in addition a class of actions that we undertake in order to satisfy our noumenal nature—not for the sake of any purpose those acts accomplish but rather in accordance with the principle they embody. Only such actions are moral, Kant reasoned, and they must be undertaken from duty rather than from inclination.[18] Against the teleological character of utilitarian ethics, Kant's ethics is deontological. The principle in accordance with which we act as moral agents is Kant's familiar categorical imperative or universalizability criterion, which stipulates that we must act only on that maxim that can be willed to be a universal law. In that regard, we must recognize other people as ends in themselves rather than as means furthering any ends of our own. Acting from duty in accordance with the categorical imperative, which entails the treatment of others as ends, thus constitutes ethical action. No specific action or intention, but only a good will, is unconditionally good.

The weakness of Kant's ethics lay in that relentlessly formalistic conception of morality, and the philosophers of the *via media* concentrated on its insufficiency as a guide to concrete action. In general, Sidgwick dealt with Kant only indirectly, because he concentrated his attacks on the intuitionism of Thomas Reid (who was ignorant of Kant) and William Whewell (through whose writings Kant entered British ethics). Although in *The Methods of Ethics* Sidgwick did discuss the fuzziness of Kant's notion of treating others as ends rather than means, his opposition to Kantian theory can best be inferred from his treatment of what he called "common sense morality" and the ethical rules it offers.[19] Sidgwick carefully examined the common sense precepts of justice, veracity, good faith, etc., and in every case he found them frayed around the edges. Although "perfectly adequate to give practical guidance to common people in common circumstances," these principles provide inadequate guidance in difficult cases. Moreover, when they contradict one another, no principle of reconciliation appears satisfactory. Sidgwick concluded that no intuited ethical maxims, including Kant's categorical imperative, provided "clear and precise principles for determining the extent of duty in any case." He asserted that Kant's categorical imperative was too loose, and that a volition consistent with that precept "may after all be wrong." Kantian ethics, like intuitionism in general, was overly formal. There are certain absolute practical principles, Sidgwick wrote, that are manifestly true, "but they are of too abstract a nature, and too universal in their scope, to enable us to ascertain by immediate application of them what we ought to do in any particular case." To supplement these principles, Sidgwick returned to utilitarianism, and in his own ethical theory he tried to compensate for the weaknesses of each system. As Fouillée counseled after registering similar objections to the overly formal character of the categorical imperative, Kant's "conception of the ideal must be transformed and brought back to the laws of experience." For we do not become moral in opposition to our nature, Fouillée argued, but instead through our steady development as progressive beings. Following Schleiermacher, Dilthey likewise denied the legitimacy of

Kant's rigid separation of pure and practical reason, and he argued that ethics must be built up from experience rather than from universal maxims.[20]

Green accepted Kant's characterization of the good will as the only unconditional good, and he considered Kant's categorical imperative to be a better formula "for the rule on which the ideally just man seeks to act" than Bentham's utilitarian calculus. Yet Kant's deontologism remained too abstract to satisfy Green. Like Fouillée, he supplemented it with a teleological notion of self-fulfillment through the concrete creation of a form of life, an ideal taken from Hegel, and he offered an Aristotelian alternative to Bentham's psychological hedonism and Kant's categorical imperative. Green subordinated duty to purpose, as utilitarians did, but he followed Aristotle (and Hegel) in defining purpose with reference to self-realization in society and history. He characterized the egoistic psychology of Bentham's philosophy as the principal impediment to the fostering of community, which he considered the ultimate end of individual development.[21]

Green's and Sidgwick's revisions of intuitionist and hedonist ethics testify to the convergence of ethical reasoning. They recognized one another's contributions to the clarification of ethical discourse, and the stridency of their debates should not obscure the extent of their agreement. Much of Sidgwick's discussion of Green consists of clarification, charges that Green misunderstood him, and denials that Green's own ethics could better solve difficult issues such as the various combinations of pleasures and pains. By the same token, in his *Prolegomena to Ethics* Green admitted that Sidgwick's treatment of the conception of desire constituted an advance on customary utilitarian discussions of that idea. Yet Green protested that we aim more toward the development of our moral capacity than toward pleasure, even given Sidgwick's idea of pleasure as an object of rational instead of purely sensual desire. Green consistently maintained that we must have an ideal standard of perfection toward which we strive. He characterized his standard in concrete terms as the construction of community, but he derived that idea from his metaphysical notion of an eternal divine consciousness. Sidgwick, by contrast, tried to establish his ethics on a more empirical basis. The common sense rules of morality, Sidgwick contended, do not reveal "any reference to perfection of character as end. The evils that these rules aim at preventing are pain, and the loss of the material means of physical well-being . . . the good that they aim at distributing is of the same kind."[22]

Dewey's successive discussions of Kant chronicle his progression from Green's idealism toward the concentration on praxis characteristic of his mature ethical theory. In *Outlines of a Critical Theory of Ethics* (1891), he recapitulated Green's critique of Kant, and he traced the overly abstract quality of the categorical imperative to Kant's unwarranted division between the noumenal and phenomenal realms.[23] Two years later, in "Self-Realization as the Moral Ideal," Dewey extended his earlier argument and maintained that Kant had stood ethics on its head. "Instead of saying that an act is moral only when done from consciousness of duty, we should say that it is immoral (because partial) as long as it is done merely from a sense of duty, and becomes moral when done for its own concrete sake." Dewey was beginning to move toward an emphasis on the entire ethical act and away from both the limited Kantian focus on motive and the corresponding—and equally limited—utilitarian focus on intent, a tendency at least partly attributable to his familiarity with James's *Principles of Psychology*.[24] That inclination became more pronounced in Dewey's later writings, in which he conceived of social reform as the transformation of ethics from abstraction to reality. In *Reconstruction in Philosophy* (1920), for example, he pointed out that a number of philosophers had rejected the narrow vision of Benthamite utilitarianism and recognized that the good is universal and objective, not just private and particular. Too often, however, "like Plato, they have been content with a metaphysical universality, or, like Kant, with a logical universality." The philosopher's goal, Dewey insisted, should involve more than such abstractions: "Communication, sharing, joint participation are the only actual ways of universalizing the moral law and end." Such universalization requires the transformation of actual social conditions, "the extension of the area and range of those who share in a good."[25] Kant's criterion, although a valuable corrective to the individualistic focus of Bentham, failed to provide a measure for specific decisions and actions, which must be directed toward real increases in collective happiness. Like Sidgwick, Dewey supplemented the categorical imperative with a universalistic utilitarian concern for the consequences of behavior; like Green, he conceived of such ethical action in terms of self-realization.

All of the philosophers of the *via media* agreed that moral philosophy must try to integrate Kant's concern for motives with the utilitarians' concern with intentions. They also shared the conviction that neither a wholly individualist interest nor an exclusive interest in maximizing the aggregate of pleasure is sufficient for making difficult decisions. While they all concentrated on the central ethical problem of reconciling the personal desire for happiness with the demand that individuals contribute to the common good, they differed in assessing the likelihood of resolving that conflict. Their disagreement reflected two different conceptions of ethical activity. Green, Fouillée, and Dewey believed that self-realization requires integrating individual preferences with the needs of the community, whereas Sidgwick, Dilthey, and James doubted that tragic collisions between self-interest and the requirements of justice could ever be prevented.

2. The Conflict Between Prudence and Justice

Any discussion of these philosophers' positive contributions to ethical discourse must begin with Sidgwick, whose *Methods of Ethics* is a classic of moral philosophy. As an attempt to construct a normative ethics, it has not been surpassed in the century since it was written. Excellent commentaries examine the details of Sidgwick's analysis, and I will attempt only to highlight certain themes illustrating Sidgwick's contribution to the convergence of ideas in ethics, particularly his delineation of the principles of prudence, justice, and rational benevolence.[26] If I seem to use Sidgwick's moral philosophy as a touchstone in discussing the ethical ideas of the other philosophers of the *via media*, that strategy is predicated not only on Sidgwick's stature as an ethicist but also on his historical role: *The Methods of Ethics* provided the standard against which James, Green, and Dewey gauged their own ethical writings.

Sidgwick designed *The Methods of Ethics* to synthesize the best from the utilitarian and intuitionist theories of ethics. Both traditions exhibited weaknesses that could be eliminated only by infusing into each some elements of the other. To use Sidgwick's image, the truth lies between the Scylla and Charybdis of intuitionism and utilitarianism.[27] He maintained that the utilitarians' standard of maximizing pleasure must supplement the principles of common sense morality, viz., justice, prudence, and benevolence. As suggested in the discussion of Sidgwick's critique of Kant, he believed that general moral rules are too abstract to provide guidance in specific situations. Beyond completing the moral principles of intuitionism, Sidgwick wrote, utilitarianism also provides a principle of synthesis and a way to bind the "unconnected and occasionally conflicting principles of common moral reasoning into a complete and harmonious system.[28] Utilitarianism, by itself, lacked sufficient grounding, but together with the rules of common sense morality it could offer a sound ethical standard.

Sidgwick's synthetic purpose has occasionally been overlooked, an unfortunate but understandable tendency given the peculiar history of *The Methods of Ethics*. In its original form, the book included numerous historical references illustrating Sidgwick's deliberate attempt to bring together ideas from different sources. Each successive edition, however, contained fewer of these historical references. Sidgwick's discussion of his development of Kantian ideas, for example, all but disappeared after the first edition. Sidgwick believed ethics to be a progressive discipline, and he thought that consideration of the historical debate and the gradual emergence of a consensus of experts played an important part in advancing moral philosophy. Each time he revised the book, however, he covered more carefully the tracks of the traditions he followed, and as a result the later editions of *The Methods of Ethics* only partly reflect that concern.[29]

"Hedonism and Ultimate Good," an essay Sidgwick wrote three years after the publication of *The Methods of Ethics*, demonstrates his conviction that philosophers were moving toward the acceptance of certain basic ethical principles. Sidgwick described developments in "Intuition, Utilitarianism, and Evolutionism" that pointed toward agreement, and he concluded that "this convergence of several distinct arguments has had, I think, a considerable effect on contemporary thought; and probably a large majority of reflective persons are now prepared to accept 'Common Good' as the ultimate end for which moral rules exist."[30] Sidgwick organized *The Methods of Ethics* around that concept of the common good toward which he believed philosophers were converging. Before analyzing that idea, however, he cleared the way by discussing the logic of ethical discourse, the combination of intuition and reason in ethical judgment, and the separation of psychological hedonism from ethical hedonism. Sidgwick then presented what he considered to be the three principal competing methods of ethics: intuitionism, or common sense morality (which in some ways resembled Kantian ethics); egoistic hedonism; and universalistic hedonism or utilitarianism. In order to arrive at a satisfactory theory of morality, Sidgwick presented several "self-evident moral principles." While these have been the subject of such intense controversy that commentators do not agree about even the number of principles he intended to prescribe, three main principles can be isolated: justice, prudence, and rational benevolence.[31]

Sidgwick stated each of these principles in several ways, but the following seem to me the most adequate. The principle of justice, which Sidgwick explicitly attributed to Kant,[32] incorporates a basic sense of fairness, an intuition of equality, and Kant's categorical imperative: "Whatever action any of us judges to be right for himself, he implicitly judges to be right for all similar persons in similar circumstances." The second principle, prudence, dictates that a person ought to look after his "own greatest happiness." Finally, according to the third principle of rational benevolence, "It is right and reasonable for me to do what I believe to be ultimately conducive to universal Good or Happiness." Sidgwick derived this principle of rational benevolence from two axioms: first, "The good of any one individual is of no more importance from the point of view (if I may say so) of the Universe than the good of any other," and second, "As a rational being I am bound to aim at good generally—so far as it is attainable by my efforts—not merely at a particular part of it."[33] By proclaiming these three principles as the heart of his ethical theory, Sidgwick tried deliberately to combine insights from Kant's theory of rational duty with the utilitarians' hedonistic theory of value as pleasure. The two systems, he asserted, are to be a certain extent interdependent rather than mutually exclusive.

In "Hedonism and Ultimate Good," Sidgwick described how these three principles draw intuitionist and utilitarian ethics together:

> The fundamental intuitions of conscience or the practical reason on which one school (Kantians and intuitionists) have always laid stress, are merely the expression in different aspects or relations of that ideal subordination of individual impulses to universal ends on which alone Utilitarianism, as a system of ethics, can rationally rest. Thus the essence of Justice or Equity, insofar as it is absolutely obligatory, is that different individuals are not to be treated differently, except on grounds of universal application: which grounds, again, are given in the principle of Rational Benevolence, that sets before each man the good of all others as an object of pursuit no less worthy than his own.[34]

Common sense morality must turn toward the principles of utilitarianism to settle conflicts, and general utilitarianism can establish itself only on the intuited egalitarian principle of common sense morality. While we intuitively recognize our duty to obey moral principles, the moral principles we obey are justified by their usefulness in promoting the common good. Sidgwick thus incorporated motives and intentions, duty and happiness, in his ethics much as the radical theory of knowledge fused sentience and activity. In J. B. Schneewind's apt phrase, rational benevolence expresses the demands of reason on desire. As the keystone of Sidgwick's ethics, that principle of benevolence attempts to satisfy the requirements of rationality preeminent in Kantian epistemology and ethics by bringing them into the framework of real desires for happiness, the preeminent consideration of British empiricism and utilitarianism.

Yet the principle of rational benevolence may not entirely resolve the conflict between the principles of justice and prudence. The reasonable requirements imposed by the self do not always neatly coincide with the reasonable requirements of one's sense of equity. This difficulty, rooted in the two dimensions of the individual as a private consciousness and a member of a community, admits no easy solution, and Sidgwick agonized over it throughout his career. Sidgwick's anguished conclusion to *The Methods of Ethics* reveals his uncertainty. He denied that he could offer any "practical solution of this fundamental contradiction," and he admitted that the ultimate reconciliation of duty and self-interest extends beyond the limits of practical reason. In cases of genuine conflict, he suggested, we can at best accept as a moral imperative the duty to maximize general happiness, a hybrid hypothesis "logically necessary to avoid a fundamental contradiction in one chief department of thought." He declined to speculate on the validity of metaphysical or religious claims to verify that hypothesis. Instead he compared it revealingly to the "edifice of physical science." Sidgwick admitted that those who accept scientific propositions as ultimately true might legitimately demand an equally solid basis for their ethical principles. But if, on the other hand, as Sidgwick wrote in his tortured closing sentence,

> we find that in our supposed knowledge of the world of nature propositions are commonly taken to be universally true, which yet seem to rest on no other grounds than that we have a strong disposition to accept them, and that they are indispensable to the systematic coherence of our beliefs—it will be more difficult to reject a similarly supported assumption in ethics, without opening the door to universal scepticism.[35]

In other words, we can establish our ethical principles only pragmatically on a foundation of "relative certainty," to use Dilthey's phrase, and we must acknowledge the fiduciary aspect of our claim that they are true. *The Methods of Ethics* thus culminates in an acknowledgment of human finitude and a Jamesian "will to believe" in the principle of benevolence rather than an irresistible demonstration of its validity.

James's scattered writings about ethics strongly resembled Sidgwick's arguments in *The Methods of Ethics*. I have already referred to James's preference for the strenuous mood of duty over the easy going mood of utilitarianism; it is instructive of the intractability of this problem that his discussion of the inevitable conflicts between the two is as labored as Sidgwick's. In "The Moral Philosopher and the Moral Life," James emphasized the antagonism "between the ethics of infinite and mysterious obligation from on high, and those of prudence and the satisfaction of merely finite need." Like Sidgwick, he denied that the conflict between those demands could be resolved in the absence of a religious appeal, but James was less reluctant to proclaim the attractiveness of faith for pragmatic moral purposes: "The strenuous type of character will on the battle-field of human history always outwear the easy-going type, and religion will drive irreligion to the wall." James offered as his final conclusion that "the stable and systematic moral universe for which the ethical philosopher asks," and in which self-interest and duty might be reconciled, "is fully possible only in a world where there is a divine thinker with all-enveloping demands."[36] James, like Sidgwick, denied the possibility of solving the problem without recourse to a nonhuman truth. He could discover in practical reason no path toward its solution.

That much of James's ethics is familiar. The full extent of his debt to Sidgwick's *Methods of Ethics* has not been recognized, however, perhaps because the link establishing the connection appears in *The Principles of Psychology* rather than in any of James's essays that focus specifically on ethics. In "Aesthetic and Moral Principles," the penultimate section of his final chapter, he attempted to account for ethical decisions and his analysis followed Sidgwick precisely. He argued that moral judgments can be reduced neither to mere habit nor to the force of public opinion. What then is the source of moral judgments? Consider the judgments of justice, or equity, James suggested. "Instinctively, one judges everything differently, according as it pertains to one's self or to someone else. Empirically one notices that everybody else does the same." Gradually, however, one comes to realize that "nothing can be right for me which would not be right for another similarly placed," that the "fulfillment of my desires is intrinsically no more imperative than that of anyone else," and that "what it is reasonable that another should do for me, it is also reasonable that I should do for him." With that dawning judgment, James concluded, "the whole mass of the habitual gets overturned."

James cited as the only source for this analysis the section of *The Methods of Ethics* in which Sidgwick advanced the principles of justice, prudence, and rational benevolence in their clearest form. It should be apparent, although it has not previously been pointed out, that James modeled his discussion of moral judgment on Sidgwick's formulation of these principles. James also echoed Sidgwick's analysis of the conflict between the principles of justice and prudence and the impossibility of reconciling them satisfactorily in the principle of rational benevolence. He contrasted the "logical stickler for justice" with "the man who goes by tact and the particular instance," and he maintained that each is right in some cases. In short, there is no easy reconciliation of duty with desire; no general rule can provide an answer in cases of genuine conflict.[37] As I will argue in the next chapter, commentators have tended to infer from some of James's fragmentary remarks that he sacrificed the demands of justice, or equity, for the rights of the individual. But as his discussions of the contrasts between the easygoing and strenuous moods in "The Moral Philosopher and the Moral Life" and his treatment of the demands of prudence and justice in *The Principles of Psychology* indicate, he recognized the depth of the difficulty. Like Sidgwick, James denied that philosophy could solve the problem of reconciling individual pleasure with the common good; he attributed a more modest capacity to practical reason.

James and Sidgwick claimed that an irreconcilable conflict looms between the dictates of personal desire and the common good. Fouillée, Green, and Dewey, on the other hand, believed the tensions could be eased if not entirely dissolved. They considered individual happiness impossible outside the context of social responsibility. They defined ethical behavior in terms of self-realization, by which they meant the continuous refinement of desire to bring personal wants into conformity with social needs. In concluding his discussion of Sidgwick's "remarkable" *Methods of Ethics* in his *Critique des systèmes de morale contemporains* (1906; cited hereafter as *Critique of Contemporary Systems of Morality*), Fouillée applauded Sidgwick's courage in choosing to remain "suspended mid-way between the a priori intuitionism of the rationalists and evolutionary utilitarianism." That position was unnecessarily precarious, however, because a means of bridging the gap between prudence and justice is available in every individual's potential for progressive moral development.[38] While James and Sidgwick dismissed attempts to identify personal desire and community welfare as "mere postulates of rationality," to use James's phrase, the possibility of that identification was essential to Fouillée's, Green's, and Dewey's ethical theories. Fouillée expressed this "surprising union of opposites" in these words: "I will be most free in the act in which I attach myself to another: it is only if I can renounce myself that I will be myself. The highest *individuality* therefore will be the highest *universality*."[39] Green stated a similar proposition somewhat differently. Denying Sidgwick's distinction between justice and prudence, he contended that all virtues are really social; "or, more properly, the distinction between social and self-regarding virtues is a false one."[40] Virtuous activity both satisfies the agent and also benefits society. If it fails to meet either of those criteria, Green refused to classify it as virtuous. Thus Green subsumed under a principle resembling Sidgwick's rational benevolence all conflicts between prudence and justice.

Personal pleasure, according to this point of view, has little to do with ethics. While the good may involve pleasure incidentally, Green maintained, it cannot be identified with pleasure. Ethical activity is not directed toward desirable objects but toward an ideal of personal development to which objects may contribute. Ethical behavior is gauged according to this ideal rather than the maximization of pleasure. The germ of morality lies in consciousness, which includes in its awareness of self an awareness of others and a sense of responsibility toward their well-being. According to this view, which Fouillée and Green shared, personal happiness depends on the happiness of others, and benevolence is the summum bonum. A passage written by

Fouillée, which Guyau selected as the epigraph for his biography, reveals the distance separating this conception from hedonism: "The being who thinks and who loves can be really happy only if everyone else is happy, except in the part he contributes to making them happy."[41] According to this view, a purely personal self-satisfaction is contradictory. In his *Ethics of idées-forces*, Fouillée insisted that a germ of voluntary altruism, which he characterized as the fundamental *idée-force* because it links the self with the other by an indissoluble bond, lies at the heart of consciousness. Morality finds a positive foundation only in the reconciliation of the social and even the universal with the individual, and Fouillée intended his ethical writings to uncover that foundation. The positive principle of morality, he asserted, must be "the virtual universality which is inherent in self-consciousness," and which reveals that the fullness of life for oneself involves others as well.[42]

Fouillée considered his *Ethics of idées-forces* a corrective to the individualism of both Kantian and utilitarian ethics and the opposite extreme of socialization represented by Comtean positivism. He emphasized the development of individual character and personality, and he contended that such development can occur only in a community. Society provides the field, while the individual is the source, of the voluntary action that alone possesses an ethical quality. Ethical individuals create a community characterized by *solidarité*, the condition Fouillée considered the goal of both ethical and political action. His ethical theory focused on individual development instead of duty or personal pleasure, development occurring within a social framework but not submerging individuality inside community.[43] In similar fashion, Green asserted that the individual develops morally only through action directed toward social needs. In his *Prolegomena to Ethics*, he wrote, "Only through society is any one enabled to give that effect to the idea of himself as the object of his actions, to the idea of a possible better state of himself." In a passage reminiscent of Fouillée's characterization of the awareness of an "other me," another subject, in immediate experience, Green contended that "some practical recognition of personality by another, of an 'I' by a 'Thou' and a 'Thou' by an 'I,' is necessary to any practical consciousness" of self-development. In short, only through society can the individual personality find fulfillment.[44] Green, like Fouillée, went beyond denying the existence of conflict between the satisfaction of individual desires and responsibility to society. He posited the identity of personal and social interest, the principle of rational benevolence, as the root of his ethics and his social and political theory.

Sidgwick acknowledged that Green's denial of competition was the most attractive feature of his ethics. Yet as Sidgwick pointed out, Green's argument, although appealing, was unclear. Green, as well as Fouillée, tended to swing between wider and narrower conceptions of the good, describing it first in broad, sociopolitical terms, then as a function only of the goodness of the individual will. When Green emphasized the noncompetitive character of his ethical ideal, he concentrated on individual virtue. By contrast, when discussing his wider cultural ideal, he referred to such practical social duties as securing the "real opportunity of self-development" for the poor. If individual virtue is the key to ethics, Sidgwick maintained, then the most unrelenting competition cannot interfere with the exercise of virtue on the part of the weakest competitor. If, on the other hand, ethics requires the realization of all scientific and artistic capacities, as Green sometimes claimed, then the quest for such realization constitutes "the main motive of the keen struggle for material wealth which educated and refined persons generally feel themselves bound to keep up, for their children even more than for themselves." If virtue is conceived as wholly personal, competition presents no problem, and yet that moral ideal exhibits as abstract a quality as Kant's categorical imperative. Alternatively, if the range of true goods includes the development of artistic and scientific abilities and the unending pursuit of knowledge of all kinds, it is difficult to imagine a noncompetitive good.[45] Some real goods can by virtue of their scarcity be distributed only unequally, as Green seemed to admit in his treatment of justice. Thus the problem of reconciling personal desires and the desires of others reappears. As I have pointed out, Sidgwick admitted his failure to resolve the conflict between personal satisfaction and the common good. He also denied that Green succeeded where he had failed.

Sidgwick's version of utilitarian ethics differed from the ideas of Green and Fouillée on the question of personal development and on the possibility of fully reconciling individual satisfaction and the common good. Undaunted by their disagreements, Dewey tried to mend them in his ethics. No better illustration of the convergence of ideas among these philosophers exists than Dewey's ultimately futile efforts, which he abandoned in his later work, to harmonize the modified utilitarianism of James and Sidgwick with Green's ethics of self-realization. In both Dewey's *Outlines of a Critical Theory of Ethics* and his and Tufts's *Ethics*, he approached ethical issues with an eye toward synthesis, discussing various theorists' contradictory analyses and attempting simultaneously to minimize and reconcile their differences. This strategy led Dewey to cite both Green and Sidgwick as sources for his ideas on various issues without admitting the extent to which their ideas differed. Dewey's chapter on "Conduct and Character" in *Ethics* typifies his approach. He first contrasted Kant's emphasis on the pure will with the utilitarians' focus on consequences. He then tried, following Sidgwick's *Methods of Ethics*, to combine these two, but his synthesis at this stage of his thinking owed more to Green than to Sidgwick. Dewey offered the idea of self-realization as a solution to the difficult problem of weighing motives against intentions: "The distinction of 'inner' and 'outer' is one involved in the *growth of character and conduct*." Only if character were not changing constantly, only if conduct were a fixed because isolated thing, "should we have that separation of the inner and the outer which underlies alike the Kantian and utilitarian theories."[46] By hitching character to the dynamic process of self-realization, and by placing ethics within the framework of the radical empiricist conception of experience and the theory of voluntary action, Dewey believed he could end the long-standing division between the right and the good.

Dewey specifically linked his connection of Green's and Sidgwick's ideas to his analysis of the unity of experience and activity. Both Kant and Bentham, Dewey wrote, mistakenly split a voluntary act which is single and entire into two unrelated parts. By separating motive from intention, ethical philosophers misconceived the entire process of ethical activity. "A voluntary act is always a disposition, or habit, of the agent passing into an overt act, which so far as it can, produces certain consequences."[47] Dewey extended that argument, which built upon his analysis of the reflex arc and his insistence on the unitary nature of volition and act. He contended that will and result must be considered in combination and in the context of the progressive development of character. Dewey's moral philosophy was consistent with his instrumentalism. He conceived of ethical activity, like all activity, in terms of problem solving. In situations of "felt difficulty," Dewey argued, progression toward further integration can be achieved only in praxis.

Two passages from Dewey's *Outlines of a Critical Theory of Ethics* clarify this elusive argument. First, from the analysis of the contrast between Kantian and utilitarian ethics, it is apparent that the end is neither the procuring of particular pleasures through satisfying various desires, nor is it action from the mere idea of abstract law in general. It is instead the "*satisfaction of desires according to law.*"[48] That much of Dewey's analysis echoed Sidgwick's *Methods of Ethics*; he added to it the conception of self-realization taken from Green's *Prolegomena to Ethics*:

> If we gather together the results of our observations of hedonism and of Kantianism we get something like the following problem and solution in outline. The end of action, or the good, is the realized will, the developed or satisfied self. This satisfied self is found neither in the getting of a lot of pleasures through the satisfaction of desires just as they happen to arise [Bentham], not in obedience to law simply because it is law [Kant]. It is found in *satisfaction of desires according to law* [Sidgwick]. This law, however, is not something external to the desires, but it is their own law. Each desire is only one striving of character for larger action, and the only way in which it can really find satisfaction (that is, pass from inward striving into outward action) is as a manifestation of character [Green].[49]

In light of his persistent efforts to draw together Sidgwick's and Green's ethics, it is hardly surprising that Dewey considered the conflict between individual interest and the common good a pseudo-problem. The moral end, he wrote, is entirely social. Responding to Sidgwick's challenge to Green, Dewey asserted that "intellectual and artistic interests *are themselves* social, when considered in the completeness of their relations." In short, all real goods, including intellectual and artistic development, must involve "interest in the well-being of society."[50] By that sleight of hand, however, Dewey merely reaffirmed Green's position without directly confronting the problem of the unequal distribution of scarce goods. Given his conceptualization of the issues in terms of individual development instead of pleasure, he did not meet the force of Sidgwick's argument. That disagreement, whether rooted in honest or willful misunderstanding, distinguishes Dewey's ethics and his social theory from the ideas of Sidgwick and James, and it points toward one of the perennial questions of politics: is individual character sacrificed or fulfilled in the integration of the personal will with the common good?

Dewey, Green, and Fouillée believed that self-realization requires the progressive growth of character through ethical action motivated by a desire to advance the common good *and* carefully calculated to advance social goals effectively. Only by following the principle of rational benevolence can the individual realize his full moral potential. Dewey stated this ethical postulate concisely. "In the realization of individuality there is found also the needed realization of some community of persons of which the individual is a member; and, conversely, the agent who duly satisfies the community in which he shares, by that same conduct satisfies himself." Obligation, as Dewey conceived it, corresponds to social satisfaction, while freedom provides self-satisfaction. Not only do they not conflict, they are interdependent and inseparable. The individual can find fulfillment only "as a member of a community. In this fact are found both freedom and duty."[51] From the perspective of James and Sidgwick, that analysis seemed a naive attempt to solve an intractable problem by defining it away. Concluding his treatment of ethics in *The Principles of Psychology*, James wrote, "Where harmonies are asserted of the real world, they are obviously mere postulates of rationality, so far as they transcend experience. Such postulates are exemplified by the ethical propositions that the individual and the universal good are one, and that happiness and goodness are bound to coalesce in the same subject."[52] While such propositions assume harmony, experience presents us with painful choices, and in every genuinely forced moral decision there is a sacrifice of one principle in order to satisfy another. When the demands of prudence collide with the demands of justice, there is no choice that does not exact a tragic price. In ethics as in epistemology, the *via media* led away from the comfort of familiar systems and toward the uncertainty of constant experimentation. Whether applying the principle of rational benevolence would help to resolve conflicts between the right and the good remained an open question to be answered not a priori but only in experience.

3. The Historicity of Ethics and the Burden of Responsibility

The difference between the moral philosophies of Sidgwick, James, and Dilthey on the one hand, and Fouillée, Green, and Dewey on the other, manifested itself equally in their analysis of the historical nature of ethics. All six theorists agreed that ethical theory develops historically, but the conclusions they derived from that premise contrasted sharply, and their disagreements carried over into their political ideas. They shared the conviction that ethics cannot be transformed into a set of unchanging propositions, and they likewise denied that ethics can be purely descriptive. In Sidgwick's words, ethics is the study of "principles of right conduct which the study of social facts as such cannot alone give, but which it is the business of ethics to give."[53] James similarly contrasted science, which "can tell us what exists," with ethics, which discloses "what is good, or would be good if it did exist."[54] Dilthey distinguished the human sciences principally according to their study of meaning and value, concerns that differentiate the objects of study of the *Geisteswissenschaften* from those of the *Naturwissenschaften*.[55] In his *Prolegomena to Ethics* and his *Lectures on the Principles of Political Obligation*, Green stressed the gap between describing how people really act and establishing an adequate theory of obligation.[56]

Because Dewey is usually treated as the exemplar of naturalism in twentieth-century moral philosophy, the distance separating judgment from description in his writings deserves particular emphasis. Such disciplines as anthropology, ethnology, and psychology, Dewey pointed out, "simply *describe*, while the business of ethics is to *judge*." As they are usually pursued, the social sciences "do not take into account the *whole* of action, but simply some of its aspects—either external or internal. Ethics deals with conduct, its end, its real meaning." Ethics, Dewey concluded, aims to detect "the element of obligation in conduct, to examine conduct to see what gives it its worth."[57]

Dewey did not abandon that conviction in his later writings, as the final chapter of *The Quest for Certainty* (1929) makes clear. There Dewey rejected all claims for intuited universal values while emphasizing that the alternative was not simply "setting up as values enjoyments that happen anyhow." Instead we need to reflect critically on the "conditions under which objects are enjoyed" and "the consequences of esteeming and liking them." He concluded that the fundamental problem with "the current empirical theory of values is that it merely formulates and justifies the socially prevailing habit of regarding enjoyments as they are actually experienced as values in and of themselves." Throughout his career, Dewey insisted that the application of critical intelligence is required for ethical judgment. As he emphasized in an important passage in *The Quest for Certainty*, "What is needed is *intelligent* examination of the consequences that are actually effected by inherited institutions and customs, in order that there may be *intelligent* consideration of the ways in which they are to be *intelligently* modified" in order to generate different consequences.[58] What Dewey meant by intelligence is as elusive as it is crucial for understanding his idea of judgment, and I will return to it in the conclusion of this chapter. Here I want merely to indicate how the radical idea of experience as meaningful ruled out the possibility of a strictly descriptive ethics—for Dewey as for the other philosophers of the *via media*—just as decisively as it ruled out the possibility of a positivistic psychology.

Yet paradoxically, as I have noted, these thinkers rejected the idea that an ontological distinction exists between the realms of fact and value. There can be no source of value judgments except experience, and there can be no approach to experience that is not itself value-laden. Dismantling this distinction mooted the question of whether universal intuited ethical norms or empirical evidence of desires serves as the ultimate ground of values. Consistent with their ideas about knowledge and activity, these radicals denied that there could be final answers to questions of value any more than there could be final answers to questions about truth. All value claims must be generated by real desires, and the consequences of satisfying those desires must be examined and evaluated critically. Like knowledge of any sort, ethical knowledge begins and ends in experience. But unlike merely partial, descriptive inquiries into either natural phenomena or human behavior, ethics as the philosophers of the *via media* conceived of it involves the careful and ongoing adjudication of competing value claims according to their meaning in specific situations. Ethics must therefore be radically empiricist; it must be sensitive to the provisional quality of value judgments and the historicity of all experience. Viewed from this perspective, disputes concerning the primacy of intuition, naturalism, or noncognitivism seemed merely to perpetuate illegitimate distinctions and misconceptions of experience as divisible into abstract intuition, cognition, and emotion, which these thinkers considered complementary and inseparable aspects of immediate experience. In his notes on the "moral universe," James argued that "all past events and all actual existing facts are wholly subject to the intellectual judgment, without being at the same time withdrawn from the emotional judgment. Only in both spheres, the judgment we make today of what is today, is liable to be rectified by what we learn tomorrow."[59] Charting their characteristic mediating course, these mavericks refused to accept any maxim that could not be tested through experience.

Further complicating their paradoxical refusal to allow ontological distinctions between fact and value even as they refused to allow the reduction of ethics to the description of desires, they maintained that history is the only source of critical judgment concerning ethical principles. While they denied that norms simply reflect what has existed or what exists, they nevertheless agreed that, in Sidgwick's words, "our view of what ought to be, must be largely derived, in details, from our appreciation of what is." Although Sidgwick did not consider the axioms of ethics—prudence, justice, and benevolence—historically conditioned, he believed that common sense morality, which provides the basis for the exercise of historical judgment, does develop historically.[60] The study of ethics must proceed from the critical application of the historical sensibility to the questions of the right and the good. Fouillée described his emphasis on accumulated experience as the distinctive feature of his theory of morality.[61] Green stressed in his *Lectures on the Principles of Political Obligation* the argument he had advanced in his *Lectures on the Philosophy of Kant*: the existing ethical rules of society, which embody the practical experience of generations, must provide the content necessary to fill out Kant's overly abstract categorical imperative. Only critical inquiry into the adequacy of accepted procedures can provide a firm footing for moral philosophy.[62] Dewey, in *Democracy and Education*, proclaimed as the first condition for determining "the criteria of good aims" that "the aim set up must be an outgrowth of existing conditions."[63]

The importance of a historically sensitive and empiricist approach to ethics received particular attention in James's essay "The Moral Philosopher and the Moral Life," in which he maintained that "the words 'good,' 'bad,' and 'obligation'" have "no absolute natures, independent of personal support. They are objects of feeling and desire, which have no foothold or anchorage in Being, apart from the existence of actually living minds." With no metaphysical foundation to support ethical principles, they can be established only pragmatically by appealing to experience. Consequently, "there can be no final truth in ethics any more than in physics, until the last man has had his experience and said his say."[64] Ethics develops over time and changes as different actors embrace different ethical principles and act on them; not surprisingly, James deemed all detailed casuistic scales illegitimate.

Responding to James's enthusiastic remarks concerning his *Outlines of a Critical Theory of Ethics*, Dewey endorsed James's analysis of obligation in "The Moral Philosopher and the Moral Life" as "the best and simplest statement I have seen." His argument in *The Quest for Certainty* revealed its lasting imprint on his thinking: "A moral law, like a law in physics, is not something to swear by and stick to at all hazards; it is a formula" whose "soundness and pertinence are tested by what happens when it is acted upon." Although philosophers fear "that adherence to standards external to experienced objects is the only alternative to confusion and lawlessness," just as scientists thought at one time, in fact the "test of consequences is more exacting than that afforded by fixed general rules," and it offers the only prospect for development and improvement of our ethical ideas.[65]

James offered as the most universal principle of ethics an apparently simple statement that has been the subject of much controversy: "*The essence of good is simply to satisfy demand*." That demand, James argued, "may be for anything under the sun." His description of the good in those terms has prompted a number of commentators to characterize James's ethical ideal as an uncomplicated utilitarian summing of pleasures. "The guiding principle of ethical philosophy," James wrote, is simply "to satisfy at all times *as many demands as we can.*" His argument seems at first to conform to Bentham's standard, the greatest good of the greatest number, yet its significance cannot be accurately assessed without reference to James's distinction between the easy going and strenuous moods. Although his position remained sufficiently ambiguous to make any final judgment difficult, it seems James meant to characterize utilitarianism as a baseline for morality and to contrast the strenuousness of benevolence as a higher ethical standard.[66] Evidence for this interpretation is contained in James's unpublished lecture notes for 1888–1889. "I firmly believe that we have preferences inexplicable by utility," he wrote, "preferences for certain kinds of behavior, as consistency, veracity, justice, nobility, dignity, purity, etc., etc." Like Sidgwick, James believed that such intuitive preferences derive from immediate experience; they are apparent to us "from a *psychological* point of view." The problem, as James admitted, again following Sidgwick, emerges from the collisions between competing preferences, "for many of them exclude each other. The whole difficulty of the moral life consists in deciding, when this is the case, which good to sacrifice and which to save."[67]

In the same way that James's pragmatism involved an implicit social verification of truth, he argued that collective experience offers the best guide to ethical principles when different demands conflict, or when prudence seems irreconcilable with justice. In "Humanism and Truth," he wrote that "the only *real* guarantee we have against licentious thinking is the circumpressure of experience itself, which gets us sick of concrete errors." The satisfaction of demands is not the subjectivist or hedonist standard it appears to be at first, because the notion of what works pragmatically requires a broader frame of reference than the isolated individual. James's ethics is social and historical in scope; the workability of moral principles and specific actions must be validated by the community over time.[68]

Viewed in this light, the relation between James's historical sensibility and his ethics comes into focus. As he wrote in "The Moral Philosopher and the Moral Life," "those ideals must be written highest which prevail at the least cost, or by whose realization the least possible number of other ideals are destroyed." In a passage that ties together history and the strenuous mood, James proclaimed that "the course of history is nothing but the story of Men's struggles from generation to generation to find the more and more inclusive order. Invent some manner of realizing your own ideas which will also satisfy the alien demands—that and that only is the path of peace!" James recognized in the historical process a progression from a more individualistic toward a more social orientation in moral philosophy, a gradual movement from prudence to justice. Still, he refused to counsel the adoption of any abstract, universally applicable standard by which individual activity could be judged. Morality must grow from life; it cannot be imposed dogmatically, since history, which James described as "an experiment of the most searching kind," has "proved that the laws and usages of the land are what yield the maximum of satisfaction to the thinkers taken all together." For that reason "the presumption in cases of [ethical] conflict must always be in favor of the conventionally recognized good."[69]

With Sidgwick, James believed that we can never hope to attain any ultimate moral ideal, and even the progressively more inclusive ethics of the strenuous mood must remain indefinite. Within those limits, the standard provided by history, which is available for the critical student of ethical development to explore, offers the best available normative measure, because history discloses how people create values. We do not find them in being but bring them into being and test them in experience. Ethics is thus an empirical and historical discipline, whose truths are disclosed gradually through a process of trial and error, and it must be critical in much the same way that epistemology must be critical. The moral philosopher cannot penetrate beyond experience in order to uncover ethical principles in ontology; he can aspire only to relative certainty.

Dilthey too refused to seek refuge from the uncertainty of the historical view of ethics by accepting a subjective theory of morality. He believed that history offers a gauge, albeit an imprecise one, for measuring the adequacy of ethical demands, because it reveals the consequences of various choices. Dilthey's analysis of the good as the object of demand also paralleled James's. "A value is for me what I have experienced in feeling as valuable," Dilthey wrote. A norm does not have absolute validity, it only "holds good" in experience.[70] In other words, it works in the pragmatic sense. The historical sensibility turns away from abstraction toward expressions of collective lived experience in historically developing ethical codes. Recognition of the relativity of all history enables the philosopher to see the generally valid in the relative and to "recognize reality as the yardstick for progress into the future."[71] Dilthey considered historical study prerequisite to ethical theory. The prime consideration for restoring moral philosophy from its descent into abstraction and dogmatism, Dilthey insisted, "is the introduction of historical facts and their utilization by the comparative method."[72]

While all of these thinkers shared the conviction that ethics must be estab-lished on an empirical basis and endlessly revised by testing consequences in experience, their applications of the historical sensibility to ethical thinking reflected their contrasting tragic and heroic moods. Sidgwick, James, and Dilthey believed that ethics poses a series of dilemmas admitting no satisfac-tory resolution. The principles of prudence and justice, both forced upon our reason by experience, inevitably collide. As Sidgwick constructed his argument, each individual intuitively understands that he has a primary and unconditional duty to maximize the general happiness, and he knows that he can further his individual happiness only by increasing the happi-ness of everyone. The individual understands equally well, however, his primary and unconditional duty to maximize his individual happiness, and he recognizes that he should contribute to the general welfare only inasmuch as his contribution does not detract from his own happiness. For that reason, the values of individual happiness and the general good are irreconcilable.

James reached a similar conclusion. "No philosophy of ethics is possible in the old-fashioned sense of the term," he declared. "Everywhere the ethical philosopher must wait on the facts." There can be no final resolution of the central ethical dilemma between personal satisfaction and the general good, and "the highest ethical life ... consists at all times in the breaking of rules which have grown too narrow for the actual case." Abstract rules offer only limited assistance in making moral decisions, "for every real dilemma is in literal strictness a unique situation; and the exact combination of ideals realized and ideals disappointed which each decision creates is always a universe without a precedent, and for which no adequate previous rule exists." The awareness that ethical codes develop historically offers small solace, then, because it reveals the open-endedness of all moral questions. No easy answers exist, and choices necessarily involve the sacrifice of a cherished value. The moral philosopher needs to know what part of his ideals must be compromised. Tension persists between the ideals of individual free-dom and the maximization of unity, and no point of perfect balance can be maintained. Either individuality is sacrificed for the sake of peace, or the richness of freedom is enjoyed at the cost of chaos.[73]

Like Sidgwick and James, Dilthey was acutely aware of the conflict among the moral imperatives we intuitively recognize as binding. He discussed these ethical principles in his essay "The Nature of Philosophy" (1907). "There is a hierarchy of obligation which descends from duty to the moral demand of kindness, devotion to others and personal improvement."[74] Counterparts to these principles may be found in *The Methods of Ethics*, and Dilthey likewise argued that they must supplement one another. Dilthey's principle of duty corresponds roughly to Kant's categorical imperative; both are abstract and universal. The moral demand of kindness resembles rational benevolence, devotion to others resembles the felt obligation of justice, and the principle of personal improvement resembles prudence or rational egoism. These values have been ranked and combined in different ways in different eras, Dilthey pointed out, and our challenge is to examine critically the process whereby these principles become codified as cultures develop historically. Ethical theory develops gradually through use, and it offers only general and imperfect guidelines for moral choices. Its justification is pragmatic rather than a priori.[75]

Dilthey maintained that accumulated experience provides the only source of ethical principles. As I have noted, he believed that life does not mean anything other than itself, that there is nothing in life that points to a meaning outside it. The historical process reveals the consequences of various values over time, and it is thus possible to regard history as a source of immanent critique in ethics as in the other human sciences. Directing the critical faculties of mind to the historical process discloses an alternative to skepticism and subjectivism: "The final conclusion of the mind is not that all the world-views through which it has passed are relative but that it is sovereign over them all."[76] While that realization liberates the individual to exercise his freedom, it also imposes on him the responsibility to act according to his own estimate of the optimum combination of ethical principles in each situation. To use James's image, the historical sensibility frees the moral judgment to decide which part of the ideal to butcher. Dilthey, Sidgwick, and James despaired of fully harmonizing contradictory ethical imperatives, yet they salvaged from their loss of certainty a sense of freedom and an acceptance of responsibility.

Fouillée, Green, and Dewey escaped such anguish by accepting two ideas central to Aristotelian ethics: telos and praxis. Green repeatedly proclaimed self-realization or self-development as his ethical ideal. He acknowledged that his vision of the telos of ethical activity derived from Aristotle and from Plato. Notably, Green's ethics contains a concept of the eternal state of being that provides a model for our ethical behavior, a Platonic idea conspicuously absent from Aristotle's ethics—and, of course, from Dewey's. The Greek conception of disinterested virtue as the ethical ideal, according to Green, marked "the great transition," and Christian thinkers picked up that idea and attached it to their conception of history as a continuous progression toward a divine ideal. This Augustinian fusion of ethics and history, which Hegel reinvigorated in his philosophy, provided a framework for individual moral development.

Green's ethics thus combined Greek, Christian, and idealist ideas about morality and history as teleology; from his point of view, personal concern for the common good constitutes the culmination of a progression centuries old.[77] Green concluded his *Lectures on the Principles of Political Obligation* by affirming, "My duty is to be interested positively in my neighbor's well-being." Both ethical principles and historical progression dictate that conclusion. "The establishment of obligations by law or authoritative custom, and the gradual recognition of moral duties," Green contended, "have not been separate processes. They have gone on together in the history of man." The evolution of legal institutions and the awareness that the will is moralized through social action reinforce each other. As political developments slowly come to embody moral sentiments, "more complete equality of rights is gradually secured to a wider range of persons."[78] Over time, Green argued, conceptions of the good have developed away from earlier notions of exclusiveness and toward spiritual conceptions in which all may share, and indeed in which all must share, if this process of development is to come to fruition. As noted in the preceding section, Sidgwick challenged the adequacy of Green's attempt to reconcile individual desire with social needs by describing the good as a spiritual activity, but it is clear that Green admitted no distinction between the idea of personal fulfillment and the general welfare either in individual life or over the course of historical development. The development of morality, in Green's words, "is founded on the action in man of an idea of true or absolute good, consisting in the full realisation of the capabilities of the human soul." Conceived in those terms, the moral impulse differs decisively from a desire for pleasure.[79] From the outset it involves "a demand for some well-being which shall be common to the individual desiring it with others." Thus no fundamental conflict between individual and social demands can arise.

Dewey shared Green's Aristotelian vision of self-development ending in harmony between the individual and society. Even after he moved out of Green's orbit, Dewey's critique of the overly abstract character of idealist philosophy did not carry over into a revision of the teleological character of his ethics.[80] Dewey characterized moral conduct in his and Tufts's *Ethics* as "activity called forth and directed by ideas of value or worth." He defined the moral end as self-realization which conceives "the self to be realized as universal and ultimate, involving the fulfillment of *all* capacities and the observance of all relations." That conception of self-realization, Dewey maintained, includes altruism, "since the 'universal self' is realized only when the relations that bind one to others are fulfilled." Moral ideals must not be considered only as individual virtues, however, because moral activity also "sustains a whole complex system of social values; one which keeps vital and progressive the industrial order, science, art, and the State."[81] Dewey, like Green, considered ethics and social development to be mutually reinforcing, and he likewise dismissed the idea of conflict between individual and social goods. Indeed, Dewey specifically declared that such conflict can be resolved within a teleological conception of ethical development. When ends are genuinely incompatible, he insisted, the only common denominator available is a decision concerning what sort of character is to be most highly prized.[82] Dewey's ethics points toward the further development of social responsibility as the goal of individual moral growth, but he refused to posit a single end of moral development. He emphasized instead the plurality of goods toward which individuals might reasonably direct their attention, and he declared that "growth itself is the only moral 'end.'"[83]

Dewey claimed to reject all proposed candidates for the summum bonum because the idea violated his conception of historical development and personal growth. His protests notwithstanding, however, he attributed to the idea of democracy, the application of intelligence, and the method of instrumentalism a normative quality, and they replaced for him the Platonic or religious conception of the eternal consciousness that figured so prominently in Green's moral philosophy and in Dewey's early writings. It is impossible to exaggerate the importance of the democratic ideal in Dewey's thought, for democracy provides the means by which individual development can be synchronized with the common welfare.[84] Dewey first linked ethics with a democratic standard in *The Ethics of Democracy* (1888). He proclaimed the inadequacy of the traditional Anglo-American atomistic view of society, a conception inconsistent with the idea of individual experience as social. He then argued that, since only in a democracy do all citizens participate equally, democracy alone allows the complete realization of all individuals' ethical potential. Dewey's concluding remarks reveal the quasi-mystical character of his democratic ideal:

> Democracy is an ethical idea, the idea of a personality, with truly infinite capacities, incorporate with every man. Democracy and the one, the ultimate, ethical ideal of humanity are to my mind synonyms. The idea of democracy, the ideas of liberty, equality, and fraternity, represent a society in which the distinction between the spiritual and the secular has ceased, and as in Greek theory, as in the Christian theory of the Kingdom of God, the church and the state, the divine and the human organization are one.[85]

Democracy provides an unstable ethical standard, however, because it contains an inherent indeterminacy. Since all individuals can stake equal claims on the polity, the course of its development cannot be determined in advance. Democracy provides a flexible mode of ethical life rather than an explicit ethical norm, and it thus satisfies Dewey's maxim that growth is the only end.[86] As late as 1892, in the address entitled "Christianity and Democracy" delivered before the Christian Students' Association at the University of Michigan, Dewey continued to acknowledge explicitly the religious foundations of his faith in the democratic process as the vehicle of divine progress on earth. But he was already in the process of shifting his ground from religion to instrumentalism, from Green to James, and after the early 1890s free inquiry and natural intelligence assumed the role previously played by Dewey's religious faith. Unless that transition is understood, his unshakable confidence in the progressive, self-correcting quality of the democratic project is inexplicable.

Attempting to explain the origins of his ethics in a letter he wrote to James in 1891, Dewey credited the energetic and charismatic journalist Franklin Ford with "whatever freedom of sight and treatment there is in my ethics." It was Ford, Dewey wrote, who "identified the question of inquiry with, in philosophical terms, the question of the relation of intelligence to the objective world—is the former free to move in relation to the latter or not?"[87] Presumably, being "free to move" enables intelligence to explore options and test consequences with sufficient flexibility and insight to insure the proper functioning of the instrumentalist method. But it must be emphasized that inquiry, even within a democratic community of free intellects such as the group of reform-minded intellectuals with whom Dewey became associated in Ann Arbor and Chicago, remains only a procedure. Dewey's confidence that the valuings of such a community are legitimate comes from the transposition of his faith from divine purpose to human potential.

Dewey's instrumentalism offers only a method of answering ethical questions. No specific moral guidelines can be derived from his injunction to analyze all moral situations intelligently with reference to both the principles involved and the consequences of an act. Dewey suggested only how we are to go about solving moral problems; he did not claim to prescribe courses of action for the specific situations we encounter in experience. His position on this point was consistent and unambiguous. In his *Outlines of a Critical Theory of Ethics*, he denied the desirability of any absolute ethical standard. All moral principles, he argued, lack sufficient flexibility to meet the requirements of life. We need only "a method of action," for which Dewey nominated an instrumentalist version of Aristotle's golden mean of virtue. Aristotle recommended deciding the proper course of action according to shifting circumstances and an ideal of personal development. What was his notion of "the right time, occasion, person, purpose, and fashion," Dewey asked, if not "the complete individualization of conduct in order to meet the whole demands of the whole situation, instead of some abstraction?"[88] Instrumentalist ethics focuses on the situations in which felt difficulties are resolved in favor of more complete harmony, and that precludes any attempt to lay down specific ethical maxims.

Whereas both Kantians and utilitarians mistakenly sought to find universally applicable rules for determining the right and the good, Dewey maintained that "the object of moral principles is to supply standpoints and methods which will enable the individual to make for himself an analysis of the elements of good and evil in the particular situation in which he finds himself." A moral principle, Dewey declared, can be only "a tool for analyzing a special situation, the right or wrong being determined by the situation in its entirety, and not by the rule as such."[89] The assertion that each situation is unique and therefore requires its own rule may seem, Dewey admitted in

Reconstruction in Philosophy, "not merely blunt but preposterous." Yet the pragmatic method dictates nothing more specific than shifting the burden of morality from rules to intelligence. That procedure, Dewey emphasized, "does not destroy responsibility; it only locates it."[90]

Dewey based his instrumentalist ethics on his democratic ideal: he relied on each individual to use his own moral judgment responsibly and on the community to ride herd over outlaws. He argued that the sole restriction on individual choices lay in the challenge of testing them in the long run in a social context. Only the guidelines drawn from past experience validated (or invalidated) in future experience furnish us with ethical standards. Ethics can be but a method of inquiry. Its specific content varies as individuals collectively alter their ethical choices over time. We must reflect on the results of our actions in order to assess their moral content, and only in a democracy, Dewey believed, can collective ethical estimates be effectively translated into positive legal codes. Although a formal, prescriptive ethics is impossible, the need for an ethics remains. As we encounter difficult choices, Dewey advised, we can best discern the path toward self-realization by applying the instrumentalist method rather than by looking for applicable rules. Each individual must shoulder the burden of responsibility.

Dewey's ethics, like Green's, begins and ends in praxis. Both asserted that existing moral standards offer the most solid foundation available for moral theory, and they agreed that the individual can determine what course of action contributes to fuller ethical development only by both consulting the values of his culture and using his own intelligence to test those values in unprecedented situations. As Green maintained in an important passage in his *Prolegomena to Ethics*, existing ethical codes represent the culmination of historical development, and they provide "a source of new practical direction when applied by a conscience, working under a felt necessity of seeking the best, to circumstances not previously existent or not considered, or to some new lesson of experience."[91] That passage reveals, first, the identity Green posited between the telos of historical and moral development, and second, the similarity between Dewey's idea of felt difficulty and Green's statement of felt necessity as the origin of ethical reflection. Although the application of intelligence to ethical situations is an idea properly associated with Dewey's ethics, it can be traced, as can Dewey's teleological perspective and his organic ideal, to Green's *Prolegomena to Ethics*.

Green designed his *Prolegomena to Ethics* to demonstrate the inadequacy of Kant's categorical imperative, despite its superiority to the pleasure-pain calculus of hedonism, by showing that pure intentions are a necessary but not sufficient condition in determining the good. Moral development requires praxis, Green insisted; the good will must translate its desires into reality by working to realize a more universal form of social life through social and political action. Dewey likewise considered the idea of praxis an essential part of his ethics. Whereas James agonized over the inevitable betrayal of some ideal in all ethical choices, Dewey stressed the incremental progress to follow from the conscientious application of instrumental procedures to moral dilemmas. Although no hint of an ultimate resolution to ethical problems appears in Dewey's moral philosophy, neither does his work exhibit the anxiety and the sense of loss that characterize James's writings. Dewey believed that the conception of ethics in terms of self-realization and praxis eliminates the antinomy between individual and social responsibility and between happiness and duty, a conviction expressed in the revealing contrast he drew between his moral philosophy and both hedonism and intuitionism.

Hedonists erred in assuming the identity of the desired and the desirable, Dewey pointed out, as "a direct or immediate unity, while in reality, it exists only in and through activity; it is a unity which can be attained only as the result of a process." Dewey did not deny the possibility of uniting personal pleasure with the good of universal happiness, but he maintained that these values could be harmonized only through critical reflection and the application of intelligence to action. Against Kant's claim that desires can never be brought into conformity with what is right, and that the right can therefore be only a pure and abstract good will, Dewey argued that while "there is no direct, or natural, identity of desire and law," their identification is not an impossible task. Again he insisted, "the problem is solved in the exercise of function"; desire and law synchronize in praxis. "Flowing in the channel of response to the demands of the moral environment"—i.e., drawn into conformity with the ethical ideal of self-realization—the desires "unify, at once, social service and individual freedom." This unification of desire and duty, of good and right, is accomplished only to the extent that "the desires are socialized. A want is socialized when it is not a want for its own isolated and fixed satisfaction, but reflects the needs of the environment."[92] While deciphering such passages is a difficult business, I believe that Dewey aimed to connect the right and the good in such a way that neither had priority over the other. If the right finally seemed to be that which promotes the good, the good must be reevaluated constantly according to instrumentalist principles.

Dewey claimed to be a naturalist because he denied that any source except experience could provide guidance concerning ethical problems. Yet he insisted that the evidence of history be examined intelligently. "Past experiences are significant in giving us intellectual instrumentalities of judging," he wrote in *The Quest for Certainty*, but these "are tools, not finalities. Reflecting upon what we have liked and have enjoyed is a necessity. But it tells us nothing about the value of these things until the enjoyments are themselves reflectively controlled, or, until, as they are recalled, we form the best judgment possible about what led us to like this sort of thing and what has issued from the fact that we liked it." This passage raises the perennial problem of whether what we desire is therefore desirable or merely desired, the question of the legitimacy of linking "ought" to "is." Sidgwick resisted that identification and resorted to intuition as the source of value; Dewey accepted it because he found in the radical idea of immediate experience, conceived as social and meaningful, the warrant for his conviction that experience itself discloses sufficient information about values to serve as the foundation for judgment. Summing up his argument in *The Quest for Certainty*, Dewey contended that values "may be connected inherently with liking, and yet not with *every* liking but only with those that judgment has approved, after examination of the relation upon which the object liked depends." Decisions must always be made in contexts laden with meanings, contexts embodying a series of prior choices reflecting the interplay between individual desires and social obligations. Just as the radical theory of knowledge emphasized the immediate awareness of meanings and the immediate connection of the self with the community, so Dewey's instrumentalist ethics broke down the distinction between individual choices and their cultural matrix. "Thus we are led to our main proposition," Dewey concluded: "*Judgments about values are judgments about that which should regulate the formation of our desires, affections, and enjoyments.*"[93] Dewey's recurrent and puzzling references to unities, harmonies, and socialized wants must be understood in light of his attempt to connect thinking, willing, and acting with the individual's ongoing cultural and historical context. Given their common appreciation of the meaningful quality of immediate experience, Sidgwick's intuitionally based utilitarianism and Dewey's naturalism were linked by their conviction that ethics must be guided by accumulated experience and by their commitment to an experimental, open-ended approach to value.

Both Sidgwick and Dewey refused to give priority to any substantive concept of justice, preferring instead to stress the desirability of a certain method of ethics. Their procedural ethical theories were consistent with their theory of knowledge; the differences between Sidgwick's tragic mood and Dewey's heroic mood reflected their different perspectives on history. Whereas Sidgwick, like James and Dilthey, could find no way to reconcile the contradictory demands of prudence and justice, Dewey, like Green and Fouillée, contended that ethical activity directed toward a goal of social harmony provides a means by which the individual can develop his full potential and gradually resolve the conflict between personal desire and social responsibility. These competing ethical orientations had far reaching implications, not only for these thinkers' own political ideas but also for the theories of social democracy and progressivism. For beyond the difference in mood lay the troubling question whether, in politics, the commitment to procedures rather than substantive principles would lead to progress or prevent it.

5

From Philosophy to Politics

1. The Politics of the *Via Media*

While empiricists and idealists disputed the nature of experience and utilitarians debated ethical questions with intuitionists, the noisy collisions of liberals and socialists drowned out the murmur of philosophical discourse during the 1870s and 1880s. Bentham's heirs championed the free market economy to defend individual freedom and personal property; socialists of diverse lineage advanced a rich variety of ostensibly scientific and admittedly utopian analyses of social conflict and methods of reconciling selfish individuals to the common good. At both ends of the spectrum, advocates of laissez-faire liberalism and Marxist socialism presented variations on the theme of inevitability in historical development. Moreover, although cherishing contradictory conceptions of the social ideal, both champions of the free market and Marxists considered economics the engine behind social development. They believed that the economy, whether ruled by the invisible hand or the dialectic, obeyed inviolable laws grounded in ontology and manifested in politics and society. While reactionaries or utopians might temporarily impede their progress or alter their course, the rules of the free market or the struggle over the means of production would ultimately shape the future. Liberals and Marxists challenged characterizations of their ideas as fatalistic, yet representatives of both traditions emphasized the imperatives of larger historical processes over individual activity. Their contrasting visions of change underlay their competing political programs.

Strong elective affinities connect conceptions of knowledge and responsibility with conceptions of politics, and the historical bond between these categories of thought is indisputable. The cautious empiricism of British epistemology spawned a tradition of prudent liberalism, democratic radicalism flowed out of the confident rationalism of the Enlightenment, and revolutionary socialism emerged from the German tradition of idealism that gave birth to Hegel as well as the young Hegelians who reversed his celebration of the state and called for its abolition. Specific theories of knowledge may not necessarily entail specific ethical or political theories, but historically these ideas have reinforced one another and yielded more or less coherent systems of thought. The congruence between epistemology, ethics, and politics was particularly clear in the philosophy of the *via media* and in the ideas of certain theorists of social democracy and progressivism. It is that historical connection, which in this case does reflect a logical relation among their ideas, that I intend to explore.

I am not claiming that a certain philosophical perspective is either a necessary or a sufficient condition for adopting a certain political stance. Just as there were other roads to socialism besides the one leading from Hegel to Marx, there were numerous forks in the road to progressivism and social democracy, some of which bypassed philosophy altogether. Conceding that theory and practice are enmeshed in a tangled web wherever historical change occurs, I am concerned with the slow, unsteady working out of an intellectual revolution, the gradual reshaping of political ideas to fit with altered conceptions of knowledge and responsibility. While not all the philosophers who arrived at such positions became social democrats or progressives, and not all social democrats and progressives grounded their politics on the philosophy of the *via media*, a number of thinkers made precisely that move from philosophy to politics. I will examine why they thought their new conception of experience ruled out certain political arguments and explain why they judged a new set of political ideas, the ideas finally elaborated in the theories of social democracy and progressivism, congruent with their radical analysis of how we know and what we are to do.

In this chapter I will discuss the efforts of Dilthey, Green, Sidgwick, Fouillée, and James to extend their theories of knowledge and ethics into social and political analysis. Because this generation reached intellectual maturity in the 1870s and 1880s, their ideas reflected a substantially different social reality from the world that dawned in the 1890s and witnessed the emergence of social democracy and progressivism. John Dewey participated more fully in the latter phase of this transformation than did the older philosophers of the *via media*, and for that reason I will examine his political writings when I discuss progressivism in Chapters Nine and Ten. Dewey's contributions to epistemology and ethics were very much part of the reorientation in philosophy accomplished by the older generation, but his ideas about politics belong to the twentieth century, and their significance can be better understood in relation to a later stage of political debate. The older generation, through their attempts to come to terms with the inchoate urban-industrial societies developing in Germany, France, Britain, and the United States, worked to establish a bridgehead from the midcentury world of liberalism and socialism to the territory of the welfare state to be occupied by social democrats and progressives. Their political writings reflect the

dislocation of rapid socioeconomic change and also the uncertainty characteristic of their philosophical work.

These thinkers were not all equally concerned with political ideas. James
only infrequently turned his attention to politics, and his writings about social
questions were few, scattered, and more on the order of desultory
meditations than systematic arguments. Dilthey also concentrated on philosophy far more than on politics. Yet James's and Dilthey's political ideas,
despite their limitations, suggest another dimension of the radical theory of
knowledge that helps to illuminate the path leading to the ideas of social
democracy and progressivism. By examining their views on politics with
some care, I do not intend to elevate them to the status of political philosophers. Clearly they were not. I want only to indicate the direction in which
their ideas ran, because their political inclinations—recognizable in the more
subtle tones and shadings of their writings—point away from certain political
positions and toward others not yet established when they wrote. Those
impulses found expression in social democracy and progressivism.

Because Green, Sidgwick, and Fouillée wrote more extensively about
politics, the political implications of the philosophy of the *via media* are more
clearly apparent in their work. They self-consciously and painstakingly drew
connections between knowledge, responsibility, and reform, and their political writings represent an important, intermediate step in the convergence of
socialism and liberalism toward social democracy and progressivism. Unlike
many who preceded them and many who followed them, these thinkers
insisted that the most important questions of politics cannot be framed in
terms of wealth, status, or power, but remain properly and irreducibly philosophical questions about values: questions about how people ought to live as
members of a community, questions for which there can be no final answers.
Thinking about the prospect of the welfare state before its creation, they
admitted misgivings that have prompted later thinkers to dismiss their ideas
as anachronistic expressions of an outdated sensibility. Their perspective,
paradoxically outside the political struggle that gave birth to the welfare state
yet informed by the radical conceptions of knowledge and obligation that
indirectly helped bring it into being, provides valuable insights into the
possibilities and the limits of political action as a solution to the cultural
problems of an urban-industrial society.

In the concluding pages of his *Critique of Contemporary Systems of
Morality*, Fouillée concisely stated the chain of reasoning that led the philosophers of the *via media* from epistemology to ethics and from ethics to politics. Discarding misleading conceptions of experience inherited from
associationists and rationalists, he argued, we must begin with a frank
admission of uncertainty. From the fact of individual consciousness aware of
itself as socially and historically situated, but not altogether determined, we
must understand how individuals build up beliefs from personal and cultural
experience tested repeatedly in practice, and this experience must form the
basis of ethical judgment. From that historically sensitive and pragmatic
vantage point we can proceed to formulate political arguments, but we must

relinquish the hubris of pretending that our knowledge about politics can be more than provisional. Moreover, we must admit the potential incommensurability of competing ideals.[1]

Sidgwick concluded the chapter "Justice" in *The Methods of Ethics* by striking a similar chord. The quest for ideal justice has followed two paths, Sidgwick reasoned, because there seem to be two distinct conceptions of it, embodied in the "Individualistic and the Socialistic Ideals of a political community." Liberals elevate "the realization of Freedom as the ultimate end and standard of right social relations," but their notion of freedom is too shallow to yield a solid basis for social construction because it violates our sense of justice. Socialistic ideals, on the other hand, appeal to our feeling of fairness, but they are too utopian and imprecise to guide social policy.[2] Although the same differences of tone that distinguished Fouillée's confidence from Sidgwick's doubt about resolving ethical dilemmas surfaced in their treatments of politics, they both sought to harmonize discordant political arguments by selecting and combining ideas from different traditions in a radically new form, echoing again the theme of convergence.

The radical theory of knowledge precluded both laissez-faire liberalism and revolutionary socialism. Fouillée, Sidgwick, Green, Dilthey, and James grounded individual freedom in immediate experience, and they rejected attempts to account for individual interest on either purely hedonistic or economic grounds. The content of the will as they understood it reflects both personal and historical development; choices vary with conditions but cannot be reduced to them. Immediate experience invalidates the claims of determinism, for while freedom is circumscribed by history, individuals rather than anonymous processes ultimately shape social change. As James argued in "Great Men and Their Environment," societies develop from the interaction of two distinct factors: first, the individual, "deriving his peculiar gifts from the play of physiological and infra-social forces, but bearing all the power of initiative and origination in his hands"; and second, "the social environment, with its power of adopting or rejecting both him and his gifts." Ignoring either element results in misunderstanding, for the community "stagnates without the impulse of the individual," and at the same time "the impulse dies away without the sympathy of the community."[3]

Rooted in the radical notion of experience as fundamentally social, this concentration on both individuals and their community characterized these thinkers' unclassifiable attitude toward society and politics. Doctrines of social organicism, which attracted so many of their contemporaries, never appealed to them. They refused to hypostatize society and ignore individuals. As Fouillée argued in *Contemporary Social Science*, Comtean positivism, socialism, and other collectivist doctrines that "elevate society at the expense of the individual" are self-contradictory, because "it is not by adding zeroes to zeroes that an effective total is obtained." In a typical formulation, he maintained that "the most comprehensive social idea is clearly the one capable of reconciling both the greatest individuality of each member and the greatest solidarity of all the members" of society. Individuals acting voluntarily mold societies, not vice versa; the social organism is based on choice and not necessity.[4] Just as Fouillée rejected the Comtean vision, so Green maintained his distance, in his political thinking, from the Hegelianism that gave an idealistic flavor to his metaphysics. The individual can never cede to the society or the state his individual liberty, "for there can be no right to mere life, no right to life on the part of a being that has not also the right to use the life according to the notions of its own will."[5] These renegades were to advocate policies considerably more communitarian than those associated with liberal individualism, but at the heart of their thinking about society and politics lay a fundamental commitment to individual voluntarism.

This generation linked freedom with the responsibility to act, and also with the necessity of testing political arguments pragmatically. The *Geisteswissenschaften* are the "sciences of acting man and the practical world," Dilthey insisted. Philosophy has a "right to exist" only insofar as it has an effect on the way people live, and only by testing theory in practice can its adequacy be determined.[6] To consider abstract ideals apart from specific practical activity seemed to Fouillée a nominalist fantasy.[7] Political activists, James maintained, by participating in the hurly-burly of practical politics, are "deciding through actual experiment by what sort of conduct the maximum amount of good can be gained and kept in this world. These experiments," he concluded in good pragmatic fashion, "are to be judged, not a priori, but by actually finding, after the fact of their making, how much more outcry or how much appeasement comes about." This crucial but overlooked statement ties James's pragmatic theory of truth directly to his political outlook. No "closet solutions," as he put it, "can possibly anticipate the result of trials made on such a scale." Ideas about society, like all abstract ideas, can be validated only in practice. "The anarchists, nihilists and free-lovers; the free-silverites, socialists, and single-tax men; the free traders and civil service reformers; the prohibitionists and the anti-vivisectionists; the radical Darwinians with their idea of suppression of the weak"—all must test their ideas before the community.[8] While James himself was no radical politically and embraced the genteel democratic liberalism characteristic of his class and his era, he never attempted to enshrine his values as a timeless and universal social ideal. Indeed, he unambiguously and repeatedly rejected such attempts. In his essay "On a Certain Blindness in Human Beings," he argued that his philosophical creed "commands us to tolerate, respect, and indulge" those who live differently from ourselves, "however unintelligible" their ways may be to us. "Hands off," James insisted, when dealing with social diversity, for "neither the whole of truth nor the whole of good is revealed to any single observer."[9] The adequacy of such broad-mindedness when applied to political questions is a subject to which I will return.

In politics as in epistemology and ethics, James committed himself to no particular substantive program but instead to a style of inquiry: an open, free ranging quest for the most satisfactory solution to specific problems arising from concrete circumstances. His faith concerned not the results of the political struggle as much as its method, not the outcome of the game but its rules. So long as all claims to truth receive a fair hearing, James concluded, "the pure philosopher can only follow the windings of the spectacle, confident that the line of least resistance will always be towards the richer and the more inclusive arrangement, and that by one tack after another some approach to the kingdom of heaven is incessantly made."[10] James's vagueness was deliberate. He denied that the particular twists along the road of social progress could be specified in advance of the actual political struggle among competing reformers for alternative ideals. While he believed that society would tend increasingly toward a more democratic and socialistic form, he never tried to chart a single course to utopia. The truth in social questions, like all truth, can emerge only from the collective experience of generations testing various hypotheses in practice.

By emphasizing the community's role in validating ideas about social and political organization, the pragmatic theory of truth reinforced the conception of the relation between self and other contained in the radical empiricist reading of immediate experience. Because the philosophers of the *via media* recognized that we are immediately aware of "the conceptual commutability of all egos," in James's words, they were able to see behind the illusion of liberal theory that society constitutes only a convenient, artificial combination of isolated and egoistic individuals.[11] While this idea may seem at first to contradict the analysis of individual voluntary action, closer examination reveals their consistency. Individuals must choose and act, but they act as beings conscious of their membership in a community, and that community is constantly testing the viability of their ideas and their actions. To underline an argument advanced earlier, it is a mistake to overlook the social dimensions of the pragmatic theory of truth. Pragmatism, James insisted, has a "stronger hold on reality than any other philosophy" precisely because it is "essentially a *social* philosophy, a philosophy of 'co,' in which conjunctions do the work."[12] Individual voluntary action remains the engine driving society, but the social nature of individual consciousness and the necessity of testing ideas by bringing them before the bar of social experience rule out the standard forms of liberal individualism.

Fouillée claimed that radical individualists like Nietzsche and Stirner on the one hand, and radical collectivists like Comte and Marx on the other, misconceived the relation between individuality and society. The synthesis that "reconciles these two terms," according to Fouillée, discloses that "man is defined at the same time by his individuality and by the social forces with which he is in solidarity."[13] Fouillée's concept of *solidarité*, which inspired a generation of French social reformers, derived from his antidualist analysis of immediate experience and from his pragmatic doctrine of *idées-forces*. Green grounded his *Lectures on the Principles of Political Obligation* on a similar understanding of the relation between individuality and community. "As to the sense given to freedom," he wrote, "it must of course be admitted that every usage of the term to express anything but a social and political relation of one man to others involves a metaphor." All attempts to establish individual rights by recourse to a social contract among presocial, free individuals rest on a fiction that might serve a certain polemical purpose but bears no relation whatsoever to experience. "Natural right," in the sense of a "right in the state of nature which is not a state of society, is a contradiction. There can be no right without a consciousness of common interest on the part of members of a society."[14] This awareness that obligations immediately accompany rights distinguished Green's thinking from that of earlier liberals, and it relied upon the prior rejection of any meaningful notion of individuality independent of membership in a community.

The conclusion these thinkers drew about values from their understanding of the mediation of experience in language also found expression and political application in their writings. "A common humanity," Green declared, "of which language is the expression, necessarily leads to the recognition of some good as common," and that recognition provides the seed from which social intercourse develops into political organization.[15] Dilthey maintained, "Every word, every sentence, every gesture of politeness, every work of art, and every historical action," in short, all the expressions of culturally mediated experience, "are only comprehensible because a community binds the expresser with the interpreter." We live, think, and act in the context of a community, and we can understand only by virtue of that shared context.[16] If individual experience were not social, it would be impossible to understand the expressions of experience by which we achieve knowledge of the human condition and debate its future.

By acknowledging the social dimension of immediate experience, expression, and understanding, these philosophers contributed to a larger development in American and European thought: the decline of the political as a category distinct from the social. Dilthey argued in the *Introduction to the Human Sciences* that there is nothing to be gained from attempting to separate state from society for purposes of analysis, because neither exists in fact without the other. Theory should square with experience, and in experience the social and the political are indissolubly linked.[17] As political and social categories coalesced, arguments typically associated with conservative theorists could be appropriated for more progressive uses. The awareness that experience is social alerted theorists to the pervasive interaction between the individual, the society, and the polity. Thinkers whose intellectual roots lay in the tradition of liberal individualism began to recognize the importance and desirability of social cohesion as they became more sensitive to the role of community in political life, and they also turned increasingly to history both as a source of information and as a value in its own right. Arguments from community and history, long standard weapons in the arsenal of theorists like Burke and de Maistre, began to appear in the writings of those advocating change rather than the preservation of tradition.

Paradoxically, the association of the individual with society in the radical theory of knowledge coincided historically with the disappearance of stable communities in the late nineteenth century, as the United States, Britain, France, and Germany became increasingly urbanized, industrialized, and interdependent societies. Traditional forms of social cohesion broke down, and in their place appeared webs of functional dependencies connecting anonymous individuals. As the foundations of community eroded, the task of strengthening social bonds in an increasingly depersonalized world took on greater significance. Social cohesion could no longer stand on the bedrock of religious faith, and the search for new sources of solidarity carried thinkers in a variety of directions. While some proclaimed the dawning of a new age inspired by science and ordered according to the biological imperatives governing human behavior, others invoked lingering preurban and pre-industrial values to denounce the fruits of modernity, and still others offered utopian visions predicated on projections of the unlimited bounty industrialization was expected to yield.[18]

The philosophers of the *via media* found in the historical sensibility an alternative to these approaches, a double-edged critical realism that made them simultaneously realistic about the impossibility of resisting the rising tides of urbanization and industrialization yet skeptical of modernization's beneficence. They faced up to the most troubling problem of modern social organization: the inverse relation between the need for and the availability of automatic social controls. Comparatively simple societies tend to have elaborate cultural codes, based on generally accepted values that regulate personal relations among relatively few people. By contrast, more complex interdependent societies, which rely more heavily on the smooth functioning of accepted guidelines to control depersonalized social intercourse, have the least stable basis for constructing such controls. In a passage written in 1887 that found echoes in Green's *Lectures on the Principles of Political Obligation* and in Fouillée's *La Démocratie politique et sociale en France* (1910; cited hereafter as *Political and Social Democracy in France*), Dilthey listed the characteristics of the new age emerging in the late nineteenth century and expressed these theorists' guarded hopes and fears:

> A science which transforms life; an industry which is world wide in scope; machines, work as the sole basis of the social order; war against the parasites of society, for whose leisure others have paid the cost; a new and proud feeling for the human mastery which has subjugated nature and promises to diminish the blind working of passion in society: these are the basic traits of a world era whose dark and awesome outlines arise before us.[19]

Technology was transforming social structure and cultural values, but the shape of the society and culture that would replace them remained shrouded in doubt.

Because these thinkers' political ideas reflected the dramatic social and economic changes of the late nineteenth century, those changes require some amplification. While socioeconomic conditions by themselves can scarcely explain complex intellectual responses, as the range of contradictory intellectual currents in the late nineteenth century illustrates, the philosophers of the *via media* were attuned to the importance of social change. Because understanding their writings about politics and society requires at least some familiarity with the structural changes that occurred between 1870 and 1920, a brief excursion into economic development is necessary.

After 1870 industrialization and urbanization entered a new phase, which economic historians have designated the second industrial revolution to distinguish it from the coming of industry to Britain over a century earlier. This second wave struck more rapidly and spread more broadly than its predecessor. By 1920 the United States, Germany, and France had joined Britain as substantially industrialized nations, but the pattern of change varied, and the differences shed light on important dissimilarities at the level of ideas. During these years the economies of all four nations evolved in different ways from the comparative chaos of entrepreneurial capitalism to the more advanced stage of organized capitalism.[20] With varying degrees of tacit or explicit government cooperation—with the United States and Germany representing the respective extremes and Britain and France at the intermediate positions along the spectrum—industrial and financial enterprises combined to dominate organized economies and to shape consumption and production patterns. Greater urbanization accompanied this process of economic maturation as both population and economic power became more centralized. In short, American and European societies became increasingly interdependent, by which I mean that complex urban-industrial societies involved individuals in unprecedently complex patterns of relations extending beyond personal and community ties to distant bonds no less real because of their obscurity.[21]

The second phase of the industrial revolution was generated by commercial and transportation improvements that brought down the cost of food, freed income for increased consumption of industrial goods, and increased sales to city dwellers hungry for new consumer goods. Although innovative mechanical processes in textiles, chemicals, iron, steel, and countless other industries revolutionized the world economy, these new technologies did not pay immediate dividends. The period from 1873 to 1895 has been called the "great depression" because industrial expansion was slowed by an unprecedented, steady fall of prices and a consequent shrinking of profits. In the closing years of the nineteenth century, this hiatus ended, giving way to a season of extended prosperity when the harvest of industrial growth began to be reaped. This economic renascence came at the cost of replacing small industrial enterprises with a new breed of mammoth corporations both horizontally and vertically integrated, which flexed their considerable muscle in both the economic and political arenas. These juggernauts signaled the arrival of a new phase of capitalist development.[22]

Although the breadth and pace of its progress varied, a trend toward the concentration of industry is discernible in the United States, Germany, France, and Britain during these years. Britain, which entered the industrial era a century earlier than the other three nations, showed signs of exhaustion, as both scientific and technical innovation slowed dramatically. Several generations of cautious businessmen had profited from the accumulated knowledge and capital of early industrialization, and the rapid progress of the late nineteenth century left a suddenly antiquated British economy mired in increasingly obsolete technologies. France also lost ground even while moving ahead. Although France developed gradually toward a more indus-trial economy, in 1914 over forty percent of the population was engaged in agriculture, as opposed to less than eight percent in England and Wales. Moreover, much of French manufacturing remained semiartisanal; of the workers in the clothing and textile industries, which employed forty percent of those involved in manufacturing in 1914, more than half worked at home. Compared to the United States, Germany, and Britian, France never experi-enced an industrial revolution; the shift from farming to manufacturing occurred only very gradually. The persistent values of Catholicism and feudalism in a society in which prestige ranked above profits combined to limit the appeal of capitalism, and the relatively static quality of French society also inhibited the concentration of industry, so that small firms survived in economic sectors from which they were disappearing in other industrialized nations.

Germany industrialized late but quickly, free from the encumbrances hindering Britain and surging with a dynamism lacking in France. Following national unification, the government actively promoted large-scale indus-trialization. In the heavy industries of iron, steel, and coal, and even more strikingly in the new chemical and electrical industries, Germany coupled scientific and technological breakthroughs with innovative production tech-niques to pass both France and Britain as an industrial power. Both the nature of Germany's industrial enterprises, most of which were capital inten-sive, and the involvement of the government, which preferred dealing with a few large firms, contributed to the organization of the German economy within a highly centralized and rigidly hierarchical structure that reflected the prominence of the landed aristocracy and the absence of an entrepreneurial bourgeoisie. The United States also industrialized rapidly, as seemingly limit-less resources, combined with technological innovations, compensated for the comparative scarcity of labor and propelled America to preeminence among the world's industrialized nations. By 1919, three-fourths of the wage earners in manufacturing in the northeastern United States worked in factories with more than one hundred employees, and thirty percent worked in giant plants employing over one thousand workers. By contrast, one-third of the French workers in manufacturing in 1914 worked in shops with less than ten employees, and more than half still worked in factories employing fewer than one hundred workers.[23] The American experience, like the German, seemed to indicate that industrial power and industrial concentra-tion went hand in hand.

The rapid growth of trusts and cartels, whether through formal mergers or informal pools, represented merely the logical conclusion of the second industrial revolution. As technology evolved, the scale of manufacturing grew. Increased size necessitated increased commitments of capital, bankers naturally demanded more security, and industrialists consequently turned toward combination and cooperation to minimize risks by consolidating control over markets and stabilizing production. American corporate mergers and pools provided the template for European cartels, syndicates, and *comptoirs*. During the 1880s and 1890s, trusts emerged as the dominant forces in the sugar, beef, oil, and financial sectors of the American economy, and the process culminated symbolically in the creation of the U.S. Steel Corporation, which combined iron and steel companies controlling sixty percent of the entire industry's production. Such giant enterprises loomed even larger in Germany, where they planned price agreements, organized supplies of raw materials and divided their markets with government approval and even assistance. In France and Britain, industrial combination was both less popular and less necessary. The independence of industrialists made cartels unattractive; their reliance on less restrictive gentlemen's agreements made them unnecessary.[24]

The effect of these developments on real income has been obscured by the unreliability of the available data, but recent studies suggest that wages did reflect the turn-of-the-century economic boom. In Britain and France, real wages appear to have risen from 1850 to 1900, and then to have tapered off to a slower rate of growth until World War I. In the United States and Germany, real income rose steadily throughout the late nineteenth century and into the second decade of the twentieth. Although estimates of income distribution are even more speculative, in all cases the working-class share of national income seems not to have increased substantially, and it may even have declined in the course of industrial expansion.[25] Not surprisingly, contemporaries only imperfectly understood that the general increase in prosperity among the populations of industrialized nations occurred simultaneously with the continuing immiseration of industrial workers compared to other economic groups. Although the working classes improved their status in absolute terms, their position deteriorated relative to those in the middle and upper economic strata. Observers had difficulty distinguishing real from relative deprivation, which helps to account for the diversity of political responses in the late nineteenth century.

Contemporaries did recognize, however, that whatever the quantitative significance of industrialization in economic terms, it was part of a larger qualitative change in the scale of life that inevitably involved increased interdependence. Frederick Taylor's dream of transforming workers into finely meshing cogs in a series of industrial gear wheels was a nightmare to those who did not share his vision of scientific management. Although industrial productivity might translate into greater wealth, it seemed to dictate a set of standards antithetical to cherished values of voluntarism and independence. Much of the brilliance, and much of the poignancy, of modern social theory derives from efforts to reconcile older humanist ideals with what appeared to be modern industrial imperatives.

Beyond altering the social structure by increasing interdependence, the waves of economic and social change that swept across the United States and Europe in the late nineteenth century also left a more subtle psychological residue. The industrialized and urbanized mode of life involved the replacement of magic and mystery by precisely calculable and strictly functional procedures, a less obvious but equally pervasive fact of modern life. James's lament concerning the "irremediable flatness" squeezing from life its "rare old flavors" was to be elaborated in Max Weber's concept of rationalization, his word for the process whereby the increasingly technical orientation of an interdependent and functionally ordered society came to characterize a "disenchanted" world. Intellectuals committed to voluntary action properly understood rationalization as a threat to autonomy, and for them no less than for those who viewed it somewhat more optimistically, economic and social interdependence stood out as the dominant feature of the modern landscape.

Although they viewed these developments with a mixture of uneasiness and dismay, the philosophers of the *via media* considered it part of their responsibility to confront the reality of their world instead of projecting their personal preferences onto it. As Sidgwick wrote, when examining contemporary society the theorist cannot possibly begin "*de novo* either for man as he is (abstracting his morality), or for man as he ought to be and will be. He must start, broadly speaking, with the existing social order, and the existing morality as part of that order." This historical sensibility precluded elevating abstract social or political ideals with no foundation in social and political experience. It further ruled out cataclysmic change as a method of attaining goals, and at the opposite end of the spectrum denied that history conforms to an unalterable pattern. The only tendency exhibited by history, as these thinkers understood it, is the tendency to build upon itself as a long-term project of pragmatic truth testing by trial and error. In Sidgwick's words, theorists trying to settle the question of "divergence" from the social code "must consider chiefly the immediate consequences of such divergence."[26]

Given those limits, revolution appears to be a utopian fantasy that turns into a practical disaster, and only moderate reform stands any chance of success. When Sidgwick's generation thought of revolution, they did not think of the democratic revolutions of the eighteenth century but of the catastrophic failures of 1848 and the commune of 1871. Revolution meant something different to them than it meant to their grandparents or their grandchildren. While they resisted the conclusion drawn by self-styled social Darwinians who preached a doctrine of inevitability in human affairs—whether inevitable struggle or inevitable progress—they subscribed to the idea that evolutionary change was more desirable than revolutionary cataclysm, which they considered horrible and ultimately futile.[27] "Revolutions do not change men," Dilthey wrote; moreover, "revolutions cannot create a new society." Regardless of the slogans invoked and the changes attempted, "the constellation of powers" in a society does not change overnight. It is apparent "to the historical sense that the historical ethos of a people" should not be "hurt and dissolved by the intervention of a radical theory." Because of their theory of history and their experience with revolutions that failed, the philosophers of the *via media* refused to allow any dissociation of means from ends. They denied that history could disclose any irresistible trend toward a particular social system capable of justifying revolutionary enthusiasm.

None of these philosophers accepted a theory of class struggle, but they offered different reasons for rejecting it. Green's conception of society as an organism in which various parts played contributing roles excluded Marx's analysis from the outset, as did Fouillée's doctrine of solidarity. Sidgwick and Dilthey focused on the inadequacy of Marx's labor theory of value (which they appear to have misunderstood as a labor theory of prices). Sidgwick cited the work of William Jevons and Alfred Marshall, while Dilthey relied on that of Gustav Schmoller and Adolf Wagner, but they reached the same conclusion: Marx's economic theory was insufficiently historical because it did not recognize the shifting social determinants of value. Although marginal utility theory and the historical economics of the *Verein für Sozialpolitik* were hardly identical, they provided Sidgwick and Dilthey with roughly similar reasons for rejecting Marxist economics: it was not derived, they argued, from empirical study, but rather was deduced from Marx's dialectical philosophy of history.[28]

Neither did they accept the invisible hand of the classical liberals' political economy, which they considered an equally unwarranted attempt to elevate a set of abstract propositions beyond experience and enshrine them as eternal truths. The nineteenth century was running away from the false utopia of laissez-faire, Sidgwick believed, and liberals who tried to halt its progress labored in vain.[29] Dilthey summarized the implications of the historical sensibility for social theory in his analysis of the late nineteenth-century *Weltanschauung*. The most basic feature of the age, he maintained, "is its realism and the worldliness of its interests." Linked with this realism was acceptance of methods taken from the physical sciences, which alerted man to his mastery over nature and encouraged him to try to control his fate. As a result of its scientific orientation and an increasing sophistication about economics and politics, the nineteenth century lost its faith "in the immutable order of society." Dilthey argued that industry and commerce, which initially accounted for the emergence of the bourgeoisie, had begun to carry forward inexorably the demands of the working class. As the individualism that had been developing since the Reformation was coupled with the use of the scientific method, "the subject who made these changes changed himself." Enlightened rulers' limited gestures at reform were increasingly "replaced by the sovereign will of the people to give themselves their economic, political, and social order." Liberated from idealist delusions and awakened to history, freed from magic and enlightened by science, and fired by a commitment to individual liberty and political, economic, and social democracy, the German people had at last set the stage for "free action ruled by thought."[30] History revealed the general direction of social change, but it did not disclose an internal dynamic or a transhistorical agent or process whose imperatives individuals must obey. History cannot prescribe standards of universal applicability for the sociopolitical order; these must emerge from, and be chosen by, society itself.

That analysis of history and society was shaped by these philosophers' ethical theory. Just as ethics takes its form from experience and develops historically, so political theory can only trace the outline of the future from the shape of the present. More circumspect even than Minerva's owl, the philosophers of the *via media* carefully delimited the scope of political thought. They found no grounds either for Hegel's celebration of the existing state as the culmination of a divinely inspired dialectic or for Marx's inverted Hegelianism. They refused to collapse the ideal into the real in their ethics, and a certain dissatisfaction, a certain pointing beyond the present, was therefore implicit in their ideas. They did not adequately define the political consequences of this attitude, in part because they concentrated more on questions of knowledge and responsibility than on reform, and in part because, for James, Dilthey, and Sidgwick at least, the tension between "is" and "ought" was an inescapable part of the human condition. They understood rational benevolence to be a limiting concept; they never expected the individual, to say nothing of society as a whole, to overcome completely the conflict between personal desire and social justice. Sidgwick contended that the conflict between defenders of the status quo, who argued that "expectations arising naturally out of the existing social order" should not be disregarded, and radicals seeking to bring about "a distribution of the means of happiness more in accordance with ideal justice," is a conflict "permanently latent in the very core of Common Sense." Yet Sidgwick did not adopt the resigned attitude toward injustice that such a conclusion seems to imply. He counseled the use of "this notion of Justice as a guide to different kinds of utilities; and in so far as these are incompatible," we should "balance one set of advantages against the other, and decide according to the preponderance."[31] Whether that formula suggests a substantive doctrine of justice or a tie-breaking procedure seldom to be invoked depends upon how one reads Sidgwick's blending of deontological and utilitarian considerations. It indicates clearly, though, that Sidgwick considered conflicts between competing values inevitable both in politics and in ethics. His outlook did not end in quietism or hopelessness, it merely disclosed the boundaries of reason and the tragic quality of life.

The Aristotelian ethics of Fouillée and Green, besides pointing toward a generally more optimistic conclusion, also pointed more directly toward political reform. In the *Ethics of idées-forces*, Fouillée contended that his conception of individual ethical development synthesized ideas from socialism and individualism. While only a genuine community of cooperative individuals could provide a sphere for ethical behavior, such ethical behavior always resulted from the voluntary action of individuals. While socialism overlooked the latter element, Fouillée charged, individualism, whether Kantian or utilitarian, deemphasized the role of community. His ethics, and his theory of solidarity, fused the two approaches.[32] Green, as indicated previously, likewise excluded the possibility of any conflict between self and community in genuine ethical behavior. "All virtues," he declared, "are social; or more properly, the distinction between social and self-regarding virtues is a false one." The individual's capacity "of conceiving a good as the same for himself and others, and of being determined to action by that conception, is the foundation of rights. No right is justifiable or should be a right except on the ground that directly or indirectly it serves this purpose." Beyond its clear parallels with Fouillée's doctrine of *idées-forces*, this analysis suggests the political significance of Green's ethics. For Green maintained, conversely, that "every power should be a right, i.e. society should secure to the individual every power, that is necessary for realising this capacity" to act ethically. He considered rights to be innate or natural in the same sense in which according to Aristotle the state is natural, "not in the sense that they actually exist when a man is born and that they have actually existed as long as the human race, but that they arise out of, and are necessary for the fulfillment of, a moral capacity without which a man would not be a man."[33] From Green's perspective, the state should assume the responsibility of securing for individuals the necessary rights and conditions enabling them to develop their moral capacity. In the context of industrial, interdependent economies and societies, the gospel of laissez-faire could no longer satisfy Green's conditions. He thus advocated political reform not only, or even primarily, for economic or social purposes, but in order to facilitate moral development.

The philosophers of the *via media* adopted a moderate reformist stance in politics because they considered it consistent with the uncertain, experimental, pragmatic, and historically sensitive spirit of their epistemology and ethics. In an important essay, "The Economic Lessons of Socialism" (1895), Sidgwick sketched out the principal features of their position. Liberal political economy had learned much from socialist economic theory, Sidgwick wrote, and the two schools were no longer as far apart as they once were. Adam Smith and his disciples had promulgated a gospel with two parts, one concerning the production, exchange, and division of wealth independent of government interference, and the other purporting to demonstrate that this process naturally led to the most desirable consequences. As a result of its collisions with socialist ideas, liberal theory had been forced to concede that the two principal tenets of its creed had no necessary logical connection with each other. The description of economic processes must be distinguished from the justification of their effects. This gradual development culminated in the writings of John Stuart Mill. In the later editions of Mill's *Principles of Political Economy*, Sidgwick pointed out, Mill was "completely Socialistic in his ideal of ultimate social improvement." Sidgwick then quoted a passage from Mill's *Autobiography*: "I look forward to a time," Mill wrote, "when the produce of labour, depending, in so great a degree as it now does, on the accident of birth, will be made by concert on an acknowledged principle of justice."[34] As Sidgwick correctly perceived, the apostasy of James Mill's son, and Bentham's prize pupil, held enormous significance for the future of liberal theory. When the author of *On Liberty* endorsed in principle the ideal of socialism, he signaled as no other individual could have done the convergence of the values of individualism and community. The philosophers of the *via media* carried forward Mill's attempt to combine liberal and socialist ideas to create a new and more fruitful approach to political problems. While their own political writings did not bring these ideas to maturity, they planted the seeds from which the theories of social democratic and progressive theory would develop.

2. Political Reform and the Role of Intellectuals

During the course of his extraordinarily prolific career, Alfred Fouillée wrote eleven books related to social and political reform, most of which built upon essays he contributed to French popular and philosophical journals. Impressed by Fouillée's political insight and sympathetic with his radical republicanism, the managing editor of the *Revue des deux mondes*, Ferdinand Brunetière, asked Fouillée in 1902 why he had never played a more active role in politics. His legendary eloquence and his personal magnetism might have carried him far; the Third Republic certainly enjoyed no surplus of talented politicians. Fouillée's response expresses the ideal of the intellectual as critic characteristic of the philosophers of the *via media*. He consistently refused "any intervention in current politics," Fouillée explained, because he believed he could "be of service to liberty more surely by defending it in purely philosophical books. Excuse me, my dear friend," he concluded, "if I keep myself completely for my work and if I continue to hold myself to the influence—restrained, no doubt, but clearly defined—that it can exert in its modest sphere." Fouillée considered the intellectual's role distinct from the activist's. While he expressed his political views frequently and forthrightly in his essays and his books, he believed as a matter of conviction rather than convenience that his responsibilities required him to maintain his independence from "*toute politique militante.*"[35]

Dilthey likewise wrote extensively about social problems without personally entering the world of political action. The intellectual's task, he wrote in 1878, is "to educate and lead" the *Zeitgeist* "with the insights of a deeper seeing science." Fulfilling that duty required maintaining the independence that makes such "deeper seeing" possible, a perspective unavoidably lost by those engaged directly in political wrangling.[36] Similar convictions about the philosopher's proper work lay beneath the refusals of Green and Sidgwick to accept offers to stand for Parliament. Both believed that their most significant contributions to society were their books; commitments distracting them from that work, however important they might be, represented threats more than opportunities.

Although sensitive to criticism of his detachment, James cherished a similar ideal. In an address delivered in 1902 at Harvard, he argued that "the mission of the educated intellect in society" is to remain critical of all popular passions, even though he realized that "this judicial and neutral attitude . . . is generally unpopular and distasteful." He was perhaps the first American to adopt with pride the epithet hurled at the defenders of Dreyfus—"*intellectuel!*"—taking as a badge of honor what was intended as a reproach. "The intellectual critic as such knows of so many interests, that to the ardent partisan he seems to have none," James admitted. Yet he persisted in his belief that resisting involvement in political struggles is required in order to maintain the intellectual independence that "keeps things in their proper places in the scale of values." Beyond the importance of detachment for the sake of perspective, James further insisted that thinkers ultimately prove more influential by concentrating on ideas than by participating in political activity. As he wrote to the Polish patriot and philosopher Wincenty Lutoslawski, "to help a revolution to *success* one has to be of coarser clay—to have the head of a buffalo, as Cavour said of Garibaldi." Philosophers, James counseled his friend, should devote themselves to "theoretic writing." "You ought to save your gifts for life long use as a professor," he advised Lutoslawski in a letter reminiscent of Fouillée's explanation to Brunetière, "and let your influence constantly but not extravagantly distil from your lectures throughout long years."[37] Certainly James himself, along with the other philosophers of the *via media*, adopted that strategy. Over the course of several decades their ideas exerted a considerable, and in some cases decisive, influence on the generation of reformers who followed them. Although they produced essays and books rather than legislation, the shape of the political universe in the twentieth century reflected in part the impact of their ideas.

Another aspect of their detachment from politics, which is also apparent in the moderate, reformist political atmosphere they helped to inspire, was their characteristic uncertainty about knowledge and values, the verso of their steadfast resistance to dogmatism. Their sensitivity to historical variation made them politically broad-minded, perhaps to a fault. As Sidgwick explained in his *Elements of Politics*, "There is scarcely any widely spread political institution or practice—however universally condemned by current opinion—which has not been sincerely defended as conducive to human happiness on the whole." Or as James put it in *The Will to Believe*, "There is indeed nothing which someone has not thought absolutely true, whilst his neighbor deemed it absolutely false."[38] That perception of diversity is valuable as a barrier against fanaticism, but unless accompanied by some substantive values it can be incapacitating. Their doubt was as much a part of their legacy as their detachment, and its consequences ultimately proved less salutary.

In short, the philosophers of the *via media* were not reformers. While the importance of their bourgeois status in shaping their attitude toward politics should not be minimized, neither should their conception of their responsibility as intellectuals be ignored. From the perspective of later thinkers more committed to political struggles, their contributions of speeches, essays, and well-reasoned letters to the editors of popular newspapers and magazines seemed decidedly timid. They were part of a transitional generation, wedged between the preachers who came before them—and who were, in the cases of Green, Sidgwick, Dilthey, and, in a sense, James, their fathers—and the more politically active intellectuals who followed them. They protected their independence as a matter of principle, but they did not limit their writing to matters of limited technical concern, as did the academic philosophers who completed the professionalization of higher education. It is instructive that philosophy and social science diverged, both institutionally and intellectually, shortly after this generation died. Philosophers gravitated increasingly toward the study of language and logic and left the questions of value and society to social scientists, who in turn gradually shifted their focus from broader philosophical questions to the description of individual, social, and political behavior. The heart of political philosophy, the analysis of the connections between knowledge and responsibility and politics, was abandoned.[39]

The members of this generation also felt the weight of religion more heavily than did their successors. Their concern with the evaporation of religious faith prompted them to emphasize the necessity of individual moral uplift as the basis of social reform. Some twentieth-century analysts have interpreted that focus as a quaint vestige of earlier sensibilities, which invalidates their ideas by placing them on the other side of the great divide that separates modern secular thought from what preceded it.[40] While the decline of religion no doubt caused these thinkers more anxiety than it causes many intellectuals today, the challenge of finding an acceptable substitute for the religious ethos as a foundation for social values has not been satisfactorily met. These philosophers offered individual moral reform, to be effected largely by education but also through political action, as a means of bridging the gap between the religious ethos and the ethical humanism they hoped would emerge to replace it. The tendency to label their emphasis "tenderminded" might be resisted by reflecting on the adequacy of twentieth-century efforts to provide an alternative. Ironically, no one contributed more potent weapons to the destruction of traditional religious values than the thinkers responsible for the radical theory of knowledge, but their role in shattering those comforting yet no longer tenable certainties only heightened their uneasiness about the world they helped create.

Education represented to these philosophers the key to social change. Fouillée emphasized in a series of books that universal education is "the first condition" of all constructive political change in a democracy. Educational reforms are the "least utopian and most fruitful of all social reforms" leading to the goals of "Fraternity and Reparative Justice" toward which the Republic should aim. In a culture dominated by the reactionary forces of the church and the lingering authority of the aristocracy, agitation for specific reforms is futile without the creation of an educated populace freed from superstition and responsive to calls for change.[41] Green and Sidgwick criticized the elitist structure of British education for perpetuating class distinctions, and they advocated broadening the reach of the school system in order to foster responsible citizenship and end the pervasive "flunkeyism," to recall Green's word, that infested British culture. Green was the first Oxford tutor to serve as a Town Councillor in Oxford, and he worked diligently to establish the Oxford High School for Boys as an alternative for those who were unable to attend an elite secondary school. Green argued that the British educational system, like its German counterpart, should also accommodate students interested in pursuing technical training instead of the traditional classics curriculum. Education should extend to everyone in order to eliminate gradually "the demarcations of class, to give a freedom of self-elevation on the social scale other than that given by money"—to create, in effect, a more meritocratic society. The concern of Green and Sidgwick with the quality and scope of education also manifested itself in the activities of the ethical societies they belonged to and helped to shape, and their interests thus filtered into the wider stream of English reform activity in the late nineteenth century.[42]

In his lecture "The Social Value of the College Bred" delivered in 1907, James called for the educated members of American society to exercise their valuable "critical sense" in the interest of guiding the nation away from "stupid prejudice and passion." By spreading the steadying hand of education throughout society, rather than confining it to a privileged elite, intellectuals might alter the course of the nation's progress. In time, the "ceaseless whisper of the more permanent ideals, the steady tug of truth and justice," James concluded, "*must* warp the world in their direction."[43] Cultivating the independence of mind and the critical spirit they prized seemed to these thinkers the most important guarantee of political progress, and for that reason they placed the highest priority on creating a well-educated democratic citizenry. Yet by trying to foster an attitude toward politics rather than advocating specific policies, and by working primarily to engender a spirit of critical inquiry, they undercut the entire notion of glittering "permanent ideals" such as "truth and justice," to use James's words, or "Fraternity and Reparative Justice," to recall Fouillée's. Their radical epistemology dislodged all abstract ideas from suprahistorical platforms and made them subject to pragmatic truth testing. Moreover, the culture's ability to differentiate between pragmatic truth, socially verified, and merely popular ideas, may have presupposed the critically alert citizenry they hoped to create through education. This problem too was part of their legacy to the theorists of social democracy and progressivism.

Beyond their emphasis on education and their belief that intellectuals should maintain their independence, these philosophers did not become more directly involved in party politics for another reason as well: the peculiarly amorphous shape and flimsy substance of European and American politics during the 1870s and 1880s, when they formed the political attitudes they maintained for the rest of their lives. Their unwillingness to participate in politics, in other words, reflected in part the nonresponsiveness of their political systems to those who shared their reformist inclinations. The political developments of the 1860s and 1870s, including the triumph of the Union in the American Civil War, the suppression of the movement for Irish independence and the French Commune, and the creation of the German Reich, all contributed to more powerful and more centralized state authority. Urbanization and industrialization added momentum to these centripetal tendencies, more slowly but even more significantly altering the shape of late nineteenth-century life. In Great Britain, the United States, France, and Germany, these forces combined to create irresistible political, social, and economic tensions that eventually manifested themselves in the emergence during the 1890s of dramatically different political configurations, more appropriate to the organized capitalist economies and increasingly urban societies that were coming to maturity. The 1870s and 1880s were thus a period of rapid socioeconomic change and political disorientation, as political systems adapted in various ways to keep up with—or to keep from completely losing control over—the revolutionary reshaping of social reality. The enlarged scale of institutions and the increased complexity of human relations invited or even necessitated an expanded role for government. But in the transitional phase from the mid-nineteenth to the early twentieth century, politicians were as puzzled by these developments as anyone else, and political parties responded only slowly to their altered circumstances. The political homelessness of the philosophers of the *via media* was shared by other intellectuals of their generation, who were less attuned to questions of epistemology or ethics but were equally sensitive to the inadequacy of available political options. Their dislocation reflects not only their political uncertainties, important as they were, but also the peculiar shallowness of party politics in these years.

In Britain, the United States, and France, the gulf dividing political rhetoric from political reality was exceptionally wide during this period. Innovative techniques of campaigning introduced during the late nineteenth century mobilized voters around issues whose largely symbolic quality masked the more fundamental cleavages in the electorate and the genuine interests of politicians. While invocations of high principle surrounded debates on tariffs, civil service reform, and the interests of the working man, politicians concerned themselves more with the immediate challenge of getting and keeping power by dispensing patronage, peddling influence, or buying votes outright, than with substantive issues.[44] Although the ideals of liberalism espoused by politicians such as Gladstone, Cleveland, and Clemenceau might seem to have been compatible with the moderate reformism of these philosophical radicals, the liberal creed began to appear outdated by the late 1870s, and a decade later it was perceived by an increasingly large number of intellectuals as anachronistic.

The British electoral reforms of 1884 broadened the franchise and appeared to mark the triumph of liberalism. But ironically the wind left the Liberal party's sails only a year later, when reform-minded Liberal Unionists such as Joseph Chamberlain bolted from the party and gravitated toward Conservatism in the aftermath of Gladstone's embrace of Irish home rule. This infusion of constructive as opposed to laissez-faire liberal policies—and middle-class, Nonconformist, business oriented politicians—enabled the hybrid Conservative party to expand its constituency and dominate British politics for the remainder of Victoria's reign. Despite the ardor of political campaigning in an era in which appeals to community were gradually being supplanted by appeals to class interest, when in power both parties made haste very slowly. In the United States, Republicans and Democrats played out a similar shadow dance of high ideological drama with rather less substantive significance. The party system in the post-Civil War years featured elaborate and effective campaigns to get out the vote, highly charged rhetoric designed to spark party loyalty, largely symbolic issues bearing little relation to real social and economic problems, and faceless politicians more or less interchangeable with one another. As James Bryce put it in *The American Commonwealth*, "Neither party has any principles, any distinctive tenets. Both have traditions. Both claim to have tendencies." But in fact, Bryce concluded, "All has been lost, except office or the hope of it."[45] Liberal Democrats claimed to stand for incorrupt government, equality of opportunity, and an open, competitive economic system free of government interference—principles resembling those of Gladstone's Liberal party—but that kind of liberalism no longer offered solutions to the problems facing the nation by the time of Cleveland's presidencies.

In France, the liberal republicans who dominated the politics of the Third Republic from 1879 to 1899 earned, by virtue of their vacuous ideology, the apt label Opportunists. French liberals likewise substituted invocations of principle, in this case Republicanism against the threat of monarchism, for creative responses to real issues, waging a putative war to preserve the Republic from its enemies instead of presenting constructive policies to cope with socioeconomic changes. Republicans, in Clemenceau's words, aimed "to release man from the chains of ignorance" and to liberate him "from religious, political, and economic despotism." After thus setting him free, they would "set no limits but those of justice to his freedom of initiative."[46] This too, like the creeds of Gladstone and Cleveland, was wisdom from an earlier age, appropriate for an industrializing rather than an industrialized economy and an embattled rather than entrenched bourgeoisie. After these freedoms were secured in the early 1880s, such phrases rang hollow. Laissez-faire principles appealed to small entrepreneurs but had little to offer the increasingly large segment of society, including peasants as well as proletarians, in France as in Britain and the United States, for whom independence was no longer possible. For them, interdependence translated into powerlessness and poverty.

The fuzzy ideological divisions between parties in the 1870s and 1880s mirrored the confusion of policy-makers about the proper response to new social conditions; the focus on symbolic issues corresponded to fundamental cleavages in the electorate that had more to do with long-standing cultural differences than with particular questions of policy. In Great Britain, Liberal strength derived primarily from small towns rather than the countryside, from villages where settlement patterns had been open rather than closed, and generally from areas in which the Church and the aristocracy had exercised comparatively less control than in rural areas, where Nonconformism and Liberalism made fewer inroads. Conservatives also appealed to working-class distrust of government economic reforms, which workers judged intrusive and expensive, and to their hatred of immigrants and other foreigners, whom they perceived as threats to national interests. The Conservative party's resurgence in the late 1880s and the 1890s was closely linked to the backlash of working-class Protestants, who were bitterly opposed to the Irish as Catholics, aliens, and competitors for their jobs. A similar fault line divided native-born American workers affiliated with the Republican party from immigrants and members of "liturgical" or "ritualist" religions such as Catholicism. Without constructing a reified and one-dimensional "religious man" to replace such ahistorical worthies as "economic man" or "psychological man," it seems fair to say that religious and ethnocultural divisions played a large part in determining the outcomes of the closely contested elections of these years. In France, deeply entrenched cultural patterns of resistance or acceptance of monarchy, religion, authority in general, and change itself, patterns that tended to vary by region and by group, manifested themselves in political affiliations that proved remarkably durable. The issues dividing the right from the left in French politics had to do primarily with the church and the Republic, and liberals who were trying to hold the middle ground in an undeclared religious war appealed, with only limited success, to moderates from both camps.

If religious and ethnic divisions during these years help to account for the largely symbolic quality of politics, the importance of political scandals is another mark of the relative unimportance of substantive issues. Indeed, in the United States and France scandals were perhaps the most prominent feature of the political landscape. The pocket lining of government officials in the Credit Mobilier and Whiskey Ring scandals, the influence peddling and bribery of the Daniel Wilson and Panama affairs, all underscored the sordidness of public life. In time, recurrent scandals contributed to widespread dissatisfaction with the political process and led indirectly to the reorganization of political systems, along class lines in Europe and along functional interest group lines in the United States, a development with wide-ranging but very different implications in different nations. The distinct odor of corruption surrounding the political process, the artificiality of the elections, and the irrelevance of many of the issues suggest that the refusal of reform-minded intellectuals to enter the political arena was perhaps merely a sensible response to a nonsensical charade. Surveying the last three decades of the nineteenth century, Henry Adams remarked that he could find "little but damaged reputation" in American politics. "The period was poor in purpose and barren in results."[47]

Politics in Germany during these years, of course, followed a different path. The reasons behind and the consequences of the impotence of liberals in Germany illustrate the distinctive quality of German national development. They also illuminate the problematic relation between the centralization of authority, the existence of an independent bureaucracy, and the vitality of democratic government. Whereas politicians elsewhere engaged in elaborate and highly symbolic battles of dubious importance, in Germany issues of genuine cultural, political, and economic significance were resolved in the 1870s and 1880s. But decisions concerning religion, the role of parties, and the process of industrialization were not hammered out by representative institutions. Instead the Reich took shape according to designs carefully laid out by Bismarck and his allies among the industrial and agrarian elites.

The inverted whiggism that inevitably dominates German historiography emphasizes the impotence of democratic liberalism in an attempt to trace twentieth-century fascism to nineteenth-century sources, and German liberals' characteristic weakness for strong authority is nowhere more apparent than in the formative years of the Empire. The tension between liberals' desire to represent the people and their desire to secure a powerful state was resolved by exchanging the independent liberalism of the early 1870s for an illusion of power in subservience to Bismarck's will. First by supporting the repressive measures of the anti-Catholic *Kulturkampf*, then by acquiescing in Bismarck's antisocialist legislation in 1878, the National Liberal party aligned itself with the coalition of Junkers and large industrialists that dominated German society and provided the core of Bismarck's strength. Liberals' fears of reaction and revolution overshadowed their interest in democracy; as a result they found themselves outflanked on the right by the Centre party and on the left by the Social Democratic party. Bismarck's economic package of 1879, which coupled tariffs on grain with tariffs on iron, satisfied both large-scale agriculture and industry. It also cemented the National Liberals' alliance with the elements of German society, and the policies, that liberals had traditionally anathematized. That final demonstration of the National Liberals' ideological bankruptcy and their absorption into the ruling conservative coalition prompted the "secession" of left-leaning liberals and the formation of a progressive alliance independent of the National Liberals, but both liberal parties' electoral strength sagged throughout the 1880s.

The effective powerlessness of the Reichstag, together with Bismarck's "reforms" of the Prussian civil service that purged the bureaucracy of liberals and fastened it more tightly to his authoritarian and antidemocratic policies, further demoralized German liberals. Their decline was matched by the dramatic increase in the popularity of conservative and revolutionary parties. The centralization of power in Germany under Bismarck's strategy of *Sammlungspolitik* (coalition politics) was thus accompanied by the simultaneous and fateful corruption of the democratic process and the polarization of the voting public. Ironically, German liberals were initially attracted to Bismarck because he seemed to offer an effective barrier against the perceived threat to *Bildung*—the ideal of cultivation cherished by the German middle class—represented by the rise of the uneducated masses. By sapping the vitality of liberalism, however, their erstwhile protector guided the German bourgeoisie down a path leading to feverish consumption and the slavish imitation of aristocratic values, the antitheses of the *Kultur* they claimed to embrace. The authoritarianism of the Junkers and the Prussian officer class replaced the cultivation of the professor and the civil servant in the pantheon of liberal values. The latent antidemocratic quality of the concept of *Bildung* was exposed, and accentuated, by the openly elitist ideals of the aristocracy that liberals increasingly espoused. Thus despite its ostensibly democratic institutions, government in imperial Germany became a tool of elite domination.[48]

German liberals since the Enlightenment had looked to the bureaucracy as the best hope for accomplishing their purposes. As Bismarck transformed the civil service into an instrument of oppression, they became increasingly suspicious of its power. Among those few liberal intellectuals who expressed dissatisfaction with the National Liberals' support of Bismarck's policies, a group including, along with Dilthey, such figures as Rudolf Haym, Hermann Baumgarten, and Theodor Mommsen remained skeptical of the progressive potential of the national state; their reservations distinguished them from those who joined Heinrich von Treitschke in celebrating the authoritarian Reich as the embodiment and expression of the German people's greatness. Consistent with his radical distrust of all received truths, Dilthey wrote of himself and his handful of allies: "We comport ourselves skeptically toward all transcendental propositions—and without these a political dogma can be neither constructed nor criticized." Dilthey prized political independence and noninvolvement as emblems of intellectual integrity. His position exemplified the aloofness of German academic liberals from politics, the fatal gap, as Friedrich Meinecke wrote, "between the political and the intellectual life of Germany."[49]

By the end of the nineteenth century, the German bureaucracy constituted a threat to liberalism because no democratic traditions existed to check its excesses; in the United States, by contrast, genteel intellectuals believed that the excesses of democracy could be controlled only by developing a more independent and efficient bureaucracy. The enthusiasm of American liberals such as E. L. Godkin, Charles Eliot Norton, and George William Curtis for civil service reform sprang from their perception, shaped by the writings of such British thinkers as John Stuart Mill and Matthew Arnold, that the tawdriness and corruption of politics could be eliminated only by educating the electorate and improving the quality and integrity of government administrators.[50] These Victorians' uneasiness about the cultural impli-cations of democratic society was part of their legacy to the generation of Green, Sidgwick, and James, and a similar ambivalence manifested itself in these philosophers' attitudes toward politics. Their emphasis on civil service reform was a reasonable response to the sorry state of electoral politics in the 1870s and 1880s, although the unwillingness of either party to formulate programs of social reform may simply have reflected a popular desire for unchecked economic growth. James's decision to join the Mugwumps' protest against the Republicans' selection of James G. Blaine as their presi-dential candidate in 1884 reflected his dissatisfaction with the alternatives presented by both parties. He would vote for any Democrat, he explained, "in order to get the present fossil Republican party permanently killed, and to be able four years later to drive out the Democrats in the same way in the name of a new national party with something of an intellectual character in purposes, which will devote itself to civil service and economical reform, and perhaps ultimately to certain constitutional changes of which we are in pressing need."[51] While the final phrase remains enigmatic because of James's failure to elaborate his political ideas in any detail, that comment suggests his inclination toward nonpartisan, moderate reform, and his emphasis on improving the quality of government administration.

James seems to have moved leftward in the 1890s, but his willingness to support William Jennings Bryan in 1900 probably sprang more from James's anti-imperialism than from economic radicalism. He wrote from Italy in 1900 that "Bryan has in him many elements of a very great man, I believe, and I shall vote for him, whatever happens, if I am at home." The juxtaposition of those two final phrases suggests James's simultaneous sense of conviction—"whatever happens"—and ironic detachment—"if I am at home." Throughout his life he viewed public affairs, when he turned his attention to politics at all, from that unsteady perch between commitment and independence. Unfortunately, the traces of James's political preferences are too faint to provide more than a tentative outline of his ideas. Although he lamented Bryan's advocacy of free silver, for example, it is impossible to determine whether he thought Bryan's economics dangerous or silly, or whether he simply considered his political strategy unlikely to succeed.[52]

The blend of elitism and reformist sympathies apparent in James's scattered musings about politics shows up in the more systematic writings of his friend Sidgwick, whom James invited to Harvard in 1899 specifically to lecture on economics and politics instead of more narrowly defined philosophical questions. In his *Elements of Politics* Sidgwick emphasized the importance of instilling in legislators "a keen *concern* for the interests of the various elements of the community for which they legislate," an aim to be attained by more frequent elections and the use of the initiative and referendum. Undercutting the democratic sentiments of such recommendations, however, Sidgwick argued that members of Parliament ought not be paid. In that way "the class of persons who possess a moderate amount of wealth may have a practical influence on legislation out of proportion to their numbers," thereby securing the fusion of oligarchy and democracy that Aristotle recommended to minimize class conflict. Sidgwick claimed that his general view of politics derived from the writings of Bentham and J. S. Mill. Given his understanding of Mill's shifting attitude toward socialism, however, that ostensibly revealing admission slips back into the ambiguity of Mill's own problematic mixture of cultural elitism and economic democracy.[53]

These philosophers' focus on education, their reluctance to participate in a political process they considered ineffective, and their emphasis on the importance of government administration echoed themes expressed by an earlier generation of liberals. These arguments, as I have noted, were encapsulated in John Stuart Mill's concluding remarks in his *Autobiography*. Mill realized that institutional changes alone could never effectively alter individual values: "To render any such social transformation either possible or desirable, an equivalent change of character must take place both in the uncultivated herd who now compose the labouring masses, and in the immense majority of their employers." Although Mill did not despair of the capacity of individuals to act for the good of the community instead of pursuing their individual interests exclusively, he cautioned that "education, habit, and cultivation of the sentiments" would be necessary to accomplish that conversion. Mill professed his belief that "interest in the common good" is not incompatible with "the essential constitution of human nature," but he never succeeded in reconciling his apostasy from liberalism with his psychological hedonism, his atomistic empiricism, or his classical economics.[54]

The philosophers of the *via media* were better equipped intellectually to complete the revolution Mill had begun. Their revisions of liberal individualism ran parallel to, rather than away from, their radical theory of social experience and their understanding that the developing values of the community give emotional meaning to the lives of individuals. Mill's endorsement of moderate socialism signaled the end of an era in the history of liberal theory. Although his successors shared his misgivings about the adequacy of political and economic solutions to cultural and philosophical problems, they provided the philosophical basis for the shift from liberalism to social democracy and progressivism. Their political writings testified to their divided allegiance between older and newer versions of liberalism, and between more elitist and more egalitarian conceptions of society, but in the political ideals they sketched, a later generation of activists would find an outline for their own ideas.

3. Resurrecting the Common Good

In the eyes of those who tried to mediate between liberalism and socialism, one problem dominated late nineteenth-century political theory. It was an old problem, central to Aristotle's *Politics*. As a political animal, man joins with his fellows for two reasons: self-interest and common purpose. Unfortunately these often conflict, and the interest of the community may be neglected as individuals look after themselves. Partisans of laissez-faire liberalism and Marxism accepted such conflict as a natural and even necessary part of historical development with ultimately beneficial consequences. They dismissed efforts to solve Aristotle's problem as counterproductive interference with either the quiet dexterity of the invisible hand or the noisy self-destruction of capitalism. The philosophers of the *via media* helped to alter the discourse of politics by returning to the classical problem of reconciling individual interest with the common good. They argued that the new world of interdependence and their new ideas of individuality and responsibility rendered prevailing political concepts obsolete, and they explored new ways of thinking about the role of the state appropriate to a radically different social reality and radically different ideas about man. They challenged prevailing conceptions of personal rights, social equality, and the responsibility of government, taking language suited to the seventeenth- and eighteenth-century world of emerging bourgeois individualism and reformulating it for the world of organized capitalism. By resurrecting the classical ideal of integrating private and public interest and suggesting novel strategies to achieve it, this generation turned away from some of the central ideas of modern political thought, and in doing so they began the process of reorienting the discourse of politics that culminated in the theories of social democracy and progressivism. Because they challenged inherited ideas so decisively, it is misleading to characterize them simply as representatives of the various national traditions from which they sprang. But in order to understand the importance of their contributions to the shaping of twentieth-century thinking about political problems, it is necessary to sketch briefly certain features of the British, American, French, and German political traditions. This outline, brushed with the broadest of strokes, will illuminate these philosophers' intellectual background and reveal the contestational quality of their ideas. Although they could scarcely be said to have solved the problem of reconciling individual interest and the common good—indeed, they were not certain it could be solved by politics—they helped to reformulate it in the context of industrialization, democracy, and a newly active state, so that those who came after them could set to work on an old problem with a new set of intellectual tools.

Green and Sidgwick both challenged the body of ideas supporting liberal capitalism, ideas that had dominated British political culture since the seventeenth century. Thinkers drawing on Hobbes and Locke constructed and successfully promoted a theory of liberal individualism that linked freedom with acquisition, liberty with property, and politics with strict noninterference.[55] Eighteenth-century elaborations of political economy further reinforced Britain's liberal consensus, and the Benthamites formed these ideas into an amalgam of empiricism and utilitarianism, market economics, and liberal politics that dominated nineteenth-century British political culture. In politics and economics as in philosophy, the goal lay less in finding justice through active creation than in removing unnecessary obstructions. Liberals contended that the political ideal would emerge automatically through the unbridled pursuit of individual interest; British liberalism deemed any more transcendent conception of justice and social cohesiveness an illusory distraction from the achievement of the greatest number's greatest good.[56] From the decade of the 1830s, liberals preached the gospel of laissez-faire. Prior to the rise of industrial labor classes, the pursuit of individual self-interest within the market economy seemed to provide an adequate theory of political obligation; only when faith in the market broke down was the suzerainty of liberalism challenged. Even then, however, British political culture exhibited the moderation that had been its trademark since the liberal consensus was forged in the seventeenth-century revolutions. That reasonableness, within the context of a prevailing liberal tradition, helps to explain much of the substance as well as the style of British political thinking.

In one sense, Sidgwick and Green broke decisively with liberalism by denying that economic considerations should dominate discussions of politics. Since the seventeenth century, political liberty had been identified with noninterference in the acquisition of property, and this characteristic distinguished British liberalism from earlier political theory. In the writings of James Harrington one can already discern the equation that was to become standard by the nineteenth century: classical citizenship minus virtue plus money equals liberalism. By their transformation of empiricism and utilitarianism, Green and Sidgwick put an end to the collapse of social and political theory into economics. In the late nineteenth century, at least in part as a result of their efforts, possessive individualism and the market began to lose their grip on British thinking, and justice again appeared as a subject that could not be subordinated to economics. Simultaneously the ideal of autonomy, conceived in liberal theory as political independence and possession of property, had to be reformulated for an interdependent world in which limited government could no longer adequately safeguard it.

The liberal consensus that dominated British politics from the seventeenth century until the close of the nineteenth century also prevailed in American political culture. Although dissenting voices did proclaim more communitarian ideals derived from Protestant pietism, civic humanism, and Scottish moral philosophy, American experience and ideas harmonized to create a set of liberal institutions and a theory of liberal politics in which fears of conspiracy by centralized power against economic and political liberty could grow into revolution. While it is clear that the blend of Lockean and Scottish rational intuitionism fueling Jefferson's Declaration of Independence contained a distinctive ethical element not reducible to property holding, those who formulated the new nation's Constitution effectively guaranteed the continuation of the liberal consensus by appropriating radical democratic rhetoric to express moderate political principles quite different from those Jefferson embraced. Their strategy obscured real social antagonism and foreclosed the development of viable positions either left or right of the political center. By identifying the principles of possessive individualism with republicanism, the creators of the American Republic transformed the Jeffersonian impulse of ethical democracy and obviated genuine conservatism and genuine radicalism as political options, an achievement that insured dominance of the liberal consensus at the cost of impoverishing American political debate.[57]

As British liberal theory discounted justice, so American liberalism, which received its classic formulation in *The Federalist*, denied to politics any transcendent function. Although Madison aimed to secure an ethical republic by constructing a mechanism whereby the wicked and foolish would elect the virtuous and wise to represent them, his emphasis on balancing countervailing pressures obscured that larger ideal. Individual and group interests could be reconciled through a process of bargaining. Faction, which classical theorists anathematized as destructive of the common good, appeared in *The Federalist* Number Ten as a means of preventing tyranny in the great Republic by deflecting inevitable class antagonisms. American liberal theorists, ingeniously amalgamating the competing concepts of natural law and liberal individualism in Harrington, Locke, and the commonwealthmen, likewise inadvertently opened the door, by concentrating on the preservation of property, for the eventual definition of politics in terms of economic rather than ethical goals. Like Jefferson, Madison sought to harness man's baser instincts on behalf of nobler ideals, but as the nation developed, the acquisitive impulses they had tried to direct toward constructive republican ends overflowed the narrow channel of virtue.[58]

Although vestiges of civic humanism continued to surface in the rhetoric of Jacksonians chastising corruption, Whigs clamoring for order, and Republicans denouncing slavery, the ideal of the virtuous republic was sacrificed in exchange for the "main chance." No more than Locke does Madison deserve responsibility for the eventual replacement of ethics by economics in liberalism, but by the end of the Civil War that transformation was substantially complete: William Graham Sumner and Stephen J. Field were now the spokesmen for American liberalism. The ethical character of the Republic that Jefferson and Madison wanted to preserve was submerged. Only the distrust of state authority survived from the legacy of civic humanism. Power exercised by government continued to be interpreted as evidence of corruption; reform consisted of removing any chance of turning citizens into clients dependent on the state. The moral content had been drained from the republican rhetoric, but the form of argument, with its emphasis on autonomy and its identification of independence with property, remained unchanged. The largely symbolic quality of late nineteenth-century politics, as I have already noted, illustrates the nearly unanimous desire to clear the field for capitalist expansion. In the final decades of the nineteenth century, that consensus began to show signs of decay. Radical challenges from agrarian and labor dissidents registered the mounting dissatisfaction of some Americans with champions of an ideology that no longer appeared suitable for an industrial age.[59]

While James did not play a direct role in transforming American liberal theory, he acknowledged the legitimacy of radical attacks, and he interpreted the struggle being waged over the nation's political future as a sign of health. James had little patience with efforts to enforce a liberal consensus, because he believed that experiments in social policy should be judged by their appeal and their results—in other words, democratically. James denied the liberal contention that the pursuit of personal interest insures optimal social benefits. The public interest, like the ethical ideal, emerges from the concrete struggle among competing conceptions of the good. Norms cannot be imposed on a polity any more than they can be imposed on an individual; they must be chosen voluntarily and validated in action by the community. As I have noted, James described history as the ongoing effort "to find the more and more inclusive ideal."[60] In the late nineteenth century it was becoming increasingly clear that Americans' quest for such an ideal was carrying them beyond the limits of possessive individualism. Just as their British counterparts insisted that the market no longer automatically assured desirable, or even acceptable, social results, so American radicals accused liberals of overlooking the unpalatable consequences of their ideology in a world grown increasingly interdependent. As James wrote near the end of his life, "Stroke upon stroke, from pens of genius, the competitive regime so idolized" in the 1880s, at the peak of laissez-faire, "seems to be getting wounded to death.

What will follow will doubtless be something better." Without claiming for himself any personal role in this transformation, he averred that he had never before seen "so clearly the slow effect of [the] accumulation of the influence of successive individuals in changing prevalent ideas."[61] But James did more than simply bear witness to the reorientation of American thought. Through his radical empiricism and his pragmatism he helped to nurture the seeds of a new political sensibility, which reached fruition in the writings of John Dewey and other like-minded American radicals between 1890 and 1920, by insisting that knowledge begins in the uncertainty of immediate experience and that all ideas must remain subject to continuous testing in social practice.[62]

The characteristics that caused American political culture to resemble Britain's, viz. its liberal tradition and the late nineteenth-century challenges to liberal ideals, distinguished the United States and Britain from France. The American revolution consolidated a liberal tradition that matured both in thought and institutions throughout the colonial period. In France, however, as Edmund Burke understood, the Revolution marked a decisive break. In part because it seemed to manifest the ideas of democratic radicalism expressed in Rousseau's *Social Contract*, the French Revolution inaugurated a new era. Although the distinction between the two traditions has been muted by the tendency of both revolutionaries and reactionaries to lump them together, Anglo-American liberalism differed from continental democratic radicalism. Liberalism was a philosophy of prudence, born in anxiety and nurtured by dissatisfaction with the idea of human perfectibility. Its outlook derived from the stark vision of Hobbes; by contrast, democratic radicalism was a product of the Enlightenment's confident rationalism.[63]

Whereas Sidgwick, Green, and James charted their course according to the prevailing values of liberal consensus, Fouillée faced a political culture characterized by polarization. Throughout the nineteenth century, democratic radicalism, which fueled the Revolution and infused French republicanism with its egalitarian ideas, confronted a powerful opposition committed to the values of monarchy, religion, and social hierarchy. This dissensus distinguished French from American and British politics at one level, but an even more significant difference concerned the basic identification of morality with politics that French republicans like Fouillée inherited from Rousseau and Michelet. Liberty, equality, and fraternity served as more than slogans; they represented a social ideal whose prestige grew throughout the nineteenth century as the Revolution evolved into a cult. Anglo-American liberal theory tended to separate politics from ethics and to subsume the political realm into the economic, but Rousseau's heirs made morality contingent on politics.

Rousseau argued that man has the opportunity to develop his ethical potential only in civil society. From this premise he criticized existing political arrangements for inhibiting moral maturation. The difficult and paradoxical character of Rousseau's ideas derives largely from his attempt to reconcile this tension between man's natural but premoral sociality and his civilized but immoral individualism. Rousseau designed his problematic concept of the general will to bring private wills into conformity with an ideal of social responsibility, and that fusion of individual and community interest—which Rousseau himself occasionally deemed impossible—filtered into French republican ideology as the aim of the Revolution and the ultimate goal of politics. Moreover, as Rousseau had sought to establish his classical ideal of virtue and social solidarity by starting with a postclassical concept of will and then using the procedures of modern science to establish the nature of politics, so his heirs tended to idealize personality, to deify science, and to scorn religious orthodoxy. The legacy of Rousseau thus included a misty vision of social integration with ethical as well as political dimensions, and a paradoxical joint commitment to personal authenticity and scientific method.[64]

The division between republicans and monarchists, and Montesquieu's and Rousseau's ideas concerning the association of ethics and politics in society, lay behind Fouillée's political ideas. His American and British counterparts could use communitarian ideas derived from the Christian tradition to indict liberal capitalism, but in France the Catholic church was an arm of monarchism and reaction. Instead of finding allies among churchmen, French republicans confronted the clergy as enemies on practically every social, political, and economic issue. James and Green both associated Christianity with socialism, James because of his father's identification of the two, and Green because of the influence of Dr. Thomas Arnold. The American social gospel movement and the English ethical societies also emanated from established religious traditions of nonconformity and social criticism. In France, however, republicanism, to say nothing of the more radical posture represented by the doctrine of solidarity that Fouillée preached, entailed anticlericalism.[65]

Second, Fouillée could and did appeal to the tradition of the Revolution and the ideas of Rousseau in arguing that political action had an ethical dimension. While the liberalism of Clemenceau muted the critical thrust of republicanism by minimizing its egalitarianism, during the early years of the Third Republic the Opportunists' individualistic version of liberal democracy reflected the significance of property and the clamor for economic independence in France. By the 1890s, however, as French society became more interdependent and dissatisfaction with laissez-faire increased, Fouillée and other radical critics were able to invoke a lively tradition of ideas with roots in Rousseau's *Social Contract*. While Anglo-American radicals faced the difficult challenge of exploding a well-fortified liberal consensus in order to establish the legitimacy of their social ideal, Fouillée needed only to appeal to the heritage of the Revolution. Whereas Anglo-American liberalism seemed to culminate naturally in laissez-faire, in the French republican tradition, negative government, individualism, and the subordination of social and political questions to economics represented only a temporary aberration.[66]

The distance separating the two traditions mirrored the distance between Locke and Rousseau, and Green's sympathetic assessment of the general will suggests the desire of his generation to draw liberalism and democratic radicalism together. Green argued that although both the idea of natural rights and the idea of an original contract are fictions lacking historical foundation, they can be useful in political theory, and he considered Rousseau's approach to such problems particularly important. The concept of the general will he judged "the permanently valuable thing in Rousseau," and he dismissed attempts to find latent absolutist tendencies in the idea. "What Rousseau meant was that the general will, as defined by him and as exercised under the conditions which he prescribes, was the only sovereign *de jure*." Given the practical difficulties involved in translating the will of all into the general will, Rousseau "would have recognized in the ordinary states of his time a sovereign *de facto*." The best available approximation of the general will, Green understood, is simply the law. "It is more true . . . to say that law, as the system of rules by which rights are maintained, is the expression of a general will than that the general will is the sovereign." Although certain laws may be imposed that conflict with the general will, in a republic the general will eventually reasserts itself. For Green, as for Rousseau, citizenship involves integration of self with community as the price of virtue, a notion with ethical as well as political significance.

In a passage echoing his contention that in true ethical behavior there can be no conflict between the demands of prudence and justice, a sentiment Aristotle shared, Green declared, "A right against society, in distinction from a right to be treated as a member of society, is a contradiction in terms." Invoking the classical ideal of citizenship much as Rousseau tried to do, Green insisted that "the proper question for each citizen to ask himself in regard to any proposal before the assembly is not, Do I like or approve it? but, Is it according to the general will? which is only another way of asking, Is it according to the general interest?" The idea of a common good somehow distinct from the summing of individual interests challenged the prevailing doctrines of liberalism in the late nineteenth century. It was an understanding that linked Green less closely with Locke than with Aristotle and Rousseau— and with Fouillée, who wrote in *Political and Social Democracy in France* that "the true democratic problem . . . is to expose the general interest, which is by no means the simple sum of individual or group interest."[67] While Locke, like Madison, originally aimed to temper individualism with rational intuitions of natural law, defenders of liberal capitalism such as Spencer and Sumner discarded such fuzzy notions and defined justice as the result of the unrestricted pursuit of individual interest. Anglo-American dissidents challenging that doctrine joined French radicals like Fouillée in returning to Rousseau, and beyond him to Aristotle, for an ideal of citizenship comprising duties as well as rights, an ideal of the common good transcending the good of any individual. Unlike Rousseau, however, who doubted whether the civilized maturity of the citizen is compatible with the demands of virtue, Green and Fouillée believed that freedom could be made responsible through politics.

In Germany, the absence of any revolutionary heritage and the presence of a centralized state after 1871 compounded the problems of polarization and instability. These two features, an anemic liberal tradition and an autocratic state, set Germany apart from France, Britain, and the United States. As in epistemology and ethics, the search for the source of modern German political ideas leads to Kant. In his early writings, Kant showed little interest in the "mob," but after reading Rousseau, and especially after the French Revolution, he turned his attention to the rights of humanity and the quest for human freedom. In *The Critique of Pure Reason*, Kant had split the world of experience into the noumenal and the phenomenal, and he restricted freedom and morality to the former sphere. But throughout the 1790s he wrestled with that division, and in his final writings he sought to escape it by offering politics as the way to realize freedom and morality in actuality. He posited freedom, equality, and autonomy as political counterparts of the ethical principles appended to his categorical imperative, and politics became for him the junction of freedom with necessity, morality with nature, and noumena with phenomena.

Against the Anglo-Americans' separation of ethics from political economy, Kant insisted that "in *objective* or theoretical terms, there is no conflict whatsoever between morality and politics." Whenever a problem arises, "morality can cut through the knot which politics cannot untie." Kant's conclusion to this section of *Perpetual Peace: A Philosophical Sketch* (1795) indicates that interpretations of his thought as a straightforward justification of despotism and political acquiescence are mistaken: "The rights of man must be held sacred, however great a sacrifice the ruling power may have to make. There can be no half measures here; it is no use devising hybrid solutions such as a pragmatically conditioned right halfway between right and utility. For all politics must bend the knee before the right."[68] The problem, however, involved the status of authority in "*subjective*," or practical terms, in which conflicts between politics and morality are constant. While Kant looked forward to the day when the state would serve as a context for ethical action, as a guarantor of social conditions within which individuals would be treated as autonomous and equal citizens, as ends rather than means, he failed to settle the question of obedience to the state prior to the achievement of such a republic. Although ideally "right" was to be the rule of reason as embodied in law, in eighteenth-century Prussia the law expressed the will of the monarch. Kant thus called for monarchs to "rule autocratically, and . . . govern in the spirit of republicanism." But this resolution offered the people, although nominally sovereign, no effective check on the state, and it transferred responsibility for realizing individual liberty to an autocrat. Kant took this step because he feared disorder at least as much as tyranny. Indeed, his horror of anarchy assumed almost apocalyptic dimensions: "If public legal justice perishes it is no longer worthwhile for men to remain alive on earth."[69] By thus justifying autocracy as a means of securing autonomy, Kant unintentionally paved the way for the transformation of the *Rechtsstaat*. He had intended to solve the problem bequeathed to contract theory by Locke and Rousseau, the problem of reconciling the idea of natural law with the idea of the people as sovereign. By trying to accommodate his hopes for the law to his fears of its abandonment, however, Kant left open the possibility of identifying existing power with morality. From Kant's original treatment of the state as a hypothetical embodiment of ethical right, his successors developed the idea that the authoritarian state actually embodies both law and morality. That extension of the dual significance of the word *Recht* robbed Kant's political theory of its radical character and made it safely assimilable into the tradition of German thought from Luther to Pufendorf, a tradition defining freedom in terms of obedience.

The idea of the *Rechtsstaat* as it developed in the nineteenth century distinguished German political thinking from Anglo-American liberalism and French republicanism in a fundamental sense. The positive law of the German state was imbued with an ethical quality absent in English, American, and French political thought. The autocratic state thus became a moral agent charged with the realization of liberty, which was conceived not as freedom from restraint, as it was elsewhere, but instead as the "inner freedom" of ethical self-direction in compliance with duty as determined by the state. This concept colored German ideas about politics in tones that clashed with the revolutionary ideal of French republicanism. Whereas French republican theory located sovereignty in the people and harnessed the state to the popular will, in German thought the people were considered subordinate to the ethical and legal state. The idea of popular sovereignty never took root in Germany, perhaps because there was no successful bourgeois revolution. In 1848, the Frankfurt Assembly met amid the rumblings of mob violence, but instead of turning popular turbulence into a weapon to be used against the autocratic state, the Assembly called on the Prussian army to put down the mob. In France, the bourgeoisie relied on the lower classes to carry forward the Revolution, but the German bourgeoisie perceived the people as a threat, and as Luther had done three centuries before, they recoiled from mass action and joined forces with the aristocracy. The failure of the 1848 Revolution had a triple significance for German liberalism: it confirmed the suspicions of German intellectuals that their ideal of *Kultur* could not be reconciled with practical political action involving the uncultivated masses; it cemented the alliance between German liberals and the aristocracy in support of the autocratic state; and it marked the disappearance of the idea of popular sovereignty so crucial in Anglo-American liberalism and French republicanism.[70]

Hegel extended Kant's argument by connecting morality with legality in real rather than hypothetical politics, entrusting the Prussian bureaucracy, which he envisioned as the "universal class" and the instrument of the world spirit, with the defense of the public interest. The doctrine of the *Rechtsstaat*, latent in the connection between individual freedom and state authority in the philosophies of Kant and Hegel, received explicit formulation in the writings of Robert von Mohl. As an alternative to the arbitrary police state serving as an arm of autocracy, the idea of the state as the embodiment of law exerted a powerful magnetic force across a broad range of German political thinking.[71] Not only were conservatives attracted to its promise of stability and liberals drawn to it in the hope of protecting individual rights, revolutionaries repelled by the identification of the bourgeois state with ethical right gravitated toward another version of the doctrine. For even Marx, who found beneath the pretensions of ethical philosophy only the hot air of bourgeois self-justification, ultimately grounded his philosophy not on objective ontology, as he claimed, but on an ideal of self-determination and social cohesion with distinctively Kantian overtones. Just as Marx stood Hegel's philosophy on its head and yet remained a Hegelian, so Marx's politics merely inverted the doctrine of the ethical and legal state without challenging its essential identification of politics with an again implicit if no longer hypothetical moral ideal.[72] Although Marx enshrined the proletariat instead of the enlightened autocrat as the carrier of liberation, dialectical materialism identified "is" with "ought" as decisively as Hegel's philosophy of history equated the rational with the real. Marx pointed toward the dictatorship of the proletariat, while Hegel envisioned the Prussian state as the culmination of the progress of liberty, but in important respects their ideas were only opposite sides of the doctrine of the *Rechtsstaat*. Thus both socialists and liberals in Germany inherited legacies that magnified the role of the state well beyond its modest dimensions in Anglo-American liberalism and French republicanism. Since this concept dominated German political theory, politics tended to be identified with moral as well as legal right.

As part of his emphasis on the critical function of the human sciences, Dilthey dissented from the concept of the ethical state, which he believed embodied an overly transcendental notion of politics. Ironically, to the extent that theorists such as Green and Fouillée sought to redirect liberalism toward an ideal of the common good that fused politics with morality, their goal resembled the doctrine Dilthey rejected. While Dilthey endorsed much of Schleiermacher's romanticism, he disavowed the belief that "the state joins the individual to the universal good and the divine order." He maintained a critical attitude toward both the state, which German liberals celebrated as the embodiment of *Geist*, and toward the proletariat, which Marxists looked to for redemption through revolutionary praxis.[73] The German tradition, which most closely linked politics with morality, produced in Dilthey, and later in Max Weber, acute critics of the classical idea that politics is a search for the common good. Kant's refinement of Rousseau's general will emphasized the gap separating practical politics from the ultimate aim of the ideal republic, and that analytical distinction, coupled with the evidence of overwhelming state authority in the German empire, alerted Dilthey to the powerful undertow of autocracy in the *Rechtsstaat*.

These thinkers' political ideas represented a step beyond liberalism toward a more egalitarian and progressive version of the earlier ideal of civic humanism, an ideal centering on the autonomy and virtue of every citizen and the Aristotelian notion that all human goods must be pursued in association. Anglo-American liberalism departed from this ideal by defining independence in terms of property holding rather than virtue, and by transforming politics from a public search for the common good into an unrestricted battle among competing individuals.[74] Heirs of the civic humanist ideal in the eighteenth and nineteenth centuries tended to advocate limiting the state, whose increased authority they identified with corruption of the citizens' ability to govern themselves, and to define independence as the opportunity to accumulate property. As the consequences of that economic struggle became increasingly unpalatable, however, a number of thinkers, including the philosophers of the *via media* and their successors, sought to recover the broader goal of civic humanism while discarding their predecessors' program for its achievement. They argued that in order to achieve the ideal of autonomy in an interdependent world, the liberal equation of independence with property holding and the liberal aversion to active government would have to be altered. This meant redefining the right to property, the meaning of freedom, and the role of the state in light of a perspective on history that interpreted change as neither necessarily corrupt, as did self-styled defenders of republican virtue, nor necessarily progressive, as did whigs and Marxists in their very different ways.

Green, Fouillée, and James all gave particular twists to the traditional liberal defense of property. Green and Fouillée both preferred an elaborate, quasi-Hegelian justification that connected owning with being. Green argued, following Hegel closely, that the appropriation of property is "an expression of will; of the individual's effort to give reality to a conception of his own good; of his consciousness of a possible self-satisfaction as an object to be attained." He claimed that the power to appropriate material things is prerequisite to moral development. That power carries the individual beyond himself and affords him the opportunity to use property in a moral way, thus contributing to the progressive moral development of humanity.[75] Fouillée opposed the abolition of property proposed by "collectivists" because it denied the "justice of private property as an extension of manual labor and especially mental labor." He contended that the ideal of collectively administering all property while preserving the liberty of individuals was a dream resting on a contradiction. This idea, he wrote, separates persons from things artificially, "as if people could survive without disposing of things." In order for that to be true, he maintained, "there would need to be a society of pure spirits. In fact, the person is not free when his liberty does not end in the property of things."[76] In contrast to Marx's treatment of his ideal of unalienated labor, Fouillée's analysis of the connection of property to work and the necessity of expressing one's freedom in material things did not involve completely restructuring the productive and distributive processes in order to fulfill the individual's need to labor productively. James's brief discussion of property in *The Principles of Psychology* underscores this distinction. James asserted that an "instinctive impulse drives us to collect property; and the collections thus made become, with different degrees of intimacy, parts of our empirical selves. The parts of our wealth most intimately ours are those which are saturated with our labor."[77] James maintained that the desire for property is rooted in the desire to work productively; like Green and Fouillée, and unlike Marx, he also believed that the individual could forge that bond without the total abolition of liberal property rights.

Yet these philosophers' defense of property differed substantially from the standard liberal case resting on the idea of natural rights. According to Green, property rights become illegitimate when one person's possession of property "interferes with the possession of property by another; when one set of men are secured in the power of getting and keeping the means of realising their will, in such a way that others are practically denied that power. In that case, it may properly be admitted that 'property is theft.'" The right to property is not merely abstract; the individual must have the actual power to realize his will in practice. The unrestricted property right, Green claimed, can interfere with that exercise of will:

> The rationale of property, in short, requires that everyone who will conform to the positive condition of possessing it, *viz.* labor, and the negative condition, *viz.* respect for it as possessed by others, should, so far as social arrangements can make him so, be a possessor of property himself, and of such property as will at least enable him to develop a sense of responsibility, as distinct from mere property in the immediate necessaries of life.[78]

Green admitted that the free exercise of liberal property rights can preclude the appropriation of property by some individuals, and, unlike eighteenth- and earlier nineteenth-century liberal theorists, he considered the resulting arrangement to be unjust. As he wrote in *The Prolegomena to Ethics*, the conflicts between the desires of different men tend to be eased by social arrangements, such as the convention of buying and selling. "But the cases in which no such settled means of compromise is available, and in which therefore A cannot gratify his particular desire for pleasure without depriving B of a chance of gratifying his, occur constantly enough to show us what is the natural tendency of a desire for pleasure, if left to itself," viz. conflict.[79] As indicated in the discussion of ethics in Chapter Four, Green rejected utilitarianism for precisely the same reason. As part of its primary responsibility, "the removal of obstacles," the state must limit the exercise of individual property rights in order to secure for all individuals the effective right actually enjoyed by the more fortunate members of capitalist societies at the expense of the less fortunate. As a result of the right to unrestricted property accumulation, then, the effective right to accumulate property had become restricted, and the state must protect the disadvantaged from being trampled under institutionalized oppression masquerading as liberty. Rights are neither abstract nor absolute; they must always be considered relative to the dual criteria of the common good and actual power relations. If either of those measures indicates good reason for limiting individual rights, then the state is not only justified but obligated to intervene so that the larger object of enabling individuals to develop fully may be attained.

Green thus adapted as an instrument of political criticism a staple of conservative political theory from Plato to Hegel. But whereas earlier thinkers had invoked the idea of subordinating the individual will to the common good to uphold order and authority, Green put it to a different use. In a lecture he delivered in 1880, "Liberal Legislation and Freedom of Contract," Green drew the distinction, since popularized by Isaiah Berlin, between the Benthamites' notion of negative liberty and the positive liberty that he endorsed. Dissenting from the standard liberal definition of freedom as the absence of legal restraint, Green maintained that liberty is "a positive power or capacity of doing or enjoying something worth doing or enjoying." That conception of freedom, consistent with the theory of voluntary action connecting experience and will to activity, entailed an aggressive if nonprogrammatic attitude toward progressive social reform. According to Green's view, freedom is not merely formal. If a right is to be effective instead of abstract, individuals must actually be able to exercise it. As the question "can people actually accomplish x?" supplanted the earlier liberals' question "is x forbidden by law?" in the minds of social critics, attitudes toward both freedom and the role of the state changed. Conceived in relation to the pragmatic theory of truth, the principle of positive liberty did not involve particular political policies as much as it suggested using the state in a flexible way to secure effective rights for individuals in interdependent societies.[80]

Sidgwick shared Green's conception of effective rights, and he also advocated the extension of state authority to limit the accumulation of property. He reasoned, as did Green, that property holding had become sufficiently concentrated to restrict the freedom of others: "The institution of private property as actually existing goes beyond what the individualistic theory justifies. Its general aim is to appropriate the results of labour to the labourer, but in realizing that aim" it has put the propertied classes "in a position of diminishing the opportunities of the unpropertied in a manner which . . . renders a demand for compensation justifiable on the strictest individualistic grounds." Sidgwick's call for compensation thus rested on his individualism, or more specifically, on the coupling of the theory of voluntary action with the conviction that individuals must be able to act effectively. He broadened his conception of property rights to include what has been called "the right not to be excluded by others,"[81] and he drew an interesting distinction between the freedom to use and the freedom to own. "If freedom is understood strictly," Sidgwick contended, "I do not see that it implies more than his right to non-interference while actually using such things as can only be used by one person at once." He distinguished that right from "the right to prevent others from using at any future time anything that an individual has once seized," which he deemed "an interference with the free action of others beyond what is needed to secure the freedom, strictly speaking, of the appropriator." That limitation on the exercise of property rights, although as vague in its implications for policy as Green's argument, directly challenged the liberal conception of freedom. For that reason it represents something of a landmark in the transformation of British political thought.[82]

Fouillée also subscribed to the idea of restricting the right to appropriate property. In *L'Idée moderne du droit en Allemagne, en Angleterre et en*

France (1878; *The Modern Idea of Law in Germany, England, and France*), he declared, "Absolute and unlimited liberty conceived as *laissez-faire, laissez-passer, laissez-mourir*, which would lead to political and economic atomism, is only apparent freedom." Although ostensibly devoted to equal rights for all, such a system only consecrated "the monopoly of the strong over the weak."[83] When the French Revolution pronounced all men free, equal, and brothers, in effect it prepared the way for plutocracy. For with the abolition of aristocratic measures of superiority, wealth emerged as a substitute symbol of privilege, and subsequent efforts to regulate the power of property by collective bargaining stumbled under the weight of accumulated disadvantages. "Bargaining strength being unequal, the freedom to assert one's strength necessarily led to such immense de facto inequalities that liberty and equality remained Platonic ideas."[84] Fouillée's elaborate analysis of property in *La Propriété sociale et la démocratie* (1884; *Social Property and Democracy*) typified the radicalism and the vagueness of these thinkers' ideas. After examining both purely individualist and purely collectivist perspectives on property in his opening chapters and judging both inadequate, Fouillée argued that all property contains simultaneously, at least in theory, "an individual part and a social part," since without individual labor and consumption nothing could be produced or enjoyed, and without the contributions of our predecessors and our community none of the fruits of cultural and economic development would ever come to maturity. Only in contrast to extreme arguments concerning individualism and collectivism could such ideas have meaning, Fouillée conceded, yet given the fury of the battles between liberals and socialists, there was virtue in stating the obvious: both the unbending defense of personal property and the unrelenting attack on it went too far.[85]

In *The Methods of Ethics*, Sidgwick provided a clear statement of the question that troubled all of these theorists: "Can it be fair for any class of persons to gain competitively by the unfavourable economic situation of another class with which they deal?" Like Green, Fouillée, and James, he answered that question in the negative. "And if we admit that it would be unfair," he asked, then "where do we draw the line?"[86] The drawing of that line represented to these theorists the principal challenge of modern politics. They could all agree that the concept of individual property rights must be broadened, but how far the range ought to be extended, how radically conditions ought to be altered, and by what means, this generation failed to resolve. Fouillée aptly characterized their goal as "the progressive equalization of conditions," and he further contended that "democracy will certainly become more and more social and even socialist in the most general sense of the word." In his essay "What Makes a Life Significant?" James articulated a similar conviction that society must "pass toward some newer and better equilibrium, and the distribution of wealth has doubtless got to change." He restated that faith, which united the philosophers of the *via media*, in "The Moral Equivalent of War": "I devoutly believe," he wrote, "in the reign of peace and in the gradual advent of some sort of socialistic equilibrium."[87]

Yet none of these philosophers adequately translated these abstract principles, which involved a broader conception of liberty requiring progressive social and economic equalization, into specific political programs. As I have emphasized, they believed that the form of the emerging society should be determined by democratic means. They knew that such political whittling is agonizingly slow, and they denied in principle that the final shape of the polity could be outlined in advance. Taken together, their broader conception of property rights, their idea of positive freedom, and their commitment to the gradual equalization of social conditions did contain certain implications for policy, but the two options that presented themselves, although they appeared at first to be mutually reinforcing, were not necessarily consistent. The first was a modest redistribution of wealth, to be achieved principally through progressive taxation. The second involved the various regulatory, insurance, and income-support mechanisms that have come to be associated with the welfare state. The latent conflict between these two strategies, which this generation did not perceive, was to become a focal point in the writings of social democrats and progressives.

As a means of equalizing the burden of government and at least potentially redistributing wealth through a gradual process, progressive taxation exerted a strong appeal. As Sidgwick argued in *The Elements of Politics*, for example, its equity and efficacy could hardly be denied. Yet he repeatedly expressed the ambivalence that has become a standard feature of twentieth-century politics, and his doubt was emblematic of his generation's attitude toward the proper means of translating their principles into policy. Sidgwick feared that given prevailing values, excessive taxation to equalize wealth might impair production by reducing incentives, and thus the equality of incomes effected by such redistribution might become "an equality in poverty." This "danger of loss to the whole community," he reasoned, necessitated a gradualist approach to the problem of inequality. Successfully balancing the goals of equity and productivity seemed to him a delicate project, and for that reason he remained uncertain about such redistribution.[88] But even provisional support for progressive taxation marked a radical break from the liberal creed, a departure resting on the heretical claim that in industrial societies wealth is not a personal but a social product. The wave that eventually carried progressive taxation into law on the eve of World War I in England, France, and the United States was only beginning to gather momentum when the philosophers of the *via media* tentatively endorsed the principle of broader individual property rights. Yet their ideas about social experience and social responsibility helped provide the philosophical impetus for social democrats and progressives who eventually institutionalized the idea of redistribution through state intervention.

Use of the state to cope with problems stemming from industrialization and interdependence originated in Germany between 1883 and 1889, and gradually spread across Europe to the United States. Through a process too complicated to explain or even to trace here, such measures as industrial regulation, and insurance against sickness, old age, unemployment, and disability, gradually became part of modern government.[89] These measures did not necessarily contribute to the kind of solution anticipated by Green, Sidgwick, James, and Fouillée. For as Burke argued in theory and Bismarck proved in practice, the essence of conservatism is timely reform, and the welfare state has tended only to mask, and thereby to perpetuate, the institutionalized inequalities these radical philosophers recognized as the core of modern social conflict. Committed to democratic procedures and to a strategy of gradualism in political reform, they called for a new conception of rights and for progress toward greater political, social, and economic equality. The welfare state was in its infancy when they wrote, and they did not discuss it in any detail. But with the exception of Dilthey, who because of the threat he perceived in Bismarck's paternalism was wary of what he called "the tyranny of the state," they did advocate the expansion of government responsibility.[90]

Their recommendations concerning the best course of action, however, remained vague. That vagueness stemmed only in part from their uncertainty regarding the consequences of progressive taxation and the provision of social services by the welfare state. Their ambivalence also had deeper roots, extending into their conception of experience as social, historical, and value-laden, and their conviction that individual life involves the interweaving of sensation and reflection, thought and action. They were skeptical of efforts to remove from individuals the responsibility to make their own choices and to act; consequently, they resisted the larger claims of those who looked to the state for straightforward answers to social problems. In their politics as in their epistemology and ethics, they tried to mediate between extremes, and their recommendations manifested a similar degree of uncertainty.

Sidgwick's *Principles of Political Economy* and *Elements of Politics* typified their approach. In much the same way that he used the principles of utilitarianism and common sense intuitionism to supplement one another in *The Methods of Ethics*, so he invoked the principles of socialism for those cases in which "the individualistic basis" of liberalism tended "to be inadequate to produce the attainable maximum of social happiness." Because he believed that individuals can care for themselves better than governments can, he ruled out all comprehensive schemes of social reconstruction, and he endorsed the extension of state authority as a "supplementary and subordinate element in a system mainly individualistic." Sidgwick discussed three methods of coping with poverty: regulated private alms giving, which he associated with France; public relief, the typical English response; and compulsory insurance, which Germany adopted under Bismarck. In characteristic fashion, he recommended "a careful combination of the three methods" as "the practically best plan." As for choosing among them, he suggested only that the choice should depend on "the actual extent and effectiveness of voluntary association among the citizens," and on the amount of "philanthropic effort and sacrifice habitually devoted by private persons to the supply of social needs.

While such counsel may seem less than enlightening, Sidgwick considered anything more specific undesirable, because political answers cannot be determined to advance from any set of abstract guidelines. Policies must be rooted in experience and tested and refined in practice. Freely acknowledging his failure to provide "general principles on which the nature and extent" of collective action such as welfare legislation or nationalization might be determined, he defended caution as the best approach to political change. "It would hardly be possible to work out a system of detailed practical rules on the basis of these principles," he confessed. But he considered that feature of his politics a strength rather than a weakness, because it reflected recognition of "the extent to which the construction of such a system ought reasonably to be influenced by the particular social and political conditions of the country and time for which it is framed."[91]

That conclusion, methodological rather than substantive in its approach to the political process, was consistent with the enlarged empiricism and the historical sensibility Sidgwick shared with the other philosophers of the *via media*. They were committed to flexibility not because they lacked convictions about political issues but because they considered the willingness to adapt a virtue—an indication of intellectual honesty rather than an evasion of responsibility. They believed in experimentation in questions of social policy not because it was expedient but as a matter of principle, as the political corollary of their radical empiricism. Politics begins and ends in the uncertainty of experience, not in abstractions, and these thinkers unflinchingly faced the realization that reformers could no longer proceed effectively with elaborate agendas made up in advance. Unlike conservatives who shared their caution, they were committed to progressive change; unlike revolutionaries who shared their ideals of genuine freedom and greater equality, they were committed to a strategy of incremental reform.

There is a myth, for which A. V. Dicey is principally responsible, that Green preached a gospel of "collectivism" that distinguished him clearly from liberal "individualists"—even renegade individualists like Sidgwick.[92] Like most myths, this one has some basis in fact: Green did emphasize, as part of his focus on the reality of relations in human experience and the ontological priority of the infinite system of relations, the importance of the state as a collectivity of individuals. Yet Green's writings about politics do not reveal the unabashedly antiliberal attitude often attributed to him. He shared instead the uncertainty of Dilthey, James, and Sidgwick about the desirability of government interference in the economy, and his primary aim, like theirs, was to facilitate individual moral development. Thus, like James and Sidgwick, he supported temperance movements enthusiastically, and he considered poverty a problem of immorality as much as economics. Green did not proclaim an unambiguous collectivist creed. In his words, "the effectual action of the state, i.e. the community acting through law, for the promotion of habits of true citizenship, seems necessarily to be confined to the removal of obstacles." Admittedly, that counsel distinguished Green from his predecessors, because he declared that "there may and should be included [in the course of removing obstacles] much that most states have hitherto neglected." But he never clearly specified what steps the state should take beyond providing universal education. While Green pointed British liberals in the direction of collectivism—and it is difficult to overestimate the importance of that reorientation—his vision of the scope of the state's responsibilities never extended much beyond his portentous but vague call for the institution of those "restraints which the public interest requires."[93] Despite their different emphases, what is significant in the writings of Sidgwick and Green about politics—as in their epistemology and ethics—is the extent of their convergence. They can be classified as exponents of "individualism" and "collectivism" in order to emphasize their differences, but such categories obscure their pivotal roles in the convergence of both traditions toward a position midway between the laissez-faire liberalism of Bentham and the social organicism of Hegel.

Perhaps because Fouillée traced his lineage to the republican ideals of the French Revolution and to the philosophy of Rousseau, he had a vision of government responsibility broader than that associated with British liberalism, and he advocated the expansion of the government's social and economic role with more confidence than did the other philosophers of the *via media*. As an heir to revolution, he also refused to identify the real with the rational and to enshrine the status quo as the embodiment of a cosmic destiny. Yet Fouillée presented the mandate for government action in terms as imprecise as those of Sidgwick and Green: "State intervention is justified in matters in which private initiative and voluntary association prove fundamentally incapable of either guaranteeing the exercise of individual rights, or of implementing a practical corollary of both social justice and the public interest."[94] That declaration clearly assumed two ideals, effective freedom and classical citizenship, both involving more than the pursuit of private gains, but Fouillée also invoked the values of private initiative and voluntary association as the foundation of social activity. He pressed for government response only when those liberal shibboleths no longer sufficed.

Fouillée did nevertheless envision a more positive role for the state. Writing in 1884, immediately after Bismarck instituted his national program of sickness and accident insurance, Fouillée proposed for France an elaborate system encompassing old age pensions, child support in cases of the premature death of a parent, and insurance for sickness, accidents, and unemployment. He justified this comprehensive scheme on the basis of social solidarity: since we all depend on one another in our increasingly industrialized world, we should all look after one another. Sensitive to fears that such measures would turn citizens into vassals—which seems to have been Bismarck's intention—Fouillée denied that his proposal was state socialism with a French accent. Embodying the revolutionary principles of liberty, equality, and fraternity in an interdependent age, it did not promise social control but social justice. Fouillée did not hesitate to play on the passions of national rivalry, however, while trying to discount fears of paternalism. He concluded his argument with an appeal to his compatriots not to allow Germany once again to surpass them, as had already happened in the diverse spheres of education and warfare. Although France was slow to take up this challenge, Fouillée continued to call for expanding the role of government "in the provision of services which have become so general that they concern all citizens in the same way as the postal services." He envisioned the nationalization of "large companies"—a rather vague category—for the sake of the public interest, he recognized the need for what is now termed the democratization of the workplace, and he called on the government to regulate the hours and conditions of work and to improve the machinery of collective bargaining.[95] A mixed economy, Fouillée believed, would suit the facts of interdependence and solidarity prevailing in the late nineteenth century, but he refused to specify in advance the exact mixture of state, private, and co-operative enterprise that he considered desirable.

Socialists' attitudes toward Fouillée reflected the ambiguity of his writings. While revolutionaries understandably dismissed him as a bourgeois reformer, others pointed out that a candidate endorsing Fouillée's program of industrial democracy and national insurance "would be classified among the socialists, although not among the collectivists and communists." Fouillée's ideas about revolution validate that judgment. He reasoned that since the French people already controlled their state by law as a result of revolution, it remained only for them to assert their control in fact. Revolutionaries overlooked the potential for substantive change made possible by democratic government, and they further ignored the progress of labor unions in improving the working classes' living conditions. Laborers' real incomes had been rising steadily since the Revolution, Fouillée contended, and their further progress required only the continued organization of the working class along the lines of English and American trade unions. "One can conclude," Fouillée wrote optimistically in *Political and Social Democracy in France* (1910), the last book he wrote about politics, that a degree of social progress "is already accomplished and tends to accelerate in France: the diffusion of wealth among the people and greater equalization of property." He anticipated that continued improvement would emerge from that "fundamental condition of stability, morality, and well being."

Fouillée's analysis of reform and revolution remained constant throughout his long career. Thirty years earlier, in *Contemporary Social Science*, he drew the connection between history and political progress that marked the thinking of all the philosophers of the *via media*. "The true social science is at the same time 'radical' and prudent," he wrote. It is "radical because it is convinced that the future holds in reserve forms of social life superior to everything that the hardiest reformers can imagine, prudent because it knows that it must take into account the past and only modify the political organism by degrees." There is no better statement of the reasoning that led these mavericks to call for constant, progressive change while preferring "evolution over revolution" as the means to achieve it. Although revolutions are sometimes necessary, Fouillée argued, they are inevitably tragic; whenever possible, and certainly in a democratic state such as the Third Republic, reformers should work for gradual change. Because democracies achieve unanimity only rarely, reformers must recognize "the necessity of transitions," and their strategy must be a combination of radical goals and prudent steps, a blend of ethical ideals and historical sensitivity.[96]

Although his analysis of industrial democracy carried him further from liberalism than the other philosophers of the *via media*, Fouillée shared their conviction that the problem of poverty was moral as well as economic and political, and he denied that unionization or the extension of government regulations to the private sector could by themselves solve the problems stemming from industrialization and urbanization. Together these constituted an important but inadequate response to the challenge facing France in the late nineteenth century. Fouillée insisted that there was already sufficient wealth in France to eliminate most existing poverty; the problem lay in its misuse. The vices of alcoholism, gambling, and prostitution loomed as large in Fouillée's analysis of society as did economic problems. "Happiness is not simply a question of the stomach," he declared. "The brain and the heart play the principal role. That truth applies as well to capitalists as to workers." Personal reform must accompany economic and political reform or all of the reformer's efforts are futile. Expressing an attitude he shared with James, Dilthey, Sidgwick, and Green, Fouillée proclaimed that "the social question is also a moral question,"[97] and that statement referred not only to the ethical element of political reform but also to the ethics of individual behavior.

The same sentiment that inspired Green to warn against the numbing effect of "paternal Government" on the "self-imposition of duties" and "the play of disinterested motives" prompted Fouillée to hope that equality of rights before the law would not hinder the cultivation of unique gifts by exceptionally talented individuals. "True equality," he insisted, "is precisely the equal power for each individual not to be identical to every other; it is the equal right to inequalities of every sort, in all that is compatible with similar rights for others."[98] While Green and Fouillée stressed the individual's responsibility toward the community, and they anticipated an increasingly close identification of personal interest with the common good, they also recognized the danger of interpreting the public interest in a manner that would restrict the healthy expression of individuality. Although on the surface such fears may seem to express a longing for romantic individualism, they are equally suggestive of a radical democratic critique of the paternalism of the welfare state and the homogeneity of mass society, a critique premised on the dual principles of autonomous citizenship and moral responsibility.[99]

These thinkers realized that beyond the boundaries of justice lies the sphere of responsibility and benevolence. While they considered social, economic, and political reform important, such steps did not exhaust the challenges each individual faces in giving meaning to his life. James addressed this issue in his essay "What Makes a Life Significant?" which sheds light on this general attitude toward the limits of reform and suggests another reason for James's disengagement from politics. He began by painting a pleasant picture of his experience on a recent visit to that quintessentially American experiment in popular culture and self-education at Chautauqua in upstate New York. He described it as "a foretaste of what human society might be, were it all in the light, with no suffering and no dark corners," and he admitted to being "held spell-bound by the charm and ease of everything." Yet on leaving Chautauqua and "emerging into the dark and wicked world again," he felt curiously relieved to be back in the outside wilderness, "with all its sins and sufferings." In a revealing passage, he explained why the taste of utopia had gone sour. He confessed that the order at Chautauqua was "too tame," its culture "too second-rate," and its goodness "too uninspiring." He finally tired of the "atrocious harmlessness of things" there, and he longed to recover the "element of precipitousness" he found in ordinary life.

Those remarks reveal more than cultural elitism, although that is certainly apparent. They also manifest James's deep respect for the uniqueness and moral capacity of every individual. He scorned platitudinous romanticizing over the lives of the masses as well as blustery Victorian paeans to individual heroes. More than the stoic endurance of drudgery or grand displays of bravery, James valued the coupling of courage and perseverance with an "inner ideal" that could give meaning to each individual's struggle for life. This union of principle and action requires the exercise of "the active will, if we are to have *depth*, if we are to have anything cubical and solid in the way of character." Ethical principles must be fused with steadiness of purpose "for a life objectively and thoroughly significant to result." Only in voluntary action, in the combination of dedication and determination, does the individual make his life worth living. It is in this context that James's comments on late nineteenth-century class conflict must be understood. He maintained that the "unhealthy and regrettable part" of that struggle "consists solely in the fact that one-half of our fellow countrymen remain entirely blind to the internal significance of the other half." The conflict in itself was not altogether undesirable, because it contributed to changing the inequitable distribution of wealth. But James judged economic problems less significant, ultimately, than the ethical problem of persuading individuals to view each other as human beings—as *ends*, to adopt Kant's terminology, rather than *means*. Class position itself does not determine the value of life, and those entirely bound up in economic conflicts ignore "the fact that happiness and unhappiness and significance are a vital mystery."

James did not dismiss the importance of economic reform. He denied only that such measures, necessary and desirable as they might be, would dissolve the problem of deciding what our values are and how we are to live. In *The Varieties of Religious Experience* he applauded the "sound antipathy for lives based on mere having" that lay at the heart of much anticapitalist sentiment. He expressed his hope that the democratic spirit of egalitarianism would gradually erode "man's usual acquisitiveness" and enrich the spirit of "humanity" that declines "to enjoy anything that others do not share." Yet James cautioned that the eventual triumph of egalitarianism and socialism, both of which he anticipated, could no more fully guarantee "significance" to the lives of individuals than the presence of elitism and capitalism could fully prevent it. For "the solid meaning of life," James insisted, is "always the same thing,—the marriage, namely, of some unhabitual ideal, however special, with some fidelity, courage, and endurance—with some man or woman's pains. And, whatever or wherever life may be, there will always be the chance for that marriage to take place." James did not intend those remarks to undercut his endorsement of social change; there is nothing anywhere in his writings to warrant that conclusion. He intended only to suggest the limited effect of all political, social, and economic reforms, because the larger significance of life does not depend altogether on its context. "The changing conditions of history touch only the surface of the show," he maintained, "and no outward changes of condition in life can keep the nightingale of its eternal meaning from singing in all sorts of different men's hearts."[100]

It is true that James did not write much about politics, but it was not because his interests did not extend to political questions. His interests simply extended beyond politics to philosophy. He was unable to find in his radical empiricism or his pragmatism any but provisional answers to the questions that concerned him, and he was unable to find in any institutional changes solutions to the perennial challenge of benevolence. The analytical acuity that enabled him to penetrate the complexities of knowledge and value, suffering and joy, proved politically corrosive. James cautioned against placing excessive faith in the efficacy of social reform, because philosophical problems cannot be solved by political or economic means. Individual choice, and the strength to hitch the will to a cherished principle, together determine the significance of life.

All of the philosophers of the *via media* considered political reform a necessary but not sufficient step in the recovery of a classical ideal of citizenship involving not only autonomy, conceived as effective rather than merely formal freedom, but also moral responsibility, manifested in carefully chosen steps toward greater equality by broadening the role of the state. Yet just as their perspectives concerning ethics and the achievement of justice ranged from the heroic to the tragic, so their political outlooks differed. Fouillée, for example, contended that the most bitter class struggles could be eased "if labor and capital, instead of fancying themselves enemies, were convinced of the necessity of their union." While that seems to resemble the spirit of James's remarks on class conflict, however, Fouillée concluded that such solidarity could indeed be achieved. Although he and Green did emphasize the irreducible moral quality of reform, they believed that history was moving slowly but steadily toward the greater integration of individual and social purpose, and they were confident that politics could eventually serve as the locus of their ultimate resolution.

Fouillée proposed the notion of the "quasi-contract" to explain how the blending of personal and community interests could be accomplished. Locke, Rousseau, and Kant had correctly indicated the purpose as well as the artificiality of all actual governments through their theories of a hypothetical social contract, but they had misconceived the nature of individuals by postulating a mythical presocial experience as preliminary to common life.

Such thinkers as Hegel, Comte, and Spencer had in different ways made the opposite error of exaggerating the social inclinations of individuals in their organic conceptions of the state. Rather than overlooking the social dimension inherent in immediate experience, as the contract theorists did, or overlooking the inescapably personal quality of individual life, as the social organicists did, Fouillée claimed that his theory of the "quasi-contract" fused the essential elements of individuality with society, liberty with fraternity, and utility with justice. As civilization has developed, he argued, people have become increasingly sensitive to the dual aspects of experience as they have become increasingly aware of their interdependence. From the fact of their solidarity they have begun to realize that their freedom must be balanced against their obligations, that their rights as citizens derive from the shared commitments of all the members of their community.[101] The understanding of experience as social and historical implied for Green and Fouillée a politics of enlarged liberties and enlarged responsibilities, a concept of citizenship reminiscent of Aristotle's but established on radically new foundations.

James and Sidgwick recognized the desirability of a harmonious blending of prudence and justice in politics as in ethics, but the ideal seemed to them to recede over the next horizon with every step of social progress. Whereas Green and Fouillée asserted that the problem of economic competition, which both identified as the primary source of social conflict, would diminish gradually through the further development of social interaction, Sidgwick maintained that "on some momentous questions—such as the distribution of taxation—the political interest of the mass of the poor is *prima facie* opposed to that of the rich." As noted above, Sidgwick examined Green's treatment of competition and judged it incoherent. If the only good, Sidgwick pointed out, is a good with respect to which competition is impossible, viz. a good of personal moral development, then the problem vanishes, and it is difficult to see how competition can lead to social conflict. Yet that solution defines the range of true goods so narrowly as to conflict with common sense. Experience indicates that we do prize certain material goods that cannot be infinitely shared. Thus if some scarce goods can, and indeed must, be unequally distributed, competition for them will persist, and reconciling the conflicting claims of individuals seems impossible. The problem, as Sidgwick conceived it, is inherent in the human condition; no amount of historical progress or social reform can solve it.[102]

Sidgwick believed that the fundamental questions of life are philosophical, and thus like James he denied that such questions as competition, at root an ethical problem of balancing the claims of prudence and justice, can ever be settled by social policy. Life inevitably presents us with a series of dilemmas, and no course of action, taken either by individuals or by society, can prevent the sacrifice of one genuine good in order to satisfy another. Sidgwick doubted that a workable scale could ever be devised for accurately measuring desert. In the absence of such a measure, social peace would be impossible, because nearly everyone would feel either inadequately rewarded for his own special contribution to the common good or dissatisfied with the system of preexisting inequalities that could prevent less advantaged members of society from sharing its rewards. While James conceded in *The Varieties of Religious Experience* that a just community, "in which there would be only sympathy and fairness" instead of competition and inequality, would be perfectly adapted to the virtues of a saint, he remained skeptical whether human society could ever reach a condition in which saints might thrive rather than suffer. "We have, in short," Sidgwick wrote, "to give up as impracticable the construction of an ideally just social order, in which all services are rewarded in exact proportion to their intrinsic value." For no such "intrinsic value" is disclosed in experience; we have only clashes among competing and incommensurable interpretations of it. Moreover, Sidgwick concluded regretfully, common sense "scarcely holds with a method to be possible: for though it considered Ideal Justice to consist in rewarding Desert, it regards as Utopian any general attempt to realize this ideal in the social distribution of the means of happiness."[103] That sober judgment reveals Sidgwick's doubt, a doubt James shared, about the possibility of attaining the degree of social harmony that Green and Fouillée cherished and anticipated. James and Sidgwick favored progressive social change, but they believed that the value of life relates to its physical conditions as color relates to form. They maintained that life is imbued with meanings that flow from history and culture, and its value is determined less according to material conditions than by individual will and activity.

The philosophers of the *via media* thus expressed their political ideas in the distinct keys of anticipation and skepticism. But none of them counseled inaction, because they considered social change desirable, although not inevitable. While they disagreed about the prospect for attaining harmony, they agreed about the course of action most likely to lead in that direction. They challenged the identification of politics with economics, insisting that a broader conception of autonomy required the destruction of liberals' identification of freedom with unrestricted property rights. Just as they linked individual experience with social and cultural context and individual responsibility with community membership, so they conceived of politics as the attempt to achieve, as nearly as possible, the harmonious integration of autonomous individuals. They conceived of autonomy, however, not in the standard liberal terms of acquisitiveness and independence from the threatening forces of corruption represented by government, but instead as citizenship, an ideal involving positive freedom secured by an active, democratic state designed to provide a context of equality for the moral development of all of its members.

This vision of politics, of course, was hardly new. It mirrored the classical image of the correlative rights and duties of the republican citizen. What was new about it, and what made it radical philosophically and ambiguous politically, was its derivation and its limits. It originated not in a priori notions of reason, virtue, or justice, but instead in a new conception of experience and a new awareness of uncertainty. Using the tools of radical empiricism and the experimental method of pragmatism, these thinkers fashioned a theory of social action stressing the reciprocal relation between individual choices and historically developing cultural values. According to that theory, moral and political principles are not brought to experience but grow from it; like all ideas, they are subject to endless testing in practice. Change, which according to the classical view inevitably signaled decline, is interpreted as a sign of vitality. Flexibility and innovation, based on collective experience but expressing the imagination of reflective individuals, are methodological principles consistent with the ongoing quest for the most satisfactory way of organizing social life. Expediency is a matter of principle, responsiveness to new demands a responsibility. Steady, incremental change through the democratic process, with all its confusions and imperfections, is the political expression of this philosophical creed. These ideas, moderate, meliorist, democratic, and sensitive to the possibility that no perfect reconciliation of liberty and equality can be attained, are the consequences of pragmatism for politics.[104]

By altering ways of thinking about liberty and equality, and by arguing that the responsibility of the state must be expanded to insure effective freedom in the context of interdependence, the philosophers of the *via media* helped to reshape the discourse of politics for the twentieth century. Victorian critics such as Arnold, Renouvier, and Godkin simply lacked the intellectual tools to construct a new framework for politics in the emerging urban-industrial world of the late nineteenth century. They disliked what they saw, but they were unable to offer constructive alternatives. In a variety of ways, indirectly through their writings about epistemology and ethics and directly through their writings about politics, Dilthey, Green, Sidgwick, Fouillée, and James helped to make available a new way of understanding a new world.

As philosophy their ideas were persuasive, but as politics they were problematical because they neglected the persistence of power. The theory of voluntary action and the ethics of rational benevolence stressed the connection between will and responsibility, yet in the shift of focus from the individual to the polity the relation between volition and action changes. The individual can and must choose, and as he acts according to his choice he becomes a person of a certain kind. But whether government policy in fact reflects the collective decisions of free individuals is not a philosophical but a political question; it reflects power as much as—or perhaps instead of—popular desires. The philosophers of the *via media* resisted efforts to specify in detail the political strategy that could carry forward the ideas they advocated. Although they denied in principle that the consideration of means could be separated from the consideration of ends, their writings about politics evaded a series of questions that eventually resurfaced as it became apparent that radical impulses could be deflected harmlessly into insubstantial reforms. How are we to perceive and effect the public's will in a context of social and economic inequality? Given unequal access to information, should the people make decisions or ratify decisions made by elites? Finally, and perhaps most unsettlingly for a democracy, does the reorientation of individual wills toward social responsibility depend on education, or does it depend on the popular exercise of effective economic and political power?

In a passage expressing both the characteristic urge to mediate and an acute sensitivity to the connection between individual choice and social cohesion, Fouillée described the convergence of liberals, socialists, and Marxists toward a common awareness. "From all sides, and by all paths, we will return sooner or later to this fundamental conception of eighteenth-century French philosophy: the social order must rest on the harmony of free wills."[105] Whether free wills can achieve harmony, however, and whether harmony can survive free wills, are among the most difficult questions of politics. Totalitarians have begged the first question and answered no to the second; liberal pluralists have begged the second question and answered no to the first. But neither the authoritarian enforcement of harmony at the expense of freedom nor the liberal toleration of freedom at the expense of harmony approximates the classical ideal these philosophers tried to establish on radical premises. Although they disagreed about the prospect of integrating individual free choice with the public purpose, they insisted that the democratic achievement of substantive reforms culminating in a more egalitarian society requires nothing less than the construction of such a social order. How a generation of social democrats and progressives assimilated their ideas and tried to translate them into politics, how they succeeded in changing the surface of the political landscape while failing to alter the underlying distribution of power, and what their failure has meant for twentieth-century politics, is the subject of Part Two of this study.

PART TWO

6

From Socialism to Social Democracy

1. The Origins of Social Democracy

The theory of social democracy was born when socialists adapted new ideas about knowledge and responsibility to the new world of organized capitalism. From backgrounds as disparate as Marxism, Christian socialism, and utopian socialism, a number of dissenters began in the 1880s to alter the fabric of socialist philosophy and socialist politics. Advancing arguments similar to, although not always directly patterned after, those woven by the philosophers of the *via media*, they contended that individual experience, conceived as radically social and unavoidably uncertain, provides the only basis for knowledge. They also emphasized the importance of history as a source of judgment, and they insisted that ideas must be tested in practice. Unlike earlier socialists who doubted the potential of representative institutions and incremental changes, these thinkers bleached the apocalyptic vibrancy from socialism and dyed their ideas in the softer shades of reform. While they preserved the substance of the cooperative and egalitarian ideals characteristic of earlier socialists, they stretched these values across a different framework of strategies designed to lead gradually from existing conditions to the eventual realization of their aims. In short, they wanted to extend the democratic principles of participation and equality from the civil and political spheres to the entire society and the economy, to accomplish without revolution the transformation from liberal democracy to social democracy.

Socialism traveled from the periphery to the center of politics at different speeds in different cultures during the years from 1870 to 1920, and the pattern of development is rich in paradoxes. The socialist party most consistently committed to revolution attracted the largest number of voters, yet it exercised almost no power in government. The party most firmly committed to defending the existing republican government from its enemies on the right refused to allow its members to participate in the government it pledged to protect. The party least successful in attracting voters operated in an environment dominated by nonsocialist parties committed, at least intermittently, to genuine progressive reforms sought by most socialists. Finally, the socialists most committed to working within existing nonsocialist parties ended up being swallowed by a new, powerful, and ostensibly socialist party that ultimately betrayed their hopes.

These features of German, French, American, and British socialism, respectively, suggest some of the complexities involved in trying to compare the shifting fortunes of socialists in four nations over a period of fifty years. Rather than tracing their political progress and the intricacies of socialist infighting, I will concentrate on a process of intellectual convergence within the broader pattern of diversity by examining six thinkers who played decisive roles in reshaping socialist theory into the new form of social democracy: German revisionist Eduard Bernstein (1850–1932), American economist Richard T. Ely (1854–1943), British Fabians Beatrice Webb (1858–1943) and Sidney Webb (1859–1947), French socialist Jean Jaurès (1859–1914), and the most prominent radical in the American social gospel movement, Walter Rauschenbusch (1861–1918). These six belonged to a different generation from the philosophers of the *via media*, and they had a rather different vision of their responsibilities as intellectuals. While all of them had a serious interest in philosophy, all devoted their attention more to social and political analysis and activity than to epistemology or ethics. Yet their ideas about the uncertainty of knowledge and the centrality of questions of value were crucial in their revision of prevailing socialist theory, and it is precisely that connection between ideas about philosophy and politics that I want to demonstrate. Viewing these political ideas in relation to their philosophical presuppositions reveals that social democratic theory was not simply an ideology expressing what had become politically expedient but was instead a manner of rethinking socialism consistent with radically new ideas about what we know and what we are to do. While these social democrats' ideas may have suited political and socioeconomic circumstances at the turn of the century—although that familiar assumption is questionable in light of the storm of criticism showered on them from both within and outside the socialist movement—their cautious, reformist, and democratic outlook also manifested a profound change from the confident mood and millennial perspective of utopian socialists and Marxists alike.

In the next chapter I will examine the politics of social democracy; in this chapter I want to explore these social democrats' challenge to socialist theory and its connection with the epistemological and ethical ideas formulated by the earlier generation of radical philosophers. That connection was in some cases direct, explicit, and acknowledged, while in others it was veiled and unrecognized. But in all cases—indeed, particularly where lines of personal influence are lacking—it illustrates the convergence toward a certain conception of experience in terms of its social, historical, and cultural context. I should emphasize that I am not interested primarily in tracing the influence of the philosophers of the *via media* on the theorists of social democracy. What is more striking, and more important historically, is the congruence between their ideas. While the earlier generation concentrated on philosophy and sketched their political ideas rather faintly, and the later generation stressed politics and left only traces of underlying philosophical positions, there is a distinctive continuity between the two groups' philosophical and political ideas, and uncovering that continuity reveals the theoretical foundation on which social democratic politics rests.

Before examining the philosophy of social democracy, however, I want to outline the careers of its creators and locate them in their quite different political traditions. These thinkers were acutely sensitive to the rootedness of their own and all other ideas. As Bernstein wrote in his memoirs, ideas "do not fly down from heaven; they are historical phenomena which originate in given conditions and alter with these conditions." In order to understand the challenge represented by social democracy in its various national forms, and to understand the different roles its partisans played, it is necessary first to scan the larger contours of socialism as it developed in the nineteenth century. Bernstein pointed out that "it is only abstract theories that are in the full sense of the word international; any application of them to real life is more or less coloured, in this country or that, by the national spirit."[1] The genesis as well as the fate of social democratic theory illustrates the accuracy of those remarks.

In Britain the roots of socialism stretched back to the humanitarian paternalism of Robert Owen. Owen's socialism dovetailed with romanticism to present an alternative to the relentlessly efficient rationality of liberal individualism, a creed whose inability to satisfy emotional yearnings would receive poignant confirmation in John Stuart Mill's *Autobiography*. By mid-century, however, Owen's cooperative ideals had been eclipsed by the vigorous growth of the competitive ethos expressed in Benthamite radicalism, and native British socialism seemed to wither in the shadow of a burgeoning capitalism. Concurrently, British trade unionism developed rapidly, but as labor organized it absorbed the liberal ideology and concentrated on securing limited concessions from capitalists instead of launching a broader challenge. As trade unions won skirmishes they became increasingly committed to a reformist strategy, and as a result the more radical socialist movements gathering momentum on the continent attracted little attention among British workers. Although the British labor movement was developing considerable political muscle from 1850 to 1883, when Marx was working in London, working-class demands were usually either accommodated or effectively muffled within the echo chamber of Britain's liberal consensus. Even when labor began to assert itself as an independent political force toward the end of the nineteenth century, it operated as a Trojan horse within the Liberal party instead of besieging it from outside the walls.

Not until the 1880s did socialism enjoy something of a renaissance in

Britain, and even as it grew it exhibited traces of the unbridled civility so characteristic of British public life. The dogmatic Marxist revolutionism of H. M. Hyndman's Social Democratic Federation made little headway despite the fact that Britain seemed to approximate Marx's model of capitalist development more closely than did any other nation in these years. More successful was the Independent Labour party of Keir Hardie and J. Ramsay MacDonald, which became increasingly moderate as its alliance with the trade unions tightened and its focus narrowed to issues of immediate concern to industrial workers. Diverse organizations espousing varieties of "ethical socialism" also gained ground. Attracting support primarily from the lower middle-class "salariat" of clerks, civil servants, teachers, and journalists, these groups grafted the romantic utopianism of the Owenites and the Christian humanitarianism of the Nonconformist tradition onto the stem of British liberalism. From the seeds of that hybrid emerged the Fabian Society.[2]

The ethical societies not only provided fertile ground for the dormant strains of earlier British socialism, they also nourished the ideas of social reform emanating from Green's idealism and Sidgwick's expanded utilitarianism. The spirit of social service manifested in settlement houses such as Toynbee Hall, founded in 1884, was also fed by widely publicized exposés of urban poverty and by the popularity of Mrs. Humphry Ward's inspirational novel *Robert Elsmere*. The ethical societies served as the institutional juncture where all of these reformist impulses intersected. Sidgwick was a prominent member of the Cambridge Ethical Society and also a popular lecturer at the London Ethical Society, an organization founded after Green's death that served as an outlet for the ideas of younger, reform-minded Oxford idealists such as D. G. Ritchie and J. H. Muirhead. In 1886 Sidgwick noted in his diary that "the main current of new feeling among thoughtful young men during the last few years" was running toward "socialistic enthusiasm," and he helped to channel those impulses toward social reform in his addresses to the ethical societies.[3]

Such humanitarian sentiments, intensified by the ideas of moral responsibility preached at Cambridge by Sidgwick and at Oxford by Green, motivated the founders of the Fellowship of the New Life, an organization formed by followers of the idiosyncratic philosopher Thomas Davidson. On November 7, 1883, the Fellowship passed its first resolution: "That an association be formed whose ultimate aim shall be the reconstruction of society in accordance with the highest moral possibilities." According to the minutes of the meeting, when debate shifted to "the special way in which this end was to be effected by the Society," the harmony immediately dissolved into such discord that "it was considered desirable to appoint a committee to draw up and submit proposals to the next meeting." Having proclaimed an ideal of cooperation, the Fellowship promptly disintegrated; on January 4, 1884, dissidents formed the Fabian Society, a body born of disagreement and nourished for a century on a rich but unsteady diet of ideas and acrimony.[4]

Sidney Webb did not begin his long association with the Fabians until the next year, when he first spoke before the society, but after he joined he quickly established himself as one of the most active and influential members. Webb was in many respects a typical Fabian: a product of an evangelical family, a struggling but intellectually alert member of the lower middle class, a pilgrim searching for a political home and a secular faith in the uncharted territory beyond John Stuart Mill's vaguely socialistic radicalism. Unable to accept a scholarship to Cambridge because of financial constraints, Webb completed his law degree in 1886 by taking night classes at London University while working full time in the civil service. Webb's doggedness more than his brilliance distinguished him among the little flock of solitary collectivists who made up the Fabian "old gang." George Bernard Shaw and H. G. Wells were more imaginative and far more gifted writers, William Clarke was more astute philosophically, and Graham Wallas was more sensitive to the fuzzy connections between politics and psychology. But if the Fabian Society's contentiousness was part of its institutional strength, the organization also proved to be an intellectual centrifuge, through the years spinning off many of its most energetic members into a political void instead of gathering them into a coherent school of thought.

Webb remained the Fabian Society's center of gravity, powerful enough to attract numerous followers but unable to prevent the more independent minded, such as Shaw, Wells, and Wallas, from careening off into irregular orbits of their own. While it has been suggested that the narrowness of Webb's vision, and his success in concentrating the energies of the Fabian society on specific issues instead of broader goals, prompted the departure of various Fabian luminaries who looked to socialism for personal salvation rather than gradual social change, I will argue that Webb's emphasis on proximate steps rather than ultimate goals stemmed from dual commitments central to social democracy: the awareness that all knowledge is uncertain and all political ideas are therefore provisional, and the dedication to democratic politics as a process of collective truth testing whose results cannot be specified in advance. "There will never come a moment when we can say '*now* Socialism is established,'" Webb argued in a lecture delivered in 1887. He was commited to an unending democratic process of widening and deepening the conscious acceptance of more collectivist social and economic values by all of the people, and he denied in principle that such acceptance could be attained except through a slow process of ethical and political regeneration.[5] Webb's empiricism was not narrow but radical; his emphasis on gathering data and working for incremental change reflected his appreciation of the contingency of knowledge. Although he passed through a Comtean phase that permanently altered his perspective from liberal individualism to organic collectivism, he had shed the positivists' confidence in ultimate certainties as inconsistent with empiricism and democracy by the time he proclaimed himself a socialist in 1886.

Webb's reputation as an indefatigable researcher brought him into contact with another earnest young social investigator, Beatrice Potter, who was at first as impressed with his knowledge as she was unimpressed with his person. Raised in a wealthy family with exceptionally wide-ranging

contacts—her father counted among his friends not only fellow Tory industrialists but also such figures as Spencer and Huxley—Beatrice Potter
received a far better education than did most English women of her generation. She turned away from Society to study society after the experience of
living with cousins who worked in a cotton mill awakened in her a sharp sense
of industrialization's consequences. She gained further firsthand knowledge
of English poverty assisting another cousin, Charles Booth, on a large-scale
research project documenting living conditions in London's East End, and
when that task was completed she began studying the British labor movement. Seeking help with sources on the development of cooperatives, in
January, 1890, she became acquainted with Sidney Webb. He was already
familiar with her work on Booth's survey, and she admired his contribution
to the phenomenally successful *Fabian Essays in Socialism* (1889). But while
Sidney appears to have been immediately attracted to Beatrice, her first
description of him in her diary suggests her initial ambivalence. He was
a "remarkable little man," she wrote, who "struts even when he stands ...
But I like the man. There is a directness of speech—an open-mindedness,
an imaginative warm-heartedness which should carry him far. He has
the self-complacency of one who is always thinking faster than his
neighbours."

As their letters during a two-year courtship reveal, Sidney wooed
Beatrice with the same relentness, and some of the same awkwardness, that
characterized all of his efforts. But in the end his combined tenacity and
sincerity did indeed carry him far. Six months after confessing to Sidney that
she considered herself incapable of love, because her painful rejection by
Joseph Chamberlain in 1886 had left her "uninjured as a worker" but
hardened like "a bit of steel," she agreed to marry Webb. She respected him
for his "self-devotion for the 'Common Good,'" and she expected that their
marriage would be "based on fellowship—a common faith and a common
work." Their union would enable her to continue her work instead of subordinating herself to the career of another, as would have been the case with
Chamberlain, and the chance to fulfill her own ambitions while leading a
productive life outweighed the "renunciation of self" she felt was involved in
her reluctant decision to become Mrs. Sidney Webb.[6]

A person of unusual grace and a writer of graceful prose, Beatrice was in
both respects the opposite of Sidney. Their "partnership," to use the oddly
impersonal yet appropriate word they used for their marriage, linked the
powerful will and steady mind of an attractive patrician with the powerful
mind and steady will of a scruffy civil servant. Beatrice combined the humanitarian impulses of Tory paternalism with a deep sense of moral uplift and
social cohesion, while Sidney joined to a radical democratic sensibility an
inclination toward carefully directed social engineering. Together they were
a formidable pair. Prolific writers and tireless persuaders, they produced
numerous pamphlets for the Fabian Society and a variety of books on social
problems. Although none of the Fabians' publications matched the
popularity of the original *Fabian Essays in Socialism*, nearly three million

copies of various Fabian Tracts were issued to the public between 1890 and 1922.

As publicists the Webbs preferred to maintain their independence from political parties, adopting a strategy of "permeation" designed to persuade politicians of various inclinations on specific issues of policy and more general principles of government. In addition to these activities, Sidney served from 1892 to 1911 as an elected member of the London County Council, and Beatrice served from 1905 to 1909 as an appointed member of the Royal Commission on the Poor Law. Drawing on a sizeable bequest from a Fabian sympathizer, the Webbs founded the London School of Economics in 1895 to provide progressive education for prospective civil servants. In 1913 they established *The New Statesman* as an outlet for their ideas. Consistent with their commitment to permeation, and reflecting their isolation from all parties that was the other side of that strategy, they proclaimed in the first issue, "We shall be bound by no ties of party, class, or creed."[7]

It was not until World War I that the Webbs became closely affiliated with the Labour party, whose prospects they had consistently underestimated. In 1918 Sidney wrote a manifesto entitled *Labour and the New Social Order*, which served as a framework for Labour party policy in the postwar years. Two years later the Webbs provided a comprehensive statement of their general perspective in *A Constitution for the Socialist Commonwealth of Great Britain.* Also in 1920 Sidney first stood for election to Parliament as a Labour party candidate, and in 1922 he was elected. Throughout their long careers, the tension between the Webbs' elitist and egalitarian impulses remained undiminished, and their oscillation between those poles puzzled their contemporaries as much as it has troubled later commentators. Did the Webbs want ethical regeneration or institutional efficiency? Did they want a democratic society or a society organized by experts? In short, did they want to reform Great Britain or run it? While their answers at times seemed clear-cut, examination of the overall pattern of their writings renders a simple judgment impossible. They represented a new amalgam of humanitarian socialism and democratic liberalism in British thought and politics, and their ambiguities and uncertainties reveal some of the most difficult problems of social democratic theory.

What is clear, however, is that the erosion of religious faith and the rise of a scientific ethos powerfully affected the Webbs; their attempt to translate their feelings of moral responsiblity into political action was typical of many intellectuals of their generation. In a passage that expressed this attitude, Beatrice Webb explained how the late nineteenth-century *Zeitgeist* carried her to a definite conclusion: "From the flight of emotion away from the service of God to the service of man, and from the current faith in the scientific method, I drew the inference that the most hopeful form of social service was the craft of a social investigator."[8] A similar conclusion was drawn by many of her contemporaries in the United States, who found outlets for their ambitions in a variety of protest movements that sprang up between 1880 and 1920.[9] As in Great Britain, these reformers relied less on Marx than on a tradition shaped by religious dissent and by the moral emphasis of civic humanism and Scottish philosophy. The most influential voices challenging industrial capitalism in the 1880s and early 1890s, ranging from Henry George's single taxers and Edward Bellamy's nationalists to Terrence Powderly's Knights of Labor, Charles Macune's alliancemen, and William Jennings Bryan's silver crusaders, spoke the language of ethical renewal rather than class warfare. Even Lawrence Gronlund, America's first expositor of Marx, reasoned that proletarian revolution made little sense in America; those such as Daniel DeLeon who argued otherwise enjoyed as little success in the United States as Hyndman did in Great Britain.

Despite the persistent violence that marked conflicts between labor and capital, American workers, like their British counterparts, remained comfortably within the bounds of liberal politics. This paradox of unruly workers and a politically inert working class has long puzzled both Europeans and Americans. In 1906 Werner Sombart asked "Why is there no socialism in the United States?" and every year the list of answers to his question grows longer. Yet the essential elements of an explanation can be traced to the absence in late nineteenth-century America of precisely those characteristics Marx isolated as prime contributors to the proletariat's evolution as a revolutionary class. First, although its share of the national income seems to have changed negligibly, the American working class enjoyed a steadily rising standard of living. Most American workers, in contrast to Marx's dictum, had considerably more to lose than their chains, and their political conservatism reflected their relative prosperity. Second, universal manhood suffrage and a lively tradition of popular participation (if not effective control) in politics limited working-class disaffection from the American political system. Third, whereas Marx interpreted all social and intraclass divisions as transparent smokescreens designed to obscure the proletariat's vision of its fundamental unity, and he believed that the working class would unite to liberate itself, discordant competition among ethnic groups effectively drowned out appeals to American working-class solidarity. Finally, Marx believed that workers' consciousness of themselves as the universal class would eventually emerge from their pauperized condition to liberate them from the illusion of satisfaction in having property rather than being free. This realization, he reasoned, would convert the proletariat to the revolutionary ideas of laboring creatively, productively, and cooperatively, in which condition alone workers might fulfill their potential as unalienated "species beings." Yet the ideology of materialism, the faith in upward mobility, and the ability of American workers to adapt their own cultural forms to the pressures of industrial capitalism and create a satisfying sphere of private life have combined to limit the appeal of a more socialized set of values. This constellation of economic, political, social, ideological, and cultural factors together suggest why the American working class seldom ventured beyond the liberal consensus.[10] Social democratic theory in the United States thus emerged from a background of ethical reformism rather than revolutionary political action.

As in Great Britain, ethical socialism provided the institutional as well as the intellectual framework for the individuals who worked to shift American socialist thinking away from millennial utopianism and revolutionary Marxism. Significantly, the founder of the American Fabian League and publisher of the short-lived *American Fabian* was William Dwight Porter Bliss, a peripatetic organizer and publicist in the second gospel movement, which was responsible for bringing social democratic ideas to America. Like the Webbs, the most prominent figures in the social gospel looked to ethics as much as economics to explain social problems. The various English and American ethical societies and Christian socialist organizations were closely affiliated with each other, and these reciprocal institutional influences mirrored the movement of ideas back and forth across the Atlantic. While the language of socialism was never as prominent in the United States as in Europe, the limited penetration of socialism into American thought during the progressive period was largely due to the work of those who tried to adapt socialist ideas to the liberal political culture of America in a theory of social democracy. These thinkers were the American counterparts to the Webbs, because more than any representatives of the American socialist parties they made a moderate version of reformist socialism a legitimate part of political discourse.[11]

Three phases may be distinguished in the rise of the social gospel. During the 1880s basic themes were introduced, and ideas from European socialists and reformers made their way into discussions of economics and politics. The next decade saw the coming of age of the social gospel and increased receptivity to radical Christian socialist ideas. Finally, from 1900 to 1915 the movement rode the wave of progressive reform to dominant positions in various religious denominations.[12] Two of the most prominent theorists of the social gospel, whose periods of intellectual activity and popular influence reflected this progression, made pivotal contributions to the development of American social democratic theory: Richard T. Ely and Walter Rauschen-busch. Ely stood at the crossroads of the social gospel, the labor movement, the professionalization of social science, and the politics of progressivism. In that position he became prominent in the 1880s and 1890s; he became a casualty when those forces later collided.[13] Rauschenbusch, in contrast to many of his contemporaries who as reformers found themselves preaching without pulpits, followed the path taken by six generations of his ancestors into the ministry. Although socialism was for him less a substitute for his faith than a supplement to it, he found personal fulfillment in a life dedicated as much to social action as to spiritual consolation, and his contribution to American culture had less to do with theology than with reorienting religious attitudes toward politics.[14]

In their intellectual development, Ely and Rauschenbusch followed parallel paths. After childhoods spent in evangelistic families, both went as young men to study in Germany, Ely at age twenty-three in 1877, Rauschen-busch at age eighteen in 1879. Ely intended to continue studying philosophy, his major subject as an undergraduate at Columbia. His first mentor at the

University of Halle was Rudolf Haym, a friend of Dilthey's and one of the leading figures in the small group of liberal German academics. Haym's influential book *Hegel und seine Zeit* (1857) had been among the opening salvos in the late nineteenth-century assault on Hegel; in its conclusion Haym recommended a return from Hegel to the critical philosophy of Kant. Ely later recalled the decisive influence of Haym's skepticism, which "did a great deal to influence me to abandon my youthful idealistic purpose of seeking the absolute truth." Having originally embarked on his German excursion to find confirmation for William Hamilton's modified common sense realism—a reflection of the limits of his own and his advisors' knowledge of German idealism—under Haym's corrosive influence Ely's confidence in such ideas crumbled, as did his confidence in his capacity to master the intricacies of post-Hegelian German thought. Disenchanted with philosophy, he turned to the increasingly prominent historical approach to economics, which seemed compatible with the anti-idealist ethos he had adopted from Haym. After studying economics with Johannes Conrad at the University of Halle, he left to complete his Ph.D. with Karl Knies at Heidelberg. Ely not only learned methods of economic research in Germany. When he returned to the United States in 1880, he also brought with him, in his words, "the idea of relativity as opposed to absolutism and the insistence upon exact and positive knowledge," as well as a commitment to "the ethical view of economics taught by Conrad, by [Adolf] Wagner, and above all by Knies."[15] Ely's conviction that economics must be historical rather than deductive, and his belief that academic study should not be divorced from social responsibility, were to make him both influential and controversial.

Germany held fewer mysteries for Rauschenbusch, who had spent several years there as a child while his father, a professor at the Baptist Rochester Theological Seminary, did research. His stay in Germany from 1879 to 1883, combining rigorous training in classical and modern languages with more light-hearted traveling around the continent, helped to shape his later career, for his reading of Schleiermacher and his comparative study of religious mythologies persuaded him that religion begins in individual experience rather than theology. That conviction helped to prepare him for his role in the larger process of shifting American Protestantism away from its preoccupation with theology toward a broader emphasis on the religion of personal commitment and humanitarianism, a process in which his advocacy of the social gospel played a prominent part.[16] Upon returning to the United States, he completed his studies at the University of Rochester and the Rochester Theological Seminary, then accepted as his first assignment a congregation of recent German Baptist immigrants in the Hell's Kitchen section of New York City. This experience, like Beatrice Potter's exposure to the rigors of life in London's East End, converted Rauschenbusch to political radicalism. He recalled in 1913 that his social ideas did not come from the church but from his "personal contact with poverty." When he saw "how men toiled all their life long, hard, toilsome lives, and at the end had almost nothing to show for it; how strong men begged for work and could not get it in hard times; how the little children died," those experiences "set a great beacon fire burning."[17] Rauschenbusch actively supported Henry George's mayoral campaign in 1886, and in 1889 he established the Christian socialist newspaper *For the Right* to express his blend of religious and political arguments for radical social change.

Ely's return to the United States was similarly cathartic. In contrast to the sparkling cities of Germany, New York City presented a dreary spectacle of dirt and disease that prompted Ely to concentrate his research on the conditions of labor in America. He accepted a teaching position at the Johns Hopkins University in 1881, and the eleven years he spent there were the most productive of his life. Several of the books he published in the 1880s, notably *French and German Socialism in Modern Times* (1883), *Recent American Socialism* (1884), and *The Labor Movement in America* (1886), were landmarks not only because Ely applied the methods of German historical economics to American conditions, but also—and perhaps more significantly—because they illustrated his growing affiliation with the American labor movement and his sympathetic attitude toward socialism. Ely also lectured and wrote in support of economic and political reform. In 1887 he was the first academic economist to address a national labor convention when he spoke before the American Federation of Labor, and as a member of the Baltimore and Maryland tax commissions he strongly advocated progressive taxation. He courted leaders of the social gospel, both more moderate figures such as Washington Gladden, Lyman Abbot, and Josiah Strong, and radicals like W. D. P. Bliss and Rauschenbusch. Ely's books, particularly *The Social Aspects of Christianity and Other Essays* (1889), written in his characteristically lean, unmuscular prose, became required reading at seminaries as well as university departments of economics. In 1892 Ely left Johns Hopkins for the University of Wisconsin, where he and other social scientists exerted considerable influence on the "Wisconsin idea" of political reform that served as a prototype for national progressivism. He was at the height of his influence when he arrived in Madison. Sidney Webb, who had met Ely on a trip to the United States in 1889, assisted him in preparing what became one of his most important books, *Socialism and Social Reform* (1894), and when the book appeared Webb helped arrange for a British edition and added it to the Fabian Society's list of recommended books.[18]

Rauschenbusch's reputation also spread in the 1890s. When he traveled to Europe in 1891 to do research for the book that would become *Christianity and the Social Crisis* (1907), perhaps the most important single expression of social democratic ideas produced by the social gospel movement, he stayed with the Webbs, and in his political addresses he referred to the international dimensions of the shift of socialist thinkers away from revolutionary strategies toward the sort of reformist socialism he advocated.[19] In 1897 Rauschenbusch left New York to teach at the Rochester Theological Seminary, where he remained until his death. As one of the most widely respected partisans of the social gospel, he was consulted by both Theodore

Roosevelt and Woodrow Wilson, and he appreciated the paradox of American radical reformers' access both to the public and to politicians despite the absence of a powerful socialist party. In the United States, he explained in 1901, "the current of socialist thought and sentiment does not run in the channel of socialist parties, but is leavening the ideas of the people and will transform our social organization in the direction of socialism quietly and gradually. If dogmatic socialists choose to sit on the fence and criticize the men who do this work, that is their look-out. The work will be done," he concluded, with an undercurrent of scorn running beneath the expression of regret, "almost as fast anyway."[20]

Those words summed up the attitude of Ely as well as Rauschenbusch and suggested the awkwardness of their alliance with moderate reform movements. They were sympathetic to socialism, but they saw little future for American socialist parties. They were impatient with the tendency of politicians to temporize, but they understood the real constraints imposed by American politics. Like the Fabians, Ely and Rauschenbusch had little impact on the working class they aimed to assist. Their influence extended primarily to those reform-minded members of the urban middle class who formed one of the several muddy currents of progressive sentiment in the pre-World War I period. In their years of greatest notoriety they stood near the far left of the American political spectrum, less radical than some socialists but more radical than most progressives, calling for changes of a sort that received greater—although still limited—support during the New Deal. Social democracy was less central in the United States than in Europe between 1890 and 1920, and in different ways Ely and Rauschenbusch paid a price for their radicalism.

Neither was a prophet without honor. Ely's *Outlines of Economics* went through six editions, and in the early twentieth century it may have been outsold among economics books only by Adam Smith's *Wealth of Nations*. Rauschenbusch's *Christianity and the Social Crisis* sold fifty thousand copies and was translated into eight languages.[21] Yet their prominence notwithstanding, both operated under pressure to moderate their messages. After Rauschenbusch sent the completed manuscript of *Christianity and the Social Crisis* to his publisher in 1906, he left immediately for a year of research in Europe, afraid that reaction to the book's radicalism would endanger his position at Rochester. "I expected there would be a great deal of anger and resentment," he explained, and he was astonished when reviewers praised the book and the public hailed him as a political messiah.[22] Ely, who was seven years older than Rauschenbusch, was less fortunate. Although not exactly the social gospel's John the Baptist, Ely was hounded by critics when he proclaimed the coming of radical political change in the 1880s and 1890s. His letters are sprinkled with apparently exaggerated references to the power and vindictiveness of his enemies. But when he was forced to stand trial before the University of Wisconsin Board of Regents in 1894, on charges of teaching dangerous economic doctrines, it became clear that his fears were not without foundation. Although vindicated at his trial, which will be discussed in greater detail in Chapter Seven, Ely emerged from the experience chastened. For the next two decades he skated cautiously across the thin ice separating respectable reformism from unacceptable radicalism, and after World War I he took refuge on the high ground of more conventional political and economic ideas.

Throughout his career Ely tried to balance the weight of his professional ambitions against his political activism. His colleagues at Johns Hopkins were puzzled by a political radical who was also an academic empire builder, and that incongruous combination likewise marked his decisive but politically ambiguous role in establishing the American Economic Association. When he moved to Wisconsin he vowed to make the university "equal to any in the country," in part by establishing a civil academy for the same educational and political reasons that motivated the Webbs to establish the London School of Economics three years later. But the burden of unstable personal finances and unsteady professional prestige eventually wore Ely down. Ironically, the celebrity he enjoyed when controversial vanished when he became conventional, and in the 1920s the profession that had grudgingly respected his radical writings on labor economics ignored his solid but unexciting contributions to land economics, a field he helped to create.[23]

In the book that confirmed his status as the most thoughtful and influential spokesman of the social gospel, *Christianizing the Social Order* (1912), Rauschenbusch singled out Ely as one of the "pioneers of the social gospel," one whose spirit had "kindled and compelled" Rauschenbusch's ideas about social justice and social democratic politics. Because Rauschenbusch did not begin to attract national attention until the peak of reformist enthusiasm was reached, he did not encounter the abuse he expected. Despite the similarity of their ideas, Rauschenbusch was spared the public spectacle of a heresy trial such as Ely's. Not until he opposed American participation in World War I was he subjected to attacks as vicious as those launched against Ely, but those attacks took their toll. As he wrote in 1918, "the world is full of hate, and I cannot expect to be happy again in my lifetime."[24] Unfortunately for a nation that would need antidotes to the self-satisfied cynicism of the 1920s, his words were prophetic: two months later he was dead.

Rauschenbusch was saddened by the suppression of dissent in America during World War I not only because it silenced his voice during his last year of life, but because he cherished the principles of free inquiry and free expression as the foundations of his patriotism and his faith. In a letter written in 1886 to support a friend being pressured from his teaching post by conservative Baptists, he argued that the absence of authoritarian creeds was the distinctive feature of dissenting Protestant denominations. Baptists "have never put the future under bond to the past"; by accepting only the Bible as a guide for faith, he wrote, "We have taken as a standard the record of very manifold and often divergent experiences of God's grace and truth." Diversity characterized the American religious tradition, and it helps to account for the importance of the social gospel in spreading social democratic ideas in the United States. Whereas in Great Britain Christian socialism faded prior to

1914, before the authority of an established Church and the conflict between reformers' enthusiasm for social action and traditional religious notions of sin and salvation, in America the affiliation between religious and political dissent was itself something of an established tradition.[25] When the more radical partisans of the social gospel preached brands of social democracy alien to American liberalism, no strictly religious sanctions were available to silence them.

The distinctive place of religious dissent in American political culture comes even more sharply into focus when the social gospel is viewed in relation to the religious war between Catholics and republicans in later nineteenth-century France. Despite efforts by moderate conservatives to rally monarchists and Catholics to the Third Republic, the virulent anti-clericalism of French positivists and the equally virulent anti-republicanism of such militants as the Assumptionist Fathers made such a truce impossible. In contrast to the social gospel, spawned by the boisterous contentiousness of American religious pluralism, social democratic ideas in France emerged from a cultural background dominated by religious polarization, which persisted until the final separation of church and state in 1905. Within this context, French socialists adopted an ambivalent attitude toward the Third Republic. After 1871, Marxists following Jules Guesde filled the vacuum created in French socialism by the exile of the Blanquist and Proudhonian leaders of the Commune. But the Guesdists carried only part of the French left with them. Other socialists deliberately moderated their radicalism because they felt a certain loyalty to a Republic they considered at least a partial embodiment of their own ideals. Further complicating their uncertain allegiance was the persistent oscillation of French socialists between alliance with the small but militant organized labor movement and the larger but less cohesive forces of the republican bourgeoisie. French socialism lacked strong ties to the working class partly due to France's comparatively slow industrialization and partly due to the anarchist tendencies evident in some sectors of the proletariat, which forced French socialists to compete with more radical parties for the loyalty of labor. Despite this confusion, the unquestioned leader of French socialism during the early years of the Third Republic was Guesde, an intense and intolerant revolutionary whose wild eyes, long hair, and flowing beard seemed to confirm the worst fears of the bourgeoisie while conjuring memories of romantic heroism among his fervent disciples. Guesde's relentless insistence on discipline and centralization did not suit those socialists who traced their roots to Fourier or Saint-Simon instead of Babeuf, however, and in 1882 Paul Brousse engineered a rebellion against Guesde, leading a band of renegades aptly dubbed *possibilistes* away from revolutionary slogans and toward moderate reformism. By the 1890s, the squabbling among French socialists had reduced the movement to six apparently irreconcilable factions unable to accomplish anything in the face of a rightward tilting Republic. Rich in ideas and enthusiasm but lacking a reliable constituency or a cohesive program, the French left seemed lost in a weird ritual of self-immolation.[26]

The individual most responsible for distracting French socialists from their obsessive infighting and giving them a sense of direction was Jean Jaurès (1859–1914). His inexhaustible determination, irresistible personal warmth, and undeniable dedication to an ideal of social justice made Jaurès an imposing figure in French politics; his breadth of learning and depth of insight made him a political theorist of major significance. More successfully than any other architect of social democracy, Jaurès coupled intellectual originality with oratorical genius and political guile. The product of a struggling petit bourgeois family, he preserved the religious spirit he absorbed from his mother, although like many of his generation he discarded its doctrinal form. After distinguishing himself as a student at the Ecole Normale Supérieure, Jaurès embarked on a teaching career, but he was soon drawn into politics. When he was elected to the Chamber of Deputies in 1885, he later recalled, "I knew only two things—the Republic on the one side and the royalist-clerical reaction on the other."[27] The zealous antirepublicanism of French conservatives had sparked his initial engagement in politics, and in his early years in the Chamber he identified himself as a centrist republican committed to the defense of the regime from its enemies on the right. Defeated in the conservative resurgence of 1889, Jaurès accepted a teaching position in Toulouse and became active in municipal politics.

He also returned to his postponed academic work. In 1891 he completed his thesis, *De la réalité de la monde sensible* (cited hereafter as *On the Reality of the Sensible World*); a year later he submitted a supplementary thesis, *Les Origines du socialisme allemand* (*The Origins of German Socialism*). Perhaps because of the pivotal role Jaurès later played in French politics, historians have tended to underestimate the importance of these two early works, which represent his most ambitious statements of the philosophical foundation of his socialism. In the first of these studies he tried to construct a theory of knowledge drawing upon aspects of a pluralistic idealism and an enlarged empiricism; in the second he tried to reconcile different varieties of socialism.[28] His synthetic enterprise, which bore a striking resemblance to the efforts of the philosophers of the *via media*, illustrates clearly the continuity between the earlier generation's radical epistemology and the radical politics of social democracy.

Consistent with his understanding of how knowledge is attained, a combination of experience and critical thinking led Jaurès from bourgeois republicanism to socialism. While working on his theses he spent long hours discussing philosophical and political ideas with Lucien Herr, the young librarian at the Ecole Normale who converted a number of young intellectuals to socialism. These conversations doubtless influenced Jaurès's thinking, but his philosophical writings display such originality that attempts to trace his ideas to a single source are unpersuasive. In addition to his reading and reflection, his exposure to the exploitation of miners and glass workers in the town of Carmaux, near his home town of Castres— particularly the galvanizing experience of the miners' strike of 1892— convinced Jaurès that the protective legislation he had favored for workers was not enough. When he returned to the Chamber of Deputies in 1893, having been elected to represent Carmaux because of his support for the miners' struggle, he promptly joined the parliamentary alliance of socialists.[29] Jaurès emerged as a major figure among socialist thinkers as a result of his celebrated debate that year with the Marxist Paul Lafargue, in which Jaurès criticized dialectical materialism and advanced an original blend of idealism, realism, and democracy as the essence of his socialism. Striking a chord that would harmonize with the ideas of the Webbs, Ely, and Rauschenbusch, Jaurès emphasized the importance of ideals such as justice and equality and denied the adequacy of a purely economic interpretation of human behavior. From a combination of philosophical analysis and personal experience, he created a French version of social democratic theory.[30]

Jaurès's efforts to serve as a political mediator working for unity among France's bickering political factions paralleled his attempts to combine ideas from different traditions. The courage he displayed in the Dreyfusard crusade first propelled him to national prominence. Although his position cost him his seat in the Chamber of Deputies by enabling his opponents to portray him convincingly in anticlerical garb, Jaurès persisted, and the articles he wrote in 1898 for *La Petite République*, published later that year in book form as *Les Preuves*, helped demolish the rickety case against Dreyfus. Amidst the turbulence stirred up by the Dreyfus affair, Jaurès reaffirmed his republicanism the following year by supporting the ministry of René Waldeck-Rousseau, a government that included the moderate socialist Alexandre Millerand, a friend and political ally of Jaurès's. Although it seemed unsteady at first, the Waldeck-Rousseau government marked a turning point for the Third Republic, a shift away from the liberalism of the Opportunists toward the progressivism of coalition governments dominated by leftist Radicals and moderate socialists. The issue of socialist participation in a nonsocialist government, an expedient accepted by Jaurès to preserve the Republic, became a major issue in the international socialist movement. Its resolution, to be discussed in Chapter Seven, helped to determine the tactics, and ultimately the fate, of social democratic politics.

While out of political office Jaurès supplemented journalism with scholarship. Thwarted in his attempt to teach a course on "the principles of socialism in relation to the ideas of individuality, morality, art, and religion" at the Sorbonne, he plunged into the production of a multivolume socialist history of France. His contributions, covering the years of the Revolution and part of the Franco-Prussian War, were greeted enthusiastically by non-socialist historians as well as socialists. He brought to his historical studies not only the political acumen of an experienced parliamentarian and the verbal dexterity of a gifted orator, but also a sophisticated philosophy of history and a tireless devotion to the sources that historians of the Revolution continue to find impressive.[31]

Jaurès returned to the Chamber of Deputies in 1902. Reflecting the prestige won by his defense of Dreyfus and his contributions to the socialist press, he was elected one of four vice-presidents of the Chamber. During the next three years he supported the campaign waged by the ministry of Emile Combes to limit the participation of the Catholic church in French education. Jaurès believed that the church no more than the army should dominate French life, and prohibiting the clergy from teaching in public schools seemed to him a necessary step toward democratic and nondogmatic education. Unlike many of his allies in this battle, however, he was not opposed to religion itself. His wife was a fervent Catholic, and when she wanted their daughter Madeleine to receive her first communion in 1901, Jaurès cooperated despite the charges of duplicity that tumbled down on him. That such a trivial incident could become a *cause célèbre* merely confirmed to Jaurès the poisonous atmosphere pervading French politics. Not until church and state were finally separated in 1905, an accomplishment made possible by the participation of the *Bloc des gauches* organized by Jaurès, did he moderate his anticlericalism and turn his attention entirely to socialism.

That year the divided French socialist movement united to form a single party, the SFIO (Section française de l'Internationale oùvrière). For the next decade Jaurès tried to keep the party from lurching too far into revolutionary syndicalism or from dissolving into bourgeois republicanism. He had as an outlet for his ideas the newspaper *L'Humanité*, which he founded in 1904 and continued to control even after the Socialist party became the majority owner of the paper in 1906. But the veneer of unity provided by the SFIO covered cracks that ran deep. Given the predilection of French intellectuals for doctrinal precision, preserving even the appearance of agreement proved difficult, and as Europe began to slide toward the trenches of World War I, disputes among competing factions became increasingly common. The declaration of principles Jaurès drafted for the Toulouse Congress of the SFIO in 1908 illustrates the problems he faced. A masterpiece of artfulness, the declaration offered an unobjectionable set of ultimate ideals and a menu of strategies designed to satisfy any palate. Guesdists could enjoy the projected final coming of collectivism; syndicalists appreciated the acknowledgment that a general strike might prove useful in appropriate circumstances (although that condition meant, for many members of the party, that it would never be useful); and everyone else could savor the party's continuing commitment to work in the short term, through parliamentary channels, for specific, limited reforms. Whether shrewd or sophistic, declarations of this sort kept the party together: in Toulouse, all but one of the 326 delegates voted to accept Jaurès's statement of principles.[32] As issues of foreign policy began to overshadow intraparty maneuvering after 1911, the importance of such exercises in obfuscation faded for Jaurès. Imperialist competition was hardening into international rivalry, and governments assumed increasingly menacing postures to satisfy bloodthirsty patriots. With a dense fog of nationalism descending over France, Jaurès embarked on what he called "the grandest of battles, the affirmation of peace."[33]

When two Serbian nationalists assassinated the Austrian Archduke Francis Ferdinand on June 28, 1914, Europe found the key that two

Moroccan wars and two Balkan wars had failed to uncover; all the tumblers fell smoothly into place, and the door to catastrophe swung open. Prodded by Jaurès, the SFIO proclaimed on July 16 that it would use all the means at its disposal—including the revolutionary general strike, which Jaurès had previously opposed but now endorsed as the weapon of last resort against war—to prevent the outbreak of fighting. Willfully misinterpreting Jaurès's dedication to peace as treason, the nationalist press shrieked its outrage and demanded his head. Ironically, he understood the revolutionary consequences of a general war more clearly than did its partisans. As he predicted in his address to the delegates of the Second International in Brussels on August 29, "When typhus finishes the work begun by bullets, disillusioned men will turn on their rulers, whether German, French, Russian, or Italian, and demand their explanation for all those corpses. Then the unchained Revolution will cry out to them: 'Begone, and ask pardon of God and men!'" But Jaurès did not see that prophecy fulfilled. On the evening of July 31, while sitting in a café discussing the next day's issue of *L'Humanité* and his plans to "expose everyone responsible for this crisis," he was murdered. Jaurès's killer, a zealous but unstable drifter sympathetic with the rabid nationalists who branded Jaurès a traitor, sought to transform an empty life by performing a single meaningful act of incalculable significance, a pattern of political assassination that has since become numbingly familiar. Although he surely could not have prevented the eruption of war, Jaurès was perhaps the one individual who might have led France to a different sort of peace.[34]

Yet there was a sad aptness in Jaurès's death on the eve of global conflict. For the world that dawned in August 1914 was a world of revolution and fascism in which Jaurès would have been a stranger. It is fruitless to speculate whether the spirit of moderation, optimism, and idealism that illuminated his radical vision of politics might have survived had he been available to defend it; in fact, it died when he did. Understandably, "*Ils ont tué Jaurès!*" remains a rallying cry for the French left. When François Mitterrand laid a wreath at Jaurès's tomb after his inauguration in 1981 as the first socialist president of France's Fifth Republic, he was trying to resurrect a collective memory of hopes that were buried with Jaurès. Not in the seventy years since his death have his ideals found a spokesman of his stature.

When Germany invaded Belgium three days after Jaurès's assassination, the international solidarity of the French and German working classes shattered. The proletariat's universal brotherhood, solemnly and repeatedly proclaimed for twenty-five years at the meetings of the Second International, vanished in the face of pleas to defend the fatherland. The most persistent denials of nationalist loyalty had come from Europe's most powerful socialist party, the German SPD (Sozialdemokratische Partei Deutschlands). When the moment of decision came, however, the SPD delegation in the Reichstag voted unanimously in favor of war credits, and leading German socialists scrambled to keep up with the party's rank and file in declaring their enthusiastic support of German war aims. Among those who eventually

committed political suicide by bolting from the party and advocating a nego-
tiated peace was the leading German theorist of social democracy, Eduard
Bernstein (1850–1932). Typical of his career, Bernstein's decision to join the
Independent Social Democratic party in 1917 was motivated by a deep sense
of conviction and marred by bad timing. Too late to serve usefully as a har-
binger yet too early merely to register a fait acompli, Bernstein ultimately
found himself classified with the "back stabbers" saddled with responsibility
for Germany's defeat. From the time he first left his native Berlin in 1878 until
he left the Reichstag in 1928, it was Bernstein's fate to be almost constantly
out of step with either his party or his nation or both. Although he ranked
with Karl Kautsky and Rosa Luxemburg among the most influential theorists
of his generation in Germany, he lost most of the battles he fought during his
lifetime, and it is only recently that his work has again begun to receive serious and sympathetic attention.[35]

The combination of a small income and a large family meant that Bernstein's parents, who were nonpracticing Jews, were unable to afford the cost
of educating all of their fifteen children. Eduard went to work as a bank teller
at age sixteen without completing secondary school, and what education he
received later came from his own reading. Distracted by his interest in poetry
and drama, he considered abandoning the bank for a theatrical career,
although whether as actor or dramatist he could not decide. During the early
1870s he became more seriously interested in socialism, and he formed a discussion club that brought him into contact with the wealthy socialist
sympathizer Karl Höchberg. Impressed with the young man's energy, Höchberg asked Bernstein to serve as his assistant in his travels as secretary of the
socialist periodical *Die Zukunft.* Although leaving the bank's security for a
temporary position seemed a reckless step, Bernstein was intrigued by the
adventure and set off for Switzerland in 1878. He would not set foot in Germany again for twenty-two years.[36]

Bernstein's evolution during those years in exile oddly paralleled that of
the German socialist movement from which he was isolated. In 1878
Bismarck announced his antisocialist legislation, and the embryonic socialist
movement, whose more and less revolutionary Eisenacher and Lassallean
portions had united only in 1875, was forced to go underground. Having been
formally declared enemies of the state by Bismarck, German socialists
became just that. Like many German socialists, Bernstein was converted to
Marxism by these repressive measures, which made it impossible for him to
return to Germany and continue his work in the socialist press, and by reading Engels's *Anti-Dühring*, a book that seemed to make sense of the German
state's hostility and offered a revolutionary alternative. Engels's volume,
translated into English as *Socialism: Utopian and Scientific*, not only
provided a response to Eugen Dühring, an economist with anti-Semitic
inclinations who believed a strong labor movement could transform capitalism without revolution, but more importantly offered an exposition of
Marxism more concise and comprehensive than anything Marx himself
wrote. It was also, unfortunately, a simplification, and it served as a

sourcebook for those who wanted to praise Marxism (or bury it) without bothering to study Marx's writings.

August Bebel, the leading political figure among German socialists, selected Bernstein in 1880 to serve as editor of the party's Zurich-based international socialist newspaper. But he feared that Bernstein's association with the bourgeois Höchberg would make him suspect to Marx and Engels, so Bebel personally escorted Bernstein on a pilgrimage to London. There Bernstein passed the masters' inspection by demonstrating that he was even more radical than most of the party's publicists, and with the blessing of Marx and Engels he assumed the influential post of editor of the *Sozialdemocrat.* In 1888 he was deported from Switzerland, an unambigous if unwelcome tribute to his notoriety. He settled in London, became a close friend of Engels's, and continued to trumpet the message of orthodox Marxism above the voices beginning to whisper their misgivings about international proletarian revolution.[37]

A gradual process of radicalization led the SPD to declare allegiance to revolutionary Marxism in the Erfurt Program of 1891, and that process reflected the peculiarities of German development. In contrast to the United States and Great Britain, in Germany revolutionary socialism as a political force antedated trade unionism. Because the German proletariat was thoroughly politicized by the time the state recognized labor's right to organize, the political party of the working class created the trade unions. In America and Britain radical politics tended to develop from the labor movement, or in the case of the Populists from agrarian unrest. On the continent trade unionism developed into socialism; in the United States and Great Britain socialism remained largely trade unionist. While the sequence of development was the same in both France and Germany, industrialization in France was so slow, and so limited in scope, that the proletarianization of the working class that fed the growth of the SPD in the 1880s and 1890s did not occur. Moreover, in France the barrier to socialism represented by the continuation of artisanal work patterns was reinforced politically by the perpetuation of anarchist tendencies on the one hand and republican sympathies on the other. By contrast, the structural disadvantages built into the German constitution, especially the class voting system and the limited power of the Reichstag, denied socialists the opportunity to exert political influence equal to that of the French left even as the SPD grew in popularity. During the years of the antisocialist laws, from 1878 to 1890, the party leadership fastened itself to a fiery rhetorical position from which the German working class, by virtue of its slowly but perceptibly improving economic situation, gradually drifted away.[38] It was into that widening gap between the party's history and its official philosophy of history that Bernstein was to insert the German version of social democratic theory, revisionism.

The difference between the economic progress and the political powerlessness of the working class reflected the uneven rates of industrial and social development in Germany between 1870 and 1914. Economic change accelerated as the bourgeoisie adapted to the new possibilities of transforming the nation into an industrial power, but political change sputtered to a halt as Bismarck worked to satisfy the Junker elite that formed the basis of his power. The Junkers, trying to preserve their ability to determine the shape of politics as their economic power shrank, allied with rising industrialists in the broad coalition politics that protected Germany's upper class from the demands of an increasingly well-organized but still politically impotent working class.[39] The interventionist state was thus developed in Germany not in response to democratic pressure from below but precisely in order to forestall such democratization by offering the carrot of social insurance plans and economic expansion together with the stick of repressive legislation.

Against the anvil of this *Sammlungspolitik*, German socialists hammered the SPD into a revolutionary party during the 1880s. The rigid resistance of combined agrarian and industrial elites to democratization hardened the attitude of workers already suspicious of the state, and the depth of the division of German society and politics prompted at least some workers to construct their own countersociety in opposition to the official culture of Wilhelmine Germany. Between the SPD and the trade unions, German socialists provided an elaborate alternative social world to satisfy many of the economic, cultural, and political needs of the proletariat. Despite the formal split between this workers' subculture and the world of the bourgeoisie, however, no distinctive values developed independently of the dominant culture from which workers were excluded. Committed to a strategy of "revolutionary waiting," which trumpeted their opposition without committing them to extralegal challenges to the state that might arrest the growth of their institutions, the leaders of the SPD often found that the pariah status they used to build the party and the unions undercut their efforts to construct a viable set of substantive cultural norms. Instead workers merely aped the bourgeoisie they claimed to scorn. Beneath their proclaimed allegiance to the party, "negative integration" wedded them to a society whose state they held in contempt.[40] Neither the British Labour party, the French SFIO, nor the various American political protest movements (including the Populists) offered their members the all-encompassing system of counterinstitutions available to German workers. The difference showed up in the relative levels of rebelliousness in their rhetoric more than it manifested itself in action. But as the German experience after World War I demonstrated, the wounds inflicted on national solidarity by repressive policies and revolutionary rhetoric left scars that refused to heal. In an environment infected by authoritarianism, the attempt of the Weimar Republic to graft democratic politics onto German political culture had little chance of success.

The commitment of German socialists to revolution may have derived clearly from the state's refusal to acknowledge the legitimacy of even their limited appeals, but whatever its source, the strategy of revolutionary waiting locked the party into an awkwardly passive position strikingly inconsistent with its goals. Marx had earlier excoriated German liberals for accepting Kant's idealization of liberty in the *Rechtsstaat*; by the 1890s Bernstein was accusing Germany's self-styled Marxists of reenacting that crime. Marx blamed German liberals for accepting a political situation "in which liberty is still a matter of imagination and sentimentality. Out of too much reverence for the ideas they are not being realized."[41] In the case of the SPD leadership, Bernstein claimed, too much reverence for the idea of history's automatic dialectical progress prevented them from realizing the goal of socialism. The missing link in their Marxism was praxis, which Marx had emphasized but "orthodox Marxists" in the 1880s and 1890s overlooked. As a result, the SPD had become a fraternal brotherhood burdened with eschatological rhetoric, a party that professed to be able to account for the past and predict the future but was puzzled by what to do in the present.

Bernstein calculated his revisionism to expose the inconsistencies of this orthodoxy. He based his assault, appropriately enough, on the unacknowledged Kantian aspects of Marx's thought. As Bernstein understood, Marx hitched Kant's antinomies to the dynamism of historical change by appropriating Hegel's dialectic, and he sought to reconcile them through praxis. Yet Marx's epistemology and politics ultimately rested on the ideal of man as a species-being, a concept of both ethical and political dimensions that indirectly restated Kant's categorical imperative and again pointed to the coherence of Marx's thought with an inverted ideal of the *Rechtsstaat*. Bernstein's revisionism was thus an attempt to examine critically the identification of ethics and politics that distinguished German political thought, in its socialist as well as its liberal mode, from American, British, and French ideas. Bernstein's challenge to Marxism must be understood within the framework of a highly polarized political culture, a party that called for revolution but acted to construct a self-sufficient subculture, and the intensely self-righteous tone of political discourse in Germany. In different ways all of these factors conspired to limit the appeal of revisionism.

No sooner had the SPD proclaimed its official revolutionary doctrine in 1891 than Bernstein began to question it. Like most of the exiled German socialists in London, Bernstein thought little of the ostensibly Marxist Social Democratic Federation and its leader Hyndman; unlike most of the Germans, Bernstein respected the Fabians. His arrival in England coincided with the publication of *Fabian Essays in Socialism*, and his letters to Kautsky reveal that as early as 1891 he was becoming attracted to the Fabians. He was sympathetic with their empirical orientation and their reformism, which he considered complementary and appealing alternatives to the method of "speculative deduction" and the dogmatic revolutionism espoused by Marxists.[42] The first public display of Bernstein's Fabian-inspired apostasy came in 1895, the year of Engels's death, in an enthusiastic afterword Bernstein contributed to his wife Regina's translation of the Webbs' *History of Trade Unionism*. This open declaration of sympathy for a non-Marxist version of socialism came as a surprise in Germany, but among Bernstein's colleagues in London his "funny respect for the Fabians," as Engels described it in a letter to Bebel, had been an open secret for several years.[43]

Bernstein's growing skepticism about orthodox Marxism extended from philosophy to strategy. In a letter to Kautsky written in 1895, he claimed that

German socialists "do no more than bourgeois radical parties elsewhere." The difference "is that we usually conceal this from ourselves and speak a language that is out of alignment with our actions and our capacities." Although Kautsky was scarcely persuaded by such arguments, he encouraged Bernstein to develop his ideas systematically, and between 1896 and 1898 he published in *Die Neue Zeit* a series of articles in which Bernstein elaborated his revisionism. Since Bernstein was a member of the inner circle of Marx and Engels—he had even been named by Engels as one of his literary executors—his heresy of moderation rocked the ideological foundations of the SPD as no previous challenge to orthodox Marxism had done. He published his expanded articles under the title *Die Voraussetzungen des Sozialismus und die Aufgaben der Sozialdemocratie* (*The Presuppositions of Socialism and the Tasks of Social Democracy*, translated into English as *Evolutionary Socialism*), which catapulted Bernstein into a prominent position in the battle raging in the 1890s over the future of socialism as theory and practice.[44]

Bernstein's debt to the Fabians in general, and to the Webbs in particular, is no longer in doubt. Although Bernstein thought it useful to deny the British roots of his ideas when he finally returned to Germany in 1901, neither his Fabian friends nor his German critics doubted that Bernstein saw the world, as Rosa Luxemburg put it, "through 'English spectacles.'" Indeed, the decisive moment of Bernstein's revisionist epiphany may have occurred during a lecture he delivered before the Fabian Society on January 29, 1897. According to a detailed report of the lecture appearing in *Fabian News*, Bernstein offered a spirited defense of orthoxdox Marxism and a strident rebuke of reformers. The working-class movement in England, he concluded, "would be all the stronger through its isolation if an earthquake could remove the Haldanes and Dilkes, the Webbs and the Shaws." Defiant as those words appear, however, it was Bernstein rather than the Fabians who converted as a result of this encounter. As he later wrote to Bebel, Bernstein became aware during his attempt to answer the Fabians' common sensical questions about economic and political conditions that he was engaged in an ultimately futile rescue operation. In their attempt to show that Marx had foreseen, and Marxists could explain, developments clearly inconsistent with the ideas expressed in *Capital*, socialists were swimming against a current growing steadily more powerful.[45]

Bernstein's desire to deny the Fabians' influence stemmed from the hostile reaction his ideas received in Germany, where even those engaged in nudging the SPD toward reformism denounced his work. His failure to attract supporters seems puzzling in light of the clear trend toward moderation in the activities of the SPD during the 1890s, and it illustrates dramatically the importance of the party's revolutionary rhetoric in preserving its self-image. Accentuating German socialists' sense of themselves as outlaws was the threat represented by the Subversion Bill of 1895 and the Penitentiary Bill of 1897, the attempts by Wilhelm II to reinvigorate the antisocialist campaign allowed to lapse after Bismarck's fall from power. The emperor's vow to destroy the SPD proved empty when the Reichstag rejected his proposals, but his scare tactics further widened the gap between the members of his ruling coalition and the working class. Confronted with the prospect of renewed repression in Wilhelm's *Sammlungspolitik*, German socialists understandably considered Bernstein's criticism of the class struggle misguided and his moderate reformism naive. While plausible in Great Britain, France, and even the United States, where social democrats made limited progress around the turn of the century, such ideas ran into the roadblock of class politics in Germany.

At party congresses in Hannover in 1899 and in Dresden in 1903, revisionism was formally condemned as "a policy of accommodation to the existing order" that "would turn a party that was revolutionary in the best sense into one that would be content to reform bourgeois society." Bernstein was not expelled from the party, and he was able to muster enough votes to serve almost continuously in the Reichstag from 1902 until 1928, but his status as a theorist remained shaky. From Ignaz Auer, the party secretary who advocated reformism in practice but refrained from justifying it with theory, on the right flank, to Rosa Luxemburg, the radical responsible for the most influential of the challenges to Bernstein in her *Sozialreform oder Revolution?* (1899), on the left flank, Bernstein's ideas attracted attacks from every angle with in his own party. The vote for his condemnation at Dresden, 288 to 11, demonstrates the unpopularity of his theory just as clearly as the actual evolution of the SPD from 1891 to 1914 demonstrates the accuracy of his analysis.[46] The party continued to invoke Marx's name as it gravitated toward Bernstein's strategy. The failure of Weimar, which certainly reflected the polarization of German politics as much as it reflected the mistakes of the SPD leadership, can be traced at least in part to that disjunction.

Bernstein titled his memoirs *My Years of Exile*, and although the book covers only his years in Switzerland and England, the phrase fits his entire career. In a sense he was always an exile, as much when he returned to Germany as when he was away. It was his fate always to fight on enemy terrain, where he did not know the contours of the battlefield, his opponents' intellectual and political supply lines were shorter and stronger than his, and their ability to muster reinforcements underscored his isolation. Not surprisingly, therefore, it was also his fate always to lose. Yet his defeats notwithstanding, he deserves the attention he has recently received. Despite his inability to persuade German socialists to turn from sterile dogmatism to fruitful uncertainty, from frozen revolutionism to flexible reformism, and despite his limitations as a theorist, he understood the problems of orthodox Marxism and the futility of revolutionary waiting. He tried to point the SPD toward a political strategy that, had it succeeded, might have enabled Germany to develop after World War I as it has after World War II, in the direction of social democracy rather than fascism. Given the shape of German history, however, his failure was hardly his fault, for in a climate so hostile to the ideas of moderation, equality, and democracy, it is difficult to see how he could have succeeded.

The European and American theorists who tried, with varying degrees of success, to reclaim socialism from its utopian and orthodox Marxist proponents were almost exact contemporaries. Bernstein, born in 1850, was the oldest of them; Rauschenbusch, born in 1861, was the youngest. Without exception, they completed their most important theoretical work between 1885 and 1915. As I have indicated, they drew their ideas from a wide array of sources reflecting different national traditions and personal predilections, but they shared a desire to reconcile the differences between the various strands of socialist theory. Jaurès provided perhaps the most ambitious statement of this goal in his thesis *The Origins of German Socialism.* He endeavored to show the compatibility of idealism with empiricism in the development of German philosophy, and to trace the roots of socialist theory beyond Hegel to Fichte, Kant, and even Luther. He argued that if Marxists would recognize their origins in philosophical idealism, they might disengage themselves from doctrines of objectivistic materialism and inevitability, and socialists of other persuasions might be more inclined to ally with them. Viewed in light of their origins, he wrote, "dialectical socialism is in harmony with moral socialism, German socialism with French socialism." Moreover, Jaurès predicted that "the hour is approaching when they will converge, when all the forces of conscience, when the aspiration for dignity and genuine freedom, will unite with the immanent dialectic of history and the universe."[47]

That idea of convergence loomed large in the theory of social democracy, and it manifested itself in these thinkers' sense of participation in an international movement and in the web of personal connections that tied them together. As I have noted, Bernstein's revisionism was nourished by the Fabians. Ely and Rauschenbusch both acknowledged their debt to the Webbs, and Rauschenbusch noted that he "used Bernstein freely" in his public lectures on political reform. The *Fabian News* turned to Bernstein for reports on German socialism after he left England. When the Webbs set up a series of lectures under the title "Socialism Restated" in 1913, they arranged for Jaurès to preside over the session on politics. The *Revue de Paris,* which published some of Jaurès's most important essays, including "Socialism and Liberty," stressed the Fabians' influence in English politics and solicited a lengthy essay by "one of the most talented and most remarkable men" of the time, Sidney Webb. When the Fabian Society published Tract # 29, *What to Read on Social and Political Subjects,* in 1901, the list included, among others, books by Green, Sidgwick, L. T. Hobhouse, Bernstein, Ely, and the Webbs; five years later Jaurès was added to the list. The Fabian reading room subscribed to only two daily newspapers, the progressive *Manchester Guardian* and Jaurès's *L'Humanité.*[48] Such examples could be multiplied to weave a tighter pattern of connections, but I want only to suggest that the partisans of social democracy recognized the international dimensions of the intellectual and political processes that were bringing together and moderating different strands of socialism. I do not want to exaggerate these thinkers' influence on one another or minimize their awareness of the limits imposed on different socialist movements by distinctive national conditions.[49] Instead

I intend to examine, by analyzing their contributions to the creation of a transatlantic community of discourse, the convergence of their ideas concerning the sources, strategy, and ideals of social democracy.

2. The Critique of Socialist Reason

In November of 1898, as the storm generated by his revisionism was gathering force, Bernstein explained his goals in a letter to Kautsky. Bernstein believed that socialism, locked into a deterministic, scientistic version of Marxism by Engels and Bebel, badly needed a Kant. Just as Kant designed his three critiques to rescue philosophy from the opposite traps of dogmatism and skepticism, so Bernstein intended to provide, in his words, "a critique of socialist reason." Kant had uncovered the conditions of experience and demonstrated the impossibility of metaphysics; Bernstein wanted to expose the shallow positivism of so-called scientific socialism in order to show the impossibility of certain knowledge concerning social and political questions. In much the same way that Kant had banished such notions as God and the good from the realm of knowledge but preserved them as regulative ideas, Bernstein at once denied the inevitability of socialism while affirming its desirability. Like Kant, he shattered cherished claims to certainty. Like the philosophers of the *via media*, he argued that extending a thoroughgoing empiricism to all of our knowledge means that our admission of uncertainty must be unconditional.[50]

Although only Bernstein spoke in terms of a "critique of socialist reason," the spirit of his criticism was characteristic of these social democrats' approach to the questions of knowledge and action. They believed that socialists should abandon the pretense of science as a shield for their political ideas. Rejecting prevailing conceptions of scientific socialism as objectivist and reductionist, they contended that socialists could proceed in the critical spirit of postpositivist science and philosophy only by remaining open-minded and constantly reexamining their assumptions. Just as reason can never be pure because the mind cannot escape the conditions of its knowing, so socialism can never be the pure science that such self-styled guardians of Marxist orthodoxy as Kautsky, Guesde, Hyndman, and DeLeon claimed it could be. If socialism is to become critical, it must avoid dogmatism and acknowledge the limits of all knowledge. Socialists must drop their smug confidence in the inevitable triumph of the proletariat and get on with the business of gathering ammunition for the ongoing political struggle to accomplish their goals. Bernstein, Jaurès, Rauschenbusch, Ely, and the Webbs adopted a radically empiricist approach to politics, a philosophical perspective strongly resembling that of the philosophers of the *via media* in its appreciation of knowledge as a continuous process of truth testing and its recognition of the historical and qualitative dimensions of understanding.

Only Jaurès carried his examination of the conditions of knowledge into a detailed analysis of consciousness itself. As early as 1882, Jaurès staked out an epistemological position similar to the radical philosophers' doctrine of immediate experience. He denied that science could explain the evolution of living consciousness, yet at the same time he considered idealism a rejection of the world's existence. "With brute matter and its movement," he argued, "you cannot explain the smallest fact of animal or human consciousness, the slightest sensation." Jaurès contended that between the movement of the acoustic nerve and a sound, between a vibration of the optic nerve and the color blue, and between the tearing of a tissue and a sensation of acute pain, there is no comprehensible connection. "So science cannot by itself explain the bases of the universe."[51] In his search for a satisfactory theory of knowledge, Jaurès advanced a sophisticated analysis of pure experience.

In the first of his two theses, *On the Reality of the Sensible World*, he launched a critique of idealist and empiricist epistemology. He denied the adequacy of either sensation or consciousness, independent of the other, as a source of knowledge. The awareness of the unity of existence, which is part of what we call knowledge, does not derive entirely from information given by our senses. Yet Kant's concepts of time and space as abstract are inadequate because they are too far removed from the objects of concrete experience. The mind contributes the "substantial unity" of phenomena that we experience, but it constructs the world only in intimate connection with external reality, as the difference between dreams and real experience shows. Like the radical theorists of knowledge, Jaurès maintained that experience cannot be understood according to the standard distinction between mind and matter. He substituted for both the empiricist and idealist dualisms a conception of immediate experience as the junction of sensation and reflection. "The consciousness tied to the brain is not at all isolated from the world, but, to the contrary, it is tied to the world." Attempts to extract consciousness from the material world or to reduce it to sensation falsify experience, Jaurès contended, because we can approach an understanding of how we know only in the unity of subjective and objective, mind and matter.[52]

Jaurès's treatment of Bergson, who was a classmate of his at the Ecole Normale, reflects the congruity between his ideas and the radical theory of knowledge. He criticized Bergson's excessive emphasis on intuitions, and he cited as a corrective to Bergson the writings of Fouillée on the role of ideas in activity. "It is necessary that energy, at the same time that it exercises itself in different ways, be brought to a certain unity of direction and form by consciousness." Our feeling of effort, then, is not simply muscular, Jaurès insisted. It also involves, as "M. Fouillée has quite ingeniously and quite firmly demonstrated," the activity of the psyche.[53] By thus endorsing Fouillée's concept of *idée-force*, in contradistinction to Bergson's more amorphous notion of *élan-vital*, Jaurès signaled his affinity with the radical reading of immediate experience as the intersection of subject and object in the socially and historically situated context of individual life.

Bernstein, as part of his attempt to become the Kant of social democracy, tried to analyze the conditions of knowledge to steer socialism away from

Engels's simple-minded positivism. Unfortunately, because he lacked Jaurès's philosophical training and also his acuity, Bernstein's efforts were less successful. In a series of appreciative if hardly enthusiastic essays on the neo-Kantian philosopher F. A. Lange in 1892, Bernstein began to challenge the grander claims of Marxists concerning the metaphysical status of their materialism. Following Lange, and Kant, he suggested that our yearning for positive knowledge outside the phenomenal realm should not be confounded with actual knowledge in such matters. Knowledge cannot extend beyond the sphere of experience, Bernstein cautioned, and socialists who overstepped that boundary were no more realistic than those they ridiculed as speculative philosophers.[54] Bernstein elaborated this criticism in his essays in *Die Neue Zeit* and in *Evolutionary Socialism*, but he was unable to persuade either Marxists or neo-Kantians. Bebel chided him for creating bitterness in the party by raising fundamental doubts about the philosophical adequacy of dialectical materialism; Karl Vorländer, a leading neo-Kantian, wondered whether Bernstein really understood either Lange or Kant.

Bernstein may have been correct that socialism needed a Kant, but his efforts to fill that gap, particularly insofar as his analysis of the conditions of knowledge was concerned, must be judged a failure. He hoped his counsel of cautious empiricism would engender a more critical attitude among socialists whose self-satisfaction stood in the way of productive activity. Given the outlaw status of the SPD, that message could scarcely have been less welcome. As the socialist Lily Braun remarked after listening to Bernstein in 1901, "We had expected a prophet of a new truth, and instead we saw before us a doubter."[55] She identified precisely the thrust of Bernstein's argument, that there is no truth that should not be doubted, but it was an argument no one in the German socialist movement was prepared to hear. As first Engels and then Kautsky boiled Marxism down to a kind of positivism for the proletariat they lost much of its richness, but the doctrinaire revolutionism that remained was the lifeblood of the SPD. When Bernstein challenged that dogma with his proclamation of creative uncertainty, he found himself alone in his dissent.

Anglo-American social democrats ventured less deeply into the tangled forests of neo-Kantian *Kritik*, both because of their predispositions and because an undoctrinaire empiricism was more prevalent in the British and American political traditions. The Webbs believed that people with widely different philosophical views could support their politics provided they made a compelling case for their ideas, and they consciously avoided theoretical issues in their quest for information. As they wrote in the preface to the final two volumes of their massive ten-volume history of English local government, they believed that political theory, like biological theory or "theoretical mechanics," must proceed from a solid empirical basis. In addition to studies of economic or political theory, "there is room for a detailed study of the form and life-history of the social institutions in which the theoretic conceptions are actually manifested."[56] In their tireless devotion to the pursuit of such knowledge, they seldom provided a single demonstration where a dozen might do, and they never tried to substitute deft arguments for bulky evidence. To the Webbs, less was never more.

Ely and Rauschenbusch argued in a similar spirit, if less exhaustively, that social analysis must rely on empirical study rather than deductive reasoning. The long-standing emphasis of capitalists on a hidden hand and of Christians on another world proved doubly damaging. It allowed the church to ease into the prevailing "narrow, negative, individualistic attitude" almost by default, and that orientation antagonized those who should be attracted to Christianity by its professed commitment to the dignity and brotherhood of all men.[57] Only by returning from disembodied theological disputes to the stuff of social reality could churchmen exert any influence, and for that reason Ely and Rauschenbusch attempted to prod Christians away from a preoccupation with salvation and to turn their attention toward their communities. At the same time they hoped to persuade socialists to reconsider their programmatic approach to social change. On the basis of their commitment to what Rauschenbusch called "a continuous and progressive unfolding of the truth," these American social democrats argued that socialists should look critically at the sources of injustice and the steps that might realistically be taken to solve immediate problems. As Christians looked beyond experience and focused on eternal life, so socialists concentrated on ultimate solutions and ignored the piecemeal reforms that might nudge society closer to their eventual goal. Both groups should embrace the "idea of relativity," as Ely termed it, and maintain a "large tolerance" for "the spirit of enquiry," in Rauschenbusch's phrase, because blind obedience to prevailing ideas would condemn society to stagnation.[58] Only Jaurès among these theorists of social democracy advanced a sophisticated analysis of immediate experience, but all of them championed an expanded and open-ended empiricism as the only source of knowledge safe from the delusions of dogma.

They also subscribed to the cluster of ideas I have designated the theory of voluntary action. In *The Social Aspects of Christianity* (1889), which signaled the beginning of the radical phase of the social gospel movement, Ely stressed the role of individual volition in social construction and economic development. "The economic life of man," he maintained, "is to some considerable extent the product of human will." No invisible hand or underlying dialectic determines human choices, although existing conditions limit the range of available options. Viewed in this light, political economy occupies a position "midway between physical or natural science and mental science. It is a combination of both." Ely expanded that argument in *An Introduction to Political Economy*, where he again distinguished his ideas from the emphasis on inevitability typical of both classical and Marxist economics. While admitting the importance of historical circumstances in economic development, he emphasized that "the changes which continually take place in our economic life are in great part the product of human will, for this will of ours is a chief economic factor."[59] Social development follows no laws automatically, because individual choices help to shape social interaction. Rauschenbusch stated this position succinctly. Stressing the connection between voluntarism and praxis, he contended that "character is formed by action, but after it is formed, it determines action. What a man says and does, he becomes; and what he has become, he says and does."[60] This conception of the reciprocal relation between volition and activity, which echoed the analysis of Fouillée, James, and Dewey in particular, recurred in social democratic theory. Although historical circumstances limit options, choices forge character, and character powerfully affects the direction of social change.

Given his conception of the role of consciousness in knowledge, Jaurès understandably rejected all attempts to deny the active force of individual volition. He contrasted the French emphasis on the freedom of the individual, an idea whose roots he traced to Descartes, with the German concentration on the connections binding the individual to the universal order in both its human and divine spheres. That difference manifested itself, Jaurès contended, in French and German politics. Characteristically, he suggested that a more fruitful course, both philosophically and politically, lay in the combination of these alternative conceptions of the individual. A philosophy equally sensitive to the importance of individual volition and social responsibility, it seems, would combine Kant with Rousseau. The goal of socialism, as Jaurès conceived it, is justice, "which is taking on an ever larger and more definite meaning. It has come to signify that in every man, in every individual, humanity ought to be fully respected and exalted to its complete stature." What is involved in that ideal? "True humanity can only exist," according to Jaurès, "where there is independence, active exercise of the will, free and joyous adaptation of the individual and the whole."[61] Justice requires positive freedom, the independent exercise of volition. Bernstein's similar emphasis on individual freedom of choice was among the most dramatic of his departures from orthodox Marxism. In contrast to the determinism preached by Kautsky, he insisted that a part of human activity can only be accounted for by the intervention of a certain individual creativity. In the "sovereignty of the human spirit as opposed to the forces of nature," Bernstein saw irrefutable evidence of volition.[62]

Beatrice Webb's writings illustrate the combination of empiricism and voluntarism with a pragmatic theory of truth. In her opening remarks in *Our Partnership*, she claimed that both she and her husband were "scientists and at the same time socialists." They "failed to find in the universe anything that was supernatural, or incapable of demonstration by the scientific method of observation, hypothetical generalization and experimental or other form of verification." Later in the book, however, quoting from her diary dated March 13, 1910, she expressed her belief that Shaw and other Fabians such as H. G. Wells "go wrong, from the standpoint of realism in its best sense," in completely ignoring religion. "By religion," she continued, "I mean the communion of the soul with some righteousness *felt to be outside and above itself.* This may take the form of conscious prayer; or the unconscious form of ever-present and persisting aspirations—a faith, a hope, and a devotion to wholly disinterested purpose."[63] This statement seems to contradict her unqualified endorsement of the scientific method, but it harmonizes with

Ely's and Rauschenbusch's ideal of the social gospel, with Jaurès's respect for the "common beliefs that bind souls together and attach them to the infinite,"[64] and with Bernstein's notion of socialism as an ideal, "a piece of the beyond."[65] Was there a contradiction between these social democrats' commitment to empiricism and their references to the religious or humanitarian sentiment animating social reform?

The resolution of that paradox lies in their appreciation of the importance of values in human activity, and in their understanding that the truth of such values cannot be established outside the arena of social practice. It is clear from passages in her diaries that Beatrice Webb was familiar with James's writings; she mentioned reading *The Principles of Psychology* and *The Will to Believe* in particular. Like the other theorists of social democracy, she and her husband sought to broaden empiricism by connecting it to pragmatic principles of truth testing. In a discussion of the conflict between "the Ego that denies" and "the Ego that affirms," she admitted that one part of her steadfastly believed that "with regard to the purpose of life, science is, and must remain bankrupt; and the men of science to-day know it." The goal toward which we must aim instead "depends on a human scale of values, a scale of values which alters from race to race, from generation to generation, and from individual to individual. How each of us determines our scale of values no one knows."[66] The importance and irreducibility of values was an integral part of social democratic theory.

These theorists accepted the pragmatists' conception of the fiduciary quality of all knowledge, and they recognized the connection between, and also the independence of, pragmatic methods and social values. As Beatrice Webb wrote elsewhere in her diary, "We differ from the Benthamites in thinking that it is necessary that we should all agree as to ends, or that these can be determined by any science." Since that passage was written less than a month after her reading of James's *Will to Believe*, it is possible that such ideas were directly connected in her mind with James's pragmatism. But the question of influence notwithstanding, her judgment of the difference between science as a technique for determining ends and as a method of analyzing means clearly parallels the pragmatists' arguments, particularly those of Dewey's instrumentalism: "Science and the scientific method can be applied," she wrote, "not to the discovery of a right end, but to a discovery of a right way of getting to any particular ends."[67] Science should guide our investigations and our considerations of practicality, but we must derive our values from another source. In other words, we must choose. Bernstein contended that "what is specifically socialistic" in socialism "is only one thing: the view of ethical or legal right." But the claims of Engels to the contrary notwithstanding, such a perspective "is no science."[68]

Rauschenbusch and Jaurès both traced the belief among socialists and bourgeois professionals in the scientific status of social and political values to the lingering prestige of positivism, which blinded its adherents to the contingent quality of their belief by glorifying as science what was merely a species of dogma. Because socialist ideas were formulated at the height of positivist enthusiasm, Rauschenbusch pointed out, naturalism and materialism were associated in much socialist thinking. "Thus we have the tragic fact that the most idealistic mass movement of modern times was committed at the outset to a materialistic philosophy with which it had no essential connection." Speaking to the graduating class of the Rochester Theological Seminary in May, 1914, he affirmed the pragmatic principle that "all study should result in wisdom and validate itself in action." We must learn "to couple the critical instinct with modesty and reverence," because we can "at most approximate the truth and will never reach it perfectly."[69] Like the Benthamites, orthodox Marxists assumed that social values are unproblematical because they are scientific. The theorists of social democracy challenged that conception and insisted that the question of ends cannot be identified with the question of means, that norms embody the choices we make personally as individuals and collectively as a culture. They reflect our values, not simply the nature of things.

The Webbs encapsulated this set of ideas about the need for a broadened empiricism and the irreducibly qualitative aspect of human experience in their inaugural issue of *The New Statesman* in 1913. After explaining their commitment to independence from "ties of party, class, or creed," they affirmed the ideal of community responsibility toward which they were aiming. "The world movement toward collectivism is altogether above and beyond party, and our belief in it rests neither upon dogma nor upon a desire to support any sectional interest." Committed to an ideal for which they made no scientific claims, they argued against Benthamites, Marxists, and positivists that "social problems may not be—indeed, are not—susceptible of scientific analysis," because "human beings are not to be weighed in balances nor measured with micrometers." Nevertheless, they concluded, "unless there can be applied to them at least something of the detachment of the scientific spirit," social problems "will never be satisfactorily solved."[70] That manifesto could have served for all the theorists of social democracy, who were committed to the desirability of socialism without pretending to have an irrefutable warrant for their choice of values, and who believed that the collection of empirical data about social and political issues might contribute to the political struggle for progressive change.

Believing as they did in voluntary action, these social democrats rejected all doctrines of inevitability in human affairs. As Sidney Webb put it, the *Zeitgeist* passes no acts of Parliament and erects no municipal libraries.[71] Individuals do the choosing and acting that drives history, not vice versa. Bernstein characterized orthodox Marxists as Calvinists without God, believers in a predetermined materialist future ruled by the dialectic. He considered the doctrine of historical inevitability a debilitating feature of German socialism. Derived from a blend of Hegelianism, which Bernstein did not understand fully, and mechanistic materialism, which he understood but rejected, the idea of inevitability, Bernstein claimed, had no place in Marx's own philosophy. What Marx achieved as a critic of capitalism, he achieved in spite of rather than because of the dialectical method. Bernstein found his apostasy on this issue particularly painful. He either did not appreciate or could not face the extent to which his revision of Marx's use of the dialectic constituted a rejection of Marx. In a letter to Kautsky written in 1927, he revealed both the tenuousness of his grip on the heritage of Marxism and how tenaciously he continued to hold on to it. He protested that he had never turned away "from the fundamental concepts of the Marxist view of history" but had merely opposed certain interpretations and applications of it. Far from rejecting the essence of Marxism, he had sought only to revise the conclusions Marx and Engels reached in too great haste "as a consequence of their being seduced by the Hegelian dialectic, which after all is not integrally connected to the theory."[72] Whether that judgment was a disingenuous effort at self-justification, a willful distortion, or a simple misreading of Marx, it illustrates Bernstein's desire to be understood as a loyal follower of Marxism, a disciple correcting minor details of the master's theory to reflect changing circumstances.

While Bernstein's treatment of the dialectic as extraneous to Marxism was erroneous, his criticism of orthodox interpreters' emphasis on inevitability made a certain amount of sense, because Marx's writings were ambiguous concerning the place of political activity in a system driven by economic imperatives. In *Evolutionary Socialism*, Bernstein carefully distinguished Marxism from natural science. "Philosophical materialism or the materialism of natural science," he wrote, "is in a mechanical sense deterministic. The Marxist conception of history is not. It allots to the economic foundation of the life of nations no unconditioned determining influence on the forms this life takes." Marx's own brand of economic determinism did differ to a degree from the views of Engels and even more strikingly from the ideas of some of his later followers. But when Bernstein suggested that "the point of economic development attained today leaves the ideological, and especially the ethical, factors greater space for independent activity than was formerly the case,"[73] he was no longer merely clarifying Marx's ideas, he was denying them. For whatever relative roles Marx may have assigned to voluntary action and the economic system in driving the engine of history, it is clear that he did not believe their structural relation shifted over time. By arguing that ideas and ideals were playing an increasingly important role in history, Bernstein unwrapped the armature of Marx's philosophy. As Rosa Luxemburg wrote about Bernstein's Marxism, "We have here, in brief, the explanation of the socialist program by means of 'pure reason.' We have here, to use simpler language, an idealist explanation of socialism. The objective necessity of socialism, the explanation of socialism as the result of the material development of society, falls to the ground."[74] Luxemburg understood better than Bernstein that by denying the identification of "ought" and "must" in the dialectic he renounced the major premise of Marx as well as Hegel. When Bernstein substituted the categorical imperative for the imperatives of the dialectic, he went further "back to Kant," and further away from the Hegelian foundations of Marxism, than he cared to admit. By exchanging the doctrine of inevitability for the idea that socialism is desirable rather than necessary, he separated himself decisively from the Marxist tradition.

Jaurès, who maintained throughout his career that both individual choice and economic conditions contribute to historical change, denied extreme forms of both materialist and idealist analysis. It is difficult to go beyond that general statement, however, because Jaurès's successive treatments of this issue in different contexts contradict one another. In 1894, in his debate with the French Marxist Paul Lafargue, "Idealism and Materialism in the Conception of History," Jaurès held that dialectical materialism provides a one-eyed vision of change. He proposed the alternative of fruitful mediation, which he claimed as the prevalent view of historical development: "There is not, in fact, a single idealist who denies that we cannot realize a higher human ideal without a prior transformation of the economic system; and on the other hand, there are few advocates of economic materialism who do not end by calling on the ideal of justice and right."[75] Marx himself, according to Jaurès, relied on precisely that kind of synthesis.

Six years later, Jaurès seemed to reverse his position. After Bernstein's heretical essays had appeared in *Die Neue Zeit* and *Evolutionary Socialism* had been published, Jaurès delivered an address on Bernstein and the evolution of socialist method. In the controversy between Bernstein and Kautsky, he declared, "I am on the whole with Kautsky." Yet several factors complicate the interpretation of his apparently unambiguous remarks. First, Jaurès wanted to distinguish himself from Bernstein in order to protect his stature in the French socialist movement from Guesde's criticism. Already recognized as a moderate, he understandably feared the consequences of being labeled the French Bernstein. Second, Kautsky's own position in the German socialist movement during the 1890s resembled Jaurès's rather than Guesde's. Kautsky was a moderate in the SPD, flanked on the left by radical revolutionaries and on the right by reformists uninterested in theory at all, and by placing himself "*dans l'ensemble de Kautsky*" Jaurès did not repudiate revisionism as decisively as it might appear. He did, however, shore up his left flank against his critics in the French socialist movement. But the third and principal reason Jaurès turned his back on Bernstein had to do with the latter's economic analysis, a question to be addressed in the next section. Jaurès did take the occasion to affirm the role of economic factors in history more decisively than Bernstein had done. While acknowledging the importance of ideas and volition, he contended that individual action "is limited by economic conditions and is finally subordinated to economic conditions." He concluded firmly that "it is the economic system that is the basis" of historical change.[76]

Jaurès softened his stance in a letter to Bernstein several months after this address, but he still contended that Marx's "method of historical materialism, when . . . it is not debased by absolute childishness, as Lafargue has done here and Franz Mehring in your country, is an excellent guide."[77] To Jaurès, however, historical materialism did not imply strict mechanistic determinism, as he explained in "Question de méthode: 'le Manifeste communiste' de Marx et Engels" (cited hereafter as "The Question of Method"), a document that further complicates the unraveling of his attitude toward Bernstein and the question of inevitability. Jaurès abruptly dismissed Marx and Engels's theory of revolution as "the result of worn-out historical hypotheses." In the *Communist Manifesto* they had predicted that the proletariat would come to power by riding the crest of a bourgeois revolution, but Jaurès maintained that the working class ought to mobilize politically behind the socialist party and actively promote democratic reform instead of merely waiting for revolution.[78] As Jaurès once again struck the chord of voluntarism and praxis, he endorsed an antifatalistic idea of social action resembling Bernstein's revisionist criticism of orthodox Marxism. The differences that remained between these two theorists, in sum, had more to do with economic analysis and socialist strategy than with their ideas concerning voluntary action and the inevitability of revolution.

Ely and Rauschenbusch both agreed that while social progress is desirable—Rauschenbusch even considered it "divine"—it is not inevitable. They too stressed the necessity of voluntary social action, and they contrasted their vision of change with Marx's dialectical materialism. Ely provided the clearest statement of their critique in *Socialism and Social Reform*: Every student of society now admits the influence of economic conditions, he wrote, "but to make everything depend upon economic forces, is shutting one's eyes to other forces, equally great and sometimes greater; and one must be blind to historical and actual phenomena who would make religion merely a product of economic life." Religion, he continued, is an "independent force, often sufficient to modify and even to shape economic institutions." Socialists who subscribe to a determinism "as inflexible as cast iron" overlook the significance of voluntary action and thus misunderstand the nature of social change. Society, Ely insisted, "is not an automaton. That society has some option, some choice, and a conscience to which an appeal can be made, is a fact, if there is any such thing as a fact at all." Employing a form of argument characteristic of these social democrats, Ely relied on empirical evidence to establish the significance of choice in human action. As his argument illustrates, empiricism and voluntarism did not contradict but rather reinforced one another in social democratic theory.[79]

By removing the filter of necessity from the socialist vision of change, these thinkers hoped to clarify the need for political action. They wanted to trade the orthodox doctrine of inevitability, with its implications of passivity that manifested themselves in the strategy of revolutionary waiting, for Marx's idea of praxis, and thereby to infuse a spirit of reformist activism into the socialist movement. According to Ely and Rauschenbusch, this new energy could begin to flow through the entire polity only after three dissimilar but equally debilitating misconceptions were corrected. First, orthodox economists must shift their focus from the descriptive question of how economies function to the normative question of how they ought to function; political economy must become, in Ely's phrase, ethical economics.[80] Second, the Christian church must reverse the process, which began shortly after Christ's death, matured in the writings of Augustine, and continued into the nineteenth century, of fixing its eyes on another world. Christians must appreciate that Christ's message was not confined to the speculative or meditative realm. Not only was Jesus "the first real socialist," Rauschenbusch insisted. "He was more; he was the first real man." He preached the gospel of brotherhood, whose message for the industrial age "is to make over an anti-quated and immoral economic system."[81] According to this reading of the gospel, Christianity offers social reconstruction as the path to salvation. Third, dogmatic socialists must discard their own millennialism. Like Chris-tians who judge the situation on earth hopeless and for that reason ignore it while waiting for the apocalypse, such socialists believe that it is folly to work for reforms because "any apparent improvements are promptly captured by the devil and only make things worse." Gathering around themselves a party of true believers committed to waiting for the revolution, these dreamers ignore Marx's own emphasis on praxis as the only way to transcend the tension between the subjective and objective aspects of the dialectic.[82] By insisting on the reintroduction of the subject to socialist theory, the theorists of social democracy returned to a forgotten Marx, and they could legiti-mately claim to be resurrecting a vital component of his philosophy by stress-ing the necessity of human activity.[83]

In the same manner that they attempted to resolve the conflict between choice and inevitability by insisting that human action is conditioned, but not wholly determined, by material factors, so social democrats dealt with argu-ments concerning the individualistic or social nature of man by resorting to a companion strategy similar to that employed by the philosophers of the *via media*. Arguments about man's nature are misconceived, they maintained, because there is no possible way to test hypotheses regarding the supposedly natural state of a presocial individual. As Beatrice Webb wrote, "The plain truth is that to apply the antithesis of 'natural' and artificial to social action is sheer nonsense." Everything that happens in human history "is equally 'natural'; its very happening makes it so."[84] Ely insisted that men have never come together in a state of nature, "and then by the formation of a State passed out of a condition of nature into an organized political existence." Instead the state grows up naturally, spontaneously. "Men are born into the State, and the State is one of the forces making them what they are. The basis of the State is human nature, and the State is the natural condition of men." Social democratic theorists assumed the rootedness of the individual in society; they were never tempted by arguments for a natural individualism. They agreed with Ely when he wrote that man is "inextricably bound up in state and society."[85] In short, if we employ an empirical test, Rauschenbusch argued, the datum that "man is a social being is the fundamental fact" of social science.[86]

If man cannot be separated from his social and political matrix, then neither can he be removed from the historical process. The theorists of social democracy recognized that the individual is born into history, and they con-ceded the futility of attempting to freeze the fluid process of social develop-ment in order to examine it. Conditions change, and people contribute to those changes and respond to them by altering their values and their activities. Whereas Marx declared that the class struggle drives the historical process, and orthodox Marxists insisted that the proletariat would inevitably replace the capitalist ruling class through revolution, social democrats disputed the necessity of both class warfare and revolution. Marx's ideas, which derived from metaphysical postulates without any basis in experience, must be replaced with a less grandiose, more empirically oriented view of history.

Jaurès provided the most ambitious attempt to construct a social democratic philosophy of history. In 1894 he tried out his ideas in an address before a group of socialist students. In human history, Jaurès said, there is "not only a necessary evolution but an intelligible direction and a progress towards the ideal." It would therefore be a mistake to consider the materialist and idealist conceptions of history as opposites. "They merge in a unique and indissoluble development, because, though one cannot consider man apart from his economic relationships, neither can one consider economic relationships apart from man," who brings with him to life projects and ideals. "While history is from one aspect a phenomenon evolving in accordance with mechanical laws, it is at the same time an aspiration working itself out within the framework of an ideal."[87] Those remarks prefigured Jaurès's mature understanding of the historical process. In his history of the French Revolution, he followed a kind of historian's *via media*: "In history, we have to take into account both economic evolution and human greatness. Thus our interpretations of history will at the same time be materialistic with Marx and idealistic with Michelet."[88] The intricate interweaving of those two threads in Jaurès's historical writings manifested his belief that social change results from "self-conscious egotism, the impersonal dialectic of history, and the profound conscience of humanity."[89]

Jaurès contrasted his ideal with orthodox Marxism and utopian socialism. He acidly characterized Engels's *The Condition of the Working Class in England* as a piece of dogmatism masquerading as history. In a typical formulation, he accused Engels of a mechanistic materialism culminating logically in an obstinately conservative politics. To Engels, as to reactionaries, all social and political progress under the present system seemed impossible.[90] Historical determinism ended in paralysis, Jaurès believed, and the politics of late nineteenth-century orthodox Marxists validated his claim. At the same time, however, he distinguished his attitude toward history from the ideas of such utopian socialists as Fourier, Saint-Simon, and Proudhon. Progress toward the socialist goal cannot spring from dreams, he warned: "No, socialism is not an academic and Utopian conception, it is ripening and developing in closest touch with reality."[91] Ideas without social and political roots are as lifeless as a mechanistic theory that leaves no room for praxis.

It is difficult to assess the role Jaurès's faith in progress played in his theory of history. He praised Michelet's republicanism while he criticized as romantic the visions of Fourier and Saint-Simon. His parable "Moonlight," first published in *La Dépêche de Toulouse* on October 15, 1890, illustrates the problematic nature of his ideas about progress. Jaurès described a walk he took late one night with a young friend, to whom he related his vision of a socialist future:

> All men will know the fullness of pride and joy, and they will feel that they are cooperators in the universal civilization. . . . They will have better understanding of the hidden meaning of life, whose mysterious aim is the harmony of all consciences, of all forces, and of all liberties. They will understand history better and will love it, because it will be their history, since they are the heirs of the whole human race.

While his young friend acknowledged the attractiveness of the socialist ideal, he protested that such a goal could be realized without revolution or any abstract thing called socialism because the world tends naturally toward greater cooperation. "Come let the universe be," he advised Jaurès in the closing passage of the tale. "It contains joy enough for all. It is Socialistic after its own fashion."[92] I emphasize this fable because it illustrates the conflict in the social democrats' theory of history. Jaurès did not challenge his friend's affirmation of the universe's natural tendency toward cooperation because he too believed that the larger historical process was guiding mankind in the direction of socialism. He agreed that the universe itself is socialistic, if only after its own fashion. That confidence in a fundamental progressive principle embedded in human history underlay Jaurès's social democratic theory, and his efforts to combine the historical theories of Marx and Michelet must be understood within that larger framework.

A similar faith in progress animated the writing of the other social democratic theorists, and it complicates their analysis of historical determinism. They denied that history unfolds according to Marx's scheme and affirmed that individual choices play a decisive role in shaping historical development, but they nevertheless believed that society is evolving gradually toward socialism. Although those three propositions seem inconsistent, these eclectics tried to juggle them in their writings about history while maintaining their equilibrium as social activists. They inhaled the evolutionary theory that filled the intellectual atmosphere of the late nineteenth century without fully appreciating the complexities involved in applying Darwinian theory to human development. They stressed the role of values and praxis in their critique of orthodox Marxist historical theory, yet they did not consistently relate that lesson to their own faith in social progress. The Webbs considered the extension of democracy toward socialism "irresistible," Bernstein dubbed his theory "organic evolutionism," and Rauschenbusch grounded his idea of change in "the modern comprehension of the organic development of human society." While they tried various strategies to legitimate claims for progressive social evolution, in the end their historical theory rested on their socialist faith. Like Fouillée, Green, and Dewey, they maintained, together with Jaurès, that the universe itself is moving in the direction of socialism.[93]

These social democrats realized the ethical quality of their social ideals. As commentators from widely different perspectives have pointed out, the decisive factor distinguishing them from Marx was their explicit emphasis on morality. Marx believed his philosophy to be objective and scientific; he insisted that his vision of the communist future was rooted in the facts of human existence and the laws of economic development. By contrast, these straying socialists rested their case on the conviction that socialism represents an ethically superior ideal.[94] They advocated socialism not because it *must* be but because it *ought* to be. They preached social action not because of the dialectical materialist interpretation of class struggle but because they considered the individual's acceptance of social responsibility to be morally desirable. Although the positivistic overlay Engels slapped on Marx's ideas rendered them even more distinct from arguments of this sort, Marx himself also rejected such ethical appeals as mawkish and unreliable expressions of bourgeois sentimentality. Although social democrats did not minimize the importance of economic factors in historical development, and they did not approach social questions in a utopian spirit, their conception of science included an awareness of the meaningful and inherently value-laden quality of human experience. They did not try to free their socialism of values; instead they faced this issue directly and acknowledged that all ideals are tied to social experience and cannot claim universal validity independent of their usefulness. Like the philosophers of the *via media*, they contended that "the social question is a moral question," to use Fouillée's phrase. As I will indicate in the next chapter, their emphasis on ethics represented simultaneously one of their greatest potential sources of strength and the greatest immediate weakness of social democracy as a political program competing with Marxism and liberalism for popular support.

Beyond the general recognition of moral considerations in social democratic theory, many of these thinkers' specific ethical ideas ran parallel to the mediating ethics of rational benevolence. When Bernstein recommended a return to Kant, he did not counsel acting from duty to the exclusion of any concern for an act's effects. Instead he argued, in *Wie ist wissenschaftlicher Sozializmus möglich? (How Is Scientific Socialism Possible?)*, that Kant's excessively formal ethics lacked "direct connections with actual life in its concrete reality." He advised that the systematic application of such ethical precepts to the "social conditions created by modern industrial evolution" constitutes "the task of modern socialism from the ethical point of view." Sounding a familiar note, he concluded, "This task implies a work of synthesis, and it is this synthesis that constitutes for me the true social ideal." Unfortunately, Bernstein's ability to provide that synthesis in ethics did not match his ability to perceive its necessity, and after he was verbally thrashed by both Marxists and neo-Kantians for his efforts as an ethicist, he never returned to such matters again. When Jaurès traced German socialism to the ethical ideas of Kant and Fichte, he likewise emphasized that socialists should place a higher value on the consequences of action than had earlier philosophers who concentrated solely on the purity of intentions. When Sidney Webb spoke of the new moral world he envisioned, he stressed the "general recognition of fraternity, the universal obligation of personal service, and the subordination of personal ambition to the common good," a set of values neatly summed up in Beatrice Webb's call for a spirit of "thoughtful benevolence."[95]

The clearest indication of the similarity between the mediating spirit of the ethics of rational benevolence and the ethical views of social democratic thinkers came in Ely's explicit use of Sidgwick's ideas in *Social Aspects of Christianity*. Ely maintained, using Sidgwick's *History of Ethics* as a guide, that benevolence was Christianity's most important contribution to the development of ethical theory. He proclaimed the desirability of combining utilitarianism with ethical systems concentrating on "the duty to love and serve one's fellows," but instead of developing that insight, which was after all Sidgwick's own aim, he dismissed all secular ethical theories because they left him "suspended in the air." As an alternative he suggested a return to the principle of benevolence, which led Christ and his followers "to the heart of the social questions of their time" and lay at the heart of the social gospel movement.[96] Ely thus offered faith as the justification for an ethics of benevolence, and his affirmation echoed with firmer conviction, if no more solid foundation, the tentative arguments Sidgwick advanced at the conclusion of his *Methods of Ethics*.

When the theorists of social democracy turned their attention to philosophical issues, they advanced arguments consistent with those of the philosophers of the *via media*. With the exception of Jaurès, they tended to state those arguments in rather less sophisticated form, but the positions they staked out and tried to defend were strikingly similar to the radical empiricism, the historical sensibility, and the social idealism of the earlier generation. In short, while they dug less deeply into epistemological and ethical questions, the theoretical foundations they laid down for their political arguments strongly resembled the radical philosphers' ideas about experience, freedom, and values. All of these social democrats enlisted in the empiricist camp by affirming that social experience, despite its imprecision and ambiguity, provides the only available source for understanding human affairs. They unanimously endorsed the theory of voluntary action, and they tied the selection of values to the continuing communal project of pragmatic truth testing. They rejected as inaccurate both purely materialist and purely idealist interpretations of history, emphasizing the role of choice and praxis in steering social development within limits set by broad economic, political, and cultural constraints. Finally, they conceived of social action in moral terms, and they blended intentionalist and consequentialist considerations in their ethics. Rauschenbusch encapsulated these ideas in an address he delivered before a group of working men at the Rochester Labor Lyceum in 1901. "Anybody who sneers at moral ideals and turns socialism purely into a stomach question," he concluded, "has picked up a few rags of the materialistic philosophy and misleads you in flaunting them before you. He takes the soul out of socialism," and snaps "the mainspring of its strength."[97]

These renegade socialists agreed with the radical empiricists that all of our knowledge is value-laden and that no source of knowledge other than the fund of collective experience, open-ended and uncertain, is available to supply ideas and ideals for social action. Yet precisely because that realization destroyed dogmatism, it opened a world of possibilities for those committed to the struggle for justice. For they understood the achievement of their aims as a project to be accomplished not once and for all by the flash of apocalypse or revolution, but instead through the steady and unending efforts of communities to live up to their own ideals, and they saw in that knowledge a spur to action and a cause for hope.

3. Rethinking Economic Theory: Where Marx Went Wrong

Social democratic theory rested not only on a critique of socialist reason but on an equally radical critique of socialist economics. While these theorists disagreed about important issues such as the labor theory of value, they derived from their economic analyses similar conclusions regarding the implications for politics of late nineteenth-century economic conditions. They rejected as false Marx's predictions that: (1) capitalism would result in the immiseration of the proletariat, (2) capitalist economies would experience increasingly severe crises, and (3) capitalism would concentrate capital in the hands of the ruling class. They observed that organized capitalism had developed contrary to Marx's expectations. Economic conditions in the 1890s pointed away from Marx's theory of proletarian revolution, and toward the effective exercise of political power by the working classes and their reform-minded allies in the bourgeoisie. That process, social democrats believed, might eventually culminate in the peaceful triumph of socialism. These theorists declared wholehearted allegiance to no single economic tradition, preferring instead a creative blend of ideas taken from Marx, the neoclassical economists, the marginal utility theorists, the German historical school, and such idiosyncratic and nonsystematic thinkers as Henry George and Philip Wicksteed.[98]

When Bernstein arrived in London in 1888, he believed fervently in the economic ideas of Marx and Engels. He denigrated the Fabians as "the English socialists of the chair," linking them with German academics like Gustav Schmoller and Adolf Wagner whose state socialism the German left anathematized. Scornful of bourgeois historical economics, Bernstein declared his fidelity to the orthodox party line. During the next few years, however, his ideas altered dramatically, a change suggested in his letters to Kautsky and manifested in an essay that appeared in *Die Neue Zeit* in 1892. The ideas of Marx and Engels could only be considered valid, he asserted, as long as they were not proven wrong by more recent scientific investigations. His postscript to the German edition of the Webbs' *History of English Trade Unionism* in 1895 evidenced his increasingly heterodox approach to economics, but his stance was still that of a friendly critic rather than an ally of the Fabians. An undated fragment in Bernstein's papers suggests why he changed his mind during the next few years. It is unfortunately impossible to know whether he was trying to capture the spark that later fired his revisionism or merely trying to distill the essence of his ideas when he scribbled these phrases on an envelope, but they are revealing in either case: "Peasants do not sink, middle class does not disappear; crises do not grow ever larger, misery and serfdom do not increase. There *is* increase in insecurity, dependence, social distance, social character of production, functional superfluity of property owners."[99] As those notes suggest, the economic prosperity of the late nineteenth century was decisive in shaping Bernstein's revisionism. Marx's theory was disproved, Bernstein contended, by the ability of capitalist economies to extricate themselves from the prolonged economic slumps that were supposed to bring their doom. In 1924, looking back on the process by which he slipped from orthodoxy into heresy, Bernstein acknowledged that facts, not "doctrinal criticisms," compelled him to correct his premises.[100] Evidence that contradicted theory corroded his faith in Marxism; from the resulting uncertainty emerged his revisionism.

In his preface to *Evolutionary Socialism*, Bernstein quoted the letter he wrote to the SPD Congress assembled in Stuttgart in 1898, in which he expanded the ideas contained in the fragment already cited. He proclaimed his apostasy boldly: "I set myself against the notion that we have to expect shortly a collapse of the bourgeois economy," because the "number of members of the possessing classes is today not smaller but larger. The enormous increase of social wealth is not accompanied by a decreasing number of large capitalists but by an increasing number of capitalists of all degrees." He considered the political significance of these economic developments self-evident. Socialist parties should "organize the working classes politically and develop them as a democracy," and they should "fight for all reforms in the State which are adpated to raise the working classes and transform the State in the direction of democracy."[101] Bernstein's political reformism sprang directly from his economic analysis, and the furor that his ideas provoked had as much to do with his interpretation of capitalism as with his recommendations for party strategy.

What role did Fabian economics play in Bernstein's conversion? That question is difficult to answer, in part because identifying Fabian economics is no easy matter, and in part because Bernstein himself minimized the Fabians' influence on his intellectual development.[102] Exhaustive studies of Bernstein's relations with Fabianism have demonstrated conclusively the close similarity between his economic ideas and those of the Webbs, Shaw, and especially Wallas, but attempts to locate his conversion in the early 1890s overlook the evidence that he was still engaged in trying to defend orthodox Marxism from the Fabians when he lectured before the Society in 1897. It is true that by that time he had already begun to publish his controversial essays in *Die Neue Zeit*, but that incongruity merely illustrates again Bernstein's awkward tendency to be slightly out of step at every stage of his development.[103]

Just as Bernstein played down his encounters with the Fabians to protect himself from his German critics, so the Fabians played down their encounters with Marx's writings to protect themselves from their British critics. Contrary to earlier interpretations, however, which the Webbs encouraged because of their desire to be viewed as *English* socialists, it is apparent that both of the Webbs were well acquainted with Marx's work. Four incomplete manuscripts in Beatrice Webb's personal papers, entitled "The Economic Theory of Karl Marx," which have been traced to 1886, give evidence of a careful reading of Marx. Sidney Webb's notes for lectures delivered in 1885 and 1886 at the Working Men's College and the City of London College indicate an even more thorough knowledge of *Capital*.[104] These documents also reveal that the Webbs were critical of Marx from the outset. Sidney characterized Marx's economic method as "abstract intuitive"; he considered it less empirical, and therefore less useful, than even the work of Ricardo. Webb much preferred the theoretically sophisticated, historically sensitive, and empirically accurate "concrete deductive" method of Mill, Marshall, and Sidgwick. He considered it most significant that these economists showed increasing sympathy toward socialism, and he argued in Fabian Tract # 15, *English Progress Toward Social Democracy* (1890), that Sidgwick's essay "Economic Socialism" was conclusive evidence that "the main principles of socialism are a plain deduction from accepted economic doctrines, and in no way opposed to them." British radicals did not need Marx for inspiration, Webb believed, when the most respected of their own economists, including Sidgwick, "that most careful of men," endorsed the sort of moderate socialism the Fabians favored.[105]

A further indication of Webb's familiarity with and resistance to Marxist economics, and of Bernstein's converse familiarity with and resistance to Fabian economics, is a letter Webb wrote to Bernstein in 1895. Responding to Bernstein's criticism of the Webbs' *History of English Trade Unionism*, Webb admitted that he was "a worse heretic than you suppose," because he had already read the studies by Marx and Engels that Bernstein confidently recommended as a tonic for his ailing economic understanding. Their disagreement was not, Webb continued, simply due to his ignorance of Marx, as Bernstein supposed, but was instead "a difference of judgment. We must 'agree to disagree,'" he concluded, on questions of economics. Thus, even as Bernstein was preparing to expose himself to his party's censure for the sympathetic treatment of Fabianism in his afterword to the German edition of the Webbs' book, he was being chided by Webb for excessive orthodoxy in his defense of Marx's economic doctrines.[106]

Like Webb, Ely was more enthusiastic about Sidgwick's economics than Marx's, and like all of these social democrats, he collected economic ideas from various sources. Typically, he contrasted the rigidity of laissez-faire economic theory, which dominated academic economics in the United States during the late nineteenth century, and the equally inflexible doctrines of German Marxists, with the empirical approaches of Sidgwick and Marshall on the one hand and the German historical economists on the other. Ely was especially enamored of his mentor Karl Knies, and he sprinkled his writings with references to Knies's ideas. He quoted Knies's dictum that "the theory of political economy is the generalization of truths recognized up to a certain point of time, and this theory cannot be declared complete either as respects its form or substance."[107] Like Sidgwick, the economists of the German historical school recognized not only the historicity but also the ethical quality of economic theory. Ely endorsed their contention that the classical economists' treatment of labor as a commodity betrayed the humanity of the worker and of the economist, and he insisted that economics must include an explicit consideration of the need for social reform. According to Ely, neither economics nor any other social science could evade its responsibility to promote "the moral and intellectual elevation of mankind."[108]

Ironically, only Jaurès, who based his philosophy less on economic arguments than did any of the other theorists of social democracy, dissented from this catholic approach to economic theory. In his address "Bernstein and the Evolution of Socialist Method," Jaurès defended Marx's economic theory in general and the labor theory of value in particular. "After hard study," he declared, "and after examining the attacks against the theory of surplus value, I find that it stands up very well. The fact always remains that the capitalist can only draw profit from part of his workers' toil."[109] His claims of hard study notwithstanding, there is little in Jaurès's writings to suggest that he considered economic theory except as an afterthought. The exploitation of workers by the capitalist system inflamed his egalitarian sensibility, and he never felt it necessary to examine carefully specific issues of economic theory. While he confidently asserted the adequacy of the labor theory of value in his critique of Bernstein, for example, he made no effort to prove the point.

It has sometimes been overlooked—notably by Jaurès—that Bernstein did not completely reject Marx's labor theory of value. Instead he followed the Fabians Shaw and Wallas in attempting to graft onto it elements of marginal utility theory. "Economic value is androgynous," he suggested; "it contains the element of utility (use, value, demand) and cost of production (labor production)."[110] Ultimately, Bernstein contended in *Evolutionary Socialism*, both Marxist and marginal utility theory must be recognized as mere tools of analysis without objective basis in economic conditions. They are abstract assumptions, he insisted, enabling us to make sense of different aspects of price and value. "Such abstractions naturally cannot be avoided in the observation of complex phenomena," Bernstein admitted. "How far they are admissible depends entirely on the substance and the purpose of the investigation." Beneath his arguments lay a sophisticated understanding of the relation between economic methods and social and political values, an understanding infrequently demonstrated either by Marxists or their opponents. "At the outset," he maintained, "Marx takes so much away from the characteristics of commodities that they finally remain only embodiments of a quantity of simple human labor," when in fact value reflects other factors as well. "As to the Böhm-Jevons school," on the other hand, "it takes away all characteristics except utility." It seemed obvious to Bernstein that both theories overlooked certain features of the economic system, and he proclaimed that both "the one and the other kind of abstractions are only admissible for definite purposes of demonstration, and the propositions found by virtue of them have only worth and validity within defined limits."[111] Whether the labor theory of value and marginal utility theory can simply be added together, however, as Bernstein, the Webbs, and Ely implied, remains problematical. A century after Beatrice Webb wrote in "The Economic Theory of Karl Marx" that "labour is only one source of value" and pointed out that "use value, desire, and quantity of materials must also be taken into account," the search for a unified theory of value that would do justice to those various factors remains alive. Typically, Bernstein correctly perceived the inadequacy of the prevailing orthodoxy in his treatment of economic theory; the synthesis he proved unable to provide has remained elusive.[112]

These theorists of social democracy concurred with Bernstein's more basic challenge to Marxist theory: his contention that nineteenth-century economic history disproved many of Marx's predictions. The appearance of the idea of social democracy coincided with the prosperity that the industrialized world enjoyed from around 1895 until World War I. Faced with the undeniable fact of rising living standards, Marxists found themselves hard pressed to demonstrate the impoverishment of the masses in industrial capitalist economies. More sophisticated arguments concerning relative immiseration still lay in the future, and the overblown rhetoric of catastrophe offered no explanation for the economic boom of the century's closing years.[113] Prosperity threatened the doctrines preached by orthodox Marxists as nothing else could, and the rigidity of their thinking during this crucial period made them vulnerable to the arguments of social democracy.

As Beatrice Webb wrote when the English economy was still sputtering in 1895, "Times of physical want and mental despair are either the seed times of angry revolutionary feeling or of colourless despairing quietude." She recollected that "it was not until the dark years of 1881–85 were well over that *constitutional socialism*, as distinguished from *revolutionary socialism*, began to grow. It was no coincidence," she suggested, that progressive parties thrived "in the years of the greatest prosperity. We must educate and wait for fat years."[114] In a sense, social democracy was a theory of and for "fat years." It first took shape philosophically, and it gained momentum politically during a period of peace and prosperity in the United States and Europe. It rested on the assumption of steady progress and democratic reform that would have appeared as naive to the generation of 1848 as it appeared to many who abandoned it in the years of war and depression that followed.

Jaurès admitted that the economic position of the working class was improving, and he described Marx's catastrophe theory as "a Hegelian transposition of Christianity." Just as Jesus "humbled himself to the lowest depth of suffering humanity in order to redeem humanity as a whole," Jaurès wrote, so for Marx, "the proletariat, the modern Saviour, had to be . . . degraded to the depth of social historic annihilation" before it could redeem mankind. Jaurès considered all of this a delusion. "Marx was mistaken," he explained, because he did not realize that a politically powerful working class could promote its interests in a democratic state without sinking into the abyss from which Marx expected its revolutionary consciousness to rise. Because the proletariat has not been impoverished by industrial capitalism, Jaurès continued, "it has also become puerile to expect that an economic cataclysm, menacing the proletariat in its very existence," will ignite the socialist revolution.[115] Like Bernstein, he believed that the maturation of capitalism made economic crises less likely rather than inevitable. As Bernstein wrote in *Evolutionary Socialism*, "The problem of crises cannot be solved by a few well-preserved catch-words" pronounced out of reverence for Marxist doctrine. He could see in the emerging industrial world "no urgent reason for concluding that such a crisis [leading to revolution] will come to pass for purely economic reasons."[116]

Marx had predicted the development of corporate capitalism and the rise of trusts, both of which were in their infancy when he wrote *Capital*, but he interpreted these trends as steps toward the socialization of work and ownership and as contributions to the ultimate destabilization of capitalism. The social democrats' critique of these ideas appeared first in Sidney Webb's and William Clarke's contributions to *Fabian Essays in Socialism*. Bernstein developed it in greater detail in *Evolutionary Socialism*, and Rauschenbusch echoed Bernstein's analysis—and used his evidence—in "Dogmatic and Practical Socialism." First, they argued that the appearance of trusts and cartels enabled capitalists to control the economy more efficiently by concentrating power in fewer hands, thus rendering a cataclysmic collapse less likely. Second, they claimed that the spread of joint stock companies separated ownership from management, diffused prosperity among a larger number of stock holders, and created a new class of managers whose technical expertise and relatively disinterested attitude made them a stabilizing force.[117]

Bernstein aimed his final assault on Marxist economics at the argument that capital would become more concentrated in a mature capitalist economy. He presented an impressive array of statistics (whose accuracy now seems doubtful) to bolster his argument that, despite the concentration of power in certain economic sectors, property in general was more widely diffused in the late nineteenth century than before. Based on evidence from American, British, French, and German industry and agriculture, he concluded that "it is thus quite wrong to assume that the present development of society shows a relative or indeed absolute diminution of the number of members of the possessing classes." To the contrary, "their number increases both relatively and absolutely."[118] Bernstein maintained that capitalism was able to sustain its equilibrium through the greater concentration of wealth and power attained by the formation of cartels, trusts, and large corporations. On the other hand, paradoxically, it successfully distributed property among an ever wider range of small capitalists in both industry and agriculture. This two-sided progression contributed to the eventual development of socialism by preparing both the economy and the minds of individuals for the socialization of property. For as some enterprises became larger and larger, people became more accustomed to the scale that nationalized industries would assume, and as property was more and more widely diffused, class lines began to blur and the possibility of a classless society increased. "Far from society being simplified as to its divisions compared with earlier times, it has been graduated and differentiated both in respect of incomes and of business activities."[119] This process, Bernstein confidently asserted, was preparing the way for the eventual emergence of socialism.

Ely and the Webbs strongly endorsed this argument, which became one of the standard features of social democratic economic analysis. As the process of industrial evolution continues, Ely explained, the division of labor becomes increasingly elaborate. From this condition, however, he drew a conclusion directly opposite from Marx's: as economic dependence increases, interclass solidarity grows. Ely wrote enthusiastically in 1886 that "men form more truly than ever before a social and industrial organism, whose numberless parts are in infinite variety of manner interdependent. Infinite interrelations! Infinite interdependence!" Such interdependence would nurture a spirit of cooperation rather than class warfare, these thinkers believed, and that spirit might lead eventually to socialism. Whereas Marx had argued that only the proletariat could become the "universal class" by virtue of its propertylessness, social democrats argued that the inner logic of capitalist development led to the socialization of the petite and haute bourgeoisie as well as the working class. Interdependence manifested itself in economic forms fostering cooperation, and thus capitalism itself could develop gradually, if constant pressure were exerted by democratic political action, toward a socialist economic system.

The Fabians first laid out this chain of reasoning in their Tract # 4, *What Socialism Is*, published in 1886. "The Great Industry," as they termed the economic system emerging from the second industrial revolution, by "rendering all branches of production mutually interdependent, has socialised labour and paved the way for co-operation." This "conscious growth of social feeling" among the people as a whole contributed to the steady increase of support for government "interference on behalf of the exploited class." As "education and political power" further awakened the mass of the population to the "possibility of changing their social condition by legal methods," the twin processes of industrial evolution and political democratization together would lead eventually to socialism. Confirming the continuity of Fabian thinking on this issue, the Webbs reiterated this argument thirty-six years later in their conclusion to the second edition of *Industrial Democracy*: "The very fact that, in modern society, the individual thus necessarily loses control over his own life, makes him desire to regain collectively what has become individually impossible."[120] From the fact of interdependence, these social democrats reasoned, would flow not the destructive flood Marx anticipated but instead a surge of social responsibility among members of all classes.

Jaurès and Rauschenbusch too hoped for such an end to social conflict, but they were perhaps less optimistic than the others concerning its achievement. The emergence of corporate capitalism, in Rauschenbusch's words, "marks a long stride toward social cooperation," because it signals a new stage in the slow "evolutionary process by which a great cooperative system will eventually be built up." The increased interdependence of the organized capitalist system encouraged, even demanded, a more collaborative social spirit. The more complex society becomes, the less viable is self-reliance as an objective and the more trust in others becomes a necessity. But during the transitional phase from individualism to socialism, Rauschenbusch cautioned, it will be necessary to guard against the atavistic tendency to wield power for personal profit rather than communal good. As society becomes increasingly interdependent, and more power is concentrated in fewer hands, "the more difficult it is to watch over the fidelity of all the trustees, and the greater is the temptation of a trustee or steward to divert the trust to his own use."[121] Sophisticated industrial societies must be especially vigilant, because the very processes that in the long run can contribute to the socialization of values and, at least potentially, of wealth as well, make possible in the short run ever more effective exploitation of the working class. That fear, that the scientifically trained managers would themselves become bulwarks of the system these social democrats expected them to steer skillfully in a more communal and egalitarian direction, seems to have troubled Ely, Bernstein, and the Webbs less than it troubled Rauschenbusch and Jaurès, and that difference manifested itself also in their political ideas, as I will indicate in the next chapter.

The economic theory of social democracy pointed toward moderate political reform. All of these theorists denied that either the invisible hand cherished by liberal political economy or the inevitable capitalist breakdown predicted by Marx corresponded to the reality of material prosperity and continued exploitation in the late nineteenth century. They discerned in the logic of capitalist development a progression toward prosperity, stability, and a wider diffusion of property, and they saw in those tendencies cause for optimism rather than despair. As workers were freed from the bondage of poverty through the unwitting efforts of capitalists pushing to increase production, they were being prepared for citizenship in the cooperative societies of the future. Workers had won the right to participate in the political process, and they now faced the challenge of turning their political freedom, and their equality before the law, into economic freedom and economic equality. As industrial capitalism matured, people became more interdependent in fact; the task of social democracy consisted of transferring that interdependence from a competitive to a cooperative basis. Social democrats calculated their strategy of political reform toward reaching that goal.

7

Social Democratic Politics

1. Reform Strategy and the Tactics of Liberal Alliance

On a fine October day in 1901, Jaurès watched in wonder as a manned airship flew over Paris. Two fellow spectators did not share his enthusiasm. One denounced the spectacle as an attempt to whitewash a recent scandal by flying around the Eiffel Tower, a preposterous effort to glamorize a monstrosity "built with stolen Panama money." The other was enraged by what he considered a cheap bourgeois trick to amuse the masses, a new kind of bread and circuses, and he vowed to establish a "group of Revolutionary Aeronauts, in other words, of aeronauts who will wait until the Revolution is accomplished before they invent balloons." Their contempt for the grandeur of the achievement saddened and puzzled Jaurès.[1]

The theorists of social democracy were tired of waiting for the revolution. They thought the working class could maneuver political democracy toward socialism, and they advised the people to take the controls. Against calls for revolution, social democrats advocated what Jaurès termed "revolutionary evolution." Their goals remained revolutionary: they envisioned a radical reordering of society according to principles of equality and cooperation. But they believed that socialism could triumph only through gradual change and that those who saw counterrevolutionary plots in the most harmless events impeded progress toward liberation. By resisting steps that contributed to the eventual triumph of cooperation over individualism, proponents of proletarian revolution betrayed the ideals of socialism out of reverence for a romantic shibboleth.[2]

Their simultaneously voluntarist and evolutionary mentality prompted the theorists of social democracy to prefer reform to revolution. Marx revealed himself as "a slave of doctrine," to use Bernstein's phrase, when he proclaimed the necessity of revolution; a more perceptive view of history discloses that societies change only slowly.[3] The gradual accumulation of partial reforms contributes more to the socialist cause than the revolutionary waiting advised by orthodox Marxists. In *Fabian Essays in Socialism*, Sidney Webb marked his distance from Marx's philosophy of history when he declared that "no philosopher now looks for anything but the gradual evolution of the new order from the old, without breach of continuity or abrupt change of the entire social tissue at any point during the process."[4] By that time Webb had shed his positivist skin, but he still approached politics with a Comtean view of society as an organism. Three decades later, the Webbs reaffirmed their commitment to "the inevitability of gradualness" in *A Constitution for the Socialist Commonwealth of Great Britain*, which they wrote at the request of Camille Huysmans, then secretary of the International Socialist Congress. The Webbs contended that each society can only reconstruct itself "on the lines of its own past development, and out of the social materials that are for the time being, available." Socialists who posited a universal historical process overlooked unique features of political development in individual nations. In Britain, the Webbs insisted, the idea of socialist revolution was a fantasy: only by using the "forms of democratic structure," they wrote, "moulded to fulfill the new requirements and rearranged so as to express the Socialist purpose," could socialists make progress.[5] Social evolution involved gradual change through democratic reform, not revolutionary cataclysm.

These social democrats' retreat from revolution reflected political developments in the late 1880s and 1890s. During these years social reform was on the march in Europe and the United States, and each new victory strengthened these thinkers' conviction that the time had come for socialists to exchange their dynamite for chisels. Developments in French, German, and American politics described in the first manifesto issued by the Fabian Parliamentary League in 1887 illustrated the slow but significant steps being taken by progressive reformers, evidence that "rendered it imperative" for English socialists likewise to work for moderate change. Those more concerned with their effectiveness than their doctrinal purity, the Fabians concluded, should concentrate on realistic political reforms.[6]

These theorists took their cue from concrete political circumstances. Reformist legislation weakened the hold of laissez-faire policies in the United States and Europe during the closing decades of the nineteenth century, and although much of this sentiment emanated from the bourgeoisie rather than the working class, the theorists of social democracy argued that progressive measures served the proletariat's interests regardless of their source. They wanted the working classes to ride the current of political reform as far as it could carry them before abandoning their middle-class allies. As long as legislation moved in the direction of socialism they interpreted it as an opportunity rather than a threat. The rhetoric of orthodox Marxists notwithstanding, the working classes of America and Europe seemed to be prospering and developing stronger feelings of national identity, a trend reflected in their increasingly moderate political attitudes. Their moderation in turn contributed to the further success of reform legislation from which they benefited, and this process provided ammunition for the social democrats' argument that socialism could be achieved through reform rather than revolution.[7]

It was precisely this argument that infuriated orthodox Marxists. Although many of the specific measures Bernstein advocated had received the support of others in the SPD, his denial of the feasibility—and even the desirability—of revolution enraged his former allies. In his most notoriously provocative formulation, which he first offered in his essays in *Die Neue Zeit* and defended steadfastly in *Evolutionary Socialism*, Bernstein proclaimed that the final goal of socialism, whatever it may be, "means nothing, the movement everything." Bernstein believed that the larger processes of historical change, political, social, and economic, were carrying the world ineluctably toward socialism by requiring greater cooperation as a result of increased interdependence. As the principle of equal participation establishes itself at the center of political democracy, he reasoned, it draws toward itself all the elements of social and economic organization as a magnet attracts scattered pieces of iron; democracy obviates the necessity and forecloses the opportunity of political catastrophe by delivering to the people as a whole the power previously exercised by the ruling class.[8]

This argument disturbed socialists of different persuasions for different reasons. According to such revolutionaries as Rosa Luxemburg, revisionism undercut the glamorous myth of a final victory that fired proletarian sensibilities. Partisans of revolutionary waiting like Kautsky feared that Bernstein's ideas might threaten the party's united front in opposition to the Wilhelmine Reich, the principle of opposition that sustained the elaborate social and economic institutions provided by the SPD. Even self-professed reformists such as Ignaz Auer, who agreed with much of the thrust of Bernstein's revisionism, feared that attempts to provide theoretical justification for the flexible approach to politics actually adopted by the SPD would undercut the party's commitment to socialist principles and open the door to political opportunism. Viewed strictly as strategy, revisionism appeared to almost everyone in the SPD a dangerous challenge to socialism.

But Bernstein's analysis represented more than simply the banal recommendation that the party pursue narrow, achievable political aims, which was the meaning many of his critics ascribed to his message. Instead Bernstein presented an entirely different conceptualization of socialism based on an entirely different idea of social experience. By asserting that the final goal of socialism meant nothing and the movement everything, he was not calling simply for more astute political maneuvering by party leaders. He was instead challenging the philosophical basis of Marxism. Bernstein sought to replace the misty vision of communism as an ultimate aim with a radical view of democratic socialism as a continuous struggle toward a cooperative society, a process that would never be completed. This notion of social and political development manifested Bernstein's decidedly non-Marxist historical sensibility, his sense of the human project as an unending search for clearer understanding. Revolution might establish a different economic system, but it could not provide answers to the philosophical questions about society and politics that must remain open.

By discounting the apocalypse of proletarian revolution, then, Bernstein did not challenge merely the strategy of the SPD, he denied the more fundamental contention that the final goal of socialism could ever be specified in advance or reached once and for all. He conceived of socialism as a struggle toward ideals of freedom and equality, and from that perspective fostering democratic principles in society appeared more important than preserving revolutionary enthusiasm. As he wrote to Rosa Luxemburg, democracy, not revolution, would accomplish socialism: "The conquest of democracy is an indispensable rule of social emancipation."[9] It is in this sense that Bernstein cherished the movement and ignored the final goal, because he considered the institutionalization of democratic principles at once prerequisite to and the vehicle of socialism. For him, as for the other theorists of social democracy, socialism was less doctrine than process, less a question of ends than a question of means. Accused by orthodox Marxists of selling out their ideals, these social democrats scorned their opponents' fidelity to revolutionary dogma as a retreat from the challenge of mobilizing constituencies for political battles. In the absence of capitalism's impending collapse, the rhetorical pose of orthodox Marxists masked a basic unwillingness to face political reality. Such revolutionaries preferred the security of familiar received truths to the uncertain prospect of forging a democratic socialist society.

Social democrats denied in principle that socialism could be achieved by revolution, because they believed that only a process of painstaking democratic development could prepare society for the transition from one economic and social system to another. Moreover, they contended that the millennialism of revolutionaries blinded them to the perpetually problematic quality of social and political organization—after as well as before the advent of socialism. As a matter of strategy, social democrats believed that democracy made possible progressive reforms that earlier socialists considered impossible in a capitalist society. As early as 1883, Ely argued in *French and German Socialism in Modern Times* that the future of socialism lay in the direction of reform rather than revolution. He reiterated that conviction two years later in "Recent American Socialism," where he distinguished between the objectionable rhetoric of American socialists and the legitimacy of their legislative programs. While he branded the residual advocacy of revolution "damnable," he nevertheless found much of value in the platforms of such groups as the Federation of Trades and Labor Unions. The identification of socialism with revolution was weakening, he concluded, and he applauded the severing of an ideal that Christian reformers like himself could endorse from the "schemes of destruction" too often spun by wild-eyed American socialists. In the preface "To Workingmen" in *The Labor Movement in America* (1886), Ely counseled moderation. "If your demands are right, if they are reasonable, then you will win," he advised. "The world will listen even to socialism, if properly presented." The secret of a successful strategy is threefold: *"Educate, Organize, Wait*. Christ and all Christly people are with you for the right. Never let go that confidence." Even when he was at his most enthusiastic about the prospects of socialism, Ely always distinguished carefully between reform and revolution. The latter could lead only to "large loss of life, estrangement of classes, incalculable destruction of property, and a shock to the social body," whereas the former might lead gradually in the direction of socialism.[10]

Like Bernstein and Ely, Sidney Webb linked the principle of gradual social development with the strategy of democratic social action. "The irresistible progress of democracy," he wrote in *Fabian Essays in Socialism*, is the "main stream which has borne European society towards Socialism during the last 100 years." Socialist strategy must be democratic, "acceptable to the majority of the people," and gradual, "causing no dislocation, however rapid may be the rate of progress." Socialists should emphasize the ethical dimension of their ideas, Webb insisted, and those Marxists who dissociated themselves from religious and moral arguments not only alienated potential allies but blunted one of the sharpest features of the socialist critique of capitalism.[11] Balancing a strategy of evolution against their goal of socialism proved a difficult challenge for the theorists of social democracy. To liberals they were dangerous revolutionaries, to revolutionaries they were traitorous pawns serving the interests of liberal capitalism. This pressure from right and left induced social democrats to adopt different strategies for different circumstances, which left them even more vulnerable than most political thinkers to charges of opportunism and inconsistency. Flexibility, however, was the keystone of their politics.

In *Christianizing the Social Order*, Rauschenbusch offered a characteristic social democratic hedge. "Let us 'go slow'," he cautioned, "but let us hurry up about it." That blend of patience and fretfulness typified social democratic strategy. Rauschensbusch further contended that, compared with earlier, more utopian socialisms, Marxism "is a great philosophy of patience," and those not caught in a petrified version of Marx's ideas have abandoned the expectation of society's breakdown "and accepted a program of evolutionary tactics." Rauschenbusch thus acknowledged Bernstein as the legitimate heir to Marx, and he also expressed his own commitment to the social gospel as a kind of revolutionary evolution. He commended the shift of the SPD from revolutionary extremism to parliamentary democracy, and he tried to persuade American socialists to follow their lead. "The old days of hand-to-hand fighting are gone," he wrote, "and no streets were ever less adapted for barricades than American streets." Although force may seem to lead directly to the promised land, "in reality it may be the longest way of all." Radicals must always consider the long reactions that follow force. "The idea that violence can suddenly establish righteousness is just as utopian as the idea that moral suasion can suddenly establish it."[12] The work of substantial social reconstruction is agonizingly slow, and there are no shortcuts.

Rauschenbusch also invoked the German example in *Christianity and the Social Crisis*. Although no class benefits from social catastrophe, idealists should not try to limit the working class to the use of moral suasion, or be repelled "when they hear the brute note of selfishness and anger." For the class struggle always manifests itself, eventually, in the field of politics. Just as the bourgeoisie uses political means to advance its interests, so should the working class use the leverage their political power gives them. After all, argued Rauschenbusch, Bismarck's resort to state socialism illustrates that dominant classes initiate political reform only when motivated by fear. As socialists have shifted their focus from ultimate ends to proximate means, he concluded, so all Christians should think less about salvation or damnation and more about their social responsibilities. The Christian social ideal, like the socialist ideal, could be achieved only if its partisans changed their orientation "from catastrophe to development" and adopted a strategy of reform.[13]

The intensity of the infighting in the French socialist movement led Jaurès to offer the most ingenious (or most tortured) version of social democratic strategy as simultaneously revolutionary and reformist. In his discussion of *The Communist Manifesto* in the "The Question of Method," he compared the "stroke of physical force" envisioned by Marx and Engels to the alternative strategy of revolutionary evolution. If "the democracy is prepared, if the proletariat can, by legal measures alone, induce it to develop the first revolutionary institutions in a communistic direction, we have in the legal conquest of the democracy the sovereign method of revolution." Other approaches to socialism, Jaurès declared, reverted to the time when the proletariat was still too feeble to adopt other than "artificial means of obtaining a victory." In other words, given the rise of democracy, evolution becomes the most effective method of genuine revolution.[14]

In the statement of purpose Jaurès drafted in 1908 for the SFIO, he attempted to advocate moderation and extremism with equal fervor:

> Precisely because [the socialist party] is a party of revolution, precisely because it has not paused in its continuous campaign against capitalist and bourgeois property, it is the most active party of reforms . . . the only party which can turn every reform into the starting point for more far-reaching, more extensive conquests.[15]

The identification of reform with revolution was typical of social democrats' strategy: they mediated between bourgeois and Marxist positions and tried to appeal broadly to moderate elements both to their right and to their left. This strategy did not reflect political opportunism, as critics charged; instead it was consistent with these thinkers' fundamental convictions. They prized flexibility because they considered it the political corollary of their epistemological uncertainty. Like the philosophers of the *via media*, they insisted that political steps must be taken one at a time. Because democratic reforms embody the will of the people, they cannot be outlined in advance. Because experience begins in uncertainty and is tested in practice, politics must be tentative and experimental. The theorists of social democracy cherished an ideal of socialism that was vague precisely because it was democratic; they considered it impossible to specify the shape of the society that people would choose to construct.

In general, these thinkers advocated the specific reforms included in the platforms of major socialist bodies. Comparison of the German Social Democratic party's Erfurt program of 1891, the French Socialist party's Tours program of 1902, the program of the Fabian Society (revised in 1900), the American Socialist Labor party platform, and the Declaration of Principles of W. D. P. Bliss's Society of Christian Socialists (1889) reveals that all of these organizations advocated roughly the same measures.[16] Bernstein helped to draft the portion of the Erfurt program concerning political strategy and specifically endorsed it in *Evolutionary Socialism.*[17] Jaurès was the principal advocate of the reformist program adopted in 1902 by the French Socialist party. The Webbs played a dominant role in shaping Fabian policy, and Ely and Rauschenbusch allied themselves with Bliss's various organizational efforts.[18] Thus the congruence between these official party programs and the positions taken by the theorists of social democracy should come as no surprise.

These specific reforms can be divided into three general categories: the political process, the welfare state, and public ownership of the means of production. First, while democratic reformers had made considerable progress in removing restrictions from the political process itself, certain impediments remained. In France and Germany, these included rights taken for granted in England and the United States, such as freedom of speech, freedom of assembly, and freedom of religion. In all of these nations, social democrats also advocated equality for women in the workplace, in the democratic process, and in the family. Finally, they supported such measures as the initiative and the referendum in the hope that they might make governments more responsive to the popular will, although these ideas never generated in Europe the enthusiasm they evoked in the United States. Such measures represented, in Rauschenbusch's words, the "reconquest of political liberty," an effective challenge to "political oligarchies" shielded from popular pressure by insufficiently democratic processes.[19]

The second category of social democratic reforms consisted of the regulatory and social service measures that have since become integral parts of the liberal capitalist welfare state. Included in this group were the four elements of the Webbs' "national minimum" scheme, which they introduced in *Industrial Democracy* (1897) and promoted tirelessly thereafter. The Webbs wanted the government to provide a floor of services, a national minimum standard beneath which no one would be allowed to sink in the areas of work, housing, health, and education. Most of the measures advocated by the theorists of social democracy fell within one of those categories. Reforming the conditions of work was the first item on this agenda, and the crusade for an eight-hour workday, which originated in the United States in the mid-nineteenth century, provided the initial focus. Gradually, however, moderate socialists and labor organizations broadened their scope to include recognition of the right to unionize, establishment of state operated employment bureaus, regulations covering health and safety in the workplace, prohibition of child labor, and the institution of a minimum wage.[20] Calls for universal, state supported, secular education also echoed through social democratic literature. These theorists inherited the Enlightenment's faith in the liberating power of knowledge, and they believed that freeing workers from ignorance ranked in importance with helping them earn a living wage. Social democrats believed that revolutions, especially evolutionary revolutions, are won in the minds of the people, and they considered education the opening wedge in their campaign to reorient public thinking toward greater cooperation.[21]

These social democrats were ambivalent about the purpose, the funding, and the ultimate implications of welfare measures such as Disraeli's health, housing, and factory legislation and Bismarck's insurance schemes. Did such measures ameliorate working-class living conditions sufficiently to merit support on strictly humanitarian grounds? Did they contribute to the development of a socialized public consciousness or merely pacify the masses? Did they carry the people toward socialism or bolster the capitalist system by siphoning off radical sentiment? Although puzzled and troubled by such questions, the theorists of social democracy tended to view the extension of government services as a step in the right direction, a necessary but far from sufficient commitment by the state to help those ravaged by industrial capitalism. Such ideas attracted support from across the political spectrum. Indeed, the breadth of their appeal contributed to their ambiguity; Disraeli and Bismarck clearly had different motives from the Webbs and Bernstein for supporting the welfare state.[22] Most social democrats nevertheless endorsed the principle stated concisely—with full recognition of its paradoxical implications—in the first official response by the SPD to Bismarck's initiative in 1883, a resolution adopted unanimously by the party congress. The party resolved "to safeguard energetically the interests of the working class in respect of all proposals concerned with the economic position of the people, from whatever motives they were advanced, without at any time renouncing the totality of the socialist demands." Although criticized as an inadequate palliative, the welfare state received grudging support from most social democrats, who despite their misgivings could not bring themselves to oppose measures promising at least a moderately better standard of living for the working class. Social democrats reasoned that such legislation committed the state to the principle that the community must shoulder the responsibility to care for all of its members, a principle whose importance outweighed all negative considerations. Regardless of imperfections in specific schemes, and despite the possibility that they would prove counterproductive, extensions of social insurance and economic regulation affirmed society's duty to aid its least advantaged members. Acceptance of that principle signaled at least a partial break from capitalism and a limited victory for cooperation.[23]

To socialists' charges that supporting the bourgeois state could never advance their cause, these renegades responded with the logic of social democracy. As Rauschenbusch stated their reasoning, opposition to the state could be justified when the state expressed only the will of an aristocracy. But the more democracy makes the state and the people "identical in extent and interest," he wrote, the less should the state be feared. "Under true democracy state action comes to mean action of the People for their own common good, and why should we fear that?" The faith that socialism would be achieved by extending democratic principles to society was central to social democratic theory, and it accounts for these thinkers' cautious optimism concerning the prospects of the welfare state. In Rauschenbusch's words, "As the state becomes democratic, the old situation is reversed. The people now desire an extension of state function and the aristocratic class fear it."[24] These social democrats believed that once the public made the state an instrument of their will, progress toward socialism would be rapid. Such notions as false consciousness and hegemony were not part of their intellectual arsenal; they expected that the extension of democratic principles from politics to society would culminate logically in socialism.

The years since World War I, of course, have revealed the dual flaws in this reasoning. First, the popular appeal of fascism and then anticommunism has rivaled and at times dramatically exceeded the appeal of democratic socialism; second, the institutionalization of the welfare state has diminished rather than intensified public interest in radical reforms. Social democrats assumed that democratic politics would be egalitarian and eventually socialist, but the twentieth century has proved them poor prophets. As the living conditions of the working classes in Western Europe and the United States have improved marginally, and as the range of integrative mechanisms has expanded to include not only universal suffrage but schools, varieties of social insurance, and reforms of some of the worst abuses of industrial capitalism, the promise of socialism seems to have lost some of its luster next to the glitter of welfare capitalism. The theorists of social democracy admitted no contradiction between their strategy of moderation and the socialist ideals they cherished, but the chain leading from democracy to socialism is evidently weaker than they thought.

The third category of social democratic reform involved the cornerstone of socialism: public ownership of the means of production. Consistent with their cautious outlook, these thinkers envisioned a series of modest, incremental changes rather than the wholesale transformation of the economy from capitalism to socialism. Although Bernstein had participated with Kautsky in writing the Erfurt program under Engels's watchful eye, he later rejected its call for the immediate dismantling of private enterprise and the institution of a completely socialized economy. Not only could the state not manage the total manufacture and distribution of products, Bernstein argued in *Evolutionary Socialism*, it "could not even take over the whole amount of medium and large enterprises." As for local authorities, they "could socialize at most those businesses which produce, or which perform services, locally for that locality." In short, the scope of practicable socialization would be narrowly circumscribed to what the German historical economists grouped together as natural monopolies, including for example utilities, natural resources, railroads, and the postal service. Beyond that sphere, Bernstein opposed immediate expropriation of capital and suggested instead a gradual transfer of ownership from capitalists to workers, a transfer facilitated by the progressive separation of management from ownership in joint-stock corporations.[25]

While their emphases varied according to national differences, all of these social democrats shared Bernstein's skepticism concerning the extent of public ownership and the desirable rate of change from one economic system to another. They advocated a flexible, experimental approach to this problem, and they were confident that time was on their side. Sidney Webb was fond of describing what he considered a typical "individualist town councillor," whose life and opinions were in such conflict that eventually his sympathies were certain to shift toward socialism. Such an official, according to Webb,

> will walk along the municipal pavement, lit by municipal gas and cleansed by municipal brooms with municipal water and—seeing by the municipal clock in the municipal market, that he is too early to meet his children coming from the municipal school, hard by the county lunatic asylum and the municipal hospital, will use the national telegraph system to tell them not to walk through the municipal park, but to come by the municipal tramway to meet him in the municipal reading-room, by the municipal museum, art-gallery, and library, where he intends . . . to prepare his next speech in the municipal town hall in favor of the nationalization of canals and the increase of Government control over the railway system. "Socialism, Sir," he will say, "don't waste the time of a practical man by your fantastic absurdities. Self-help, Sir, individual self-help, that's what has made our city what it is."[26]

Although Webb's tale might equally well suggest that individualist ideologies can survive the existence of quite an extensive system of government services, social democrats found in such parables evidence that the process of socialization would continue regardless of anachronistic bourgeois attitudes.

The enthusiasm of European social democrats for municipal socialism filtered into the writings of Ely and Rauschenbusch. Ely cautioned, however, that the persistence of individualism limited the appeal of socialized agriculture, commerce, and manufacturing in the United States. Rauschenbusch likewise judged natural monopolies "the irreducible minimum which must come under public ownership," but he was generally less sanguine than Ely concerning the efficiency of private enterprise.[27] Both of them repeatedly criticized the idea of independent regulatory agencies, and their lack of faith in this weapon brandished by American reformers distinguished them from many progressives less sympathetic to socialism. Such efforts to tame the lions of corporate capitalism were not only futile, Ely argued, they had the added disadvantage of confirming the American public's low estimate of government authority by limiting the efficiency of private enterprise without limiting its power.[28] Drawing on Ely's analysis of regulation as the worst of both worlds, Rauschenbusch endorsed nationalization rather than regulation to cope with the worst abuses of corporate power. "We fritter away precious time by dallying at the halfway house of mere public supervision," he warned. "The outside interference of government officers will prove inefficient, meddlesome, and irritating. We must come to public ownership sometime," Rauschenbusch concluded, "and anyone whose thinking parts are in order ought to see it by this time."[29] While social democracy may have worn a comparatively moderate guise in the United States, its advocates nevertheless proposed considerably more radical measures than did most American reformers for dealing with concentrations of economic power.

These thinkers' preference for experimentation revealed itself not only in their strategy of revolutionary evolution, it was equally apparent in their approach to the most vexing tactical question they faced: alliance with the progressive wings of liberal parties. By surveying the various problems they faced in different political situations, I intend to demonstrate the complexity of drawing general conclusions about the role played by social democrats in shaping twentieth-century politics. Certain incidents illustrate with particular clarity the contrasts among the political cultures of Great Britain, France, Germany, and the United States, and I will concentrate on those specific issues rather than attempt to survey the larger patterns of political conflict between moderate socialists and reform-minded liberals. In general, given the polarization of German politics and the liberal consensus dominating American politics, the problem of cooperation between socialists and liberals paradoxically appeared less complicated in both of these nations than it did in Britain and France. In Germany, social democrats were kept so far outside the political mainstream that they did not confront the choice of allying with more moderate political elements until the first decade of the twentieth century. In the United States, by contrast, no viable political force existed outside the two-party system (with the exception of the Populists, who never appealed to the urban working class), and social democrats were forced to ally with liberals or resign themselves to oblivion.

The Webbs' attitude on this question illustrates its problematic character in the context of British politics. During the early years of the Fabian Society, the organization followed Sidney Webb's lead and advocated a policy of "permeation." "Until a fitting opportunity arises for putting forward Socialist candidates to form the nucleus of a Socialist Party," to use the language of the Fabian Parliamentary League's manifesto in 1887, Fabians officially opposed as futile efforts to establish an independent third party. Instead they pledged themselves to support "those candidates who will go furthest in the direction of Socialism," generally Liberals whom they tried to permeate with social democratic ideas and pull to the left. This policy encountered resistance within the society. Some members favored independent action such as that taken by the Social Democratic Federation; others were more inclined toward anarchism than toward any organized political activity. But eventually the Webbs' tactic of permeation prevailed.[30]

Since English politics was in a state of flux during the late nineteenth and early twentieth centuries, and the Liberal party wandered between its traditional laissez-faire policies and the "new liberalism" of progressive theorists like L. T. Hobhouse, the Webbs' strategy was not unrealistic. Sidney Webb perceived as early as 1891 the shift in British politics that historians have only recently begun to understand: the transformation of the Liberal party into a class-based, labor oriented amalgam of traditional liberalism and social democracy. People did not yet realize, Webb argued, "that the Tory Party is now a Whig party, and that those Liberals who are only Whigs . . . are just as bad as the so-called Tories. The Radical Party will never do any good," he concluded, until it discarded its older leaders and conformed to the new political reality "by adopting and carrying out the Workers' Political Program"—i.e., social democratic policies of the sort advocated by the Fabian Society. A decade later Webb sharpened this analysis still further, and his argument conforms neatly to the interpretation of the pre-World War I period now accepted by most students of British politics. Webb described the "steady alienation from Liberalism of the great centres of population," notably London and Lancashire, which were no longer enthusiastic in their support of laissez-faire but were "flatly opposed to it." Why? In short, Webb concluded, "we have become a new people," with new political attitudes and allegiances, as "we have become aware, almost in a flash, that we are not merely individuals, but members of a community." The shift in politics to a class-based party system merely reflected the realization of interdependence, a new way of "thinking in communities."[31]

That Webb's analysis now appears so incisive makes the Fabians' dramatic reversal of tactics in 1893 even more puzzling. Their decision, announced breathlessly in an article entitled "To Your Tents, Oh Israel!" explained their impatience with timid Liberals and seemed to commit the Fabian Society to supporting the struggling Independent Labour party. But in 1896, believing the ILP doomed to extinction, the Webbs and Shaw led the Society back to the tactics of permeation. Those liberals they chose to permeate, however, were the liberal imperialists who supported the Boer War, and when they faded from prominence, the Webbs found themselves more than ever isolated on the left, victims once again of their consistent weakness for betting on the wrong horses in British politics. While in the abstract the tactics of permeation may have been appropriate for sharpening what the Webbs correctly identified as the increasingly social democratic sympathies of the changing Liberal party, the Fabians' clumsy political maneuvering limited their effectiveness.[32]

The Fabians moved only fitfully into alliance with the Labour party, which emerged from the explosions of World War I as the legitimate heir to the Liberal party and the apparent champion of social democracy. Searching for a usable past in his introduction to the 1919 edition of *Fabian Essays in Socialism*, Sidney Webb claimed that during its early years the Fabian Society tried "persistently to get on foot an independent political party, which would hold Socialist views and adopt a definitely Socialist programme." He went so far as to claim that the Fabians tried to persuade the trade unions and trade councils to form such a party, "to which we promised whatever personal assistance we could give." The record, however, does not support such self-congratulation. The Webbs in fact directed their efforts primarily toward permeation, and these remarks must be judged an attempt to obscure the failure of the Fabian Society, following the Webbs' advice, to predict accurately the political future of the British left. Eventually the bond between the Fabian Society and the Labour party became quite strong, but that bond was not forged until the Labour party had become the dominant force in Britain embodying social democratic ideas.[33] Furthermore, because the Labour party relied upon the trade unions for the core of its electoral support, it tended to be far more concerned with issues of immediate interest to industrial workers than with the broader question of restructuring British society.

Zigzagging of that sort typified the complicated relations between social democrats and liberal parties, and their wandering paths reflect their uncertainty concerning the political viability of such partnerships. Jaurès consistently advocated any alliances that might help the cause of revolutionary evolution, but his equally steadfast loyalty to the French socialist movement, which did not always share his tolerance of bourgeois radicals, makes his progress appear as inconsistent as the Webbs'. Jaurès prized effectiveness more than consistency, and he calculated his tactical moves to make the most of unsteady bourgeois support for desirable reforms. He believed that the long-term success of the working class depended on the strength of the socialist party, and he cherished unity on the left as wholeheartedly as he desired concrete political action. Since he was thus pulled in opposite directions, occasionally at the same time, he sometimes appeared to lose his balance. He alternated between active support of reform-minded liberals and complete separation from them, however, less because his convictions wavered than because they conflicted. Jaurès claimed that his attitude toward cooperation with nonsocialist groups derived from Marx's counsel that socialists should ally with the proletariat against the bourgeoisie, and with the bougeoisie against the aristocracy and the church. Jaurès was animated by that principle: he consistently interpreted progressive reforms, even when sponsored by the bourgeoisie, as a greater challenge to the squirearchy and the priesthood than to the purity of the socialist movement. Only his intense yearning for socialist unity kept him firmly attached to the movement when his socialist allies rejected what he judged useful coalitions.[34]

Jaurès first committed himself to an alliance with nonsocialist progressives in 1895, when he urged socialists to stand behind the new Radical ministry of Léon Bourgeois. Moderate socialists like Alexandre Millerand and René Viviani enthusiastically supported such cooperation, and even revolutionaries such as Guesde and Edouard Vaillant did not actively oppose it. Jaurès, at least for the moment, seemed able to draw together radicals and socialists who had long been at each other's throats. But his success was short-lived. For reasons to be discussed in my analysis of Bourgeois's ministry in Chapter Nine,[35] this alliance fell apart before the entrenched forces of reaction. While the socialists stood firm behind Bourgeois's proposal for a graduated income tax and helped push the measure through the Chamber of Deputies, the more conservative Senate defeated the plan and voted to censure the Bourgeois ministry. Rather than challenging the Senate, as Jaurès advised, Bourgeois chose to resign, and the fragile socialist-radical coalition disintegrated.

The next major test of Jaurès's commitment to cooperation with progressives came in the midst of the Dreyfus affair. In 1899, attempting to rally all shades of leftist opinion behind the Republic, René Waldeck-Rousseau extended an offer to Millerand to join his ministry. Millerand's willingness to participate in a nonsocialist government unmasked the split personality of the socialist movement and strained Jaurès's divided loyalties. The Guesdists and their allies were ready to run Millerand out of the party as a traitor, while Jaurès defended the principle of participation and tried to persuade Millerand's critics to "fight not from a futile distance, but from the very heart of the citadel." The French socialist congress of 1899 wrestled over this issue at length without reaching a final decision. The resolution they adopted contained enough contradictions to allow both the defenders and opponents of "ministerialism" to claim victory or at least vindication.[36]

It is in the context of this dispute over ministerialism that Jaurès's criticism of Bernstein's revisionist economics in 1900 must be understood. Having come under fire for endorsing Millerand's participation in a bourgeois government, Jaurès badly needed to renew his credentials as a bona fide revolutionary, and by claiming to stand with Kautsky against Bernstein, he confirmed his radicalism in the eyes of his fellow French socialists. Yet as I have suggested, Jaurès did not criticize revisionism itself as thoroughly as has sometimes been assumed. Bernstein did stand in relation to Kautsky roughly as Jaurès stood in relation to Guesde, and an overly harsh critique of revisionism would not have helped the cause of moderation in France, a cause to which Jaurès was firmly committed.[37] Thus Jaurès tried to play off the Guesdists against the revisionists without alienating either faction of the international socialist movement, and for several years it appeared he would succeed.

A similar modus vivendi had apparently been reached in Germany by the turn of the century. While differences between Bernstein and his critics persisted, both factions in the SPD appeared willing to let the controversy simmer. Emboldened by the party's success in the 1903 elections, however, Bernstein recommended that the SPD exercise its constitutional prerogative by claiming the first vice-presidency in the Reichstag, a step, ironically enough, that Jaurès himself had taken in the Chamber of Deputies a year earlier without incident. But again Bernstein's international perspective served him poorly; his respect for Jaurès's acumen and his enthusiasm for the Webbs' idea of permeation caused him to misread the German political situation. From his perch in the Reichstag Bernstein believed that the time was ripe for permeating German liberalism with socialist ideas, but he was looking at the German middle class through Sidney Webb's pince-nez. In Britain much of the support for Fabian ideas did indeed come from the lower middle-class salariat of teachers, journalists, clerks, and government officials. Bernstein had come to know this white-collar class well in London, and he believed that their German counterparts would prove equally sympathetic to social democratic ideas if the SPD would only jettison its revolutionism and present itself as a responsible party of reform. Bernstein was convinced that ideas and class interests together shaped political consciousness, and he considered the exclusive concentration of German socialists on the prole-tariat unnecessarily limiting. "Party strife is not identical with class struggle," he contended, "and in our socially complex society there is a large stratum whose class interests are not as clear-cut as those of manual workers and who would therefore seek to be bound to the SPD by bonds of idealism."[38] As an explanation of Fabianism in Britain, and of Jaurès's appeal in France, that argument was perceptive. As an assessment of German politics, it was a fantasy.

The lofty status historically accorded bureaucrats and government officials in Germany meant that white-collar workers identified with elites rather than proletarians, and they proved remarkably uninterested in social reform throughout the pre-World War I period. Moreover, the corporatist tradition that had moderated class cleavages in German society was undercut during the late nineteenth century by the "reforms" of the bureaucracy insti-tuted by Bismarck, so that the protection of the poor assumed traditionally by the guilds and corporations crumbled at precisely the moment when industrialization intensified the problems confronting the German working class. The elitist identification of the German salariat, together with the sharpening of political polarization effected jointly by Bismarck's strategy of *Sammlungspolitik* and the SPD party leadership's reductionistic approach to the class struggle, made nonsense of Bernstein's Fabian-inspired strategy. In Germany, for many of the same reasons liberalism attracted so few champions, permeation failed because of the impermeability of the middle class.[39]

Given the level of antagonism in German politics, Bernstein's apparently modest proposal concerning the vice-presidency blew the lid off the revision-ist controversy. One of the most reform-minded figures in the SPD, Ignaz Auer, branded Bernstein's suggestion "an act of imbecility and a tactlessness of the first order." Bernstein's recommendation smacked too much of Millerand's ministerialism to suit Kautsky and Bebel, and they launched an attack against Bernstein at the party's congress in Dresden, which climaxed in a strongly worded rebuke of revisionism and the principle of socialist-liberal cooperation. Despite the severity of the Dresden resolution, Bernstein was not drummed out of the party, as Rosa Luxemburg and her allies had hoped, and he continued, albeit more quietly, to promulgate his revisionist ideas.[40]

Their success at Dresden prompted Kautsky and Bebel to risk a confron-tation with Jaurès on the questions of cooperation, participation, and mini-sterialism at the Amsterdam Congress of the Second International in 1904. Fresh from the Dreyfus affair and still struggling to preserve the Third

Republic from the combination of monarchist and clerical reaction, Jaurès brought his considerable international prestige to the defense of alliances between socialist parties and progressive liberals. Because he knew in advance that he could not muster enough votes to carry the congress with him, he departed from his familiar role as mediator and lashed out at the SPD's attempt to dictate tactics to the international socialist community. For once Jaurès had nothing to lose. For that reason his speech at Amsterdam merits particular attention, because he expressed in it his convictions rather than his keen sense of what would prove most advantageous politically.

Addressing himself to the representatives of the SPD, Jaurès declared that socialists must not scorn reforms representing "important steps towards liberation." If socialists would accept their responsibility to participate actively in the political process, democracy could carry the banner of socialism. "It would be foolhardy, even criminal, to abandon the amorphous, heterogeneous, inconsistent democratic mass to its own devices," Jaurès insisted, and in France, as in England, that perception of the volatile electorate was accurate. Because German socialists were unable to translate their electoral strength into effective political power, they wanted to impose a similar restriction on more successful socialist parties. "Why? Because you cannot act either as revolutionaries or parliamentarians." The only power of the SPD was rhetorical, because the proletariat in fact possessed little revolutionary potential and its party exercised negligible legislative influence. It was a simple fact of history, Jaurès pointed out, that despite their bluster German socialists had no revolutionary tradition. "They never conquered universal suffrage on the barricades. They received it from above." It mattered little whether the SPD participated in the Reichstag or not, Jaurès noted, because "your Parliament is only a pseudo-Parliament." It would not matter even if the SPD achieved an absolute majority in the electorate or in the Reichstag, because representative institutions in Germany remained impotent.[41]

Although (or perhaps because) Jaurès's charges rang true, the Amsterdam congress passed resolutions calling for united socialist parties and condemning revisionism, reformism, and ministerialism. The principle of socialist-liberal alliance appeared to be defeated decisively. Yet just as Bernstein and his followers continued to work for reform without calling themselves reformists, so Jaurès, although he submitted to the International's dictates by formally allying with the Guesdists and breaking with progressive republicans, did not stop agitating for moderate reforms supported also by liberals. Neither did he concede either the legitimacy of the Amsterdam resolution or the accuracy of its authors' assessment of socialist tactics. In a stinging series of articles in *L'Humanité* from September 5 to September 16, 1904, Jaurès painstakingly traced the contrasting histories of the French and German socialist movements from the French Revolution through the nineteenth century. He insisted that "differences of context and tradition" made it impossible for the French and German proletariats to follow precisely the same tactics. Whereas French socialists exercised meaningful political power in a Republic because of the rights won by the French people through successful revolutionary struggles, in Germany nationalism and democracy did not go hand in hand. Indeed, historically they contradicted each other, so that each triumph for nationalism had been a defeat for democracy. The German nation itself was only a gift from the Prussian aristocracy to the people, and it was hardly a gift without strings. Twisting the knife one last time, Jaurès pointed out that the real challenge for German socialists was the conquest of popular sovereignty, because without democratic government the "bourgeois abortion of the German revolution" in 1848 would be followed by an abortion of the proletariat.[42]

The incisiveness of such arguments notwithstanding, both Bernstein at Dresden and Jaurès at Amsterdam lost crucial battles over their reformist tactics in 1903 and 1904. The German and French socialist movements preserved their threatened purity as revolutionary parties, in rhetorical pose if not in fact, and they spurned the heretical idea of cooperating with bourgeois parties. The discontinuity between rhetoric and reality had different consequences in Germany and France, but in both nations the adherence to a program of nonalliance isolated socialists from any potential supporters among the bourgeoisie. Bernstein's defeat prefigured the decline of moderation in the SPD, and after World War I the party divided into revolutionary and conservative factions that contributed to the fatal polarization of Germany in the 1920s. After Kautsky split decisively from Rosa Luxemburg in 1910, he tried to carve out a centrist position between her revolutionism and Bernstein's revisionism. His centrism, however, united the party at the cost of incapacitating it. Against the radicals, he insisted that the SPD was a "revolutionary, not a revolution-making party." Against the revisionists, he opposed compromising the integrity of the proletariat and therefore refused active participation in government. Kautsky thus fell between two stools, and only blind faith in the inevitability of socialism obscured the political powerlessness of his strategy, a powerlessness born of romantic fantasy and ultimately confirmed in tragic failure.

By contrast, the united French Socialist party created in 1905, the SFIO, developed into a constitutional party, the advance guard of democracy, rather than the narrow vanguard of the revolution Guesde pretended it was. In the years leading to World War I Guesde may have been the party's titular head, but its spiritual direction came from Jaurès. In France the seeds of social democracy recovered after Amsterdam, but in Germany's arid political climate they languished. Still, I would not argue that Bernstein and Jaurès might have led the German and French socialist parties to democratic victories had their tactics been adopted. Although it is impossible to know what success less revolutionary parties might have had, the SPD and the SFIO in fact had little luck attracting lower middle-class voters from the centrist and right-wing parties from 1905 to 1914. The cleavages between socialists and liberals in Germany and France ran far deeper than did such divisions in Britain, and the Fabians' puzzled amusement over the wrangling at Amsterdam indicated that their perception of the problems facing continental socialists was no less fuzzy than Bernstein's vision through the Webbs' lenses.[43]

In the United States, the question of an alliance between social democrats and left leaning liberals took on a different significance for two reasons. First, the pressure that theorists like Ely and Rauschenbusch had to fear came not from the left, as it did in France, Germany, and to a lesser extent England, but from the center of the political spectrum. If American moderates perceived social democrats as revolutionaries, their chance to effect substantive change would vanish. Whereas in Europe social democrats worried about maintaining their legitimacy as radicals in order to preserve their power base in the working class, in the United States excessive radicalism guaranteed powerlessness, and Ely and Rauschenbusch were careful not to sever their ties to responsible political opinion. Second, the traditional identification of religious sentiment and social reform in the United States meant that Ely and Rauschenbusch did not have to turn away from religion to find support for social democracy. Particularly in France, but also in much of Germany, religion equaled reaction, but that connection did not hold in the United States because of the heritage of nonconformism and the historical inclination of at least some religious leaders toward political activism. As Rauschenbusch wrote in *Christianizing the Social Order*:

> Many Socialist leaders misread the situation in America because they are obsessed by theories developed in Europe on the basis of the bad experience which Democracy has had with the Roman Catholic Church and with the Protestant State Churches. They know too little of religious history to be aware that religion is a very different thing in England and America where it has been loved and sustained for centuries by the free sacrifices of the plain people in their own little religious democracies.[44]

These two characteristics of American social democracy, springing from the moderation of American politics and the strong identification of reform with religion, reinforced one another, and together they help to account for the differences between the tactics of Ely and Rauschenbusch and those of European social democrats.

Ely and Rauschenbusch realized that the American labor movement would determine the fate of social democratic ideas, and both actively supported labor organizations. Ely was an enthusiastic partisan first of the Knights of Labor and later of the American Federation of Labor, and Rauschenbusch likewise advocated mobilizing the working class to work for economic change. Both tried to put the American reform movement into a broader frame of reference by comparing American trade unions to their German and British counterparts. In 1891 Ely pointed out that Bismarck's repressive legislation had so thoroughly radicalized the German working class that moderate reforms appeared less attractive than revolution, and three years later, in the preface to *Socialism and Social Reform*, he compared the situation in the United States to that in Germany twenty years earlier. He concluded that while Germany had done much to improve the condition of the working class through social insurance, such steps always came so late "that the masses have received the impression that the action was forced by fear, and did not proceed from a real, sincere desire to benefit the less fortunate portions of the community." Only if the American polity acted decisively, Ely warned, could polarization along German lines be avoided. "It is not by any means too late for us to escape the situation in which Germany finds herself," in which the center was a political no-man's-land. "However it may be in Germany, the policy of social reform is still practicable among us; but we must always bear in mind the high ideal which socialism has placed before the masses of the people, and which they have absorbed." Ely's counsel was clear: if the nation failed to meet the legitimate demands of the labor movement, the United States too might find itself torn apart by class warfare. America's liberal consensus made peaceful change possible, but the opportunity to preserve it could be grasped only if reformers raised their sights beyond "timid, halfway measures" and pushed for substantial social change.[45]

Rauschenbusch drew a similar conclusion for America from the different situation in Britain. The vitality of the center in British politics accounted for the absence of substantive change, because no socialist movement exerted sufficient power to "enforce remedial measures" of the sort instituted by Bismarck. Taken together, these comparative perspectives suggested that nonresponsiveness to social problems could lead to either of two extremes: the poisonous acrimony of Germany or the inert gentility of Britain. To save the United States from both conditions, Ely and Rauschenbusch believed their political goals might be reached through the influence of a labor movement sufficiently disciplined to resist unrealistic revolutionary appeals and sufficiently dedicated to resist succumbing to limited concessions on wages and hours. Somewhere between the romantic vision of Terence Powderly's Knights of Labor and the blinkered business unionism of Samuel Gompers's American Federation of Labor lay a conception of working-class activism combining James's notion of an "inner ideal" with the requisite "active will" and "fighting virtue." Just as "the idealistic movement" of the social gospel alone "would be a soul without a body," Rauschenbusch wrote, so labor's "economic class movement alone would be a body without a soul."[46] Only if ideals could be made real through genuine reform, only if American society were responsive in ways that Germany and Great Britain in their opposite ways were not, could the labor movement exert sufficient leverage in American politics to carry forward social democratic principles. In light of the repeated failures of third parties, an independent working-class party seemed unrealistic and unnecessary; the challenge was to reorient the economic and political thinking of the entire culture in order to avoid a German-style politics of confrontation or a British-style politics of co-optation.

The difference between American and continental European political culture is reflected in the opposite fates of Bernstein and Jaurès on the one hand and Ely on the other. While the European social democrats were forced at Dresden and Amsterdam to curb their efforts to cooperate with liberals, Ely was brought before a committee appointed by the University of Wisconsin Board of Regents on charges of economic heresy. Significantly, he cleared his name, and kept his position, by denying the charge that he was a socialist, and much has been made of his alleged recantation.[47] Because he drifted gradually from radicalism to respectable reformism and then to conservatism, Ely has been accused of allowing his ambition to get the better of his convictions. I do not dispute the importance of Ely's perception that his reputation for radicalism obstructed his further academic advancement, but several other features of this incident are noteworthy. I believe that Ely wanted honestly—and accurately, it should be emphasized—to distinguish his version of socialism, which was consistent with the moderate, reformist politics of European social democrats such as the Webbs, Jaurès, and Bernstein, from the violent millennialism that generally passed for socialism in late nineteenth-century America. In his writings and at his trial, Ely stressed the gulf separating parliamentary socialism from the fire-breathing revolutionism associated in American popular rhetoric with the epithet "socialist." Thus Ely's defense did not require him to compromise his principles, because the principles he defended, from the 1880s until he left the progressive camp after World War I, remained reformist instead of revolutionary. His principles were the principles of social democracy, the unconventional ideas for which Bernstein and Jaurès were censured by orthodox socialists. Although Ely's refusal or inability to establish his political ideas as a legitimate version of socialism may have helped perpetuate the truncated and impoverished political discourse characteristic of American public life, he could hardly have altered that feature of American political culture at his hearing. His defense, or his recantation, only illustrated the larger difficulty of establishing an acceptable social democratic position even within the context of the radical wing of the social gospel movement. Ely tried to redirect Christianity from its otherworldly orientation, and he tried to rescue socialism both from the materialsm that handicapped its understanding of the role of individual activity in historical development and from the revolutionary strategy and isolationist tactics that impeded its political progress. He was no more successful in either of these efforts than was Bernstein in reorienting the SPD, although they failed for opposite reasons.

Ely's trial illustrates the difference in the political significance of social democratic theory in continental Europe, Great Britain, and the United States. In France and Germany, social democracy sprang from socialist roots, and its partisans had constantly to demonstrate their radical credentials to preserve their legitimacy against attacks by anarchists in France and orthodox Marxists in Germany. By contrast, in Great Britain and especially in the United States, social democracy represented the left wing of responsible liberal discourse. Consequently American and British social democrats tried, with varying degrees of success at different times, to ally themselves with progressive movements whose strength extended beyond the working class and the labor movement into the liberal politics of the middle class.

Both at the level of theory and at the level of strategy, the theorists of social democracy were in substantial agreement, but their choice of tactics—or rather the tactics forced upon them—varied in ways that reflected the dissimilarities of their political cultures.

2. Democracy and the Problem of Expertise

What role should bureaucracy play in government? The Benthamites believed that the machinery of the state would be less important as the principles of laissez-faire became better established. Once the restrictions on the social machine were removed, nothing more than occasional fine tuning might be required. Marx reached a similar conclusion: after an interim period during which the proletariat would consolidate its control, the state would wither away. The theorists of social democracy, consistent with their other criticisms of Bentham and Marx, considered such notions utopian. Indeed, as the state became increasingly subservient to the will of the people, social democrats expected it to play a larger role. The state as they envisioned it would surely be democratic, yet given the intricacies of modern interdependent societies, the smooth functioning of government would require considerable expertise. Democracy implied decentralization and equalization of authority, while reliance on highly trained officials imperiled those values because it involved a measure of centralization and elitism. The theorists of social democracy found themselves pulled toward opposite poles.

They recognized the desirability of decentralization as a democratic ideal. As Ely wrote in *Socialism and Social Reform*, "all active agitators of socialism want a democratic state, because they wish that control of the collectivity over the economic life should be exercised in behalf of the masses. They are all not merely socialists, but democrats." It is for the same reason, Ely continued, "that all socialists are working for the decentralization of government. They look upon the present state as too highly centralized." Yet he admitted that socialists "do not find it everywhere equally necessary to lay emphasis upon their democracy," and in some cases that lack of emphasis seems to have stemmed from a deeper ambivalence about the role of the expert in functionally organized and highly differentiated societies.

What the Fabians called municipalization, in contrast to nationalization, appealed to social democrats because of their interest in decentralizing power. The Fabians and the partisans of the social gospel in the United States in particular advocated municipal socialism wherever possible as a means of countering the concentration of authority in a centralized state. As Sidney Webb pointed out in his introduction to the 1919 edition of *Fabian Essays in Socialism*, once the Fabians discovered "the important part to be played in the Socialist State by its various democratically organized and practically autonomous Local Governing Bodies," they became less enamored of state socialism and "came very vividly to appreciate the significance of municipalities' manifold functions." Municipalization defended society from "the hypothetical tyranny of a single national employer, inevitably 'bureaucratic' in character, no less than from the incubus of an all-pervading uniformity of social life." Most of the Webbs' own historical research had to do with town government, and their political activities centered around the London County Council. They consistently advocated a broad diffusion of power and strong local self-governments as essential checks on centralized authority.[48]

Despite their persistent criticisms of state socialism, however, social democrats feared that no socialist state could survive without a large and powerful army of bureaucrats. The unchecked authority that would accompany central economic planning and the coordination of government services in a socialist state disturbed them, yet they could conjure up no viable alternative to the exercise of monopoly power in organized capitalism. Municipal authority, desirable as it might be, had limits in a well-integrated economic system, and the residual power vested in a central state bureaucracy clouded their dreams of a decentralized democracy. The ominous outlines of a bureaucratized state were already coming into focus in the late nineteenth century; as early as 1905 Robert Michels began to publish the articles that laid the groundwork for his *Political Parties* (1911). Michels's familiar law of oligarchy put into explicit form the nightmare of social democratic theorists. Every system of leadership, Michels declared categorically, "is incompatible with the most essential postulates of democracy." In other words, inasmuch as the modern state, socialist or otherwise, requires political parties and administrative bureaucracies, it contradicts democratic principles by concentrating authority. Or as Michels put it in formulating what he considered the fundamental sociological law of political parties, "it is organization which gives birth to the dominion of the elected over the electors, of the mandatories over the mandators, of the delegates over the delegators. Who says organization, says oligarchy." Michels was only one of a number of sociologists and social psychologists who challenged the viability of modern democracy at the turn of the century, and their work cast doubt on the social democratic faith in decentralization as a democratic counterweight to the threat of bureaucracy.[49] Neither Bernstein, Jaurès, Ely, Rauschenbusch, nor the Webbs successfully resolved the conflict between expertise and popular control. Yet their different assessments of this problem and its solution illuminate not only their contrasting views of historical development but also the different lessons they derived from their nations' political experience.

Bernstein considered democracy the heart of socialism, as he explained in a letter to Kautsky in 1898. "I could very well have written, and what is more I originally wanted to write, that socialism for me finally means democracy, self-government." Bernstein broke from Marxism in large part because he could not endorse the SPD's strategic accommodation with the powerlessness of the proletariat in politics and in industry. Orthodox Marxists considered this condition of utter dependence a necessary phase in the degradation of the working class, a phase integral to the production of its revolutionary consciousness; Bernstein considered it deplorable. He believed that German socialists should work to improve the competency of workers in their jobs and as citizens so that they might gradually assume greater responsibilities. Unless the working class developed the capacity to administer the economy and the state, Bernstein reasoned, a dictatorship of the proletariat would be a nightmare of authoritarian incompetency, and democratic socialism would remain a dream. Bernstein noted in *Evolutionary Socialism* that the centralization of authority arises inevitably from the division of labor in an interdependent society. While he hoped that eventually such concentration of power might become superfluous, he acknowledged that "for the present it cannot be dispensed with in democracy." Bernstein had little sympathy for the notion of direct democracy, which he considered unworkable in a modern nation-state. "The so called coercive associations [*Zwangsgenossenschaften*], the state and the communities, will retain their great tasks in any future I can foresee," he wrote. Bureaucracy had arrived with urbanization and industrialization, and even the most far-reaching efforts toward municipalization could not do away with the need for centralized national authority of a sort that would remain at least a potential threat to popular government.[50]

Characteristically, Jaurès was more expansive about the prospects of democracy in a socialist state and more unclear about how such a system would operate. He simply asserted that a socialist state would no longer stand in adversarial relation to the people, and that the tension between administrative authority and the popular will would therefore disappear. Among several vague descriptions of this hope, the most detailed was a series of articles published in *La Revue socialiste* between March, 1895 and May, 1896, in which Jaurès outlined his vision of the collectivist future and dismissed the problem of bureaucracy in a socialist state as a fantasy projected by capitalists. When the ruling class controls the economy and the state, he argued, administrators serve the interests of capital, but as soon as the people control industry and government, the opposition between bureaucracy and democracy will end. When expertise serves everyone instead of simply those with power, those in positions of authority will no longer have interests different from those over whom they exercise authority. This formulation has a certain neatness about it, but it clearly begs the question it attempts to resolve. In his more sober moments, as I will indicate later in this chapter, Jaurès himself admitted doubts about whether the public interest could be so deftly secured.[51]

Ely's discussions of democracy and bureaucracy exhibit the ambivalence to be expected from one involved simultaneously in the professionalization of economics and the effort to extend workers' rights. On the one hand Ely deplored the excesses of capitalistic authority. Paternalistic attempts to deal with the problem of industrialization, such as the experiment at Pullman that initially intrigued American reformers, offended his democratic loyalties. On the other hand he distrusted the masses and doubted their ability to govern themselves. He indicted the architects of laissez-faire capitalism for systematically degrading the working class, yet he maintained that the "one indispensable condition of permanent improvement in the lot of laborers is their moral elevation." Like numerous reformers of his generation, Ely could not sort out his indignation concerning the exploitation responsible for workers' grim living conditions and his impatience with workers who were unable to untangle themselves from those conditions. Ely wanted to reshape the economy and reform behavior, and the two aspirations sometimes carried him in opposite directions. "As far as my general social philosophy is concerned," he wrote in self-defense during his Wisconsin ordeal in 1894, "I am a conservative rather than a radical, and in the strict sense of the term an aristocrat rather than a democrat." As if acknowledging that such comments hardly jibed with his writings or his activities, Ely noted, "When I use the word 'aristocrat,' I have in mind of course not a legal aristocracy, but a natural aristocracy." In order that such a meritocracy, to use our word for it, should be a reality rather than a dream, he concluded that this natural aristocracy should dedicate itself wholeheartedly to the "special service" of social reform along egalitarian lines.

By such verbal sleights of hand did Ely try to reconcile his belief in self-government with his doubts that the people, unaided by trained advisors (such as professional economists), could make informed political judgments. He considered the anti-intellectualism that he perceived in Populism and the labor movement as serious a threat to working-class liberation as were concentrations of economic power. Part of Ely's hesitancy about socialism, as I have noted, had to do with strategy: in the American lexicon, the label social-ist served more often to denounce than to describe. But his reticence stemmed also from his double-sided skepticism about the opposite dangers of nondemocratic government and the dangers of mob rule. His uncertainty about trusting the people ironically reflected his judgment of their non-responsiveness to radically democratic ideas; those doubts about the people's self-confidence prompted him to emphasize expertise as a guiding force. To suggest that Ely was therefore interested in social control more than social reform, or efficiency more than equality, introduces a pair of distinctions that Ely himself, and those of his contemporaries who considered them-selves reformers, would not have recognized. Like most of those involved in the progressive reform movement, he believed that democratic government required expertise in order to deal with complicated social problems effec-tively and responsibly.[52]

The difficulties implicit in that viewpoint are particularly apparent in the Webbs' writings. Ever since the publication of H. G. Wells's *The New Machiavelli* in 1911, critics have emphasized the elitism allegedly lurking beneath the Webbs' appeals to democracy. While there is much to be said for this argument, the problem of uncovering the Webbs' allegiance is thornier than some of their critics suggest. The tension between the Webbs' awareness of their own extraordinary talents and the needs of the public is present throughout their writings, but it is just that, a persistent tension. In other words, they never allowed their sense of their abilities to eclipse completely their egalitarianism. A passage in a letter Sidney wrote to Beatrice six months after their first meeting nicely illustrates this characteristic blending of attitudes: "A fearful responsibility has been laid upon us both," he began earnestly. "We have the ideas which can deliver the world. We have, to some extent, even the opportunity of making these heard and accepted."[53] Glimmering in that marvelously unselfconscious juxtaposition are not only Webb's limitless confidence in his and Beatrice's abilities and the soundness of their democratic ideas, but also his rather more limited confidence in the public's ability to appreciate the egalitarian principles so clear to him.

Sidney Webb gave a more detailed demonstration of his uncertainties in six lectures he delivered on the subject of democracy in 1896. First he argued that direct democracy was only a "primitive expedient"; the Swiss cantons illustrated how such arrangements resulted in political domination by leading families. In his second lecture he contrasted the talented elite and the untutored masses. He argued that such devices as the rotation of office robbed society of its richest resources by violating the organic principle that would assign to each part of society the responsibility it was best equipped to perform. He further counseled the use of competitive examinations to select executive officials. Next he challenged the initiative and the referendum, two measures generally popular with social democrats. He doubted that the public could really understand the intricacies of legislation, and thus he advised against giving them what amounted to a veto over the decisions of their elected representatives. Fourth, Webb denied the delegate theory of democracy and argued that elected officials had at least as great a responsibility to instruct their constituencies as to follow their wishes. As specialists in the craft of legislation, legislators should instruct the people. Finally, Webb contended that government could function effectively only if it could attract qualified public officials, and he recommended that experts be induced to serve by attractive salaries and the opportunity of permanent employment, both of which might lure the talented away from the private sector.[54]

These lectures suggest that Webb was at least as interested in efficient government as in democratic government. He characterized his social ideal as "a discreetly regulated freedom," a phrase whose patina of self-righteousness and superiority has prompted Eric Hobsbawm to describe the Webbs' ideas as "antiliberal." As Beatrice Webb recounted in the diary she kept of their trip to the United States in 1898, the awkward institutions and the amateurish officials of American democracy appalled them. Sidney wrote to Shaw, only half in jest, that if "the American nation would sell all it has, and buy with the price the Fabian Executive" to run its government, "it would make a good bargain!"[55] The Webbs sincerely believed that experts (such as themselves) who believed in democracy could govern the people more effectively than the people could govern themselves, and that conviction raises doubts about the legitimacy of considering the Webbs democrats at all.

The attribution of elitist sensibilities to social democratic and progressive reformers has become a recurrent theme among historians and social critics. As some of the Webbs' remarks suggest, the urge to reform can become an urge to control, and the sensitivity to differences of opinion may be lost in the quest for efficiency. Yet the Webbs' emphasis upon the role of the expert did not stem from a secret longing for aristocratic government. Rather they believed, as did Ely, that interdependent societies require independent analysts to separate narrow self-interest from the general will. In short, they thought democracy could survive in the twentieth century only if it could find a new path toward the public interest. Ely and the Webbs argued that the liberal pluralist model of democratic politics as a competition among special interests was no longer viable because of the concentrations of power in organized capitalism. Democracy required a new method of promoting the common good, and these American and British social democrats nominated their elite corps of experts to do that job.

During the early 1890s, Beatrice Webb later wrote, she and Sidney began "developing a new view of Democracy" in which elites played an important part.[56] They offered a thorough exposition of their ideas in *Industrial Democracy* (1902), and their understanding of the implications of inter-dependence figured prominently in their argument. In a complex society, they reasoned, the division of labor accelerates, and jobs require ever greater expertise. While this principle of functional differentiation pervades industry, the political process continues as before, with disastrous results. "It is the supreme paradox of democracy that every man is a servant in respect of the matters of which he possesses the most intimate knowledge, and for which he shows the most proficiency, namely the professional craft to which he devotes his working hours," while at the same time "he is a master over that on which he knows no more than anybody else, namely, the general interests of the community as a whole. In this paradox, we suggest, lies at once the justi-fication and the strength of democracy."

The Webbs accepted popular control as the essence of industrial democ-racy. They insisted that its exercise was more problematical in politics than in economics, however, and that the issue became more difficult as the scope of government expanded. Just as "progressive specialization" marked the modern economy, they argued, so politics should recognize the necessity of preparing specialists to serve as advisors in government. Far from advocating the removal of power from the people's hands, the Webbs wanted only to provide the public with better information to use in making decisions about policy. Only impartial administrators, whose personal fate did not hang in the balance, could help the public to recognize the costs and benefits of alter-native courses of action:

> It is only when the resources of the nation are deliberately organised and dealt with for the benefit, not of particular individuals or classes, but of the entire community; when the administration of industry, as of every other branch of human affairs, becomes the function of specialized experts, working through deliberately adjusted Common Rules; and *when the ulti-mate decision on policy rests in no other hands than those of the citizens themselves*, that the maximum aggregate development of individual intellect and individual character in the community as a whole can be attained [emphasis added].

The intervention of experts, the Webbs believed, could free industrial democracy from anarchic wars between labor and management. When special interests clashed, emotion, personal interest, and economic power determined the outcome, and the interests of the public were poorly served. Given their focus on technical knowledge and expertise, it may seem surprising that the Webbs never ceded to such advisors the final decision-making authority on questions of public policy. But they were unambiguous on this decisive issue: "Not even the wisest of men can be trusted," they concluded, "with that supreme authority which comes from the union of knowledge, capacity, and opportunity with the power of untrammelled and ultimate decision."[57] Advisors, the Webbs concluded finally, should only advise; the people should judge. *Industrial Democracy* thus ended with a ringing endorsement of democratic control over expert officials.

When the Webbs had the chance to apply these ideas to British politics after Beatrice was appointed a member of the Royal Commission on the Poor Law in 1905, however, their commitment to popular government appeared less steady. The Webbs' unsuccessful attempt to torpedo David Lloyd George's National Insurance Plan of 1911 illustrates the darker side of their elitism. During her exhaustive research on the Poor Law from 1905 to 1907, Beatrice became convinced that the insurance proposals suggested by Liberals newly converted to social reform were inadequate to solve the problem of destitution. She resolved to offer an alternative plan, which was detailed in a massive Minority Report published by the Fabian Society in 1909. The Webbs opposed the Liberals' scheme, which Lloyd George and Winston Churchill patterned after the German model constructed by Bismarck, because it relied on contributions to be collected from workers on a regressive scale, and because it did not confront the causes of poverty but dealt only with its effects. These objections were consistent with their general social democratic strategy, which sought to go beyond such palliatives to redistributive forms of taxation and more basic restructuring of the economy. As part of the plan the Webbs championed, however, they called for the institution of compulsory labor exchanges empowered to organize, train, and provide jobs for the able-bodied unemployed regardless of the prospective workers' own desires, and critics have understandably charged that such efforts overstepped the fuzzy boundary separating social reform from social control.[58]

Beatrice Webb's letters and memoirs support such an interpretation of the Minority Report. In a letter to her sister written in 1904, a year before her appointment to the Royal Commission on the Poor Law, she explained that she had in mind a set of strictures "devised by the most cold-blooded scientific expert wholly absorbed in the intellectual problem of getting erring mortals into the right state of body and mind." That chilling prospect surfaced again four years later, in the heat of the battle over the competing insurance proposals, when she wrote in her diary: "I tried to impress on [the commissioners] that any grant from the community to the individual, beyond what it does for all, ought to be conditional on better conduct and that any insurance scheme had the fatal defect that the state got nothing for its money—that the persons felt they had a right to the allowance whatever their conduct." In her struggle for the Minority Report, her patrician sensibilities overpowered her humanitarianism; she remained too deeply interested in moral and cultural uplift to accept the idea of unconditional government assistance. Even after passage of the bill had at last been secured in 1911, she continued to protest. Malingering could not be staved off "except that the amount given is so wholly inadequate" that only the very worst workmen would choose to claim the insurance and stay out of work. Her conclusion suggested the hard edge of her own approach: "No attempt is made" in the government's plan, she lamented, "to secure an advance in conduct, in return for the increased income." Not surprisingly, the Webbs' scheme elicited little enthusiasm from the working class; its conditional relief was reminiscent of the Speenhamland Law of 1795 that had pauperized rural England. The idea of offering insurance against misfortune in exchange for improved behavior testifies to the astringency of Beatrice's character and the intensity of her commitment to enforcing social responsibility. She was willing, even eager, to commit the community to a far-reaching system designed to secure a national minimum standard of living for everyone, but she insisted that obligations accompany such privileges.[59]

Viewed in light of the ethical conception of politics at the heart of social democratic theory, the Webbs' plan seems less puzzling, if no less disturbing, because it appears rooted in the idea that every individual owes a debt to society that may not be ignored. Lloyd George's plan, by contrast, followed the well-worn liberal path: respecting the freedom of individuals, he made no effort to constrain individual behavior according to prescribed community standards. When labor leaders endorsed the Liberals' plan and rejected the Webbs', they reaffirmed their long-standing resistance both to a broader conception of personal responsibility and to broader economic changes. Floating beyond the threatening specter of detention houses was the Webbs' dream of a society in which individuals freely acknowledged their inter-dependence and internalized the ethics of rational benevolence, a nation whose citizens accepted their obligations to the community willingly. Although that vision was clouded by the power such a scheme would have made available for misuse by obdurate bureaucrats, I believe the Webbs' Minority Report expressed not so much a latent authoritarian impulse as their conviction that the Liberals' insurance plan would fail to address the basic economic problem of inequality, and that it would instead have the effect expected by Churchill: "With a stake in the country in the form of insurance against evil days," he predicted, echoing Bismarck, "the workers will pay no attention to the vague promises" made by socialists.[60]

The furious propaganda campaign the Webbs launched in support of the Minority Report not only alienated their former allies in both the Liberal and Labour parties, it also disenchanted many Fabians who considered the campaign an object lesson in the futility of permeation. While the Webbs withdrew to lick their wounds on a year-long trip around the world in 1911, the Fabian Society began drifting closer to the Independent Labour party of J. Ramsay MacDonald. The Webbs had invested too much energy in the struggle for a comprehensive plan of social reconstruction to endorse the ILP's more modest aims. When they established *The New Statesman* in 1913, they immediately set about the task of redefining their political ideas to recover the larger vision of socialism from the trade unionist focus of MacDonald and his sympathizers in the Fabian Society. The result was a series of essays on the question "What is Socialism?" which emphasized that socialism, as the Webbs conceived it, was *not* simply tinkering with technical issues of administration or organization. Instead it required, to use the title of the fourth essay in this series, "Participation in Power and the Consciousness of Consent." To be effective, reform must be "the outward and visible manifestation of an inward and spiritual grace." What is needed is not merely a change of institutional arrangement but a more profound "change of heart, impelling us to a change of 'values,' permitting, in fact, the gradual reconstitution of society on the basis of public service instead of on the basis of the desire for riches." Such a transformation of values must be guided by "the scientific method" and "the best political science of the time," but mere information by itself is inadequate to the task; new values must accompany this new knowledge. Finally, in order that social reconstruction will have a lasting effect, it must be democratic, involving "participation in all social power by every adult citizen and a universal consciousness of consent in the community as a whole." These essays, which provide a splendid summary of the Webbs' social democratic theory, demonstrate conclusively that their interest in reforming behavior must be understood in the context of their fundamental commitment to a society resting on "a universal consciousness of consent." Empirical study, joined with ethical regeneration, can make possible the creation of a genuinely democratic society. That reasoning lay at the heart of social democratic theory.[61]

During the course of World War I, the Webbs became more closely associated with the Labour party, and after the war ended they helped prepare the party's new manifesto. As contemporaries understood, however, that affiliation merely confirmed the reverse permeation the Webbs had feared: Labour had captured the Fabians rather than vice versa. Given the limited concessions sought by the trade unions that dominated the Labour party, the inclusion of an explicitly socialist plank in the platform represented nothing more than a symbolic concession to those who longed for ethical regeneration instead of better wages and hours legislation. The lower middle class salariat originally attracted to the moral socialism of the Fabian Society was swallowed up by the Labour party, and the Fabians' ideal of a cooperative community served no more than a rhetorical function in party policy during the interwar years. Although now formally linked with the Labour party, the Webbs continued to envision a more thorough restructuring of British society than their party seemed willing to consider. Their *Constitution for the Socialist Commonwealth of Great Britain* (1920), written almost two decades after *Industrial Democracy*, indicates the persistence of the Webbs' desire for a new social spirit and their reliance on disinterested elites as a safeguard of the common good. Disturbed by the increasingly apparent tendencies toward centralization in state authority accentuated by the war, they proposed an elaborate system of checks and balances in which government officials were to play a vital but carefully limited part. The "disinterested professional expert" who performs administrative and research tasks, they cautioned, should have "no power of command and no right to insist on his suggestions being adopted. His function is exhausted when his report is made." Decision-making power should remain in the hands of the public, which, having access to the best information attainable, should be both more informed and more effective in asserting its will.

The Webbs were unpersuaded by arguments that a "humane or well-meaning" aristocracy was needed to rein in the excesses of a public whose weakness for hysteria received considerable attention in the aftermath of World War I. "What is wrong with the world to-day," they concluded, "is not too much Democracy but too little, not too many thoroughly democratic institutions but too few."[62] The Webbs repeatedly endorsed the principle of democracy in their work, and while they emphasized the need for experts in democratic government, they did so from the conviction that social analysis enables the people to govern themselves with a clearer understanding of the consequences of their decisions. This is not to suggest that the Webbs resolved the tensions between popular control and elite manipulation. They did not. Their faith that expertise could be kept separate from influence exhibited little appreciation of the subtle shift from knowledge to power that is part of politics in the twentieth century, when expertise carries its own authority.

It is instructive that the Webbs and Ely showed somewhat greater confidence in the ability and the disinterestedness of bureaucrats than did Bernstein. Whereas in Germany government officials identified themselves with the military and the aristocracy rather than the masses, in Great Britain and America white-collar workers did not inherit the same prestige or power. In contrast to German bureaucrats, who governed with little interference from the untutored subjects under their care, the government officials envisioned by Ely and the Webbs were to demonstrate the skill of their German counterparts without exercising the same autocratic power. Impressed by the efficiency of German officials but oriented toward democratic values, Anglo-American social democrats expected the administrators of their government to be very much like themselves: talented, conscientious, and sincerely dedicated to their perception of the common good. They saw no conflict between highly trained bureaucrats and lively democratic government, because they thought greater expertise would make possible more sophisticated public debate and more efficient execution of the public's will. They did not suspect what later experience has shown about the insulation of administrators from public pressure and their vulnerability to private power. In short, they simply did not perceive the depth of the conflict between bureaucracy and democracy.[63]

The theorists of social democracy believed that the challenges facing their societies could be met by extending democratic principles from politics to the economy and the society. The triumph of socialism, they argued, meant eliminating the legal and institutional supports undergirding privilege. If the popular will could express itself freely, then a cooperative, self-governing society would eventually emerge. In 1885, during his first political campaign, Jaurès articulated this animating spirit of social democratic theory. After comparing various systems of government, he concluded that only a "regime of popular control, discussion, and freedom" can "err without irreparable harm." In such a state "a mistake can be corrected, because every man can make his criticisms known and help to reshape national policy." The gradual shift from a capitalist to a socialist economy was a necessary but not sufficient condition for the transformation these thinkers sought. Democracy was the more fundamental requirement, because as Jaurès pointed out, in a democracy a social process of pragmatic truth testing can operate freely.

Bernstein stressed a similar argument in *Evolutionary Socialism*. Although his experience in England suggested that bureaucrats could be Fabian socialists like Sidney Webb instead of Prussian aristocrats, he remained worried about concentrating power in the state. "Democracy is a condition of socialism," he insisted; "it is not only the means but also the substance." Specifying the shape of the socialist future was impossible for that reason, but these thinkers accepted such uncertainty as the price of their democratic convictions. Although the public might move fitfully, or perhaps not at all, in the direction of socialism, no alternative path was available. Unless the people freely adopted the principles of cooperation and equality, unless they endorsed the Webbs' principles of "participation in all social power by every adult citizen and a universal consciousness of consent in the community as a whole," government authority and the public interest would continue to strain against one another.[64] Whether expertise and the common good could be made to pull together in the harness of social democracy was a question these thinkers answered in different ways, and the differences reflected their national historical experiences and their visions of the possibility of social harmony. The Webbs, Ely, and to a certain degree Bernstein, all of whom placed somewhat greater emphasis on the role of elites, also exhibited more confidence in the ultimate resolution of conflict in socialist society. Jaurès and Rauschenbusch, who distrusted experts and prized democracy above efficient administration, were less optimistic. The reason for that difference is to be found in their political ideals.

3. Liberty, Equality, and Fraternity Reconsidered

The theorists of social democracy affirmed the eighteenth-century triad of liberty, equality and fraternity. These ideals, however, required rethinking, both in light of social and economic developments that altered their significance in the world of organized capitalism, and in light of new conceptualizations of individual and cultural experience. Liberty and equality must be made effective rather than merely formal, these thinkers insisted, because interdependence limited the exercise of rights guaranteed to individuals by law. Their ideal of social cohesion, the voluntary blending of private wills with the public interest, resurrected the classical emphasis on the intimate relation between autonomy, cooperation, and virtue. The conception of liberty as freedom from oppression served a constructive function in the eighteenth century, Ely pointed out, by fueling the fires of revolution and capitalism. But as the forces unleashed by bourgeois revolutions matured, the world in which the values of the Enlightenment were useful disappeared. By the late nineteenth century, the threat to liberty appeared in economic rather than political guise. The ideal of laissez-faire, the "absence of all social regulations," meant in practice "the unrestricted tyranny of the strong."

Social democrats appreciated the twin ironies of liberalism's historical connection with industrialization. First, as modern economies matured, the values that underlay their expansion became socially dysfunctional. Individual property rights lost their progressive significance and became barriers to the further expansion of freedom. In Rauschenbusch's words, "Capitalism set out as the opponent of privilege and the champion of freedom; it has ended by being the defender of privilege and the intrenchment of autocracy." Second, with industrialization came both the potential to eradicate poverty and the creation of a kind of poverty more debilitating than that characteristic of preindustrial societies. The customs that limited competition in the early modern era crumbled before the irresistible force of industrial development, and "new economic theories were developed which sanctioned what was going on and secured the support of public opinion and legislation for those who were driving the machine through the framework of the social structure."[65] The resulting disjunction between the possibility of general prosperity and the reality of class division preoccupied these theorists. While they resisted the temptation to find in "plenty" the solution to social conflict—a temptation to which thinkers as different as Marx and Henry George succumbed—they did insist that steps toward harmony could be taken only by resolving the paradox of poverty created by progress.

By the end of the nineteenth century the negative concept of liberty had become a pretense shielding privilege. Jaurès maintained in *The Origins of German Socialism* that the poor were not free regardless of their legal rights, because they were bound by the oppression of hunger, and in his later writings he presented several variations on this theme. "To conceive of freedom only in its negative aspect," he wrote in 1903, would make the inhabitant of Constantinople, "not subject like the Parisians to regulations over hygiene and roads, not forced to send his children to school, a free citizen, while we are the victims of tyranny." Sidney Webb was fond of compiling lists of the regulations that liberated rather than enslaved British citizens, and he drew the same conclusion: liberal shibboleths concerning negative freedom from government were meaningless; actual barriers presented by poverty were a more serious impediment to liberty. "If Liberty means every man being his own master," the Webbs wrote in *Industrial Democracy*, then it is clearly inconsistent not so much with democratic reforms as with "the crowding together of population in dense masses, division of labour, and we think, civilization itself." Libertarian fantasies never tempted social democrats, because they believed that the pastoral dream of complete freedom becomes a nightmare, in the reality of the industrialized world, for everyone except the wealthiest members of society. As interdependence had replaced independence as a condition of social life, so positive liberty had to replace negative liberty as an ideal. Viewed from this perspective, freedom is not "any quantum of natural or inalienable rights," the Webbs insisted, "but such conditions of existence in the community as do, in practice, result in the utmost development of faculty in the individual human being." As a result of economic changes, freedom conceived as government noninterference had become a hollow promise. A society in which a minority of citizens held "all the opportunities of livelihood in its arbitrary control," Rauschenbusch wrote, while the great majority were without property and "without an assured means of even working for a living," was a society in which freedom had been strangled rather than secured.[66]

Liberals customarily began with the assumption that freedom from political control was the primary objective; given rights, individuals could shape their lives as they chose, and from their own labor they could obtain property. Socialists, Ely pointed out, had a different conception of liberty because they concentrated on economic rights rather than political rights. They wanted everyone to have "a voice in the control of industry, and not be subjected to the rules of others." Beyond this difference in focus, Ely pointed out, lay a difference in social analysis. Socialists "perceived that the chief restrictions upon freedom of movement at the present time are economic in nature, and in this they are quite correct." Jaurès drew a similar contrast between the path followed by liberals from political to economic liberty and the "*marche inverse*" of socialists, but he emphasized that whereas liberals tended to downplay the importance of a "moral ideal" in their concentration on personal freedom, socialists refused to separate ethical from social and political considerations. This dual emphasis on moral as well as institutional reform, which was one of the distinctive features of social democratic as opposed to both Marxist and laissez-faire liberal theory, was the foundation of Rauschenbusch's social gospel. "Our moral and legal theories about the rights of the individual in using the resources of nature and in operating his tools to get wealth," Rauschenbusch pointed out with reference to the liberal theory of the social contract, assume a small population and simple methods of agricultural and craft production. Although once legitimate and useful, the personal rights based on those assumptions "will have to be resocialized" to fit a new reality and new ideas of responsibility. Not socialized but "resocialized," Rauschenbusch insisted; he contended that liberal individualism represented only an aberration from the longer trend toward cooperation.[67]

The people won their political freedom by marching behind the banner of liberalism, but they could be liberated from their economic bondage only by shifting their allegiance to a positive ideal of freedom. Drawing on the writings of Green and Fouillée, social democrats emphasized the individual's freedom to act effectively rather than his freedom from being acted upon by government. "True liberty means the expression of the positive powers of the individual," Ely wrote. Like Green and Fouillée, he argued that such liberty could be secured not by a policy of laissez-faire but by the active promotion of effective rights through the intervention of government. Social democrats denied emphatically that their expanded idea of freedom, or the expanded role they envisioned for the state to guarantee it, in any way challenged essential individual rights. Expressing an argument reminiscent of Hegel or Green, Webb wrote that preserving "individual liberty to do other than the *right* course" merely reflects society's ignorance and the ability of the powerful to protect their interests. Jaurès insisted in a thoughtful essay, "Socialism and Liberty," that a collectivist society "will give the fullest scope to liberty, to all liberties; it is for them, more and more, the necessary condition." He stressed elsewhere that "justice is inseparable from liberty," and that socialism, as he conceived of it, was above all a method "to obtain through the fullness of freedom the greatest possible efficacy of human energies."[68] This concept of positive freedom carried with it an altered notion of the right to private property.

Liberal property rights meshed with the world of Locke and Bentham, but they clattered noisily against the framework of urban-industrial society. The very institution of private property was merely an "intermediate and necessary stage of evolution between two forms of communism," Rauschen-busch claimed; the family, the school, and the church operated on communal principles, and he expected such forms of organization to become increasingly prominent. Just as the city water system replaced the community water well and the backyard pump, so the capitalist system would be replaced eventually by the socialization of the economy. Rauschenbusch used the idea of "stewardship," which other advocates of the social gospel such as Ely also invoked, to express his conception of property. Those who own property, he argued, hold it for society as stewards. By asserting their absolute claim to property, liberal individualists usurped society's presumptive right to ownership, and society must reassert its claim and remind stewards that they are guardians of a trust which the people can revoke. Rauschenbusch did not propose doing away with private property. He insisted only that property be used to maintain and develop life rather than the other way around. While ownership should be the means and life the end, capitalism reversed those priorities and forced the people to serve the interests of capital.[69]

None of these theorists sought to abolish private property. They all wanted to expand the role of public ownership through municipalization and nationalization of certain industries and all natural monopolies, but they did not envision a society without personal property. "Far from being hostile to the institution of private property," the Webbs wrote in their *Constitution of the Socialist Commonwealth of Great Britain*, "it would necessarily be one of the fundamental objects of a Socialist Commonwealth so to broaden the base and extend the benefits of private ownership as continously to increase its aggregate amount." Social democrats accepted the idea of private ownership, but they protested that, in the Webbs' words, "to extend private property to the ownership of the instruments of production is a perversion of the institution." While the liberal concept of property rights may have seemed sensible in the early phase of industrialization, by the late nineteenth century it had become apparent "that with free competition and private property in land and capital, no individual can possibly obtain the full result of his own labor." Thus, as Sidney Webb wrote in *Fabian Essays in Socialism*, public ownership should supplant private ownership of the means of production, and "private property in land and capital will inevitably go the way of the feudalism which it superseded."[70]

Jaurès tied these ideas together. The individual is born into society with certain vested rights, he maintained, including the "free use of the means of labor that have been accumulated by human efforts." Although the value of property derives from its social character, the concept of liberal property rights overlooks the relation and allows individuals to appropriate for themselves what should remain a community resource. Property thus becomes exclusive, and rather than benefiting society it becomes a source of personal profit. Liberal theory extends to everyone the formal right to obtain property, but gradually the accumulation of capital enables one class to use property to enrich itself while other classes are excluded. Thus, the exercise of liberal property rights slowly robbed workers of their right to property. In industrial capitalism, Jaurès wrote, because the ownership of the means of production is in the hands of a single class, it is "a power of exploitation and oppression." By transferring the ownership of capital to all citizens, socialists sought to transform capitalist property into social property and return property rights to the community from which they originate. The social ownership of property, he insisted, "is merely opportunity of action brought within the reach of all."[71]

Ely made a similar case in his widely read text *Introduction to Political Economy*, where he argued that moderate socialists "make no war on capital, strictly speaking," because only fools would kill such a golden goose. "What socialists object to is not capital but the private capitalist. They desire to nationalize capital and to abolish capitalists as a distinct class by making everybody, as a member of the community, a capitalist; that is, a partial owner of all the capital in the country."[72] That passage illustrates Ely's persistent attempts to defang socialism for American audiences by minimizing its threat to all but the most wealthy segments of society. That image of a society in which everyone is his or her own capitalist was close to the center of the social democratic vision. Although only Bernstein elaborated the idea of socialism as a wildly expanded joint-stock corporation with all citizens as shareholders, schemes of that sort were common among those who shared his belief that corporate capitalism pointed the way toward a more socialized but equally productive economy.

The transformation of the idea of liberty from negative to positive culminated in calls for the socialization of property. Social democrats developed the argument suggested by the philosophers of the *via media*: the interdependent world of the late nineteenth century rendered the conception of negative freedom obsolete. The formal right to accumulate property without legal interference was useless in a world marked by increasing economic oppression. For when some individuals could enter the game with enormous advantages, the equality that ostensibly accompanied individual freedom in liberal theory faded from ideal to illusion. The theorists of social democracy wanted to restrict private ownership of the means of production in order to extend private ownership of personal property to a wider range of people. By limiting the property rights of capitalists, they were fond of saying, they could broaden the property rights of the people. Unlike some of their socialist predecessors and some of their contemporaries, they believed in a middle course concerning property. They wanted only to outlaw ownership of land and capital and to preserve personal property that could not be used to produce further wealth. That distinction shelters in its ambiguity a Pandora's box of difficulties, but these thinkers' unwillingness to specify the scope of acceptable property was consistent with the open-endedness of their general approach to such questions. This vagueness, although disconcerting, was rooted in their conviction that more specific answers to such questions could only be provided over time through a democratic process of social experimentation.

These thinkers' commitment to positive freedom prompted them to deny that the welfare state could serve as more than a temporary accommodation on the way toward socialism. I have already indicated that they supported welfare legislation as a positive step even though they recognized its potentially counterproductive implications. In *Evolutionary Socialism*, Bernstein declared allegiance to the principle that "the modern proletarian is indeed poor but that he is no pauper. In this distinction lies a whole world, the nature of our fight, the hope of our victory." Social insurance was acceptable only as a stopgap measure; paternalism was no substitute for equality. Rauschenbusch drew a simple but instructive analogy to contrast charity and welfare with the more comprehensive solution he preferred. The head of an asylum for the insane, Rauschenbusch wrote, used a simple test to distinguish the sane from the insane. He took patients to a basin of water under a running faucet, gave them dippers, and asked them to empty the water from the basin. "The insane merely dipped and dipped. The sane turned off the faucet and dipped out the rest."[73]

Social democrats endorsed the welfare state for the same reason they supported progressive taxation; namely, as a symbolic commitment to the principle of community responsibility. But they insisted that such measures made sense only in the mad world of capitalism. It would be more sensible, they reasoned, to close off the source of poverty. Social democrats considered liberty impossible without equality, so they reversed the priorities of liberalism and rated equalization of wealth above preservation of unrestricted property rights. They faced what Jaurès called the "essential truth" that despite professed guarantees of equal rights, a small group of individuals, "privileged by education and wealth, exercises decisive political and economic power."[74] Since the concentration of power precluded the exercise of positive freedom, social democrats hoped to transform equality of opportunity from a slogan to a fact by working to achieve at least approximate equality of condition through the gradual redistribution of wealth.

These theorists' ambivalence regarding the role of elites in democracy resurfaced in their discussions of equality. Given the existence of inequality either in capacity or in opportunity, the Webbs wrote, "a free struggle among unequal individuals, or combinations of individuals, means the permanent oppression and degradation of those who start handicapped, and inevitably results in a tacit conspiracy among the more favored classes to maintain or improve their own positions of vantage at the cost of the community at large." Yet the Webbs lapsed into fuzzy language in describing what constitutes genuine equality, insisting only "on the need for a conscious and deliberate organization of society, based, not on vested interests or the chances of the fight, but on the scientifically ascertained need of each section of citizens."[75] Unfortunately, they failed to specify who is to determine, and by what ostensibly scientific measure, the "needs of each section of citizens." The people, presumably, would make such decisions democratically, but given the importance the Webbs assigned to elites in the formulation of public policy, the precise manner in which such decisions would be made remains unclear.

Ely maintained that the ideal distribution of rewards would lead "to the maximum satisfaction of wants, that is, distribution in accordance with needs. This means equal distribution among equals, but unequal distribution among those who are unequal; and, as a matter of fact, inequalities among men, in capacity and requirements, are immense." That passage reveals Ely's tortured indecision on the issue of distribution that Sidgwick and Green disputed. He seemed first to endorse an uncomplicated utilitarian summing of pleasures to attain the "maximum satisfaction of wants," but when he defined that end as "distribution in accordance with needs," he suggested immediately not only that needs differ but that some, as Sidgwick pointed out to Green, can only be satisfied at the expense of others, as in the case of developing extraordinary artistic or perhaps even administrative or intellectual capacities. How are these incommensurable needs to be weighed, particularly when inequalities of ability and desire are acknowledged, as Ely did? Unfortunately, it is impossible to determine precisely what Ely or the Webbs understood by equal distribution. Although Ely on the one hand described the goal of socialism expansively as the "most perfect development of all human faculties in each individual," a phrase worthy of Green at his most grandiloquent, on the other hand he warned that this "means anything but equality. It means the richest diversity, for differentiation accompanies development." When Ely described the aim of political economy as "such a production and distribution of economic goods as must in the highest practicable degree subserve the end and purpose of human existence for all members of society," he meant to offer more than a truism. But in the absence of more specific content for the chestnut about the "end and purpose of human existence," his statement seems to shrivel toward meaninglessness.[76]

Its potential significance, however, emerges from the more thoughtful arguments formulated by Jaurès and Rauschenbusch, whose writings indicate that social democracy had another face besides that presented by Ely and the Webbs. Jaurès's passionate republicanism and Rauschenbusch's social Christianity sprang from deeply egalitarian sensibilities. Rauschenbusch consistently emphasized that effective freedom and self-development depend on the equalization of wealth and power. "Approximate equality is the only enduring foundation of political democracy," he declared in *Christianity and the Social Crisis*. That foundation, "which is one of the richest endowments of our American life, is slipping from us" as a result of the excesses of liberal individualism. "Actual inequality," Rauschenbusch maintained, "endangers the sense of equality." With industrialization, "the extremes of wealth and poverty are much farther apart than formerly, and thus the poor are at least relatively poorer." Since people have unequal capacities, their inherent inequalities of talent will inevitably be reflected in some inequality of possessions. Yet beneath superficial inequalities of intellect, Rauschenbusch insisted, lies "the fundamental endowment of human personality, and in that we are all equal." Responding to charges that socialists embraced an unrealistic ideal of perfect equality, he protested that he wanted only approximate equality. The least society can do, he contended, is refrain "from perpetuating and increasing the handicap of the feebler by such enormous inequalities of property as we have now." The assertion that such inequalities mirror actual differences in ability was idle talk, which became "more absurd with every year as we see great fortunes grow." Rauschenbusch had little patience with those who feared that equality would restrain ability under the numbing hand of mediocrity. "If ability can be held down it is not very able," he suggested to defenders of privilege, and he volunteered to join a crusade for the emancipation of the strong should the time of their oppression ever come.[77]

He presented an even stronger statement of this argument in *Christianizing the Social Order*: "Men can have no fraternal relations until they face one another with a sense of freedom and of equal humanity. Despotism is always haunted by dread, and fear is not a symptom of the prevalence of fraternity." He then offered the standard social democratic justification of redistribution: "We are told that democracy has proved a failure. It has in so far as it was crippled and incomplete. Political democracy without economic democracy," he concluded, is "a form without substance." As that statement suggests, the meaning of social democrats' demands for redistribution cannot be found outside their commitment to democratic decision making. Whether there will be ways to achieve distributive justice for all members of society despite their unequal abilities and diverse interests cannot be answered in the abstract, in advance of the effort to test different options democratically. Seen in the context of the theory of voluntary action and the pragmatic theory of truth, Ely's hedge concerning the "highest practicable degree" to which political economy can "subserve the end and purpose of human existence" appears less evasive than decisive. For only within a framework of equality can the various needs of different individuals be weighed fairly; only in a vigorous democracy can alternative ways of meeting competing demands be tested and progressively refined. No adequate formula can be specified, as James put it, "before the last man has had his experience and said his say," because the possibility always exists that new ideas originating in new experiences will prove instructive.[78] Distributive justice must remain a challenge to be met by communities struggling to establish a structure of rewards that takes into account inequalities of ability and differences of interest while at the same time providing incentives for effort and initiative. Like the philosophers of the *via media*, the theorists of social democracy denied in principle that answers to such questions can be offered in advance of flexible, social experimentation. Perhaps more emphatically than the earlier generation, however, they insisted that no fair test is possible outside the context of approximate equality and democratic decision making.

As Rauschenbusch indicated in the summary of his argument in *A Theology for the Social Gospel*, economic, political, and ethical objectives interlocked in these ideas:

> An outlook toward the future in which the spiritual life is saved and the economic life is left unsaved is both unchristian and stupid. . . . Our chief interest in any millennium is the desire for a social order in which the worth and freedom of every last human being will be honored and protected, in which the brotherhood of man will be expressed in the common possession of the economic resources of society; and in which the spiritual good of humanity will be set high above the private profit interests of all materialistic groups.[79]

The final part of that passage suggests another important element distinguishing social democracy from Marxism in theory as well as strategy: denial of the class struggle. Whereas Marx had located the conflict between the bourgeoisie and the proletariat in the heart of society, social democrats saw only a disjunction between law and economics, between democracy and capitalism, which could be resolved by political action. Marx dismissed social reform as chimerical because he believed that no extension of democratic rights could alter the fundamental tension rooted in the historical struggle for control over the means of production. These revisionists argued that history reflects human will as much as socioeconomic imperatives, and they were not persuaded that the pathology of capitalism would resist the therapy of political reform. They reasoned that as capitalism emerged from feudalism through the fusion of initiative and economic development, so a socialist system might grow from late nineteenth-century European and American society.

For some of the same reasons that they rejected Marx's historical and economic analysis, social democrats altered his theory of class conflict. They denied that the middle classes were sinking into the proletariat. They argued that the evidence suggested instead a broader, more complex system, with numerous gradations within and among classes, an arrangement that complicated Marx's concept of class struggle. As a result, they intended to construct a coalition of various classes as an end as well as a means. "The true aim of the best socialism," Ely wrote, "is that general social amelioration which proposes to sacrifice no class, but to improve and elevate all classes." That approach to social change, which attracted Americans like Ely and Rauschenbusch from liberalism to the cause of social democracy, caused orthodox Marxists to accuse Bernstein, Jaurès, and the Webbs of abandoning Marx entirely. Social democrats believed, with Ely, that "it is not by any means necessary to make socialism a purely working-class movement." The question of socialism, after all, concerns all classes of society: "It is by no means evident that wage-earners will obtain greater benefit than any other social class. ... What is called an 'all-classes socialism' is stronger than a working-class socialism." Ely regretted the development in Germany of a class-based socialist movement, to which he correctly attributed the peculiar disjunction between rhetoric and reality in German socialism, and he contrasted that situation with the more broadly based socialism he saw developing in England and hoped to develop in the United States.[80]

By conceiving of socialism as an ethical ideal rather than an inevitable result of capitalist exploitation, social democrats abandoned Marx's identification of socialism with the working class. Bernstein characterized the idea of class as a "purely abstract concept," and he thus challenged the foundation of *The Communist Manifesto*. Whereas Marx consistently criticized the idea of solidarity as a cynical and self-serving trick the bourgeoisie played on the proletariat, Bernstein believed that socialism would emerge as an expression of the will of all of the people, a manifestation of the extension of popular sovereignty from politics to economics and society.[81]

Social democracy, in short, involved the integration of individual, group, and class interests with the larger interest of society as a whole. Marx had said that the proletariat would become the universal class by passing through the fires of immiseration. Social democrats, although they steadfastly supported proletarian demands, believed that no single class served as the exclusive carrier of the general will. In Jaurès's words, socialism is "destined for the benefit of all." For that reason, "it must be prepared and accepted by almost all, practically indeed by all; because the hour inevitably arrives when the power behind an immense majority discourages the last efforts to resist its will." Socialism could be achieved only by mobilizing all classes around an ideal of social integration. Although rooted firmly in their commitment to improving the condition of the working class, the ideal of these thinkers, like their strategy and tactics, transcended narrow conceptions of the proletariat. Socialism, as they envisioned it, could not be the work of a revolutionary vanguard; it had to be achieved peacefully and democratically if it were to be achieved at all. In Jaurès's words, "the noblest thing about Socialism is precisely that it is not the regime of a minority. It cannot, therefore, and ought not to be imposed by a minority."[82]

Because of their commitment to an ideal extending beyond the limits of the working class, social democrats were skeptical of the role of producers' cooperatives and trade unions in a projected socialist future. The Webbs provided the template for such analyses. They contended that "the needs and desires of the consumers should be the main factor in determining the commodities and services to be produced," and for that reason they challenged the claim of guild socialists that trade unions should control industrial production. Because manual workers bring no special knowledge to the problem of determining what should be produced, and because they are trained to perform particular services, the Webbs argued, "they are even biased against the inevitable changes in demand which characterize a progressive community." While workers should not be required to concede their right to strike, neither should they be allowed to govern themselves independently, because "no man can be trusted to be judge in his own case."[83] Producers would naturally seek better than average pay, conditions, and hours for themselves, so their interests would run counter to the interests of society as a whole. Bernstein adopted the Webbs' posture toward cooperatives in *Evolutionary Socialism*.[84] Citing as evidence Beatrice Webb's *The Co-operative Movement in Great Britain* (1891), Bernstein argued that whereas consumers organize to protect the general interest, producers organize primarily to advance their own interest and as a result, producers' cooperatives can operate as a divisive force in any economic system.[85]

Beyond that structural difficulty, these thinkers perceived in the late nineteenth-century labor movement distressingly individualistic values. Segments of the working class retarded the progress of socialism by their resistance to interclass solidarity. While some genuine collectivists participated in the British labor movement, the Webbs wrote in *Industrial Democracy*, they were matched by conservatives, who exhibited an "abiding faith in the sanctity of vested interests" and "a strong presumption in favor of the *status quo*," and individualists, who confidently placed "the welfare of the community under the guardianship of self-interest" and only wanted to organize labor in order to challenge the self-interest of capital. The Webbs considered it reckless to entrust workers possessing such antisocialist values with control over production in their sectors of the economy.[86] Given the values of American labor, Ely believed, workers' control over production, pricing, and profit would end in chaos, because no sense of solidarity had yet emerged to moderate the pursuit of individual self-interest. The roots of possessive individualism ran too deep in the American value system to permit any group to police itself. Perhaps surprisingly, Bernstein applied the same analysis to the German labor movement. He argued that the German workers' associations were neither socialistic nor democratic. "Far from being a suitable form for removing the capitalist from the field of modern large industries," he contended, "they are much more a return to pre-capitalist production."[87] The contrast between the German labor movement, with its origins in medieval workers' associations, and the American labor movement, marked by strikingly dissimilar individualistic values, has occasionally been offered to explain the uneven progress of socialism in Germany and America. The appearance of this argument in both Bernstein's and Ely's, as well as the Webbs', analyses of workers' control suggests once again the convergence of ideas in social democratic theory, and it underscores the centrality of their opposition to Marx's class analysis.

An undercurrent of ambivalence regarding the proper balance of state authority and popular control ran through these theorists' discussions of the tension between producers and consumers in the socialist economy of the future. Articles Jaurès wrote in 1895–1896 for *La Revue socialiste* testify to his concern about the bureaucratic threat to democratic prerogatives. "A central planning commission could not possibly wield all the power or resolve all the problems" in a socialist state, Jaurès wrote. "The government would have to decentralize, granting both autonomy and initiative to local groups." In the industrial sectors, unions of the same trade would federate locally and elect delegates to a national planning commission. The authority of local and regional federations and councils would be limited, however, to avoid an economic *imperium in imperio*. The central planning commission, "elected, composed of representatives of both the separate industries and the nation as a whole, would have the final authority to allocate resources, to ensure proper investment, and to determine prices and wages." Thus Jaurès, who began by conceding the undesirability of vesting ultimate authority in a central planning commission, appeared to take refuge in the very concentration of bureaucratic power he set out to avoid. Centralization appeared to offer the only escape from the kinds of conflict described by the Webbs, Bernstein, and Ely. Evidently trapped in an analytical cul-de-sac, he bravely announced his confidence that, through the dynamic shifting of responsibility from local to central authority and back again, sensibilities might be honed in such a way that self-interest might fit snugly into the common good. For Jaurès, the democratic nature of the entire process, as he envisioned it, would prevent both excessive inefficiency and authoritarianism. Expertise would never be disconnected from popular control. As he concluded, with characteristic ebullience, through such a process a socialist society might eventually become "both disciplined and free, centralized and varied, planned and spontaneous."[88] Although a certain amount of centralization would be necessary, it could be controlled if economic decision making, like political decision making, were thoroughly democratic.

Like the philosophers of the *via media*, Jaurès, Rauschenbusch, Ely, Bernstein, and the Webbs prized positive liberty and social equality. They embraced an ideal of justice as the fair, democratically determined distribution of opportunities and rewards for all members of society. The difference between the confidence of Green and Fouillée and the skepticism of Sidgwick and James concerning the possibility of achieving those goals has been traced to their competing visions of ethics and their competing ideas of historical development. Placed in that context, the theorists of social democracy all conceived of morality as self-realization and history as the triumphant, if erratic, march of progressive principles. Yet another difference cut across their epic mood. As I have emphasized, Ely, Bernstein, and the Webbs put more faith in elites. With the guidance of expert administrators, they believed, the people should be able to advance steadily toward the social democratic ideal of justice defined as social solidarity.

Ely repeatedly affirmed his confidence that "men's interests are inextricably intertwined" in the industrialized world. "The sooner the idea of social solidarity, which is not only a doctrine but also a real fact, is recognized in all its ramifications, the better it will be for us." He denied that individual interest inevitably conflicts with the common good. "Social solidarity means the oneness of human interest; it signifies the dependence of man upon man, both in good things and in evil things. Social solidarity means that our true welfare is not an individual matter purely, but likewise a social affair: our weal is common weal; we thrive only in a common wealth." Echoing Green and Fouillée's theme of self-development as the harmonizing of personal with community interest, he declared, "We fulfill our own mission and develop our own true individuality, not in isolation, but in society, and by bringing ourselves in body and mind into harmony with the laws of social solidarity." He tried to reassure those who discerned in such ideas the subordination of personal freedom to the will of the whole: "This view, however, does not imply a conflict between the development of the individual and the development of society. Self-development for the sake of others is the aim of social ethics. Self and others, the individual and society, are thus united in one purpose."[89] Clearly bound up in those statements were the concepts of individual experience as social, ethical action as rational benevolence, and politics as the quest for justice.

Ely carried that gospel with him when he left Johns Hopkins for the University of Wisconsin, and he played a major role in the political revival that was Wisconsin progressivism. His protests to the contrary notwithstanding, he never effectively solved the problem of identifying the interests of the individual with those of the community. Instead, just as Sidgwick accused Green of doing, he shifted between broader and narrower conceptions of social responsibility. At times he called for the radical transformation of society and the socialization of the means of production, but occasionally he retreated to vague jeremiads calling for a spirit of cooperation and justice. Like Green, he never faced the central problem of institutionalizing his idea of distributive justice, and as Sidgwick predicted, in the long run the price of such ambiguity turned out to be political ineffectiveness.

The Wisconsin progressive movement, which sprang from the experience of interdependence galvanized by the depression of the 1890s, embodied many of Ely's ideas. Progressives' awareness that society was becoming more organic in fact nourished their conviction that it should become more cooperative in spirit. Wisconsin progressives echoed Ely's recommendation that solidarity replace individualism as a primary social value. Reform sentiment emanated from consumers who realized that their freedom was being challenged by corporate arrogance, and this popular sensibility found expression in a political activism focused on a quest for the public interest.

The people's sense of themselves as a community derived primarily from two sources, the social gospel and the new social science; in both of these spheres Ely was the dominant figure.[90]

While tracing the dissemination of social democratic ideas falls beyond the scope of this study, I want to emphasize the consistency between the arguments advanced by Ely and the ideology of Wisconsin progressivism, because I believe that the same ambiguity apparent in Ely's treatment of the integration of individual and public interest eventually crippled progressivism in Wisconsin. Ely never adequately explained how elites should bring the quest for personal profit into conformity with the common good. Like Green and Fouillée, he asserted only that government must advance the public interest by balancing competing private interests. Unfortunately, as historians of progressivism have repeatedly demonstrated, the reforms instituted in the name of the public interest often served ironically to protect the excesses of privilege and power they were designed to control, and politicians' invocations of the common good served merely as a rhetorical gloss to deflect public attention from private power.[91]

It would be a mistake to see in America's progressive reform legislation a mirror image of social democratic ideas. As I have suggested, Ely advocated considerably more radical measures than the American polity ever endorsed. He was, for example, an incisive critic of that peculiarly impotent weapon much favored by progressives, the regulatory agency, and he championed, albeit inconsistently, far greater equalization of political, social, and economic conditions than the majority of Americans proved willing to support. As a partisan of professionalization among economists, Ely worked to raise the level of competence as well as the status of American administrators in the public and private sectors of the economy. But inasmuch as he advocated administrative solutions to social problems, he contributed indirectly to the insulation of elites from public pressure and helped to perpetuate rather than transform organized capitalism. The theory of social democracy rested on the idea that socialism could be achieved by extending democratic principles from politics to the economy and society. Ely's emphasis on elites betrayed that central premise.[92] The Webbs' writings exhibit a similar tendency to compromise democracy by relying on experts to advance the public interest. In his contribution to *Fabian Essays in Socialism*, Sidney Webb endorsed the ideal of social solidarity in words quite similar to Ely's. "The community must necessarily aim, consciously or not, at its continuance as a community; its life transcends that of any of its members; and the interests of the individual unit must often clash with those of the whole." In such instances of conflict, society must assert its will, for "without the continuance and sound health of the social organism, no man can now live or thrive; and its persistence is accordingly his paramount end." Although individuals will always look after their own interests, "where such action proves inimical to the social welfare, it must sooner or later be checked by the whole, lest the whole perish through the error of its members."[93]

Hardy individualism no longer sufficed in an interdependent world.

Individuals who proved unable to harness their personal desires to the public purpose, social democrats believed, must be compelled to serve the community. If the natural identification of individual and public interest is assumed, that prospect seems harmless enough. But when the logic of social democracy, so cogent in the abstract, ran aground on public apathy or opposition, the prospect of force seemed a viable option. The antidemocratic implications of the Webbs' approach to social integration surfaced frequently enough, as in the debate over Lloyd George's insurance plan, to suggest the problematic nature of their emphasis on elites. They maintained in *Industrial Democracy* that the community must stand above all its constituent parts. "To its elected representatives and trained Civil Service is entrusted the duty of perpetually considering the permanent interests of the State as a whole." In the pursuit of the public interest, none of the decisions affecting the economy, personal behavior, health, and welfare "can be allowed to run counter to the consensus of expert opinion representing the consumers on the one hand, the producers on the other, and the nation that is paramount over both." The Webbs' goal, like Ely's, was to protect the public interest from the threat of private power, but like Ely they came close to vesting the ultimate authority to determine the common good in a presumably benevolent body of experts, an all too human successor to Rousseau's divinely inspired lawgiver. Midway between the appearance of *Industrial Democracy* in 1897 and her appointment to the Royal Commission on the Poor Law in 1905, Beatrice insisted in her diary that the Fabians preferred "a society in which there is a considerable variety" when it comes to questions of taste and the end of government, questions that cannot be "determined by any science," and yet if the persistence of such variety threatened the enforcement of the common good, one cannot but wonder which value the Webbs would have chosen to sacrifice. In the conclusion of their *Constitution of the Socialist Commonwealth of Great Britain*, they argued that "the greatest obstacle to social amelioration" is not, as many suppose, "any failure in public spirit." The challenge instead is "to induce the whole body of citizens . . . to realise the imperative need for a rapid development of science in its widest sense, alike in the discovery of new knowledge and in the universal dissemination of scientific methods and thinking."[94] The Webbs emphasized the need for experts because they valued empirical social analysis so highly. They considered the public well-intentioned but simply ill-informed. There is a difference between the dissemination of new knowledge and the manipulation of a public necessarily dependent on those responsible for informing it, but that difference can become muddled when those intending to guide society assume the authority to determine what is in the "permanent interests of the State as a whole."

Bernstein patterned his idea of government on the Webbs' model of industrial democracy. The Marxist idea of the withering away of the state reminded Bernstein of anarchism instead of democracy, and he considered it atavistic in an interdependent world requiring active government. Rather than maligning political institutions, he chided the advocates of revolution, socialists should turn their attention to making those institutions serve the common good. Like the Webbs and Ely, Bernstein embraced an ideal of personal development that left no room for any contradiction between the individual and society. "The aim of all socialist measures," he reassured his readers, "even of those which appeared outwardly as coercive measures, is the development and the securing of a free personality. Their more exact examination always shows that the coercion included will raise the sum total of liberty in society, and will give more freedom over a more extended area than it takes away." A socialist society, Bernstein blithely assumed, would necessarily protect the public interest: he expressed little concern about enforcing the requisite "coercive measures." He judged Engels's conception of the state as inherently repressive "absolutely inadequate." Although perhaps appropriate to describe the state in "certain stages of development," such a notion "does not at all do justice to the role of the state in its more highly developed form."[95] Modern democracy necessarily relies on bureaucrats to administer a complex state apparatus, but in a socialist state, Bernstein believed, such officials would serve rather than control the people.

Despite their similar conception of the guiding role to be played by elites in a socialist democracy, the ideas of the Webbs and Bernstein had sharply contrasting significances in British and German political development. Although the Fabians claimed to exert considerable influence by redirecting the thinking of both liberals and labor leaders toward social democratic ideas, recent historians have minimized their direct effect on British law and politics.[96] The Webbs' conception of ethical politics, as much as their intellectualism and the public's perception of their elitism, guaranteed that they would only skid across the surface of the emerging class-based party system. Their demand for a spirit of cooperation, together with the stigma of anti-liberalism attached to some of the measures they championed, limited their appeal to a working class oriented more toward liberal individualism and immediate economic demands than to the Webbs' vision of a socialist commonwealth. The Labour party was more concerned with proximate reforms than with attempts to foster the sort of fraternal spirit the Webbs believed must accompany institutional changes. The British welfare state, as it has evolved through the twentieth century, has come to embody part of the institutional form but little of the ethical substance of social democracy.

Bernstein promulgated ideas very similar to the Webbs', but he had only limited success in Germany for nearly opposite reasons. Although the German trade unions and many SPD politicians actually adopted policies identical to those Bernstein advocated, the party formally repudiated revisionism. The reasons for this disjunction between theoretical rigidity and practical flexibility lay in the polarization of German political culture. Despite persistent denials by both left-wing and right-wing spokesmen, there was in the late nineteenth and early twentieth centuries considerable cooperation between labor and capital, and between socialist and liberal politicians, particularly at the local and regional level. Whereas in the United States cooperation of this sort was central to the operation of both the economy and politics, in Germany it was officially condemned as collaboration with the enemy by leading figures at both ends of the ideological spectrum. In the United States, the AFL evolved toward a kind of business unionism, and management experimented with varieties of welfare capitalism; independent progressive reform movements lost momentum when both the Republican and Democratic parties proved willing to incorporate the rhetoric if not the spirit of reformers' demands into their platforms and sometimes even into their policies. The presence of consensus, which fed liberal reforms while it starved more substantive changes, was as important in America as its absence was in Germany. In the United States, as a result, the radicalism of social democracy was first diluted by the pluralism of the political system, which spread reformers' energies through a wide range of channels, and then harmlessly swallowed up by an omnivorous liberalism. In Germany, Bernstein's revisionism was chewed up and spit out by a culture that found broad-based, reform-oriented, democratic politics unpalatable.[97] While all of these social democrats encountered a certain amount of resistance, none was vilified as was Bernstein, first by the repressive regime that exiled him, then by the party that censured him, and finally by both sides at once when he dared criticize German war aims in World War I. His failure symbolized the larger tragedy of German politics, which began to unfold shortly after Bernstein left the SPD. With the fate of German socialism hanging in the balance between opportunist bureaucrats and revolutionary Leninists, the centrist position represented by Bernstein's social democracy was the first to vanish in the quicksand of postwar German politics.

Rauschenbusch and Jaurès also endorsed social solidarity as their ideal of justice, but their writings exhibited a more consistently democratic quality than did those of Ely, Bernstein, or the Webbs. Significantly, they linked their unqualified commitment to popular government with skepticism concerning its ability to meet their goals. Ely, Bernstein, and the Webbs contended that the people, given the proper guidance by elite administrators, could successfully realize the social democratic ideals of positive freedom, approximate equality of condition, and social solidarity. Rauschenbusch and Jaurès, however, conceded the limits of political, social, and economic reconstruction, and they demonstrated greater sensitivity to the persistence of conflict. This is not to say that the ideal of fraternity did not appear in their writings; they merely acknowledged that securing the common good through the political process would remain a perennial challenge. As Rauschenbusch put it, "The ideal situation is created when self-interest and the common interest run in the same direction, and selfishness of its own will bends its stout shoulders to the yoke of public service."[98] While he believed that the key to that identification lay in a revitalized Christianity, he judged individual regeneration an essential but only preliminary step toward lasting social reconstruction. The cooperative spirit must be institutionalized in socialism, which would "embody the principle of solidarity and fraternity in the fundamental institutions of our industrial life. . . . Such a social order would develop the altruistic and social instincts just as the competitive order brings out the selfish instincts."

Rauschenbusch accepted James's counsel in "What Makes a Life Significant?" regarding the desirability of greater respect between classes in capitalist society, but he affirmed more determinedly than did James the establishment of a social foundation for such mutual respect in the substantial equality of power. The conscious effort of individuals to understand one another was inadequate "to offset the unconscious alienation created by the dominant facts of life which are wedging entire classes apart." While practicing the ethic of benevolence could set society on the road toward solidarity, its beneficent effects could be perpetuated only by establishing the principle of benevolence as the legal as well as the spiritual basis of economic and political interaction. At the same time, Rauschenbusch insisted with equal conviction that attempts to minimize the importance of "the sense of justice, the ideal of brotherhood, the longing for a truer and nobler life" in the movement for social reform were equally misguided. Such efforts transformed "one of the sublimest movements the world has ever seen into the squealing of a drove of pigs." If American workers narrowed their focus to purely economic issues and lost sight of the broader spiritual goals of the social gospel, Rauschenbusch warned, they would "cut the heart out" of genuine democratic reform.[99] Only by linking legitimate social and economic demands to more amorphous but equally important ethical ideals could progress be made.

Jaurès dressed a similar argument in anticlerical garb. In contrast to Rauschenbusch's recurrent references to Christian principles, Jaurès scorned the invocation of Christian piety by capitalists as a cruel deception perpetuating injustice. "Capitalism is covered over in this society with Christian kindness and generosity, like a foul-smelling factory in a sweet-smelling forest. It depends on the direction of the wind whether one detects the nauseating odors of the factory or the sweet perfumes of the forest." He stressed the dramatic difference between the values ostensibly embraced by Christians and the oppressiveness of the capitalist system those values were used to justify. While advocates of the social gospel tried to close that gap by turning Christianity into a weapon of reform, Jaurès contended that the disjunction between principles and reality had incapacitated institutionalized Christianity. In contrast to Christian social activists who invoked religious values to criticize the excesses of capitalism, Jaurès contended that capitalism itself had undermined religious ideals so completely that they could no longer offer any real resistance to the system of privilege and exploitation they had defended for centuries. Socialism, not the salvation of capitalism, would serve to unify the City of Man and the City of God, for it would provide in the form of a just society an outlet through which the genuinely religious sentiments of humanity might flow. "We can say today that there is no religion," he wrote, "and, in the truest sense, there is no community." Capitalism was killing them both. "Traditional Christianity is dying, philosophically, scientifically and politically." He defined the socialism that would take its place as "a moral revolution expressed through a material revolution."[100]

Jaurès looked toward socialism to revivify the faltering values of community and benevolence that had been poisoned by capitalism and by its apologists in the Catholic church. The line that divided opponents from partisans of religion also divided republicans from monarchists in nineteenth-century France. As a result, class lines were blurred, and the spirited republicanism of the French middle class was shared by the bureaucracy, which developed a democratic tradition quite unlike the authoritarianism of German state officials. To French republicans such as Jaurès, bureaucracy was neither the demon feared by the German left nor the savior awaited by many British and American reformers. It was merely an arm of the republican citizenry, a highly trained elite with strongly egalitarian sympathies. The petite bourgeoisie was as important in the French socialist movement as it was originally in the Fabian Society, but the SFIO was able to retain this part of its constituency, and much of its idealism, whereas the Fabians surrendered both when they adopted the distinctly trade unionist orientation of the Labour party. Jaurès's anticlericalism, his egalitarianism, and his idealism made him the personification of democratic socialism for a broad section of the French public. Unfortunately for the fate of the political ideas he advocated, his death came at precisely the moment when first the strains of war and then the success of the Russian Revolution tugged at the delicate fabric of the SFIO coalition. Under the pressures exerted by nationalism and revolutionary enthusiasm, the French left slowly unraveled.

Beneath their defense of socialism as the best means of advancing the common good, serious misgivings shaded Rauschenbusch's and Jaurès's discussions of the socialist future. They were uncertain fraternity could be secured by any institutional changes. This difference mirrors the one I have already noted between the more and less democratic emphasis of the theorists of social democracy, and the congruity is more than coincidental. There was an element of hubris in the confidence that Ely, Bernstein, and the Webbs placed in elites as democratic guides. The administrators envisioned by these theorists were patterned, it seems safe to say, on themselves. They also bore an unsettling resemblance to the guardians in Plato's *Republic*: lacking personal ambition and unsullied by class or group loyalty, they were expected to exercise unfailingly good political and economic judgment and to perceive clearly the public interest. Whether the public would reach its own decisions on the basis of their counsel, or merely endorse their judgments, is the question raised but unanswered by their writings.

By contrast Rauschenbusch and Jaurès, who put their faith in the democratic process, did not claim to have a solution for the problem of harmonizing private interest and the common good. The societies they envisioned would continue to face this central political challenge, and their awareness of its perennial nature set them apart from their fellow social democrats. "In asking for faith in the possibility of a new social order," Rauschenbusch insisted, "we ask for no Utopian delusion. We know that there is no perfection for man in this life: there is only growth toward perfection." It is part of the Christian message "to seek what is unattainable. We have the same paradox in the perfectibility of society." Rauschenbusch understood that in a democracy the people must make their own decisions, and he understood the frailty of reason and benevolence. "We shall never have a perfect social life, yet we must seek it with faith. We shall never abolish suffering. There will always be death and the empty chair and heart." Conflict, cruelty, and loss are not part of the capitalist condition only, they are part of the human condition, and socialism will not bring down the curtain on tragedy. "The strong will always have the impulse to exert their strength, and no system can be devised which can keep them from crowding and jostling the weaker."[101] No social or economic transformation, and no corps of administrators, can guarantee justice.

Jaurès shared this tragic sensibility. Despite his faith in democracy, he at times despaired of ever achieving his goals. "I have often compared socialism to the heart," he once wrote. "It has, like the heart, pulsations, rhythm, alternate movements of expansion and contraction." That image conveys the special quality of Jaurès's thought. It expanded with hope in the proletariat, in the possibilities of liberal alliance, in the ultimate triumph of socialism, and in the possibility of achieving a just society; and it contracted with doubt regarding the weakness and cupidity of all men. A note of poignancy marked all of Jaurès's work, and it surfaced even in his more theoretical writings. In his thesis *On the Reality of the Sensible World*, for example, he ruled out the possibility of complete social harmony. It is the persistence of tension, he argued, that "renders the life of the world so dramatic. The battle is never fully won."[102] Yet neither is it ever fully lost, he added, and throughout his life he was drawn to politics by his fascination with that struggle and his commitment to the victory, even if it could be only tentative, of his principles.

Politics is a struggle for power in any economic system, and because life imposes choices it involves competition regardless of how society is organized. As Sidgwick demonstrated in his discussion of Green's attempt to replace a competitive system with a cooperative, organic arrangement, the finite nature of certain prized items necessitates the general acceptance of a principle of distributive justice. Insuring that acceptance without resorting to coercion requires the conversion of society to an ideal of rational benevolence as much as it requires the institutionalization of socialism. Ely, Bernstein, and the Webbs, like Green, never explained how that most vexing of political questions could be solved. By isolating the issues of bureaucracy and justice, however, they clarified the essential elements of the problem and established the terms of the debate that has been at the center of twentieth-century politics.

Like Rauschenbusch, Jaurès believed that the quest for social justice must extend beyond personal benevolence to political action; like James, he also believed that there is more to life than the battle for social and economic change. In 1911, Jaurès delivered a lecture on Tolstoi in which he described his own deepest hopes for the revolution. Jaurès's ideas about knowledge and values reverberate in a passage that expresses his sense of the human project as a philosophical as well as a political quest:

· In our narrow, confined existence, we tend to forget the essence of life. . . . All of us, whatever our occupation or class, are equally guilty: the employer is lost in the running of his business; the workers, sunk in the abyss of their misery, raise their heads only to cry in protest; we, the politicians, are lost in daily battles and corridor intrigues. All of us forget that before everything else, we are men, ephemeral beings lost in the immense universe, so full of terrors. We are inclined to neglect the search for the real meaning of life, to ignore the real goals—serenity of the spirit and sublimity of the heart. . . . To reach them—that is the revolution.[103]

Jaurès and Rauschenbusch understood life as a series of challenges. Just as we should be able to appreciate its grandeur before the revolution—and enjoy the spectacle of airships above Paris—so we should expect to face painful decisions after the advent of socialism. There can be no recourse to elites, because no individual or group of individuals can perceive final truths where human life is concerned. Socialism must be democratic because life is open-ended. Answers are to be discovered by the tempering of social experience rather than the application of administrative skill. Even after the revolution, society will still be composed of—and governed by—men, not gods. At its most incisive, then, social democratic theory as formulated by Rauschenbusch and Jaurès embodied the radical commitment to open-ended, pragmatic decision making consistent with the radical empiricism of the philosophers of the *via media*. More directly than Ely, Bernstein, or the Webbs, they confronted the ultimate uncertainty of judgment and refused to take refuge in the false reassurance of expertise. For them socialism remained a goal with ethical as well as social and economic dimensions, an ideal that could be approached only through the steady development of that most unsteady instrument of change, democracy.

8

From Liberalism to Progressivism

1. Drifting from Liberalism

Progressivism was a body of ideas cut loose from its moorings in the liberal tradition. Although social democrats transformed essential elements of the socialist creed, they thought of themselves as heirs to the legacy of socialism, responsible for revitalizing rather than recreating that tradition. Progressives were less sure of their role. In their search for a new philosophical foundation, which I will examine in this chapter, they renounced the atomistic empiricism, psychological hedonism, and utilitarian ethics associated with nineteenth-century liberalism. In order to construct the political theory of progressivism, which I will discuss in Chapters Nine and Ten, they also discarded the idea of possessive individualism, broadened their political allegiance to include the working class along with the bourgeoisie, and embraced the ideals of equality and community to supplement the customary liberal commitment to individual freedom. Having left behind much of their philosophical and political heritage, they traveled uneasily along the border of socialism. "We are unsettled to the very roots of our being," the young Walter Lippmann wrote in the classic articulation of their perplexity, *Drift and Mastery* (1914). The socioeconomic and intellectual revolutions of the nineteenth century altered human relations decisively, and as a result, Lippmann explained, his generation did not know "how to behave when personal contact and eternal authority have disappeared. There are no precedents to guide us, no wisdom that wasn't made for a simpler age." Theory was out of phase with reality. "We are 'emancipated' from an ordered world. We drift."[1]

The maneuvers accomplished by a generation of renegade liberals determined the direction of that drift. Shifting the weight of the intellectual baggage they carried, jettisoning ideas that were no longer useful, and riding the political currents prevailing between 1890 and 1920, they transformed liberal theory into progressive theory. From a doctrine based on the idea of natural rights and culminating in the idea of a noninterventionist state, these thinkers turned the old liberalism into a new liberalism, a moral and political argument for the welfare state based on a conception of the individual as a social being whose values are shaped by personal choices and cultural conditions. In France, Great Britain, Germany, and the United States, a number of intellectuals and political reformers worked to alter the terms of liberal discourse. Not only did their ideas and programs vary according to national political traditions, even within each nation quite different ideas competed for preeminence. Without claiming that these thinkers were either the most influential or the most representative of those who could legitimately be considered progressives, I will focus on six individuals whose ideas attracted considerable attention during these years, thinkers whose political positions rested on epistemological and ethical ideas similar to—and in important respects influenced by—those advanced by the philosophers of the *via media*. Certain strands of progressive theory were extensions of the radical theory of knowledge and the ethics of rational benevolence into politics. Those are the ideas I want to examine, in order to demonstrate that the convergence of at least some social democratic and progressive thinkers reflected not merely a marriage of political convenience but an alliance based on common principles.

For the purposes of this analysis, then, these were the most important theorists of progressivism: Léon Bourgeois (1851–1925), whose doctrine of solidarity inspired a wave of social reform legislation in France; Leonard T. Hobhouse (1864–1929), whose efforts to redefine liberalism helped persuade Britain's Liberal party to exchange laissez-faire for state activism; Max Weber (1864–1920), whose multidimensional contributions to the discourse of progressivism are often overlooked or misinterpreted because of the failure of these ideas to flourish in Germany; Herbert Croly (1869–1930) and Walter Lippmann (1889–1974), editors of the most important organ of American progressive thought, *The New Republic*; and finally John Dewey (1859–1952), whose writings about politics and society illustrate most clearly the continuities between the philosophy of the *via media* and the politics of progressivism. In this section I will outline these individuals' careers (with the exception of Dewey, whose professional progress is traced in Chapter One), examine their efforts to reconcile science with religion or positivism with idealism, and indicate the similarities between their ideas about knowledge and action and those of the generation of radical philosophers who inspired them.

The various designations applied to these thinkers and their allies in the late nineteenth and early twentieth centuries testified to their transformation of the liberal creed. Of these labels, which included the new liberalism, left liberalism, and social liberalism, none captured the novelty and the amorphousness of these ideas better than the term progressivism. Just as social democracy suggests a departure from revolutionary and utopian collectivism more clearly than does a phrase like liberal socialism, so is progressivism free from the idea of a self-guiding market economy and the negative conception of liberty associated with variations on the theme of liberalism. If the extension of democracy from the political to the socio-economic realm was the quintessential social democratic principle, so the graduated—or progressive—income tax, which represented a radical departure from liberalism by establishing the ability to pay as the legitimate measure of the individual's responsibility to the common good, was the central doctrine of progressivism.

A brief etymological excursion illustrates both the appropriateness and the difficulty of using the rubric of progressivism. The word "progressive" first entered British political discourse in the late 1880s, when social and municipal reformers adopted it to designate their "advanced" position while distinguishing themselves from the imperialism of the Liberal party at the national level. When a group of intellectuals with inclinations similar to those of Hobhouse constituted themselves into a Rainbow Circle (either because they represented different shades of liberal opinion or, as now seems more likely, because they originally met at London's Rainbow Tavern), they decided to name the journal they established in 1896 *The Progressive Review*. Weber found a political home for the only time in his life in the short-lived Progressive People's party, founded in 1910; and Croly and Lippmann identified themselves with the "progressive movement" when that term first became widespread during the campaign to elect the Progressive party's presidential candidate, Theodore Roosevelt, in 1912.

Yet the appearance of neatness is deceptive. *The New Republic* largely discontinued its use of the word progressive after 1916, and the progressive label all but disappeared in Britain and Germany after World War I. The French use of the term indicates even more clearly the perils of using static categories for slippery historical phenomena. In the 1880s *progressist* connoted a leftist republican position, but during the 1890s Opportunists appropriated it for their more moderate politics. By 1910 *Progressists* occupied seats on the right of the Chamber of Deputies, and the word itself had become a rather awkward synonym for reaction.[2] The question of imperialism raises an entirely different set of problems, since British progressives denounced the Liberal party as excessively expansionist while German progressives denounced the National Liberal party as insufficiently expansionist. American progressives, to complicate matters further, ranged themselves on all sides of foreign policy issues: some applauded Theodore Roosevelt's jingoism, some endorsed Wilson's internationalism, and others clung tenaciously to the nation's traditional isolationism. I appreciate the depth of these difficulties. I concede that I am using the term progressivism as a matter of convenience, as an ideal typical comparative construct that will enable me to discuss similarities and differences among these thinkers and their national intellectual and political traditions. It makes more sense, even within a single nation, to discuss progressivisms in the plural than to attempt an inclusive definition of an essential or normative progressivism. By using the word I am not arguing that only these thinkers merit designation as progressives. They represent one species among many of a political genus that was well populated in the years from 1890 to 1920, and they figure prominently in this analysis not because of their typicality but because of the unusual incisiveness of their ideas.

The first individual to make substantial contributions to the theory and practice of progressivism was Léon Bourgeois. His book *Solidarité* (1896; cited hereafter as *Solidarity*) became the bible of France's Radical Republicans during the years of their greatest political strength; it provided the rationale for an impressive array of social reforms enacted between 1896 and 1912. The ideal of social solidarity, Bourgeois explained, derived from two sources that had long been strangers to one another but were now being "brought together and combined in all advanced nations: the scientific method and the ethical idea." Drawing on Christianity, liberalism, positivism, and Darwinian biology—and perhaps most importantly on the work of Fouillée— he articulated a philosophy designed to satisfy the bourgeois economists' concern for liberty and the socialists' concern for justice, a philosophy of reconciliation between ideas, parties, and classes. In *La Solidarité humaine* (1914), he linked this new way of thinking to the new intellectual and moral world accompanying the new economic world created by industrialization. Gradually, France was shaking itself free from outworn controversies and awakening to the fact of interdependence. From that realization of the "ineluctable solidarity of things" slowly dawned the recognition of the "necessity of a solidarity of obligations and rights, without which no human society could live in harmony and peace."[3] Although not a profoundly original thinker, Bourgeois did possess a quick and supple intelligence, and his theory of solidarity was more substantial than his critics have charged. His ideas grew as much from his familiarity with Fouillée's writings as from his perception of the ideological needs of French radicalism. While solidarity may have served to appease the middle classes and the proletariat, it was intended not merely to end class warfare but also to end the conditions of poverty and inequality that provoked it. Bourgeois understood that the depleted intellectual resources of the republican tradition could no longer fuel an effective campaign of reform, and he conceived his doctrine to provide a coherent justification for the expansion of state authority required to meet the demands of a culture no longer served by the slogans of 1789.

Whereas Fouillée crafted his philosophy of *idées-forces* in the solitude of his study, Bourgeois hammered out his ideas in the workshop of party politics. Born in Paris in 1851, he left a promising legal career in 1876 to enter government administration. Lacking friends as powerful as his ambitions, he parlayed his insatiable appetite for work and his considerable personal charm into a spectacularly successful career. He rose rapidly through a series of administrative posts to become the prefect of Albi in 1882. There he successfully mediated one of the earliest of the increasingly bitter strikes of the Carmaux mine workers, demonstrating a gift for arbitration that would later be put to an even more formidable test. His talents were recognized and his efforts repeatedly rewarded. In 1888, leaving his post as the prefect of police in Paris, he ran successfully against General Boulanger for a seat in the

Chamber of Deputies representing Chalons sur Marne. He thus entered national politics as part of a new generation of Radicals who took for granted the survival of the Republic and moved quickly toward a new style of social reform. In Bourgeois's case, however, his zeal was tempered by shrewd political instincts, which kept him from fighting battles he could not win, and by a temperament more reflective than is typical of successful politicians, which enabled him to construct an arsenal of ideas for his party. These characteristics, together with oratorical and administrative skills rarely combined in one individual, made him uniquely *ministrable*. From 1890, when he was named minister of the interior, until his death in 1925, Bourgeois held a succession of high offices, including minister of education, minister of labor, minister of foreign affairs, president of the Chamber of Deputies, and President of the Senate.[4]

He also collected critics. When he was named by President Félix Faure to form the Third Republic's first all-Radical government in 1895, the left's hopes were as wild as the right's fears. Bourgeois's reformist position was well known, and he unhesitatingly declared his support for a progressive income tax to fund a system of social insurance against sickness, unemployment, disability, and old age. That platform incorporated the most important demands of the *Comité central d'action républicaine*, an umbrella group formed in 1894 to unify the badly splintered left leaning republican parties and resurrect a spirit of "republican solidarity." It also offered an agenda that moderate socialists like Jaurès could support, and the left, *mirabile dictu*, united behind the Bourgeois ministry. Not surprisingly, this coalition met stiff resistance in the more conservative Senate, which voted consistently against major and minor initiatives of the government in the hope of bringing it down. Bourgeois's supporters advised him to force a constitutional crisis by challenging the prerogatives of the Senate, but instead he resigned. Although he vowed in his final speech to continue the struggle against reactionary obstructionism, Bourgeois's resignation represented to Jaurès and his allies an abdication of the responsibility Bourgeois assumed as premier of the first Radical government. Many socialists believed the Radicals had betrayed their trust, and the future prospects of a union of socialists and left-wing republicans dimmed in the shadow of that disillusionment.[5]

Motivated by a desire to clarify the ideas informing his political program, Bourgeois set to work shortly after his resignation on the series of essays that first appeared in the *Nouvelle Revue* and then, in revised form, as *Solidarity*. The ideal of solidarity was hardly novel; it has been traced to the Stoics, to early Christian writers, to medieval legal thought, and more proximately to the otherwise quite dissimilar ideas of Comte and Renouvier. Yet the argument Bourgeois formulated to establish the legitimacy of his ideas differed dramatically from all of these. Instead of proceeding from premises concerning natural law or natural rights, he relied on the radical empiricism of the philosophers of the *via media*. We must, he insisted, "put aside all completed systems of thought," whether religious, scientific, or positivist. We must treat "all schemes of law, history, and politics as relative and always susceptible of revision." In place of a system Bourgeois offered a method of inquiry, in place of certainty he offered the challenge of continuous experimentation. We can no longer pretend to grasp the truth, he argued; instead "we must submit even the oldest and most venerable institutions to the test of free reason and verification in experience." This was the pragmatism proclaimed by Fouillée, the replacement of dogma by hypothesis, the substitution of empirical testing for deductive reasoning.

Although Bourgeois's vision was broadened by science, it was not conventionally scientific—at least not in the sense that positivists understood science. He maintained that a genuine empiricism must attend to the multidimensionality of experience, including "physical, intellectual, and ethical realities." Moreover, an adequate investigation of human affairs must acknowledge that man is at once "a being of passion, reason, and conscience," a creature of culture "born from the historical process and living in a social milieu to which he stands in a reciprocal relation."[6] It would be difficult to find in the writings of Green or Sidgwick, Dilthey or James, Dewey or Fouillée, a passage encapsulating so neatly the radical theory of knowledge, the theory of voluntary action, the awareness of the multifaceted nature of man's sociocultural experience, the historical sensibility, and the emphasis on ethics as an empirical and historical project. The philosophy of the *via media* comprised all of those elements, and together they provided the foundation on which Bourgeois constructed the theory he presented in *Solidarity*.

From 1897 until 1914, solidarity was one of the most widely discussed topics among French intellectuals. Philosophers, economists, political theorists, legal historians, and members of the fledgling guild of sociologists all gathered at annual conferences sponsored by the Ecole des Hautes Etudes Sociales; from their discussions a flurry of articles and books appeared in the first decade of the twentieth century. These thinkers went off in a variety of directions, ranging from Emile Boutroux's spiritualism to Emile Durkheim's brilliantly idiosyncratic version of positivism.[7] None of those associated with solidarity as an intellectual movement, however, presented more incisive arguments for the relation between progressive politics and radical empiricism than did Bourgeois, and none played an equally significant role in political reform.

Meanwhile Bourgeois's own interests were shifting from domestic to international politics. In 1899 he represented France at the first international disarmament conference; when offered the opportunity to head another ministry later that year he refused. His decision frustrated Jaurès, who remarked bitterly that "the angel of arbitration has flown off to the Hague" at yet another moment when the Republic badly needed his skills as a mediator. Given the intensity of the conflict then raging over the Dreyfus affair, however, Bourgeois might plausibly have judged the chances of settling France's cultural civil war rather less promising than the chances of achieving immediate universal disarmament. Despite more auspicious circumstances in 1902, when the Dreyfusard landslide swept Bourgeois to the presidency and Jaurès to the vice-presidency of the Chamber of Deputies, Bourgeois again turned down the offer to serve as premier. His growing preoccupation with foreign affairs during these years of the "Radical Republic," when an alliance of social democrats and progressives dominated French politics and accomplished such important reforms as the first significant wages and hours legislation and the separation of the church and the state, puzzled many of his fellow Radicals.[8]

Bourgeois shared their satisfaction with these successes, but he understood that the prospects of continued progressive reform would depend on continued international peace, and the evidence of increasing tension alarmed him. From the time he became minister of foreign affairs in 1906 until he was awarded the Nobel Prize in 1920 as the "father of the League of Nations," he concentrated on achieving international solidarity: first focusing on international arbitration, then on the creation of the league. He insisted at the end of World War I that a punitive peace was unwise as well as unjust, and he warned that a league without an international army to enforce its decisions would be worse than useless. In both cases his counsel was ignored.[9] Not only did war end progressive reform in France by destroying the middle ground in which solidarist measures had begun to take root, it also poisoned French foreign policy. The humane but prudent internationalism Bourgeois preached was drowned out by competing choruses celebrating, on the one hand, the mystical promise of peace, and on the other, the nationalist demand for retribution. In the wake of the league's failure and the debacle of World War II, it is understandable that today the "father of the League"—who warned against making it powerless—is more often ignored than venerated. Nations seldom celebrate their Cassandras.

Bourgeois was a favorite of British progressives, who saw in his theory of solidarity and his opposition to imperialism convictions that mirrored their own. In a lengthy review published in December, 1896, the editors of *The Progressive Review* greeted the appearance of *Solidarity* with enthusiasm. The disappointment British progressives felt at the Senate's defeat of the Bourgeois government was mitigated by the opportunity it provided for this theorist and politician, "the ablest now living in France," to contribute "to the newer political philosophy which is remoulding thought." Whereas ethical imperatives and scientific data, democratic principles and economic realities, were generally considered contradictory, Bourgeois established their consistency "not by suppressing facts," but by discovering that science emphasizes the "inter-dependence of all living beings upon one another." This recognition of "solidarity in the world is consequently the true teaching of science, and this must modify the narrow and crude conception of the individualist and also effect the needed reconciliation between science and ethics." Bourgeois's argument was doubly important. It established "a satisfactory rational ground for ethical conduct" in two ways: first, in its conception of man as social, and second, in its conception of science as broadly cultural rather than narrowly positivistic. This philosophy led directly to "the new politics, in which the ends before us will be, not the enforcement of 'natural rights,' but the obligations laid upon us from the fact of association."

So closely did *Solidarity* resemble the new liberalism espoused by British progressives, the reviewer concluded, that "the body of doctrine thus stated will be familiar" to most readers of *The Progressive Review*.[10] Mired in a bog of Tory reaction, Britain in 1896 was ten years away from the sort of progressive legislation the Bourgeois ministry pursued, albeit prematurely; it was not merely the articulation of these ideas but also their apparent political vitality that electrified British progressives. Just as Bourgeois was able to chide his countrymen for falling behind Germany in the provision of social insurance, so British progressives used the example of their counterparts across the Channel to prod the Liberal party to keep pace.

Among those who created the British version of progressivism, Leonard T. Hobhouse contributed the most detailed elaboration of the philosophy undergirding the new politics. He was born in 1864, the youngest of seven children whose father, an evangelical clergyman, did his best to keep the modern world away from his congregation and his family. Hobhouse had already shed his father's religious enthusiasm and Tory politics by the time he left school for Oxford in 1883. Although Green died the year before Hobhouse arrived, the idea of social activism lingered in the atmosphere of the university. Hobhouse became caught up in a variety of political controversies, debated contemporary issues fervently, and served as president of Oxford's Radical Society. Yet as he wrote with a hint of apology in a letter of 1884, "I am a little speculative by nature, and am always in danger of caring more for knowing truth than for doing good." After earning a First in Greats and winning a prize fellowship at Merton College, his desire for truth got the upper hand, and he scuttled a planned sojourn working with London's poor at Toynbee Hall to pursue a career in philosophy at Oxford. He returned to his own college, Corpus Christi, as an assistant tutor in 1890, then was elected a Fellow there four years later. Hobhouse's experiences at Oxford decisively shaped his outlook. He encountered philosophical idealism and Fabian socialism through Green's disciple D. G. Ritchie, he became acquainted with scientific research through six months of work in Oxford's physiological laboratory, and he acquired an abiding respect for Aristotle through his performance of the Greats Tutor's changeless duties.[11]

Yet deep currents of anxiety flowed beneath the surface of his life at Oxford. In 1887 he experienced the first of a series of severe nervous breakdowns that afflicted him until his death in 1929. Like William James, Hobhouse was to produce a body of work characterized by a tone of indomitable optimism strikingly different from his own repeated experiences of incapacitating depression. Hobhouse later recalled that during these years he began to find Oxford a "rather misty out-of-the-world place"; in response he formulated a plan that should be familiar by now, a plan to integrate knowledge from both science and philosophy with his interest in social and political reform. Whereas the generation of Green and Sidgwick had wrestled with the competing demands of religion and science, Hobhouse's contemporaries faced, in his words, the "conflict between the scientific and the ethical points of view." Their reconciliation required weaving together several strands of thought: first, the idea of natural selection, freed from Spencer's politics and returned to Darwin's biology; second, the "social and ethical outlook of Green," loosened from its idealistic trappings and conceived as an "'empirical' rather than a 'metaphysical' truth"; third, the "requirements of liberty as set out by Mill"; and finally, "the Comtist conception of Humanity." In other words, Hobhouse wanted to synthesize empirical science with idealist philosophy, liberal individualism with positivist collectivism.[12] This was a tall order, although a typical one for social democrats and progressives of his generation, and the psychological toll it exacted was frequently as heavy as the burden it imposed on the imagination.

In order to achieve a psychological equilibrium between his impulses to know truth and do good, Hobhouse did attempt to balance his scholarly commitments with political activity. Sidney Webb wrote to Beatrice in 1892 of his "overwhelming admiration" for Hobhouse, and while Beatrice may have been exaggerating when she wrote three years later that "Leonard Hobhouse is recruiting for us at Oxford," his genuine affinity with Fabianism was manifested in his first book, *The Labour Movement* (1893). Hobhouse employed Green's arguments concerning positive freedom and endorsed Beatrice Webb's assessment of the importance of the cooperative movement. Reviewers noted these similarities, which testify to the fuzziness of the distinction between Green's liberal followers and Fabian socialists in the early 1890s.[13] That alliance dissolved as Hobhouse and others worked out their theory of progressivism and the Fabians appeared to shift their focus from moral regeneration toward administration and imperialism. Attempts to assign Hobhouse a place in the "liberal" or "socialist" camp, however, are misleading because he, like Green and the Webbs, was struggling to escape those ideological categories.

His philosophical work also resists conventional classification, as his second book, *The Theory of Knowledge* (1896), demonstrates.[14] Even though Hobhouse later turned his attention increasingly toward politics and sociology, he acknowledged that philosophy had "the first claim" on him, and he always thought of himself principally as a philosopher. His ideas have been described as empiricist, idealist, realist, rationalist, and materialist, but that confusion merely underscores his unconventionality. He subscribed to important aspects of the radical theory of knowledge, and unless that connection is appreciated his philosophical writings seem either inconsistent or eccentric. When J. S. Mackenzie reviewed Hobhouse's *Theory of Knowledge* in *Mind*, he pointed out that it was "the first treatise we have had in English dealing explicitly with Epistemology as such." Mackenzie understood better than some of Hobhouse's later critics that he advanced neither a standard empiricist nor a standard idealist conception of knowledge:

> Mr. Hobhouse's view, as I understand it, is that the primary fact of consciousness is an immediate datum of sense which is at the same time the "assertion" of an objective reality—an assertion which is, as it were, valid in its own right, and subject to no correction or modification in the subsequent development of knowledge.

Hobhouse argued, in other words, that experience precedes the division of subject from object, and that immediate experience provides an irreducible baseline for knowledge. As Mackenzie noted, Hobhouse bolstered his analysis of experience "by reference to the psychological theory of Professor James."[15] The similarities between *The Theory of Knowledge* and *The Principles of Psychology* are striking. Hobhouse insisted that knowledge is "dependent on sentience and thought" together. He emphasized that "though thought and feeling may influence and modify each other, the beginning of knowledge implies the operation of both." He criticized Hume and Kant alike for abstracting from the connections between the knower and the known in immediate experience, and he turned to James for a corrective to their dualism, noting that it would be pointless for him "to attempt to add anything to Professor James's masterly discussion" of this issue. Hobhouse paid particular attention to James's account of the stream of consciousness because he considered it an antidote to Bradley's idealism, which was among his principal targets in *The Theory of Knowledge*. Hobhouse believed that Green had answered Hume on the relatedness of experience, but he valued James's account of the continuity of consciousness more highly than Green's. Because the pieces of experience we encounter through our senses are immediately experienced as parts of a pattern, as Green suggested and James confirmed, there is no need to resort to Bradley's metaphysical explanations.

Hobhouse also followed James's affirmation of uncertainty. Despite our best efforts to synthesize information from the physical sciences and such human sciences as poetry and politics, our knowledge must always be tentative. Its imperfections notwithstanding, such uncertain knowledge is the best we can do. It discloses "reality, not seen through a glass darkly, nor still worse—projected in some distorted plane of our own vision, but so far as it goes, and however limited it may be, true, genuine reality seen face to face."[16] Much as Hobhouse's epistemology resembled James's, however, their ideas differed on a matter of basic importance. James had admitted to Dewey the significance of the difference between their backgrounds in empiricism and Hegelian idealism, which flavored their philosophies despite their considerable similarities. Dewey's concept of inquiry as progressive, integrative, and purposive owed an important debt to Aristotle and Green; Hobhouse's epistemology likewise contained an element of idealism that distinguished his ideas from James's and rendered them more similar to Dewey's. Although Hobhouse claimed always to resist Green's metaphysics, he began in *Mind in Evolution* (1901) to infuse notions of progress and harmony into his epistemology. This process culminated in *Development and Purpose* (1913), in which he treated mind less as a Jamesian field than as a Hegelian *Geist*. He contended that personal experience, like biological evolution, evidences a teleological character: From the "two opposite starting points" of science and philosophy, he maintained in his conclusion, "we have arrived at the conception of a conditional purpose as constituting the core of the world-progress."[17] Hobhouse's mature philosophy thus displayed a directional quality more reminiscent of Aristotle, Green, and Dewey than James, and that similarity carried over into his ideas about history and politics.

The relation of Hobhouse's ideas to James's pragmatism is as difficult to unravel as the relation between the philosophies of James and Fouillée, and for some of the same reasons. In *The Theory of Knowledge*, Hobhouse offered an account of epistemology similar to James's and especially to Dewey's. In his 1904 essay "Faith and the Will to Believe," he criticized an unnamed doctrine comprising two principal ideas: "The first is, that by believing a thing we make it true; the second is, that we can believe in a thing without asking ourselves seriously whether it is true or false." Hobhouse understandably rejected such an analysis, which was a considerable distortion of James's meaning in "The Will to Believe," but the arguments he presented in support of what he called an alternative view nearly paraphrased James's own argument. We need not "take the world precisely as reason shows it," he admitted; we should sometimes "give weight to the element of feeling as well." For the feeling of belief can be compelling, and feeling is after all "the forerunner of thought."[18]

James, thinking himself ill-suited for the role of straw man, wrote to Hobhouse in protest. "Don't you think it a *tant soit peu* scurvy trick to play on me," he wrote, to offer "a beautiful duplicate of my own thesis in the 'Will to Believe' essay . . . in the guise of an *alternative and substitute* for my doctrine, for which latter you, in the earlier pages of your charmingly written essay, *substitute a travesty* for which I defy any candid reader to find a single justification in my text?" Yet James's general reaction was less unfavorable than these remarks suggest. He asserted that the difference between his view and Hobhouse's was largely a matter of emphasis: "You say identically the same things; only, from your special polemic point of view, you emphasize more the dangers [of the will to believe]; while I, from *my* point of view, emphasized more the right to run their risk." James closed his letter on a less argumentative note, admitting, "I like and admire your theory of Knowledge so much, and you reduplicate (I *don't* mean *copy*) my views so beautifully in this article, that I hate to let you go unchidden."[19]

James seems to have considered Hobhouse an ally even if Hobhouse himself was reluctant to concede as much, and Hobhouse's later writings lend support to James's assessment. In the "Philosophy of Development," Hobhouse returned to the question of knowledge and presented two arguments consistent with pragmatism. First, he pointed out that knowledge derives from the "evolution of thought . . . by comparison and analysis of results," a gradual process by which thought learns "to accommodate itself" to reality. Our mental pictures do not necessarily coincide with external reality; only testing in experience can validate them. Second, Hobhouse focused on the necessity of assimilating all new data of experience with our preexisting stock of attitudes and beliefs, a central idea in James's philosophy, which implies that our knowledge is a body of shifting ideas that reflect new experiences.[20] Like many of James's critics, Hobhouse shied away from James's more extreme formulations, but his own writings on the role of will and belief in knowledge and action paralleled the central arguments of James's pragmatism.

Although Hobhouse maintained a lifelong commitment to philosophical inquiry, and his political writings cannot be understood without reference to the philosophy that informed them, he severed his professional affiliation with the world of philosophy when he left Oxford in 1897. C. P. Scott, the editor of the left leaning *Manchester Guardian*, habitually raided Oxford for talent, and when Henry Sidgwick's brother Arthur recommended Hobhouse to him as "quite the ablest of our younger Greats men, and a strong Liberal and progressive of the best type," Scott immediately sought to recruit Hobhouse for the paper. Hobhouse was vulnerable for several reasons. His fragile health was poorly suited to the rigors of Oxford's weather, his pride was wounded by what he interpreted as lukewarm reviews of his *Theory of Knowledge*, and his political views were unpopular in the increasingly conservative atmosphere of the university in the mid-1890s. He continued his scholarly activity after taking a position with the *Guardian* (*Mind in Evolution* appeared in 1901), but he devoted most of his time and energy to political journalism. Loosening his connection with Scott's paper in 1902 gave him more time to write for the *Speaker* and the *Nation* as well as the *Guardian*, and his work for these papers landed him a position as the political editor of the London *Tribune*. His responsibilities in this job severely taxed the imperious Hobhouse's limited patience and his unsteady nerves. When the *Tribune*'s ownership shifted to America and its tone slipped from progressive to merely popular, Hobhouse abandoned ship. Although he succeeded in writing *Morals in Evolution* (1906) during these years, the attempt to juggle sustained research and steady journalism finally exhausted him. He returned to the academic fold in 1907, becoming the first professor of sociology in Great Britain when he accepted the Martin White Chair at the University of London.[21]

Throughout the decade of his most intensive journalistic activity, Hobhouse never lost sight of his broader aim. In one of his first contributions to the *Manchester Guardian* in 1897, he contended that "there will be no steady and continuous social progress until an adequate progressive theory is reconstituted to suit the needs of our own time." His own writings during these years offered precisely that sort of theoretical justification for the reformist program being worked out by Liberal politicians. In 1902, he complained that the "present decadence of Liberalism" could be traced "to the weakening of the intellectual basis upon which the reformers of an older generation founded themselves." The Benthamites succeeded only because they harnessed their social activism to their philosophical radicalism. Politics without philosophy wandered aimlessly from crisis to crisis; only a clear theoretical vision could give direction to the vague impulses of progressivism. Hobhouse provided the most lucid and the most influential statement of that direction in *Liberalism* (1911), which appeared at the climax of five years of Liberal legislation informed by, if not always fully consistent with, the principles of progressivism he and his allies had been advocating since the

1890s.[22] *Liberalism* drew upon, and tried to draw together, the ideas of Mill and Green, and in the conceptions of freedom, the common good, and harmonious social progress he presented there, Hobhouse provided a new lexicon for twentieth-century liberalism.

The rest of Hobhouse's writings provide a rather melancholy postscript to his brilliant early work. He shared Bourgeois's enthusiasm for international arbitration—he described the Hague tribunal as a step toward "the actual realization of internationalism"—and he was equally devastated by the outbreak of World War I. His hopes for peace and progress became increasingly desperate as their plausibility evaporated; from the perspective of the 1920s, his pioneering work in sociology and anthropology seemed overly optimistic as well as ethnocentric. Yet he refused to allow his personal pessimism, which frequently dragged him into such deep depression that he was unable to work, to intrude on his philosophical commitment to hope. In a letter he wrote in 1927, he revealed the conflict between the two sides of himself and the pain of feeling drawn "quite deeply and keenly in opposite ways." He tried to persuade himself to persevere: "'Your arguments are all pretty poor,'" he reported chiding himself, "'but your meaning's right. It is absolutely true that the world is neither mechanism nor spirit, but a spiritual struggle for wholeness or harmony in discordant parts. . . . You'd betray your ideas if you gave up,'" he concluded, "'because though a poor thing it's the best you can do. You don't express them well, but nobody else expresses them at all.'" Although nearly four decades separated that letter from William James's equally impassioned claim that "all is nature *and* all is reason too," the same search for a *via media*, and the same spirit of resolution in the face of despair, is apparent in both passages.[23] Like James, Hobhouse refused to trade his uncertainty for the cynicism that seduced many of his contemporaries. In a review of Mill's *Letters* written in 1910, Hobhouse explained the source of Mill's intellectual vitality and revealed his own deepest conviction:

> In one point, Mill was greater than all the thinkers of his century. They thought they knew. He had taken to heart the message of the oracle to Socrates. Also, he had early learnt that, since truth is not a system that emerges complete from the workshop of one mind, but is the slowly wrought achievement of many generations, the most useful work is not that which counterfeits finality, but that which furthers the collective effort.[24]

Hobhouse offered his own work in precisely that spirit. His appreciation of its tentativeness is often overlooked, because he guarded his belief in progress despite the overwhelming evidence of modern barbarism. But like Socrates—and Mill—he knew how little he knew. His hope was born not of naive optimism but of resistance to despair, and the difference, although seldom acknowledged, is decisive.[25]

The years of the Radical Republic in France and the Liberal resurgence in Great Britain also saw the rise of a lively reform movement in the United States. In 1897, in the aftermath of McKinley's landslide victory over Bryan,

The Progressive Review lamented the fate of "the most distracted and help less body of political Radicalism in the world," which in the United States had "no place to lay its head." Fifteen years later, both major parties were struggling to outbid the renegade Progressive party for the loyalty of American voters. Clearly a dramatic transformation had occurred in the interim. After returning from a visit to the United States in 1911, Hobhouse tried to explain "the New Spirit in America" by emphasizing the emergence of "a heightened social consciousness, and a singularly broad and generous interpretation of social duty and the common good."[26] As a political phenomenon, American progressivism was more multifaceted than either solidarity or the new liberalism, and it is impossible to describe it accurately as a simple analog to either of those movements. It comprised a variety of different constituencies agitating for different and often incompatible reforms, and that diversity helps to explain the wide range of interpretations historians have offered to account for its appearance and its achievements. Several progressive factions competed with one another in America. One worked to secure greater efficiency through political reforms designed to streamline government and make it less susceptible to democratic influence. Another aimed to reduce concentrations of economic power through antimonopoly legislation. A third sought to accomplish a kind of national purification through nativism and prohibition. Finally, there was a variety that resembled French and British progressivism, a variety emphasizing, as Hobhouse indicated, a new spirit of "social consciousness," a heightened awareness of the individual's "social duty," and a new conception of the government's central role in securing the "common good." The most important theorists affiliated with this wing of American progressivism, who contributed the new ideas of knowledge, responsibility, and reform that it embodied, were Herbert Croly, Walter Lippmann, and John Dewey.[27]

The career of Herbert Croly illustrates the convergence of ideas from opposite directions and the relation between a certain philosophical perspective and a commitment to progressive political ideas. His father David Croly embraced Comte's positivism with a fervor perhaps unique in the United States, and Herbert was one of the few American children formally baptized, according to Comte's prescribed ritual, into the service of the Goddess Humanity. Born in 1869, Croly was five years younger than Hobhouse; like Hobhouse, he rebelled against his father's strict beliefs as soon as he left home. His progress, however, departed in substance from the pattern it followed in form: the religion he was trying to escape was positivism; he found liberation in the quasi-religious idealism preached at Harvard by Josiah Royce and George Herbert Palmer. During his first two years in college, 1886–1888, Croly wrote lengthy letters home explaining his dissatisfaction with Comte and his enthusiasm for Royce. Unfortunately, these letters have not survived, but Croly's apostasy can be inferred from his father's part of the correspondence, which reveals his anguished attempts to persuade his son not to abandon his positivist faith. Herbert was preparing to pursue a career in philosophy, though, and he could see less and less value in the simplistic "laws of science" Comte and David Croly revered.[28]

Croly left Cambridge in the spring of 1888 to serve as his father's private secretary, and he remained there until David Croly's death a year later. He inherited a part interest in the *Real Estate Record and Builder's Guide*, and he wrote for the magazine until 1892, when he married and returned to Harvard. Many of Croly's articles during these years concerned politics; one in particular indicated the drift of his ideas. The modern world had already undergone two revolutions, he wrote in August, 1890, first the Protestant Reformation and then the democratic revolutions of the eighteenth century. The organization of labor and capital in his own day constituted a third revolution, an industrial revolution whose outcome would almost certainly not satisfy either workers or industrialists. "Some middle way between the clash of interests," he concluded, "will no doubt be found to the advantage of all concerned." As he was predicting confidently the triumph of a political *via media*, however, his personal quest for its philosophical counterpart seemed further than ever from fulfillment. A nervous breakdown in January, 1893, prevented him from completing his first semester back at Harvard, and he withdrew for two years of isolation in Cornish, New Hampshire, and travel in the eastern United States and Europe. Although the scaffolding of an explanation for Croly's collapse is rickety because of his lifelong reluctance to discuss it, an associate later remarked that "his oldest friends could tell of a profound spiritual crisis he went through in revolt against Auguste Comte, the god of his father." As was often true in such psychological crises, Croly's intellectual conflict, intensified in this case by the added strain of his father's death, also involved a vocational conflict. Croly continued to envision himself as a professor of philosophy, but he lacked clear evidence of his likely success as well as a clear sense of the ideas capable of reconciling positivism with idealism.[29]

He returned once again to Harvard in 1895. This time he remained for four years, studying philosophy with Royce, Palmer, Santayana, and James, and also taking courses in aesthetics and religion. Although he performed adequately, he left Harvard without earning a degree. The 1898–1899 *Catalog* noted his "marked excellence of the second rank," and such faint praise evidently matched his teachers' lack of enthusiasm for the ever-silent Croly. He sailed again to Europe, at least ostensibly in order to continue his studies. When he returned to New York in 1900, however, he had resolved to become a journalist rather than a philosopher. What happened to his earlier ambition? There is no contemporary evidence, but letters Croly wrote in 1913 advising Felix Frankfurter against accepting a teaching position at Harvard suggest at least Croly's retrospective view of his decision. With a disingenuousness that now discloses the insecurity he hoped to mask from his younger friend, he confided that he had spent six years at Harvard "as a graduate student." His experience convinced him that becoming a professor "is almost like becoming a Bishop," because your "freedom of movement is hampered, and what is worse, you are almost committed to thinking along certain lines." Perhaps more revealingly, he warned Frankfurter of the perils of pedagogy: "The necessity of teaching tends to make one a routine thinker."[30] Since the examples of the equally idiosyncratic Royce, Santayana, and James could have only demonstrated the opposite, it seems likely that the particular danger of teaching was less the potential intellectual stultification than the requirement that one face students regularly. For Croly, whose intense aversion to meeting strangers became legendary, and who habitually spoke in a voice so quiet that it reduced normal conversations to traded whispers, the prospect of holding forth in lecture halls must have seemed unattractive if not overwhelming. Although he never developed a particularly fluid prose style, as a journalist Croly was at least able to communicate his ideas without having to talk about them.

Despite the very real importance of these considerations, an even more imposing obstacle stood in Croly's way. He confessed in an unpublished autobiographical fragment written in the mid-1920s that "a lack of dialectical ability" prevented him "from thinking out satisfactory reasons for choosing among conflicting doctrines." His professors at Harvard, particularly James and Santayana, "pulled me in different ways," and despite his best efforts he became "the victim of an incoherent eclecticism." Like Richard Ely before him, Croly seemed unable to reconcile idealism and empiricism, and that failure prompted him to discontinue his philosophical studies. Also like Ely, he found the ideas that resolved his earlier confusion in the style of political analysis he cultivated as an alternative to philosophy.[31]

Croly's first sustained efforts as a journalist only hinted at the ideas brewing in his imagination. As a contributor to the *Architectural Record*, a magazine founded as a companion to the *Real Estate Record and Guide*, he wrote haphazardly about developments in contemporary architecture. During these years, the only significant theme identifiable in his writings concerns the restraints imposed on the artist's independence by modern democratic culture. Croly feared that "wherever the genuine artist comes into contact with the public he is placed on the defensive." Only the gradual improvement of public taste through cultural education might solve that problem. Croly tied the specific difficulties of the artist to the broader American predilection for the multitalented handyman, whose lack of training limited his expertise but insured his independence. Americans, Croly argued, had long considered distrust of the expert part of their democratic faith.[32] Finding a way to harmonize the special skills of the superior talent with the popular demand for equality, Croly believed, was the particular challenge facing American culture.

"If one wants to do some solid thinking," Croly counseled Frankfurter in 1913, "it is not necessary to retire to a college town for the purpose." Croly was doing some solid thinking himself while he was churning out articles for the *Architectural Record*, and in 1905 he cut back the time he devoted to the magazine in order to do some solid writing as well. The result was *The Promise of American Life*, which he worked on steadily from 1905 until its appearance in 1909. The book contained Croly's solution to the conflict between the independent individual and the democratic community, his celebrated formula for achieving Hamiltonian ends through Jeffersonian means. Dozens of periodicals reviewed the *Promise* enthusiastically, and its success immediately established Croly as the most important theorist of American progressivism. Theodore Roosevelt's magazine, the *Outlook*, devoted two articles to the book, the first praising it as "an unusual and remarkable work," the second contrasting its generous Hamiltonian nationalism to the more limited Jeffersonian vision of Woodrow Wilson. Croly was understandably overwhelmed by this reception. He wrote cautiously to Learned Hand that the *Promise* "is essentially a reconnoitering expedition into territory hitherto not very well occupied in this country; and I cannot expect to hold my ground unless I obtain support." Hand assured him that he need not worry, warning instead that Croly's followers were in some danger of canonizing him, and prophesying that myths would soon proliferate surrounding Croly's powers as he began to "take on the form of the Sun-God."[33]

The most powerful myth about Croly involved Theodore Roosevelt, who found in the *Promise* a convincing rationale for the expansion of government authority he favored. When he ran for president in 1912 as the Progressive party candidate, Roosevelt adopted Croly's phrase "the new nationalism" as his campaign slogan. According to public perceptions, Croly's book converted the colonel to progressivism and inspired him to challenge his handpicked successor, William Howard Taft, for the presidency. Roosevelt fed such rumors simply by doing nothing to squelch them. In fact, Croly did help to write the Progressive party platform, and he also produced position papers on the trust question for use in the campaign. The public no doubt exaggerated Croly's influence, although historians' later attempts to minimize it may be no less inaccurate. Not only did Roosevelt agree with Croly's argument in the *Promise*—after all, Croly singled him out for praise as a "nationalist" reformer—there is clear evidence that he actually read the book carefully as well. The association between Croly and the colonel was close, and the lines of influence ran in both directions, from their first contact in 1910 until after the election of 1912. At that time, Croly declined Roosevelt's offer of a permanent position in the Progressive party, because he wanted to maintain his independence.[34]

Croly enjoyed the reflected glare of Roosevelt's celebrity, but he suffered no blindness about his own importance in American politics. "I am getting down to work again," he wrote Learned Hand after Wilson's election, "& don't propose to be interrupted until Christmas—unless the country really needs me—which it won't."[35] Croly kept a firm grip on his ego throughout this heady time, quietly accepting the degree Harvard finally awarded him in 1910 without questioning the university's motives or its timing. In 1913 he received an invitation to deliver Harvard's Godkin lectures, and in 1914 they were published in revised form as *Progressive Democracy*. Although it failed to attract as much attention as *The Promise of American Life*, *Progressive Democracy* was a much more solid book. The *Promise* teetered unsteadily not only between Hamilton and Jefferson but also between science and mysticism. Croly concluded with a frequently quoted plea for a "democratic St. Francis," and he challenged every citizen to become "something of a saint and something of a hero." The book's hybrid quality has enabled Croly's numerous interpreters to argue plausibly that the *Promise* was influenced primarily by Hegel, James, Santayana, Royce, Comte, David Croly, or the novelist Robert Grant (whose inspiration Croly himself emphasized). One can in fact identify traces of all these thinkers' ideas in Croly's work, and if that characteristic helped account for the book's popularity at the time of its publication, it also undercut the coherence of its argument.[36]

Progressive Democracy, on the other hand, reflects clearly and un-questionably the influence of James and Dewey, and it presents a more penetrating analysis of the problems confronting America as well as a less fuzzy vision of their solution. In the *Promise* Croly was still working his way through the "incoherent eclecticism" of his formative years; in *Progressive Democracy* he resolved his long-standing intellectual conflict by adopting the philosophy of pragmatism. Croly himself recognized his progress, and he was disappointed when the book made fewer waves than its less coherent predecessor. He wrote to Roosevelt that *Progressive Democracy* was designed to supplement the *Promise*, and he admitted his "wish that the two books had been combined into one."[37]

The books do resemble each other: they present similar analyses of American history and similar reformist programs. They differ principally in the disappearance of the earlier, quasi-mystical reliance on heroes, which lent a peculiar tone to the otherwise quite straightforwardly democratic analysis of the *Promise*. Although Croly's commitment to democracy was fundamental and unwavering, it is true that the fulfillment of the *Promise*'s prescriptions occasionally seemed to depend on the sensitive, dynamic indi-viduals who lead rather than the unimaginative masses who follow. In *Progressive Democracy*, Croly replaced that residue of faith in a Comtean priesthood with a more clearly manifested faith in the democratic will, a faith inspired by pragmatism. A passage at the beginning of the chapter "Industrial Democracy" encapsulates the ideas Croly derived from James and Dewey about knowledge and action. Democracy, he wrote,

> assumes an intrepid and inexhaustible faith in the humanity of an ideal of individual and social fulfillment. It assumes the ability of the human will, both in its individual and its collective aspects, to make an effective contribu-tion to the work of fulfillment. It assumes the ability of the human intelligence to frame temporary programs which will provide a sufficient foundation for significant and fruitful action. It anticipates that as a result of such action a progressive democracy will learn how to be progressively democratic.[38]

It is instructive to put those words in the framework of the radical theory of knowledge and the theory of voluntary action presented by the philosophers of the *via media*, in order to show, in Croly's words, how his vision of democracy was "necessarily opposed to intellectualism and allied to

pragmatism." First, knowledge is never a simple reflection of the world outside us. It inevitably contains a fiduciary element; its verification requires us,
in James's phrase, to "trade on each other's truth." Second, neither this pragmatic knowledge nor the sort of progress stemming from it is automatic.
Third, our intelligence cannot yield definite answers to social questions; it
only enables us to construct possible solutions to the situations of "felt
difficulty" that we encounter in experience, solutions we must then test
in practice. Finally, no abstract scheme of progress can be presented
in advance; as individuals and as a society we can only tackle our problems instrumentally, through the admittedly imperfect mechanism of
democracy.

Croly insisted that "the value of the book, so far as it has any, will consist
not so much in the attainment of definite conclusions as in the spirit which
characterizes the attempt to reach them," a virtual paraphrase of James's
defense of his method in *Pragmatism*.[39] In a world without certainty,
the traditional American reverence for the Constitution as the source of all
political wisdom was foolish. Croly urged Americans to unshackle their
imaginations from the "presumably permanent body of constitutional law"
and have the courage to experiment with "a social program which will not
make any corresponding pretensions to finality." The only "permanent
element in the life of the community will be derived," Croly concluded, from
"the democratic faith and ideal," from "the creative power of the will, which
insists, even though its brother, the reason, cannot ascertain."[40] Only if we
adopt a pragmatic outlook, in other words, can we survive without the
comfort dogma offers. For the framing and testing of hypotheses, only
democracy provides the appropriate political framework. Croly had come a
long way from his father's faith in Comte. The positivists' assertion of inevitable progress had become a pragmatic faith in fragile human wills, science no
longer yielded definite knowledge but only an experimental method, and
social guidance came from democratic participation rather than from a
priesthood of sociologists. In short, Croly had traded the positivists' claims to
certainty for the pragmatists' fertile doubt.

In the late summer of 1913, while Croly was working on the lectures that
became *Progressive Democracy*, he encountered an angel who changed his
life. Although accounts of visions are notoriously unreliable, Croly later
reported his version of what happened. While he was delivering his standard
diatribe against the Jeffersonian progressivism that Louis Brandeis was proclaiming at that time in *Harper's Weekly*, one of Croly's listeners suggested he
spread his message by starting his own magazine. When Croly wondered
aloud about finances, the angel assured him she would attend to such matters.
From that conversation, and many others Croly had with his angel, Dorothy
Whitney Straight, and her husband, Willard Straight, *The New Republic* was
born.[41] Croly now had a regular outlet for his ideas, just as Jaurès had in
L'Humanité, the Webbs had in *The New Statesman*, and Hobhouse had,
briefly, in the London *Tribune*. The Straights shared Croly's political views
and his enthusiasm for their friend Theodore Roosevelt, and they gave Croly

a free hand to shape the magazine. In the fall of 1914, he began putting together a staff to fill its pages.

Because Croly wanted his magazine to "throw a few firecrackers," he was looking for writers who not only shared his brand of pragmatic progressivism but also showed a certain feistiness. In Walter Lippmann he found both. As Croly explained to Learned Hand shortly after Lippmann had agreed to come aboard *The New Republic*, Lippmann had "real feeling, conviction and knowledge to give a certain assurance, almost a certain dignity to his impertinence, and of course the ability to get away with impertinence is almost the best quality a political journalist can have." Only intelligence and the ability to write were more important, and Lippmann possessed those in even greater abundance. He graduated from Harvard in 1910, the same year the university got around to awarding a degree to Croly; aside from that coincidence, the two men had very little in common. Unlike the stolid Croly, Lippmann as an undergraduate displayed the mercurial brilliance and sharp wit that would earn him more admiration than affection throughout his life. While at Harvard, he delighted in challenging the pretense of gentility that shielded economic privilege, and one of his articles on that subject caught the attention of William James. Charmed by Lippmann's irreverence and impressed by his thoughtfulness, James invited Lippmann to take tea regularly at his home, and Lippmann wrote enthusiastically to his parents that these weekly sessions with James were "the greatest thing that has happened to me in my college life." Lippmann's family was wealthy and cosmopolitan, but it was also Jewish, and not everyone at Harvard was as open-minded as James, whom Lippmann later eulogized as "perhaps the most tolerant man of our generation." Like his classmate John Reed, however, Lippmann weathered his experience of rejection from the university's clubby world. Largely because of his iconoclasm, he even attained a sort of celebrity before he left Cambridge. Irony was only one element at work when Reed introduced him to a gathering of undergraduates as "the future President of the United States."[42]

Lippmann completed the requirements for his degree in three years. Concentrating particularly on philosophy, he earned the respect of the usually aloof Santayana, who invited him to stay on a fourth year as his teaching assistant. With his rapid progress and the attention of a patron, Lippmann appeared poised for the successful career in philosophy that eluded Croly. But he felt drawn toward another world. As founding president of the Socialist Club at Harvard, and as a card-carrying, dues-paying member of the Fabian Society, he was immersed in radical political activity. He enrolled in a seminar taught by visiting professor Graham Wallas, whose study *Human Nature in Politics* (1908) challenged the competence of the ordinary citizen and left a lasting mark on Lippmann's political sensibility. Lippmann likewise impressed Wallas, just as he had James and Santayana; in a striking illustration of his generation's expectations for the young man, Wallas dedicated his next book, *The Great Society* (1914), to his former student. After a brief stint muckraking with Lincoln Steffens, Lippmann joined the socialist administration of

Mayor George Lunn in Schenectady, New York, only to find that these radicals, once in office, exchanged the sabers they flashed in their rhetoric for jackknives. As progressives were to discover with numbing regularity, the politicians they supported proved to be more interested in reelection than reform. Lippmann had no patience with the temporizing required to juggle constituencies. He was elated, he reported to Wallas soon after his resignation, that his political career was "so compressed that I can already look back upon it." After delivering an indignant indictment of Lunn in the socialist weekly *Call*, he was ready for other things.[43]

The first item on his agenda, he wrote to Wallas in July, 1912, was "what may be a little book—at least a series of essays, and no small part of it is aimed at popularizing your *Human Nature in Politics*." When it appeared in 1913, *A Preface to Politics* was a sensational success. It represented Lippmann's attempt to combine James's philosophy and Freud's psychology with Wallas's politics, and he wrapped that untidy package in the cleverly offhand style typical of the prewar innocents' rebellion. Of the fiddles Van Wyck Brooks claimed to hear tuning up all over America, Lippmann's was among the most dazzling. He was the enfant terrible of New York City's little renaissance, bubbling over with a confidence born of precocity that enabled him to float freely from his parents' home on Manhattan's Upper East Side to Mabel Dodge's bohemian salon. Lippmann explained to Wallas that the idea he wanted most of all to communicate in his first book was James's idea of uncertainty. The "great difficulty in all complicated thinking" is "to understand that the concept is a rough instrument that stands in the place of adequate perception." "James always felt," Lippmann continued, that "the epistemological problem, especially . . . has tremendous consequences" for the world of political practice, and the challenge lay in explaining the political implications of this new understanding. In *A Preface to Politics*, Lippmann announced that the modern age required "a different order of thinking. We cannot expect to meet our problems with a few inherited ideas, uncriticized assumptions, a foggy vocabulary, and a machine philosophy." Paraphrasing James's *Pragmatism*, he contended that "our primary care must be to keep the habits of the mind flexible and adapted to the movement of real life. The only way to control our destiny is to work at it." Although the forces of life may appear coercive, "nothing is entirely inevitable. There is always some choice, some opportunity for human direction."[44]

Achieving that human direction was the subject of Lippmann's next book, *Drift and Mastery*. Randolph Bourne expressed the feeling of his generation when he said that this was "a book one would have given one's soul to have written." As a piece of social analysis, it was the masterpiece of the prewar period. Having swept up and thrown out the scraps of irrationalism cluttering *A Preface to Politics*, Lippmann presented in their place a brilliant exposition of the consequences of radical empiricism for political thought and action. His prose flowed so smoothly, and his arguments proceeded so effortlessly, that the philosophical depth of *Drift and Mastery* was easy to overlook. It appeared on the surface to be simply a book of topical political commentary, discursive rather than analytical, a vivid illustration of the era's unfocused impulses. Yet beyond its preferences for regulation over trust-busting, for Roosevelt over Wilson, it was also much more. After fifty years of cultural anxiety about the replacement by science of religion, Lippmann was able to examine that phenomenon with a detachment and an acuity unavailable to those who felt more sharply the loss of a faith Lippmann never really had. His age had "lost authority and retained the need of it." His contemporaries were "freer than we are strong," and had "more responsibility than we have capacity." Facts only smiled ironically on any "monumental creeds" his generation might try to invoke. In their "giddy and reeling universe," it was time "to cast aside the old thickset forms of their thinking for suppler experimental ones." Although such thinking was uncomfortable, since it provided "none of the harmony outside which men desire," it was "more accurate than settled principles can ever be." Still, there was a cost: "the repose and sublimity and the shelter of larger creeds" were gone forever.[45]

Lippmann offered science as the mastery capable of directing all this drift. His escape from Nietzsche's conclusion has attracted much criticism: did Lippmann not realize that scientists make mistakes? Indeed he did. In fact, it was precisely the ability of science to acknowledge its mistakes—instead of trying to hide them, as philosophers and social theorists often do—that attracted him, just as it attracted James and Dewey, to the discipline of scientific inquiry. Intersubjectivity is the key to the success of the scientific community, pragmatists argued. Investigators commit themselves to the rigorous testing of one another's work instead of assuming its accuracy. Conscientiously pursued, science is the pragmatic method in action, and it inspired Lippmann's hopes even though he understood its limitations. "The power of criticizing the scientific mind," he wrote, is "our best guarantee for the progress of scientific discovery." It is when science "becomes its own critic" that it "assures its own future." Lippmann's faith in science was not naive. "Rightly understood science is the culture under which people can live forward in the midst of complexity, and treat life not as something given but as something to be shaped." This is not the science of positivism but the *Wissenschaft* of Dilthey and the experimentalism of James, the science that treats even its most firmly established conclusions as the most unstable of hypotheses.[46]

How does such science relate to politics? This equation might seem problematical, since Comte and Spencer both considered themselves scientists. But Lippmann insisted that nothing can be more unscientific than the masquerade of certainty, and only one sort of political system leaves room for, and even insists upon, doubt. "There is nothing accidental then in the fact that democracy in politics is the twin-brother of scientific thinking. They had to come together. As absolutism falls, science arises. It *is* self-government. For when the impulse which overthrows kings and priests and unquestioned creeds becomes self-conscious we call it science." The spirit of the scientific community, in its collective search for knowledge, is the "discipline of democracy, the escape from drift, the outlook of a free man." This was precisely the argument Dewey tried repeatedly to make, but he never made it more persuasively—perhaps because he never made it so clearly.

Lippmann's vision of science and democracy derived directly from the philosophy of the *via media*, even though the connection often remained implicit in his writings. He wanted to communicate with a larger audience than philosophers reached, and he wanted his message to have an impact on those who had never heard of epistemology or reflected on its consequences for their lives. He had no illusions about what he could offer them. "The only rule to follow," he advised, "is that of James: 'Use concepts when they help, and drop them when they hinder understanding.'" Thought must not be petrified in inherited forms; "Mastery in our world cannot mean any single, neat, and absolute line of procedure." In a passage James would have been proud of, he warned that his vision of the democratically-determined future

> is not a fixed picture, a row of shiny ideals which we can exhibit to mankind, and say: Achieve these or be damned. All we can do is to search the world as we find it, extricate the forces that seem to move it, and surround them with criticism and suggestion. Such a vision will inevitably reveal the bias of its author; that is to say it will be a human hypothesis, not an oracular revelation. But if the hypothesis is honest and alive it should cast a little light upon our chaos. It should help us to cease revolving in the mere routine of the present or floating in a private utopia. . . . The day is past, I believe, when anybody can pretend to have laid down an inclusive or a final analysis of the democratic problem. Everyone is compelled to omit infinitely more than he can deal with; everyone is compelled to meet the fact that a democratic vision must be made by the progressive collaboration of many people.[47]

Lippmann himself would prove unable to resist the lure of the oracular later in his career, when he surrendered his uncertainty and took refuge in the sort of "monumental creed" he ruled out in 1914. The overwhelming experience of totalitarianism had that effect on millions of people. Prior to World War I, however, before his involvement in foreign affairs demoralized him, and before his experience with propaganda showed him how easily people could be duped, his pragmatic philosophy and progressive politics made him an ideal choice for *The New Republic*.

If Harold Laski was right when he compared Lippmann's mind to a knife, Croly's resembled a pair of shears, precise but slow, which worked best when it brought together at the proper angle the edges of two ideas. Croly lacked Lippmann's sharpness and his elegance, but they complemented each other effectively. They took *The New Statesman* as their model, and their own combination of steadiness and unpredictability mirrored the Webbs' partnership as nearly, if not as deliberately, as did their attempt to steer a course between conventional liberalism and revolutionary socialism. In the circular they sent potential subscribers, the editors described their magazine in terms reminiscent of the celebrated masthead of *The Masses*: "*The New Republic* will respect no taboos, it will play no favorites, it will be confined to no set creed and tied to no political party. Its philosophy will be a faith rather than a dogma." In the speech he made, reluctantly, at a gathering of those launching the magazine in the summer of 1914, Croly announced his intention to use *The New Republic* as an educational tool for progressive reform.[48] As he and Lippmann had argued in their books, democratic change could be achieved only by introducing the public to new ideas.

Both Croly and Lippmann admitted privately their concern about the corrosive effect producing a weekly might have on their ability to write books of the sort that won their reputations, and as it turned out they had good reason to worry.[49] As Lippmann later wrote in *Public Opinion* (1922), the only one of his books to approach the quality of *Drift and Mastery*, the press is "like the beam of a searchlight that moves restlessly about, bringing one episode and then another out of darkness into vision. Men cannot do the work of the world by this light alone. They cannot govern society by episodes, incidents, and eruptions." That was one danger facing the editors in 1914, but there was another perhaps even more important. Three years earlier, Lippmann had described the "pathetic loneliness" imposed on Santayana by his refusal to descend into the life of the world around him, and he had concluded sadly that "a man can't see the play and be in it too."[50] All too soon, caught up in a drama they had not expected but could not resist, Croly and Lippmann would find themselves sucked into a world of politics so enchanting it almost completely destroyed their own ability to see.

The intoxication of power posed no comparable threat to the few German intellectuals interested in progressive politics. Indeed, the most striking feature of progressivism in Germany is its absence: there was never a significant reform movement designed to shift German liberalism toward the left. Yet there is one thinker who merits consideration as a progressive manqué, Max Weber. Weber wanted to unbuckle liberalism from laissez-faire, broaden its focus from the middle class, and secure greater social justice than was possible within the boundaries of Bismarck's *Sammlungspolitik*. Given those interests, Weber never found a political home, and he never exerted the sort of influence that Bourgeois or Croly did. His intellectual achievements, however, dwarfed those of every progressive thinker except perhaps John Dewey, and the challenges he presented to both progressive and social democratic ideas—ideas with which he felt more sympathy than is often realized—raise troubling questions about the ideas discussed in this study. Weber worked to create a viable German progressive party at those few moments when he considered its success possible, and he longed for a more liberal social democratic party of the sort that Bernstein had in mind, yet neither survived. His political frustration helped to shape his analysis of the failure of democracy and liberalism; his interpretation of rationalization and bureaucratization left him without hope for the future prospects of progressive change. Examining the most desperate of progressives is instructive precisely because his conclusions differed from those of Bourgeois, Hobhouse, Croly, Lippmann, and Dewey. Weber shared their philosophical perspective and their political ideals—indeed, the similarities may be startling because they are not part of the conventional image of

Weber, for reasons I will try to unravel—and his rejection of their conclusions is therefore particularly important in the analysis of progressive theory. The story of the twentieth century is in large part the story of Germany's divergence from Britain, France, and the United States, and the unexpected similarities and differences between Weber and the other theorists of progressivism powerfully illuminate one dimension of that divergence. Until now my analysis has concentrated on convergence; in this case the impediments to convergence are at least as important.

Interpretations of Weber are extraordinarily diverse, in part because of his multifaceted ambivalence, and in part because the breadth of his scholarly activity often escapes the narrow interests of his interpreters. Like James and Dilthey, whose work has inspired equally sharp disagreements among their followers, Weber not only relied upon a variety of intellectual sources, he resisted efforts to synthesize and insisted on holding opposite ideas in tension. His understanding cut to the heart of theoretical controversies, and he could not tolerate naive claims to reconcile the irreconcilable. He preferred to endure the doubt engendered by admitting the intractability of problems. Few of his critics have shown that strength. As a philosopher of the social sciences, he has been enshrined as the father of objective, value-free inquiry, and as the patron saint of interpretive sociology. As a political thinker, he has been vilified as a cynical *Machtpolitiker* advocating German expansion, and praised as a lonely, heroic spokesman for the values of democracy and toleration against the clamor of repression and revolution. As a sociologist, he has been cast as the bourgeois answer to Marx, the apologist of religious ideas as determining factors in history, and as the prophet of rationalization, whose analysis of modern culture leaves no room for the lingering romance of faith.[51] It is a measure of Weber's complexity that a plausible case can be made for each of these interpretations, but each presents only a partial view of his achievements, insufficiently accounts for his intellectual growth, and perhaps most importantly, overlooks his principled commitment to the impossibility of resolving these issues once and for all.

While Weber's philosophical perspective was colored by Dilthey's and Heinrich Rickert's competing arguments against the possibility of patterning social investigation on the model of the natural sciences, he wanted to filter out as much subjectivity as possible without losing sight of the necessarily hermeneutical quality of the *Geisteswissenschaften*. His political views reflected his respect for Germany's national unity and its cultural accomplishments, and he refused to surrender that loyalty in the face of the nation's failures. The distinction Weber's generation drew between the highly spiritualized and moralistic "culture" of Germany and the flattened utilitarianism of French and British "civilization" was not necessarily inaccurate or inevitably destructive.[52] There is a persistent tendency to find in all celebrations of German culture dark foreshadowings of Nazi terror. Until that understandable but unfortunate failure of historical imagination is overcome, it will be impossible to understand the nature of Weber's nationalism. His criticism of Germany's repressive politics was rooted in a commitment to the values of autonomy and responsibility he inherited from Kant. That same commitment made him equally skeptical of organized capitalism and bureaucratic socialism. Finally, Weber's sociological research convinced him that both Hegel's idealism and Marx's materialism were insufficiently dialectical. He found in his study of world religions a very different cunning of reason; the evidence he gathered concerning the prospects of charisma in a disenchanted world left him suspended between heroic resolution and despair.

The personality that produced all of these paradoxes was itself remarkably contradictory. Weber's family reproduced in chiaroscuro the tensions evident in the backgrounds of most of the thinkers discussed in this study. Born in 1864, Weber was the same age as Hobhouse, five years younger than Dewey, and five years older than Croly. The forging of the German Reich in 1870 was one of the formative experiences of his life; sharing the glory of Bismarck's achievements was as much a part of his early years as celebrating Lincoln's glory was of Dewey's. Weber's father was a prominent member of the National Liberal party, and other party luminaries and members of the German intellectual elite—including Dilthey—frequented the Webers' house in Berlin. His father was an intelligent, amiable, and self-satisfied functionary, who performed the necessary obeisances in his job and demanded the even more rigid subservience of his family in his home. Weber's mother was in some ways the antithesis of her good-natured husband. She luxuriated in self-sacrifice as only a Calvinist could, she cultivated an excruciating sense of moral duty, and she brought to her life a wonderfully limitless energy. She was as resolutely a woman of faith as her husband was a man of affairs. Max, the eldest of their six children, found himself caught in the friction between his mother's spirituality and his father's realism. Meeting the standards of one of his parents excluded the possibility of satisfying the other, and that pressure mounted as the time approached for Max to choose a career.

His first two years at the University of Heidelberg and his year of military service seemed to reinforce his father's down-to-earth orientation. Weber's academic efforts seemed futile. While he was neither the first nor the last to be driven by Dilthey to despair, Weber's inability to penetrate the hermeneutic circle prompted him to write home that he had "reached the darkest depths of stupidity—being completely unable to find even by use of a microscope any sign of brains in my head." But in 1884 Weber experienced the familiar romantic epiphany. A book by the American Unitarian William Ellery Channing, sent to Weber by his mother's sister, who shared her religious exuberance, did for Weber what Wordsworth had earlier done for Mill, Green, and James. In a letter to his mother, Weber praised the "unassailable loftiness" of Channing's philosophy and applauded "the clear, calm idealism" Channing drew "from the observation of 'the infinite worth of the human soul.'" This incident marked, Weber confessed, "*the first time* within my memory *that something religious has had a more than objective interest for me*."[53] This moment was decisive, even though Weber never shared his mother's or his aunt's religious faith, because it convinced him of the superiority of their lives of relentless commitment from a strictly ethical point of view. He became increasingly impatient with his father's banal contentment, he became increasingly maniacal in his own scholarly work, and he became increasingly uneasy about the connection between his yearnings for a life of moral worth and the rather flat fact-finding of the research that consumed his energies during these years.

Weber lived in his parents' home in Berlin from 1887 until 1893. During that period he worked long hours as an apprentice attorney, wrote his first doctoral dissertation on medieval trading companies, wrote his second dissertation (required of those aspiring to university positions) on Roman agrarian history, and also completed a massive study of farm laborers in East Prussia for the Verein für Sozialpolitik. At the age of twenty-nine, having published three impressive books on quite different subjects, he was at last prepared for a career in university teaching. Yet he was as unsure of his future as James or Jaurès or Hobhouse. With the prospect of a successful academic career at last in reach, he wrote, "I am simply not . . . a real scholar. For me scholarly activity is too much bound up with the idea of filling my leisure hours, even though I realize that due to the division of labor, scholarly activity can be carried on successfully only if one devotes one's entire personality to it." He hoped that teaching would redeem the scholarly life by providing "the indispensable feeling of *practical* activity," but his hope could not smother his anxiety. "Nothing is more horrible to me than the arrogance of the 'intellectual' and learned professions," he wrote to his fiancée Marianne Schnitger. As a scholar, he warned her, "My sphere of duty does not please me sufficiently for me to bring into our house the kind of natural happiness that comes from . . . fulfilling and *practical* work."[54]

Weber tried to achieve through political engagement the fulfillment scholarship failed to provide. He became involved with the German analog to the American social gospel, the Christian social movement, which offered a reformist alternative to the rigidity of the SPD and the sterility of National Liberalism. He became a close associate of Friedrich Naumann, one of the leading figures in radical Protestant political circles. The goal of political and social action, Weber announced to the Protestant Social Congress in 1894, must be the cultivation of "personal responsibility, the deep aspiration for the moral and spiritual goals of mankind." Improving the standard of living of the working class was but a means toward an altogether different end, the achievement of a kind of nobility that was inversely proportional to the subjective feeling of happiness prized by liberal utilitarians and orthodox Marxists alike.[55] This aim was anything but utopian. To the contrary, Weber acknowledged the persistence—even the positive value—of struggle as the essence of both domestic and international politics.

In the Inaugural Address he delivered in 1895 after his appointment as professor of economics at the University of Freiburg, he surveyed the barren landscape of German politics. The Junkers continued to covet power, but they could not provide direction because their economic decline was inevitable. The bourgeoisie, as a result of Bismarck's domination of national politics, wallowed in the "peculiarly 'unhistorical' and unpolitical mood" induced by their long-standing political impotence. Although the working class aspired to political power, their leaders were merely "pathetic experts in political triviality" who lacked "the deep instincts for power of a class which has been called to political leadership." Germany must face the challenge, Weber demanded, of asserting itself as a force in international politics; otherwise it would remain a pawn in the imperialist powers' world-historical struggle for domination. The preservation of German culture depended on the expansion of German political power, and that expansion in turn depended on economic growth and the substantive integration of the German people in a united nation only formally achieved by Bismarck in 1870.

Weber's strategy of social reform and political democratization, then, was motivated by his desire to create a stable economic and political foundation for the protection and assertion of German cultural values against the competing values of other nations. National expansion, as the British demonstrated, required the active support of the bourgeoisie and the proletariat, and Weber sought to win that broad-based assent for national power politics by involving the middle and lower classes in the political affairs of the Reich. His outlook, which resembled the liberal imperialism that attracted the Webbs and repelled Hobhouse, aligned Weber in the mid-1890s with more cynical and self-interested nationalists whose interests differed markedly from his desire to contribute to the "development of those characteristics . . . which make for human greatness," the characteristics of cultural and moral excellence he commended to the Protestant Social Congress the year before his Freiburg Inaugural. Reproducing the conflict between the models provided by his parents, Weber defended a spiritual ideal of national greatness by subscribing to a hard-headed politics of national interest. Those committed to ethical idealism, in other words, must be prepared to struggle for its success, and they must not ignore the potential consequences of that struggle. "Instead of the dream of peace and happiness," he said coldly, "there stands over the gate of the unknown future of human history: abandon all hope."[56]

This was stark counsel, and it offered Weber no greater consolation than it offered his stunned listeners. Social reform must be undertaken in order to improve the prospects of imperialism. The sacred values of individual autonomy and moral responsibility can be secured only by playing the ruthless game of power politics. If the resolution of idealism and realism required such jarring contradictions, the price might be too high. Weber's own psychological tensions were accentuated rather than relieved by his dual allegiance to moral and spiritual goals and the hard-edged politics of German nationalism. In 1897, a year after he accepted a position at the University of Heidelberg, he suffered an incapacitating psychological collapse. His breakdown occurred several weeks after a climactic argument with his father, in which he challenged his father's right to determine when and whether his mother could visit Max and Marianne. This unprecedented denial of the patriarch's prerogatives culminated in his father's departure from Weber's house and the onset of icy relations between his father and mother. It attained even greater significance when his father died while traveling with a friend a few weeks later.[57] Those circumstances may have precipitated Weber's collapse, yet his emotional trauma merely intensified an already perilous intellectual instability. Weber's deepest loyalties were split, and the strident cultural nationalism he proclaimed in Freiburg was hardly an adequate solution to that fundamental problem.

Weber's ascent from his hell of swirling guilt and mounting frustration, a climb marked by repeated relapses into complete psychic and physical helplessness, took a full five years. From the autumn of 1897 until the autumn of 1902, intellectual activity or emotional excitement of any kind produced sleeplessness and nervous exhaustion. During that time he resigned from his professorship at Heidelberg and retained only an honorary position, thereby giving up the independence he had worked so feverishly to attain while he lived in his parents' home. He became utterly dependent on Marianne, surrendering the awesome willfulness that had proved so destructive. His ordeal not only gave him a new personality, it gave him new ideas.

The first project he undertook in the course of his recovery was an inquiry into the philosophy of social science, an attempt to resolve for himself the *Methodenstreit* that was becoming a permanent feature of German academic life. Largely because Weber ruled out the possibility of the positivistic social science that many of his self-styled followers have pursued, this study has not received the attention it deserves. Initially appearing in three installments between 1903 and 1905, *Roscher and Knies: The Logical Problems of Historical Economics* was Weber's challenge to the assumptions and the methods of the dominant school of historical economists and their critics. Weber presented his case for interpretive social science by means of a polemical attack directed against positivists and intuitionists alike. Criticizing the grander claims of the *Natur-* and the *Geisteswissenschaften*, he explicitly rejected the possibility of certain knowledge beyond the barest analytical propositions or the experience of the raw immediacy of consciousness. Because Weber proceeded in *Roscher and Knies* almost exclusively by criticizing the competing positions he found inadequate, it is very difficult to determine his own epistemological stance from his fragmentary comments. Nevertheless, his most clearly formulated arguments are consistent with important aspects of the radical theory of knowledge. Neither a pseudo-scientific search for laws of social causation, nor a celebration of intuitive reexperiencing, takes into account the limits of our knowledge. The "self-evidence" of personal consciousness provides access to the conscious experience of others with no more certainty than the "so called 'axioms of physics'" account for matter; both yield only imperfect knowledge. The differences between the natural sciences and the human sciences, which will be discussed in greater detail in the next section of this chapter, are heuristic rather than ontological, as Dilthey insisted; they have to do with the purposes and methods of analysis characteristic of these different sciences, not with the degree of certainty derivable from them.[58]

Weber also adopted a theory of voluntary action considerably more complex than was apparent in his earlier work. That sensitivity to the multidimensional nature of experience became clear in the substantive and methodological studies he began in 1903, which were later published as *The Protestant Ethic and the Spirit of Capitalism*, "'Objectivity' in Social Science and Social Policy," and "Critical Studies in the Logic of the Cultural Sciences." He emphasized the necessity of taking into account objective conditions, cultural values, and emotional and psychological factors. He acknowledged that each of these elements can seduce naive interpreters into fatal simplifications, but he insisted that students of society must resist one-sided explanations. Neither pure determinism nor pure voluntarism is tenable, Weber maintained, because the most creative activity occurs within a social context that limits the individual's options, while at the opposite end of the spectrum, even conformity requires choices among varieties of acceptable behavior. An irreducible element of will intermingles with material constraints in all activity; ideals and economic interests together shape historical change. As he summed up his broad-gauged approach, "All the activities and situations constituting an historically given culture affect the formation of the material wants, the mode of their satisfaction, the integration of interest groups and the types of power they exercise."[59] Such statements have prompted interpreters to exaggerate Weber's emphasis on the role of ideas, despite his explicit warnings in the closing words of *The Protestant Ethic*: "It is, of course, not my aim to substitute for a one-sided materialist an equally one-sided spiritualistic causal interpretation of culture and history. Each is equally possible, but each, if it does not serve as the preparation, but as the conclusion of an investigation, accomplishes equally little in the interest of historical truth."[60] In a satisfactory, multidimensional approach, these two interpretive models must supplement one another.

Despite his misgivings concerning determinism, Weber rejected identifications of freedom with simple unpredictability. Those who explained volition by pointing to the impossibility of reducing ideas to a formula confused rational choice, which is the essence of human freedom, with capriciousness, which is basically irrational. The "characteristic of 'incalculability,'" he wrote, "is the privilege of—the insane. On the other hand, we associate the highest measure of an empirical 'feeling of freedom' with those actions which we are conscious of performing rationally."[61] The entire enterprise of the human sciences rests on the assumption of rational action, and Weber had no interest in dethroning Marx only to be left with Schelling.[62]

Weber's political ideas also changed after his breakdown. It is sometimes assumed that the confident nationalism he trumpeted in the 1890s found expression in World War I. Weber did initially support the German war effort, until full-scale submarine warfare, and the refusal to renounce the aim of territorial acquisition, turned him against it. But there was an important change in his attitude toward foreign policy earlier, around 1900, and even his most severe critics have rejected as preposterous the suggestion that Weber's style of nationalism was causally linked to the militaristic policies of the Second or Third Reich.[63] Weber wanted Germany to play the role of a major power in world politics, but he had no illusions that it could simply recast the map of Europe. Weber's nationalism flowed from a loyalty to German *Kultur*, but his allegiance to that ideal was tempered after 1900 by a growing appreciation of the values of other cultures, and also by an awareness that Clio, at least, is always on the side with the big batallions.

Weber also changed his mind about domestic politics. At the turn of the century, he felt moderately optimistic about the chances of achieving political democratization, social reform, and international power through a coalition of progressive and social democratic forces. When the SPD formally censured Bernstein at Dresden in 1903, however, the opening on the left sought by progressives like Weber and Naumann slammed shut. "The time is still far off when we shall be able to join hands with the urban proletariat for a solution of social problems," Weber wrote. "I hope that this will come, but for the time being there can be no question of it."[64] While he continued to participate intermittently in politics, he devoted the bulk of his time to scholarship. The 1905 Russian Revolution briefly sparked his imagination but eventually confirmed his growing suspicions about the prospects of freedom in an increasingly bureaucratized world. The differences between early and late capitalism, although considerable, only emphasized the depth of the threat facing the industrial world. The central question posed by the increasing size and complexity of the bureaucratic machinery driving organized capitalist economies and modern states, he warned, "is what we have to oppose to this machinery, so as to keep a residue of humanity free from this parcelling out of the soul."[65] He tried in his mature political sociology to find an answer to that question. He hoped the seeds of a new realism might flourish in the ground cleared by Germany's defeat in World War I, but he was skeptical about rooting the new Republic in catastrophe. Although he helped to write the Weimar Constitution, and was willing to serve in the government position to which he was nearly called, he understood the inadequacy of merely institutional solutions for problems lodged deep in German political culture. His death in 1920 saved him from watching his dream of a vigorous plebiscitary democracy under charismatic leadership turn into a nightmare.

The question of rationality became increasingly central in Weber's writings about politics and society during the last decade of his life. His comparative studies of world religions and economic systems alerted him to the varieties of rationality and the problematic nature of reason itself. But that sensitivity to the historicity of reason heightened his analytical acuity without plunging him into the nihilism that enveloped Nietzsche. Examining Weber's conclusions concerning history and values will reveal the reasons why a deepening pessimism colored his attitude toward the prospects of progressive politics, and how that attitude distinguished him from other progressive theorists. He never despaired, however, of the individual's ability to pursue meaningful goals through rational action. The cryptic comment Weber made on his deathbed, "The true is the truth," emerges from obscurity when placed in the context of his continuing search for answers that could never be final.[66] Like James, and like the other progressives who shared his ideals if not his mood, Weber believed in the quest for what is true even though he refused to believe in truth itself. He believed that the true, conceived as descriptive of a reality that is always in process and never completed, constitutes the only truth we can know.

2. Understanding Social Experience

In 1888, John Dewey observed in *The Ethics of Democracy* that "the non-social individual is an abstraction arrived at by imagining what man would be if all his human qualities were taken away."[67] That argument, fundamental to the philosophy of the *via media*, represented a direct challenge to liberal individualism and a less obvious but equally important challenge to both romantic and positivist varieties of social organicism. In this section I will examine the relation between progressive thinkers' ideas about social and historical experience and the ideas discussed in Chapter Three. In addition, I will indicate how the distinction drawn there between Green and Dewey on the one hand and Dilthey and James on the other reappeared in progressive theory. All of these progressives shared the radical philosophers' approach to interpretive social analysis. Most of them also found grounds for confidence in their study of history, and they extrapolated from the accumulated evidence of the past a scheme of continuing progress. Weber, by contrast, like James and Dilthey rather than Dewey and Green, believed that cultures sweep forward with a dull edge that leaves behind jagged and vulnerable traditions. He warned that social and economic progress comes by hacking the meaning from institutions that survive in warped forms, and he worried that the modern world of bureaucratic rationality, drained of its values, was slowly withering. After surveying these progressives' similar approaches to social inquiry, I will explain the reasons for their sharply different conclusions.

Bourgeois and Croly offered nearly identical accounts of the process that led social theorists toward a radically empirical conception of social experience. Throughout the nineteenth century, Bourgeois pointed out in *Solidarity*, philosophers retreated from the idea of the individual as a solitary being. In idealist and positivist schemes, individuals were swallowed up into different sorts of organic society. On the other hand, self-styled followers of Darwin concluded that the natural association of individuals is part of a ruthless struggle that only the strongest members of a species survive. Against those two extreme views, Bourgeois championed the doctrine of solidarity, which he derived from Fouillée's philosophy. Bourgeois's discussion of solidarity before the Ecole des Hautes Etudes sociales in 1901 mirrored with particular clarity Fouillée's analysis of the social dimensions of individual life.

According to Bourgeois, every group of men is either voluntarily or involuntarily an "*ensemble solidaire*." As individuals become increasingly interdependent, that solidarity grows. The social task consists in translating that natural solidarity into a moral solidarity by awakening individuals to the fact of their sociality and the responsibility it involves.[68] In *Progressive Democracy*, Croly argued that the "sacred individual and the sacred community" were ideas "born of a similar process of abstraction" from experience, and nurtured by "loyalty to ideal values" rather than life itself. Both Comte and Royce, in other words, were heading in the right direction when they emphasized the community instead of the individual, but they were on the wrong track. Only when psychology became social psychology, a shift for which James and Dewey were primarily responsible, did it become apparent that consciousness is "essentially social." According to Croly, a new image of society as a product of individual choice and individual action accompanied this altered conception of experience. In tandem, the new psychology and the new understanding of society illuminated the reciprocal relation between individual and social life.[69]

Hobhouse likewise emphasized the social quality of experience in *The Theory of Knowledge*. In his refutation of idealist epistemology, he argued that the "contents of apprehension are concrete and continuous," and that "qualities and relations" are part of that immediate experience. He was even less satisfied with standard empiricist accounts of knowledge. By inaccurately splitting apart a unified consciousness, British philosophers had contributed to the tendency to emphasize isolated physical stimuli, which was useful for physiologists but led philosophers toward the dead end of atomism. Efforts to deny the immediacy of social relations in individual experience, Hobhouse argued, involve a similar distortion. Our awareness of others is part of immediate experience; our reflections on life are reflections on social life. Hobhouse based his critique of utilitarianism on the impossibility of separating social values from calculations of pleasure and pain, which reflect not absolute human preferences but social mores. Hobhouse realized, as did Bourgeois and Croly, that if experience is social, then individual life cannot be considered apart from the meanings imparted to it by its cultural context. Thus the choices of the individual, although voluntary, are not expressions of the sort of pure individuality cherished by liberal theorists. Hobhouse accused idealists of collapsing the real into the ideal, and empiricists of collapsing the ideal into the real; both effectively, and improperly, identified the status quo with optimal social conditions.[70]

Weber shared the view that because experience is social, it is value-laden, and for that reason he agreed that social analysis must proceed through interpretation to uncover the meanings imbedded in social interaction. He tried to steer a path between opposite conceptions of sociology as a science patterned after physics and as an art relying primarily on the creative use of intuition. In his early methodological essays, Weber ruled out the possibility of modeling social analysis on the natural sciences for two complementary reasons. First, the object of investigation is the subjective meaning of experience for individuals, which can never be adequately explained according to causal laws. Second, the sociologist brings with him culturally influenced, subjective values and purposes, which prohibit him from reaching the sort of objectivity to which the physical sciences aspire.[71] The best sociology can hope to do, given these limits, is to *understand* individual action, and to *explain* social action by constructing ideal types. It cannot provide nomological laws of social causation.

Weber presented his mature formulation of these ideas in *Economy and Society*, the massive collection of manuscripts published posthumously in 1920. There he took an apparently more expansive view of the scientific potential of social analysis, but he remained more skeptical than some later empirical sociologists have cared to admit. In *Economy and Society*, he staked out a position midway between the positivist and intuitionist stances he rejected earlier in *Roscher and Knies*. As the definitions in his opening pages make clear, he wanted to stress the centrality of meaning in understanding social action. Because this issue has proved so controversial, and because Weber's methodology is often misrepresented, a rather lengthy quotation from these definitions is necessary:

> Sociology ... is a science concerning itself with the interpretative understanding of social action and thereby with causal explanation of its course and consequences. We shall speak of "action" insofar as the acting individual attaches a subjective meaning to his behavior—be it overt or covert, omission or acquiescence. Action is "social" insofar as its subjective meaning takes account of the behavior of others and is thereby oriented in its course. ...
> "Meaning" may be of two kinds. The term may refer first to the actual existing meaning in the given concrete case of a particular actor, or to the average or approximate meaning attributable to a given plurality of actors; or secondly to the theoretically conceived *pure type* of subjective meaning attributed to the hypothetical actor or actors in a given type of action. In no case does it refer to an objectively "correct" meaning or one which is "true" in some metaphysical sense.

Weber's awareness of the importance of subjective meaning suggests his debt to the tradition of German cultural history in general and to Dilthey in particular. Weber's use of *Verstehen* also indicates the extent of that debt. His shift in focus from history to sociology in his later years did not blind Weber to the limits imposed on social analysis by the meaningful quality of human experience. In *Economy and Society*, he acknowledged that no matter how clear an interpretation of individual action may be, "it cannot on this account claim to be the causally valid interpretation. On this level, it must remain only a peculiarly plausible hypothesis." For several reasons, including the tendency of people to disguise or misunderstand their own motives, and the impenetrability of the calculations according to which people freely select among conflicting impulses, it is simply not possible to be certain of any interpretation.[72]

Weber's most straightforward statement of the hermeneutical quality of sociological investigation appeared in his essay "The Meaning of 'Ethical Neutrality,'" where he pointed out, "Every science of psychological and social phenomena is a science of human conduct (which includes all thought and attitudes). These sciences seek to 'understand' this conduct and by means of this understanding to 'explain' it 'interpretively.'"[73] Although this argument appears to echo Dilthey's on the *Geisteswissenschaften*, it is difficult to determine the extent of Weber's reliance on Dilthey or even to assess the similarity between their ideas. Dilthey explicitly stated his agreement with Weber's early methodological writings, but Weber's elliptical references to Dilthey are more tantalizing than illuminating. Dilthey, he claimed, considered the elevation from specific to general the definitive problem of the cultural sciences, and Weber deemed that argument an exaggeration. That comment, however, like most of those concerning Dilthey in *Roscher and Knies* (where all of Weber's published references to Dilthey appear) suggests that he indicted Dilthey for crimes he did not commit. For example, Dilthey's distinction between the *Geistes-* and the *Naturwissenschaften* was only heuristic, as I have pointed out. Although Weber faulted Dilthey on this issue, he made precisely the same point in his own writings. Weber seems to have classified Dilthey as an "intuitionist," an interpretation consistent with the criticism of Dilthey in Rickert's *Die Grenzen der naturwissenschaftlichen Begriffsbildung* (1896; *Limits to the Concept Formation of Natural Science*). Dilthey accepted the legitimacy of that criticism for his early work, but he worked to overcome the problem of his later writings. Indeed, by the time Weber wrote *Roscher and Knies*, Dilthey himself had become an outspoken critic of the kind of psychologism that Weber, following Rickert, found unacceptable in such thinkers as Friedrich Gottl, who was the specific target of Weber's sharpest barbs. Weber did not differentiate Dilthey's hermeneutics from Gottl's with sufficient care, and later critics have sometimes been even less careful in their comparisons. The controversy swirling around Weber's methodology and its relation to hermeneutics indicates the extent to which he, like Dilthey, has become a symbol to both sides of a debate he hoped to end.[74]

Closely connected with the status of *Verstehen* in Weber's writings is the question of value neutrality. His ideas on this question underwent a similar process of evolution, which has fueled a similar scholarly debate. If one holds that life is meaningful, then it follows that values are integral to all experience. Thus norms cannot be factored out of experience, and a purely objective, value-free social science is excluded from the start. Yet Weber, who acknowledged that experience is value-laden, is revered by empirical sociologists as the champion of value-free sociology. This confusion seems to arise from the failure to distinguish two separate issues in Weber's thought. First, as I have pointed out, Weber denied in "'Objectivity' in Social Science" the possibility of achieving objectivity: the subjective experience of both analyst and analysand is imbued with meanings. A second issue, which came into focus a decade later in "The Meaning of 'Ethical Neutrality,'" has to do not with the metatheoretical question of understanding but with the practical question of the sociologist's role as a teacher. Weber insisted that scholars bear a responsibility not to proselytize; they must not abuse the respect accorded them as teachers by advocating their own values disguised as science. In the course of his attack against those who used their podiums as rostrums, he subtly shifted the ground of his earlier analysis. "A careful examination of historical works," he contended, "quickly shows that when the historian begins to 'evaluate,' causal analysis almost always ceases—to the prejudice of the scientific results." The scientist risks trying to account for a mistake or a decline when he is in fact merely dealing with "ideas different from his own, and so he fails in his most important task, that is, the task of 'understanding.'"[75] Although he continued to identify understanding as the sociologist's goal, Weber at least implied in that formulation that it is possible to avoid the intrusion of values in social science.

There is some evidence that after 1913, Weber departed from the position he took in his earlier methodological studies and tried to distinguish between value relationships, which he claimed can be examined objectively, and value judgments, which necessarily express the values of the sociologist. Yet if that was his aim, he failed to achieve it. Important arguments from his partisan writings, in which he freely and passionately expressed personal value judgments, appear in his ostensibly scientific political sociology.[76] The most adequate resolution of this problem, which has been offered by a number of Weber's interpreters, is the suggestion that Weber wanted not to eliminate value judgments, which is impossible according to his own premises, but only to clarify them. His emphasis on science, according to this view, was motivated by a desire to lay bare covert identifications of fact and value and to demonstrate the significance of various norms in social action and social analysis. Sociologists should contribute to the solution of social problems by making clear the values underlying different policy options rather than draping their own value judgments with the gaudy cloak of science. If this interpretation is accurate, it indicates the close similarity between Weber's ideas and those of the philosophers of the *via media* and the theorists of social democracy—particularly Bernstein, who considered Weber the only prominent theorist who understood his own ideas about the relation between science and values. If, on the other hand, Weber in his last writings did aim toward value neutrality as a goal to be realized instead of a limit to be approached, he was guilty of what has been called "self misunderstanding," a failure to follow his own methodological principles.[77]

The other theorists of progressivism, while they pursued this question less rigorously than Weber did, reached conclusions similar to his. Hobhouse pointed out that "value is also a fact, an element in reality." While a distinction could be drawn between facts and values for analytical purposes, a complete sociology should properly "embrace a social philosophy and a social science." The sociologist should aim at a synthesis of the two kinds of inquiry. Although Hobhouse, like Weber, was concerned that "grave confusions arise when issues of fact are coloured by judgment of value," he added that "when the facts are completely and accurately stated, it is reasonable to essay their valuation, and this is the proper task of social philosophy."[78] Croly advanced a similar argument. "The knowledge of individual and social life which we crave has an essentially moral character," and this knowledge cannot be attained simply by "describing, analyzing and comparing existing or past individuals and societies with one another." Such bare facts embody cultural values, and in order to understand these values we must grasp the "morally and socially creative purposes" that lie behind them. "Individuals and societies are not natural facts" but rather the products of cultural creation.[79]

These ideas about experience and understanding were consistent with a certain conception of history. Progressive theorists understood history as a reflexive process in which human choices both shape and are shaped by society. When culture and personality are recognized as products of the interaction of history and voluntary action, all meanings and values appear to be relative. Yet like the philosophers of the *via media*, these theorists discerned in history a basis for judgment. Whereas Weber could see in history no transcendental purpose, the other progressives shared the spirit of Fouillée's dictum, which Bourgeois quoted in *Solidarity*: "What one respects in man is less what he is than what he can be." Their understanding that history reflects human purposes gave them confidence that society could be revitalized through collective action. For that reason they felt little of the desperation with which many intellectuals, including Weber, greeted the modern era. They believed that Darwin preached a gospel of hope and that his science disproved Marx's history. Evolution, they reasoned, follows a pattern of progressive development. When they joined Darwinian ideas to their theory of voluntary action and their pragmatic theory of truth—ideas that may seem inconsistent without the framework of teleology surrounding their concepts of knowledge and action—they concluded that history can be made to advance in the direction of harmony. "This doesn't mean the constructing of utopias," Lippmann cautioned, echoing Hobhouse's caveat. "The kind of vision which will be fruitful to democratic life is one that is made out of latent promise in the actual world."[80] These thinkers contended that history provides the only sourcebook for social action. They understood that cultures can resist as well as support progressive schemes, but in time, they believed, the latent promise of progress could be redeemed.

These theorists' faith in progress can be—and often has been— exaggerated. They were confident that society could be steered toward greater harmony, and with the exception of Weber they believed that the larger historical pattern tended in that direction. But they explicitly denied that such progress is inevitable. Marxism, as they understood it, involved determinism, and it was thus inconsistent with the concept of voluntary action they embraced. "For while it is illuminating to see how environment moulds men," Lippmann wrote, "it is absolutely essential that men regard themselves as moulders of their environment" as well. True to his prag- matism, he admitted that while this perspective "may not be 'truer' than the old materialism" of orthodox Marxists, it is "more useful. Having learned for a long time what is done to us, we are now faced with the task of doing." Referring to the renegades who forged the theory of social democracy, he noted that "all over the world socialists are breaking away from the stultifying influence of outworn determinism." The philosophy replacing that determinism, Lippmann concluded, is "one of deliberate choices." History may be progressive, but it remains a project. It does not propel itself; it is driven forward by man. In Dewey's words, "Progress is not automatic; it depends upon human intent and aim and upon acceptance of responsibility for its production."[81]

The study of history was central to Hobhouse's sociology. He was equally critical of theories of inevitability whether offered by idealists, evolutionary naturalists, or dialectical materialists. Marx's "false interpretation of history," Hobhouse wrote, mistakenly emphasized the blind dynamics of economic development rather than the conscious efforts of individuals and groups. "The progress of society, like that of the individual," he countered, "depends ultimately on choice." This progress "is not 'natural' in the sense in which a physical law is natural, that is, in the sense of going forward automatically from stage to stage." He then added a qualification revealing his debt to Green and his affinity with Dewey. "It is natural only in this sense, that it is the expression of deep-seated forces of human nature which come to their own only by an infinitely slow and cumbersome process of mutual adjustment." Hobhouse believed that man has a purpose which is realized in gradual progress toward cooperation. In Hobhouse's view of history, Green's concern for organic wholes took on a pragmatic cast in the validation of different cultural hypotheses in collective experience. His conclusions about progress toward cooperative social action derived from that reading of history, a reading almost identical to Dewey's. There has been, and there will continue to be, the widest diversity of forms through which this cooperative urge is expressed. Conceived as a large-scale pragmatic test of truth, however, the entire human enterprise is progressive. Hobhouse wedded the idea of freedom to purpose. In *Liberalism* he made that union explicit: "True harmony is an ideal which is perhaps beyond the power of man to realize, but which serves to indicate the line of advance." As the study of history and anthropology demonstrates, freedom leads in many directions. The "course that will in the end make for social harmony" is only one option among many. Nevertheless, Hobhouse concluded, it can serve as a benchmark for judging the "line of advance."[82]

This conception of progress did not descend from heaven in the shape of the *Weltgeist*, it emerged from the radical theory of knowledge. Even in his later writings, in which a metaphysical fog obscured many of his earlier ideas, Hobhouse returned to the source of his historical sensibility in his epistemology. According to Hobhouse, knowledge is a quest for ever-better congruence among all the pieces of experience, with the goal being a harmonious set of ideas. "We are led, then, to view human thought as an organic structure maintaining itself by the mutual support of its parts, growing, and modifying itself as it grows, through the constant assimilation of fresh experience."

When we reason, in other words, we engage in "the continuous and comprehensive effort toward harmony in experience." Viewing all of history in light of this conception of rationality, Hobhouse concluded that experience is always "either in harmony with feeling, that is, supported by the feeling which it excites, or at odds with it, and this relation directly determines our immediate impulse."[83] As Green talked about a unifying consciousness at the core of experience, and as James talked about the "directly felt fitnesses between things," so Hobhouse derived from his view of the most minute elements of experience a vision of history as the gradual integration of knowledge and the incremental achievement of cooperation, not as part of an inevitable process, but as part of an ongoing project.

Weber's multidimensional methodology of social inquiry likewise led him to reject exclusively idealist and exclusively materialist theories of history. His reputation as the Marx of the bourgeoisie has, however, distorted his intention to supplement rather than supplant Marx's interpretation of the role played by economic factors in history. Just as Marx did not subscribe to the deterministic model of change proclaimed in his name by those who forgot his reminders about praxis, so Weber did not deny the importance of objective conditions. Although he stated categorically that "the so-called 'materialistic conception of history' as a *Weltanschauung*, or as a formula for the causal explanation of historical reality, is to be rejected most emphatically," he also considered "the economic *interpretation* of history" indispensable. He even worried that its heuristic value might be underestimated when reaction set in against the "boundless over-estimation" of materialism characteristic of late nineteenth-century thought.[84] *The Protestant Ethic and the Spirit of Capitalism* is only the best known of Weber's efforts to demonstrate the subtle interplay between economic and cultural factors in historical development. He envisioned all of his historical studies as correctives to one-dimensional accounts. In his essay of 1892 on the condition of East Prussian farm workers, he emphasized the connection between the desire to improve their material conditions and the "powerful and purely psychological magic of 'freedom,'" a less easily measured but equally decisive factor in the phenomenon of migration.[85] Two decades later, in "The Social Psychology of the World Religions," one of his most general, reflective essays, he provided a striking formulation of his view of history:

> Not ideas, but material and ideal interest, directly govern men's conduct. Yet very frequently the "world images" that have been created by "ideas" have, like switchmen, determined the tracks along which action has been pushed by the dynamic of interest. "From what" and "for what" one wished to be redeemed and, let us not forget, "could be" redeemed, depended upon one's image of the world.[86]

As a student of comparative history, Weber understood that a wide variety of world images have served as history's switchmen. His typology of social action in the early sections of *Economy and Society* reflected that awareness of diversity. He posited four forms of rational action: (1)

Instrumentally rational action "is determined by expectations as to the behavior of objects in the environment and of other human beings; these expectations are used as 'conditions' or 'means' for the attainment of the actor's own rationally pursued and calculated ends." (2) Value-rational action is governed by belief in "the value for its own sake" of some behavior, generally ethical or religious, without concern for the means or the prospects of achieving the end. (3) Affectual action is determined by emotional states, and (4) traditional action by "ingrained habituation." Different kinds of behavior, and different kinds of social interaction, follow from the adoption of these different kinds of rationality.

Weber considered the first type, instrumental rationality, typical of modern Western society. Interpreters disagree about whether he also considered it normative, but since he defined voluntary action as rational action according to the calculation of means and ends, it is arguable that he judged only such instrumentally rational action really free. If he did treat instrumental rational action as superior to the other forms, however, it is apparent from his definition that such activity must involve the selection not only of means, as some of Weber's critics argue, but also of rationally calculated ends. There are strong similarities between this concept of instrumental rationality, conceived in terms of the rational calculation of ends as well as means, and both James's pragmatism and Dewey's instrumentalism; it is therefore not surprising that all three should be criticized for neglecting ends and concentrating on means. But that interpretation makes as little sense in Weber's case as in James's or Dewey's. Weber emphasized that these forms of rationality almost always overlap in social action, even though he conceded that it is possible for actors to concern themselves entirely with means and to treat ends simply "as given subjective wants and arrange them in a scale of consciously assessed relative urgency," as is the case, to use his example, in "the principle of 'marginal utility.'" But he was aware of the difficulties involved in such purely technical calculations. To treat that acknowledgment as indicative of a reductive disinclination to consider value orientations integral to instrumental rationality therefore seems to me a misinterpretation of Weber that neglects the opposite conclusion drawn in his substantive work. From his earliest investigations until his death, Weber concentrated on the interplay between people's interests and their images of the world, and that interplay is an essential part of his concept of instrumental rationality.[87]

The integral relation of technique to value in instrumental reasoning must be understood in order to appreciate the pathos of rationalization, the concept that has long been recognized as the centerpiece of Weber's interpretation of modern history. The secular world is ruled by scientific conceptions of natural causality in which the questions of meaning that remain essential to human experience play no part. Religious cosmologies provide answers that cannot meet the requirements of modern science; the game is simply played by different rules, the rules of purely formal, or technical, rationality. Recent commentators have emphasized the close connection between Weber's studies of Calvinism and his studies of non-Western religions, thus clarifying the peculiar solution to the problem of theodicy that contributed to the elective affinity Weber discerned between Calvinist and capitalist rationality. Whereas world-fleeing religions such as Hinduism and Buddhism focus the attention of believers on magic and resignation, Calvinism—far more than Judaism, early Christianity, or Lutheranism—motivates believers to devalue institutional avenues to salvation, to master the valueless world as an instrument for divine purposes, and thereby to demonstrate their membership among the elect. Thus, through an elaborate working out of its own immanent logic, a religion with roots in the idea that all men are brothers proved uniquely suited to the creation of an economic system that takes Cain and Abel as the model of brotherhood.

In the course of modernization during the centuries since the Reformation, however, the instrumental rationality that Calvin's followers employed in their efforts to master the world gradually inverted the means and the end of individual behavior. The Protestant ideal of a calling no longer provided the justification for capitalist rationality. Instrumental rationality now reigned without the religious cosmology that determined the ends to be pursued. The quest for material goods, which the Puritans envisioned as a light cloak that the saint could throw aside at any time, became instead an iron cage. Thus instrumental reason, which Weber identified with voluntary action, ironically contributed to the enslavement of the individual in modern society. If the ultimate value of Christianity no longer claimed the loyalty of a disenchanted age, it was even more difficult to challenge the means-end inversion encouraged by modern capitalism. Weber's concept of individuality, which plays such an important (if ambiguous) part in his political thought, must be understood in this context. Given the vacuity of capitalism's ultimate value—the creation of material goods and the satisfaction of the individual's desire for pleasure—the individual cannot find fulfillment by directing his actions toward the end enshrined by the world of his work. Individuality, as Weber understood it, requires for its satisfaction something more than allegiance to the empty norm of bureaucratic efficiency. Rationality, finally, cannot be merely the calculation of means, it must also involve their relation to consciously chosen ends. Carving out a space in which the individual can exercise his freedom represented to Weber the central challenge of philosophy and politics in a secular world; I will examine the strategy he recommended when I return to his ideas about responsibility and reform.[88]

Like James and Dilthey, Weber argued that the historical drama has no meaning beyond that brought to it by its actors and interpreters. He described culture as "a finite segment of the meaningless infinity of the world process, a segment on which human beings confer meaning and significance."[89] Thus Weber brought all values, including Kant's and Marx's different notions of critique, before the bar of historical analysis. Also like James and Dilthey, he admitted the historicity of his own ideas. He maintained that we create our own meanings and values, and he likewise found in that recognition a kind of freedom. It will be recalled that Dilthey considered the historical sensibility a source of immanent critique, a foundation for transcendental historicism. Weber staked out an even more radical position. It is man's fate not to know the meaning of the world, even though our investigations may give us an ever clearer image of its development. That is why "*Weltanschauungen* can never be the product of progressive experience and why the highest and most stirring ideals can become effective for all times only in a struggle with other ideas that are just as sacred to others as our ideas are to us."[90] Whereas James and Dilthey contended that freedom represents the obverse of relativism, and the historical sensibility provides a basis for the critical exercise of a radically liberated individuality, Weber perceived in modernization a challenge to freedom. As the process of rationalization advanced, it sucked from instrumental rationality the meaningful, rationally chosen values that made it the embodiment of voluntary action. The remaining shell, Weber feared, while it might resemble instrumental rationality on the outside, was empty of any human purpose. James and Dilthey believed that the historical sensibility might awaken the individual to a new sense of responsibility by confronting him with the fact of his freedom, and they hoped the shock of that realization might shake loose new sources of creativity. By illuminating the process whereby men create meanings, Weber admitted, history could liberate them to choose their own values, but he was skeptical about the exercise of such a radical freedom. It imposed a burden of responsibility only a few individuals could carry.

Because the world is disenchanted, Weber argued, the individual has no basis for accepting as absolute any transcendent values, including the values of science, progress, or even the apparently modest and empirically based concept of history as a source of immanent critique. All of his values must be his own. "Men have to substitute purpose for tradition," Lippmann wrote in *Drift and Mastery*, "and that is, I believe, the profoundest change that has ever taken place in human history. ... In endless ways we put intention where custom has reigned. We break up routines, make decisions, choose our ends, select means." The uncanny resemblance between that passage and the distinction Weber drew between instrumentally rational and traditional action does not make Lippmann a Weberian; it merely testifies to the understanding progressive theorists shared regarding the profound consequences of their intellectual independence. Such freedom requires individuals to make their own choices; Lippmann, like Dewey, Hobhouse, Croly, and Bourgeois, was confident that such choices could be made rationally to advance the cause of social cooperation. Indeed, according to Lippmann, such deliberate instrumental calculations are "what mastery means: the substitution of conscious intention for unconscious striving."[91] Neither he nor the other progressives believed, as Weber did, that rationality itself, if institutionalized on a sufficiently large scale in bureaucratic hierarchies, could impede progress toward that goal. The individual attempting to exercise his freedom, Weber contended, finds himself in an age in which even charisma has been routinized, and his attempts to act freely through purposively rational action are futile because the purposes he serves have no human significance. Modern capitalism thus denies the individual the opportunity to achieve satisfaction by burying the promise of apocalypse beneath the relentless progress of rationalization. Weber's interpretation of the bleak prospects for freedom explains his cultural pessimism. He shared James's and Dilthey's belief that the historical sensibility liberates the individual from all conceptions of transcendence and imposes on him responsibility for his own values and actions. But unlike those progressives who had a teleological conception of human purpose and historical progress, he could not draw from his historical studies any confidence about the exercise of freedom in a disenchanted world.

3. The Problem of Ethics in a Disenchanted World

When Max Weber agreed to deliver a public lecture in Munich on January 28, 1919, on the topic of politics as a vocation, he knew he would be stepping into the eye of a hurricane. Conditions were chaotic in the newly proclaimed Bavarian Republic, organized three months earlier by revolutionary socialist Kurt Eisner in defiance of Germany's refusal to end the war. Weber had already lectured on science as a vocation, and he tried to persuade his friend Friedrich Naumann to discuss the possibility of finding in politics a genuine vocation (*geistiger Beruf*), as the organizers of the lecture series put it, which neither hid from the world nor bowed to it. But when Naumann declined and the organizers of the series considered inviting Eisner in his place, Weber volunteered. Weber had nothing but contempt for Eisner, whom he used in *Economy and Society* to illustrate the archetypal charismatic demagogue, and whose power emerged, in Weber's words, from a "bloody carnival that does not deserve the honorable name of a revolution." Because Weber could not abide the thought that Eisner's vision of political activity as personal catharsis might gain even greater notoriety—and perhaps even a degree of scholarly legitimacy—through a formal public lecture, he agreed to speak on the subject himself.

His listeners did not know what to expect. Some of them looked to him for the leadership Germany would need in order to survive after the abdication of the Kaiser and the declaration of the armistice. The nation seemed in danger of choking on its own rage and bitterness. A student who had heard Weber speak in November on Germany's new political order expressed the attitude of at least some Germans when he wrote: "On you, Herr Professor, the political hopes of the best people are pinned, as far as I can tell. And, to put it plainly, my greatest desire would have been to see you in the post of the Reich Chancellor.... We badly need you as a leader." On the other hand, the crowd gathering to hear his address also contained critics. Members of Munich's bohemian underground, militant communists, and supporters of Eisner had jeered Weber's earlier speech, and they expected to hear the same old bourgeois temporizing about moderate democratization, the importance of a republic, and the need for national strength and unity. Weber's lecture, scheduled to be delivered three weeks after the Spartacist uprising that rocked Berlin, and two weeks after the government counteroffensive that left Rosa Luxemburg and Karl Liebknecht dead and the German left in shambles, came at a decisive moment.[92] In the cross fire between revolution and reaction, what wisdom could Weber offer about politics as a vocation?

He began on an inauspicious note. "This lecture, which I give at your request, will necessarily disappoint you in a number of ways." For he intended not to talk about the daily news, but instead to reflect on the more universal quality of political life. After surveying the different forms of political authority, he distinguished officials who live *off* politics from politicians who live *for* politics. Despite the indispensable role officials play, they do not, indeed cannot, have a vocation for politics. Their primary duty is obedience to the commands of others, namely, those leaders who can, although they rarely do, pursue politics as a vocation. Weber was himself a charismatic figure. His public speeches had an explosive power generated as much by his own brooding presence as by his considerable talent as a writer. In his books, Weber made no effort to refine his prose, which uncompromisingly reproduces the complexity of the ideas he wanted to express. He scorned scholars who affected artfulness in their academic work. Confusing *Wissenschaft* with *Literatur*, they ended up producing neither. In his public addresses, though, he skillfully distilled his political sociology into a blend of anecdote, abstraction, and exhortation. In "Politics as a Vocation," he built slowly toward a final question that was as arresting as it was unanticipated: "What is the true relation between *ethics* and politics?"

He contrasted two familiar approaches to the problem. The "ethic of conviction" (*Gesinnungsethik*) is the unconditional requirement of single-minded selflessness, typical of all religious ethics and stated in familiar form in the Sermon on the Mount. The "ethic of responsibility," by contrast, requires that means and ends be weighed together. These two alternatives may be equated, roughly but not inaccurately, with the deontological ethics of Kant and the utilitarian ethics of Bentham, the former concerned with the purity of the will and the latter with the consequences of the act. From an ethical perspective, political activity is always problematical because "the decisive means for politics is violence" (*Gewaltsamkeit*). Neither Buddha nor Jesus nor Francis of Assisi chose a life of politics, although the effectiveness of their apolitical lives was and is obvious, precisely because they eschewed the violence essential to political activity. "The genius or demon of politics lives with the God of love," according to Weber, "in an inner tension, which can at any time erupt into irreconcilable conflict." The ethic of conviction forbids compromises, but as a result of complying with its stringent requirements, one's goals may be "damaged and discredited for generations, because the responsibility for *consequences* is lacking." In short, there is a fundamental contradiction between the ethic of conviction and the ethic of responsibility, and anyone considering politics as a vocation confronts that dilemma. There can be no escape, Weber concluded, and for that reason the most important requirement for the ethical pursuit of a political career is a special kind of "trained ruthlessness in viewing the realities of life, and the ability to face such realities and to measure up to them inwardly." That was not the advice of a cynical *Machtpolitiker*, as it may at first appear. It was instead an eloquent and unflinching acknowledgment of the very real conflicts between ethics and politics.[93]

In their writings about the meaning of responsibility, all the theorists of progressivism faced the challenge of ruthless realism that Weber posed. None of them, however, presented it more starkly, or in more dramatic circumstances, than did Weber, who simultaneously renounced the self-righteousness of all partisan politics and sounded the familiar note of resolution in the face of doubt. These progressives all realized the inadequacy of deontological and utilitarian principles conceived in isolation from each other. Like the philosophers of the *via media*, they tried to examine the problems of ethics through a set of bifocal lenses that enabled them to see the intentions of actors and the consequences of their acts, and to realize the incommensurability of competing moral principles. They also shared their predecessors' conviction that no rational foundation exists for establishing an adequate system of ethics. They insisted that morality, like all cultural values, reflects experience and changes over time. As Lippmann wrote, "No moral judgment can decide the value of life. No ethical theory can announce any intrinsic good."[94] Citing Fouillée's *Ethics of idées-forces*, Bourgeois argued that we must look to experience if we wish to understand morality. Ethical norms are a product of the "general conditions of social life," and we can uncover their basis "only by studying the human person, considered not in metaphysical isolation, but in the reality of his relations with his social milieu."[95]

Their awareness of the historicity of ethics, like their understanding of cultural development, attuned these thinkers to the anguish that accompanies responsibility in a world without absolutes. Weber declared that "an epoch which has eaten of the tree of knowledge . . . must know that we cannot learn the *meaning* of the world from the results of its analysis, be it ever so perfect; it must rather be in a position to create this meaning itself."[96] In Lippmann's words, "Each man in his inward life is a last judgment on all his values. . . . No creed possesses any final sanction."[97] Ethics, as these theorists understood it, cannot be a science, it can only assist individuals in clarifying their thinking about values and help them to recognize the consequences of their choices. Individuals and societies, Croly contended, are "moral creations." Both are "essentially verbal nouns, and mean something which is going on and must continue to go on." They carry with them "the risk of failure as well as the chance of success," and it is up to individuals to choose their own values and to make their societies work.[98] Writing about Dewey's philosophy, Lippmann argued that philosophies are constructed in order to serve the purposes we choose rather than in accordance with truths we discover in being. We cannot know whether our ideas about morality are true until they are tested. So, Lippmann concluded in his typically offhand manner, "No pious mumbo-jumbo need surround any system of ideas." Traditional forms of argument, as Dewey and James emphasized, must be reversed. Ethics, instead of prescribing a course of action, must take shape through a social process of truth testing.[99]

The contrast that the philosophers of the *via media* drew between prudence and justice, and between the results of an act and the intention behind it, also surfaced elsewhere in Weber's writings. He emphasized repeatedly that we are pulled in opposite directions whenever we try to act morally. In "The Meaning of 'Ethical Neutrality,'" he pointed out that two incommensurable values conflict in ethical judgment. Should we esteem more highly "the intrinsic value of ethical conduct—the 'pure will' or the 'conscience' as it used to be called," or should we instead take into account "the responsibility for the predictable consequences" of an action? This is a question "not only of alternatives between values but of an irreconcilable death-struggle, like that between 'God' and the 'Devil.' Between these, neither relativization nor compromise is possible." In our daily activity, of course, we necessarily blend these considerations, and "the value-spheres cross and interpenetrate," but the tension between them remains.[100] This problem troubled Weber throughout his career—not merely because it was a projection of the conflict between his parents—and he was not at all sure it could be resolved.

Although the other progressives offered similar conceptualizations of the problem, they believed a solution could be found in progressive moral development. Through a certain kind of benevolent action, the individual can satisfy both the demands of a pure will and the concern with consequences by contributing simultaneously to his self-development and to the good of the community. Bourgeois, Lippmann, Croly, and especially Hobhouse argued that prudence can be reconciled with justice, because they envisioned ethics as the identification of personal good with social good. What appears to be a contradiction, Bourgeois contended in *Solidarity*, "is in reality only a superior harmony." "Apparent opposition" contributes to social growth, and through that process "the moral idea receives its formula and the theory of laws and duties its expression," not in any abstract or subjective sense, but as a concrete and objective set of principles conforming to natural constraints. The conflict between ethical principles, which logically presents a dilemma, can be resolved in life through personal growth toward an ideal of benevolent action. "First and foremost, there is an extension of the idea of responsibility," Bourgeois declared in a passage that echoes Fouillée almost perfectly. In place of the "completely individualistic conception of responsibility" we must "substitute a more complex idea." Our responsibility extends to others, and their responsibility extends to us as well. This idea of reciprocal duties, rooted in the fact of natural solidarity, is nourished by the growth of interdependence.[101]

Hobhouse followed the argument of Green's *Prolegomena to Ethics* as closely as Bourgeois followed Fouillée's *Ethics of idées-forces*. Hobhouse dismissed completely the ethical egoism assumed by utilitarians. He argued that the pursuit of individual interest ended not in harmony but in chaos. Only by attaching individual self-development of others can personal growth take on an ethical significance. He rejected out of hand Sidgwick's contention that such an ideal of benevolence might involve the compromise of a legitimate concern for prudence. "It is not any and every self-development that is good," he wrote in *Democracy and Reaction*. "Development 'as a moral being' will mean a development which harmonises with social life, and so fits in with and contributes to the development of others." This passage, typical of Hobhouse's ethical thinking, illustrates his debt to Green. Not only did Hobhouse assume the possibility of genuinely benevolent ethical action, the difficulty of which Sidgwick had emphasized in *The Methods of Ethics*, he believed that only such action could be characterized as moral. Particularly in his later writings, Hobhouse advanced an ethical philosophy that was basically a restatement of Green garbed in evolutionary terminology. The notion of progress was again central to Hobhouse's vision. Only one yardstick could be used to measure social development, the purely formal standard of progress toward benevolence. Different cultures might manifest this progress in different sorts of behavior. History reveals a general pattern of development, however, toward the eventual reconciliation of individual interest and the common good through the emergence of a broadened and deepened conception of individuality. Quite unlike the older liberal egoism, Hobhouse's more classical view focused on developing the ethical personality rather than satisfying the personal desire for pleasure. Rooted in a different psychology from that of Hobbes, his ethics grew into a different politics. Mill's inability to reconcile his hedonism with his socialism has already been noted in Chapter Five; Hobhouse's moral philosophy sprang from Green's concept of individual and social development and flowered into a progressivism distinctly different from the laissez-faire of Bentham and James Mill.[102] Whereas John Stuart Mill was tortured by his inconsistencies, Hobhouse found satisfaction in the congruence between his moral philosophy and his politics. It was not the failure of his imagination, but rather the failure of the world to live up to its promise, that eventually shattered Hobhouse's confidence in progressivism in the 1920s.

This version of ethics was strikingly similar to Dewey's. Since I have already examined in some detail the connection between his radical theory of knowledge and his ethics of rational benevolence, I will not restate that argument here.[103] It should be emphasized, however, how closely the ideas of Bourgeois and Hobhouse resembled those of Dewey. First, all three agreed that ethical theory emerges in response to difficulties encountered in experience rather than logic; they conceived of ethics as problem solving. Second, they believed that ethics exhibits a progressive quality both in individual development and in history. Third, they maintained that all real goods must involve, in Dewey's words, "interest in the well-being of society." Notions that the individual can act ethically without taking into account the social implications of an act, or by calculating its benefit strictly according to self-interest, they dismissed as delusions. Finally, all of these thinkers begged a question of basic importance. For it is one thing to define individual satisfaction and ethical growth in terms of social service, but it is quite another to construct an ideal of social welfare that will prove generally acceptable, and it is yet another to integrate individual preferences with that ideal of the common good in the political and social spheres. This difficulty will come into sharper focus when I discuss their conception of education as the key to political change.

Weber was not sure whether the modern ethos of secular rationality represented an advance or a decline from the religiosity of earlier eras. He believed that individuals in a disenchanted age face a problem of unprecedented difficulty, since they must create for themselves the values that give meaning to life. Whereas magical and religious world views provide ready-made solutions to the problem of meaning—indeed, Weber thought their appearance could be explained in terms of that purpose—in the world of science and capitalism no such answers are available. As a result the individual is alone and responsible. Contemporaries who thought they could find in science a successor to religion misunderstood the shift from a transcendental to a naturalistic world view. No ultimate sanction exists for the selection of standards. The pretense that a world of objective meaning could be uncovered by science repelled Weber, who sought in his writing and his lectures to drive home the unsettling lesson of contingency. In one sense, disenchantment meant decline, because it robbed man of confidence. But in another sense, it meant progress, because it opened the door to unprecedented autonomy. Disenchantment allowed—or forced—individuals to shape their lives according to values that are freely chosen instead of universally imposed.

Given Weber's dramatic characterization of the conflict between the ethic of conviction and the ethic of responsibility as a "death struggle," it might be supposed that he considered any reconciliation of these competing values impossible. The recurring note of desperation in much of what he wrote suggests the plausibility of such an interpretation. Yet, at least near the end of his life, he seems to have considered a limited resolution possible in a certain kind of practice, even though the two ethics remained logically distinct. He denied that the antinomy between God and the devil could be transcended entirely, and for that reason he stood nearer to Sidgwick and James than to Hobhouse and Dewey. In the closing pages of *The Methods of Ethics*, it will be recalled, Sidgwick tried unsuccessfully to establish rationally the principle of benevolence, which would reconcile the competing demands of prudence and justice, and decided ultimately to accept it on faith. Weber likewise failed to find in reason or history any foundation for ultimate standards. His failure has prompted some critics to accuse him of leveling all values by demonstrating their incommensurability. That argument confuses Weber's ideal of value neutrality, which he advanced as an antidote to the veiled advocacy of values under the disguise of science, with the promotion of value relativism.[104] He acknowledged the inevitability of collisions between competing notions of the good, but he did not conclude that all values are therefore equally legitimate. He spurned efforts to avoid the choice among values as an evasion of responsibility. Attempts to invoke a transcendental source of values and teleological conceptions of ethics seemed to him equally futile. Ultimately, he believed, individuals must choose their values on the basis of accumulated social experience, without the consolation of certainty.

Dewey, Hobhouse, and Bourgeois attempted to blend Weber's two contrasting principles in an ethics of self-development, in which individual satisfaction is defined as action both motivated by concern for, and contributing to the advancement of, the social welfare. Weber denied the possibility of that resolution, because he believed that the ethic of single-minded conviction must remain absolute or it disintegrates. But he neither counseled despair nor ended in simple resignation to the demands of the world. Instead he adopted a position close to James's ethics of the strenuous mood. However attractive the ethic of conviction may be, it is no longer possible in the modern era, because the absolute confidence, the certainty, that must inform such an ethic is no longer available. Neither traditional religious faith nor scientific pretenders to its throne can any longer provide the content for a genuine ethic of conviction. Weber nevertheless believed passionately that a moral life requires more than instrumental adjustment to the world. The individual must be responsible for the consequences of his actions, for the religious flight from the world remains open to few in a secular age. Yet unless the individual acts in service to some ideal, he sinks into opportunism and forfeits the chance to give meaning to his life. "Some kind of faith must always exist," Weber insisted, or else "the curse of the creature's worthlessness overshadows even the externally strongest political successes." Politics "is made with the head, but it is certainly not made with the head alone." Life must be fired by a will to believe, a faith in the validity of one's goals—even though that faith can have no foundation beyond individual conviction—if it is to have meaning and ethical significance. James established his ethics of the strenuous mood on his experience of freedom, his pragmatic theory of truth, and an ideal of social responsibility derived from his interpretation of life as part of a cultural project. Weber likewise refused to take refuge in the transcendental, and like James, he expressed his belief that, although competing values can never be reconciled once and for all, they fuse in the lives of heroic individuals. "It is immensely moving," Weber wrote, when an individual

> feels with his entire soul the responsibility for the consequences of his actions and thus acts according to the ethic of responsibility. At some point he says, "I cannot do otherwise. Here I stand." That is something genuinely human and stirring. For each of us who is not spiritually dead, this situation must surely be a possibility. In that sense, the ethic of single-minded conviction and the ethic of responsibility are not absolute opposites but supplements, which together constitute a genuine man, a man who can have the "vocation for politics."[105]

Weber, like James and the other philosophers of the *via media*, was convinced that ethical action must have its source in individual choices. Both the theory of voluntary action and the belief that no transcendental system can justify particular choices of values point to the conclusion that a general normative ethics cannot be prescribed. James and Weber, because they did not consider individual choices part of a teleological process, viewed each life as a separate drama. Both recognized that experience is historically constituted and delimited, and they believed that the individual should determine his values by reflecting carefully on that fund of knowledge and then make his decisions freely. This was obviously a "virtuoso ethic," whose difficulty made its general adoption impossible. Weber doubted that the power of reason, without the buttress provided by religious faith, could sustain the commitment of any but exceptional individuals to such an ethics. We cannot escape the dilemma of choosing between competing values; we are forced to decide, as James put it, which ideal to butcher. No universally applicable solution can be found in religion, science, or politics for the problem of ethics in an era of disenchantment.[106]

In ethics, then, Weber's mood of heroic pessimism distinguished him from the other theorists of progressivism, all of whom hitched the idea of individual moral growth to a larger scheme of steady, although hardly inevitable, cultural progress. Yet he shared with them one characteristic that had serious—some would say crippling—consequences for the politics of progressivism. As I argued in the conclusion to Chapter Four, the older generation of radical philosophers prided themselves on refusing to offer substantive guidelines for ethical action. They provided methods for making ethical decisions, but they denied the possibility of prescribing moral principles. Their ethics was a mode of inquiry, as Dewey made particularly clear, rather than a set of rules. Hobhouse and Bourgeois defined ethics as personal development through social service, but they declined to specify the content of that service. They could discuss ethics only in formal terms, because it must take its substance from individual choices in response to specific problems. Beneath their ethics was a faith that society is moving toward greater harmony, and their willingness to rely on the accumulated choices of individuals to advance that ideal testifies to their confidence. Weber insisted that an ethic of responsibility must be fortified by deeply felt and freely chosen personal convictions, but he too rejected any casuistic prescriptions. While his reading of rationalization as the trajectory of modern history prevented any optimistic conclusions about the prospects for the hero ethics he advanced, he shared the other progressives' belief that ethical decisions must finally rest with individuals. Values change and collide, and while Weber himself seems to have cherished an ideal resembling James's ethics of the strenuous mood, he refused to elevate that standard to the level of a universal norm.

The problematical nature of their ethical vision became apparent when these theorists directed it to politics. Their ethics, formal rather than substantive, methodological rather than prescriptive, is the crucial link connecting

their ideas about knowledge with their ideas about politics, and its significance may be underestimated or misunderstood. Unlike many of their contemporaries, these thinkers did not concern themselves with questions of
morality simply because they sought to substitute new prescriptions for those
previously supplied by religious creeds they no longer considered binding.
Rather than merely positing a substitute faith—as many of their generation
did with science, art, nationalism, physical or psychic health—they tried to do
without any sanctions whatsoever. Yet neither did they surrender to nihilism,
even though they denied the existence of any universal values.[107]

Instead they walked the fine line between metaphysical hope and cultural
despair, trying to connect their radical theory of knowledge to a politics of
substantial but gradual reform by recovering the classical idea of virtue. They
denied the attempt of earlier liberals and some early Freudians to equate
happiness with the satisfaction of impulses. Freedom, as they understood it,
was "the condition of mental and moral expansion," to use Hobhouse's
phrase, not the occasion for self-gratification.[108] They conceived of the individual as a moral being developing within a socially and historically shaped
context, a being whose fulfillment does not depend, as Hobbes and Bentham
thought, on narrowly focused personal pleasure, but rather on the sense of
satisfaction that flows from active participation in a community.

This notion of virtue, obscured in the theory of liberalism and nearly
obliterated by its practice, dominated these progressives' field of vision. Like
the philosophers of the *via media* and the theorists of social democracy, they
embraced an ideal of social cooperation. They believed that the ethos of
possessive individualism caused organized capitalism to clank noisily toward
chaos. Only a sense of social responsibility could cause personal preferences
to synchronize with the common good. These thinkers' emphasis on virtue
led them to focus on education as the most important lever of political
change. If social action is rooted in personal choices, they reasoned, social
reorganization requires reforming individual sensibilities as much as it
requires redesigning political or economic machinery. In the context of their
ideas about knowledge and responsibility, education became a talisman with
the power to transform prudence into a passion for social justice. In Chapter
Nine, I will indicate how these progressives' philosophical ideas shaped their
politics.

9

Progressive Politics

1. Political Action and Cultural Change

Cultural problems require cultural solutions. All of the ideas about experience, understanding, and virtue advanced by Bourgeois, Hobhouse, Weber, Dewey, Croly, and Lippmann ruled out the possibility of separating politics or economics from their sociohistorical context. Consistent with their philosophical premises, these progressives insisted that substantive political change in a democracy is impossible without a profound cultural change; neither can proceed without the other. The form of social organization they had in mind would require individuals to accept a wider definition of social responsibility than earlier liberals had considered possible or desirable. In the absence of a public sensibility oriented toward the community and away from possessive individualism, significant change could be achieved only if it were imposed from above. Given these social liberals' commitment to autonomy and voluntarism, that cure appeared worse than the disease. Political progress, as they understood it, cannot result from simple institutional modifications. Instead reformers must convert their communities to a new way of thinking.[1]

These thinkers all stressed the qualitative dimension of politics. If individualistic values prevail, efforts to promote the common good will inevitably fail. As part of their ethical emphasis, all of these progressives except Weber embraced a version of the doctrine of the *Rechtsstaat*, the state conceived as the embodiment of moral as well as legal right. But they gave to that idea a critical thrust lacking in German liberal thought. They believed that although the state *ought* to embody ethical principles, existing states protecting the system of privileges fostered by organized capitalism stood in the way of such an ethical politics. Possibly because he saw at first hand the kind of power that could be justified by appealing to the idea of the *Rechtsstaat*, Weber, like Dilthey, warned that the risks involved in equating politics with morality might outweigh the potential benefits. For that reason, even though he advocated many of the same policies that the other progressives favored, and he desired a society not too different from their ideal, Weber's politics differed in tone and substance from the progressivism of Dewey, Croly, Lippmann, Hobhouse, and Bourgeois. He perceived, albeit imperfectly, that the consensus implied by the conception of the *Rechtsstaat* promises repression. Once ethical right comes to be associated with reality instead of the ideal, consensus can justify crushing any challenge to the state. In a variety of ways, the identification of legal with moral right that bolstered Bismarck's policies has led other nations, including those that pride themselves on their toleration of diversity, periodically to define dissent as immoral.

The progressives who lacked Weber's acquaintance with this danger struggled to infuse an ethical quality into politics by advocating the principle of benevolence as a social value. Their efforts served, however, to provide a patina of morality for the liberal capitalist welfare states emerging in Great Britain, France, and the United States. They tried to channel the spirit of organized capitalism into a new politics of social responsibility, but by establishing the legitimacy of the *Rechtsstaat*, they succeeded only in justifying the expansion of state action. The shape of the state changed, but its purpose did not. Because these thinkers linked political reform with broadened social responsibility, they believed that education alone could accomplish the socialization of values needed for institutional reforms. Ironically, many of the specific reforms they considered less important than the reorientation of cultural norms actually did take root, but because these new institutions were not sustained by a new set of values, they did not achieve the results these progressives desired. If progressive reforms failed, and they usually did, it was not because progressive theorists separated politics from culture, but rather because political reform did not occur within the framework of a cultural transformation involving general acceptance of the ethics of rational benevolence. Addressing the Congress of the Radical Republican and Radical Socialist party, the party that served as the vehicle for the philosophy and the politics of solidarity, Bourgeois urged his allies to "remember that our politics is only the application of the highest morality, answering the deepest urges of the conscience." Natural solidarity is a fact; moral solidarity is a duty. Unless political economy is made consistent with "moral economy," "the liberty and the dignity of the person are not assured."[2]

Dewey emphasized the connection between ethics and politics at every stage of his long career. Because Dewey played a prominent role in constructing the philosophy of the *via media*, his ideas about knowledge and responsibility were discussed in Chapters One through Four rather than Chapter Eight. But as a political thinker he was part of the progressive generation, and in this chapter his ideas will again be central, as the focus of the analysis shifts to politics. Indeed, it is arguable that Dewey and Weber are the two most significant social theorists America and Europe have produced in the twentieth century, and their contributions provide the clearest evidence of the depth—and the range—of the discourse of progressivism. Dewey and Weber differed so sharply in their assessments of the prospects for progressive change that their participation in parallel progressive movements has received little attention. Although I will not attempt to minimize the extent of their disagreements, one of my primary goals is to establish the nature of their common aim and to indicate the reasons for their different conclusions about the chances of democracy in a world of instrumental rationality.

Dewey's preoccupation with linking ethics and politics is evident as early as 1884, when he was completing his graduate studies at the Johns Hopkins University. In a letter to William Torrey Harris, Dewey wrote that the greatest weakness of American philosophy in general, and of the department of philosophy at Johns Hopkins in particular, was the neglect of ethics. In his minor subject, "the theory of the state," he encountered the economists, political scientists, and historians who played such a prominent role in the professionalization of American social science, but he was disappointed to find that "there is no provision to give them the philosophic side of their own subject." As long as "social ethics in its widest sense is untouched," he concluded, "they can't get more than half the good of their own courses." Four years later, in *The Ethics of Democracy*, he established his own political position, from which he never wavered: "Democracy, in a word, is a social, that is to say, an ethical conception." There is an individualistic principle in democracy, he admitted, but it is "an individualism of freedom, of responsibility, of initiatives to and for the ethical ideal, not an individualism of lawlessness." Dewey insisted that all life has a moral dimension, whether it is viewed from the political, social, or economic perspective. "Economic and industrial life is *in itself* ethical," and it must be "made contributory to the realization of personality through the formation of a higher and more complete unity among men."[3] In *The Study of Ethics* (1894), he reiterated that argument, and he suggested that the tendency to separate politics from ethics had its source in Aristotle's *Ethics*. For the sake of analytical clarity, Aristotle attempted to distinguish two senses of the word justice: obedience to law and virtue. But Dewey maintained that "practical sense is wiser in fusing them than Aristotle in separating them." Although he did not use the word, Dewey wanted to replace the customary separation of law from right in Western political thought with a doctrine resembling that of the *Rechtsstaat*.[4]

Dewey contended that the separation of ethics from politics had contributed to the equally pernicious isolation of the individual from society in Western thought. By reuniting the political and moral spheres, he hoped also to recover the connection between individual life and social life. In the *Ethics* (1908) he coauthored with James Tufts, Dewey discussed at length the reform of prisons, criminal procedures, government administration, corruption in politics, public utilities, political parties, the machinery of government, and social legislation. His decision to include subjects customarily avoided in textbooks on ethics signaled Dewey's radical perspective on both moral and political philosophy, a view he shared with Hobhouse. In his and Tufts's *Ethics*, Dewey quoted a passage from Hobhouse's *Morals in Evolution* that drew together strands from epistemology, ethics, and politics: "The responsible human being," Hobhouse wrote, "is the center of modern ethics as of modern law, free so far as custom and law are concerned to make his own life." Moreover, "the social nature of man is not diminished either on the side of its needs or its duties by the fuller recognition of personal rights." The reason, Hobhouse continued, echoing Green, was that "so far as rights and duties are conceived as attaching to human beings as such, they become universalized, *and are therefore the care of society as a whole rather than of any partial group organization*." Dewey wholeheartedly endorsed this line of argument and noted its debt to Green. Both he and Hobhouse followed the logic that led from their theory of knowledge, rooted in individual experience and socially validated, to a broad conception of responsibility, and further to a radical critique of liberal individualism.[5] In addition, both shared the conviction that these questions must be addressed with reference to historical development, and they agreed that the emergence of urban societies and industrial economies provided the context in which the recognition of responsibility, and its projections into politics, became both possible and necessary.

In *Reconstruction in Philosophy* (1920), Dewey made explicit the political significance of his philosophical ideas. When we realize that selfhood is an active process, we understand that "social modifications are the only means of the creation of changed personalities." Once this association has been made, we can identify "the interest in individual moral improvement and the social interest in objective reform of economic and political conditions." That understanding of personal development provides a compass for our "inquiry into the meaning of social arrangements. We are led to ask what the specific stimulating, fostering, and nurturing power of each specific social arrangement may be. The old time separation between politics and morals is abolished at its root."[6] Progressive political theory was as strong as each of the links in that chain of reasoning. Ascertaining the "stimulating, fostering, and nurturing power" of political and economic institutions, Dewey contended, requires the exercise of intelligence to evaluate their ethical quality.

Hobhouse was equally persistent in harnessing social change to ethical rejuvenation. As he argued in *The Labour Movement* (1893), "If the change from individualism to socialism meant nothing but an alteration in the methods of organizing industry, it would leave the nation no happier or better than before." The goal must be conceived in moral as well as mechanical terms, and it must involve "introducing a new spirit into industry—a feeling for the common good, a readiness to forgo personal advantage for the general gain, a recognition of mutual dependence." He reiterated that analysis not only in *Morals and Evolution*, which Dewey quoted, but also in *Liberalism* and in the second edition of *The Labour Movement* (1912), where he emphasized the verso of progressivism's ethical emphasis: "Machinery—laws, administration, organization—are after all valuable only as the lever by which the moral forces of society can work. Mere reform of machinery is worthless unless it is the expression of a change of spirit and feeling."[7] Although his dissatisfaction with the elitist and bureaucratic orientation of the Fabians and the Labour party prompted him to drop his earlier endorsement of a change "from individualism to socialism," he continued to insist on the integral relation between political and ethical progress.

Their identification of politics with morality distinguished these radical intellectuals from the politicians who enacted much of the progressive reform legislation during the early twentieth century. In order to reach a clear understanding of progressive political theory—and of the limited success of progressive reforms—the gap separating theory from practice must be kept in mind. Collapsing that distinction may result in either of two misconceptions. On the one hand, these thinkers may be dismissed as unrealistic because of their ethical conception of politics, even though their grasp of the problems their cultures faced—problems encompassing values as well as institutions— was in certain respects considerably more solid than that of many later commentators. On the other hand, they may be improperly identified as the fathers of the welfare state. That argument, however, rests on three mistaken premises. First, it exaggerates the influence of theory on practice and ignores the decisive role of power in politics. Second, it misses the contestatory quality of these rebels' ideas: the assumption that the welfare state as it developed was consistent with their plans is simply untrue. Third, it betrays the naive view that the source of the problems plaguing the welfare state can be traced to the inadequacy of the ideas that inspired it rather than the particular historical forces—economic, political, and social as well as intellectual—that shaped it. Muddling through crises is the essence of politics, and failures of policy cannot be understood without careful analysis of the diverse factors involved in their formulation and their execution. Intellectuals may help to make changes possible by articulating different visions of society, but between idea and reality there falls much more than a shadow.

In "Politik als Beruf" (cited hereafter as "Politics as a Vocation"), Weber chided those who supposed that ideas could be neatly translated into political practice. Anyone entering the world of politics, the world of power and force as means, enters a world "governed by demons," and he must deal with the devil to accomplish his goals. "It is *not* true that good can follow only from good, and evil only from evil, but often the opposite is true. Anyone who fails to see this is, indeed, a political child."[8] As the history of progressivism illustrates, unintended consequences are the rule rather than the exception in political life. Intellectuals may provide the ideas that spark reform, but the translation of those ideals into practice involves the intervention of actors with a variety of motives at several different levels. The individual leaders who succeed in changing a nation's political course may have very little understanding of the ideals they claim to cherish: neither Lloyd George nor Asquith, Roosevelt nor La Follette, Waldeck-Rousseau nor Combes, and certainly neither Bismarck nor Miquel, had as clear a perception of the underlying philosophy of progressivism as they had of the reality of political power. Theirs was a courage often without convictions, and they achieved results not because they articulated clear and consistent ideas but because they manipulated the levers of politics with dexterity. They knew more about the principle of compromise than they knew about the principles of progressive theory. What is true of political leaders is even more true of political parties, which shift their rhetoric not only according to the prevailing winds of political theory but, even more directly, in order to maintain and extend their popular appeal.

The different levels of political power, the competition among existing groups with vested interests, the preferences of government officials who end up implementing programs planned by others—all of these factors complicate political life. That the final product seldom resembles the model ostensibly followed should occasion little surprise. Between the initial altruism or outrage that sparks action and the final formulation of policy, too many individuals and constituencies with too many conflicting interests are waiting in the political maze to tug and slash at an idea whose original form and direction may be wildly distorted in the process. There are identifiable reasons why political reforms failed to have the impact these thinkers hoped they would, but the explanation for their failure must be sought in the detailed examination of progressive politics rather than the easy dismissal of progressive ideas.[9] There is nothing evasive about pointing out the distance between the ideals of these theorists and the reality of the welfare state. To point out the irony of progressive reform is not to offer apologies for its shortcomings, it is merely to account for what may otherwise appear either sinister or bewildering by directing attention to the complex dynamics of political history.

The kind of moral regeneration required for the substantive change these theorists sought can occur only slowly. Together with Croly, they counseled "patient agitation rather than any hazardous attempts at radical reconstruction." Radical reform could not "be permanent, or even healthy," until "public opinion has been converted to a completer realization of the nature and extent of its responsibilities." The proper strategy would yoke "certain very moderate practical proposals with the issue of a deliberate, persistent, and far more radical challenge to popular political prejudices and errors." Consistent with this approach to political action, these Fabians of liberalism resisted the idea of a permanent class struggle. The principle of social responsibility must be accepted by all, or at least almost all, before reform can be effective. In a speech Weber gave to Austrian officers in Vienna in 1918, which was among his most detailed treatments of specific political issues, he stressed the futility of revolutionary mass action. He applauded social democrats like Bernstein who understood that revolution, while capable of bringing civil war, could not create a genuine socialist society. Weber had doubts about the possibility, and even the desirability, of achieving a *Rechtsstaat* under socialism or capitalism, for reasons to be discussed later. But given his understanding of the intertwining of religion, politics, and economics in cultural development, his fear that violent revolution would end only in chaos seems understandable. Like the theorists of social democracy, progressives wanted change, but they wanted to make haste slowly.[10]

Despite their emphasis on moral regeneration as a necessary condition for political change, these radicals did not neglect less amorphous measures. The graduated income tax, based on the idea that everyone owes a debt to society proportional to his ability to pay, was perhaps the quintessential progressive reform. Departing from older approaches to the problem of raising revenues, which in France, for example, exempted the nobility and imposed relatively heavier burdens on those less able to pay, progressives like Bourgeois sought to tax all income, including rent, on a sliding scale. American and British progressives likewise rallied to this cause.[11] Typically, there was no popular agitation for an income tax in Germany. None was necessary: it was enacted by Finance Minister Miquel in 1891. But the first party Weber felt capable of supporting wholeheartedly, the short-lived Progressive People's party, advocated in its first platform of 1910 a more extensive system of graduated income and estate taxes.

Perhaps the sharpest debate over progressive taxation came in France, where the Bourgeois ministry stood—and fell— on its proposal for an income tax. Jaurès was among the most enthusiastic supporters of Bourgeois's plan, and the speech he gave in the Chamber of Deputies on March 21, 1896, was among his most powerful. He acknowledged that the mere presence of a progressive income tax would not touch the concentration of capital and power. Yet he defended the principle of graduated taxation, even at the cost of antagonizing segments of the French socialist movement. If we support the income tax, he declared, "it is simply because it introduces into our fiscal legislation a deep concern for man, a deep concern for human and social reality." It was, finally, neither a socialist tax nor a capitalist tax, it was simply "a human tax," which took into account the actual inequality of wealth and the human equality of all citizens. Jaurès implored the left to stand behind it as a symbol of the assault against privilege. Bourgeois delivered his own equally impassioned plea five days later. He made it clear that the survival of the first all-Radical government in the Third Republic would depend on this issue, and he urged the fragmented French left to present a united front. Emotions ran high, and when the measure passed the Chamber on March 27, *La Petite République* hailed it the next day in a banner headline proclaiming "*DEFAITE DE LA REACTION.*" The celebration proved premature, however, as Bourgeois still had to carry the income tax through the gauntlet of the more conservative Senate. There, together with his ministry, it quietly expired.[12]

Despite their defeat, neither Bourgeois nor Jaurès abandoned the idea. Bourgeois hammered away at it in almost everything he wrote, and it is possible to argue that the entire movement of solidarity sprang from his tireless efforts to clarify the idea of ethical duty embodied in the concept of progressive taxation. Jaurès was equally persistent. On July 12, 1914, speaking

before the Chamber of Deputies, he presented variations on his entire reper-
toire of arguments supporting the income tax. His devotion to this cause, he
pointed out, testified to the tenacity of France's propertied classes: the
income tax had also been the subject of his first speech in the Chamber thirty
years earlier, and nothing had changed in the interim. "But where, gentlemen," he concluded, "is one to learn patience if not in parliaments?" Nineteen
days later Jaurès was dead. What proved to be his last substantial speech in
the Chamber, like his first, was futile, and his assassination gave a bitter edge
to the tone of gentle mockery in the speech that turned out to be his farewell
address. The income tax was not instituted in France until 1917, and then
only because the requirements of the war that Jaurès and Bourgeois struggled
to prevent at last made it inescapable.[13] In no nation did graduated taxation
fulfill these thinkers' hopes as a method of redistributing income. It did at
least imply, however, that wealth is a social product, and that the distribution
of social burdens should bear some resemblance to the distribution of social
rewards.

The reforms that established the welfare state were more ambiguous.
Either such measures could advance the ideal of responsibility by institutionalizing the community's duty to care for its members, or they could
merely deflect dissatisfaction from more radical reforms by offering palliatives. Progressives generally followed the social democrats' reasoning on this
question: as long as the state represented repression, any expansion of its
power constituted a threat, but the rise of democratic government enabled
the state to serve its citizens rather than vice versa. "In democracy," Dewey
wrote, "the governors and the governed are not two classes, but two aspects
of the same fact—the fact of the possession by society of a unified and
articulate will. It means that government is the organ of society." Hobhouse
offered a similar analysis. Once the people "could look upon the Government
as their servant and the acts of government as their acts, it followed necessarily that the antagonism between democracy and governmental action fell
to the ground."[14]

While this group of progressives endorsed the expansion of government
services with far greater enthusiasm than many of their contemporaries could
muster, they remained sensitive to the problematic nature of the welfare
state. They supported the measures that the Webbs advocated to secure a
"national minimum" in the categories of health, housing, education, and
work. In *Drift and Mastery*, Lippmann appropriated the Fabians' terminology,
proclaiming that "a minimum standard of life below which no human being
can fall is the most elementary duty of the democratic state." In his lecture "La
Solidarité et la liberté," read at the International Congress of Social
Education in 1900, Bourgeois presented the solidarists' shopping list:
insurance against sickness, accident, unemployment, and old age; universal
free education; and the maintenance of life for all who are unable to care for
themselves. Hobhouse endorsed similar measures in *Liberalism*. He also
stipulated that such programs should be funded from general tax revenues,
instead of contributions, so that participation would be universal. Otherwise,

he reasoned, if the wealthy were able to exclude themselves from a system they did not need, a certain opprobrium might accompany the receipt of these benefits, and the purpose of the system of services would be undermined. Although they appreciated the limited nature of these reforms, progressives applauded them as signals of what Croly called "the adoption of a new outlook, the beginning of a new life." Thus a limited program securing national minimum standards of living "would consequently be radical and revolutionary in implication, even though it were modest in its expectation of immediate achievement."[15]

Despite their hopes that the first steps toward the welfare state might evince and encourage a new sense of community, these partisans of the activist state also appreciated that social service legislation might prove counterproductive. Germany's early encounter with state sponsored insurance gave Weber a particularly sharp insight into this problem. He conceded the desirability of the immediate results achieved by Bismarck's scheme, but he contended that the long-term political cost of such gains was too high. Germany's welfare provisions reached only those not politically integrated into the Reich: the infirm, the aged, the disabled, and veterans. It contributed nothing to help "those sound in body and mind defend their interests soberly and with self-respect." In fact, Bismarck's paternalism drained the nation's political vitality. The "sentiments of honor and solidarity are the only decisive moral forces for the education of the masses," Weber wrote, and "for this reason these sentiments must be given free rein." Only by struggling to achieve its goals can a nation mature politically. As a result of his autocratic rule, Bismarck "left behind him a nation without any political sophistication, far below the level which in this regard it had reached twenty years before."[16] As Germans grew accustomed to state action independent of any popular participation, their political will atrophied. The major impediment to Germany's further democratization after World War I, in fact, was not the persistence of the military-Junker oligarchy, Weber argued, but the torpor of the nation's political culture.

Because these progressives stressed the themes of moral harmony and community, their position has occasionally been confused with the authoritarian organicism of much conservative theory. They insisted, however, that there was a decisive difference. They conceived of social integration as the product of individual action tempered by an ethic of benevolence, and they contrasted that idea to the paternalism they identified with conservative notions of community. Rather than imposing on the individual a set of pre-existing standards or rules of behavior, they believed that the state should manifest the values of autonomous individuals conscientiously fulfilling their social responsibility. Legitimate heirs of republican liberalism, whose form they altered in order to perpetuate the spirit of autonomy, these progressives criticized paternalism as a challenge to the political integrity of the citizenry. Providing for the material needs of an individual need not constrain his freedom, Hobhouse wrote, "if you leave him to roam unfettered in the larger field of mental and spiritual development." The "organization of all the material basis of society," such as the welfare state offers, merely "forms the foundation of the wider life" of freedom.[17] Without minimum standards of existence, in short, liberty is an illusion; only if those material needs are met through the sacrifice of the individual's moral autonomy does the social service state become an obstacle rather than an avenue to freedom.

In part due to Croly's cautious support of Mussolini in the early days of fascism, when *il Duce* was quoting William James and promising a pragmatic commitment to efficiency without repression, critics have been tempted to read protofascist tendencies into Croly's pre-World War I writings. His straightforward critique of authoritarianism in *Progressive Democracy* shows the inaccuracy of that argument. A system of social services purchased at the price of undemocratic government "is not worth what it costs," he warned. "It makes no difference how benevolent the intention of the government may be or how wise its legislation. The program which is carried out by such means will do nothing to make the people worthy of their advantages. The result will be either popular servility or organized popular resistance or both." The similarity of that analysis to Weber's is as evident as its applicability to the German case. Like Weber, Croly used Bismarck as the prime example of the paternalism he mistrusted. "The country in which a benevolent government has succeeded in carrying out the most comprehensive social policy of modern times," he pointed out, contains a party of revolution that lacks effective political power but routinely wins the support of one-third of the electorate. Croly was certain that paternalism only impedes democratic mobilization and polarizes society. Those who characterize him as a collectivist with protofascist tendencies jump from a few of the more mystical passages in *The Promise of American Life* to a conclusion that Croly explicitly and repeatedly repudiated. Croly maintained that the proletariat can emerge as a potent force only through "a series of conflicts in which the ground is skillfully chosen and permanent defeat never admitted." He was talking about political rather than revolutionary battles, to be sure, but he insisted that freedom "would not amount to much" if it were handed down to the people by the state or by employers' associations. Workers must instead win their struggles "in the same way that every modern nation has earned or protected its independence—that is, by warfare appropriate for the purpose."[18] Croly was no insurrectionist, but neither was he a partisan of welfare capitalism, benevolent state socialism, or government by elites. Like Weber, he criticized efforts to co-opt the working class; unlike Weber, he was confident that progress could come through democratic political action.

These progressives were wary of welfare legislation because of their philosophical commitment to voluntarism. It is now evident that many of the devices presented in the guise of social assistance have served to legitimate inequality, and others have become tools for covert or overt social control. Yet arguing from that evidence back to the intent of these radicals is bad logic and worse history. By dismissing as conservative all efforts that did not lead to the overthrow of capitalism, such arguments wander into the no-man's-land of tautology: according to that standard, all attempts to reform the state rather than destroy it are by definition reactionary. As historical analysis such criticism is even less satisfactory, since it ignores the context in which this generation wrote. What may appear tame from a later vantage point appeared unmistakably radical at the time, as even a cursory reading of contemporary debates indicates. One of Dewey's early essays both demonstrates the distance between progressive and conservative theory and reveals the source of these ideas in the theory of voluntary action. "A true social interest is that which wills for others freedom from dependence on our *direct* help, which wills to them the self-directed power of exercising, in and by themselves, their own functions. Any will short of this is not social but selfish, willing the dependence of others that we may continue benignly altruistic." In the age of industrial capitalism, charity was anachronistic, a transparent rationalization of inequalities for which there could be no such easy atonement. "The idea of 'giving pleasure' to others, 'making others happy,' if it means anything else than securing conditions so that they may act freely in their own satisfaction, means slavery."[19]

There were many apostles of efficiency, welfare capitalists, and unreconstructed aristocrats who endorsed variations of the solution Dewey opposed. But such architects of social control should not be confused with these theorists of progressive democracy. Much of the confusion surrounding the ideas of these intellectuals, and much of the disagreement concerning their historical significance, derives from the multiple uses to which their pragmatic concept of experimentation was put by many of their contemporaries and their successors whose values differed dramatically from theirs. The sharp divisions historians have drawn between humanitarian moralists and manipulative scientists, however, bear little resemblance to the rather more complicated debates of these years, when the edges between social reform and social control were blurred by the simple inability to see into the future.[20]

Until now I have emphasized the similarities between these progressives and the theorists of social democracy. Significant as that convergence was, the liberal roots of progressivism surfaced in discussions of the social ownership of the means of production. The distance separating these two groups, however, was considerably smaller than that separating revolutionary socialists from laissez-faire liberals. Bourgeois, for example, claimed to oppose only collectivism, not socialism. Hobhouse considered himself a partisan of "liberal socialism." Croly affirmed that his "proposed definition of democracy is socialist."[21] Despite these inclinations toward socialism, differences of substance as well as emphasis divided even the most socialist of liberals from the most liberal of socialists. Those differences had to do with conceptions of freedom, which will be discussed in Chapter Ten, and with the consolidation of economic power in the state. Weber provided the most cogent explanation of progressives' fears on this issue. In his speech on socialism in 1918, he explained the rise of revisionism almost exactly as Bernstein did in *Evolutionary Socialism*, but he drew quite a different conclusion. Whereas Bernstein and other social democrats believed that the trend toward the concentration of power in corporate capitalism and the rise of a new class of managers would eventually lead to social harmony and public ownership, Weber argued that such developments would only ensure the domination of society by bureaucrats. The process of rationalization, he contended, would frustrate equally the desire of socialists for justice and the desire of capitalists for efficiency. He based his analysis on the now familiar concept of status groups, which he formulated most clearly in *Economy and Society*. Class power, or what he called "'economically conditioned' power," is not identical with power as such. "On the contrary, the emergence of economic power may be the consequence of power existing on other grounds. Man does not strive for power only in order to enrich himself economically. Power, including economic power, may be valued for its own sake." Weber reasoned that social conflict would survive the destruction of capitalism. The locus of struggle would simply shift, for regardless of the economic system, he concluded, "politics means conflict."[22]

The gradual elimination of private capitalism is theoretically conceivable, Weber admitted, but he cautioned that such a change would have little impact on "the steel frame of modern industrial work." The highest levels of industrial management might be integrated into the state bureaucracy without appreciably changing the individual worker's experience in his job. Working conditions in the state owned Prussian mines and railroads, Weber pointed out, scarcely differed from those in private industries. Now it is surely true that there are bureaucracies and bureaucracies, and Weber may have begged important questions by offering Prussian bureaucrats as prototypical. Yet his argument rested less on the notoriously rigid discipline in those state socialist industries than on a structural problem. The position of labor under socialism, he contended, would be even worse than under capitalism. Public and private bureaucracies can, at least in principle, check one another's excesses, whereas in a socialist state they "would be merged into a single hierarchy. This would occur in a much more rational—and hence unbreakable—form." The worker's dependence would thus be increased, for while labor may challenge capitalist power through unionization, there can be no court of higher appeal to arbitrate grievances against the state. Democratic socialism, organized around groups of consumers rather than producers, seemed to some progressives and socialists a viable alternative to bureaucratic state socialism, but Weber brusquely dismissed such plans. "No one has the slightest idea," he scoffed, where the leaders of such a system would come from, "nor where the interested parties might be found to bring it into being in the first place; for experience has shown that consumers as such are only to a very limited extent capable of organization."[23] Here Weber's despair over the depoliticization of Germany clearly shaped his analysis. He doubted the people's ability to mobilize around a nonpartisan public interest, and that pessimism separated him from the other theorists of progressivism and social democracy.

The emergence of precisely those public-spirited groups of consumers, whose organizational capacities Weber denigrated, played a decisive role in the rise of solidarity in France, the new liberalism in Britain, and progressivism in the United States. This popular insurgency, in fact, may help to account for the confidence Bourgeois, Hobhouse, Croly, Lippmann, and Dewey expressed concerning the prospects for meaningful change within capitalism. These thinkers believed that private power can be brought under public control without resorting to government ownership of industry. They shared Weber's skepticism regarding the consolidation of economic power in the state, and for that reason they preferred experiments in economic regulation to complete nationalization. Hobhouse objected to "official socialism," his euphemism for Fabianism, because it relied on "a class of the elect, an aristocracy of character and intellect which will fill the civil services and do the practical work of administration." Lippmann shared that mistrust of bureaucratic socialism, but after meeting the Webbs in 1914, he denied that they were guilty of such elitism themselves. Nevertheless, he became increasingly suspicious of "the pretense of Socialists that they alone are the agents of progress," an assumption "contradicted by the plain facts of everyday life."[24] Bureaucratic government promised order at the expense of spontaneity and diversity, and these progressives preferred less drastic measures not because they were enamored of administration, but rather because they feared an even more oppressive bureaucratization would accompany a socialist solution to the problems of industrialization. Unlike many of their critics, these thinkers believed that political experimentation is the fulfillment of democracy rather than its circumvention.

In the United States, in particular, where the independent regulatory commission was such a prominent part of progressive reform, many progressives championed regulation because they judged it more democratic than the alternative of bureaucratic socialism. Because regulation has clearly served different purposes than they expected, it is important to recover the reasons behind their original enthusiasm. Hobhouse argued that the need for legislation to counter the power of monopolies was more pressing in America than Britain, but he contended that such action, far from infringing on older liberal ideas, was simply "a necessary means to their fulfillment." Croly, Lippmann, and Dewey agreed that trusts had arrived in America to stay, and that summoning the ghost of Thomas Jefferson would not alter the shape of organized capitalism. The only reasonable response was creative adaptation, and to them regulation seemed attractive because it offered the flexibility they desired. Managed competition, from their perspective, seemed an attractive alternative to imposed order. But regulation was from the start a risky business. Would regulatory agencies' independence free them from private power for democratic purposes, or vice versa, and who would determine which was which? Over the past century, the French, British, and American experiences with regulation have been mixed, reflecting the complicated interplay of vested interests that enter into the governmental process and the different abilities of self-interested industries and less narrowly focused consumer groups to sustain intense political activity over long periods of time. Eventually, the public enthusiasm that generated much reform in the pre-World War I period flagged, and the machinery that survived came to serve purposes very different from those progressive theorists had in mind.[25]

Regulation was a gamble, as progressives understood. In *Drift and Mastery*, Lippmann noted the difference between the open-ended view of reform pragmatists accepted and the orthodoxy of dogmatic revolutionaries. "They are God's audience," he wrote, "and they know the plot so well that occasionally they prompt Him." Not only did progressives deny they knew history's plot, they thought the actors were making it up as they went along, and they endorsed regulation in that spirit of improvisation. Many radicals, Lippmann argued, were insufficiently radical, and thus fell victim to "the panacea habit of mind." Their good ideas became fixed ideas. Once they discovered a reform they liked, they became convinced that "some one change will set everything right." But neither the short ballot, the single tax, woman suffrage, nor the socialization of the economy could deliver all their partisans promised. Unfortunately, he concluded, "men will do almost anything but govern themselves." That simple demand lay at the heart of progressive political theory. The later transformation of the independent regulatory agency into a well-oiled gear in the corporate capitalist economy, like the transformation of the welfare state into an effective tool legitimating the perpetuation of inequality, does not demonstrate the inherent inadequacy of regulation. Instead it reflects the persistence of power and the failure of citizens to sustain their commitment to active participation in democratic government. Weber doubted that the public could bring a highly rationalized industrial economy under popular control, as the other progressives trusted they could do. Democratic governments can only continue to wager that faith against his doubt. "Efficiency will never be a popular cause," Lippmann wrote in 1916, "until it is tied securely to radical liberalism."[26] The last seven decades have confirmed that prediction, although hardly as Lippmann hoped.

The optimism progressive reformers expressed for the chances of democratic change reflected the instability of political conditions in Europe and the United States during the first two decades of the twentieth century. With party alignments in flux and the state's role rapidly expanding, the prospects for progress looked good. Particularly in the immediate prewar years, coalitions of moderate socialists and left liberals succeeded in achieving what appeared to be important gains. A brief survey of political developments during these years should indicate why progressives were hopeful, and why their hopes were not fulfilled.

In the United States, the progressive era was marked by the rapid formation and dissolution of coalitions around different and often contradictory causes. Because conditions and constituencies varied over time and across the nation, attempts to generalize about the essence of progressivism are futile. Different groups mobilized around at least four identifiable sets of reforms, and they allied with each other in puzzling ways. Moreover, many individuals enlisted in several of these crusades, their zeal overshadowing their occasional inconsistency. Perhaps the most familiar band of progressives centered their attention on antimonopoly legislation and found their most influential spokesman in Woodrow Wilson. In some ways diametrically opposed to such progressives were the midwives of organized capitalism, those advocates of scientific management and the associative state who rallied around Teddy Roosevelt. They sought a bureaucratic revolution, which would streamline American government and the American economy under the guidance of university trained professionals and social scientists. Yet another collection of activists who considered themselves progressives aimed to swab America's decks through a series of measures including prohibition, immigration restriction, and racial segregation, a program that would reverse the nation's slide from grace and return it to its original lofty status as a bastion of white Anglo-Saxon Protestantism. Finally, there was a contingent of progressives less interested in trust-busting, organizational revolutions, or reforming cultural behavior than in public welfare measures, labor legislation, and social responsibility. It was this group that subscribed to the ideas that Croly, Lippmann, and Dewey expressed.[27] Obviously this faction had no monopoly on the rhetoric of fairness; one could look long and hard without finding a good word for selfishness or injustice in the speeches of any of these very different groups of progressives—or their opponents, for that matter. Yet different progressives persistently emphasized different issues, and one segment did congregate around the position occupied by those who edited and wrote for *The New Republic*.

As these competing groups of reformers were wrestling over the nation's future, another development altered the shape of American politics. What historians term the third party system, inaugurated with Lincoln at the start of the Civil War, collapsed during the 1890s, and its successor emerged during the early years of the Progressive Era. The Civil War party system, characterized by symbolic, largely artificial issues, persistent corruption, and high voter turnout, reflected in its stability a nearly perfect balance between America's principal ethnocultural groups. Two different pressures upset that precarious equilibrium. The rapid transformation of America into an urban-industrial society rocked the machinery of politics and created openings for a new generation of administrators, who redefined the purpose and redesigned the shape of government. Simultaneously, an electorate incensed by recurring scandals and incompetent politicians finally lost confidence—and interest—in electoral politics. "Suppose you were an idiot," suggested Mark Twain. "And suppose you were a member of Congress. But I repeat myself." A less deftly expressed but equally deep dissatisfaction with party politics caused the public to turn with increasing frequency to single-issue interest groups to accomplish political reforms. As a result, the polity briefly opened up to accommodate a new breed of political managers and a new style of political activity. It was during this transitional phase, between the politics of party professionals and the professionalization of party politics, that progressive reform flourished and progressive theory took shape.[28]

The inchoate form of the new political world helps to account for the rapid shift of loyalties that led to charges of opportunism against *The New Republic* crowd. Prior to 1912, Croly and Lippmann enthusiastically supported Roosevelt as the embodiment of their ideals, an energetic advocate of expanded government authority and a defender of the public interest. Yet after Wilson's election, when he showed the flexibility these thinkers prized so highly—and perhaps even more when he showed an interest in consulting them about policy—Croly and Lippmann came around to the view that Wilson, not Roosevelt, was their best hope. Indeed, as president his efforts on behalf of social welfare legislation corresponded more closely to the principles of *The New Republic* than to the principles of the New Freedom expressed in his campaign speeches. At the height of progressive enthusiasm, the contagion of reform infected both parties, and because their brand of progressivism in fact differed on important issues from both Roosevelt's and Wilson's varieties, Croly and Lippmann's shift of loyalties was simply a response to Wilson's evident change of heart—and TR's increasingly strident jingoism—rather than a betrayal of their political principles.[29] Wilson confirmed their belief that experience provides the best guidance concerning effective democratic reform, and they were confident about the future because they believed the American people shared their vision. Even after World War I indicated how easily public sentiment could be manipulated, a lesson that would gradually erode Lippmann's democratic faith, these progressives' hopes died hard. "In spite of all appearance," Lippmann wrote at the conclusion of World War I, a decisive majority of Americans

> is progressive to radical. That which in 1912 went to the making of liberalism in all parties but the Republican rump and the Bourbon Democracy is not extinguished and cannot long be frustrated. It swung the election of 1916 for Wilson, and it is abroad today. As a party the Bull Moose is dead, as a way of behaving it will not down. For it represents the persistent dream of all Americans, that whatever Europe's experience may be, here at least obstinacy and fanaticism shall not have their way; here at least citizenship shall overpower class.[30]

That stubborn faith in the reforming spirit of a new citizenship sustained Croly and Dewey as well as Lippmann. They believed that most Americans agreed with them about the need for radical democratic reform, "in spite of all appearances," and that belief has been an enduring part of their legacy to the American left.

In contrast to Croly and Lippmann, who twice found themselves courted by presidential candidates claiming to share their convictions, Max Weber had difficulty finding any kindred spirits in German politics. I have already outlined Weber's odyssey from National Liberalism through the wilderness of various left liberal parties, a journey that did not lead him to a real political home until after World War I. Attempts to forge a coalition between revisionist segments of the SPD and progressives failed repeatedly in the 1890s, but for a brief period in the early twentieth century the prospects for such an alliance appeared brighter. Weber understood that in Germany, as in the

United States and Great Britain, the decisive factor in creating a progressive political movement would be white-collar workers. In Germany, however, these voters' traditional subservience to authoritarianism impeded the growth of an independent political sensibility. In 1907, and again in 1912, members of the SPD and the Progressive party were instructed by party leaders to vote on the second ballot for one another's candidates if that candidate supported the extension of the franchise. SPD voters appear to have followed those directions, but middle-class voters could not bring themselves to vote for candidates representing the party of the working class. What success the Bülow Bloc attained in 1907, moreover, came by pulling progressives toward the right rather than pulling liberals toward the left. In a speech Weber gave on the subject of extending the franchise in 1907, he ridiculed the fears of those he privately called the "faint-hearts" of his own class. Bringing socialists to power would have the salutary effect, he argued, of strengthening the revisionists against the revolutionaries, a necessary step toward the unification of left leaning parties. Weber supported the Progressive People's party when it was formed in 1910, but he was not optimistic about its prospects unless an arrangement could be made with the SPD. The continuing disagreements between socialists and left liberals, even after their success in the 1912 elections, made clear that Weber's skepticism was well founded. An alliance from Bebel to Bassermann was never a real possibility in prewar Germany. Progressives attempted to stress the common interests of their potential working-class and middle-class constituencies as consumers and taxpayers, precisely the strategy successfully employed by many American progressives, but in Germany such appeals were drowned out by more strident pleas for class loyalty.[31]

Weber explained the continuing intensity of the antagonism between the bourgeoisie and the proletariat in Germany during the course of a wide-ranging address he delivered at the Congress of Arts and Science held in St. Louis in 1904. Neatly packaging several standard interpretations of American uniqueness as he went, Weber argued that the absence of a feudal past and the presence of free land, material prosperity, and safe borders, all combined to differentiate the United States from European nations. What distinguished Germany just as decisively from Great Britain and, to a lesser degree, from France, was the depth of its authoritarian heritage, particularly in Prussia. "The class of rural landowners of Germany," he pointed out, provided more than the political leadership of the largest German state. "These Junkers imprint their character upon the officer corps, as well as upon the Prussian officials and upon German diplomacy." In short, whatever vestiges of authoritarianism survived in Germany, he concluded, "result directly or indirectly from the influence of these upper classes." A year later, he complained about "the disastrous political influence of the leaders of heavy industry." The *Sammlungspolitik* of industrialists and aristocrats effectively excluded all other segments of the German population from political participation. The polarization of the bourgeoisie and the proletariat facilitated the acquiescence of the public required for the success of that policy. The "*cowardice* of the bourgeoisie in the face of 'democracy,'" Weber proclaimed at the end of 1917, enabled Germany's oligarchy to preserve its bureaucratic rule without any challenge from below.[32] In other words, it was the political impotence of precisely those emerging professional classes central to American progressivism that accounted for the absence of progressivism in Germany.

After World War I Weber played a political role himself. He participated, although less fully than he would have liked, in writing the Weimar Constitution. He was active in the German Democratic party, which came closer to embodying his democratic liberalism than did any other party during his lifetime. He was even nominated for a seat in the Reichstag, but a complicated series of events involving bureaucratic snafus, misunderstandings, and Weber's own arrogance prevented him from being elected. It seems unlikely that Weber would have succeeded in politics anyway: he was equally scornful of the unbending adherence to principle and the willingness to compromise. He complained that Germany's political parties were too rigid ideologically, and he compared them unfavorably to political parties in the United States, which were devoid of principle but politically effective. Yet he resisted such accommodations to circumstances himself, as he explained shortly before his death, because while "the politician *must* make compromises—the scholar must not whitewash them."[33] Despite the occasional temptations that came his way, Weber realized that science, not politics, was his vocation.

Because Bourgeois was the consummate political insider, it might seem his impulses were the opposite of Weber's, but he had misgivings about politics that were rooted in a similar discomfort with the necessity to compromise. Criticism of his decision to resign in 1896, a decision that he considered an act of principle, scarred him permanently. I believe his increasing interest in international arbitration reflected not only a genuine commitment to the cause of peace but also a desire to avoid battles of the sort that brought down his ministry. He remained active in politics, to be sure, but less as a party leader than as a source of ideas and a reliable administrator. On May 5, 1896, less than a month after his farewell address as premier, Bourgeois called for the formation of a "progressive democratic party," which would be open to all shades of republican sentiment and closed only to those of the reactionary right who defended entrenched privilege, and to those of the revolutionary left who denied legitimacy to any form of personal property. In a speech to the Chamber of Deputies two years later, he argued that France would continue to be divided into two camps, one conservative and the other republican. During these years, in his speeches, his essays, and in *Solidarity*, he was trying to uproot the French bourgeoisie from the petrified liberalism of Opportunism.

Bourgeois was not alone in his desire to shift the fulcrum of politics from dead center to the left. At the turn of the century a deep and long-lasting realignment of French politics occurred, a realignment confirmed in the emergence of the Radical Republican and Radical Socialist party, which was after 1902 the largest party in the Chamber of Deputies. The single most important source of the ideas animating this party was Bourgeois's *Solidarity*. At the party's first congress in 1901, he was named president by acclamation, and in his address he emphasized the connection between social experience and social responsibility, between natural solidarity and ethical solidarity, and between these ideas and the program of social insurance—to be funded by a progressive income tax, of course—that he believed the party should endorse. A year later he reiterated these arguments and added a sharp rebuke of the Progressist party in power for resisting many of the reforms radicals and socialists sought. By 1903, the tides had shifted leftward, and Bourgeois was writing to the party congress as president of the Chamber of Deputies, expressing his "faithful devotion" to the party and its ideal of "social solidarity."[34]

But progressivism in France was as complicated as progressivism in America, and the apparent success of Bourgeois and his fellow radicals masked underlying problems. Party realignment did launch reformers into positions of power, as moderate liberals retreated into alliance with conservative parties. Much of the success progressives enjoyed during these years, however, stemmed from the willingness of radical liberals and moderate socialists to unite in the face of the Dreyfus affair. Their mutual affection ran less deep than their animosity for the reactionaries against whom they joined forces. Moreover, French radicalism, like American progressivism, had different meanings for different people. For the masses, particularly outside Paris, the new party represented merely the continuation of republicanism by other means, and the French public remained more interested in long-standing local issues. For professional politicians, the emergence of a new party meant the opening of new positions, and the scramble for places seldom originated in passionate commitment to the ideals of solidarity. For the well-educated, advantageously situated individuals who directed radicalism, the chance to govern provided an opportunity to bring order to chaos. For many of them, the goal of socioeconomic and political rationalization seemed more proximate, and perhaps even more important, than the goal of social justice. Finally, for intellectuals like Bourgeois, the Radical Republic afforded a chance to see their theories tested in practice. Not surprisingly, a steadily widening gap opened between the dream of solidarity and the reality of continuing social conflict. A certain discouragement set in as reforms failed to meet expectations, particularly after 1905, when the separation of church and state was accomplished and the French Socialist party was instructed by the International to shun cooperation with bourgeois reformist parties. As in the American case, during a chaotic phase the French polity opened to allow the infusion of new ideas and new policies from a new generation, then snapped shut and settled back into inaction. Illustrating this change, Bourgeois's letter to the party congress in 1906 struck a melancholy note; in it he completely ignored the socialists whom he had sedulously cultivated for the preceding decade. The fragile coalition was coming apart at the seams connecting its middle-class and proletarian pieces. As late as 1909, Bourgeois could still claim plausibly that all the ministries since his own, regardless of their specific party affiliations, stood for similar principles of social reform, although they pursued those goals with varying degrees of intensity and success.[35] That contention was becoming shakier, however, and there were signs that French radicalism was collapsing from exhaustion.

Bourgeois's own frustration with politics mounted, and his desire to escape politics for the less hectic world of scholarship intensified. When Jaurès and Aristide Briand tried to persuade him to declare himself a candidate for the presidency of the Republic in 1912, Bourgeois at first accepted their offers of support and then abruptly declined to run. Again his allies were puzzled, but it appears he struck a deal with Raymond Poincaré, whereby he agreed to support Poincaré for the presidency in exchange for the latter's support of Bourgeois's bid to become a member of the Académie Française. Bourgeois reportedly told Anatole France that he "did not care a damn about the presidency of the Republic, since his sole ambition was membership in the Academy." Poincaré's candidacy, of course, was successful; Bourgeois's was not.[36]

Historical speculation is cheap, but this bargain obviously had enormous implications. Had the "angel of arbitration," to use Jaurè's double-edged phrase, not sold his soul—or at least mortgaged his political prestige—to the patriot from Lorraine, France's position in the summer of 1914, and Europe's future in the spring of 1919, might have been very different indeed. Despite his talent for politics, Bourgeois generally followed an ethic of single-minded conviction rather than an ethic of responsibility. Again and again, he withdrew from struggles he was not confident he could win on his terms. He disliked the kind of pitched battles that Jaurès, for example, relished, and he avoided them whenever possible. At the moment when his willingness to devote himself wholeheartedly to politics might have made an incalculable difference, although he could scarcely have known it at the time, he chose to withdraw to the world of ideas. As the careers of Bourgeois and Jaurès illustrate, the lines dividing prudence from evasiveness, and courage from recklessness, are difficult to trace.

Hobhouse, like the other theorists of progressivism, resisted the call of politics as a vocation. As a prolific journalist he attained a certain prominence, and several times safe Liberal seats were offered him if he would stand for Parliament. Each time he refused, in his son's words, because "he would not undertake the necessary subservience to party principles." Hobhouse was as temperamentally unsuited to politics as Weber was. His contempt for those less able than he—and for those who disagreed with him—made him a difficult partner in any cooperative venture. As a theorist he was valuable; as a party man he would have been hopeless. Viewing the transformation of Liberal policies from the vantage point of 1911, he emphasized the infusion of new ideas from idealism and socialism that gave the Liberal party a new vitality and a new direction. During the 1890s, he argued in *Liberalism*, the old party system began to break down under the pressure of industrial unrest. Fueled by the writings of Henry George on the one hand and William Morris on the other, Britain became receptive to more radical ways of thinking.

"Meanwhile, the teaching of Green and the enthusiasm of Toynbee were setting Liberalism free from the shackles of an individualist conception of liberty." Finally, the Fabians "brought Socialism down from heaven and established a contact with practical politics and municipal government." Because of foreign policy issues, first the Irish question and then the Boer War, "the party fissure took place on false lines." Alliances that formed around the questions of Unionism and imperialism obscured the steady growth of a new political sensibility, which the cooperation of liberals and labor clearly evidenced. Progressives won important victories in 1900, 1906, and particularly 1910, by which time they had effectively captured the Liberal party for their reformist purposes. Hobhouse believed that labor, liberals, and even some conservatives were converging toward a new political position, a new liberalism that reconciled the demands of the working class with the desires of the middle class. Few developments in British political history, he wrote in 1910, "are more remarkable than the way in which a practicable social policy commanding wide agreement has crystallised itself in the last two or three years."[37] In the years immediately preceding World War I, Hobhouse could see no reason why this progressive alliance should not continue to flourish.

Historians now share his assessment of the prewar political situation. It is generally agreed that, through progressivism, the Liberal party effectively adapted itself to the altered conditions of urban-industrial Britain. Yet strains were apparent in the coalition even in the years of its greatest success, and these eventually contributed to the replacement of the Liberal party by Labour after the Liberals were discredited by the debacle of the war. First, the lingering adventurism of the liberal imperialists continued to sour many progressives on the party, and their worst fears seemed confirmed during the course of the war. Second, the Liberals' tenacious resistance to enfranchising women seemed anachronistic to many progressives. Third, the legacy of laissez-faire hung over the party's policy toward trade unions, and despite the sympathy for labor organizing expressed by intellectuals like Hobhouse, important segments of the party still tried to resist the rising tide of labor activism. These rifts cut across class lines, and they indicate the inadequacy of attempts to present the prewar Liberal party as a clear prototype of the postwar Labour party. Progressives altered the shape of liberalism in significant ways, and there is a great deal of similarity and a great deal of continuity evident in the programs advocated by Hobhouse and the Webbs, for example, both before and after the war. Yet the spirit of the old liberalism continued to mingle with the spirit of the new liberalism, and the resulting mixture was as unstable as the progressivism of the United States or France.[38]

There was a realignment of parties in Great Britain, just as in America and France. But in none of these nations was the realignment caused by the progressive reforms that are sometimes offered to explain them. In the United States the formation of the industrial party system in the 1890s predated the upward shift in the location of decision making that has made twentieth-century electoral politics so insulated from, and so unimportant to, the American people. In France, the realignment of parties in 1899 resulted at least as much from the furor over Dreyfus as from any of the measures instituted by the parties of radical republicanism. And in Great Britain, the shift toward a class basis for politics actually was completed before 1914, even though its accomplishment was obscured first by the fissures in the Liberal party and then by the rapid triumph of Labour after the war. In short, in none of these nations did the phenomena of reform and realignment fit neatly with one another. The transformation of political systems, like the translation of political principles into practice, rarely proceeds neatly, and attempts to simplify either process lead only to distortion.

In sum, political developments during this period seemed on the surface to run parallel with, and even to embody, the thrust of progressive thinking. In the United States, France, and Great Britain, reform movements inspired by these ideals, and comprising more and less radical groups of liberals and social democrats, cooperated to create social service institutions, and regulatory measures, which together appeared likely to file down the roughest edges of organized capitalism. But these steps were only preliminary. Continued progress depended on nourishing parties committed to moderate but meaningful change, which required strengthening the political center and dragging it leftward. Progressivism, dependent for its success on political as well as intellectual convergence, had to avoid being crushed, to use Hobhouse's image, between the grindstones of plutocratic imperialism and revolutionary socialism. When the Labour party appeared in the 1920s as the most promising vehicle of progressive ideas, Hobhouse acknowledged the continuity between prewar new liberalism and postwar Labour policy. He was afraid, however, that the party's roots in the working class would prevent it from becoming the focus of the all-classes radicalism he and the other progressives considered indispensable to the achievement of their goals.[39] The editors of *The New Republic* had equally mixed feelings about the Labour party. They judged it "the first genuinely national party in the history of democratic politics," but they were unsure that it could bridge the gap between Britain's classes. Croly nevertheless longed for such a party in America. Following hard on the disintegration of Roosevelt's Progressive party as a major force came the disgrace of Wilson's Democratic party, first by its violation of civil liberties and then by its acquiescence in the unjust peace proclaimed at Versailles. American progressives, who seemed in 1912 to be commanding the heights of national politics, found themselves after the war fighting a holding action against a counteroffensive launched by both major parties. As Croly wrote sadly in 1919, his earlier hopes for a consensus supporting the ideas and policies of reform now seemed dreamlike. Instead of deciding between two varieties of progressivism, as Americans had done as recently as 1912, the United States now joined Europe in facing a choice between "the tyranny of Bolshevism or the anarchy of unredeemed capitalism."[40]

The great war and its aftershocks shattered the politics of progressivism on both sides of the Atlantic. First, the political economy of total war discredited government intervention in the economy. Not only did the cause of war become increasingly unpopular as the sacrifices it required grew, the blend of compulsion and voluntarism seemed just bitter enough to displease almost everyone involved, regardless of their political affiliation, unless they profited from it personally. Second, the repression employed by ostensibly liberal governments to enforce support of their foreign policies discredited Wilson's Democratic party, Clemenceau's Radical Republican party, and Lloyd George's Liberal party. Finally, the Versailles Treaty mocked the high-minded justifications that Allied leaders offered during the war to explain their own excesses. European progressives like Bourgeois and Hobhouse were as enthusiastic about the idea of a League of Nations as Wilson was; they had been discussing it long before he arrived on the scene. The passionate commitment of *The New Republic* to Wilson's policy of a just peace reflected the editors' personal involvement in its formulation: Wilson lifted the phrase "peace without victory" from one of Croly's articles; he borrowed the language of the most delicate of the Fourteen Points from a report written by Lippmann.[41]

Progressives supported the war only because of the peace they believed it could bring. While they showed more respect for the war's opponents than did their governments, they did not accept the condemnation of war *per se* as immoral. In the essay "Conscience and Compulsion," which appeared in *The New Republic* in July, 1917, Dewey challenged the responsibility of pacifists in an argument similar to the one Weber later offered in "Politics as a Vocation." It was one thing to oppose the war and seek to mobilize sentiment in support of an international organization that would ensure future peace, as Jane Addams and others did. But pacifists who simply folded their arms and resolved to wait until the horror passed drew Dewey's fire on instrumentalist grounds. If in moments of crisis, Dewey reasoned, "the moving force of events is always too much for conscience, the remedy is not to deplore the wickedness of those who manipulate events." Instead, responsible critics must work to "connect conscience with the forces that are moving in another direction. Then will conscience itself have compulsive power instead of being forever the martyred and the coerced."[42] Dewey counseled, in short, a combination of convictions and responsible action, a willingness to test one's principles in the hurly-burly of practical politics, which was consistent with his ethical theory and with the conception of conscientious engagement Weber presented as his political and ethical ideal.

The tragedy of Wilson's failure at Versailles, like the tragedy of reformers' failure to reach their goals in domestic politics, does not demonstrate the folly of these theorists' efforts or invalidate their ideals. They realized immediately that the treaty betrayed their principles, and they denounced the Versailles accords as the prelude to another war. Bourgeois, who had worked so diligently for the cause of international arbitration, understood that the peace would not survive without an army to enforce it. Given his misgivings about the league as it took shape, and his fears about its impotence, there was a bittersweet quality to his acceptance of the Nobel Prize in 1920 for his efforts to construct an institution whose actual form deeply disappointed him. Hobhouse complained that the treaty was a futile gesture, "just a formal bond" pledging the victors to maintain, and the defeated to endure, an arrangement that was "intrinsically unjustifiable." Dewey was equally critical: "When the war aims were gained," he wrote, "the peace aims were lost." Lippmann spoke for all of these radicals when he confessed, in a letter to Ray Stannard Baker, "For the life of me I can't see peace in this document." *The New Republic* put the point more bluntly: "The Treaty of Versailles is impossible of execution and will defeat itself."[43]

Critics of these progressives' support of the war, like critics of their support of domestic reforms, often misinterpret the nature of that support because they lose sight of its critical edge. In Croly's first editorial on the war, he emphasized the importance of the conflict for the United States and outlined the nation's options. If the treaty at the war's conclusion "is one which makes for international stability and justice, this country will have an interest in maintaining it. If the treaty is one which makes militarism even more ominously threatening, this country will have an interest in seeking a better substitute." That was the position of *The New Republic* throughout the war, and the editors backed Wilson precisely because of the settlement he aimed to secure. That was also their position in 1919, and the reasons for these Americans' opposition to the treaty were fully consistent with their reasons for supporting America's participation in the war. Like many other crusades during these years, the crusade for a just peace failed. But that does not mean that it was from the start an imperialist venture, nor that its failure was inevitable, nor that intellectuals were naive for supporting a president who was only tilting at windmills. "The ideals of the United States have been defeated in the settlement," Dewey wrote, not because the ideal of peace without victory was unworthy or flawed, but "because we took into the war our sentimentalism, our attachment to moral sentiments as efficacious powers, our pious optimism as to the inevitable victory of the 'right,' our childish belief that physical energy can do the work that only intelligence can do, our evangelical hypocrisy that morals and 'ideals' have a self-propelling and self-executing capacity."[44] Inasmuch as Croly, Lippmann, and Dewey assumed that ends could be achieved without attention to means, they betrayed their own philosophical pragmatism; their failure, in short, lay not with their ideals or their methods but with their inability to live up to them in political action.

Finally, the defeat was not really theirs, because the decisions at Versailles were not theirs to make. But if they expected that their support of the war ensured the success of their values at its conclusion, then they were, in Weber's phrase, only political children, because they remained innocent of how often evil follows from good in politics. They were so deeply demoralized after the war because they had allowed their enthusiasm to soar so high before the peace. The problem was not their pragmatism; it was instead their neglect of the argument that was the essence of their pragmatism: ideals without the will and the intelligence to secure them are useless. Even so, Versailles was difficult for them to swallow. It effectively ended the careers of Croly and Hobhouse as creative progressive theorists, pushing them over the edge of radical empiricism and off toward fuzzy versions of mysticism and metaphysics.[45] Although the turn of events at the war's end crushed these progressives' hopes, it ironically confirmed their pragmatic conception of the relation between ideas and activity. It illustrated why the reform of political machinery, whether domestic or international, must be considered only a springboard to further, more far-reaching, cultural changes. In the absence of those changes, the promise of liberation contained in the welfare state rang hollow, and the ideal of international peace turned to dust in the hands of vengeful statesmen.

2. Progressive Education

The theorists of progressivism were realists. They understood that tinkering with political institutions would not accomplish the radical cultural transformation they sought. Like the philosophers of the *via media*, they stressed the importance of education in social change. Only if changes in values accompany political, economic, and social reforms can such reforms be more than cosmetic. But these progressives also saw the need for an efficient corps of administrators to run the more active state they considered necessary. Unfortunately, there was at least a potential contradiction between a well-educated, politically active citizenry and a well-educated, politically active bureaucracy; radical liberals disagreed about how, and even whether, that conflict could be resolved. It is on this question that the differences between Weber and the other progressive theorists become decisive, and the gap separating his arguments from theirs has stretched forward into contemporary discussions of democratic education and bureaucratic government.

The need for education became more pressing, these thinkers reasoned, as political life became more democratic and social life more interdependent. No conscious effort on the part of individuals, Dewey wrote, but instead the blind working of economic processes, widened "the area of shared concerns" throughout the eighteenth and nineteenth centuries. To sustain and extend the resulting opportunities for "greater individualization," on the one hand, and a "broader community of interest," on the other, would require a "radical change in education." The fact of interdependence undercut the liberal ideal of individualism, but sheltering a core of personal integrity from the intrusions of the community, and coaxing reluctant individualists to accept their share of the social burden, challenged the resources of educational systems more attuned to freedom than to responsibility. Dewey conceived of education as the centerpiece of democratic life throughout his career. This particular formulation of his argument appeared in *Democracy and Education* (1916), a book on educational theory that he described, appropriately, as "the closest attempt I have made to sum up my entire philosophical position."[46] Dewey's instrumentalism did culminate logically in his philosophy of education, which was the most carefully conceived, and certainly the most influential, of these progressives' writings about educational issues.

Dewey first articulated his unconventional ideas about education in lectures he delivered at the University of Michigan in 1892, which he encapsulated five years later in an essay entitled "My Pedagogic Creed." "I believe that education is the fundamental method of social progress and reform," Dewey contended categorically. "I believe that all reforms which rest simply upon changes in mechanical or outward arrangements, are transitory and futile." Cultural change can occur only through the cultivation of "social consciousness," which requires that education take a trip along the *via media*. In his educational writings, as in his philosophy and politics, Dewey sounded the theme of convergence. His conception of education, he pointed out, relied on "both the individualistic and socialistic ideals. It is duly individual because it recognizes the formation of a certain character as the only genuine basis of right living." In other words, individuals can fortify their personalities for lives of virtue only by freely choosing to fulfill their responsibilities. "It is socialistic because it recognizes this right character is not to be formed by merely individual precept, example, or exhortation, but rather by the influence of a certain form of institutional or community life upon the individual." The content of ethics, then, is shaped by culture, but it is up to individuals to adopt and advance those values. "The community's duty to education," Dewey concluded, "is, therefore, its paramount moral duty."[47]

What Dewey meant by progressive education has been so distorted by generations of well-meaning but ill-equipped educational administrators that its original significance has been almost entirely lost. As he explained in *School and Society*, an apparently simple book that has long been misunderstood, his idea of the "child-centered school" involved anything but catering to the whims of children. Discipline was at the heart of Dewey's vision of fostering intelligence, but it was a radically different sort of discipline. Instead of passing information to mute pupils, he instructed teachers to engage children's native enthusiasm by connecting learning to life. Before the urban and industrial revolutions flattened children's experience at home, Dewey wrote, every day raised a multitude of questions about man's relation to nature and the individual's relation to those around him, questions that grew from children's experiences and could often be answered by their own independent investigations and encounters. Educators outside that environment confront new challenges. Since industry removes work from the home and makes man an appendage of his machines, it is more difficult to encourage children to develop the imagination and intelligence earlier generations saw in use all around them daily. The goal of education, then, must be to assist children in exercising their natural capacities by placing them in situations where their minds are put to work, not filled with data. This requires the complete reconstruction of the curriculum and the method of instruction. In a memorable passage, Dewey explained the problem with existing schools and the solution he envisioned:

The child comes to the traditional school with a healthy body and a more or less unwilling mind, though, in fact, he does not bring both his body and mind with him; he has to leave his mind behind, because there is no way to use it in the school. If he had a purely abstract mind, he could bring it to school with him, but his is a concrete one, interested in concrete things, and unless these things get over in school life he cannot take his mind with him. What we want is to have the child come to school with a whole mind and a whole body, and leave school with a fuller mind and an even healthier body.[48]

This conception of education was firmly rooted in Dewey's radical theory of knowledge. Thinking, conceived in this way, does not occur in a vacuum, or in Descartes's stove. It arises, as Dewey put the point in *School and Society*, "from the need of meeting some difficulty, in reflecting upon the best way of overcoming it, and thus leads to planning, to projecting mentally the result to be reached, and deciding upon the steps necessary and their serial order." This experience of problem solving, this "concrete logic of action," comes well before the sort of logic required for "pure speculation or abstract investigation," and it provides the best means of developing the mental habits necessary for conceptual thought. In *Democracy and Education*, Dewey offered a rather more technical definition of education: "It is that reconstruction or reorganization of experience which adds to the meaning of experience, and which increases ability to direct the course of subsequent experience." Although it is difficult to sift the meaning from that formulation without shaking the words, embedded within the idealist jargon of Hegel and Green is an idea with revolutionary implications. The teacher's goal, Dewey believed, is not to train students to perform familiar tasks in time-honored ways, but to help them learn to solve unanticipated problems with imagination, not to impart bodies of knowledge but to develop the capacity to think.

Dewey's own woolly style is at least partly responsible for the distortions of his meaning by self-styled progressive educators. He expressed himself, as Oliver Wendell Holmes, Jr., put it, much as "God would have spoken had He been inarticulate but keenly desirous to tell you how it was."[49] Nevertheless, hidden in the thickets of his prose was an emphasis on developing the most difficult of all abilities to acquire, the ability to reason independently, without the assistance of inherited methods or the reassurance of knowing that a correct answer always exists. The discipline of thinking, as Dewey understood it, places enormous demands on teachers and students, because it requires exercising the radical intellectual freedom entailed by pragmatic philosophy.

Croly and Lippmann both endorsed Dewey's pedagogic creed. In *A Preface to Politics*, Lippmann asserted that the real work of politics "lies deeper than parties and legislatures," because it requires the reorientation of culture that is possible only through education. In *Drift and Mastery*, he scoffed at the folly of attempting to find political solutions to complicated and unfamiliar social problems. Reform is "necessarily an educational process," he insisted, because it demands the long-term, intelligent engagement of the mass of citizens rather than the pulling of a few switches and levers by politicians. Lippmann's own adventures in the world of politics had come to grief for precisely this reason: the failure of the socialist administration in Schenectady taught him "a sharp object lesson in what always results when we turn from education to politics, when we seek to win votes rather than to make converts." Education, as Lippmann understood it, may begin in school, but it must continue through citizenship. Without it, reform is doomed.[50]

In *The Promise of American Life*, Croly was even more emphatic about education, describing it as the focal point of progress. "The real vehicle of improvement" in a democracy, he insisted, is neither political organization nor institutional change. "It is by education that the American is trained for such democracy as he possesses; and it is by better education that he proposes to better his democracy." Consistent with the other indications of the influence Dewey exerted on Croly's *Progressive Democracy*, this later book also demonstrates clearly that Croly had come to share Dewey's vision of what would constitute such an education. He presented educational reform as the necessary precondition of other reforms: "Once this underlying condition is fully and candidly accepted, then a fair chance exists of uniting disinterested and aspiring people upon a practicable method of accomplishing the purpose" of radical change. In his conclusion, Croly endorsed the counsel of "the wisest of modern educators," viz. Dewey, who taught that "'the only way to prepare for social life is to engage in social life,'" first in school and then as an active citizen.[51]

Bourgeois's treatment of education was similar to the Americans' approach. "The goal of education is to create social beings," he wrote in *Solidarity*; like Croly, he judged that reorientation of attitudes prerequisite to effective reforms. "The law can intervene only to facilitate, not to impose" the spirit of association from which social solidarity can develop. The reformer must devote his primary attention to education rather than law, for only education can "elevate men to the notion of social debt," the central idea of solidarist politics. Individuals must realize that "every act of mutuality and solidarity is an act of higher morality," an act of freedom conceived in the context of social responsibility and reciprocal justice.[52]

Critics have argued that these progressives' conception of education as a seedbed of radical political sensibilities led in practice to a deeply conservative kind of education, education as hegemonic social control. The problem, according to this analysis, was the introduction of policy issues, which have no business in education, into the school. It is certainly true that education has frequently been used for that purpose, but these theorists did not believe that a certain set of reform measures ought to be proselytized in classrooms. Instead they sought to instill in individuals an awareness that because experience itself is social, the standard, individualist conception of citizenship is flawed. They believed that the awareness of interdependence might prompt individuals to recognize their social responsibilities, and they believed that the awareness of uncertainty might engender a critical attitude toward authority. Without aiming for a form of education as political indoctrination, they were confident that a fertile variety of political action would spring from that new way of thinking. Croly concluded *Progressive Democracy* by repudiating the idea of education preached by "social conservators," who try to convince the individual that he must restrain himself and abide by the rules established in his interests by a governing minority. Progressive theory, by contrast, demands that the people be freed from external restraints and expects that they will then freely choose to be responsible. If they do not, democracy cannot succeed. Whereas conservatives view education as a means of coaxing people to accept injustice stoically, Croly insisted, early Christianity and modern psychology both urge the liberation of creative individuality.[53]

There is nothing intrinsically reactionary about education for citizenship, so long as the conception of citizenship is democratic, open-ended, and centered on the dual ideas of voluntary action and community responsibility. The presence of those two ideas at the heart of progressive thinking distinguished these intellectuals' conception of education—and their political ideals, as I will argue in Chapter Ten—from conservatism. These social liberals focused on community, but they believed that community must be the product of autonomous individuals' interaction. Societies develop historically and do not spring from an actual or hypothetical social contract; they derive their legitimacy neither from tradition nor from a transcendental historical purpose. Social integration must be understood to flow from the free development of individuality in the direction of benevolence. It cannot be imposed from above. It must develop, in other words, from the democratic ethos of the citizenry. If progressive educational theory had a weakness, it was not its susceptibility to manipulation by conservatives for the purpose of social control. No ideas can resist perversion by resourceful minds. The problem instead had to do with logical circularity and with the shape of modern values.

The first problem was simple but fundamental: the new ideas to be instilled through education, and the institutional changes to be accomplished by this new way of thinking, both seemed to presuppose each other. For education inevitably involves institutions as well as the ideas to be communicated, and unshackling students from a false individualism and a false subservience to authority must therefore await the unshackling of their teachers. This difficulty, of course, is perennial. If the problems facing society can be traced to its individualism, as these thinkers believed, and reform must proceed by means of education, how can reformers get around the awkward fact that the educational system is imbued with precisely the values they have isolated as the source of the problem? As if to answer such criticism, Croly suggested that America should establish a "National School of Political Science," which would train public servants to spread to the public "sound progressive ideas and authentic information in relation to living political problems." Perhaps inspired by Dewey's success at the University of Chicago, Croly proposed to fund such a school by relying on a most unlikely deus ex machina, a Rockefeller-like foundation. But rather than resolving the problem, he merely removed it to a different level. The existence of such a national school, imparting to students "sound ideas" about politics, would require as a precondition the conversion it was designed to effect. If Americans could agree about the political ideas to be taught in such an institute, the desired change in thinking would already have occurred. Dewey admitted the difficulty: "The exercise and training requisite to form the habits which make the individual rejoice in right activity before he knows how and why it is right, presupposes adults who already have knowledge of the good. They presuppose a social order capable not merely of giving theoretic instruction, but of habituating the young to right processes."[54] Dewey wrestled with this problem throughout his career, but he never solved it.

Social democrats were also enamored of the idea of a national academy to train public servants. While Croly was trying to find a donor for his dream, the Webbs received a gift sufficiently large to enable them to establish the London School of Economics. The original purpose of the LSE was similar to that of Croly's "National School," but its permanence was secured only when it exchanged its radical character to become part of the University of London. Solidarists established the Ecole des Hautes Etudes Sociales in order to teach the principles of social solidarity, and the school sponsored several of the most important congresses on the social and political applications of solidarist principles.[55] Ely suggested in *Socialism and Social Reform* that the American government "should have a civil academy, surpassing in equipment the military and naval academies by as much as civil administration is more important than the army and navy, in a country devoted to the arts of peace." During his first years in Wisconsin, Ely tried to make the state university serve that purpose, but he failed for reasons that illustrate the problems involved in relying on educational institutions to accomplish the radical reorientation of social values. As recent analyses have demonstrated, attempts to use universities as instruments of social reform were frustrated by the wave of professionalization in higher education during the late nineteenth and early twentieth centuries, a process that compounded the already considerable problems confronting progressive and social democratic efforts to alter political thinking.[56]

In the midst of World War I, Croly at last had a chance to try his hand at education. A group of intellectuals who shared his dissatisfaction with the condition of American universities, which were increasingly dominated by games and clubs and increasingly distant from the ideals of liberal or progressive education, met in the offices of *The New Republic* to organize an alternative institution. They took as their models the Webbs' LSE and the Ecole Libre des Sciences Politiques in Paris. While they seemed unaware of it, the distance between the Fabians' radical concerns and the emphasis of the French on training elite administrators would quickly be mirrored in the different images its founders had of the New School for Social Research, which opened its doors in the fall of 1919. Joining Croly in this enterprise were many distinguished educators, including not only Dewey but Charles Beard, James Harvey Robinson, Alvin Johnson, and Wesley C. Mitchell. They agreed that the school should be governed by its teachers, and that there should be no entrance requirements, no degrees, no departments, and no football. But there agreement ended. One faction believed the New School should concentrate on providing informal adult education. The other, which included Croly, wanted something more ambitious. Croly expected the New School to "make social research of immediate assistance to a bewildered and groping American democracy" by training its students to serve as experts in labor relations and other social and political problems. "Thus a school of social science becomes above everything else an instrumentality both of social purpose and of social research."[57]

Despite its founders' imperfectly reconciled visions of the school's purpose, its beginning was certainly auspicious. Its faculty included, in addition to those already mentioned, such luminaries as Thorstein Veblen and Horace Kallen; among those who agreed to give lecture courses were Graham Wallas, Harold Laski, and Roscoe Pound. The appearance of stability, however, was deceptive. Almost immediately, the New School was rocked by outside critics and internal dissension. *The National Civic Federation Review* spoke for conservative opinion when it referred ominously to the dangerous, semiseditious dissenters who organized the institution. Some had been dismissed from universities for their opposition to the war; others had resigned to protest those dismissals. In short, critics charged, this was an attempt, in the apparently harmless guise of a school, to convert pro-German war propaganda into "another yet no less definite and inimical form, the propaganda of social discontent, revolution, and civil strife." Serious as such criticism was at a time when Hun-baiting was still more popular than Red-baiting, even more dangerous to the health of the New School was the bickering among its founders concerning its purpose and its future. Finally, after failing to shift the school's focus emphatically toward labor research, and frustrated by the continuing disagreements about its social role, Croly resigned. It would be difficult to find, or even to imagine, a clearer illustration of the predicament facing progressives interested in achieving reform through education. Impoverished by its inability to convince potential donors it was not too dangerous, the New School was abandoned by some of its most important supporters because it was too safe. Caught in a vicious circle, it escaped only when Alvin Johnson transformed it during the 1920s into a solid but relatively harmless center for adult education.[58]

These progressives' hopes for education faced another, equally serious problem, rooted in the same set of historical developments that made necessary the reforms they sought. No one saw this problem more clearly than Weber. Education, in his words, always provides "the most important opening for the impact of domination upon culture," and the sort of domination emerging in the twentieth century would be different from traditional forms but no less deadly in its effect on independent thinking. For professionalization, which was integral to the process of rationalization overtaking European and American societies, directly threatened the idea of progressive education. Weber pointed out that the bureaucratization of capitalism increases the need for experts. Both the logic of expertise and the actual system of selection it engenders, however, run counter to democratic principles. "Behind all the present discussions about the basic questions of the educational system," Weber warned, "there lurks decisively the struggle of the 'specialist' type of man against the older type of 'cultivated man,' a struggle conditioned by the irresistible bureaucratization of all public and private relations of authority and by the ever-increasing importance of experts and specialized knowledge." When Weber defended *Kultur* against *Zivilisation*, this was the contrast he had in mind. Progressive efforts to educate cultivated citizens would run aground on the socioeconomic imperatives leading schools and universities to train specialized experts. Unlike earlier forms of education emphasizing the creation of new souls or fully integrated ways of thinking, modern industrial societies seek "simply to *train* the pupil for practical usefulness for administrative purposes."[59] Thus progressives, in their attempt to reorient their societies' values through educational reform, were challenging not only the prevailing political conservatism of school systems but also the fundamental logic of modernity.

Although Weber recognized the obstacles preventing education from providing a path to social reconstruction, he did not despair of the contribution educators could make. In his lecture "Science as a Vocation," he argued that teachers who help students learn to think clearly perform a moral service. Disgusted by those who used their authority as professors to vent their political opinions, Weber emphatically denied that the teacher's role extends beyond the presentation of options to the recommendation of the values students should adopt. The most a teacher can do, he declared, is to "force the individual, or at least to help him, to give himself an *account of the ultimate meaning of his own conduct.*" This is no trifling matter. "I am tempted to say of a teacher who succeeds in this: he stands in the service of 'moral' forces; he fulfills the duty of bringing about self-clarification and a sense of responsibility." Among the primary goals of teaching, according to Weber, is to make students aware of what he called "'inconvenient' facts," facts that do not fit neatly into their political worldviews.[60] Like the other theorists of progressivism, he believed that education ought to concentrate on instilling habits of critical inquiry rather than particular ideas or ideologies.

I think Weber realized that the combination of autonomy and responsibility he considered part of such an independent intelligence itself constitutes a kind of ideology. But it is an ideology more methodological than substantive in nature, and therein lay a problem that would become evident in the political ideals of progressivism. If Weber shared the other progressives' view that the clarification of ideas through education might contribute to an informed and thoughtful selection of convictions, he was far less confident about the outcome of such education. His pessimism was rooted not in different political values but in a different assessment of the likelihood of realizing those values. Standing in their way he saw the professionalization and bureaucratization of modern life.

3. Bureaucracy versus Democracy

Weber postulated a contradiction between the principle of democracy and the necessity of bureaucracy. Democracy and bureaucracy grew together historically, for the extension of democratic government made necessary the creation of new administrative forms unlike those appropriate to more autocratic schemes. Eventually, however, the rationalized legal procedures that are the essence of bureaucracy created islands of autonomous power distant from democratic control. To use Weber's terminology, the formal rationality of administration collided with the substantive rationality of popular government. Democracy is designed to reflect the shifting moods of the public; bureaucracy is designed to provide continuity by establishing legal rather than personal norms. Whereas democracy changes constantly, bureaucracy resists change. Following its own technical logic, bureaucracy inherently becomes independent of control by the economy or the polity. Weber considered this tension between democracy and bureaucracy the central fact of modern government.[61]

Although the other theorists of progressivism acknowledged this problem, they considered it manageable. Bourgeois treated the question almost casually. Like most republicans in France, including Jaurès and more radical socialists, he identified the state as at least a potential source of repression, and he advocated only limited growth in the size and strength of the machinery of government. But he assumed that the people could retain control of the state so long as it remained republican. It may be that economic and political power was in fact less consolidated in France than in Germany, Britain, or the United States during these years, and the failure of Jaurès and Bourgeois to confront the problem of reconciling democracy with bureaucracy reflects that difference.[62] To British and American progressives, this question was of central importance.

Hobhouse's misgivings about the Webbs' ambiguous attitude toward elite administrators drove a wedge between him and the Fabians. In his early writings, Hobhouse expressed his sympathy with Fabianism, but during the 1890s he and other British radicals were alienated by what they perceived as the Webbs' antidemocratic tendencies. His consistent advocacy of democratic government, and the consequent shifts back and forth in his attitude toward the Fabians as their democratic enthusiasm waxed and waned, can be followed by comparing his successive treatments of this issue. In *The Labour Movement* (1893), he aligned himself with the Fabians and endorsed their democratic idea of socialism. By 1900 he had soured on the Webbs, and he commented sadly on "the wrecked Ideal of the Socialism of the 'eighties.'" In *Democracy and Reaction* (1907), Hobhouse admitted that democracy is an imperfect tool for fashioning utopia, but he judged self-government more important than efficiency. Social change requires moral fervor more than administrative skill, and it is the essence of the democratic gamble to risk the achievement of justice on the shifting desires of the people. A year later in the

Nation, he directed his criticism specifically against the Fabians. Betraying the democratic principle, "Mr. Webb and his associates" had shifted their loyalties to the notion of "a highly centralised machine, so delicately specialised in structure and so intricate and secret in working as to be incapable of any real control on the part of the electorate."

This uneasiness about the Webbs' elitism manifested itself in British progressives' criticism of the Webbs' Minority Report. Although Hobhouse admitted his preference for the Minority's approach over the Majority's continued reliance on the philosophy animating the Poor Laws, he remained skeptical about the amount of independence the Webbs planned to allow administrators in their insurance scheme. Hobhouse preferred tying the system directly to local government representatives, who would have to answer to the electorate. In *Liberalism* (1911), he complained of the Fabians' "contempt for average humanity in general," and he distinguished his own preferences from their reliance on "a class of the elect." He insisted that "liberal socialism . . . must be democratic," and "it must make its account with the human individual."[63] To fulfill those two rather fuzzy conditions, socialism must be anti-authoritarian. In that connection, Hobhouse stressed the importance of vigorous local government, which was, paradoxically, also the Webbs' primary concern. Echoing Tocqueville, Hobhouse contended that democracy depends on the decentralization of public authority, "at present crushed in this country by a centralized democracy." Hobhouse's criticism illustrates clearly the disagreements between new liberals and Fabians on the question of bureaucracy. I have already indicated why I consider the portrait of the Webbs as elitists something of a simplification. Unlike some Fabians, notably Shaw, they appreciated—albeit inconsistently—the necessity of limiting the authority of administrators, whose importance they certainly emphasized, through public control. They believed such experts could exert power and remain responsible to the public; Hobhouse insisted on formal public control to ensure that responsibility.

During the course of his career, Lippmann's hopes and fears seem to have shifted in the opposite direction from Hobhouse's. He became increasingly suspicious of democratic decision making, as his celebrated *Public Opinion* (1922) made clear. But in his early writings he displayed a strong, if idiosyncratic, commitment to democracy. In *A Preface to Politics*, he expressed his horror at the "dreadful amount of forcible scrubbing and arranging and pocketing" involved in the idea of government by experts. He reiterated that concern in *Drift and Mastery*, in which he tied the bureaucratized state to the utopian tradition running from Plato through More to William Morris and Edward Bellamy. "A real man would regard this ideal life as an unmitigated tyranny," Lippmann maintained, for "there is no democracy in utopia." He discerned a similar mistrust of popular government in state socialist schemes, which would impose benevolent government on a resisting humanity in order to "make men clean, sober, and civil-minded."[64] Lippmann endorsed Oscar Wilde's dictum that no map of the world is worthwhile without utopia on it, but he feared many reformers reserved too large a space on their maps for the bureaucrat.

The analysis of bureaucracy was one of the principal themes of Croly's *Progressive Democracy*. In *The Promise of American Life*, his juxtaposition of the Hamiltonian and Jeffersonian conceptions of the national government prompted him to emphasize the positive contribution of talented administrators, but in his later book he stressed the necessity of democratic decision making. He took issue with the "many sincere social democrats in this country, as well as in England or France, [who] regard any such dependence upon direct government with the utmost repugnance." Like Hobhouse, he contrasted their emphasis on efficiency with his own concern for popular control. He conceded that "in the near future direct popular government will increase the difficulty of securing the adoption of many items in a desirable social program," but he considered that the price of democracy. Reformers who emphasized results more than methods were "willing to have the people imposed upon in the interest of what is or is intended to be the popular benefit." Croly prized social harmony as much as the advocates of elite administration did, but he was even more firmly committed to popular government. In a crucial passage, he counseled social reformers to "be patient as well as eager and tenacious." It is necessary to wait for the people to decide, for democracy means "that social reformers must present their arguments primarily to the electorate, and welcome every good opportunity of allowing the electorate to pass judgment upon their proposals."[65] This argument, which seemed to pour cold water on the most avid activists' enthusiasm, was consistent with Croly's ideas about education. He believed there can be no short cuts in democratic change; administrative solutions cannot substitute for democratic decisions.

The commitment of Dewey, Lippmann, and Croly to democracy seems clear enough, yet it also seems inconsistent with their endorsement of regulatory agencies as a means of achieving at least some of their goals. Since regulation has proved to be neither effective nor responsive to democratic pressures, these thinkers' support of such administrative solutions has been criticized as antidemocratic. While such criticism again confuses the reasons for supporting reforms with the results reforms achieve, this question does suggest one of the paradoxes of progressive theory. If progressives distrusted bureaucrats and trusted the public, why did they agree to give regulatory commissions, by design independent of the electoral process, so much power?

The answer lies in their conception of science. Many American progressives agreed with Lippmann's argument in *Drift and Mastery* that the scientific method is uniquely attractive because it employs pragmatic principles of verification. "The discipline of science is the only one which gives any assurance that from the same set of facts men will come approximately to the same conclusion." Like pragmatism, science relies on the testing of hypotheses to establish truth. Both scientists and pragmatists, in Lippmann's phrase, "live forward," because they "read life not as something given but as something to be shaped." If science provides a model of pragmatic thinking, then that model should be applied to political problems as well. Perhaps the crucial link in these progressives' argument concerned their equation of science with democracy. "Democracy is possible only because of a change in intellectual conditions," Dewey wrote in 1899. Democracy "implies tools for getting at truth in detail, and day by day, as we go along." In short, he concluded, democracy "means an alignment with science."[66]

Just as scientists must collectively distinguish between true and false hypotheses, so societies must distinguish between true and false ideas. Not every democratic impulse is true, at least not in the pragmatic sense. It may be the genuine expression of public sentiment, but it may not "work" to the advantage of the society as a whole. It must be tested; its results must be examined. It was that process of critical analysis and intelligent evaluation, not merely the notion of popular participation, that appealed to these progressives. As students of democracy have realized at least since Plato, the popular will can as easily be unjust as just. There must be some way to keep the public sensibility from spinning down toward the despotism Tocqueville feared might be the destiny of an industrialized mass society. Progressive theorists believed they could find that gyroscope in science, because the ideal of intersubjectivity, balanced by the historical sensibility, offered them a way to extend pragmatic thinking from a few individuals to the culture as a whole. Their commitment to democracy was not naive. They did not affirm the unerring genius of the popular will, because they had too many occasions to observe the popular will in action. They were worried that virtue, which Montesquieu correctly identified as the principle of a republic, could no longer be nourished by the lively local institutions that characterized the early American nation. Only widespread popular participation could sustain democratic government, and as authority shifted upward and receded from view, political activity diminished and individuals' consciousness of their responsibilities as citizens faded. Without the virtue that democratic citizenship requires, these progressives argued, democratic government becomes simply an institutionalized scramble for private advantage through public legitimation.

The equation of democracy with science helps to explain the attractiveness of regulatory agencies, which these thinkers envisioned as the political arm of science. Using the techniques of scientific analysis, administrators would report to the people through their representatives, who would evaluate all the available options and then instruct the bureaucracy to execute the public will. The question, though, is whether such expertise, by shaping the alternatives to be discussed, slides imperceptibly but necessarily into control. Neither Croly, Lippmann, nor Dewey adequately answered that question. Croly's *Progressive Democracy* best illustrates their confusion on this issue. As I have noted, he criticized American and European reformers who relied heavily on bureaucrats. He described in detail the tendency of elites to insulate themselves from democratic control. Yet when he turned to the subject of regulatory agencies, he argued that they represent the application of scientific techniques to politics and thus constitute a step toward progressive democracy.

The resolution of this paradox lies in Croly's analysis of popular sovereignty as the defining feature of American as opposed to European politics. Bureaucracy is a threat where national unity is a product of centralized authority; in those circumstances the role of administration in government is accentuated. The reliance on bureaucracy then leads to the arbitrary exercise of power, because excesses are "sanctioned by the ominous rule that the safety of the state constituted the Supreme law." The kind of bureaucratic power Americans quite properly feared "was the product of an essentially coercive conception of sovereignty." Despite his criticism of bureaucratic government, Croly was confident things could be different in the United States. American regulatory agencies were to be subservient to the legislative branch of the government. For that reason they would not represent a threat to democratic control, but would merely facilitate the testing of various policies to determine how the common good might best be advanced. Of course regulatory agencies historically have often served a very different purpose: protecting private power while claiming to defend the public interest.[67]

Weber considered this outcome inevitable. In *Economy and Society*, he argued that the involvement of government in private enterprise would result not in the greater control of capital by the state, but in the greater control by capital of the state. The "expert knowledge of private interest groups in the field of 'business' is superior to the knowledge of the bureaucracy. This is so because the exact knowledge of facts in their field is of direct significance for economic survival." Thus government investigators are necessarily at a disadvantage in dealing with private power, and they are bound to fail. "Authorities are held within narrow boundaries when they seek to influence economic life in the capitalist epoch, and very frequently their measures take an unforeseen and unintended course or are made illusory by the superior expert knowledge of the interested groups."[68] American progressives had confidence in regulation because they believed that its informality would enable government investigators to be flexible and to become as sophisticated in their understanding of industry as the officials of the businesses they were to regulate. As a direct result of that informality, however, regulatory agencies have been unable to make law. Their flexibility has proved detrimental to their effectiveness, because it has translated into an unwillingness or inability to establish the general norms and formal procedures that are required for effective government. American progressives considered the regulatory agency a special case, an application of science to government, a unique kind of bureaucracy that did not threaten popular government. That perception was accurate: regulatory agencies have not threatened the public order. But neither have they threatened private power. As Weber realized, to the extent that a bureaucracy is effective it tends to insulate itself from outside control and to subvert the democratic process. The progressives' experiment in democratically controlled bureaucracy suggests that the converse of that principle is equally true.

Weber believed that the system of organized capitalism could lurch along toward a condition of somewhat greater justice and political vitality only if an equally formidable labor movement were counterposed to the power of capital. The state could offer no more than the enforcement of ground rules governing this necessary struggle. For precisely this reason, Weber shared Lujo Brentano's aversion to the policies advocated by the senior members of the Verein für Sozialpolitik. Unlike the historical economists of this older generation, who looked to the state for paternalist resolutions of the conflicts between private enterprise and trade unions, Weber believed that state socialism would merely deepen the sleep of German political culture. As he insisted in his Freiburg Inaugural, Germany could never advance from its subservience to the reign of officials unless the people somehow received the sort of political education most modern nations achieved through successful bourgeois revolutions. Whereas many American and British social democrats and progressives wanted the state to serve as an arbiter in the economic arena, Weber recommended the more limited role of referee. Government should neither enter the competition nor try to end it, because once government presumes to settle such matters, it either rises to assume the dominant role in society, as it did in Bismarck's Germany, or it falls into subservience to the most powerful forces in the economy.[69]

Dewey, Croly, and Lippmann were themselves skeptical of government by expert. They appreciated the need for sophisticated knowledge in modern government, but they insisted that investigators should only advise and that the people, through their representatives or through initiatives and referenda, should make policy decisions. They agreed that science cannot, and must not presume to, make value judgments. The difference between the Americans and Weber lay in the Americans' greater confidence that officials, properly restrained by law, could be made to serve the public interest. By contrast, Weber argued that bureaucrats represent a special interest themselves, and that bureaucracy thus does not serve but rather undermines democratic government. Instead of riding herd over special interests on behalf of the people, bureaucrats advance their own interest, which may or may not coincide with that of the democracy. According to Weber, "Bureaucratic administration always tends to exclude the public, to hide its knowledge and action from criticism as well as it can."[70]

Because he linked bureaucratization with the larger process of rationalization, Weber doubted that the power of bureaucracy could be controlled. The demands of an interdependent economy and society led inevitably toward greater reliance on specialized knowledge. Because the world has been disenchanted, "one need no longer have recourse to magical means in order to master or implore the spirits. . . . Technical means and calculations perform the service."[71] One of the larger ironies of this period, as the difference between Weber and the American progressive theorists illustrates, concerns the contrast between the liberating effect of the radical theory of knowledge, which frees man from dogma and emphasizes experience and volition, and the process of bureaucratization, which, by using the techniques of science, tends to usurp power from the individuals whose liberation, both intellectual and political, these theorists sought to secure. In a sense, then, their ideas about knowledge and action both entailed, and were challenged by, their ideas about reform. They focused on individual experience, validated socially by the pragmatic method, as the source of knowledge, but the generalized form of that knowledge, bureaucratic administration operating on scientific principles, undercut the people's ability to govern themselves.

His interpreters have never been able to agree about Weber's own attitude toward the contradiction he perceived between bureaucracy and democracy. It is clear he doubted it could be resolved; it is less clear he thought it should be. A number of his critics have argued that he conflated the instrumental rationality of modern bureaucracies with substantive rationality. According to this view, democracy as Weber conceived of it not only cannot effectively block bureaucratic decision making, it also lacks any basis for making the attempt. I consider that argument a mistake for several reasons. First, it overlooks Weber's fundamental values of autonomy and responsibility, values that show up in his essays and lectures even though they are often submerged in his political sociology. Second, it neglects the distinction Weber drew in "Politics as a Vocation" between the politician who lives for politics and the official who lives off politics. Weber unambiguously endorsed the independence that comes with the politician's commitment to acting responsibly, in accordance with his convictions, over the bureaucrat's willingness merely to carry out orders. Finally, although he chose to play Daedalus to Dewey's Icarus, Weber did consider himself a partisan of the democratic values that appeared from his descriptions of modern politics to be in such peril.[72]

Weber passionately affirmed the importance of struggling against the thrust of history for the values of popular government and personal liberty. "It would be extremely harmful to the chances of 'democracy' and 'individualism' today, if we were to rely for their 'development' on the 'lawlike' operation of *material* interests," he argued in opposition to orthodox Marxists. For those interests are pointing history in the opposite direction, toward industrial America's "benevolent feudalism" or toward Germany's "so-called 'welfare institutions,'" both of which in their separate ways threaten individual autonomy. "Everywhere," Weber wrote ominously, "*the casing of the new serfdom* is ready." Merely the continuation of economic, social, and political processes already in motion would end in that enslavement. Weber scoffed at those who feared that democracy would threaten social stability: "All too much care has been taken to make sure that the trees of democratic individualism do not grow to the skies. All our experience suggests that 'history' continues inexorably to bring forth new 'aristocracies' and 'authorities' to which anyone who finds it necessary for himself—or for the 'people'—can cling." For those, including some progressives, who optimistically predicted that social evolution would end oppression, Weber had little sympathy. He found it "utterly ridiculous" to suppose that "present-day advanced capitalism . . . should have an elective affinity with 'democracy' or indeed with 'freedom' (in *any* sense of that word), when the only question to be asked is: how are all these things, in general and in the long term, *possible* where it prevails?" Those of Weber's contemporaries who looked forward to the triumph of organization and the more efficient management of the masses by elites—and there were many who applauded that prospect—did not speak with such anguish about the emergence of organized capitalism.

Weber expected the pressures threatening individuality to intensify, but he considered resistance possible. The further "parcelling out of the soul," to recall his poignant description of the consequences of disenchantment, could be halted only by "the resolute *will* of a nation not to allow itself to be led like a flock of sheep. We 'individualists' and supporters of 'democratic' institutions are swimming 'against the steam' of material developments. Anyone who wishes to be the weather-vane of 'developmental trends' might as well abandon these outdated ideals as quickly as possible."[73] Weber himself, however, emphatically refused to abandon the ideals of individuality and democracy, despite their slim chances of survival in the face of rationalization. It is possible to distinguish his heroic pessimism from the antidemocratic cynicism with which it has too often been confused only if his allegiance to these ideas is appreciated. As a scholar he felt obliged to identify the unique constellation of economic, social, political, and intellectual factors that led to the development of the liberal values he cherished, and he felt compelled to point out the differences between those circumstances and the situation of the late nineteenth and early twentieth centuries. But his aversion to wishful thinking did not entail acquiescence in the demolition of freedom and popular government.

Weber's concern for the conflict between democracy and bureaucracy, and between substantive and formal rationality, led him to advance a theory of plebiscitarian leader-democracy. A democracy of this sort rests on the consent of the governed, but in contrast to a leaderless democracy run by bureaucratized parties, it concentrates a great deal of power in a single charismatic individual. It thus relies on charismatic rather than rational or traditional domination. The plebiscitarian leader controls absolutely both the administrative machinery of the state and also the party machinery, and he commands absolute obedience from the people.[74] Understandably, that view of democracy evokes a shudder in the wake of twentieth-century lessons in charismatic domination. It can be argued, however, that Weber was willing to entrust such power to a democratically chosen leader precisely because he feared bureaucracy's numbing effect more than he doubted the people's ability to select responsible leaders. An exchange between Weber and General Erich Ludendorff, which occurred shortly after the end of the First World War, illuminates Weber's thinking on this matter. Asked by Ludendorff to explain his idea of democracy, Weber replied, "In a democracy the people choose a leader whom they trust. Then the chosen man says, 'Now shut your mouths and obey me.' The people and the parties are no longer free to interfere in the leader's business." After Ludendorff commented that he could like such a democracy, Weber added a caveat: "Later the people can sit in judgment. If the leader has made mistakes—to the gallows with him."[75] Weber knew that such an emotional style of government is unstable, but he deemed it preferable to the paralysis he considered inevitable in government by bureaucracy. He emphasized that charismatic leadership must be exercised with the consent of the people. Although he recognized the dangers,[76] neither he nor his contemporaries had any idea that the people would prove willing to use the gallows not for their leader but for themselves.

Weber's attitude toward democracy must be understood within the larger context of German history. As I indicated in Chapter Five, Germany had no tradition of popular sovereignty, and liberals repeatedly put their faith in elites rather than democracy to accomplish their goals. As a result of this pattern, which persisted even after World War I, the vestiges of autocracy latent in the idea of the *Rechtsstaat* seemed to Weber likely to endure. Germany was ruled by what has been called an "open-yet-authoritarian elite," which monopolized power and made the idea of participatory democracy appear chimerical. Weber deliberately calculated his theory of leader-democracy to compensate for the people's lack of experience with self-government. Yet in a sense his own ideas only reflected the weakness of the democratic tradition in Germany, a weakness painfully manifested in the Weimar Republic's failure, which Weber did not live to see. But his own experience with German democracy did not inspire Weber's confidence. As he wrote to Robert Michels, "such concepts as 'will of the people,' genuine will of the people, have long since ceased to exist for me; they are fictitious. All ideas aiming at abolishing the dominance of men over men are 'Utopian.'"[77]

Perhaps Weber's worries about the excesses of government as *Rechtsstaat* led him to deny that anything resembling a public interest exists, or perhaps he was merely throwing in his lot with the generations of German liberals who distrusted democracy when climactic moments arrived. But Weber disagreed with those who anticipated an end to class conflict in a postwar democratic government devoted to the common good. He considered conflict essential to healthy politics, and he believed that the only hope of making progress lay in subverting bureaucratic domination by relying on the authority of a charismatic leader. "In large states everywhere modern democracy is becoming a bureaucratized democracy," he asserted in 1918. "And it must be so; for it is replacing the aristocratic or other titular officials by a paid civil service. It is the same everywhere, it is the same within parties too. It is inevitable." Given the prevalence of an open-yet-authoritarian elite, the absence of a tradition of popular sovereignty, and Weber's doubt that the trend toward bureaucratization could be arrested in any other way, it is understandable that he emphasized the importance of the leader.[78] While he denied the possibility of organizing democratic politics around a transcendent public interest, neither was he content with the conception of politics as the simple pursuit of individual self-interest. In conditions of disenchantment, he believed, only a charismatic leader could awaken the people from apathy and narrow-mindedness and instill in them a concern for public affairs. Their interest would necessarily be tied to specific values, though, and Weber considered the most important of these to be the nation itself.

With parliamentary politics under the control of party machines—as Weber's own disappointing brush with electoral politics after the war confirmed—the only alternative involved individual leadership. The choice facing Germany in 1919, he proclaimed in "Politics as a Vocation," was "between leadership democracy with a 'machine,' and leaderless democracy, in other words the rule of professional politicians without a calling, without the inner charismatic qualities that make a leader. And that means what the party rebels"—such as Weber was himself, he might have noted—"are accustomed to call the 'rule of clique.' For the moment we have only the latter in Germany." It was in order to counter the degradation of democracy to the level of horse trading by party hacks that Weber recommended concentrating power in the leader's hands. He understood that this postwar position contrasted with his earlier support of parliamentary supremacy, and he explained the difference in a speech on the *Reichspräsident* in 1919. When the authoritarian state ruled, he argued, attempts to strengthen Parliament were necessary. But "now we have a situation where all constitutional proposals have degenerated into a blind faith in the infallibility and sovereignty of the majority." Moreover, it was not a popular majority that ruled, Weber contended, but rather a majority of party professionals. This condition, an inverted but equally unsatisfactory version of Bismarck's *Sammlungspolitik*, represented the opposite, "but equally undemocratic, extreme," and as a result the pendulum had to be pulled back. "True democracy means, not a helpless surrender to cliques, but submission to a leader whom the people have elected themselves."[79] As that passage indicates clearly, Weber was eventually driven by his distrust of bureaucracy back toward the long-standing equation of freedom with obedience characteristic of German political theory. Having been himself an eloquent critic of the *Obrigkeitsstaat* in the prewar period, in his final writings he stood on the brink of endorsing the mirror image of authoritarianism and calling it democracy. It is true that Weber wanted the people to select the leader who would rule them. That difference is crucial; Weber was not looking for another Bismarck. Yet even when he was affirming the desirability of popular government, his focus on a plebiscitary leader made Weber a peculiarly German democrat.

The limits of Weber's commitment to democracy cannot be explained away. As he wrote to Michels, he was deeply skeptical of popular decision making: "It is as if one were to speak of a will of shoe consumers which should determine the technology of shoemaking! Of course the shoe consumers know where the shoe pinches, but they never know how it can be improved."[80] The contrast between that statement and Croly's discussion of bureaucratic expertise in *Progressive Democracy* illuminates the difference between Weber's democratic theory and that of the American progressives. Americans wisely distrusted delegating authority to government officials,

Croly argued. "No plebiscite can bestow authenticity upon an ostensibly democratic political system which approximates in practice to the exercise of executive omnipotence. No intermittent appeals to the people for their approbation can wholly democratize a system which approximates in practice to the exercise of legislative omnipotence." If given sufficient power, bureaucrats will use it "to perpetuate the system which is so beneficial to themselves."[81] Thus Croly insisted that democracy must do precisely what Weber doubted it could do: restrict the bureaucracy to providing information and executing the public will. That disagreement regarding the possibility of democratic government in modern society is among the major differences between Weber and the other theorists of progressivism.

During the 1920s, however, that difference diminished. Weber died in 1920, but the other progressives lived to see their hopes caught in the cross fire between an unreconstructed laissez-faire liberalism and an equally dogmatic revolutionary communism. The apparently sturdy ideas of progressivism and social democracy proved surprisingly fragile in the face of resurgent right- and left-wing ideologies. Sobered by the public's enthusiasm for extremist appeals both during and especially after the war, progressive intellectuals found their faith in democracy shaken. In his correspondence with Wallas in 1920, Lippmann referred to the rapid passage of American opinion from hysteria to disinterest, and concluded that he was kept from feeling "profound discouragement with universal suffrage" only because he regarded that year's election of Harding as "the final twitch of the war mind."[82]

Despair cut even more deeply into Croly's sensibility. During 1920 he furiously prepared a manuscript called "The Breach in Civilization," but thanks to Felix Frankfurter's advice, Croly never published it. Although only part of the manuscript has survived, what is left provides a pathetic counter-point to Weber's *Economy and Society*. Croly's theme, although less clearly defined and far less carefully developed, was similar to Weber's focus on rationalization as the central principle in modern Western history. Croly emphasized the breakdown of intellectual unity in the Reformation and the replacement of the well-ordered otherworldliness of the Middle Ages by a more secular, subjectivistic, rationalistic, and materialistic world view. The disintegration of medieval unities resulted in the rise of individualism, democracy, and science, all of which gradually loosened the grip of dogma over intelligence. Their excesses in turn led to the anarchy of capitalism and the tragedy of war. That much of Croly's analysis paralleled much of Weber's. When he turned his attention to the present and offered recommendations for the future, however, the extent of his demoralization became evident. In contrast to Weber's stoical resolution to struggle against the continuing pressures of rationalization and bureaucratization, Croly sounded a kind of retreat. As he wrote in *The New Republic*, "I see no way out of this morass except through the new affirmation of Christian truth as a way of life and the solemn belief in it by Christian peoples as more formative and sacred than any of the special gods of natural science, politics, economics and the world."[83] His confidence in radical empiricism washed away by the susceptibility of democratic masses to appeals he considered irrational, Croly gave up on the attempt to construct a moral community on the basis of collective experience. Like many others before and after him, he was driven by war from hubris to piety.

Lippmann's career followed a rather different trajectory: after the war he left the more reflective *New Republic* for greater visibility at the New York *World*. Lippmann disregarded the advice of Harold Laski, who hoped he would remain with *The New Republic* because only he could "do the great human service of bringing to maturity the ideas and hopes which struggle for expression in Herbert's mind."[84] Lippmann may have understood already that even he could not bring order to the chaotic mysticism of Croly's last years. In any case, having rubbed shoulders with the powerful during World War I, Lippmann was growing weary of political theory. The sparkle of celebrity distracted him from the deeper luster of well-crafted ideas, and he was ready to move into a different world from the one beckoning Croly.

He began this second phase of his career as explosively as he had begun the first in *A Preface to Politics*. In fact, the reputation of Lippmann's *Public Opinion* (1922) has generally cast a shadow over his earlier, more radical books, and his prewar work is sometimes dismissed as a mere prologue to his mature—i.e., less democratic—ideas. It is possible to emphasize the references to Nietzsche and Freud in *A Preface to Politics* and the references to regulatory agencies in *Drift and Mastery* in order to make such a case, but as I have pointed out, those books also contain the iconoclastic and democratic fervor that made Lippmann a participant rather than an observer in the prewar innocents' rebellion. *Public Opinion* belongs to another world, and a detailed analysis of it will have to wait for another time. Here I want only to note Lippmann's disillusionment in the 1920s with what he called the "omni-competent citizen" enshrined by liberal democratic theory. Because citizens do not see public problems in their full complexity but only through the distorting but indispensable lenses of stereotypes, they are incapable of making the intelligent choices democracy demands. In fact, because he feared that "the common interests largely elude public opinion entirely, and can be managed only by a specialized class whose personal interests reach beyond the locality," there was some question about whether Lippmann could still be considered a democrat at all.[85] His analysis seemed to point toward Plato's guardians rather than Jefferson's yeomen.

Yet Lippmann's criticism, severe as it was, did not go further than the other progressives'. In an autobiographical fragment Croly wrote in the mid-1920s, he expressed with sad conviction the disillusionment he shared with Lippmann in the postwar years: "Twenty-five years ago the vast and apparently fertile estate of political democracy looked bright with the promise of abundant harvests," Croly wrote. "I among others imputed to the thoroughly democratic commonwealth the power to contribute enormously and speedily to human welfare. It was a mistake."[86] Hobhouse, whose faith in progress seemed unshakable, also lost heart. In *The Elements of Social*

Justice, published in 1922, as was *Public Opinion*, he complained that "the power of conscious democracy is practically limited to certain critical decisions, and largely to a veto on the proposals of the bureaucrat."[87] Progressive theory appeared to be suffocating in the supposedly free atmosphere of democratic politics. What had gone wrong?

Dewey thought he knew. In a review of Lippmann's *Public Opinion* that appeared in *The New Republic*, he applauded Lippmann's analysis of democracy's problems but offered a different solution. According to Dewey, Lippmann realized that the bureaucracy he recommended to advise the public was not without its own difficulties. For that reason, Lippmann was not vulnerable to the objection that he ignored the progressives' analysis of the dangers involved in relying on elites. Nevertheless, Dewey suggested, Lippmann's solution only scratched the surface of the problem. The difficulty with democracy, Dewey wrote, "is so fundamental that it can be met, it seems to me, only by a solution more fundamental than he has dared to give." What did he have in mind? "Democracy demands a more thoroughgoing education than the education of officials, administrators and directors of industry. Because this fundamental education is at once so necessary and so difficult of achievement, the enterprise is so challenging. To sidetrack it to the task of enlightenment of administrators and executives is to miss something of its range and its challenge."[88] No other progressive could match the endurance of Dewey's confidence in education as democracy's redeemer. I have noted previously how Dewey transferred his early religious faith to democracy in the 1890s, and how he linked the pragmatic ideas of testing truth to the democratic process. I have also noted the connection between his conception of democracy as progressive social development and his flexible, open-ended ethical theory.[89] Dewey's vision of democracy focused so clearly on education because he conceived of citizenship in terms of the Greek ideal of *paideia*. Rather than reserving this ideal of personal development for a few superior individuals, however, he believed it could be extended to every member of society.

This was perhaps the essential difference separating Dewey from Weber. The virtuoso ethic Weber held out in "Politics as a Vocation" involved blending responsible public activity with personal convictions, precisely the sort of intelligent, benevolent commitment Dewey had in mind for every citizen. In an essay published in *The New Republic* shortly before his review of *Public Opinion*, Dewey admitted the challenge facing partisans of democracy while affirming the continuing vitality of the democratic ideal:

> It may be that the word democracy has become so intimately associated with a particular political order, that of general suffrage and elective officials, which does not work very satisfactorily, that it is impossible to recover its basic moral and ideal meaning. But the meaning remains whatever name is given it. It denotes faith in individuality, in uniquely distinctive qualities in each normal human being; faith in corresponding unique modes of activity that create new ends, with willing acceptance of the modifications of the established order entailed by the release of individual capacities.[90]

Dewey even conceded the difficulties involved in nurturing this species of individuality in the modern world. In *The Public and Its Problems* (1927), which can be read as Dewey's response to *Public Opinion*, he outlined the processes that "have effected uniform standardization, mobility and remote invisible relationships"—the processes Weber termed rationalization and bureaucratization. These developments contributed to the "disintegration of the family, church and neighborhood," leaving individuals isolated in a society lacking community. By the 1920s, that formulation had become standard among American and European sociologists and social psychologists, but few still drew Dewey's conclusion that the future of democratic government in such a disenchanted world remained an "unanswered question."[91]

Like Weber, Dewey chose to swim against the prevailing antidemocratic current; unlike Weber, he expected the current to shift. In an uncanny illustration of the difference between them, Dewey employed the same image Weber used in his letter to Michels but drew precisely the opposite conclusion: "The man who wears the shoe knows best that it pinches and where it pinches, even if the expert shoemaker is the best judge of how the trouble is to be remedied."[92] Without the participation of those who wear the shoes, Dewey maintained, the shoemaker's technical expertise—his instrumental rationality, in Weber's language—is useless. The public may indeed not know how to improve the fit of its shoes, as Weber insisted to Michels. But unless the public identifies the problem and determines the goal, Dewey contended—unless the public supplies the substantive rationality to guide the technician's skill—the shoemaker's talent is squandered. In that case, the correspondence between what bureaucratic government provides and what the public seeks, like the fit of shoes to feet, will be haphazard at best.

Dewey was the only progressive to survive the 1920s with his democratic faith intact. Six years after the appearance of his spirited defense of progressive ideas in *The Public and Its Problems*, Hitler and Roosevelt assumed power. It is an odd irony, which should sober anyone tempted to read the future from the past, that those two individuals' contrasting styles of charismatic leadership confirmed the contradictory assessments offered by Weber and Dewey of the future of democracy. For American politics, even at the height of the New Deal, continued to be a struggle for power among party professionals rather than a search for the public interest, and in that sense Weber was the better prophet. But in the years after Weber's death, Germany helped to demonstrate what Dewey suspected, that charisma may represent an even greater threat than bureaucracy to the survival of democratic government.

10

The Prospect of Justice

1. Freedom and Property

When the first issue of the British *Progressive Review* appeared in October of 1896, its lead editorial concluded with a ringing endorsement of a radical idea. Liberals must "assign a new meaning to liberty: it must no longer signify the absence of restraint, but the presence of opportunity." That editorial signaled clearly the distance liberals had traveled from their origins in laissez-faire. "The Benthamite philosophy and the economics of the Manchester school," the *Review*'s editors conceded, provided "a certain theoretical basis and harmony" to the Liberal party in the early nineteenth century. But times—and ideas—had changed. Completing "the task of securing genuine economic freedom" would require a broadened conception of the state to accompany the broadened conception of individuality prevailing at the century's end. "Faith in ideas and in the growing capacity of the common people to absorb and apply ideas," not the earlier liberals' restriction of government to the enlightened few, "forms the moral foundation of democracy."[1]

The idea of positive freedom was the keystone of progressive theory. Securing the independence of the individual seemed to these thinkers the central challenge of the twentieth century, and their ideas about equality and justice reflected their acceptance of the analysis of freedom advanced by Green and Fouillée. In contrast to the identification of liberty with freedom from restraint in earlier liberal theory, these social liberals maintained that in an interdependent world conditions of inequality effectively negated rights formally guaranteed by law. For that reason they adopted the idea of positive freedom.

Green was careful to distinguish his ideas of liberty from the Hegelian concept of right. It is important to recall the nature of that distinction, because it reveals the gap between positive liberty as progressive theorists understood it and the very different meaning of freedom in collectivist schemes. Green pointed out that Hegel saw the individual's relation to the state in a manner quite alien to English thought. Hegel conceived of the state as "objective freedom," and he defined individual freedom as obedience to such a state. He contended that in the state, "reason, the self-determining principle operating in man as his will, has found a perfect expression for itself." The individual "who is determined by the objects which the well-ordered state presents to him is determined by that which is the perfect expression of his reason, and is thus free."

While that paraphrase of Hegel initially appears to flutter between paradox and meaninglessness, it is possible to see beneath it the shadow of the doctrine of the *Rechtsstaat*. Because the state embodies both legal and ethical right, the individual finds freedom by subordinating his will to the commands of the state. Green valued the idea that freedom is not an entirely personal affair, but he cautioned that Hegel extended an important argument too far. It is nonsense to describe the state as free, Green insisted. We "cannot significantly speak of freedom except with reference to individual persons," for only individuals can exercise freedom, and "therefore the realisation of freedom in the state can only mean the attainment of freedom by individuals through influences which the state . . . supplies." It is a mockery to speak of the state as the realization of freedom when the state permits individuals to endure poverty and injustice. In Hegel's political philosophy, "The difference between the ideal and the actual seems to be ignored, and tendencies seem to be spoken of as if they were accomplished facts."[2] Green was among the first English philosophers to appreciate the attractiveness of the *Rechtsstaat* as an ideal. By insisting that the ideal must not be confused with reality, however, he gave a critical edge to the idea of the *Rechtsstaat*. Green believed that any conception of freedom without individual choice at its foundation is a distortion.

It is necessary to emphasize this point because of the repeated misuse of the idea of positive freedom in the twentieth century. As Green employed the term, and as the progressives who followed him understood it, positive freedom means liberation. They considered the idea of forcing anyone to be free a contradiction in terms. Although they realized that laws are intended to deny certain kinds of behavior, they never confused restrictions of freedom with freedom itself. Their commitment to the theory of voluntary action prompted them to emphasize individual freedom, and their opposition to paternalism reflected this conviction. The other side of the radical theory of knowledge, the awareness that experience is social, led them to redefine freedom in positive terms. That conception of freedom, as I have indicated in discussing its use by the philosophers of the *via media* and the theorists of social democracy, was closely tied to an ideal of autonomy conceived within the framework of community. All of these thinkers understood that freedom has both individual and social dimensions. In contrast to many conservatives and collectivists, they rejected definitions of freedom as subservience to an external purpose. In contrast to earlier liberals, who were committed to a theory of possessive individualism, they insisted that freedom also involves responsibility.

Dewey and Hobhouse both presented elaborate analyses of the distinction between positive and negative freedom, but their arguments added little to the account Green provided in "Liberal Legislation and Freedom of Contract" (1880).[3] Like Green, they contended that liberty involves the right not to be excluded by others, and that principle entailed a reorientation from formal to effective freedom as the ideal of progressive theory. This insight derived not only from Green but also from Sidgwick, as Dewey's lectures on political philosophy in 1892 clearly demonstrate. In those lectures, Dewey referred repeatedly to the treatment of rights in Sidgwick's *Politics*, particularly emphasizing "*the negative and the positive aspects of rights*" and the importance of keeping both aspects in view.[4] Dewey elaborated these early arguments in his and Tufts's *Ethics*, maintaining that "in its external aspect, freedom is negative and formal." But such freedom from restraint is "only a condition, though an absolutely indispensable one, of effective freedom." Positive freedom, on the other hand, requires: "(1) positive control of the resources necessary to carry purposes into effect, possession of the means to satisfy desires; and (2) mental equipment with the trained powers of initiative and reflection."

The logical corollary of such a concept of freedom, for Dewey as for Green, was the demand for equality. Echoing arguments the philosophers of the *via media* presented in the 1880s, Dewey pointed out that "historical conditions have put the control of the machinery of production in the hands of a comparatively few persons." The forces unleashed by liberalism ended in a concentration of property and power that effectively denied the freedom of the working class. Broadening the scope of freedom required the gradual equalization of social conditions through the intervention of government. The original impetus of liberalism was the bourgeoisie's desire for equality, but during the course of capitalist expansion the liberal creed came to stand for a set of nominal rights actually restricting the freedom of the majority of citizens. The challenge of twentieth-century politics, Dewey wrote, "is not one of magnifying the powers of the State against individuals, but is one of making individual liberty a more extensive and equitable matter."[5]

In *Liberalism*, Hobhouse likewise connected positive freedom with equality: "The struggle for liberty is also, when pushed through, a struggle for equality."[6] Freedom is an abstraction in the absence of equal conditions, because privilege translates easily into oppression. Hobhouse, like the theorists of social democracy, denied that the abolition of inequality requires the abolition of property. In "The Historical Evolution of Property" (1914), he distinguished between property for use and property for power. The former, which involves the appropriation of things, he deemed legitimate, but the latter, which could be extended into the control of people, he wanted to reserve for society. It seems arguable that such a distinction entails social

ownership of the means of production, but Hobhouse emphasized the difficulty of distinguishing in practice between the two kinds of property, and
nowhere in his writings did he resolve this crucial ambiguity, which has
continued to vex his successors.[7]

The other progressive theorists were equally uncertain about how to
resolve this problem. The French Revolution, like the American Revolution,
was ostensibly dedicated simultaneously to freedom and to equality. Maintaining a balance between those two ideals proved increasingly difficult over
the course of the nineteenth century, however, as the actual relation between
them shifted with the rise of organized capitalism. French republicans
assumed that liberty, equality, and fraternity all triumphed as a result of the
Revolution, Bourgeois argued, but in fact it guaranteed only liberty, and its
exercise eventually undercut the other two ideals. The doctrine of solidarity
was designed to resurrect the lost elements of the revolutionaries' triad.
Bourgeois specifically ruled out the abolition of private property as a means
to that end, however, and it was primarily on this question that solidarists
differed from socialists. In his letter to the Congress of the Radical and
Radical Socialist party in Nantes in 1909, he differentiated progressivism
from both liberalism and socialism by playing a variation on Marx's theme.
"To those who say, 'to each according to his strength,' and who thus sacrifice
justice to the appearance of liberty," Bourgeois began, and "to those who say,
'to each according to his needs,' and who thus sacrifice liberty to the appearance of justice, as if justice were possible without liberty," solidarists offered
an alternative formulation: "'To each according to his associated rights in
human society,' a society that is truly contractual, where liberty will be the
reward of social responsibility fulfilled, of justice realized." That blending of
liberal and socialist principles seemed to Bourgeois's allies a perfect statement of their position. Beyond distinguishing them from parties to their left
and their right, though, which it accomplished neatly enough, that distinction
was fuzzy. Presumably, the measure of social responsibility would be the
slope of the curve of progressive taxation, and justice would be realized
through the system of social insurance Bourgeois envisioned, but the
solidarists' critics doubted such steps would suffice to secure a truly contractual society.[8]

In *Economy and Society*, Weber also offered a double-edged analysis of
freedom. Property rights in a market economy in fact guaranteed only the
freedom of those with property, he pointed out, since the working class was
placed in a dependent relation to owners of capital. He acknowledged that
liberty would have a different meaning in a socialist economy. "Which system
would possess more real coercion and which one more real personal freedom
cannot be decided, however, by the mere analysis of the actually existing or
conceivable formal legal system." That question would have to be answered
in practice, by social experimentation.[9] The charges of some of his critics
notwithstanding, Weber was genuinely committed to the value of individual
freedom. His commitment was complicated by his equally strong belief that
rationalization threatened the sort of responsible self-determination he

valued, the autonomy conceived with reference to duty that he took from Kant and Channing. In short, in conditions of disenchantment Weber was afraid of freedom and he was afraid of the end of freedom. He believed that liberty directed only by instrumental reason would prove disastrous to the cultural ideals he cherished, but he was perhaps even more concerned about the prospect of liberty disappearing altogether under the pressure of bureaucratization. In his deep devotion to the ideal of autonomy, Weber was a liberal, but as a result of the tension between his own convictions and his findings as a scholar, he was indeed a "liberal in despair."[10]

Progressives wanted to protect what Jaurès called "legitimate and essential" property rights because of their commitment to freedom, but they were no more successful than Jaurès in specifying what kind of property fit that description. Hobhouse's distinction between property for use and property for power was perhaps the most analytically useful formulation of their position, but its translation into policy remained vague. A letter Lippmann wrote in 1915 illustrates the problematic nature of this progressive impulse. His ideal, he explained, was socialistic in that it denied the legitimacy of existing property rights. Yet it could be identified neither with the socialist party nor even with government ownership of the means of production. "I think of it as a society in which social opportunity has been equalized, in which property has lost its political power, a society in which everyone has a genuine vote, not only a ballot, but a real share in economic development."[11] How to achieve that genuine equalization of social opportunity remained elusive, because progressives considered this a question to be answered by experimentation, a question for political practice rather than political theory. Decisions concerning ownership of the means of production should be made by the people democratically, and change should in any case be gradual.

This argument, pragmatic and meliorist, at first appears to beg the question, but viewed in the context of these thinkers' commitment to the social verification of truth and to democratic politics, it seems reasonable rather than evasive. These progressives understood that the question of balancing liberal property rights with the equalization of opportunity represents one of the most difficult challenges of the industrial era. They saw that unrestricted property rights contribute to the restriction of freedom by creating conditions of inequality, and they agreed that the idea of freedom must be broadened to include the right not to be excluded by others. For that reason they advocated the "progressive equalization of conditions," to use Fouillée's phrase, and they accepted his contention that "democracy will certainly become more and more social and even socialist in the most general sense of the word."[12] On the specific shape of the property rights to be guaranteed in the society that would emerge from such progressive reforms, however, they had little to say.

Progressive and social democratic ideas about individual liberty differed in emphasis. Both groups of thinkers drew on the idea of positive freedom expressed in the 1880s and 1890s by the philosophers of the *via media*. Social democrats, reflecting their socialist origins, tended to emphasize the social side of positive freedom; progressives, reflecting their liberal origins, tended to emphasize the individual side. But they all tried to balance personal liberty and social responsibility in ways that distinguished them clearly from both the socialists and the liberals who preceded them. Because their view of politics was filtered through their historical sensibility, these radicals were more sensitive than most political thinkers to the creative dynamism of individual life and the need for flexibility in social organization. Their political writings therefore exhibit a tentativeness that some critics have found unsettling or unsatisfactory. But that uncertainty manifests neither confusion nor lack of clarity; instead it is essential to their ideas. Lippmann explained this unconventional approach in *A Preface to Politics*:

> Politics is not concerned with prescribing the ultimate qualities of life. . . . If men can keep their minds freed from formalism, idol worship, fixed ideas, and exalted abstractions, politicians need not worry about the language in which the end of our striving is expressed. For with the removal of distracting idols, man's experience becomes the center of thought. And if we think in terms of men, find out what really bothers them, seek to supply what they really want, hold only their experience sacred, we shall find our sanction obvious and unchallenged.

In other words, democracy should be our guide, because it provides a better way to test experience on a large scale than any other alternative. Progressives conceived of politics in ethical terms, and their view of politics was as open-ended as their ethics. That was the reason they embraced democracy. They all believed, with Lippmann, that the focus of politics ought to shift "from authority to autonomy," although not all of them shared his optimism about the chances of achieving that goal.[13]

Because of the extent to which Croly, Dewey, and Hobhouse in particular emphasized the importance of the community, their commitment to individual freedom may be considered suspect. But each of them denied that equality or justice can be, or ought to be, achieved at the cost of positive liberty. "A socially educative faith cannot be imposed upon reluctant democracies," Croly wrote. "It is not a dogma to which the good citizens must conform or a rule which the good citizen must obey. . . . If it is not freely accepted, it is powerless and meaningless." Repression contradicted the voluntarism Croly prized. Only if individuals were to accept social responsibility freely could the goal of social cohesion be reached. Individuality is "a moral and intellectual quality"; it must be cultivated rather than coerced. Only when "personal action is dictated by disinterested motives can there be any such harmony between private and public interests."[14] Certain aspects of Croly's political vision were not clear, but on this issue he was unambiguous: justice must wait on the voluntary acceptance of social responsibility. It cannot be imposed.

In his and Tufts's *Ethics*, Dewey denied that freedom and social integration could be discussed except in terms of each other, and he acknowledged his debt to Green's treatment of these issues. He also quoted a passage from Hobhouse's *Morals in Evolution* that summarizes progressive ideas about freedom and draws together several of the larger themes of this study. It reveals the connection between the ideas of voluntarism, social experience, responsibility, and the progressive idea of freedom, and it places all of them within the context of Hobhouse's and Dewey's Aristotelian notion of individual development and their vision of history as epic. As society becomes more interdependent, Hobhouse wrote, "the individual human being becomes more and more subject to social constraint," and "the tightening of the social fabric may diminish the rights which the individual or large classes of individuals can claim." As a result of this process, liberty and social order come into conflict. But that opposition can be overcome, and in nations with progressive political movements "we have seen order and liberty drawing together again." This convergence mirrors the true relation of freedom to social cohesiveness. "The best ordered community is that which gives most scope to its component members to make the best of themselves, while the 'best' in human nature is that which contributes to the harmony and onward movement of society." Finally, the responsible individual "is the center of modern ethics as of modern law, free so far as custom and law are concerned to make his own life."[15]

That passage indicates the distinctive philosophical basis on which progressive theory rested. These ideas were not simply a convenient response to political opportunity, nor were they designed to rationalize social control. These progressives, like the theorists of social democracy and the philosophers of the *via media*, emphasized individual freedom not because they wanted to shore up a sagging liberal capitalist system but because they considered freedom a fundamental value in human experience. They were troubled by collectivist schemes that sacrificed individuality to the needs of the community. Sensitive to the need for social change, they advocated a series of economic, social, and political reforms almost indistinguishable from those advanced by social democrats. Yet they returned always to liberty, because they considered its status precarious in an increasingly interdependent world. They knew that individual freedom is an illusion under conditions of inequality, and for that reason they advocated radical, although gradual, social reform. But they also knew that equality is devalued when its cost is the repression of freedom.

2. Toward a Harmony of Free Wills

Can social order survive freedom in a disenchanted world? As I noted at the conclusion of Chapter Five, Fouillée believed he could see the first glimmerings of consensus among political thinkers from different backgrounds concerning a single idea: "Social order must rest on the harmony of free wills." Dewey, Croly, Lippmann, Hobhouse, and Bourgeois agreed with that assessment; it was the reason they expected their progressive ideals to be realized through broad-gauged reform movements attracting renegade liberals and revisionist socialists. Weber thought they were dreaming. His studies of the relation between class, status, and politics led him to doubt the possibility of such alliances, and his studies of bureaucratization made him equally skeptical about societies ever reaching consensus without having it imposed on them by autocracy. The other progressives, as I pointed out at the beginning of Chapter Nine, believed that effective reform requires ethical regeneration, and they were confident that a society dedicated to the public interest would emerge from the revolution in values accompanying a return to the classical notion of republican citizenship. They emphasized reconciling the conflicts among competing individuals and groups through cultural education and the machinery of democratic politics. Weber, by contrast, believed the conflicts between individuals and groups would eventually grind down the smooth surfaces of benevolence that make such cooperation possible, revealing the sharp edges of self-interest that make order and individuality almost always irreconcilable.

Dewey argued that the conscientious application of the pragmatic method, which he identified with the procedures of democracy, would enable society to recognize and advance common interests, and to recognize and eradicate the sources of conflict. He argued that progress should be gauged by the standard we derive from our immediate experience of life as social and from the ethics of rational benevolence. He contended in *Democracy and Education* that both of those criteria point toward democracy as a social ideal, an ideal that cannot be described in more specific terms because it will assume whatever shape the people choose to give it.[16] Croly likewise identified the possibility of justice with the politics of democracy. "Thoroughgoing democracy is unnecessary and meaningless except for the purpose of realizing the ideal of social justice," he insisted. At the same time, "the ideal of social justice is so exacting and so comprehensive that it cannot be progressively attained by any agency, save by the loyal and intelligent devotion of the popular will." The only guidelines for social and political theory come from experience, Croly and Dewey reasoned, and proposed changes must therefore emerge from, and be tested in, practice.

These progressives' goals were freedom and the public interest; because they cherished the first, they declined to specify the precise content of the second. "A democracy must be tempered first of all by and for action," in Croly's words. "Yet if it cannot combine thought with action, discussion with decision, criticism with resolution, a searching inquisitiveness with a tenacious faith, it cannot avoid going seriously astray." This formulation reveals the sort of democracy that Croly and Dewey envisioned, a democracy guided by the critical use of intelligence as pragmatic philosophers understood it. These thinkers did not place an unqualified trust in popular wisdom. They emphasized the necessity of cultural and political education to rekindle the spirit of republican citizenship. They maintained that regardless of its imprecision and uncertainty, democracy is the most effective counterweight to autocracy and the only politics consistent with radical empiricism. The prospects of democratic justice in any society, though, rise and fall with the level of its citizens' pragmatic intelligence and civic virtue. "Democracy must risk its success," Croly maintained, "on the integrity of human nature."[17]

Croly and Dewey agreed that democracy requires a willingness to accept the people's will, and they shared a faith that the people would, over time, move in the direction of progressive reform. As I noted in discussing Dewey's ethics, his entire philosophy rested on his faith in democracy. Croly's ideas had a similar basis. "For better or worse," he wrote in the conclusion to *The Promise of American Life*, "democracy cannot be disentangled from an aspiration toward human perfectibility, and hence from the adoption of measures looking in the direction of realizing such an aspiration."[18] Both Croly and Dewey saw the democratic challenge in heroic terms. They considered the people capable of meeting their expectations, but they did not believe that their ideal could ever be completely realized because they conceived of democratic life as a project that is never finished. From the pragmatic perspective, politics is an endless search for better truths. Because they conceived of individual and social growth as self-development toward a goal of social harmony, a conception rooted in Dewey's notion of experience, they considered the imperfect but progressive integration of individual and social interest possible in a democracy.

Hobhouse and Bourgeois expressed their vision of harmony by contrasting it to the original liberal idea. "The older economists conceived a natural harmony," Hobhouse wrote, whereby the hidden hand led individuals to act in such a way as to benefit society as a whole. Progressives considered that assumption overly optimistic. They contended, in Hobhouse's words, "not that there is an actually existing harmony," but only that "there is possible ethical harmony." That conviction led them toward the nonrevolutionary socialism of social democratic theorists. "The ideas of Socialism," Hobhouse wrote, "when translated into practical terms, coincide with the ideas to which Liberals are led when they seek to apply their principles of Liberty, Equality, and the Common Good to the industrial life of our time."[19] Progressivism was thus simultaneously the fulfillment of liberal and socialist ideals through the deliberate, democratic integration of personal interest and the public interest. Bourgeois likewise distinguished between natural solidarity and the ideal of solidarity. He described his goal as a "voluntary socialism," in which the older notion of freedom as the struggle between isolated individuals gives way to an idea of "association between persons working voluntarily to coordinate their activities." In short, solidarity involves the coordination of freedom with order. In order to reconcile liberty with justice, Bourgeois proclaimed, "it is not a matter of socializing all goods, but instead of socializing spirits and wills."[20]

Neither Hobhouse nor Bourgeois would concede that such socialization of freedom might involve repression. As Hobhouse put it in 1920, "the problem of freedom is not that of dispensing with all guidance and all restraint, but that of finding the lines upon which the manifold social qualities of man can develop in harmony, with the result that the restraints involved are voluntarily accepted and self-imposed." In its implication that freedom equals voluntary submission to duty, that formula recalls the ambiguity of Kant's earlier endorsement of obedience to authority as the manifestation of the individual's autonomous internalization of the categorical imperative, an idea that could lead either to Marx's objectification of freedom in the revolutionary politics of the proletariat or toward the confusion of the rational with the real in the theory of the *Rechtsstaat*. Another formulation of this argument by Hobhouse reveals this difficulty even more clearly: The "most developed community," he contended, "would be that which effectively achieves the most complete synthesis of the widest range of human activity, including within its membership the largest number of human beings, but in such wise as to rest most completely upon their free co-operation, thus expressing the whole of their vital energies as far as these are capable of working together in harmony." As Hobhouse realized, this argument was essentially a restatement of Green; as he did not acknowledge, it was thus vulnerable to precisely the criticism that Sidgwick offered regarding the inevitably competitive nature of the struggle for certain goods. From the perspective of Sidgwick or James—or Weber—the concluding qualification in Hobhouse's argument, "as far as these are capable of working together in harmony," decisively undercut its forcefulness.[21]

I have already suggested the reason why Weber did not share the other progressive theorists' confidence about achieving social harmony. He considered politics an unending struggle for power, a "hard transaction" requiring that the politician "be free of illusions and acknowledge the one fundamental fact: namely the inevitable eternal struggle of man against man." Because he believed that private interest dominates all political struggles, he considered the idea of a single public interest an illusion. The tension between "the genius or demon of politics" and "the God of love" cannot be resolved by recourse to any Aristotelian notion of personal ethical development. The conflicts between democracy and bureaucracy, between classes, between status groups, and between the competing principles of capitalism and socialism cannot be dissolved, because the overarching ideals capable of inspiring individuals voluntarily to subordinate personal desires to the public good have lost their power in a disenchanted world. The Enlightenment's faith in the natural harmony of free individuals was demolished by the persistence of class antagonism, Weber maintained. The economic development accompanying the spread of capitalism's instrumental rationality intensified rather than eliminated social conflict.[22] Weber dared only to hope that certain individuals might affirm a radically ungrounded personal conviction through the responsible exercise of political power. These virtuosos, called to politics as a vocation, could fuse their ethical convictions with their political skills in a way that calls to mind Croly's invocation of leaders combining the ideals of the saint with the steadfastness of the hero. Whereas Croly considered that combination possible, however, and expected it to invigorate American society as it percolated through the nation's political culture, Weber judged that prospect unlikely because of the constraints imposed by bureaucratization.

According to Weber, the fusion of freedom and order was made possible historically by the emergence of Puritanism, which contributed to the rise of voluntary associations that engaged individuals in politics without exacting submission to external authority as the price of their participation. For that reason, Weber argued, America provided a uniquely fertile ground for nourishing democratic institutions. In Germany, by contrast, the legacy of Lutheranism was the legitimation of violence by the state against its citizens. Whereas Lutherans were encouraged to accept the world as it is, Calvinists were inspired to struggle against the world in order to shape it according to divinely inspired ideals. While the Lutheran ethos of world resignation permeated German culture, American culture encouraged the energetic pursuit of worldly goods, justified by religious dogma, through participation in small-scale, egalitarian organizations. The theorists of progressivism shared an enthusiasm for pluralism and the voluntary political activity it encouraged. Bourgeois identified such organizations as the principal source of "social amelioration." Such groups, "consenting to the rules that one and all deem for the best, because they are in the interest of everyone," provided a model of democratic government for these thinkers. Progressives wanted merely to extend the principle of voluntary participation, and the agreement upon procedures and aims hammered out in such groups, to society as a whole, so that all individuals would be able to shape the future according to rules they helped to establish. "The development of social interest," according to Hobhouse, "depends not only on adult suffrage and the supremacy of the elected legislature, but on all the intermediate organizations which link the individual to the whole." For this reason, he maintained, the revival of local government is "the essence of democratic progress."[23] The possibility of coordinating these various bodies without trampling any of them was an article of these progressives' faith.

Croly and Lippmann likewise sought to extend to the national level the combination of lively activity and widespread participation they witnessed in local politics and voluntary associations, and that quest for a community was also at the heart of Dewey's democratic faith. Unless the sense of participation in a common enterprise characteristic of American culture in the pre-industrial era could be resurrected in the world of interdependence, these thinkers believed, it would be impossible to effect the sort of changes they sought. Although sensitive to the precariousness of community groups in an urban-industrial age, they did not grasp the significance of the reorganization of American public life during these years away from such local organizations and toward functional differentiation and professionalization. These developments shifted attention and influence away from grass roots organizations, eventually leading to the rise of interest group liberalism and the decline of progressive democracy. Compared to European nations, the American polity continued to exhibit more diversity because of the fragmentation of power inherent in its federal structure. Nevertheless, the dream of enlarging the pattern of participation in voluntary organizations, so that it could serve as a template for national politics, faded before the reality of organized capitalism, the realignment of parties, and the reorganization of power in the party system that began to emerge in the United States around the turn of the century. These maverick liberals did not realize that such developments threatened the continuation of voluntary participation in public life.[24] It was precisely this emphasis on the positive contributions to politics of the conflicts between various competing groups that led them to resist socialism, despite their sympathy with its ideals: they feared the loss of diversity and the numbing consensus that might result from the concentration of political, social, and economic power in a single sphere. But the result of the continued fragmentation of public power, which they did not anticipate, has been the increased concentration of private power and the extension of its effective management of the political realm.

Weber expected nothing less. He interpreted the continuing rationalization of capitalist economies as a challenge to the values of liberal democracy, and he considered the techniques of scientific management in particular to be the logical culmination of the application of instrumental logic to industrial processes. In such a scheme, the "psycho-physical apparatus of man is completely adjusted to the demands of the outer world, the tools, the machines." Scientific management thus represents the reductio ad absurdum of capitalist rationality, demonstrating that "discipline inexorably takes over ever larger areas as the satisfaction of political and economic needs is increasingly rationalized."[25] Under such conditions, the individual can hope only to leave traces of his freedom on the walls of rationalization that circumscribe his life. The assertion of individuality in a world of instrumental reason becomes increasingly desperate; the chances of effective political activity, motivated by genuine conviction, become increasingly remote.

Croly and Dewey countered Weber's austere portrait of freedom's prospects with a democratic faith. They believed that industrial democracy offers a solution to the problems created by the rationalization of work. "Scientific management must bring with it as a condition of its acceptance the self-governing work-shop," Croly argued. Self-determination in the workplace enables workers to turn the techniques of efficient production into tools; it places man in charge of technique. Dewey adopted a similar stance in *Democracy and Education*. If scientific management means nothing more than the organization of work for more efficient production, it is a perversion of science. "The chief opportunity for science is the discovery of the relations of a man to his work—including his relations to others who take part—which will enlist his intelligent interest in what he is doing."[26] Unless workers are involved in the decisions concerning the work they do, demands for increased efficiency, no matter how rational, are oppressive. Croly and Dewey resisted the separation between substantive and instrumental rationality. Although aware of the problem, they demanded that science be made to serve democratic purposes. "Without the help of science the human race would have remained forever the victim of vicissitudes in its supply of food," Croly admitted, but "without the advent of democracy science would have become merely an engine of class oppression and would have been demoralized in its service." While that inversion may have been true in the past, the meaning of science must be altered for the future. "Democracy must never permit science to determine its fundamental purposes, because the integrity of that purpose depends finally upon a consecration of the will."[27] Once again, it is not shoemakers who should determine whether shoes fit. The people, organized democratically, must provide technicians with the values that direct their work.

The proposition that science cannot provide answers to questions of value was central to the radical theory of knowledge. Intoxicated by their faith in democracy, Dewey, Croly, Lippmann, Hobhouse, and Bourgeois did not see clearly the difficulty cultures face in attempting to construct social and political standards to achieve harmony in a disenchanted world. As Weber pointed out, in the eighteenth and early nineteenth centuries law served both an instrumental and a substantive function, but during the course of the nineteenth century its ethical content dropped out. As a result law no longer provided a substantive norm for social behavior, and individuals found themselves caught in a web of purely formal codes without evident connection to subjective values. Freeing law from intention seemed to many late nineteenth- and early twentieth-century legal theorists a step from irrationality toward rationality; it seemed to Weber merely the replacement of substantive rationality with instrumental rationality. As a result of that change, he contended, only precedents are relevant in determining law, and only actions, not intentions, are relevant in determining guilt. In the context of such purely technical considerations, the idea of the *Rechtsstaat* becomes particularly troublesome, since the legal system lacks even the pretense of ethical right and derives its legitimacy purely from its instrumental value. Weber's historical sociology of law has led some critics to infer that he shared the legal system's equation of substantive with formal rationality, but like the misreadings of Weber as a simple *Machtpolitiker*, that interpretation neglects the critical distance he kept from the system he described. That distance is more apparent in his public lectures than in his scholarly writings. In "Science as a Vocation," he lashed out at those who assumed that the application of instrumental reason through science could yield normative guidelines:

> After Nietzsche's devastating criticism of those "last men" who "invented happiness," I may leave aside altogether the naive optimism in which science—that is, the technique of mastering life which rests upon science—has been celebrated as the way to happiness. Who believes in this?—aside from a few big children in university chairs or editorial offices. . . . Tolstoy has given the simplest answer [to the question of the meaning of science], with the words: "Science is meaningless because it gives no answer to our question, the only question important for us: 'What shall we do and how shall we live?'" That science does not give an answer to this is indisputable.[28]

Weber understood, as did the other progressives, that efficiency is but one goal among many, and he agreed that its relation to other values should be examined critically rather than taken for granted. He differed from the others in judging that sort of critical inquiry highly unlikely in the modern era. The "iron cage" of capitalism could not so easily be escaped, as he argued in the gloomy concluding pages of *The Protestant Ethic*. In a culture oriented toward purely formalized norms, "the idea of duty in one's calling prowls about in our lives like the ghost of dead religious beliefs. Where the fulfillment of the calling cannot directly be related to the highest spiritual and cultural values, or when, on the other hand, it need not be felt simply as economic compulsion, the individual generally abandons the attempt to justify it at all."[29] In a world empty of ultimate values, attempts to escape the iron cage usually prove futile.

The other theorists of progressivism disagreed. They believed that science need not serve the purposes of capitalism, although they understood the close historical connection between instrumental thinking and liberal economics. "The community as a whole will not derive full benefit from scientific achievements until all of the members share in its responsibilities and opportunities," Croly wrote. Together with Dewey and Lippmann, Hobhouse and Bourgeois, he assumed that such community participation was not only desirable but possible. The unity of scientific considerations and political values is neither a fact, as many conservatives and collectivists believed, nor an impossibility, as Weber feared. It is instead a project, which can be accomplished only through progressive democratic reform. These radical liberals were visionaries, but they realized that the sort of society they wanted could emerge only from a lengthy political struggle and a basic reorientation of values. They stressed both education and institutional change because they knew that neither alone would suffice. It is "perfectly true to declare that democracy needs for its fulfillment a peculiarly high standard of moral behavior," Croly admitted. It is even more true "that a democratic scheme of moral values reaches its consummate expression in the religion of human brotherhood." Yet there was more to progressive politics than hope. "A profound sense of human brotherhood is no substitute for specific efficiency. The men most possessed by intense brotherly feelings usually fall into an error, as Tolstoy has done, as to the way in which those feelings can be realized." Croly was sensitive to the conflict between means and ends, which Weber put in terms of the contrast between the ethic of responsibility and the ethic of conviction. Characteristically, Croly approached the problem in pragmatic fashion. As a logical problem it was intractable, he argued. Practical activity offers a kind of resolution, however, because voluntary action, conceived instrumentally, involves bringing an ideal, or what Dewey termed an end-in-view, into being. Croly envisioned politics according to that model. "Back of any work of conversion must come a long slow process of social reorganization and individual emancipation; and not until the individual is released, disciplined and purified, will the soil be prepared for the crowning of some democratic Saint Francis."[30] It was precisely the possibility of such a Franciscan politics that Weber ruled out in "Politics as a Vocation"; Croly's opposite conclusion neatly illustrates the gulf separating his position from Weber's.

Dewey discussed this problem in his presidential address before the American Psychological Association in 1899. He acknowledged its difficulty but affirmed his conviction that it could be solved in instrumental action. The modern age has brought with it a tremendous increase in our ability to shape nature to our purposes, Dewey declared. Despite that increased capacity, the realization of our aims grows increasingly "unassured and precarious. At times it seems as if we were caught in a contradiction; the more we multiply means the less certain and general is the use we are able to make of them." Still Dewey remained optimistic. He admitted that science "will never tell us just what to do ethically, nor just how to do it. But it will afford us insight into the conditions which control the formation and execution of aims, and thus enable human effort to expend itself sanely, rationally, and with assurance."[31] There can be no final resolution of the tension between means and ends in reform, just as there is no final resolution of political problems in a democracy and only imperfect release from alienation through democratic control of the workplace. But Dewey, committed to a pragmatic approach to problem solving, nevertheless considered a measure of incremental progress possible.

Even Weber believed that the ethic of responsibility and the ethic of conviction, although logically distinct, could be joined in the life of a certain sort of hero. Although he doubted the wisdom of waiting for Croly's democratic St. Francis to lead modern culture out of the darkness of rationalization, he differed from the other theorists of progressivism primarily in mood rather than convictions. Weber was far more skeptical about the possibility of realizing the ideals of individual autonomy and social harmony that he shared with the other progressives. Whatever the chances of their reconciliation in the past, routinization dragged the romantics' dreams of radical freedom and organic unity down into the dull and illusionless landscape of efficiency. The other theorists of progressivism, perhaps because they were bewitched by the seductive appeal of the *Rechtsstaat*—whose allure Weber resisted for good reasons—believed that progressive reforms could carry them closer to their ideals. Weber's reading of history, by contrast, seemed to point in the direction of nihilism, which he resisted even though all the evidence indicated the futility of such resistance. He resolved to assert his freedom through his work, despite his doubts that any larger purpose would be served by his efforts.

The idea of reconciling apparently contradictory principles was the hallmark of all the thinkers considered in this study. Although more circumspect in his assessment of its potential, Weber contributed to the effort of these two generations to transcend accepted philosophical and political categories. In certain respects, he stood apart from the other theorists of progressivism, yet the undercurrents of this thought, the values he embraced without hope, drew him in the direction of their ideas. While the sharpness of his attacks against socialism, and against attempts to use bureaucratic government as an instrument of democratic purposes, obscure the nature of his convictions, there was an important difference between what Weber considered possible in the face of history and what he considered desirable. The latter dimension of his thought repeatedly carried him toward progressivism, and he thus served as both advocate and critic of these ideas. His concluding remarks in "Politics as a Vocation" reveal his passionate ambivalence and the resolution shielding his pessimism from despair:

> Politics is a strong and slow boring of hard boards. It takes both passion and perspective. Certainly all historical experience confirms the truth—that man would not have attained the possible unless time and again he had reached out for the impossible. But to do that a man must be a leader, and not only a leader but a hero as well, in a very sober sense of the word. And even those who are neither leaders nor heroes must arm themselves with that steadfastness of heart which can brave even the crumbling of all hopes. This is necessary right now, or else men will not be able to attain even that which is possible today. Only he has the calling for politics who is sure that he shall not crumble when the world from his point of view is too stupid or too base for what he wants to offer. Only he who in the face of all this can say "In spite of all!" has the calling for politics.[32]

Weber and the other theorists of progressivism departed from liberalism in realizing that politics requires the fusion of responsibility and conviction. When John Stuart Mill became dissatisfied with laissez-faire and leaned toward socialism, he was unable to reconcile that inclination with his atomistic empiricism or his hedonistic psychology. Progressive theorists were able to complete the transformation of liberalism Mill started because they built their political ideas on a different philosophical foundation: their understanding of the social and value-laden quality of experience. As a result, they conceived of politics in terms of an egalitarian and progressive concept of civic virtue. They did not, however, make the mistake of adopting what Weber termed "that soft-headed attitude, so agreeable from the human point of view, but nevertheless so unutterably philistine, which thinks it possible to replace political with 'ethical' ideals and innocently imagines that this is the same as optimistically hoping for the best."[33] They understood that unless the reorientation of values they sought manifested itself in the reorganization of politics and the redistribution of power, change would remain a chimera. In that case, the preservation of freedom for some would mean only the more effective subordination of others; social order would not depend on the spontaneous harmony of free wills, but on the monotonous drone of enforced conformity.

3. Conclusion: Knowledge, Responsibility, and Reform

Intellectual developments during the years from 1870 to 1920 had all the neatness of a shattered kaleidoscope, and some of the same chaotic brilliance. The twentieth century's understandable preoccupation with the origins of its disasters has diverted attention from the philosophers of the *via media*, the theorists of social democracy, and the theorists of progressivism, who neither discovered the unconscious nor celebrated the violence and irrationality they found beneath the gloss of Victorian gentility. These two generations accomplished a less dramatic revolution with no less dramatic results: they transformed the ideas of revolutionary socialism and laissez-faire liberalism, and thereby helped to give birth to the political world in which we now live.

The years from 1870 to 1920 were pivotal in the development of socialist and liberal theory. Prior to 1870, the ideas of social democracy and progressivism did not exist; by 1920, they were central to the political discourse of Great Britain, France, Germany, and the United States. This set of developments is the decisive chapter in a much longer story, involving the shift from liberal republicanism to social democracy, from the world of Locke, Rousseau, Kant, and Madison to that of Crosland, Sartre, Habermas, and Rawls. The founders of liberal theory, who focused on the ideal of individual autonomy, helped to set in motion a process that ended by making freedom an end in itself rather than a means toward the end of virtue. By contributing to the creation of a world dominated by instrumental rationality and bourgeois capitalist values instead of dedicated to the idea of autonomous but responsible citizenship that attracted early liberals, liberalism eventually became a rationale for perpetuating privilege instead of an ideology of radical change; in that form it spawned the revolutionary socialism dedicated to its destruction. In the late nineteenth century, liberal and socialist ideals, and the philosophies on which they rested, were challenged by two generations of rebels who understood the irony of liberal virtue as it worked its way through eighteenth- and nineteenth-century culture, and who sought to recover the dual focus on liberty and justice that had been distorted by the fury of industrial capitalist development that liberalism made possible and then served to justify.

What were the sources of social democratic and progressive theory? These ideas grew, as all ideas do, from roots in political, social, economic, and intellectual history. Developments in the first three areas created pressures that were widely recognized by the beginning of the twentieth century, but the way to dissipate those pressures remained the subject of heated debate. Social democratic and progressive theorists presented two sets of coherent and imaginative options designed to defuse explosive conditions of inequality and oppression while avoiding the violence promised by both authoritarian and revolutionary solutions. Yet precisely because social democracy and progressivism offered a political *via media*, their origin has often been misunderstood. It is a mistake to interpret these ideas as a sign of the exhaustion of socialist energy or as liberalism's dying shudder, as a phase in the social history of intellectuals or a search for order in a newly interdependent world. Nor were they simply an expression of bourgeois class biases or an attempt to bolster organized capitalism. Social democratic and progressive ideas were put to all of those uses and more by various politicians, industrialists, engineers, and intellectuals, but that does not mean these ideas originated in the impulse to manipulate democratic cultures for antidemocratic ends.

The theories of social democracy and progressivism, at least as articulated by the individuals examined in this study, took shape as they did not only in response to socioeconomic and political conditions. They also reflected the impact of new ideas. The philosophers of the *via media* appreciated the philosophical inadequacies as well as the political problems of laissez-faire liberalism and revolutionary socialism. From different traditions they converged toward new ways of thinking about knowledge and action. The generation of political theorists and activists who inherited their dissatisfaction with prevailing ideas and politics, and their radical commitment to the fruitfulness of uncertainty, extended their radical theory of knowledge, their ideas about history, and their ethics of rational benevolence further into politics.

These thinkers' focus on immediate experience broke down subject-object dualism, and in that revolutionary rethinking of knowledge lay the seeds of a new approach to politics. The radical empiricist conception of immediate experience, which seems at first so distant from the realm of political argument, contained two complementary ideas that redefined the relation of the individual to the world beyond himself, ideas that altered perceptions of freedom and community and thus had profound implications for politics. The first of these ideas, the theory of voluntary action, revealed that freedom is an irreducible part of immediate experience that neither science nor metaphysics can challenge or explain away. In conjunction with the historical sensibility, the theory of voluntary action illuminated the cultural sources of values and pointed toward a broadened ideal of self-determination.

The second element in the concept of immediate experience, the idea that social relations are a fundamental part of individual life, altered the meaning of individuality by excluding the possibility of presocial or nonsocial experience on which so much earlier political theory relied. As the social dimension of experience came into focus, the meaningful quality of all life was revealed, and the futility of efforts to create an all-encompassing science of human affairs became apparent. The dream of a value-free science faded with the recognition that life is always value-laden. That recognition implied that politics must remain a servant to human purposes and that no values enjoy immunity from critical examination.

Social democratic and progressive politics also rested on the idea that there is no necessary opposition between the individual and society. This conviction, rooted in the analysis of immediate experience, found expression in the ethics of rational benevolence, which balances prudence against justice and motives against results. The theorists of social democracy and progressivism believed that political reform requires moral reform, and much of the confusion surrounding their emphasis on education as a necessary part of social change derives from a failure to appreciate the centrality of virtue in their political thought. Finally, the historical sensibility and the pragmatic theory of truth led these thinkers to judge democracy, with its inherent indeterminacy, a uniquely suitable method for achieving their goals.

In sum, the theories of social democracy and progressivism did not simply embody, express, or rationalize social developments by putting a gloss of ideas over the facts of economic and political change. Neither were they the incorporeal progeny of idealism and empiricism. Like all philosophy and political theory, they were born of the union between ideas and experience. Political theory changed between 1870 and 1920 not only because societies changed, but also because ideas changed. Without minimizing the importance of economic and political factors, I have tried to trace the process by which ideas about knowledge and responsibility altered ideas about politics. As Dewey wrote late in his career: "Any theory of activity in social and moral matters, liberal or otherwise, which is not grounded in a comprehensive philosophy, seems to me to be only a projection of arbitrary personal preferences."[34] There were obviously partisans of social democracy and progressivism who embraced these political programs without understanding or caring about their philosophical foundation. But the theorists discussed here shared Dewey's commitment to consistency between theory and practice, and they grounded their politics in precisely such a comprehensive philosophy.

The most important characteristic of this philosophy was its frank admission of uncertainty. These thinkers did not pretend to have solved the problems of social theory. They denied in principle that completely adequate solutions could be found. A critical attitude toward all forms of knowledge, including their own, was part of the intellectual independence they prized. Their willingness to live with doubt, however, was a sign of intellectual courage that their successors considered a kind of cowardice. As Reinhold Niebuhr wrote in 1919, the "gray spirit of compromise" pervading progressive democracy no longer satisfied a war-weary generation. "We need something less circumspect than liberalism to save the world."[35] The radicals whose caution he rejected believed that the world could not in any meaningful sense be saved, that it could only be shaped by purposeful and pragmatic social action. In the decades after 1920, their gospel of uncertainty seemed an unappealing alternative to competing millennial visions.

Not only did these skeptics deny that the world could be redeemed by faith, they also denied it could be redeemed by politics. They emphasized cultural change through education and democratization not because they trusted the popular will, but because they believed nothing less than a dramatic reorientation of values would suffice to accomplish their goals. They were right. While they may have been able to live without faith in the redemptive power of theology or ideology, their societies have proved unable to do so. The radical politics of social democracy and progressivism demanded the participation of all citizens and the pursuit of justice through constant experimentation, a cultural quest that could not be left in the hands of bureaucrats and party professionals but required the involvement of all citizens. A letter James wrote to the Polish activist and philosopher Wincenty Lutoslawski expressed his fears, and the fears of those who shared his conception of democracy as a cultural enterprise, concerning the danger of putting too much faith in reforming political institutions: "The strongest force in politics is human scheming," James warned, "and the schemers will capture every machinery you can set up against them."[36] The fate of social democratic and progressive political reforms in the last seven decades has demonstrated the wisdom of those words. Democracy's only defense against the power of private interests, as these thinkers understood, is a virtuous and active citizenry. In the absence of benevolence, politics is merely a struggle for private advantage, and when it is conceived in that way, it is inevitably dominated by those who possess power and know how to use it.

The absence of radical change in the United States, Great Britain, France, and Germany in the early twentieth century is clear, yet this does not necessarily mean the measures enacted during this period were poorly designed. It may mean only that they were poorly executed, at least when measured by the standards of social democracy and progressivism. In order to understand why, from these radicals' perspective, so many have been satisfied with so little for so long, it is instructive to recall the conception of politics discussed at the beginning of Chapter Nine. Because political life and fundamental cultural values are intertwined, they must change together. Radical reform failed to flourish after World War I because it was strangled by the roots of older, more firmly established patterns of thought and behavior that resurfaced in the harsh climate of reaction and revolution prevailing in the 1920s. The political radicalism of the prewar years did not cut deeply enough to dislodge older traditions of deference and older concentrations of power.

In their discussions of political change, these thinkers themselves provided the best explanation of the problems they faced. Bourgeois's most forceful statement of the philosophy and politics of solidarity was the introduction he contributed to Buisson's *La Politique radicale* (1908), in which he ran through the entire list of progressive reforms, then argued that these measures would be effective only if the ideas of duty and justice behind them were embraced by the entire society. Widespread agreement was crucial, Bourgeois argued, because solidarists believed in democracy as their fundamental value. They denied that anyone, including themselves, could dictate changes to the public against its will. These progressives denied the existence of the kind of certain knowledge that would justify suppressing the will of the majority in order to give the people what is good for them. Since they could appeal to no authority but experience to make their case, they could rely only on the failures of unrestrained capitalism to make the need for change evident. Moreover, progressivism was not the politics of any single group, and for that reason it could not appeal to simple self-interest. Bourgeois denied that solidarity was, as its critics on the left and right charged, simply "a moderate solution composed of approximations and reciprocal concessions." It offered rewards to, but also required sacrifices from, all members of society. Radical progressivism, Bourgeois concluded, should not be confused "with the exclusive defense of interests," whether "interests of party, sect, or class." Such radicalism was born of "the encounter of two forces becoming permanently free: reason, which searches for truth; and conscience, which longs for right."[37] The ideal of citizenship at the center of these progressives' vision could be realized only if popular ideas about knowledge and responsibility changed dramatically.

Far from establishing the transformative power of ideas in history, this study illustrates the limits of their influence. In all four nations, the disjunction between these thinkers' ideas and what has happened politically is as striking as the correspondence between their ideas and the programs of the reformist parties they helped to inspire. By 1920, the outlines of the various national forms of the corporate capitalist welfare state had been sketched out in Europe and, more faintly, in the United States. Progress toward democratic decision making, however, did not accompany that transformation. While the limited reforms accomplished during these years were not insignificant, they fell far short of these thinkers' hopes because they were pasted on the surface of cultures whose underlying values did not change. Welfare states that guarantee a minimum standard of living without challenging hierarchies of wealth and power betray rather than embody the ideals of social democracy and progressivism.

As these thinkers realized, democratic reform is an endless struggle. What is accomplished today can be undone tomorrow; what is left undone today can be accomplished tomorrow. The indeterminacy of democracy offers no basis for complacency or even confidence that progress toward positive freedom and genuine equality will continue, yet it always leaves open the possibility of such progress. Fortified by determination, that confidence can sustain hope. Even Weber, the most desperate of these critics, chose to swim against the stream of history, to be a champion of democratic institutions despite his pessimistic assessment of their prospects. The other theorists of social democracy and progressivism shared that heroic resolution regardless of their judgment of history as tragedy or epic. With James, they believed that the most probing question we face is also the most simple: "Will you or won't you have it so?" They understood that we choose our fate by our decision to confront or avoid the risks of "living on the perilous edge" of uncertainty.[38] We must accept responsibility for selecting our values and acting to realize our ideals without the comfort of a formula yielding easy answers to difficult questions. We must live with our uncertainty instead of trying to escape it. All of these thinkers envisioned a society in which equality guarantees the exercise of freedom, and in which individuals measure fulfillment against the criterion of benevolence. The twentieth century has rubbed some of the shine from their dream by demonstrating that man is capable of less than they hoped and more than they feared. The persistence of power has corroded the political institutions and the civic virtue they trusted to secure their ideals. While their victory has thus proved uncertain, their dream of democracy should survive.

Notes

Introduction

1. William James, "What Makes a Life Significant," in *Talks to Teachers on Psychology, and to Students on Some of Life's Ideals* (New York, 1901), 273–74.

2. Marc Bloch, "Pour une histoire comparée des sociétés européennes," *Revue de synthèse historique* (1928), reprinted in Bloch, *Mélanges historiques*, 2 vols., ed. Charles-Edmond Perrin (Paris, 1963), 1: 16–40; see also William H. Sewell, Jr., "Marc Bloch and the Logic of Comparative History," *History and Theory* 6 (1967): 208–18. More recent discussions of comparative history include C. Vann Woodward, "The Comparability of American History" and "The Test of Comparison," in *The Comparative Approach to American History*, ed. C. Vann Woodward (New York, 1968), 3–17, 347–56; George M. Fredrickson, "Comparative History," in *The Past Before Us: Contemporary Historical Writing in the United States*, ed. Michael Kammen (Ithaca, 1980), 457–73; and Raymond Grew, "The Case for Comparing Histories," *American Historical Review* 85 (1980): 763–78. Nor should any student of comparative history ignore the melancholy reflections offered near the end of a lifetime of comparative study by Max Weber in "Science as a Vocation," *From Max Weber*, ed. and trans. Hans Gerth and C. Wright Mills (New York, 1946), 134–35: "All work that overlaps neighboring fields," Weber wrote, "is burdened with the resigned realization that at best one provides the specialist with useful questions upon which he would not so easily hit from his own specialized point of view. One's own work must inevitably remain highly imperfect."

3. William James, *Pragmatism, The Works of William James* (cited hereafter as *Works*), ed. Frederick H. Burkhardt et al. (1907; Cambridge, Mass., 1975), 34–35.

4. This study thus has a focus different from those of the two most familiar students of this period, H. Stuart Hughes and Morton White. In *Consciousness and Society: The Reorientation of European Social Thought, 1890–1930* (1958; rpt. New York, 1961), Hughes concentrates more on the psychology of his subjects than on their ideas. His claims to the contrary notwithstanding, in *Social Thought in America: The Revolt Against Formalism*, 3rd ed. (1949; New York, 1976), White neither "causally explains" nor traces the "consequences" of historicism and cultural organicism, the two intellectual orientations he examines. Like Hughes, he does not connect these new styles of thinking with the transformation of politics. This study overlaps with those of

Hughes and White only in discussing Dilthey, Weber, and Dewey, and in all three cases I depart substantially from their interpretations—in part because I am interested primarily in the explicit connections between philosophy and politics, connections less important for Hughes's and White's conceptions of "social thought."

5. John Dewey, "The Influence of Darwinism on Philosophy," in *The Middle Works, 1899–1924* (cited hereafter as *MW*), vol. 4, *1907–1909*, ed. Jo Ann Boydston et al. (1909; Carbondale, Ill., 1977), 14.

Chapter 1. The Philosophy of the *Via Media*

1. For general conceptualizations of nineteenth-century intellectual history, see Maurice Mandelbaum, *History, Man, and Reason: A Study in Nineteenth-Century Thought* (Baltimore, 1971); Harald Höffding, *History of Modern Philosophy*, trans. B. E. Meyer (London, 1908); and Ernst Cassirer, *The Problem of Knowledge: Philosophy, Science, and History Since Hegel* (New Haven, 1950).

2. Scottish common sense realism has recently attracted considerable attention. The long-standard history of the movement is James McCosh, *The Scottish Philosophy, Biographical, Expository, Critical, from Hutcheson to Hamilton* (London, 1874). See also S. A. Grave, *The Scottish Philosophy of Common Sense* (Oxford, 1960); Douglas Sloan, *The Scottish Enlightenment and the American College Ideal* (New York, 1971); Donald H. Meyer, *The Instructed Conscience: The Shaping of the American National Ethic* (Philadelphia, 1972); Sydney Ahlstrom, "The Scottish Philosophy and American Theology," *Church History* 24 (1955): 257–72; and Terrence Martin, *The Instructed Vision: Scottish Common Sense Philosophy and the Origin of American Fiction* (Bloomington, 1968). On Reid, see his *Works*, 2 vols., ed. William Hamilton (Edinburgh, 1846–63), which also contains an essay by Hamilton on common sense and Dugald Stewart's biography of Reid. Hamilton's most important works are *Discussions on Philosophy and Literature, Education and University Reform* (London, 1852); and his *Lectures on Metaphysics and Logic*, 4 vols., ed. H. L. Mansel and John Veitch (Edinburgh and Boston, 1859–60). Compare the recent discussions of the Scottish school, and especially the contrasting estimates of McCosh, in Elizabeth Flower and Murray G. Murphy, *A History of Philosophy in America*, 2 vols. (New York, 1977); and J. David Hoeveler, Jr., *James McCosh and the Scottish Intellectual Tradition* (Princeton, 1981).

3. On Cousin and French philosophy in the mid-nineteenth century, see Paul Janet, *Victor Cousin et son oeuvre* (Paris, 1885); Theodore Zeldin, *France 1848–1945: Taste and Corruption* (Oxford, 1980), 60–63; and idem, *France 1848–1945: Intellect and Pride* (Oxford, 1980), 205–27. In addition to Cousin's *Du Vrai, du beau et du bien* (Paris, 1853), see his *Philosophie écossaise*, 3rd ed. (Paris, 1857). William Logue discusses the fate of Cousin's eclecticism in late nineteenth-century France in *From Philosophy to Sociology: The Evolution of French Liberalism, 1870–1914* (DeKalb, Ill., 1983), 17–50.

4. Portions of Fichte's *Sämmtliche Werke* (1845–46) were translated by the American philosopher William Tory Harris and published as *The Science of Knowledge* (1794; London, 1889); the passage quoted is from p. 36 of Harris's edition. See also Richard Kroner, *Von Kant bis Hegel*, 2 vols. (Tübingen, 1921).

5. On romanticism, I have found particularly useful M. H. Abrams, *The Mirror and the Lamp* (New York, 1953); and idem, *Natural Supernaturalism: Tradition and Revolution in Romantic Literature* (New York, 1971). Conflicting views of romanticism can be found in Irving Babbitt, *Rousseau and Romanticism* (1919; rpt. Austin, 1977), a polemic blaming romanticism for modernity; and Arthur Lovejoy, "On the Discrimination of Romanticisms" (1924), in *Essays in the History of Ideas* (New York, 1960), which denies that a single romanticism can be identified. Jacques Barzun, *Romanticism and the Modern Ego* (Boston, 1943), reprinted as

Classic, Romantic, and Modern (New York, 1961), is a helpful overview. On France, see George Boas, *French Philosophies of the Romantic Period* (Baltimore, 1925); and D. G. Charlton, *Secular Religions in France, 1815–1870* (London, 1963). On America, see Perry Miller, ed., *The Transcendentalists: An Anthology* (Cambridge, Mass., 1950); F. O. Matthiessen, *American Renaissance: Art and Expression in the Age of Emerson and Whitman* (New York, 1941); Michael T. Gilmore, *The Middle Way: Puritanism and Ideology in American Romantic Fiction* (New Brunswick, N. J., 1977); Paul F. Boller, Jr., *American Transcendentalism, 1830–1860: An Intellectual Inquiry* (New York, 1974); and Philip F. Gura and Joel Myerson, eds., *Critical Essays on American Transcendentalism* (Boston, 1982).

6. On Hegel I have found most useful Charles Taylor's *Hegel* (Cambridge, 1975). More general studies include Karl Löwith, *From Hegel to Nietzsche: The Revolution in Nineteenth-Century Thought*, trans. David E. Green (New York, 1964); Herbert Marcuse, *Reason and Revolution: Hegel and the Rise of Social Theory* (1941; Boston, 1964); Hayden White, *Metahistory: The Historical Imagination in Nineteenth-Century Europe* (Baltimore, 1973); and Mandelbaum, *History, Man, and Reason*. On idealism in Britain see A. J. M. Milne, *The Social Philosophy of English Idealism* (London, 1962); and in America, Henry A. Pochmann, *German Culture in America, Philosophical and Literary Influences, 1600–1900* (Madison, 1961); William H. Goetzman, ed., *The American Hegelians: An Intellectual Episode in the History of Western America* (New York, 1973); and Flower and Murphy, "The Absolute Immigrates to America," in *A History of Philosophy in America*, 2: 463–514.

7. On positivism, see Walter Simon, *European Positivism in the Nineteenth Century* (Ithaca, 1962); Frank E. Manuel, *The New World of Henri Saint-Simon* (Cambridge, Mass., 1956); idem, *The Prophets of Paris* (Cambridge, Mass., 1962); D. G. Charlton, *Positivist Thought in France during the Second Empire, 1852–1870* (Oxford, 1959); idem, *Secular Religions in France, 1815–1870* (London, 1963).

8. See Löwith, *From Hegel to Nietzsche*, 323–85; Leszek Kolakowski, *Main Currents of Marxism*, vol. 1, *The Founders*, trans. P. S. Falla (Oxford, 1978), 81–119; Frederick Copleston, *A History of Modern Philosophy*, vol. 7, *Modern Philosophy*, Part 1, *Fichte to Hegel* (Garden City, N. Y., 1963); and Part 2, *Schopenhauer to Nietzsche* (Garden City, N. Y., 1963); Flower and Murphy, *Philosophy in America*, 2: 464–74, 517–21; and John Burrow, *Evolution and Society* (Cambridge, 1968).

9. Recent discussions of Darwinism include Neal C. Gillespie, *Charles Darwin and the Problem of Creation* (Chicago, 1979); James R. Moore, *The Post-Darwinian Controversies* (New York, 1979); and Michael Ruse, *The Darwinian Revolution* (Chicago, 1979). See also Loren Eisley, *Darwin's Century: Evolution and the Men Who Discovered It* (Garden City, N. Y., 1958); Stow Persons, *Evolutionary Thought in America* (New Haven, 1950); Paul F. Boller, Jr., *American Thought in Transition: The Impact of Evolutionary Naturalism, 1865–1900* (Chicago, 1969); Cynthia Eagle Russett, *Darwin in America: The Intellectual Response, 1865–1912* (San Francisco, 1976); and Gertrude Himmelfarb, *Darwin and the Darwinian Revolution* (1959; rpt. New York, 1968).

10. Henry Adams, *The Education of Henry Adams* (Boston and New York, 1927), 451–55; Karl Pearson, *The Grammar of Science* (London, 1892); the quotation is from Pearson's introduction to the 2nd ed., 1899; Ernst Mach, *The Science of Mechanics,* in *The Changeless Order,* ed. Arnold Koslow (New York, 1967), 143.

11. Chauncey Wright, *Philosophical Discussions*, ed. Charles Eliot Norton (New York, 1877), vii–xxiii. See also Flower and Murphy, *Philosophy in America*, 2: 535–53; Mandelbaum, *History, Man, and Reason*, 28–37; Walter Houghton, *The Victorian Frame of Mind* (New Haven, 1957), 1–23; Frank M. Turner, "The Victorian Conflict Between Science and Religion: A Professional Dimension," *Isis* 69 (1978): 356–76; D. H. Meyer, "American Intellectuals and the Victorian Crisis of Faith," in *Victorian America*, ed. Daniel Walker Howe (Philadelphia, 1976),

59–77. Arnold's "Stanzas from the Grande Chartreuse," from which the quotation is taken, was first published in 1855 and appears in *Poems of Matthew Arnold*, 3 vols. (London, 1905–1907), 2:214.

12. See Nietzsche, *On the Genealogy of Morals*, trans. Walter Kaufmann and R. J. Hollingdale (New York, 1967), essay 3, sections 24 and 25; and *The Gay Science*, trans. Walter Kaufmann (New York, 1974), sections 124, 343, 347, 377. On varieties of antimodernism and decadence, see Fritz Stern, *The Politics of Cultural Despair: A Study in the Rise of the Germanic Ideology* (Berkeley, 1961); Eugen Weber, *The Nationalist Revival in France, 1905–1914* (Berkeley, 1959); K. W. Swart, *The Sense of Decadence in Nineteenth-Century France* (The Hague, 1964); and T. J. Jackson Lears, *No Place of Grace: Antimodernism and the Transformation of American Culture, 1880–1920* (New York, 1982). Norman Stone chronicles the flight from liberalism and the rise of political irrationalism in *Europe Transformed, 1878–1919* (Cambridge, Mass., 1984).

13. Dewey's appreciation of James first appeared in *The Independent*, September 8, 1910; it is reprinted in *MW*, 10: 91–97. James's comment appears in a letter to J. C. F. Schiller, April 8, 1903, reprinted in Ralph Barton Perry, *The Thought and Character of William James*, 2 vols. (Boston, 1935), 2: 375. Cf. Nietzsche, *The Gay Science*, section 228.

14. Wilhelm Dilthey, *Gesammelte Schriften* (cited hereafter as *GS*), ed. Bernard Groethuysen et al., 18 vols. (Stuttgart and Göttingen, 1914–1977), 18: 208. On Dilthey's youth and early career, see *Der junge Dilthey: Ein Lebensbild in Briefen und Tagebüchern, 1852–1870*, edited by Dilthey's daughter (and wife of Dilthey's student, the philosopher Georg Misch) Clara Misch, 2nd ed. (Stuttgart and Göttingen, 1960).

15. James to his sister Alice James, Oct. 17, 1867, in *The Letters of William James*, ed. Henry James, 2 vols. (1920; rpt. New York, 1969), 1: 108–14. Dilthey to Graf Yorck, June, 1884, in *Briefwechsel zwischen Wilhelm Dilthey und dem Grafen Paul Yorck von Wartenburg, 1877–1897*, ed. Sigrid von der Schulenburg (Halle a.d.S., 1923), 44.

16. A comprehensive bibliography of writings by and about Dilthey is Ulrich Hermann, *Bibliographie Wilhelm Dilthey: Quellen und Literatur* (Berlin, 1969). The first 6 volumes of Dilthey's *Gesammelte Schriften* contain his published writings; the other volumes comprise primarily portions of the enormous number of manuscripts he left unfinished when he died. Interpretations of Dilthey begin with Georg Misch's introduction to volume 5 of *GS*, the first attempt at a comprehensive account of Dilthey's ideas. Misch placed Dilthey's thought in a broader framework in his *Lebensphilosophie und Phänomenologie: Eine Auseinandersetzung der Diltheyschen Richtung mit Heidegger und Husserl*, 2nd ed. (Stuttgart, 1967). Postwar Dilthey studies began with Kurt Mueller-Vollmer's *Towards a Phenomenological Theory of Literature: A Study of Wilhelm Dilthey's Poetik* (The Hague, 1963), which focused on Dilthey's aesthetics, a subject also addressed in Karol Sauerland, *Diltheys Erlebnisbegriff* (Berlin, 1972); and Rudolf A. Makkreel, *Dilthey: Philosopher of the Human Studies* (Princeton, 1975). Perhaps a more important impetus in the revival of interest in Dilthey was the treatment he received in Hans-Georg Gadamer, *Truth and Method*, ed. and trans. Garrett Barden and John Cumming (1960; London, 1975), in which hermeneutics was reontologized and Dilthey appeared disguised as a forerunner of Gadamer's teacher Heidegger. Equally significant were the neo-Marxist readings of Dilthey contained in Georg Lukacs, *Die Zerstörung der Vernunft: Der Weg des Irrationalismus von Schelling zu Hitler* (Newuwied am Rhein, 1962), and the somewhat less unsympathetic interpretation in Jürgen Habermas, *Knowledge and Human Interests*, trans. J. J. Shapiro (1968; Boston, 1971). A more elaborate analysis of Dilthey from a Marxist perspective, which blithely overlooks Dilthey's explicit criticism of Marx, is Christofer Zöckler, *Dilthey und die Hermeneutik: Diltheys Begründung der Hermeneutik als "Praxiswissenschaft" und die Geschichte ihrer Rezeption* (Stuttgart, 1975). A thorough examination of Dilthey's early writings is Peter Krausser, *Kritik der endlichen Vernunft: Diltheys Revolution der allgemeinen Wissenschafts-*

und Handlungstheorie (Stuttgart, 1969), a précis of which is available in English in "Dilthey's Revolution in the Theory of the Structure of Scientific Inquiry and Rational Behavior," *Review of Metaphysics* 22 (1968): 262–80. Frithjof Rodi, *Morphologie und Hermeneutik: Zur Methode von Diltheys Ästhetik* (Stuttgart, 1969), explores the tensions between interpretations of the organic world and the world of meaning in Dilthey's hermeneutics. Helmut Johach, *Handelnder Mensch und objektiver Geist: Zur Theorie der Geistes- und Sozialwissenschaften bei Wilhelm Dilthey* (Meisenheim, 1974), emphasizes the inadequacy of viewing Dilthey as a contemplative thinker unconcerned with contemporary problems and places him in the context of late nineteenth-century social theory. A corrective to Gadamer and Habermas that places Dilthey in the Kantian tradition is Hans Ineichen, *Erkenntnistheorie und geschichtlich-gesellschaftliche Welt: Diltheys Logik der Geisteswissenschaften* (Frankfurt a.M., 1975). In English, H. A. Hodges, *The Philosophy of Wilhelm Dilthey* (London, 1952), remains a solid introduction to Dilthey. More recent general studies include Ilse N. Bulhof, *Wilhelm Dilthey: A Hermeneutic Approach to the Study of History and Culture*, Martinus Nijhoff Philosophy Library, vol. 2 (The Hague, 1980), and Theodore Plantinga, *Historical Understanding in the Thought of Wilhelm Dilthey* (Toronto, 1980). H. P. Rickman has done more than anyone to make Dilthey's writings accessible to the English-speaking public. See his editions of Dilthey's writings *Pattern and Meaning in History: Thoughts on History and Society* (New York, 1962); *W. Dilthey, Selected Writings*, cited hereafter as *SW* (Cambridge, 1976); and his analytical overview of Dilthey's ideas and his impact on modern thought, *Wilhelm Dilthey: Pioneer of the Human Studies* (Berkeley, 1979). The most comprehensive study of Dilthey in English is Michael Ermarth, *Wilhelm Dilthey: The Critique of Historical Reason* (Chicago, 1978).

17. Henry Sidgwick's "Recollection of T. H. Green," sent to Mrs. T. H. Green in a letter postmarked Aug. 3, 1882, is in the T. H. Green papers, library of Balliol College, Oxford. The standard biography of Green is R. L. Nettleship, *Memoir of Thomas Hill Green* (London, 1906). A broader account is Melvin Richter, *The Politics of Conscience: T. H. Green and His Age* (Cambridge, Mass., 1964), a thorough intellectual biography marred by its presentism. Although Richter grudgingly admits that the historical analysis of Green's philosophy requires taking his ideas seriously at least "provisionally," the swaggering toughness of Richter's analysis obstructs his understanding of Green's world. When he exclaims, for example, that Sidgwick and Leslie Stephen were, like Green, "not able to put completely behind them the teaching of self sacrifice" (120), the reader can only wonder why such earnest Victorians should be expected to have "put completely behind them" their deepest convictions. Richter's emphasis on Green's religious convictions as the key to understanding his thought is disputed by John Rodman in his introduction to *The Political Theory of T. H. Green* (New York, 1964) and challenged more forcefully by I. M. Greengarten, *Thomas Hill Green and the Development of Liberal-Democratic Thought* (Toronto, 1981), esp. 6–11.

18. Green, *Prolegomena to Ethics*, ed. A. C. Bradley(1883; rpt. New York, 1969), 2.

19. Green, *Works*, ed. R. L. Nettleship, 3 vols. (London, 1885–1889), 1: 369; 3: 117–25. Green was very fond of the Lake Country poets, and he considered Wordsworth's "Ode to Duty" the "high water mark of modern poetry" (*Works*, 3: xviii, 118–20). This poem, a departure from the self-absorption characteristic of the English romantics' early yearnings for release from alienation through union with nature, recalls in form and mood a sterner, Senecan sense of self-discipline that expresses precisely the blend of elements in Green's own outlook. Its closing lines encapsulate Green's creed:

> Give unto me, made lowly wise,
> The spirit of self-sacrifice;
> The confidence of reason give;
> And in the light of truth thy Bondman let me live!

20. Green to H. S. Holland, Dec. 29, 1868, in *Henry Scott Holland, Memoir and Letters*, ed. Stephen Paget (London, 1921), 29–30.

21. Mrs. Humphry Ward, *Robert Elsmere*, 3 vols. (London, 1888); and see idem, *A Writer's Recollections* (London, 1918).

22. Green, *Works*, 3: cxi. Green's impact on British politics is emphasized by George H. Sabine, *A History of Political Theory*, 2nd ed. (New York, 1950), and minimized by Adam B. Ulam, *Philosophical Foundations of English Socialism* (Cambridge, 1951). John Morrow, in "Liberalism and British Idealist Political Philosophy," *History of Political Thought* 4 (1984): 91–108, effectively differentiates Green's ideas from those of Bosanquet and Ritchie. Studies of Green's philosophy include W. H. Fairbrother, *The Philosophy of Thomas Hill Green* (London, 1896); Milne, *English Idealism*; and Ann R. Cacoullos, *Thomas Hill Green: Philosopher of Rights* (New York, 1974), which contains a bibliography of the secondary literature, including periodicals, dealing with Green and his ideas. The most thorough analysis of Green's philosophy is Jean Pucelle, *La Nature et l'esprit dans la philosophie de T. H. Green: la renaissance de l'idéalisme en Angleterre au XIXᵉ siècle*, 2 vols. (Louvain and Paris, 1965).

23. These quotations are from letters Sidgwick wrote in 1863 to H. G. Dakyns and in 1866 to Roden Noel, included in the autobiographical fragment dictated by Sidgwick shortly before his death and printed in Arthur Sidgwick and Eleanor Mildred Sidgwick, *Henry Sidgwick, A Memoir* (London, 1906), 9. This account, written by Sidgwick's brother and his wife, is the most thorough biography of Sidgwick. For brief accounts of his life, see C. D. Broad, *Ethics and the History of Philosophy* (New York, 1952), 49–69; Jerome B. Schneewind, *Sidgwick's Ethics and Victorian Moral Philosophy* (Oxford, 1977), 13–63; and Stefan Collini's essay on Sidgwick in Collini, Donald Winch, and John Burrow, *That Noble Science of Politics: A Study in Nineteenth-Century Intellectual History* (Cambridge, 1983), 278–307. The 6th ed. of Sidgwick's *Methods of Ethics* (1874; London, 1901) contains an autobiographical sketch.

24. Undated entry from Sidgwick's diary, ca. March, 1855, and entry from Sidgwick's journal of 1867, both in the Henry Sidgwick papers, Wren Library, Trinity College, Cambridge.

25. William James to Mrs. Henry Sidgwick, Sept. 1, 1900, Sidgwick papers.

26. Sidgwick to Mrs. T. H. Green, postmarked Aug. 3, 1882, Green papers.

27. A splendid analysis of Sidgwick's ethics in relation to earlier and contemporary ethical theory is Schneewind, *Sidgwick's Ethics and Victorian Moral Philosophy*. More broadly focused, and less tightly argued, are William C. Havard, *Henry Sidgwick and Later Utilitarian Political Philosophy* (Gainesville, Fla., 1959); and D. G. James, *Henry Sidgwick: Science and Faith in Victorian England* (Oxford, 1970). The best brief discussion of Sidgwick's moral philosophy is C. D. Broad, *Five Types of Ethical Theory* (New York, 1930).

28. Sidgwick, *Philosophy, Its Scope and Relations: An Introductory Course of Lectures*, ed. James Ward (London, 1902), 243.

29. Sidgwick, *The Methods of Ethics*, 1st ed. (London, 1874), 473.

30. Fouillée, *Histoire générale de la philosophie*, 11th ed. (1875; Paris, 1910), 528.

31. Fouillée, "Réponse à une enquête sur l'idée et le sentiment religieux," *Mercure de France* 66 (1907): 582–83.

32. Fouillée, *La France au point de vue moral*, 5th ed. (1900; Paris, 1911), 406; *Esquisse psychologique des peuples européens* (Paris, 1905), xiv.

33. Fouillée tried to explain the impact of Guyau's death on his life in one of his few surviving letters, this one to Ernest Havet, Aug. 9, 1888, Salle des manuscrits, Bibliothèque Nationale, Paris. The best biography of Fouillée is Augustin Guyau, *La Philosophie et la sociologie d'Alfred Fouillée* (Paris, 1913), written by the son of Fouillée's disciple Jean–Marie Guyau. J.–M. Guyau became Fouillée's stepson when his mother married Fouillée after the death of Guyau's father. Although A. Guyau's account is uncritical, it is nevertheless the best source of information about Fouillée's life. For an account of Fouillée's thesis defense, see Guyau, x–xiii. Renouvier is said to

have remarked that in comparison to Fouillée's eloquence, "the vaunted lessons of Victor Cousin were contemptible."

34. The most thorough analysis of Fouillée's philosophy is the magisterial study by Elisabeth Ganne de Beaucoudrey, *La Psychologie et la métaphysique des idées-forces chez Alfred Fouillée* (Paris, 1936), which includes a complete bibliography of Fouillée's voluminous writings. As Ganne de Beaucoudrey notes, the enormous quantity of material Fouillée produced may account as much as any other reason for his lack of followers: the bulk of his writings, to say nothing of the intricacy of their treatment of philosophers now even more obscure than Fouillée, presents an intimidating barrier. Among the most important of his books are *La Liberté et le déterminisme*, 8th ed. (1872; Paris, 1911), a revision of his controversial dissertation; *L'Idée moderne du droit en Allemagne, en Angleterre et en France* (Paris, 1878); *La Science sociale contemporaine*, 2nd ed. (1880; Paris, 1885); *L'Evolutionisme des idées-forces* (Paris, 1890); *La Psychologie des idées-forces*, 2 vols. (Paris, 1893); and *L'Enseignement au point de vue national* (Paris, 1891), edited and translated into English by W. J. Greenstreet as *Education from a National Standpoint* (New York, 1892). On competing contemporary philosophers, see *Le Mouvement idéaliste et la réaction contre la science positive* (Paris, 1896); *Nietzsche et l'immoralisme* (Paris, 1902); and *La Pensée et les nouvelles écoles anti-intellectualistes* (Paris, 1911), directed primarily against Bergson. Discussions of Fouillée in English include Harald Höffding, *Modern Philosophers*, trans. A. C. Mason (London, 1915); John A. Scott, *Republican Ideas and the Liberal Tradition in France, 1870–1914* (New York, 1951), 159–69; J. E. S. Hayward, "'Solidarity' and the Reformist Sociology of Alfred Fouillée," *American Journal of Economics and Sociology* 22 (1963): 205–22, 305–12; and Logue, *From Philosophy to Sociology*, 129–50.

35. The standard biographies of James are Perry, *The Thought and Character of William James*, which focuses primarily on James's philosophy; and Gay Wilson Allen, *William James* (New York, 1967), which ignores James's ideas altogether and concentrates on his illnesses. Allen leaves a peculiar impression of James as a crotchety hypochondriac who wandered around two continents wallowing in self-pity, indulging his bizarre fascination with the occult, and unable to get down to work. Although Allen's biography contains valuable material not available elsewhere, it does not do justice to James. For a portrait of one of America's most remarkable families, see F. O. Matthiessen, *The James Family: A Group Biography* (New York, 1947). Howard M. Feinstein offers a fascinating but unfortunately one-dimensional portrait of the artist (*manqué*) as a young man in *Becoming William James* (Ithaca, 1984), an insightful study that discounts James's ideas and focuses on the role of family tensions in shaping James's early years.

36. The most important sources on James's psychic crisis are his notebooks, diaries, and letters from 1867 to 1872 in the William James papers, Houghton Library, Harvard University, particularly the diary entry dated Feb. 1, 1870, and the notebook entry dated April 30, 1870. The quotations are from James's autobiographical account of his experience, disguised as the recollections of an anonymous Frenchman, in *The Varieties of Religious Experience*, 2nd ed. (1902; New York, 1929), 157–58. On the importance of Renouvier and Wordsworth, see Henry James, Sr., to Henry James, March 18, 1873, in *Letters of William James*, 1: 169–70. See also the discussions of this period in Perry, *James*, 1: 320–25; Allen, 162–70; and *Letters of William James*, 1: 144–48. Recent interpretations of the decisive years from 1867 to 1872 include Feinstein, *Becoming William James*, 298–329; Cushing Strout, "William James and the Twice-Born Sick Soul," *Daedalus* 97 (1968): 1062–82; James Anderson, "William James's Depressive Period (1867–1872) and the Origins of his Creativity: A Psychobiographical Study," Ph.D. diss., University of Chicago, 1980; and Mark R. Schwehn, "Making the World: William James and the Life of the Mind," in *A William James Renaissance: Four Essays by Young Scholars*, ed. Mark R. Schwehn, *Harvard Library Bulletin* 30 (1982): 426–54.

37. James, "What Is an Instinct?" *Scribner's Magazine* 1 (1887): 360. For a brilliant analysis

424 Notes to Pages 39–40

of Darwin's importance for James, see Robert J. Richards, "The Personal Equation in Science: William James's Psychological and Moral Uses of Darwinian Theory," in Schwehn, ed., *A William James Renaissance*, 387–425. See also Schwehn, "Making the World," 437, on Peirce's role in James's interpretation of evolutionary theory; and Philip P. Wiener, *Evolution and the Founders of Pragmatism*, 2nd ed. (1949; Philadelphia, 1972), 97–128.

38. William James to Alice Howe Gibbens, March 4, 1888, James papers. The letters from James to his wife, only recently made available to scholars, reveal an important dimension of James's personality. See also James, "Quelques considérations sur la méthode subjective," which appeared originally in *Critique philosophique* 2 (1878), and is reprinted in *Essays in Philosophy, Works* (Cambridge, Mass., 1978), 28, where James expresses a similar viewpoint.

39. On James, Sidgwick, and psychical research, see R. Laurence Moore, *In Search of White Crows: Spiritualism, Parapsychology, and American Culture* (New York, 1977); *William James and Psychic Research*, ed. Gardner Murphy and Robert Ballou (New York, 1960); Eugene Taylor, "William James on Psychopathology: The 1896 Lowell Lectures on 'Exceptional Mental States,'" in Schwehn, ed., *A William James Renaissance*, 455–79; and John J. Cerullo, *The Secularization of the Soul: Psychical Research in Modern Britain* (Philadelphia, 1982).

40. The principal sources for James's religious thought are *The Varieties of Religious Experience* and *The Will to Believe, Works* (1897; Cambridge, Mass., 1979). Among the studies and commentaries, the best place to begin is Henry Levinson, *The Religious Investigations of William James* (Chapel Hill, N.C., 1981). See also William A. Clebsch, *American Religious Thought: A History* (Chicago, 1973), 125–70; Stephen T. Davis, "Wishful Thinking and 'The Will to Believe,'" *Transactions of the Charles S. Peirce Society* 8 (1972): 231–45; Patrick K. Dooley, "The Nature of Belief: The Proper Context for James's 'The Will to Believe,'" *Transactions of the Charles S. Peirce Society* 8 (1972): 141–51; and James L. Muyskens, "James's Defense of a Believing Attitude in Religion," *Transactions of the Charles S. Peirce Society* 10 (1974): 44–54. The religious feelings hidden beneath Fouillée's anticlericalism are revealed in his letters to Ernest Havet, especially the letter of May 6, 1884, in Nouvelles Acquisitions Françaises, 24474, ff. 235–37, Salle des manuscrits, Bibliothèque Nationale, Paris.

41. James's writings are currently being published in a definitive edition by Harvard University Press, *The Works of William James*, ed. Frederick J. Burkhardt et al. It is useful to have standard editions of James's work, and particularly helpful to have some of his scattered essays gathered together. Although these volumes stagger under the weight of their elaborate scholarly apparatus—an ungainly condition that might elicit a good-natured jibe from James were he around to see it—they are invaluable guides for students of James's thought. Given the multidimensional quality of James's thinking, the inclination to accentuate one feature of it and minimize the rest appears irresistible, and it has led to the proliferation of contradictory interpretations of his thought. Perhaps in reaction to the straightforward empiricist reading of James in Perry's standard *Thought and Character of William James*, interpreting James as a phenomenologist has become a growth industry on both sides of the Atlantic. Among these studies are Johannes Linschoten, *On the Way Toward a Phenomenological Psychology: The Psychology of William James*, ed. Amadeo Georgi (Pittsburgh, 1968); and Bruce Wilshire, *William James and Phenomenology: A Study of "The Principles of Psychology"* (Bloomington, Ind., 1968), both of which concentrate on James's relation to the transcendental phenomenology of Husserl. John Wild, by contrast, distinguishes James from Husserl and places him closer to the existential phenomenology of Merleau-Ponty in *The Radical Empiricism of William James* (Garden City, N.Y., 1969). For citations of the other contributions to this burgeoning literature, see John McDermott's introduction to James's *Essays in Radical Empiricism, Works* (1912; Cambridge, Mass., 1976), xlv n. 41. These antihistorical attempts to dress James in phenomenological garb, imaginative as they may be, suggest that philosophers often bring very different considerations than historians to the study of ideas. Likewise illustrating that problem, but from the

opposite vantage point of analytic philosophy, are A. J. Ayer's *The Origins of Pragmatism: Studies in the Philosophy of Charles Sanders Peirce and William James* (San Francisco, 1968); and Ayer's introduction to the paperback edition of *Pragmatism and the Meaning of Truth* (Cambridge, Mass., 1979), both of which reveal much more about Ayer than about James. Useful correctives to such presentist views are Murray G. Murphy, "Kant's Children: The Cambridge Pragmatists," *Transactions of the Charles S. Peirce Society* 4 (1968): 3–33, and Bruce Kuklick, *The Rise of American Philosophy: Cambridge, Massachusetts, 1860–1930* (New Haven, 1977), both of which emphasize the Kantian elements in James's thought. More recent studies include Don Browning, *Pluralism and Personality: William James and Some Contemporary Cultures of Psychology* (Lewisburg, Penn., 1980); Marcus Ford, *William James's Philosophy* (Amherst, 1982); and Jacques Barzun, *A Stroll with William James* (New York, 1983).

42. James, *The Varieties of Religious Experience*, 481; *Pragmatism*, 27–28, 98. On James's attitude toward Bergson, see Perry, *James*, 2: 599–636; and Richard J. Bernstein's introduction to James, *A Pluralistic Universe, Works* (1909; Cambridge, Mass., 1977), xx–xxiii.

43. James, *The Will to Believe*, 112. This passage comes near the end of James's address "Reflex Action and Theism," which concludes with the closing lines of Tennyson's "De Profundis," a poem James also read to his classes in philosophy at Harvard. See Henry F. May to Ralph Barton Perry, June 13, 1931, in the James Papers. On Sidgwick's fondness for Tennyson, see Schneewind, *Sidgwick's Ethics*, 378 f.

44. James's image of picture painting appears on an envelope catalogued with his "Introduction [for a systematic work on philosophy]," dated 1904, in the James papers. After 1900, James frequently expressed his desire to write "a general treatise on philosophy" and lamented that his work resembled "an arch built only on one side." See *Letters of William James*, 2: 203; James, *Some Problems of Philosophy, Works* (1911; Cambridge, Mass., 1979), 5; and cf. Perry, *James*, 2: 338, 468. As Dewey wrote in a review of James's posthumously published *Essays in Radical Experience* (*MW*, 7: 143), "There is still something congenial to Mr. James's personal temperament and to his philosophy in this unfinished state. For there is nothing more characteristic of the substance of his thought than the belief that the world itself has an element of unfinishedness in it and that one of the standing errors of philosophers has been to attribute to reality a completeness which as matter of fact it does not possess."

45. See James's review of *Studies in Logical Theory*, in *Psychological Bulletin* 1 (1904): 1–5; and James's letter to F. C. S. Schiller, Nov. 15, 1903, in Perry, *James*, 2: 501.

46. In the preface to *Studies in Logical Theory*, University of Chicago Decennial Publications, 2nd series, vol. 11 (Chicago, 1903), 5, *MW*, 2: 297, the contributors acknowledged their "preeminent obligation" to James, "who, we hope, will accept this acknowledgement and this book as unworthy tokens of a regard and an admiration that are coequal." For the correspondence between James and Dewey at this time, see Perry, *James*, 2: 520–26. See also James's letter to Dewey, Dec. 3, 1903, in the general manuscript collection of Butler Library, Columbia University, in which James praises Dewey for having created "a genuine school of original thought" for which he predicts a "great future" and with which he promises his "zealous cooperation." James's reading notes on *Studies in Logical Theory*, in the James papers, further reveal his enthusiastic response to Dewey's ideas.

47. Dewey to Daniel C. Gilman, Aug. 11, 1882, quoted in George Dykhuizen, *The Life and Mind of John Dewey* (Carbondale, Ill., 1973), 26. Dykhuizen's splendid biography is the essential source on Dewey's life, more reliable than Dewey's own autobiographical essay, "From Absolutism to Experimentalism," in *Contemporary American Philosophy*, ed. George P. Adams and William F. Montague (New York, 1930) 2: 13–27. Although Dewey lived until 1952, I will follow his career only through the publication of *Reconstruction in Philosophy* in 1920. While I do not dispute the importance of later developments in Dewey's thought, for purposes of my analysis it is more appropriate to limit myself to Dewey's "early" and "middle" years; in 1920 he

was sixty-one years of age. Useful studies of the early stages of Dewey's career include Morton G. White, *The Origin of Dewey's Instrumentalism* (New York, 1943), which concentrates on Dewey's intellectual development and emphasizes, despite the book's title, Dewey's later philosophy as the optic through which his growth should be viewed; and Neil Coughlan, *Young John Dewey: An Essay in American Intellectual History* (Chicago, 1973), which is broader in scope but less helpful concerning Dewey's ideas.

48. On Dewey's experiences at Johns Hopkins, see Dykhuizen, *Dewey*, 28–43. The characterizations of Peirce and Hall are contained in letters Dewey wrote to H. A. P. Torrey, Oct. 5, 1882, quoted in Dykhuizen, *Dewey*, 30; and to William Torrey Harris, Feb. 4, 1883, in the John Dewey papers, Morris Library, Southern Illinois University, Carbondale. On Dewey's attitude toward Morris, see Dykhuizen, *Dewey*, 31–34. Dewey's attraction to idealism is discussed in light of his religious faith in Bruce Kuklick, *Churchmen and Philosophers: Jonathan Edwards to John Dewey* (New Haven, 1985), 230–33; and Flower and Murphy, *Philosophy in America*, 2: 813–22. Dewey's comments on the appeal of Hegel and idealism are in his autobiographical essay "From Absolutism to Experimentalism," 19–21. On Trendlenburg, Morris, and Dewey, see Gershon George Rosenstock, *F. A. Trendlenburg: Forerunner to John Dewey* (Carbondale, Ill., 1964), which persuasively outlines the parallels between Trendlenburg's and Dewey's ideas but fails to establish Dewey's reliance on Trendlenburg. For Dewey's comment on his attitude as a young man toward Wordsworth, see the fragment dated May 7, 1943, in the Dewey papers; and Max Eastman, "John Dewey," *Atlantic* 168 (1941): 673.

49. Morris's comments on Dewey's *Psychology* quoted in Dykhuizen, *Dewey*, 54–55. Since Dewey's *Psychology* was published in 1887, and James's letter about it to Croom Robertson in the James papers is dated, in James's handwriting, Dec. 27, 1886, he must have read the book before its publication. This discrepancy has understandably prompted some confusion. See for example Robert Crunden's essay on Dewey and Jane Addams in John D. Buenker, John C. Burnham, and Robert M. Crunden, *Progressivism* (Cambridge, Mass., 1977), 102 n. 34, where Perry is accused of having "apparently" misdated a letter dated quite clearly by James himself.

50. Dewey, "The Philosophy of Thomas Hill Green, *Andover Review* 11 (1889): 337–55; in John Dewey, *The Early Works* (cited hereafter as *EW*), ed. Jo Ann Boydston et al. (Carbondale, Ill., 1968), 3: 14–35. The ongoing collection of Dewey's writings in a comprehensive edition, directed by Jo Ann Boydston at the Center for Dewey Studies in Carbondale, Illinois, and published by the Southern Illinois University Press, is a particularly valuable contribution to American scholarship because of the obscurity of many of Dewey's writings, especially in the pre-World War I years. "No man with such universally important things to say on almost every social and intellectual activity of the day," Randolph Bourne noted in 1915, "was ever published in forms more ingeniously contrived to thwart the interest of the prospective public" (*The New Republic*, March 13, 1915, 154). The Southern Illinois University Press edition, with all five volumes of *The Early Works* and fourteen volumes of the projected fifteen volume *Middle Works*, including all of Dewey's writings through 1922, complete as of this writing, rectifies this problem. This is a splendid series of books, with introductions, notes, and appendices that are helpful but not intrusive. Jo Ann Boydston and Kathleen Poulos have also written a valuable bibliographical guide, *Checklist of Writings about John Dewey, 1887–1977*, 2nd ed. (Carbondale, Ill., 1978). On Dewey's progressive disenchantment with Green, the best discussion is in Kuklick, *Churchmen and Philosophers*, 233–40. See also Dewey to James, May 6, 1891, in the James papers. In a passage not included in Perry's quotation from this letter in *James*, 2: 516, Dewey consigns Green to James's "tender mercies" and distinguishes Green from Hegel, with whose philosophy Dewey still feels some affinity. On Dewey's estimate of Green's lasting significance for the transformation of political theory, see *Liberalism and Social Action*, The Page-Barbour Lectures (New York, 1935), 23–28.

51. Dewey, *EW*, 4: 3–12. See also Dewey, "Reconstruction," *Monthly Bulletin* (1894), *EW*,

4: 96–105; and the discussion in Dykhuizen, *Dewey*, 64–68. For the role of religion in Dewey's ideas, see Robert M. Crunden's essay in *Progressivism*, 85–93; and his *Ministers of Reform: The Progressives' Achievement in American Civilization, 1889–1920* (New York, 1982), 54–58.

52. Dewey to James, May 10, 1891, in Perry, *James*, 2: 517. Cf. Dykhuizen, *Dewey*, 65, on Dewey's use of *The Principles of Psychology* in his Advanced Psychology course beginning in 1891.

53. Dewey to H. Robet, May 2, 1911, Dewey papers. In "The Influence of William James on John Dewey's Work," *Journal of the History of Ideas* 45 (1984): 451–62, Michael Buxton contends, strictly on the basis of a close reading of Dewey's published writings, that Dewey began to shift from idealism before he encountered James's *Principles of Psychology*; Dewey's letter to Robet corroborates that argument.

54. On Dewey at the University of Chicago, see Lewis Feuer, "John Dewey and the Back to the People Movement in American Thought," *Journal of the History of Ideas* 3 (1959): 545–68; Dykhuizen, *Dewey*, 76–115; Buenker et al., *Progressivism*, 93–97; Crunden, *Ministers of Reform*, 58–63; and Steven J. Diner, *A City and Its Universities: Public Policy in Chicago, 1892–1919* (Chapel Hill, N.C., 1980). Dewey was not a prolific letter writer, and few of the letters he did write have survived. Much of what remains from his early years, however, concerns the controversy over the administration of the University of Chicago's schools. See in particular the correspondence with William Rainey Harper, in the Dewey papers, Morris Library, Southern Illinois University, and the Regenstein Library, University of Chicago.

55. In Descartes's words, the question of the manner in which a thinking soul could move matter seemed "to be the question people have the most right to ask me," a question he never satisfactorily answered. On this issue, see Anthony Kenny, *Descartes: A Study of His Philosophy* (New York, 1968), 222–26.

56. Sidgwick, *Lectures on the Ethics of T. H. Green, Mr. Herbert Spencer, and J. Martineau* (London, 1891), 3; James, *The Varieties of Religious Experience*, 489; and Dilthey, unpub. mss. from the Berlin Nachlass quoted by Ermarth, *Dilthey*, 171.

57. Dewey's précis of his dissertation, "Kant and Philosophic Method," first appeared in the *Journal of Speculative Philosophy* 18 (1884); it is reprinted in *EW*, 1: 44. See Green, introduction to Hume's *Treatise on Human Nature, Works*, ed. R. L. Nettleship (London, 1885), 1: 80–81, for the source of this line of argument. Green's introduction was originally published in 1874.

58. Dilthey, *GS*, 5: 3; and 8: 175. Cf. Hajo Holborn, "Wilhelm Dilthey and the Critique of Historical Reason," *Journal of the History of Ideas* 11 (1950): 93–118.

59. James, "The Sentiment of Rationality," in *The Will to Believe*, 61; and *The Varieties of Religious Experience*, 509. Cf. H. S. Thayer, *Meaning and Action: A Critical History of Pragmatism* (Indianapolis, 1968), 137; Wild, *The Radical Empiricism of William James*, 13; and Morton G. White, *Science and Sentiment in America: Philosophical Thought from Jonathan Edwards to John Dewey* (New York, 1972), 191–92, for further discussion of James's critique of materialism.

60. Sidgwick, "The Coherence of Empirical Philosophy," *Mind* 7 (1882): 533–43. Cf. Havard, *Sidgwick and Political Philosophy*, 14, and D. G. James, *Henry Sidgwick*, 35. Sidgwick's unpublished essay is in the Sidgwick papers. See also his essay "Is Philosophy the Germ or Crown of Science," also in the Sidgwick papers, and cf. the discussion of these essays in Schneewind, *Sidgwick's Ethics*, 52–53.

61. Fouillée, *Education*, 249–50. See also *Histoire générale*, 343–48, for Fouillée's discussion of Hume.

62. Green, *Prolegomena to Ethics*, 11.

63. Dewey, *EW*, 1: 3–8. Dewey restated his case against materialist epistemology in his essay "Knowledge and the Relativity of Feeling," *Journal of Speculative Philosophy* 17 (1883): 56–70, *EW*, 1: 19–33.

64. Green, introduction to Hume's *Treatise on Human Nature, Works*, 1: 40. See also Pucelle, *Philosophie de T. H. Green*, and Richard Rorty, *Philosophy and the Mirror of Nature* (Princeton, 1979), 76–86; 140–46.

65. Perry, *James*, 1: 551. See also Fredson Bowers and Ignas K. Skrupskelis's notes to their edition of James's *Pragmatism, Works*, 170 n. 118.35, for James's marginal notations in his copy of volume 1 of Green's *Works*, which is in The Philosophical Library of William James, Houghton Library, Harvard University.

66. James, "On Some Omissions of Introspective Psychology," *Mind* 9 (1884): 5–6. James, *The Principles of Psychology*, 2 vols. (New York, 1890), 1: 277–78. See also Ayer, *The Origins of Pragmatism*, 254–57; and John J. McDermott's introduction to James, *Essays in Radical Empiricism, Works*, xviii ff. For amplification of this argument, see pp. 74–75 below.

67. Fouillée, *L'Evolutionisme*, 140–43.

68. Dilthey, unpub. mss. from Göttingen Nachlass quoted by Ermarth, *Dilthey*, 170.

69. Dilthey, *GS*, 9: 183. See also Ineichen, *Erkenntnistheorie*, 58–68; Hodges, *The Philosophy of Wilhelm Dilthey*, 199 f.; and Makkreel, *Dilthey*, 165–67.

70. Dewey, *Leibniz's New Essays Concerning Human Understanding: A Critical Exposition* (Chicago, 1888), *EW*, 1: 319. Morton White has written that Dewey's work on Leibniz "points up very clearly" Dewey's "organic view of the world, his emphasis on activity and continuity, and his attack on dualism and formalism." White, *The Origin of Dewey's Instrumentalism*, 60–61.

71. Cf. Fouillée, *La Psychologie*, 1: 307; Fouillée, *L'Evolutionisme*, xl; and Dewey and Tufts, *Ethics* (New York, 1908), 269, *MW*, 5: 246–47, where they discuss the question with reference to Green's treatment of it in his *Prolegomena to Ethics*.

72. James, *The Principles of Psychology*, 1: 296–98. H. S. Thayer perceptively treats this issue in *Meaning and Action*, 142 f. I am also indebted to the discussion of social conditioning and "unconditioned response" in Mandelbaum, *History, Man, and Reason*, 262–69.

73. J. B. Schneewind, "Henry Sidgwick," *The Encyclopedia of Philosophy*, ed. Paul Edwards, 7 (1967); rpt. New York, 1972): 435 f. James, "Rationality, Activity, and Faith," *Princeton Review* 2 (1882): 64–69, quoted in *The Principles of Psychology*, 2: 313 f.

74. See Hodges, *The Philosophy of Wilhelm Dilthey*, 22–23; Holborn, "Wilhelm Dilthey and the Critique of Historical Reason," 110; and cf. Richard J. Bernstein's introduction to Dewey, *On Experience, Nature, and Freedom* (Indianapolis, 1960), xlv.

75. Green, "Review of J[ohn] Caird, *Introduction to the Philosophy of Religion*," *Works*, 3: 138–46.

76. Fouillée, *La Psychologie*, 1: 356; *L'Evolutionisme*, lxxxv–lxxxvii; *L'Avenir de la métaphysique fondée sur l'expérience* (Paris, 1889), 254 ff.

77. Dewey, "From Absolutism to Experimentalism," 16–21; and his letter to H. Robet, May 2, 1911, Dewey papers.

78. Dewey, "The Metaphysical Assumptions of Materialism," *EW*, 1: 3–8; "Kant and Philosophic Method," *EW*, 1:35–47. Dewey's comment comparing the Kant essay with his dissertation appears in a letter he wrote to T. R. Ball, May 28, 1888, in the Special Collections of the Milton S. Eisenhower Library, Johns Hopkins University. Cf. Dykhuizen, *Dewey*, 35–38.

79. Dewey, "The New Psychology," *Andover Review* 2 (1884): 278–89, *EW*, 1: 48–60. On Morris and Hall, see White, *The Origin of Dewey's Instrumentalism*, 34–40. See also Dewey, "The Psychological Standpoint," *Mind* 11 (1886): 153–73, *EW*, 1: 144–67.

80. Reviewing Dewey's *Psychology* for the *American Journal of Psychology* 1 (1887): 156, G. Stanley Hall wrote, "Viewed from the standpoint of facts, very few of them are satisfactory, and many we believe to be fundamentally wrong and misleading. . . . But the author is more intent on the mutual interpretation and coherence of his network of definitions than on their relation to facts." The *Psychology* (New York, 1887) has been reprinted as vol. 2 of *EW*.

81. Dewey, *EW*, 3: 14–35, 180–84.

82. Dewey, *Essays in Experimental Logic* (Chicago, 1916), *MW*, 10: 33. Several of the essays in this volume first appeared in *Studies in Logical Theory*, which Dewey sent to James with a note to the effect that Dewey considered James's *Psychology* "the spiritual progenitor" of the essays. Dewey further asked James's permission to dedicate the volume to him (Dewey's March, 1903, letter is in Perry, *James*, 2: 520 f.). James later thanked Dewey effusively for the "masterly set of essays of which we may all be proud, distinguished by good style, direct dealing with the facts, and hot running on the trail of truth, regardless of previous conventions and categories. I am sure it hitches the subject of epistemology a good day's journey ahead, and proud indeed am I that it should be dedicated to my memory." Dewey's own contribution to the *Studies*, James continued, "is to my mind the most *weighty*," and James concluded by assuring Dewey that "it is the philosophy of the future, I'll bet my life" (James to Dewey, Aug. 4, 1908, in *Letters of William James*, 2: 310).

83. James to Dewey, March 23, 1903, in Perry, *James*, 2: 521–22. See also Dewey's response of March 27, 1903, in which he admits the effects of the "continued working of the Hegelian bacillus of reconciliation of contradictories in me" (Perry, *James*, 2: 522–23).

84. James, *The Will to Believe*, 196–221. Cf. Wild's discussion of this essay in *The Radical Empiricism of William James*, 204.

85. Dilthey, *GS*, 4: 236–37, 249.

86. Dilthey's letter to his student Bernhard Groethuysen in 1904 is quoted in Hannes Böhringer, *Bernhard Groethuysen* (Berlin, 1978), 44.

87. Dilthey, *Briefwechsel*, 20.

88. Dilthey, *GS*, 5: 50–51.

89. On neo-Kantianism in Germany, see particularly Thomas E. Willey, *Back to Kant: The Revival of Kantianism in German Social and Historical Thought, 1860–1914* (Detroit, 1978); Fritz Ringer, *The Decline of the German Mandarins: The German Academic Community, 1890–1933* (Cambridge, Mass., 1969), 309–12, 335–36; and Ermarth, *Dilthey*, 73–83.

90. Green, "Lectures on the Philosophy of Kant," *Works*, 2. Green discusses Kant's *Critique of Pure Reason* on 1–81, and Kant's ethics on 83–155.

91. Green, *Prolegomena to Ethics*, 15–16; cf. 33 f., 40.

92. Fouillée, *La Psychologie*, 1: 262; 2: 115–16; *Morale des idées-forces* (Paris, 1908), liii–liv. See also Fouillée's critical treatment of Kant in *Histoire générale*, 319–413.

93. Fouillée, *Le Moralisme de Kant et l'amoralisme contemporain* (Paris, 1905), 333–34.

94. Fouillée, *Critique des systèmes de morale contemporains*, 5th ed. (1887; Paris, 1906), 79–87.

95. Ralph Barton Perry, in *James*, I: 465, argued that idealists such as Green and the American Josiah Royce "were in all cases James's philosophical adversaries," and that James "threw in his lot" with the "party of empiricism, in its hour of gravest peril." Yet as James's critique of associationism suggests, he challenged as much of empiricist psychology as he accepted. Although he traced his intellectual ancestry to British rather than German thought, it is important to understand that James drew ideas from both sources. Murray G. Murphy boldly advances the argument on the Kantian qualities of James's philosophy in "Kant's Children." Kuklick also emphasizes James's neo-Kantianism in *The Rise of American Philosophy*, but Kuklick is careful to limit his argument. In answer to his own question "Was James, then, a Kantian?" he quotes a passage James wrote in *Pragmatism*: "Superficially this [emphasis on the construction of knowledge in consciousness] sounds like Kant's view, but between categories fulminated before nature began, and categories gradually forming themselves in nature's presence, the whole chasm between rationalism and empiricism yawns" (*Pragmatism*, 120; cf. Kuklick, 272 f.). This recognition of James's critique of Kant notwithstanding, Kuklick may push James too far toward a neo-Kantian position. He seems sometimes to see James through Roycean glasses or to point to formal parallels between James and Kant that obscure substantial

differences. For an especially clear example of this difficulty, see 317–18. On balance, however, Kuklick's account seems a fair corrective to Perry's overly empiricist reading of James, and the judiciousness of his analysis is apparent from his concluding remarks on James: "Rather than being the least neo-Kantian of the major Cambridge thinkers, James was the most serious neo-Kantian of the group: in his thought the ambiguities of the Kantian position were most apparent. But the importance of these ambiguities and ambivalences only reveals the limitations of the label neo-Kantian. James was working in a Kantian problem matrix, but his own concerns, and the turnings taken by his thought, marked him as a major thinker in his own right for whom all labels must be inadequate" (334). That seems a fair assessment, although Kuklick occasionally underestimates the significance of James's criticism of Kant. The revision of Perry's interpretation has carried the resurrection of neo-Kantian elements in James's thought so far, in fact, that it now seems useful to rescue James from his rescuers and insist on his misgivings about Kant.

96. James to Royce, Jan. 15, 1882, in Perry, *James*, 1: 793; James to Renouvier, Aug. 5, 1883, in *Letters of William James*, 1: 231.

97. For a different interpretation emphasizing James's debt to Royce, see Kuklick, *The Rise of American Philosophy*, esp. 257–64; cf. James to Royce, Sept. 26, 1900, in *Letters of William James*, 2: 135–38.

98. James, *The Principles of Psychology*, 1: 182, 244–50, 274–78.

99. Ibid., 369–70; *The Principles of Psychology*, 2: 661–62.

100. James, *Psychology. The Briefer Course* (New York, 1892), 468.

101. James, *Principles of Psychology*, 2: 627. See also Flower and Murphy, *Philosophy in America*, 2: 667.

102. James's unpublished, undated article on Kant is in the James papers.

103. James, "The Pragmatic Method," an address originally delivered before the Philosophical Union of the University of California on Aug. 26, 1898, and printed in *The University Chronicle*, Sept., 1898; reprinted in James, *Essays in Philosophy*, 123–29. For further evidence that James remained critical of Kant in his later years, see his unpublished ms. "Introduction [and] Common Sense," 1904, in the James papers.

104. James, *The Varieties of Religious Experience*, 72 f.; and James, *A Pluralistic Universe*, 222–23.

105. Dilthey, unpub. mss., ca. 1880, in Göttingen Nachlass, 239, 254–55, trans. Ermarth, *Dilthey*, 144–45.

106. Dilthey, *GS*, 1: 14 f., 17; 7: 86 f., 159. See also Hodges, *The Philosophy of Wilhelm Dilthey*, xviii f.; and Makkreel, *Dilthey*, 210.

107. Dilthey's estimate of Kant's *Critique of Pure Reason* is from *Westermanns Monatshefte* 47 (1879): 126; the passage on consciousness structuring experience comes from *GS*, 5: 12. My discussion of Dilthey's critique of Kant is indebted to Ineichen, *Erkenntnistheorie*, 31–58, 70–124; and Ermarth, *Dilthey*, 149–52. See also H. P. Rickman's introduction to Dilthey, *SW*, 21 f.

108. Dilthey, *Der Junge Dilthey*, 87.

109. Sidgwick, *Lectures on Ethics*, 3. See also Schneewind, *Sidgwick's Ethics*, 58–62.

110. Fouillée, *La Psychologie*, 1: 229.

111. Dewey, *The Significance of the Problem of Knowledge*, University of Chicago Contributions to Philosophy 1 (Chicago, 1897), *EW*, 5:3–24.

112. Dewey, *Democracy and Education* (New York, 1916), *MW*, 9: 346.

113. This is James's list of attributes of the two temperaments:

TENDER MINDED	TOUGH MINDED
Rationalistic	Empiricist
(going by "principles")	(going by "facts")

Intellectualistic	Sensationalistic
Idealistic	Materialistic
Optimistic	Pessimistic
Religious	Irreligious
Free-Willist	Fatalistic
Monistic	Pluralistic
Dogmatical	Skeptical

The list appears in *Pragmatism*, 13. H. S. Thayer, in his introduction to *The Meaning of Truth, Works* (1909; Cambridge, Mass., 1975), xvii, contends that James "generally inclined to the tough-minded outlook," but Thayer's "important exceptions," viz., "free-will, religious belief, and optimism," indicate the perilous and, I believe, ultimately misleading nature of attempts to assign James to either camp.

114. Dilthey, *SW*, 133–54; from *GS*, 8: 75–118. Cf. *GS*, 4: 528–54; Hodges, *The Philosophy of Wilhelm Dilthey*, 90–105; and Ermarth, *Dilthey*, 323–38.

Chapter 2. The Radical Theory of Knowledge

1. James to Thomas W. Ward, March, 1869, is in *Letters of William James*, 1: 152–53.

2. Green and Sidgwick participated less directly in constructing the radical theory of knowledge than did James, Dilthey, Fouillée, and Dewey, and I will not discuss their ideas at length in this chapter. As indicated earlier, their critical analyses helped to undermine the foundations of idealist and empiricist epistemology, but their own positive contributions had to do more with ethics and politics than with the theory of knowledge, and they will figure more prominently in Chapters Four and Five. Indeed, because Green remained something of a metaphysical dualist, he never followed the path the others took toward a radical rejection of the subject–object dualism standard in modern philosophy. It is worth noting in this connection that Green died in 1882, eight years before the publication of James's epochal *Principles of Psychology*, and Sidgwick died in 1900, prior to the appearance of Dewey's *Studies in Logical Theory* and James's *Pragmatism*. While not erasing important differences, the fact of Green's and Sidgwick's comparatively early deaths may help to explain why they had less to do with creating the radical theory of knowledge than did the other philosophers of the *via media*.

3. This is one of two related disagreements I have with the brilliant work of Richard Rorty, who argues in *Philosophy and the Mirror of Nature* that as long as we see James or Dewey as "having 'theories of truth' or 'theories of knowledge' or 'theories of morality' we shall get them wrong. We shall ignore their criticisms of the assumption that there ought to *be* theories about such matters." I think that assessment fits Nietzsche—and his heirs Foucault and Derrida, as Rorty points out—who really wanted only to scream "no!" to the entire tradition of Western philosophy, and that is why I do not count him among the philosophers of the *via media*. But I believe that James and Dewey, along with Dilthey and in important respects Fouillée as well, wanted to set epistemology on a different course rather than destroy it altogether. They denied that it could provide certainty through any "theory of knowledge," and to that extent Rorty is correct to emphasize the radical thrust of their arguments. Yet I believe they thought philosophy, conceived along radically different and more experimental lines, could do more than that, that it could provide an imprecise compass for personal and political decision making. I will discuss that question, and my related reservations about Rorty's treatment of Dewey in *Consequences of Pragmatism* (Minneapolis, 1982), in Chapters Three, Four, and Nine.

4. James, "The Place of Affectional Facts in a World of Pure Experience," *Essays in Radical Empiricism*, 69. Cf. his essays "Does 'Consciousness' Exist?" and "A World of Pure Experience," both of which are reprinted in *Essays in Radical Empiricism*, 3–19, 21–44.

5. Dilthey, *Introduction to the Human Sciences, SW*, 164; from *GS*, 1: 14–21. Ermarth, in

Dilthey, 359–60, argues persuasively for translating *Geisteswissenschaften* as "human sciences" rather than "human studies," which is Rickman's preferred term in *SW*. I have followed Ermarth's lead. As further support for this translation, Stephen Toulmin points out that the term was introduced into German by the translator of John Stuart Mill's *System of Logic* as a rendering of the English "moral science." See Toulmin's essay "The Mozart of Psychology," in *The New York Review of Books*, Sep. 28, 1978, 57 n.

6. Dilthey, *GS*, 18: 18. For a careful discussion of this thorny issue, see Ermarth, *Dilthey*, 94–108; and Manfred Riedel, "Das erkenntniskritische Motiv in Diltheys Theorie der Geisteswissenschaften," in R. Bubner et al., eds., *Hermeneutik und Dialektik. Festschrift für H.-G. Gadamer* (Tübingen, 1970), 1:233–55.

7. Dilthey, *GS*, 1: 36–37.

8. Fouillée, *L'Avenir de la métaphysique*, 55; *L'Evolutionisme*, 289; *Histoire générale*, 487–88.

9. The earliest indication of James's inclination to move beyond subject–object dualism is in his unpublished "Idealism Notes," dated by Perry from the 1880–1884 period, in the James papers.

10. James, *The Principles of Psychology*, 1: 6, 35; 2: 336 n. Among the most incisive of the numerous discussions of James's *Principles of Psychology* is Schwehn, "Making the World," in Schwehn, ed., *A William James Renaissance*, 426–54. The reception that greeted James's *Principles of Psychology* testified to the book's ambiguity as well as the novelty of its approach. Critical appraisals varied widely, ranging from Shadworth Hodgson's accusation that James had lent support to the "so-called conscious automation theory" of materialists to the opposite extreme of James Ward's exasperation with James's "penchant for spiritualism." For a thorough discussion of the critical response to James's *Psychology*, see Perry, *James*, 2: 91–111; and Allen, *William James*, 323–36. In his autobiographical sketch, "From Absolutism to Experimentalism," Dewey pointed out that "two unreconciled strains" ran through James's *Psychology*, and he criticized James's "adoption of the subjective tenor of prior psychological tradition." As I hope to make clear, James aimed in his later work to remove the ambiguities that could support such an interpretation of his ideas. See Dewey, "From Absolutism to Experimentalism," 23–24.

11. James, *The Principles of Psychology*, 2: 451–53.

12. See Fouillée, *La Psychologie*, 1:11–13, 210, 215–16, 226, 305; and 2: 43–44.

13. James, *The Principles of Psychology*, 2: 570. For Renouvier's decisive role in shaping James's attitude toward Fouillée, see James's letter to Renouvier, Aug. 5, 1883, in Perry, *James*, 1: 694–96.

14. James's personal copies of these volumes are in the Philosophical Library of William James.

15. Fouillée, *La Psychologie*, 1: xxiv–xxxiii; *L'Evolutionisme*, 30.

16. James's 1895–1896 notebooks are in the James papers. See also John J. McDermott's introduction to *Essays in Radical Empiricism*, xxiv–xxv. Two recent studies written in a Jamesian spirit are Daniel N. Robinson, *The Enlightened Machine: An Analytical Introduction to Neurophysiology* (New York, 1980); and Richard L. Gregory, *Mind in Science: A History of Explanations in Psychology and Physics* (Cambridge, 1981).

17. Dewey, "The Reflex Arc Concept in Psychology," *Psychological Review* 30 (1896): 357–70, *EW*, 5: 96–100. This essay marked the culmination of a series of earlier attempts to articulate a functionalist psychology, beginning with "The Psychology of Infant Language," *Psychological Review* 1 (1894): 63–66; and "The Theory of Emotion," *Psychological Review* 1 (1894): 553–69; and 2 (1895): 13–32.

18. Dewey, "The Reflex Arc Concept in Psychology," *EW*, 5: 102–9.

19. Dilthey's "Ideas Concerning a Descriptive and Analytical Psychology" is in vol. 5 of *GS*;

an excerpt is included in *SW*, 88–97. The entire essay has been translated by Richard M. Zaner and published with an introduction by Rudolf Makkreel in Dilthey, *Descriptive Psychology and Historical Understanding* (The Hague, 1977), 21–120. On Dilthey's response to James's *Principles of Psychology*, see Ermarth, *Dilthey*, 176, 212–13.

20. Dilthey, *GS*, 5: 169–73.

21. Ibid., 168–69. On the role of Schleiermacher and Dilthey's reliance on, and departure from, romanticism, see H. Nohl, "Theologie und Philosophie in der Entwicklung Wilhelm Diltheys," *Die Sammlung* 14 (1959): 19–23.

22. Dilthey, *GS*, 6: 314–16.

23. Dilthey, *GS*, 8: 16. Cf. *GS*, 7: 334: "To be sure, external objects are components of lived experience. They belong to the realm of life itself."

24. James, *The Will to Believe*, 5, 22.

25. James, "Experience," reprinted in *Essays in Philosophy*, 95.

26. James, *Essays in Radical Empiricism*, 29–30. In his introduction to this volume, McDermott describes the section of this essay from which these passages are taken as "a telescoped version of James's fundamental position." See xxxiv. On this point, also cf. Linschoten, *Phenomenological Psychology*, and Richard Bernstein's introduction to *A Pluralistic Universe*, xxvi–xxix. It is this aspect of James's thought that has attracted phenomenologically inclined thinkers looking for a grandfather figure. Despite the ahistorical quality of such phenomenological readings of James, they have helped to clarify the differences between James's position and that of Husserl, who believed he could find pure objectivity in the bracketing of experience, thereby establishing the structure of consciousness on an apodictic foundation. While certain similarities exist between James and Husserl, particularly in their attack on subject–object dualism, James's radical empiricism never carried him anywhere near Husserl's transcendental reduction. For the literature interpreting James as a proto-phenomenologist, see the writings of Wild, Linschoten, Wilshire, and McDermott cited in n. 41 to Chapter One.

27. James to Warner Fite, April 3, 1906, in Perry, *James*, 2: 391–93.

28. Dewey, *MW*, 1: 113–30; esp. 121–22.

29. Dewey, *Essays in Experimental Logic*, *MW*, 10: 320–24; and "The Need of a Recovery of Philosophy," in *Creative Intelligence: Essays in the Pragmatic Attitude* (New York, 1917), reprinted in *MW*, 10: 3–48; esp. 6.

30. Green, *Prolegomena to Ethics*, 40, 69–78. Several commentators have attempted imaginatively to salvage Green's ideas, but the legitimacy of his metaphysics is irrelevant to my analysis. On this subject, see especially Pucelle, *La Philosophie de T. H. Green*, 43–142; and Milne, *English Idealism*, 89; and cf. the more critical assessments of Richter, *The Politics of Conscience*, 186; Lemos's introduction to Green's *Prolegomena to Ethics*, xiii–xxvi; and Kenneth R. Hoover, "Liberalism and the Idealist Philosophy of Thomas Hill Green," *Western Political Quarterly* 26 (1973): 550–65.

31. Green, *Prolegomena to Ethics*, 69–70.

32. James, "On Some Omissions of Introspective Psychology," *Mind* 9(1884): 1–26; "The Function of Cognition," read before the Aristotelian Society, Dec. 1, 1884, published in *Mind* 10 (1885); reprinted in *The Meaning of Truth*, 13–32. James fully understood how radically he was challenging not only associationism but also neo-Kantianism in these essays. When Renouvier scolded him for minimizing the role of an independent consciousness, his response was unrepentant. See his letter to Renouvier, Sept. 30, 1884, in Perry, *James*, 1: 697–99.

33. James, *The Principles of Psychology*, 1: 224, 239.

34. Ibid., 1: 278; and see the discussion of this point on pp. 57–58 above.

35. James, preface to *The Meaning of Truth*, 7; "A Word More About Truth," published in the *Journal of Philosophy* 4 (1907): 396–406, reprinted in *The Meaning of Truth*, 79.

36. James, "A World of Pure Experience," in *Essays in Radical Empiricism*, 21–44. In his essay "Does 'Consciousness' Exist?" James connected the idea of consciousness as a stream with his radical empiricism to explain the acquisition of knowledge: "Knowing can easily be explained as a particular sort of relation toward one another into which portions of pure experience may enter. The relation itself is a part of pure experience; one of its 'terms' becomes the subject or bearer of knowledge, the knower, the other becomes the object known" (*Essays in Radical Empiricism*, 4–5).

37. On James and Bergson, see Perry, *James*, 2: 599–636; Wild, *The Radical Empiricism of William James*, 236; and Kuklick, *The Rise of American Philosophy*, 331–32.

38. James, *A Pluralistic Universe*, 101–24, 147. James also used Bergson's *élan vital* as a corrective to Green's overly abstract approach to relations and discussed Green's critique of associationism on 126–27.

39. Cf. Dewey, "The Philosophy of Thomas Hill Green," *EW*, 5: 21–22; "The Reflex Arc Concept in Psychology," *EW*, 5: 100; *Studies in Logical Theory*; and "The Need for a Recovery of Philosophy," *Creative Intelligence*, *MW*, 10: 3–48. In a letter to B. H. Bode, March 12, 1914, in the Horace Kallen Collection at the John Dewey Center, Southern Illinois University, Carbondale, Ill., Dewey explained his decision never to have his seminal "Reflex Arc" essay, which he dismissed as "the reflex arc thing," reprinted. From the perspective of his instrumentalism, it was, he wrote, "too 'subjectivistic'—too 'psychical'—about sensations etc.—too much the stream of consciousness idea—And I never saw my way to rewriting the terminology."

40. Dewey, *Reconstruction in Philosophy* (New York, 1920), *MW*,12: 131–32. See also Bernstein, *Praxis and Action: Contemporary Philosophies of Human Activity* (Philadelphia, 1971), 208–11; and Thayer, *Meaning and Action*, 477–85.

41. Fouillée, *L'Evolutionisme*, 73; and cf. Guyau, *Fouillée*, 201–11.

42. Fouillée, *La Psychologie*, 2: 73–78.

43. Dilthey, *Introduction to the Human Sciences, SW*, 161, from *GS*, 1: xv–xix.

44. Dilthey, "Ideas About a Descriptive and Analytical Psychology," *SW*, 91, 94–95, from *GS*, 5: 151, 206–11.

45. Dilthey, *The Construction of the Historical World in the Human Sciences, SW*, 185–86, from *GS*, 7: 130–66.

46. Ibid., 210, from *GS*, 7: 189–200. For an extended discussion of this theme, see the brilliant study by Stephen Kern, *The Culture of Time and Space, 1880–1913* (Cambridge, Mass., 1983).

47. Dilthey, *GS*, 5: 177. The near identity of James's and Dilthey's ideas on this issue is striking. Compare this passage from James's *Principles of Psychology*, 1: 232–34, with Dilthey's leaf metaphor: "However we might in ordinary conversation speak of getting the same sensation again, we never in strict theoretic accuracy could do so; and that whatever was true of the river of life, of the river of elementary feeling, it would certainly be true to say, like Heraclitus, that we never descend twice into the same stream. . . . Experience is remoulding us every moment, and our mental reaction on every given thing is really a resultant of our experience of the whole world up to that date."

48. Ganne de Beaucoudrey pieces together Fouillée's various discussions of time in *Fouillée*, 251–68. James's comments appear in his letter to Bergson, Feb. 25, 1903, in Perry, *James*, 2: 608–10.

49. Dilthey, *GS*, 7: 72. My discussion of Dilthey's concept of time is indebted to Makkreel's analysis in *Dilthey*, 386–99.

50. Sidgwick and Green contributed little to this theory of voluntary action. Sidgwick admitted that we have "a distinct consciousness of choosing between alternatives of conduct," an experience we feel compelled to respect, but he concluded that the ethical importance of deciding the question of free will "is liable to be exaggerated," and he did not discuss it in detail

(Sidgwick, *Methods of Ethics*, 65–66). See also Schneewind, *Sidgwick's Ethics*, 207–8. Green adopted a more conventional defense of free will than did James, Fouillée, Dewey, and Dilthey. Although he admitted that consciousness filters the conditions of experience that impinge on the individual from the outside world, Green ultimately sought refuge in the notion of the human agent as a "free cause," a being not tied to external reality, but making decisions according to a vague awareness of "the divine self-realising principle in him" (Green, *Prolegomena to Ethics*, 81, 99, 101f., 186).

51. Dilthey quoted in Ermarth, *Dilthey*, 27.

52. Guyau, *Fouillée*, 2–3; Ganne de Beaucoudrey, *Fouillée*, 22–23.

53. Cf. James's diary entry dated April 13, 1868, in the James papers, and the more elegantly crafted imagery of his letter to Henry James of the same date in Perry, *James*, 1:270. While still in Germany, he recounted in his diary on May 22, 1868, another revealing episode: "The intuition of something here in a measure absolute gave me such an unspeakable disgust for the dead drifting of my own life for some time past. I can revive the feeling perhaps by thinking of men of genius. It ought to have a practical effect on my own will—a horror of wasted life since life can be *such*—and Oh god! an end to the idle, idiotic sinking into *Vorstellung* disproportionate to the object." Although James concluded bravely that "every good experience ought to be interpreted in practice," his uncertainties got the better of his resolution for the next two years. See James's diary in the James papers.

54. James's notebook dated April 30, 1870, quoted in *Letters of William James*, 1: 147–48. The early enthusiasm Renouvier and James felt for each other cooled after 1885, as James moved toward radical empiricism and Renouvier toward rationalism. Yet James never abandoned the voluntarism he embraced after reading Renouvier. See Perry, *James*, 1: 670–90, 696–710. Unfortunately, efforts to obtain James's medical records from McLean Hospital in Belmont, Mass., have been unsuccessful.

55. James, *Collected Essays and Reviews*, ed. Ralph Barton Perry (New York, 1920), 187, 211; and cf. Kuklick, *The Rise of American Philosophy*, 166–68.

56. James, "Reflex Action and Theism," *The Will to Believe*, 95.

57. James, "Rationality, Activity, and Faith," *Princeton Review* 2 (1882): 66.

58. James, *The Principles of Psychology*, 2: 572–73, 561–62.

59. James, "The Dilemma of Determinism," in *The Will to Believe*, 114–40. Edward H. Madden rehearses the objections to James's position in his introduction to *The Will to Believe, Works*, xxiv–xxx.

60. James, *The Principles of Psychology*, 2: 570–71. James's copy of Fouillée's *L'Evolutionisme des idées-forces* is in the Philosophical Library of William James; see esp. 186, 191–93; and James's lengthy note on p. 197. Cf. James to Theodore Flournoy, Sept. 19, 1892; and James to James Ward, Nov. 1, 1892, in Perry, *James*, 2: 177, 96–97. James's review of Fouillée's *La Psychologie des idées-forces* appeared in *The Philosophical Review* 2 (1893): 716–20. See also Fouillée's *La Science sociale contemporaine*, 134–44.

61. Fouillée, *Morale*, 277–89.

62. Fouillée, *La Psychologie*, 2: 261–67, 287–91, 304f.; and cf. *Histoire générale*, 496. Because Fouillée couched his arguments for voluntarism within a monistic idealism, and James steadfastly opposed all versions of what he termed the "block universe" of monism, it would be misleading to attempt to reconcile completely the ideas of Fouillée and James. But as I have indicated, both Fouillée and James grounded their epistemology on lived experience rather than metaphysical speculation.

63. Dewey, "The New Psychology," *Andover Review* 2 (1884): 278–89, *EW*, 1:60; "The Ego as Cause," *Philosophical Review* 3 (1894): 337–41, *EW*, 4: 95. Dewey elaborated this argument in a letter to Horace Kallen dated April 16, 1915, in the Horace Kallen Collection, Center for Dewey Studies: "I thoroughly believe but the orthodox psychology has substituted . . . a notion of

subjectivism as a set of psychical existences having nothing to do ... with active attitudes to the world.... Incidentally there seem to me to be too [*sic*] strains in James which he was never aware of in their incompatibilty. That is while he carried philosophy thru psychology to the possibility of a different standpoint there is still much in him where the terminology is that of the older tradition."

64. Dewey, *The Study of Ethics: A Syllabus* (Ann Arbor, 1894), *EW*, 4: 339.

65. Dewey, *Studies in Logical Theory, MW*, 2: 310. See also Dewey's letter to H. Robet, May 2, 1911, Dewey papers.

66. James, "Remarks on Spencer's Definition of Mind as Correspondence" (1878), *Essays in Philosophy*, 11 n., 21–22. See also Robert J. Richards, "The Personal Equation in Science: William James's Psychological and Moral Uses of Darwinian Theory," in Schwehn, ed., *A William James Renaissance*, 387–425.

67. Dewey, "The Intellectualist Criterion for Truth," in *The Influence of Darwin on Philosophy and Other Essays on Contemporary Thought* (New York, 1910), *MW*, 4: 71–72.

68. Dilthey, *Introduction to the Human Sciences, SW*, 162, from *GS*, 1: xviii.

69. Dilthey, *GS*, 5: 167.

70. Dilthey, *GS*, 7: 257.

71. Dilthey, unpub. mss. from Berlin Nachlass quoted by Ermarth, *Dilthey*, 120–21.

72. Sidgwick's journal for 1867 is in the Sidgwick papers.

73. Dewey, *Outlines of a Critical Theory of Ethics* (Ann Arbor, 1891), *EW*, 3: 254–55.

74. Dewey, "The Significance of the Problem of Knowledge," *University of Chicago Contributions to Philosophy*, 1 (Chicago, 1897), reprinted "with slight change" in *The Influence of Darwin on Philosophy and Other Essays on Contemporary Thought, EW*, 5: 20–21. Cf. Dewey's review of Ward, Kidd, Adams, and Flint, *Psychological Review* 1 (1894), *EW*, 4: 205n.; see also "Thought and Its Subject Matter," in *Studies in Logical Theory, MW*, 2: 298–315.

75. Dewey, *The School and Society* (Chicago, 1899), *MW*, 1: 93–94.

76. Dilthey to his father, summer, 1852, in *Der junge Dilthey*, 6; and Dilthey to Graf Yorck, Aug. or Sept., 1897, in *Briefwechsel*, 247.

77. Dilthey, unpub. mss. in Berlin Nachlass quoted by Ermarth, *Dilthey*, 172.

78. James, *The Principles of Psychology*, 2: 312–15.

79. James, "Reflex Action and Theism," *The Will to Believe*, 92.

80. James, *Collected Essays and Reviews*, 67. James M. Edie also argues that voluntarism and activity were linked in James's thought. In his essay "The Philosophical Anthropology of William James," Edie writes, "I believe it is by focusing on *action* as the central category of James's thought that we can best unify his insights." James's "ultimate liberation came neither from medicine nor in the form of special philosophical reasons for believing himself to be free, but in his own decision *to act. Action*, in the philosophy of James, is another word for *freedom*" (*An Invitation to Phenomenology: Studies in the Philosophy of Experience* [Chicago, 1965], 130–31).

81. Fouillée, *L'Evolutionisme*, xlii; and *La Psychologie*, 1: 115.

82. Fouillée, *L'Evolutionisme*, xlvi, 181; and *La Psychologie*, 1: 307.

83. See Fouillée, *L'Evolutionisme*, 78, 197; *La Psychologie*, 1: ix–x, 274; and a letter written by Fouillée and printed in Guyau, *Fouillée*, 105.

84. Cf. Dewey, *How We Think* (Boston, 1910), *MW*, 6: 236–37, where Dewey lists the five steps in instrumental thinking: "(i) A felt difficulty; (ii) its location and definition; (iii) suggestion of possible solutions; (iv) development by reasoning of the bearings of the suggestions; (v) further observation and experiment leading to its acceptance or rejection; that is, the conclusion of belief or disbelief."

85. Green, *Prolegomena to Ethics*, 92–93, 137, 158.

86. James drew the connection between Green's treatment of the will and Fouillée's concept

of idées-forces on p. 131 of his copy of Green's *Prolegomena to Ethics*, which is in the Philosophical Library of William James.

87. Dewey's and James's letters are in Perry, *James*, 2: 516–33; the quotation is from Dewey's letter dated March, 1903, 522–23.

88. Peirce's essay "How We Make Our Ideas Clear" (1878), which grew from the discussions of the "Metaphysical Club" that met in Cambridge and counted among its members James, Peirce, and Chauncey Wright, is generally accepted as the first statement of pragmatism. James's essay "Remarks on Spencer's Definition of Mind as Correspondence," also published in 1878, foreshadowed his own pragmatism in its references to the knower as actor and the subject's role in the creation of truth. Although Peirce did not use the word "pragmatism" in his essay, James credited him with introducing the idea into philosophical circles. See *Pragmatism*, 28f. On the relation of James and Dewey to Peirce, see Dewey's letters to James, Nov. 28, 1907, and Feb. 24, 1909, in Perry, *James*, 2: 528–31, and Perry's remarks on p. 531. See also Dewey, "The Development of American Pragmatism," *Studies in the History of Ideas* (New York, 1925), 2: 361. Although I do not deny Peirce's importance in the development of James's and Dewey's ideas, I will make no attempt to examine his philosophy here. See Thayer, *Meaning and Action*, 79–132, for an introduction to Peirce, and cf. the bibliography in Amelie Rorty, ed., *Pragmatic Philosophy* (New York, 1966), 529–31. On the Cambridge "Metaphysical Club" and the origins of pragmatism, see Max Fisch, "Was There a Metaphysical Club in Cambridge?" in *Studies in the Philosophy of Charles Sanders Peirce*, 2nd series, ed. Edward C. Moore and Richard S. Robin (Amherst, 1964); Fisch, "A Chronicle of Pragmatism," *Monist* 48 (1964): 441–66; John Smith, "Note on the Origins of Pragmatism," appendix to *Purpose and Thought: The Meaning of Pragmatism* (New Haven, 1978), 194–97; Thayer, *Meaning and Action*, 488–92; and Philip P. Wiener, *Evolution and the Founders of Pragmatism*, 18–30. On the discussions of Green's introduction to Hume by the Metaphysical Club in 1875, see Flower and Murphy, *Philosophy in America*, 2: 507–8.

89. James, "The Function of Cognition," read before the Aristotelian Society, Dec. 1, 1884, and published in *Mind* 10 (1885), reprinted "with slight verbal revision" in *The Meaning of Truth*, 13–31. James's "Note" appears on p. 32. See also *The Will to Believe*, 20.

90. See James, *The Principles of Psychology*, 2: 295, 312; and *The Will to Believe*, 14, 19–21, 23–24.

91. James, *Pragmatism*, 37, 28–32.

92. Ibid., 44, 97, 106.

93. James to his son William, April 24, 1907, in *The Letters of William James*, 2: 275 ff.

94. See Fouillée, *La Liberté*; *La Pensée*; and cf. Guyau, *Fouillée*, 217–18. James's copy of *L'Evolutionisme des idées-forces* is in the Philosophical Library of William James. See esp. lxviii, 91.

95. Dewey, "What Pragmatism Means by Practical," in *Essays in Experimental Logic, MW*, 4: 98–115; and "An Added Note as to the Practical," *Essays in Experimental Logic, MW*, 10: 366–72.

96. See James, "The Meaning of the Word Truth," first delivered at a meeting of the American Philosophical Association, Cornell University, 1907; reprinted in *The Meaning of Truth*, 117–19.

97. For a recent treatment of James's pragmatism as involving a "personal rather than social, private rather than public" test of truth, which represents a continuation of the line of analysis James tried to lay to rest in *The Meaning of Truth*, see Joseph L. Blau's introduction to *Pragmatism and Other Essays* (1963; rpt. New York, 1970), xii–xiii.

98. James, *The Meaning of Truth*, 106, 128.

99. See *Pragmatism*, 35–37, 99–101.

100. Recent discussions of James's pragmatic theory of truth include H. S. Thayer's

introductions to the editions of *Pragmatism* and *The Meaning of Truth*, in *Works*; Thayer's account in *Meaning and Action*, 148–53; Bruce Kuklick's introduction to the Hackett paperback edition of *Pragmatism* (Cambridge and Indianapolis, 1981); and David Hollinger, "William James and the Culture of Inquiry," *Michigan Quarterly Review* 20 (1981): 264–83.

101. Dilthey, *GS*, 15: 157; see also the discussion of Dilthey's pragmatic view of truth in Ermarth, *Dilthey*, 155–56.

102. The quotation from the unpublished *Breslauer Ausarbeitung* is in Bernard Eric Jensen, "The Recent Trend in the Interpretation of Dilthey," *Philosophy of the Social Sciences* 8 (1978): 424.

103. Dilthey, *GS*, 5: 42–43.

104. On this issue, see two essays by Richard Rorty, "Idealism and Textualism," in *The Consequences of Pragmatism*, 139–59; and "Dewey's Metaphysics," in *New Studies in the Philosophy of John Dewey*, ed. Stephen M. Cahn (Hanover, N.H., 1977), 45–74.

Chapter 3. Culture, Understanding, and History

1. Dilthey, *GS*, 1: 30–32.

2. Dilthey, *GS*, 5: 110, 35; 7: 359. For further elaboration of this theme, see Johach, *Handelnder Mensch und objektiver Geist*.

3. Fouillée, *La Science sociale contemporaine* (Paris, 1880), vi–xiii.

4. Fouillée, *La Psychologie*, 2: 18, 73; *Morale*, 4–10; cf. Dilthey, *GS*, 1: 30–32.

5. Dewey, *The Ethics of Democracy* (Ann Arbor, 1888), *EW*, 1: 227–49.

6. Dewey, "Psychology as Philosophic Method," *MW*, 1: 113–30.

7. See for example Thayer, *Meaning and Action*, 442.

8. James, *The Principles of Psychology*, 1: 293.

9. Fouillée, *Morale*, 10. Because of this conception of experience as immediately social, neither Fouillée, James, Dewey, nor Dilthey ever shared the difficulty faced, for example, by Husserl, who never succeeded in establishing intersubjectivity from his phenomenological foundation. They never challenged the ontological status of the components of lived experience, including other people, as Husserl did by his insistence on the *epoche* (bracketing) of experience.

10. James, *Pragmatism*, 100; cf. also 139. David Hollinger emphasizes this point in "William James and the Culture of Inquiry," 269–70. It may be surprising, given Husserl's inability to construct a bridge toward intersubjective understanding, that those analysts most sensitive to the phenomenological side of James's writings have shown the clearest insight into the social dimensions of his pragmatism. See for example Wild, *The Radical Empiricism of William James*, 85, 384; Edie, introduction to Pierre Thévenaz, *What is Phenomenology?* (Chicago, 1962), 34–36; McDermott, "A Metaphysics of Relation: James's Anticipation of Contemporary Experience," in *The Philosophy of William James*, ed. W. Robert Corti (Winterthur, 1975); and John K. Roth, *Freedom and the Moral Life: The Ethics of William James* (Philadelphia, 1969), 103. As Wild in particular has shown, Merleau-Ponty's existential phenomenology is far more similar in spirit to James's radical empiricism than is Husserl's transcendental phenomenology. For interpretations that emphasize the individualist orientation of James's pragmatism, see Thayer, *Meaning and Action*, 442; and Kuklick, *The Rise of American Philosophy*, 269 f.

11. Fouillée, *Morale*, 30; cf. *L'Idée moderne du droit*, discussed in Guyau, *Fouillée*, 151.

12. Dilthey, *GS*, 7: 132, 141. As Ermarth points out in *Dilthey*, 225–27, analysts of Dilthey have tended to over look this crucial concept. See 373 n. 73 for Ermarth's discussion of R. G. Collingwood's and H. A. Hodges's misunderstandings of Dilthey on this point.

13. Dilthey, unpub. mss. from the Berlin Nachlass quoted by Ermarth, *Dilthey*, 238–39.

14. Fouillée, *L'Avenir de la métaphysique*, 8–10; *Histoire générale*, vi–xvi.

15. Dewey, "The Experimental Theory of Knowledge," reprinted with considerable change from *Mind* n.s. 15 (1906), in *The Influence of Darwin on Philosophy and Other Essays in Contemporary Thought, MW*, 3: 118.

16. James, *The Principles of Psychology*, 1: 255. Cf. Wild, *The Radical Empiricism of William James*, 51–53, 69, 212–13; and Wilshire, *William James and Phenomenology*, 224.

17. Dilthey, unpub. mss. in Berlin Nachlass quoted by Ermarth, *Dilthey*, 203.

18. Dilthey, "The Nature of Philosophy," *SW*, 122–23, from *GS*, 5: 404–16.

19. Dilthey, *GS*, 8: 234.

20. James's Oct. 4, 1908, letter to Russell is in appendix IV of *The Meaning of Truth*, 299–300. The other quotation, which comes from a letter James wrote to Horace M. Kallen concerning Russell and G. E. Moore, is also in appendix IV of *The Meaning of Truth*, 305. Cf. James, "Two English Critics," originally published in the *Albany Review*, Jan., 1908, and reprinted in *The Meaning of Truth*, 146–53; see also *A Pluralistic Universe*, 117. A. J. Ayer, in *The Origins of Pragmatism*, interprets James's position as similar to the logical positivists' "doctrine that there are three fundamentally different types of statements which are supported in fundamentally different ways: those of empirical science which are factual, those of pure mathematics and logic which concern the relationship between ideas, and those which are moral and esthetic" (114). As Morton White has pointed out, however, in "Logical Positivism and the Pragmatism of William James," a review of Ayer's book reprinted in White's *Pragmatism and the American Mind: Essays and Reviews in Philosophy and Intellectual History* (New York, 1973), James explicitly rejected such a distinction. White concluded that James "encourages us to reject sharp positivistic distinctions between the analytic and the synthetic, between metaphysics and science, between science and morals" (120).

21. Dewey, *Essays in Experimental Logic, MW*, 10: 357–58; cf. 338–39.

22. Dilthey, unpub. mss. from the Berlin Nachlass quoted by Ermarth, *Dilthey*, 239. Cf. Ermarth's discussion, 160–64.

23. Dewey, *Experience and Nature* (Chicago, 1925), 303.

24. Dewey, *How We Think, MW*, 6: 272; see also 273–85.

25. James, *The Principles of Psychology*, 2: 80.

26. For a recent interpretation stressing the discontinuity in Dilthey's writings from his earlier "psychologistic" to his later "hermeneutic" writings, see Plantinga, *Historical Understanding in the Thought of Wilhelm Dilthey*.

27. Dilthey, "The Development of Hermeneutics," *SW*, 262; from *GS*, 5: 332–37.

28. Dilthey, *Historical World, SW*, 189–90; from *GS*, 7: 130–66.

29. Ermarth contends that "there has probably been more arrant nonsense written on this subject [of *Verstehen*] than on any key concept of modern thought and inquiry." See his thorough recounting of the debate surrounding the idea, and Dilthey's unsuccessful attempts to clarify it fully, in *Dilthey*, 241–67.

30. Dilthey, *GS*, 7: 191.

31. Dilthey, unpub. mss. from the Berlin Nachlass quoted by Ermarth, *Dilthey*, 213.

32. Dilthey, *Historical World, SW*, 176; from *GS*, 7: 87.

33. Dilthey, *GS*, 5: 332.

34. Dilthey, "The Development of Hermeneutics," *SW*, 258; from *GS*, 5: 329; and cf. *GS*, 16: 425. For an excellent discussion of this difficult issue, see Ermarth, *Dilthey*, 278–80.

35. Ibid., 261; from *GS*, 5: 332. Interpreters continue to assert that Dilthey sought through "intuition" to achieve some sort of "transposition" of the interpreter with the author at a psychological level, despite Dilthey's efforts to deny such charges. When Geoffrey Barraclough accuses Dilthey of "exalting intuition," and Martin Jay claims that Dilthey "felt the present situation of the historian could be bracketed and the distance between the past and present nullified" in the achievement of "total empathetic reexperiencing" with an author's thought world, it is apparent

that Dilthey's argument continues to be elusive. The pervasiveness of such interpretations, which I take to be misconceptions of Dilthey's position, testifies not only to the ambiguity of what Dilthey meant by *Verstehen*, it testifies also to the continuing debate about what we should mean when we are interpreting meaning to achieve understanding. Dilthey's position, which rested on the methodological hermeneutics of Humboldt and Schleiermacher, emphasized the limited focus of interpretation on meaning rather than being, and it must be contrasted with the ontological hermeneutics of Heidegger and Gadamer. Unlike those who have tried to "re-ontologize" hermeneutics, Dilthey believed that we could not move behind or beyond consciousness or history to find truth. By trying to transcend the self-consciously imposed boundaries of Dilthey's methodological hermeneutics, Heidegger, Gadamer, and their followers have tried to leap outside the radically demarcated scope of the philosophy of immediate experience in order to recover a viable metaphysics. Dilthey considered such a leap futile if not dangerous. For arguments affirming the legitimacy of Dilthey's methodological hermeneutics, see E. D. Hirsch, *The Aims of Interpretation* (Chicago, 1976); and Michael Ermarth, "The Transformation of Hermeneutics: 19th Century Ancients and 20th Century Moderns," *The Monist* (1981): 176–94. Recent analyses sensitive to Heidegger's and Gadamer's perspective include Richard Palmer, *Hermeneutics* (Evanston, 1969); and David C. Hoy, *The Critical Circle: Literature, History, and Philosophical Hermeneutics* (Berkeley, 1978). Barraclough's comment appears in *Main Trends in History* (New York, 1979), 13; see also Martin Jay, "Should Intellectual History Take a Linguistic Turn?" *Modern European Intellectual History: Reappraisals and New Perspectives*, ed. Dominick LaCapra and Steven L. Kaplan (Ithaca, 1982), 95.

36. Dilthey, *Historical World*, SW, 229; from *GS*, 7: 189–200. See also Ermarth, *Dilthey*, 244–45, 274–75, 347, on this point.

37. Dilthey, *GS*, 5: 169–73; trans. Hodges, *Wilhelm Dilthey: An Introduction* (New York, 1969), 135–36.

38. Dilthey, "The Development of Hermeneutics," *SW*, 259–60, 262; from *GS*, 5: 317–37. Dilthey brought together these arguments in a passage in *Historical World*: "Let us summarize the results of the preceding investigations about the interrelatedness of the human sciences. This rests on the relationship between experience and understanding from which three main principles have emerged. Our knowledge of what is given in experience is extended through the interpretation of the objectifications of life and this interpretation, in turn, is only made possible by plumbing the depths of subjective experience. Similarly, understanding of the particular depends on knowledge of the general which, in turn, presupposes understanding" (*SW*, 195–96; from *GS*, 7: 130–66).

39. Ibid., 230; from *GS*, 7: 189–200.

40. Dilthey, "The Development of Hermeneutics," *SW*, 260; from *GS*, 5: 332–37.

41. Dilthey, *Historical World*, SW, 192; from *GS*, 7: 130–76.

42. Dilthey, *Introduction to the Human Sciences*, *SW*, 166; from *GS*, 1: 20–21. Although Dilthey considered the controversy surrounding the distinction between the *Geistes-* and the *Naturwissenschaften* sterile, it continues to attract lively minds. See for example the provocative interchange between Hubert L. Dreyfus, Charles Taylor, and Richard Rorty in *The Review of Metaphysics* 34 (1980): 3–55. Rorty distinguishes between Dilthey's and Dewey's positions, but he concludes with a puzzling comment: "The Deweyan view I want to suggest is naturalistic in seeing no *ontological* break between human and non-human reality, but only (to put it in somewhat misleading Kantian terms) a *moral* break. This seems to me the only sort of break we need, and that it does not need to be 'grounded' on some more fundamental 'metaphysical' or 'methodological' distinction" (46). By thus conflating metaphysics and methodology, Rorty blurs Dilthey into Gadamer in a way that I consider misleading. Moreover, the insistence that the "break" is not ontological but is instead moral seems to me more similar to Dilthey's view than different from it, although the problems involved in making ethical decisions from either an

instrumentalist or a hermeneutic perspective are, as I will point out in Chapter Four, considerable.

43. James quoted in Perry, *James*, 2: 700.

44. James to Adams, Feb. 9, 1908, James papers.

45. Fouillée, *La Science sociale*, 379–88.

46. Dilthey, *GS*, 1: 107.

47. Dewey, "Progress," *The International Journal of Ethics* 26 (1916): 311–22, *MW*, 10: 234–43.

48. Dewey, "The Influence of Darwin on Philosophy," (1909), *MW*, 4: 1–8.

49. James, "Great Men and Their Environment," in *The Will to Believe*, 182–83.

50. James, *The Principles of Psychology*, 2: 669; *Pragmatism*, 104–7; and Perry, *James*, 1: 492; 2: 389ff., 462. See also Robert Richards, "The Personal Equation in Science: William James's Psychological and Moral Uses of Darwinian Theory," in Schwehn, ed., *A William James Renaissance*, 387–425.

51. James, *The Principles of Psychology*, 2: 283; 1: 233. Cf. James's later statement of this point in "A World of Pure Experience": "Personal histories are processes of change in time, and the change itself is one of the things immediately experienced. 'Change' in this case means continuous as opposed to discontinuous transitions. But continuous transition is one sort of a conjunctive relation; and to be a radical empiricist means to hold fast to this conjunctive relation of all others, for this is the strategic point, the point through which, if a hole be made, all the corruptions of dialectics and all the metaphysical fictions pour into our philosophy" (*Essays in Radical Empiricism*, 27–28).

52. Dilthey, *Historical World, SW*, 210; from *GS*, 7: 189–200.

53. James, *Pragmatism*, 97, 123. For another interpretation of James that emphasizes his historical sensibility, see Hollinger, "William James and the Culture of Inquiry," esp. 277.

54. James, "The Chicago School," *Essays in Philosophy*, 102–6.

55. Dewey, "What Pragmatism Means by Practical," *MW*, 4: 109. Cf. this passage from Dewey's syllabus for his course "Types of Philosophic Thought" (1922), in *MW*, 13: 353. Describing his instrumentalism, Dewey wrote that it "may be labelled critical radical empiricism: radical, in the sense that it recognizes the claims and traits of all the qualitative modes and organizations of experience, instead of setting up some one form as ultimate and 'real'; critical, in that each philosophy is interpreted not in terms of abstract criteria of truth and value (a method which of necessity begs the question), but of concrete historic origin, context and operation."

56. See Rickman's introduction to *SW*, 18; Ermarth, *Dilthey*, 151–52; James, *Pragmatism*, 82–83, 120; and Kuklick, *The Rise of American Philosophy*, 272–74.

57. Dilthey, *GS*, 11: 140–41; trans. Ermarth, *Dilthey*, 295. Cf. *Historical World, SW*, 181; from *GS*, 7: 130–66: "The individual person in his independent existence is a historical being."

58. James, *The Will to Believe*, 23.

59. Dilthey, "The Types of World View and their Development in the Metaphysical Systems," *SW*, 135; from *GS*, 8: 75–118.

60. Royce's celebrated lampoon of James, concerning a hypothetical pragmatist instructing a witness to tell "the expedient, the whole expedient, and nothing but the expedient," is a case in point. More serious challenges to the apparent relativism of what I have described as the historical sensibility include Maurice Mandelbaum, *The Problem of Historical Knowledge: An Answer to Relativism* (New York, 1938), 58–67; and Leszek Kolakowski, "Historical Understanding and the Intelligibility of History," trans. Henry Beitscher, *Triquarterly* 22 (1971): 103–17.

61. Dilthey, *GS*, 7: 153.

62. Dilthey, *GS*, 7: 290f.; trans. Hodges, *The Philosophy of Wilhelm Dilthey*, 314.

63. On this point, see John Wild, "Authentic Existence: A New Approach to Value Theory," in Edie, ed., *An Invitation to Phenomenology*, 59–77.

64. Dilthey, "Present Day Culture and Philosophy," *SW*, 121; from *GS*, 8: 190–205.

65. Dilthey, *GS*, 5: 338.

66. Dilthey, "Present Day Culture and Philosophy," *SW*, 120; from *GS*, 8: 190–205. See also Plantinga, *Historical Understanding in the Thought of Wilhelm Dilthey*, 130.

67. See Mueller-Vollmer, *Towards a Phenomenological Theory of Literature*, 86–87; and Ermarth, *Dilthey*, 353 ff. The meaning of the word "historicism" has become so muddled that I have deliberately tried to examine these theorists' historical sensibility without reference to the word. Originally, historicism (or historism, since the word derives from the German *Historismus*) expressed the idea that all historical phenomena are unique in their concrete individuality. In the years since Karl Popper used it in *The Poverty of Historicism* as a label for the quite different, and indeed opposite, notion of history as a grand scheme, the original meaning of the word has been submerged if not drowned. Given the current ambiguity of the term historicism, it may be best to avoid it altogether. For a discussion of the various definitions advanced for historicism, see Maurice Mandelbaum, "Historicism," *Encyclopedia of Philosophy*, 4: 22–24; and for the history of historicism, see the article "Historicism" by Georg C. Iggers in the *Dictionary of the History of Ideas*, 2: 456–64.

68. See above, pp. 99–100, for Dilthey's discussion of this issue. In a passage that expands and clarifies this position, Karl Mannheim wrote: "Human consciousness can grasp a landscape *as a landscape* only from various perspectives; and yet the landscape does not dissolve itself into its various possible pictorial representations. Each of the possible pictures has a 'real' counterpart and the correctness of each perspective can be controlled from the other perspectives. This implies, however, that history is only visible from within history and cannot be interpreted through a 'jump' beyond history, in occupying a static standpoint arbitrarily occupied outside history. The historicist standpoint [which I am labeling the historical sensibility to avoid the confusion surrounding historicism], which starts with relativism, eventually achieves absoluteness of view, because in its final form it posits history itself as the absolute; this alone makes it possible that the various standpoints, which at first appear to be anarchic, can be ordered as component parts of a meaningful overall process" (*From Karl Mannheim*, ed. Kurt Wolff [N.Y., 1971], 97).

69. Dilthey, *GS*, 13: xxxvi; *GS*, 6: 189.

Chapter 4. The Ethics of Rational Benevolence

1. Dewey's review of A. and E. M. Sidgwick's *Memoir of Henry Sidgwick*, *Political Science Quarterly* 22 (1907): 133–35, *MW*, 4: 242–45; Fouillée, *Le Moralisme de Kant*, 334.

2. James, "The Moral Philosopher and the Moral Life," *The Will to Believe*, 154.

3. Standard sources on utilitarian theory include Elie Halévy, *The Growth of Philosophic Radicalism*, trans. Mary Morris (London, 1934); J. Plamenatz, *The English Utilitarians* (Oxford, 1949); and the essays collected in J. J. C. Smart and B. Williams, eds., *Utilitarianism: For and Against* (Cambridge, 1973).

4. James, "The Moral Philosopher and the Moral Life," *The Will to Believe*, 142–43, 160–61. Cf. *The Principles of Psychology*, 1: 306.

5. James, "The Moral Philosopher and the Moral Life," *The Will to Believe*, 141–62. John Wild offers an incisive discussion of James's relation to utilitarianism in *The Radical Empiricism of William James*. See esp. 274 f., 281 f., 409 f.

6. Dilthey's lectures on ethics are contained in *GS*, 10. For his treatment of Bentham, see 30–32; and cf. *GS*, 6: 150, for an earlier assessment of utilitarianism's inadequacies. In *Erkenntnistheorie*, 162–82, Hans Ineichen provides the most thorough analysis of Dilthey's ethics, tracing

Dilthey's attempt to build from Schleiermacher's critique of Kant a set of ethical arguments sensitive to naturalism but more critically reflective than utilitarianism; cf. Zöckler, *Dilthey und die Hermeneutik*, 30–44, for a less sympathetic assessment.

7. Fouillée, *Psychologie*, 1: 21 f.; *Morale*, 241–45; cf. *Le Moralisme de Kant*, 344–45; and *Histoire générale*, 477–78.

8. Green, *Prolegomena to Ethics*, 374–82.

9. Dewey, "Intuitionism," in *Johnson's Universal Cyclopedia*, ed. Charles Kendall Adams, 4 (New York, 1894): 657–59, *EW*, 4: 123–31.

10. Sidgwick, *Methods of Ethics*, 40 f., 52. Unless noted otherwise, all references are to the 7th edition.

11. See Sidgwick's autobiographical notes in the 7th ed. of *Methods of Ethics*, xvii; and Schneewind, *Sidgwick's Ethics*, 42 f.

12. Cf. this passage from *Methods of Ethics*, 53: "It is sometimes said that whatever be the case with our present adult consciousness, our original impulses were all directed towards pleasure or from pain, and that any impulses otherwise directed are derived from these by 'association of ideas.' I can find no evidence that even tends to prove this: so far as we can observe the consciousness of children, the two elements, extra-regarding impulse and desire for pleasure, seem to coexist in the same manner as they do in mature life. Insofar as there is any difference, it seems to be in the opposite direction; as the actions of children being more instinctive and less reflective are more prompted by extra-regarding impulse, and less by conscious aim at pleasure."

13. Dewey, *Outlines of a Critical Theory of Ethics*, *EW*, 3: 259 f., 254.

14. Dewey and Tufts, *Ethics*, 85–86, 269–70, 265 n., 281–84. Dewey's contributions to this book can be identified because he and Tufts specified in their preface who wrote which sections.

15. Sidgwick, *Methods of Ethics*, 94–95. On this point see also Green, *Prolegomena to Ethics*, 169–78; and Dewey, *Outlines of a Critical Theory of Ethics*, *EW*, 3: 270–71, 274–75, where he relies on Green and distinguishes Sidgwick from Mill.

16. Sidgwick, *Methods of Ethics*, 388.

17. Dewey, *Outlines of a Critical Theory of Ethics*, *EW*, 3: 276; and *The Study of Ethics: A Syllabus*, *EW*, 4: 284–85. For further criticisms of Mill along these lines, see Fouillée, *Histoire générale*, 477–88; Dilthey, *GS*, 10: 35–36; and James's lecture notes from 1888–1889, in the James papers.

18. As Kant stated this argument, "An action done from duty has its moral worth, not in the purpose to be attained by it," as hedonism would have it, "but in the maxim in accordance with which it is decided upon." It depends, therefore, "not on the realization of the object of the action, but solely on the principle of volition" according to which, "irrespective of all objects of the faculty of desire, the action has been performed" (Kant, *Groundwork of the Metaphysic of Morals*, trans. H. J. Paton, 3rd ed. [1956; rpt. New York, 1964], 67 f., 13 f.).

19. Sidgwick, *Methods of Ethics*, 389–90; and cf. Schneewind, *Sidgwick's Ethics*, 419–20. On Sidgwick's relation to Reid and Whewell, see Schneewind, 63–74, 101–16.

20. Sidgwick, *Methods of Ethics*, 361, 262, 210, 379; Fouillée, *Le Moralisme de Kant*, 335–36, 291; Dilthey, *GS*, 10: 21–23, 41–45, 101–12.

21. Green, *Prolegomena to Ethics*, 228–29; Richter, *The Politics of Conscience*, 199, 231.

22. See Sidgwick, *Lectures on Ethics*, 123–31, 105 ff., 76–77; and Green, *Prolegomena to Ethics*, 367. For a thorough discussion of the relation between Sidgwick's and Green's ethics, see Schneewind, *Sidgwick's Ethics*, 401–11.

23. Dewey, *Outlines of a Critical Theory of Ethics*, *EW*, 3: 335–38.

24. Dewey, "Self-Realization as the Moral Ideal," *Philosophical Review* 2 (1883): 652–64, *EW*, 4: 52 n. It is noteworthy that Dewey's essay "The Reflex Arc Concept in Psychology," in which he proclaimed the continuity of stimulus and response in experience, appeared in 1896, three years after "Self-Realization as the Moral Ideal" and two years after he further developed

his critique of Kant in *A Study of Ethics: A Syllabus*. On Dewey's gradual shift away from Green's ethics, see Kuklick, *Churchmen and Philosophers* 239–40.

25. Dewey, *Reconstruction in Philosphy, MW*, 12: 197–98.

26. The best of these commentaries is Schneewind, *Sidgwick's Ethics*; also excellent is C. D. Broad, *Five Types of Ethical Theory*, 143–256.

27. Sidgwick, *Methods of Ethics*, 379. Sidgwick is often treated as an exponent of "classical" utilitarianism; see for example John Rawls, *A Theory of Justice* (Cambridge, Mass., 1971), 22–33. I believe that interpretation underestimates the extent to which Sidgwick deliberately modified what he perceived to be utilitarian principles as part of his search for a synthesis of Kantian, intuitionist, and utilitarian ethics. As William K. Frankena has argued, "It seems best therefore to regard Sidgwick as synthesizing the positions which had been opposed since early in the eighteenth century, rather than as belonging wholly or even mainly to one of them." See Frankena's splendid essay on Sidgwick in the *Encyclopedia of Morals*, ed. Vergilius T. A. Ferm (New York, 1956), 540–44.

28. Sidgwick, *Methods of Ethics*, 422.

29. Five editions of *The Methods of Ethics* were published during Sidgwick's life: 1st, 1874; 2nd, 1877; 3rd, 1884; 4th, 1890; 5th, 1893. The 6th ed., published in 1901 after Sidgwick's death in 1900, partly compensates for the alterations in the text by including in the preface Sidgwick's own "Genetic Account" of the book, which recounts his intellectual progress from John Stuart Mill through Whewell, Kant, Butler, and Aristotle, and discloses the importance of different ethical traditions in the development of Sidgwick's ideas. A 7th ed. was published in 1907. On this issue, see also Schneewind, *Sidgwick's Ethics*, 412, 424.

30. Sidgwick, "Hedonism and Ultimate Good," *Mind* 2 (1877): 32.

31. A passage in *The Methods of Ethics*, 386–87, in which Sidgwick recapitulates his argument concerning the self-evident principles, supports this interpretation: "The axiom of Prudence, as I have given it, is a self-evident principle, implied in Rational Egoism as commonly accepted. Again, the axiom of Justice or Equity as above stated—'that similar cases ought to be treated similarly'—belongs in all its application to Utilitarianism, as much as to any system commonly called Intuitional: while the axiom of Rational Benevolence is, in my view, required as a rational basis for the Utilitarian system." See also Schneewind, *Sidgwick's Ethics*, 490–95, on the various interpretations of Sidgwick's "self-evident" ethical principles.

32. Sidgwick, *Methods of Ethics*, xix.

33. Ibid., 379, 497, 507, 382.

34. Sidgwick, "Hedonism and Ultimate Good," 31.

35. Sidgwick, *Methods of Ethics*, 508–9. Sidgwick's willingness to label "self evident" principles that nevertheless conflict with one another has occasioned considerable criticism. For guidance through Sidgwick's axioms, and a careful discussion of their relation to one another, see Schneewind, *Sidgwick's Ethics*, 290–95.

36. James, "The Moral Philosopher a .d the Moral Life," *The Will to Believe*, 161.

37. James, *The Principles of Psychology*, 2: 672–75. See also James's extensive marginal notations in his copies of Sidgwick's *Methods of Ethics* and his *Outlines of the History of Ethics for English Readers* in the Philosophical Library of William James.

38. Fouillée, *Critique des systèmes de morale contemporains*, 36–38.

39. Fouillée, *La Liberté*, 337–38.

40. Green, *Lectures on the Principles of Political Obligation, Works*, 2: 550.

41. Guyau, *Fouillée*, frontispiece.

42. Fouillée, *Morale*, 4, 6, 30.

43. Ibid., 211–14.

44. Green, *Prolegomena to Ethics*, 200.

45. Sidgwick first launched his attack on Green's notion of a noncompetitive ideal in his

review of Green's *Prolegomena to Ethics*, which appeared in *Mind* 9 (1884): 169–84. He expanded it in his *Lectures on Ethics*, from which these quotations are taken; see 65–72.

46. Dewey and Tufts, *Ethics, MW*, 5: 221–40.

47. Ibid., 218.

48. Dewey, *Outlines of a Critical Theory of Ethics, EW*, 3: 292 f.

49. Ibid., 300.

50. Ibid., 315.

51. Ibid., 322, 327.

52. James, *The Principles of Psychology*, 2: 675.

53. Sidgwick, "The Relation of Ethics to Sociology," a paper read before the London School of Ethics and Social Philosophy, reprinted in *Miscellaneous Essays and Addresses* (London, 1904); see esp. 264–68. See also *Methods of Ethics*, 1–2, 33–34, 112; *Lectures on Ethics*, 1; and "Is the Distinction between 'Is' and 'Ought' Ultimate and Irreducible?" *Proceedings of the Aristotelian Society* 2 (1892): 88–107.

54. James, "The Will to Believe," *The Will to Believe*, 27. Cf. James, "The Sentiment of Rationality," *The Will to Believe*, 84–85, 88; and the following passage from the outline of James's lectures in 1888–1889: "The search constitutes philosophy, which has two subdivisions: (1) science, the principles of *fact* or what *is*, whether good or bad; (2) ethics, what is good or bad, whether it *be* or *be not*. The principles of ethics are independent of those of science." Perry, *James*, 2: 263.

55. Dilthey, *GS*, 1: 26–27.

56. See for example Green, *Prolegomena to Ethics*, 178; and cf. Richter, *The Politics of Conscience*, 176.

57. Dewey, *Outlines of a Critical Theory of Ethics, EW*, 3: 241–42.

58. Dewey, *The Quest for Certainty*, Gifford Lectures (1929; New York, 1960), 259, 272–73. Emphasis added.

59. James, notes on the "moral universe," ca. 1878, James papers.

60. Sidgwick, *Methods of Ethics*, 2. I am grateful to Jerome Schneewind for clarification of this important distinction.

61. Fouillée, *Morale*, xlvi.

62. Green, *Political Obligation, Works*, 2: 335 ff.

63. Dewey, *Democracy and Education, MW*, 9: 111.

64. James, "The Moral Philosopher and the Moral Life," *The Will to Believe*, 150, 141.

65. See Dewey to James, May 10 and June 3, 1891, in Perry, *James*, 2: 517–19; and Dewey, *The Quest for Certainty*, 278.

66. James, "The Moral Philosopher and the Moral Life," *The Will to Believe*, 152–53, 155–56. For competing interpretations of James's meaning, cf. Wild, *The Radical Empiricism of William James*, 274 f.; Perry, *James*, 2: 517; E. C. Moore, *American Pragmatism* (New York, 1961), 244; and Hollinger, "William James and the Culture of Inquiry," 269–70.

67. James's lecture notes from 1888–1889 are in the James papers.

68. James, "Humanism and Truth," *The Meaning of Truth*, 47.

69. James, "The Moral Philosopher and the Moral Life," *The Will to Believe*, 155–56.

70. Dilthey, *GS*, 7: 297.

71. Dilthey, *GS*, 8: 75–118, 190–205, in *SW*, 135, 121.

72. Dilthey, *GS*, 6: 33–34.

73. James, "The Moral Philosopher and the Moral Life," *The Will to Believe*, 158. See also John K. Roth, *Freedom and the Moral Life*, 113–14, 143.

74. Dilthey, *GS*, 5: 404–16, in *SW*, 127–28.

75. See Dilthey to Graf Yorck, Jan., 1890, in *GS*, 10: 9–11.

76. Dilthey, *GS*, 5: 404–16, in *SW*, 123.

77. See Green, *Prolegomena to Ethics*, 179–80, 272–73, 292–93, 300. For the Platonic and religious elements of Green's ethics, see also 197ff.

78. Green, *Political Obligation, Works*, 2: 552–53.

79. Green, *Prolegomena to Ethics*, 308–9.

80. Dewey's shifting estimate of Green's ethics can be traced by comparing the following: "Psychology as Philosophic Method," *Mind* 20 (1886): 153–73, *EW*, 1: 144–67; "The Philosophy of Thomas Hill Green," *Andover Review* 11 (1889), *EW*, 3: 14–35; "Green's Theory of the Moral Motive," *Philosophical Review* 1 (1892): 593–612, *EW*, 3: 155–73; and "Self-Realization as the Moral Ideal," *Philosophical Review* 2 (1893): 652–64, *EW*, 4: 42–53.

81. Dewey and Tufts, *Ethics, MW*, 5: 194, 351–53.

82. Ibid., 194–95.

83. Dewey, *Reconstruction in Philosophy, MW*, 12: 181.

84. See Arnold Brecht, *Political Theory: The Foundations of Twentieth-Century Political Thought* (Princeton, 1959), 269, for an illuminating discussion of Dewey's reliance on democracy to solve the problems of deciding between competing values.

85. Dewey, *Ethics of Democracy, EW*, 1: 248–49.

86. I will return to Dewey's concept of democracy when I examine his political ideas in Chapters Nine and Ten.

87. Dewey to James, June 3, 1891, in Perry, *James*, 2: 517–19. For the most complete account of Dewey's involvement with Ford, see Coughlin, *Young John Dewey*, 93–108.

88. Dewey, *Outlines of a Critical Theory of Ethics, EW*, 3: 325–26.

89. Dewey and Tufts, *Ethics, MW*, 5: 301–2.

90. Dewey, *Reconstruction in Philosophy, MW*, 12: 173.

91. Green, *Prolegomena to Ethics*, 337.

92. Dewey, *Outlines of a Critical Theory of Ethics, EW*, 3: 386–88.

93. Dewey, *The Quest for Certainty*, 272, 264–65. For contrasting arguments on the thrust, and the adequacy, of Dewey's value theory, see Morton White, *Social Thought in America*, 212–19; "Value and Obligation in Dewey and Lewis," in *Pragmatism and the American Mind* (New York, 1973), 158–61; and *Science and Sentiment in America*, 279; and for a different perspective, more similar to my own, cf. Thayer, *Meaning and Action*, 389–90, 405–8; James Gouinlock, *John Dewey's Philosophy of Value* (New York, 1972), 161–232; Robert L. Holmes, "The Development of John Dewey's Ethical Thought," *The Monist* 48 (1964): 392–406; the brief, incisive treatment in Flower and Murphy, *Philosophy in America*, 2: 859–74; and Murray G. Murphy's introduction to Dewey, *Human Nature and Conduct* (New York, 1922), *MW*, 14: ix–xxiii.

Chapter 5. From Philosophy to Politics

1. Fouillée, *Critique des systèmes de morale contemporains*, 389–92.

2. Sidgwick, *Methods of Ethics*, 293–94.

3. James, "Great Men and Their Environment," *The Will to Believe*, 170, 174; and cf. "The Will to Believe," 29.

4. Fouillée, *La Science sociale*, 242, 247–48; and cf. Guyau, *Fouillée*, 134–44.

5. Green, *Political Obligation, Works*, 2: 461.

6. Dilthey, *GS*, 18: 225; and see Ermarth, *Dilthey*, 27.

7. See Guyau, *Fouillée*, 143–44.

8. James, "The Moral Philosopher and the Moral Life," *The Will to Believe*, 157.

9. James, "On a Certain Blindness in Human Beings," *Talks to Teachers on Psychology*, 169. See also James's notes from the lectures he delivered in 1905 at Wellesley College and the

University of Chicago, in which he made clear the connection between radical empiricism, pragmatism, experimentation, tolerance, democracy, and social change. At Chicago, he invoked Dewey's writings to emphasize this linkage. James's notes are in the James papers.

10. James, "The Moral Philosopher and the Moral Life," *The Will to Believe*, 157.

11. James to Ralph Barton Perry, July 17, 1909, James papers, in which he praises Perry's *Moral Economy* (1909) for its "reasoned faith in radical democracy."

12. James, "The Essence of Humanism," *The Meaning of Truth*, 72.

13. Fouillée, *Morale*, 226.

14. Green, *Political Obligation, Works*: 2, 354. This weakness continues to haunt attempts to establish principles of justice on the basis of a hypothetical compact among individuals. For a penetrating critique of John Rawl's *Theory of Justice* which employs arguments similar to those Green applied to earlier social contract theorists, see Michael J. Sandel, *Liberalism and the Limits of Justice* (Cambridge, 1982).

15. Green, *Works*, 2: 445.

16. Dilthey, *GS*, 7: 146–47.

17. Dilthey, *GS*, 1: 48, 83–86. Sheldon Wolin perceptively discusses "the erosion of the distinctly political" in *Politics and Vision: Continuity and Innovation in Western Political Thought* (Boston, 1960), 290–92, 361–62.

18. On the multifaceted phenomena of antimodernism and utopianism in America and Europe, see, in addition to the sources cited in n. 12 of Chapter One, Eugen Weber, *Action Française* (Stanford, 1962); R. Jackson Wilson, "Experience and Utopia: The Making of Edward Bellamy's *Looking Backward*," *American Studies* 11 (1977): 45–60; John L. Thomas, "Utopia for an Urban Age: Henry George, Henry Demarest Lloyd, Edward Bellamy," *Perspectives in American History* 6 (1972): 135–62; and idem, *Alternative America: Henry George, Edward Bellamy, Henry Demarest Lloyd and the Adversary Tradition* (Cambridge, Mass., 1983).

19. Dilthey, *GS*, 6: 239. Cf. Green, *Political Obligation, Works*, 2: 446; and Fouillée, *La Démocratie politique et social en France* (Paris, 1910), 190.

20. The concept of "organized capitalism" derives from Austrian socialist Rudolf Hilferding, whose most important work, *Das Finanzkapital*, first appeared in 1910. The phrase refers to the combination of finance capitalism, monopoly industrialism, and a hierarchically ordered economy. Among its characteristics are the large-scale organization of production and markets, the consolidation and merger of corporations, reliance on clerical employees and managers, and increasing government interference in the economy. I will use organized capitalism as a limiting concept indicating the tendencies of the American, French, German, and British economies during the 1870–1920 period. None of the national economies demonstrated all of these characteristics, and their rates of economic change varied widely during these years, but the concept serves to highlight the direction in which they were developing. On Hilferding, see Kolakowski, *Main Currents of Marxism*, vol. 2, *The Golden Age*, 290–304.

21. Thomas Haskell discusses the concept of interdependence perceptively in *The Emergence of Professional Social Science: The American Social Science Association and the Nineteenth-Century Crisis of Authority* (Urbana, Ill., 1977), 12–17, 27–47. I do not contend that the recognition of social bonds was unique to the late nineteenth century. That awareness is as old as reflections on the human condition. I do want to argue, however, that the degree and kind of interdependence characteristic of advanced urban-industrial societies did represent a new development, one that helped to break down or alter the idea of individual autonomy prominent in some varieties of earlier social and political thought. On the social consequences of economic change, see also Kenneth Barkin, *The Controversy over German Industrialization, 1890–1920* (Chicago, 1970); and for a comparative analysis, Jürgen Kocka, *White Collar Workers in America, 1890–1940: A Social-Political History in International Perspective*, trans. Maura Kealey (London, 1980).

22. My discussion of the second industrial revolution relies on the following: David S. Landes, *The Unbound Prometheus: Technological Change and Industrial Development in Western Europe from 1750 to the Present* (Cambridge, 1969); Douglass C. North, *Growth and Welfare in the American Past: A New Economic History*, 2nd ed. (Englewood Cliffs, N.J., 1966); Robert Higgs, *The Transformation of the American Economy, 1865–1914* (New York, 1971); J. H. Clapham, *The Economic Development of France and Germany, 1815–1914*, 4th ed. (Cambridge, 1955); William Ashworth, *An Economic History of England, 1870–1939* (London, 1960); Carlo M. Cipola, ed., *The Fontana Economic History of Europe*, vol. 3, *The Industrial Revolution* (Glasgow, 1973); Charles P. Kindleberger, *Economic Growth in France and Britain, 1851–1950* (Cambridge, Mass., 1964); Karl Polanyi, *The Great Transformation: The Political and Economic Origins of Our Time*, 2nd ed. (Boston, 1957); and Patrick O'Brien and Caglar Keyder, *Economic Growth in Britain and France, 1780–1914: Two Paths to the Twentieth Century* (Boston, 1978).

23. Daniel Rodgers, *The Work Ethic in Industrial America, 1850–1920* (Chicago, 1978), 24–25; Gordon Wright, *France in Modern Times: From the Enlightenment to the Present*, 2nd ed. (Chicago, 1974), 273, 284–85.

24. See Alfred Chandler, *The Visible Hand: The Managerial Revolution in Modern Business* (Cambridge, Mass., 1977); Landes, *The Unbound Prometheus*, 245–46; and Morton Keller, *Affairs of State: Public Life in Late Nineteenth Century America* (Cambridge, 1977), 434–38. Cf. the range of perspectives presented by the contributors to Norbert Horn and Jürgen Kocka, eds., *Law and the Formation of the Big Enterprises in the 19th and Early 20th Centuries* (Göttingen, 1979); and the contributors to *Regulation in Perspective: Historical Essays*, ed. Thomas K. McCraw (Cambridge, Mass., 1981), 56–94.

25. On Britain and France, see Ashworth, *Economic History of England*, 200–1; Wright, *France in Modern Times*, 285; and Landes, *Unbound Prometheus*, 242 n. 1. On the United States and Germany, see Albert Rees, *Real Wages in Manufacturing, 1890–1914* (Princeton, 1961), 4; and North, *Growth and Welfare in the American Past*, 153.

26. Sidgwick, *Methods of Ethics*, 474.

27. See Fouillée, *La Science sociale*, 162–65, for a characteristic analysis of the inadequacy of social Darwinists' recourse to the idea of inevitability; and Fouillée, *La Propriété sociale et la démocratie* (Paris, 1884), on the undesirability of revolution and the greater promise of gradual change.

28. Dilthey, *Westermanns Monatshefte* 50 (1876): 209–15, *GS*, 6: 82. See also Sidgwick's preface to *The Principles of Political Economy* (London, 1883), v; and "The Economic Lessons of Socialism," in *Miscellaneous Essays and Reviews*, 237. Eric Hobsbawm discusses Sidgwick's aversion to Marx in "Dr. Marx and the Victorian Critics," in *Labouring Men: Studies in the History of Labour* (1964; rpt. London, 1976), 247–48. For Dilthey's attitude toward Marx, see Ermarth, *Dilthey*, 292–94; for a Marxist critique of Dilthey's position, see Zöckler, *Dilthey und die Hermeneutik*, 227–64.

29. See A. V. Dicey's letters to Mrs. Henry Sidgwick, Oct. 23 and Nov. 7, 1902, in the Henry Sidgwick papers, Wren Library, Trinity College, Cambridge, for concise expositions of Sidgwick's interpretation of the fate of laissez-faire ideals in the nineteenth century, an interpretation most fully presented in *The Development of European Polity* (London, 1903), which Eleanor Sidgwick edited for publication after Sidgwick's death.

30. Dilthey, *GS*, 8: 190–205, in *SW*, 109–11.

31. Sidgwick, *Methods of Ethics*, 447–48.

32. Fouillée, *Morale*, 211–14.

33. Green, *Political Obligation, Works*, 2: 550, 553.

34. Sidgwick, "The Economic Lessons of Socialism," *Economic Journal*, Sept., 1895, reprinted in *Miscellaneous Essays and Addresses*, 235–48. See also Sidgwick, *Principles of*

Political Economy, 499–517, in which he offers a similar analysis. The quotation from Mill appears in his *Autobiography* (1873; rpt. New York, 1960), 162.

35. Fouillée to Brunetière, Aug. 22, 1902, in Bibliothèque Nationale, Cabinet des manuscrits, N.A.F. 25038, ff. 330–31.

36. Dilthey, *Westermanns Monatshefte* 44 (1878): 335.

37. James's address, delivered January 9, 1902, is quoted in Perry, *James*, 2: 298f. James's letters to Lutoslawski, Dec. 1, 1900, and March 3, 1901, are in the Beinecke Library, Yale University. See also Richard Hofstadter, *Anti-Intellectualism in American Life* (New York, 1962), 38–39.

38. Sidgwick, *Elements of Politics*, 40; James, *The Will to Believe*, 23. For an incisive discussion of the personal and political reasons for Sidgwick's nonpartisanship, see Collini, *That Noble Science of Politics*, 305–7.

39. As philosophers ceased to be clerics and philosophy freed itself from theology and psychology, an independent discipline, more limited in scope and more strict in its definition of acceptable methods, began to emerge. This phenomenon has been ably chronicled, and I will consequently forego any extended discussion of the professionalization of philosophy. I do not intend thereby to minimize its significance. On this point see A. J. Ayer, *The Revolution in Philosophy* (London, 1956); Schneewind, *Sidgwick's Ethics and Victorian Moral Philosophy*; Sheldon Rothblatt, *The Revolution of the Dons: Cambridge and Society in Victorian England* (London, 1968); A. J. Engel, *From Clergyman to Don: The Rise of the Academic Profession in Nineteenth-Century Oxford* (Oxford, 1983); Kuklick, *The Rise of American Philosophy*; Ringer, *The Decline of the German Mandarins*; Logue, *From Philosophy to Sociology*; and the splendid collection of essays edited by Alexandra Oleson and John Voss, *The Organization of Knowledge in Modern America, 1860–1920* (Baltimore, 1979). On the professionalization of the social sciences, see Haskell, *The Emergence of Professional Social Science*; Mary O. Furner, *Advocacy and Objectivity: A Crisis in the Professionalization of American Social Science, 1865–1905* (Lexington, Ky., 1975); Burton J. Bledstein, *The Culture of Professionalism: The Middle Class and the Development of Higher Education in America* (New York, 1976); Philip Abrams, *The Origins of British Sociology, 1834–1914* (Chicago, 1968); and Terry N. Clark, *Prophets and Patrons: The French University and the Emergence of the Social Sciences* (Cambridge, Mass., 1973).

40. Perhaps the clearest example of this deprecatory tendency is Richter, *The Politics of Conscience: T. H. Green and His Age*.

41. See Fouillée, *La Propriété*, 288–89; *La Science sociale*, 374–80; *Education; Les Etudes classiques et la démocratie* (Paris, 1898); and Fouillée's letter to Ferdinand Brunetière, March 26, 1897, Bibliothèque Nationale, Cabinet des manuscrits, N.A.F. 25038, f. 319. See also George Weisz, *The Emergence of Modern Universities in France, 1863–1914* (Princeton, 1983).

42. Green, "On the Grading of Secondary Schools," in Nettleship, *Memoir*, lvii; Green, "The Oxford High School for Boys," *Works*, 3: 387–476. It is worth noting that Sidgwick was the guiding force behind the founding of Newnham College for women at Cambridge. See Sidgwick and Sidgwick, *Memoir*, 208–12; and Havard, *Sidgwick and Political Philosophy*, 56–61. On Green, see Richter, *The Politics of Conscience*, 77, 366. The ethical societies are discussed in Reba Soffer, *Ethics and Society in England: The Revolution of the Social Sciences, 1870–1914* (Berkeley, 1978), 179–89. For broader patterns of educational reform at Oxford and Cambridge, see T. W. Heyck, *The Transformation of Intellectual Life in Victorian England* (London, 1982); and Peter Gordon and John White, *Philosophers as Educational Reformers: The Influence of Idealism on British Educational Thought and Practice* (London, 1979).

43. James, *Memories and Studies* (New York, 1911), 319–20. See also Matthiessen, *The James Family*, 633–36.

44. Recent overviews of late nineteenth-century politics in Great Britain include Martin

Pugh, *The Making of Modern British Politics, 1867–1939* (Oxford, 1982); and D. A. Hamer, *Liberal Politics in the Age of Gladstone and Rosebery: A Study in Leadership and Policy* (Oxford, 1972); on the United States, Morton Keller, *Affairs of State*; and Paul Kleppner, *The Third Electoral System 1853–1892: Parties, Voters, and Political Culture* (Chapel Hill, N.C., 1979); and on France, Jean-Pierre Azéma and Michel Winock, *La IIIᵉ République: "naissance et mort,"* 2nd ed. (Paris, 1976); Jean-Marie Mayeur, *Les Débuts de la IIIᵉ République: 1871–1898*, vol. 10 of the *Nouvelle Histoire de la France contemporaine* (Paris, 1973); and especially Jacques Kayser, *Les Grandes Batailles du radicalisme: des origines aux portes du pouvoir, 1820–1901* (Paris, 1961).

45. James Bryce, *The American Commonwealth*, 2: 21, quoted in Keller, *Affairs of State*, 544. In Keller's apt description, "Between the sharp-edged politics of Reconstruction and the bitter Bryan-McKinley contest of 1896 lay a time when the issues, the very shape of American politics were fuzzy and indistinct. The brittle, mechanical devices of organizational politics prevailed over major national issues" (544). A pathbreaking comparison of American and British Democratic-Liberalism is Robert Kelley, *The Transatlantic Persuasion: The Liberal Democratic Mind in the Age of Gladstone* (New York, 1969).

46. Clemenceau quoted in Pierre Barral, *Les Fondateurs de la Troisième République* (Paris, 1968), 182. An exceptionally acute discussion of the politics of the Third Republic is Stanley Hoffmann's analysis of the "republican synthesis" and the underlying "stalemate society" in his essay "Paradoxes of the French Political Community," in Hoffmann, ed., *In Search of France* (Cambridge, Mass., 1963), 1–117. Theodore Zeldin illustrates how the institutional arrangements of French political life reinforced the stasis of the system in *France 1848–1945: Politics and Anger* (Oxford, 1979), 210–29.

47. Adams, *The Education of Henry Adams*, 294. For guidance through the dense thickets of political sociology and ethnocultural analysis, see Pugh, *The Making of Modern British Politics*, 312–15; Richard L. McCormick, "Ethno-Cultural Interpretations of Nineteenth-Century American Voting Behavior," *Political Science Quarterly* 89 (1974): 351–77; Robert Kelley, "Ideology and Political Culture from Jefferson to Nixon," *American Historical Review* 82 (1977): 531–62; Kleppner, *The Third Party System*; Zeldin, *Politics and Anger*, 1–29; and David Sumler, "Subcultural Persistence and Political Cleavage in the Third French Republic," *Comparative Studies in Society and History* 19 (1977): 431–55, an essay marred by a somewhat naive Parsonian view of American politics but offering an intriguing treatment of French political culture and useful references to local studies. On the limits of this new political history, see James E. Wright, "The Ethnocultural Model of Voting," *American Behavioral Scientist* 16 (1973): 653–74; and James R. Green, "Behavioralism and Class Analysis: A Review Essay on Methodology and Ideology," *Labor History* 13 (1972): 89–106.

48. The analysis of Bismarck's *Sammlungspolitik* as a means of perpetuating the power of prebourgeois agrarian elites through alliance with large-scale industrialists, a strategy that eventuated in expansionist policies designed to deflect attention from domestic repression to foreign affairs, derives from the work of Eckhart Kehr and Hans Rosenberg. See Kehr, *Battleship Building and Party Politics in Germany, 1848–1901*, trans. Pauline R. and Eugene N. Anderson (1930; Chicago, 1973); idem, *Economic Interest, Militarism, and Foreign Policy*, ed. Gordon A. Craig, trans. Grete Heinz (1965; Berkeley, 1977); Rosenberg, *Bureaucracy, Aristocracy, and Autocracy: The Prussian Experience, 1640–1815* (Cambridge, Mass., 1958); and idem, *Grosse Depression und Bismarckzeit. Wirtschaftsablauf, Gesellschaft, und Politik in Mitteleuropa* (Berlin, 1967). Recent elaborations of their analysis include Dirk Stegmann, *Die erben Bismarcks: Parteien und Verbände in der Spätphase des Wilhelminischen Deutschlands* (Cologne, 1970); and especially Hans-Ulrich Wehler, *Das deutsche Kaiserreich, 1871–1918* (Göttingen, 1973). On Germany and liberalism in the 1870s and 1880s, see James J. Sheehan, *German Liberalism in the Nineteenth Century* (Chicago, 1978); Gustav Seeber, *Zwischen Bebel*

und Bismarck: Zur Geschichte des Linksliberalismus in Deutschland, 1871–1893 (East Berlin, 1965); and Gordon A. Craig, *Germany 1866–1945* (Oxford, 1978), 1–278. On German political parties, see Gerhard A. Ritter, *Die deutschen Parteien vor 1918* (Cologne, 1973); and Ludwig Bergsträsser, *Geschichte der politischen Parteien in Deutschland*, 11th ed. (Munich, 1965).

49. Eckhart Kehr explored the "refeudalization of the bureaucracy" in his essay "The Social System of Reaction in Prussia under the Puttkamer Ministry," in *Economic Interest, Militarism, and Foreign Policy*, 109–31. See also Dilthey, *GS*, 16: 140; Meinecke, "Drei Generationen deutscher Gelehrtenpolitik," *Staat und Persönlichkeit* (Berlin, 1933), 136; Ermarth, *Dilthey*, 28–30; James J. Sheehan, *Lujo Brentano: A Study of Liberalism and Social Reform in Germany* (Chicago, 1966), 46–113; and Fritz Ringer, *The Decline of the German Mandarins*, chap. six.

50. On the emergence of this position in the mid-nineteenth century and its Anglo-American dimension, see David D. Hall, "The Victorian Connection," in Howe, ed., *Victorian America*, 81–94. For a vigorous and provocative defense of the genteel intellectuals and their focus on civil service reform as an appropriate response to American political realities, see also Geoffrey Blodgett, "A New Look at the Gilded Age," in *Victorian America*, 95–108; and for the interpretations he is challenging, which are more critical of the mugwump approach, see John Sproat, *"The Best Men": Liberal Reformers in the Gilded Age* (New York, 1968); and John Dobson, *Politics in the Gilded Age: A New Perspective on Reform* (New York, 1972).

51. James to R. G. Bromberg, June 30, 1884, in Perry, *James*, 2: 296–97. On the popular perception of laissez-faire policies as instrumental in economic development, see Blodgett, "A New Look at the Gilded Age," in Howe, ed., *Victorian America*, 103–5; and R. D. Anderson, *France, 1870–1914: Politics and Society* (London, 1977), 160.

52. James to Grace Norton, July 6, 1900, in Perry, *James*, 2: 252–53; cf. 312 for James's letter to Francis Boott: "I have fallen in love with [Bryan] for his character, that I am willing to forget his following . . . The worst thing said is . . . that in public affairs he is an amateur. So are you and I!" That quality, from James's perspective, counted as a strength rather than a weakness. As part of his argument that James was "self-satisfied and uncritical of the social order," an argument I consider overstated, Kuklick contends that James "viewed William Jennings Bryan's campaign in 1896 with alarm." But the letter from James to Hugo Münsterberg, Sept. 2, 1896, which Kuklick cites, is ambiguous: "The political campaign goes on admirably—splendid speeches and documents on both sides. It seems difficult to doubt the essential soundness of people where such a serious mass of discussion, pursued on the whole in such a dignified tone, is a regular incident of life. Of course, the silver party must be beaten, but they have much that is ideal on their side." These words suggest enthusiasm more than alarm, and they also suggest why James preferred to see new ideas tested pragmatically in the "hurly burly" of politics instead of decided according to a priori political principles. Lacking further evidence, it is impossible to know whether James opposed the "silver party" because of its radicalism, as Kuklick implies, or because he considered free silver simply bad economics and bad politics—an opinion some radicals shared, and a view whose insightfulness was made apparent by the shift of urban working-class voters into the Republican party during the 1890s. Cf. Kuklick, *The Rise of American Philosophy*, 313f.; and James's letter to Münsterberg in Perry, *James*, 2: 146. For a recent discussion placing James in the context of the ambivalent genteel liberalism of the Gilded Age, see Alan Trachtenberg, *The Incorporation of America: Culture and Society in the Gilded Age* (New York, 1982), 140–81.

53. See James to Sidgwick, March 22 and April 30, 1899, in the James papers; and Sidgwick, *Elements of Politics*, 357–58, 373–74, 590–92; v–vi.

54. See Mill, *Autobiography*, 162–63.

55. While the work of C. B. Macpherson has stimulated a great deal of productive thinking about the origins of liberal capitalism, it seems clear that the paternity suit he filed against Locke in *The Political Theory of Possessive Individualism: Hobbes to Locke* (New York, 1962) was

misdirected. As John Dunn and Peter Laslett have pointed out, Locke was the child of Calvinism more than he was the father of capitalism, and his discussion of property relies on a controlling idea of natural law that excludes the unrestricted exercise of possessive individualism. See John Dunn, *The Political Thought of John Locke* (Cambridge, 1969); and Peter Laslett's introduction to his edition of Locke's *Two Treatises of Government*, rev. ed. (1960; Cambridge, 1963), esp. 106–35. For Macpherson's rejoinder, see "Natural Rights in Hobbes and Locke," in his *Democratic Theory: Essays in Retrieval* (Oxford, 1973), 224–32; and his introduction to Locke's *Second Treatise of Government* (Indianapolis, 1980), vii–xxi. Macpherson and others have pointed to the inconsistency between Locke's empiricism and his recourse to natural law; for an incisive and evenhanded discussion of Locke's awareness of this problem and his attempts to resolve it—a discussion that suggests further reasons for resolving the controversy over the historical Locke in Dunn's favor—see Patrick Riley, *Will and Political Legitimacy: A Critical Exposition of Social Contract Theory in Hobbes, Locke, Rousseau, Kant, and Hegel* (Cambridge, Mass., 1982), 72–97. Riley's account, however, also suggests how the theory of possessive individualism may have developed out of Locke's ideas, even if he was not himself responsible for its creation.

56. On the rise of liberalism in Britain, the standard work remains Halévy, *The Growth of Philosophic Radicalism*.

57. This argument derives largely from Bernard Bailyn, *The Ideological Origins of the American Revolution* (Cambridge, Mass., 1967); idem, *The Origins of American Politics* (New York, 1967); Gordon Wood, *The Creation of the American Republic, 1776–1787* (New York, 1969); Joyce Appleby, *Capitalism and a New Social Order: The Republican Vision of the 1790s* (New York, 1984); and Drew R. McCoy, *The Elusive Republic: Political Economy in Jeffersonian America* (Chapel Hill, N.C., 1980). See also Louis Hartz, *The Liberal Tradition in America* (New York, 1955); and John P. Diggins, *The Lost Soul of American Politics: Virtue, Self-Interest, and the Foundations of Liberalism* (New York, 1984). In addition to the studies of the Scottish Enlightenment cited in Chapter One, see Morton White, *The Philosophy of the American Revolution* (New York, 1978), which emphasizes Jefferson's rational intuitionism.

58. On Madison and *The Federalist*, see Douglass Adair, "That Politics May Be Reduced to a Science: David Hume, James Madison, and the Tenth Federalist," in *The Reinterpretation of the American Revolution*, ed. Jack P. Greene (New York, 1968), 487–503; Marvin Meyers, ed., *The Mind of the Founder: Sources of the Political Thought of James Madison* (Indianapolis, 1973), xvii, xlviii; and Garry Wills, *Explaining America* (Garden City, N.Y., 1981). Wills's analysis of *The Federalist*, in large part an elaboration of Adair's insight into the role Hume played in Madison's theory of republicanism, is more persuasive than is his analysis of Jefferson's Declaration of Independence in *Inventing America* (Garden City, N.Y., 1978). For a review of recent literature on this issue, see Daniel Walker Howe, "European Sources of Political Ideas in Jeffersonian America," *Reviews in American History* 10 (1982): 28–44.

59. On the transformation of liberalism during the course of the nineteenth century, see especially Marvin Meyers, *The Jacksonian Persuasion: Politics and Belief* (Stanford, 1960); Daniel Walker Howe, *The Political Culture of the American Whigs* (Chicago, 1979); Eric Foner, *Free Soil, Free Labor, Free Men: The Ideology of the Republican Party Before the Civil War* (New York, 1970); Robert G. McCloskey, *American Conservatism in the Age of Enterprise, 1865–1910* (1951; New York, 1964); Kelley, "Ideology and Political Culture"; idem, *The Cultural Pattern of American Politics: The First Century* (New York, 1978); and R. Jackson Wilson, *In Quest of Community: Social Philosophy in the United States, 1860–1920* (New York, 1968). Dorothy Ross, in her essay "Socialism and American Liberalism: Academic Social Thought in the 1880s," *Perspectives in American History* 11 (1977–1978): 5–79, argues that four currents of egalitarian dissent flowed through American thought during the nineteenth century: (1) the democratic tradition of Paine, Jefferson, and Jackson; (2) the Locofocos and working-class

egalitarianism; (3) the Whigs' emphasis on the mutuality of interests and responsibilities; and (4) evangelical Christianity. Transcendentalism, the most celebrated challenge to prevailing opinion, in fact extended the radical individualism of the liberal capitalist ethos even as it repudiated its economic doctrine. Emerson's *Nature* and Thoreau's *Walden* both expressed the transcendentalist view of society as an obstacle to individual fulfillment. Whereas eighteenth-century moral philosophy emphasized the instruction of conscience by the moral sense to bring individual will into conformity with natural law, transcendentalists wanted to leap beyond conventional communities to penetrate the heart of nature and find truth in the intuitive union of self with cosmos.

60. James, "The Moral Philosopher and the Moral Life," *The Will to Believe*, 155. Cf. the following passage from the same essay, p. 156:

> A true philosopher ... must see that there is nothing final in any actually given equilibrium of human ideals, but that, as our present laws and customs have fought and conquered other past ones, so they will in their turn be overthrown by any newly discovered order which will hush up the complaints that they still give rise to, without producing others louder still. "Rules are made for man, not man for rules"—that one sentence is enough to immortalize Green's *Prolegomena to Ethics*. And although a man always risks much when he breaks away from established rules and strives to realize a larger ideal whole than they permit, yet the philosopher must allow that it is at all times open to anyone to make the experiment, provided he fear not to stake his life and character upon the throw.

61. James to Henry James, Dec. 19, 1908, in *Letters of William James*, 2: 317–18.

62. Although James was sympathetic to a wide range of social reforms, he was not himself a reformer. The straw man Perry set up in his chapter "James as Reformer" in *James* has been torched with great fanfare but less historical understanding by George R. Garrison and Edward H. Madden, "William James—Warts and All," *American Quarterly* 29 (1977): 207–21. Bruce Kuklick has pointed out that James's importance for American politics lay in his challenge to the "deterministic interpretation of Darwin that Spencer popularized. In this sense the 'pragmatism' of James (and of Royce) had implications for social and political thought; its success transformed the framework of intellectual debate in the United States and made it possible for those later interested in social and political thought, for example Walter Lippmann and Herbert Croly, to argue credibly for collective action of one kind or another. But," Kuklick concludes, "this sort of thinking had a low priority for James himself." For a variety of reasons discussed in section two of this chapter, James concentrated his energies on philosophical rather than political issues. See Kuklick, *The Rise of American Philosophy*, 311–14.

63. As Hume expressed the liberal perspective, it is "a just political maxim that every man must be supposed a knave." Although "Honour is a great check upon mankind," nevertheless "where a considerable body of men act together, this check is, in a great measure, removed." According to Douglass Adair, this sober judgment from Hume's *Essays Moral, Political, and Literary* helped to shape Madison's thinking decisively, and Hume's pessimism thus filtered into American liberal theory. See Adair, "That Politics May Be Reduced to a Science: David Hume, James Madison, and the Tenth *Federalist*," in Greene, ed., *The Reinterpretation of the American Revolution*, 497. On the French Revolution and the differences between continental radicalism and Anglo-American liberalism, see R. R. Palmer, *The Age of the Democratic Revolution. A Political History of Europe and America, 1760–1800*, vol. 1, *The Challenge* (Princeton, 1959), 119; and Wolin, *Politics and Vision*, 293–94.

64. My discussion of Rousseau is indebted to Roger D. Masters, *The Political Philosophy of Rousseau* (Princeton, 1968); Masters' introduction to his edition of Rousseau's *First and Second Discourses*, trans. Roger D. and Judith R. Masters (New York, 1964); Masters' introduction to *On the Social Contract*, trans. Judith R. Masters (New York, 1978); and Judith Shklar, *Men and Citizens: A Study of Rousseau's Social Theory* (Cambridge, 1969).

65. On Arnold, see Richter, *The Politics of Conscience*, 49; on Henry James, Sr., see Charles Howard Hopkins, *The Rise of the Social Gospel in American Protestantism, 1865–1915* (New Haven, 1940), 67.

66. On French liberalism, see Stephen Holmes, *Benjamin Constant and the Making of Modern Liberalism* (New Haven, 1984); and R. D. Anderson, *France, 1870–1914*.

67. Green, *Political Obligation, Works*, 2: 396–97, 410, 415–16; and Fouillée, *La Démocratie*, 64–65.

68. Kant, *Perpetual Peace: A Philosophical Sketch* (1795), in *Kant's Political Writings*, ed. Hans Reiss and trans. H. B. Nisbet (Cambridge, 1970), 124–25. On Kant's political writings, see also Hans Saner, *Kant's Political Thought: Its Origins and Development*, trans. E. B. Ashton (1967; Chicago, 1973); Patrick Riley, *Will and Political Legitimacy*, 125–62; and George Armstrong Kelly, *Idealism, Politics, and History* (Cambridge, 1969), 75–181.

69. Kant, *The Contest of Faculties*, in *Kant's Political Writings*, 184n. See also Leonard Krieger, *The German Idea of Freedom: History of a Political Tradition* (Chicago, 1957), 86–125, for a thoughtful discussion of Kant's role in German political theory; and Kant, *The Metaphysical Elements of Justice (Rechtslehre)*, trans. John Ladd (Indianapolis, 1965), 100. Cf. this passage from *Perpetual Peace*, in *Kant's Political Writings* (121n.): "By putting an end to outbreaks of lawless proclivities, [the government] genuinely makes it much easier for the moral capacities of men to develop into an immediate respect for right ... thus a great step is taken *towards* morality." The search for the sources of twentieth-century totalitarianism has carried some critics back to Kant, but that interpretation is as ahistorical and distorting as the treatment of Rousseau as a protofascist. In both cases such readings concentrate on the importance of discipline while ignoring the centrality of freedom—an odd mirror image of the misreadings that make Locke and Madison the fathers of liberal capitalism.

70. On the abortive 1848 revolution and its significance for the failure of German liberalism, see Sheehan, *German Liberalism*, 59–78; Donald G. Rohr, *The Origins of Social Liberalism in Germany* (Chicago, 1963), 161–62; Theodore Hamerow, *Restoration, Revolution, Reaction: Economics and Politics in Germany, 1815–1871* (Princeton, 1958), 151–54; and Otto Pflanze, *Bismarck and the Development of Germany: The Period of Unification, 1815–1871* (Princeton, 1963), 47. On the separation of German philosophy and politics during the nineteenth century, see Willey, *Back to Kant*, 26–30, 184 n.34; and Hermann Lübbe, *Politische Philosophie in Deutschland: Studien zu ihrer Geschichte* (Basel, 1963), 25, 78.

71. The problem with Hegel's philosophy of history, Fouillée pointed out in *Histoire générale*, 447–49, lay in his glorification of the state and his denial of the concept of popular sovereignty, the first principle of French republicanism. Krieger discusses Hegel's contribution to German political thought in *The German Idea of Freedom*, 125–38; he discusses Mohl on 256–61. See also Hajo Holborn, *A History of Modern Germany*, vol. 3, *1840–1945* (Princeton, 1969), 35–40.

72. On Marx's claims to an objective ontology, see Istvan Meszaros, *Marx's Theory of Alienation* (New York, 1972), 78–81. Shlomo Avineri argues that Marx's concept of man as species-being constitutes an anthropological restatement of Kant's categorical imperative. See *The Social and Political Thought of Karl Marx* (Cambridge, 1968), 86–95. See also Eugene Kamenka, *Marxism and Ethics*, New Studies in Ethics, ed. W. D. Hudson (New York, 1969), 4–30, on this point.

73. Schleiermacher quoted in Sheehan, *German Liberalism*, 41. For a Marxist critique of Dilthey as a "member of the ruling elite," see Buloff, *Wilhelm Dilthey: A Hermeneutic Approach to the Study of History and Culture*, 13–16; and cf. Dilthey's own statement of his position concerning liberal and socialist theory in *GS*, 10: 14–17.

74. On the weaving of civic humanism in the Renaissance and its unraveling in liberalism, see the competing interpretations of J. G. A. Pocock, *Politics, Language, and Time: Essays on*

Political Thought and History (1960; New York, 1973); idem, *The Machiavellian Moment: Florentine Political Thought and the Atlantic Republican Tradition* (Princeton, 1975); and Joyce Appleby, *Economic Thought and Ideology in Seventeenth-Century England* (Princeton, 1978). They air their differences in a spirited debate in the *Newsletter of the Intellectual History Group* 2 (1980); 3 (1981); and 4 (1982). Appleby has pointed out that the elitist and antiprogressive quality of civic humanism made it unattractive to many American republicans.

75. Green, *Political Obligation, Works*, 2: 517–35; *Prolegomena to Ethics*, 201.

76. Fouillée, *La Démocratie*, 207, 213–14; see also *La Propriété*, 11–25.

77. James, *The Principles of Psychology*, 1: 293.

78. Green, *Political Obligation, Works*, 2: 526.

79. Green, *Prolegomena to Ethics*, 304.

80. Green, "Liberal Legislation and Freedom of Contract" (1880), *Works*, 3: 365. In his study of Green, Richter refers to Isaiah Berlin's celebrated essay "Two Concepts of Liberty" and quotes Berlin's harsh judgment of the authoritarian tendency hidden in the idea of positive liberty. Oddly, however, Richter neglects to mention that Berlin specifically absolves Green of any protototalitarian tendencies. "Green was a genuine liberal," Berlin points out; his criticism of the idea of positive liberty has to do with its misuse by "many a tyrant . . . to justify his worst acts of oppression." Berlin does in the end opt for the negative conception of liberty as a "truer and more human ideal" than the idea of liberty as self-realization, but his analysis is considerably more balanced and sensitive than Richter's use of the argument would suggest. Cf. Richter, *The Politics of Conscience*, 204; and Berlin, "Two Concepts of Liberty" (1958), reprinted in *Four Essays on Liberty* (Oxford, 1969), 13n. Green and the other philosophers of the *via media* did not use the concept of positive liberty to disguise authoritarian urges any more than they invoked Rousseau's idea of the general will to justify oligarchic usurpation of popular sovereignty. It is essential to distinguish the social ideas of this generation from later perversions of their meaning by tyrants whose methods and aims they would have abhorred.

81. Sidgwick, *Elements of Politics*, 156. While Sidgwick did contribute to the reorientation of British political thinking, it would be a mistake to exaggerate his apostasy from liberalism. His contemporary A. V. Dicey classified him with Spencer as an advocate of "individualism"; while that judgment unduly emphasizes Sidgwick's reluctance to assert the power of the state in order to distinguish him from late nineteenth-century "collectivists," it does suggest the mediating role Sidgwick played in political as well as ethical thought. See Dicey, *Lectures on the Relation between Law and Public Opinion during the Nineteenth Century* (London, 1905), 17–18. For a recent restatement of this position, see Stefan Collini, *Liberalism and Sociology: L. T. Hobhouse and Political Argument in England, 1880–1914* (Cambridge, 1979), 20–23.

82. Sidgwick, *Methods of Ethics*, 276–79. See also his *Memoir*, 441–42, and Collini, *That Noble Science of Politics*, 302 n.60, on Sidgwick's ambivalence regarding property.

83. Fouillée, *L'Idée moderne du droit*, 382.

84. Fouillée, "Le Progrès sociale en France," *Revue des Deux Mondes* 15 (1899): 816–17.

85. Fouillée, *La Propriété*, v, 43–45.

86. Sidgwick, *Methods of Ethics*, 288.

87. James, "What Makes a Life Significant?" *Talks to Teachers*, 189; "The Moral Equivalent of War," *Memories and Studies*, 286. In *The Will to Believe*, 156, James lamented "the abuses which the institution of private property covers, so that even to-day it is shamelessly asserted among us that one of the prime functions of the national government is to help the adroiter citizens to grow rich."

88. Sidgwick, *The Elements of Politics*, 173–74, 151–52. See also his *Principles of Political Economy*, 560–71; and "Economic Socialism," in *Miscellaneous Essays and Addresses*, 200–15. Given the enormous productivity of liberal capitalism, despite the inequalities it generates, this concern was, and continues to be, legitimate. For a recent attempt to solve this problem, see

Rawls, *A Theory of Justice*, 302. Although Rawls is generally critical of Sidgwick, part (a) of his second principle of justice echoes Sidgwick's reservations concerning the relation between production and distribution. Fouillée articulated his concern for weighing equality against productivity, in terms strikingly similar to Sidgwick's, in *La Propriété*, 287.

89. Recent studies of the welfare state include W. J. Mommsen, ed., *The Emergence of the Welfare State in Britain and Germany, 1850–1950* (London, 1981); Peter Flora and Arnold J. Heidenheimer, eds., *The Development of Welfare States in Europe and America* (New Brunswick, N.J., 1981); Gaston Rimlinger, *Welfare Policy and Industrialization in Europe, America, and Russia* (New York, 1971); James T. Patterson, *America's Struggle Against Poverty, 1900–1980* (Cambridge, Mass., 1981); Roy Lubove, *The Struggle for Society Security, 1900–1935* (Cambridge, Mass., 1968); Daniel Nelson, *Unemployment Insurance: The American Experience, 1915–1935* (Madison, Wis., 1969); J. R. Hay, *The Origins of Liberal Welfare Reforms, 1906–1914* (London, 1975); idem, *The Development of the British Welfare State, 1880–1975* (London, 1978); Samuel H. Beer, *British Politics in the Collectivist Age* (New York, 1965); Maurice Bruce, *The Coming of the Welfare State* (London, 1961); Bentley B. Gilbert, *The Evolution of National Insurance in Great Britain: The Origins of the Welfare State* (London, 1966); H. Hatzfeld, *Du Paupérisme à la sécurité sociale. essai sur les origines de la sécurité sociale en France, 1850–1940* (Paris, 1971); John H. Weiss, "Origins of the French Welfare State: Poor Relief in the Third Republic," *French Historical Studies* 13 (1983): 47–77; and A. Gladen, *Geschichte der Sozialpolitik in Deutschland* (Wiesbaden, 1974). For brief overviews of the rise of the welfare state, see Asa Briggs, "The Welfare State in Historical Perspective," *Archives Européennes de Sociologie* 2 (1961): 221–58; and Calvin Woodard, "Reality and Social Reform: The Transition from Laissez-Faire to the Welfare State," *Yale Law Journal* 72 (1962–1963): 268–328.

90. Dilthey, *GS*, 6: 287. In *GS*, 11: 131, Dilthey traced to Hegel the tendency of his contemporaries to view "the state as an end in itself," an inclination that he feared could culminate in despotism.

91. Sidgwick, *Elements of Politics*, 39, 139; *Principles of Political Economy*, 533–44, 158–59, 530, 418.

92. See Dicey, *Law and Opinion*; and Crane Brinton, *English Political Thought in the Nineteenth Century* (Cambridge, Mass., 1949), 223–24. For a more balanced assessment of the political significance of Green's thought, see Dewey, *Liberalism and Social Action*, 23–26.

93. Green, *Political Obligation, Works*, 2: 514–15, 533.

94. Fouillée, *Le Socialisme et la sociologie réformiste* (Paris, 1910), 30.

95. Fouillée, *La Propriété*, 67–153; "Le Progrès social en France," *Revue des Deux Mondes* 15 (1899): 822. On the importance of these arguments for French political debate, see J. E. S. Hayward, "'Solidarity' and the Reformist Sociology of Alfred Fouillée," 205–22, 305–12.

96. See M. Van Diema's review of Fouillée's *Le Socialisme*, quoted in Guyau, *Fouillée*, 164; Fouillée, *La Démocratie*, 161–69; *La Science sociale*, 128–31.

97. Fouillée, *La Démocratie*, 199–200.

98. Green, *Political Obligation, Works*, 2: 345–46; Fouillée, *La Démocratie*, 18.

99. Michael Walzer has recently suggested the outlines of such a critique in the collection of essays *Spheres of Justice: A Defense of Pluralism and Equality* (New York, 1983).

100. James, "What Makes a Life Significant?" *Talks to Teachers*, 172–91; *The Varieties of Religious Experience*, 312–18. For different readings of James's attitude toward politics, cf. Kuklick, *The Rise of American Philosophy*, 306–14; and Perry, *James*, 2: 267–99.

101. Fouillée, "The Sense of Brotherhood, and its Role in the School," an address delivered in 1886 at the annual prize distribution of the Société pour l'Instruction Elémentaire, reprinted in *Education*, 316–22; *La Science sociale*, xi, 56–73, 420–21; and *La Démocratie*, 13. Cf. Green, *Political Obligation, Works*, 2: 410–16.

102. See above, pp. 129–30; and Sidgwick, *Methods of Ethics*, 298–99; *Elements of Politics*, 556; *Lectures on Ethics*, 65–72; and Schneewind's perceptive discussion in *Sidgwick's Ethics*, 401–11.

103. Sidgwick, *Methods of Ethics*, 289–90; James, *The Varieties of Religious Experience*, 366. For a recent discussion of the incommensurability of competing conceptions of justice in contemporary political philosophy, a discussion strikingly reminiscent of Sidgwick's analysis in *Methods of Ethics* although applied to the ideas of Robert Nozick and John Rawls instead of Bentham and Kant, see Alasdair MacIntyre, *After Virtue* (Notre Dame, 1981), 227–37.

104. David Hollinger, in "The Voice of Intellectual History in the Conversation of Mankind: A Note on Rorty's *Philosophy and the Mirror of Nature*, " *Newsletter of the Intellectual History Group* 4 (1982): 27, has asked pointedly, "if one believes what Rorty says in *Philosophy and the Mirror of Nature*, how ought one to do political philosophy?" Without suggesting that the approach taken by the philosophers of the *via media* corresponds to Rorty's own, I would argue that the position examined in this chapter is consistent with the radically hermeneutic and pragmatic ideas Rorty has advanced in *Philosophy and the Mirror of Nature* and *Consequences of Pragmatism*.

105. Fouillée, *Histoire générale*, 797.

Chapter 6. From Socialism to Social Democracy

1. Eduard Bernstein, *My Years of Exile: Reminiscences of a Socialist*, trans. Bernard Miall (1921; rpt. New York, 1961), 276, 264.

2. On the relation of the British labor movement to British political culture, see Hobsbawm, "Trends in the British Labour Movement Since 1850," in *Labouring Men*, 316–43; and Polanyi, *The Great Transformation*, 172–76. On the Owenites, J. F. C. Harrison, *The Quest for the New Moral World: Robert Owen and the Owenites in Britain and America* (New York, 1969) is standard. The British reception of Marxism is discussed in Stanley Pierson, *Marxism and the Origins of British Socialism* (Ithaca, 1973); and Kirk Willis, "The Introduction and Critical Reception of Marxist Thought in Britain, 1850–1900," *Historical Journal* 20 (1977): 417–60. On the Social Democratic Federation and its reductionist version of Marxism, see Chushichi Tsuzuki, *H. M. Hyndman and British Socialism* (Oxford, 1961). Henry Pelling, *Origins of the Labour Party*, 2nd ed. (Oxford, 1965) traces the early years of Labour's political career. I have found most useful two recent studies that relate the rise of Fabianism to these competing tendencies in British socialism: Willard Wolfe, *From Radicalism to Socialism: Men and Ideas in the Formation of British Socialist Doctrines, 1881–1889* (New Haven, 1975); and Stanley Pierson, *British Socialists: The Journey from Fantasy to Politics* (Cambridge, Mass., 1979).

3. On the ethical societies, see Gustav Spiller, ed., *The Ethical Movement in Great Britain: A Documentary History* (London, 1934); and Reba N. Soffer, *Ethics and Society in England*, 179–89. Sidgwick's diary entry is quoted in *Henry Sidgwick: A Memoir*, 440; for samples of his speeches to ethical societies, see "The Scope and Limits of the Work of an Ethical Society," an address delivered at a preliminary meeting of the Cambridge Ethical Society, May 18, 1888; and "The Aims and Methods of an Ethical Society," his presidential address to the London Ethical Society, April 23, 1893, both of which are reprinted in Sidgwick's *Practical Ethics* (London, 1898).

4. The richest source on the origins of the Fabian Society is the minutes of Fabian Society meetings, which begin with the Oct. 24, 1883, meeting of the Fellowship of the New Life. These minutes and other records of the Society are contained in the Fabian Society archive, Nuffield College, Oxford. Part One of the Fabian archive, *Minute Books and Records, 1884–1918*, is available on microfiche; Part Two, *Minutes of the Executive Committee, 1918–1960*, and the

Lectures of the Fabian Society, 1888–1960, is available on microform. On the origins of the Fabian Society, see also Edward Pease, *History of the Fabian Society* (London, 1916); Wolfe, *From Radicalism to Socialism*, 151–81; and A. M. McBriar, *Fabian Socialism and English Politics, 1884–1918* (Cambridge, 1966), 1–28, which remains the standard study of Fabianism and contains an excellent bibliography.

5. Although its concluding section is missing, the first twenty-eight pages of Webb's lecture "The Economic Basis of Socialism and its Political Programme," a lecture delivered in Dec., 1887, are in the Passfield papers, British Library of Political and Economic Science, London School of Economics. Because McBriar did not have access to this collection of the Webbs' personal papers, which is particularly valuable for Webb's early writings, parts of his account in *Fabian Socialism* are in need of revision. For an account of Webb that stresses the continuity between his socialism and the tradition of British liberalism, see Wolfe, *From Radicalism to Socialism*, esp. 183–214. In *British Socialists*, Stanley Pierson points out that not until after 1920 did the Webbs begin searching in socialism—particularly in the Soviet Union—for the sort of ultimate salvation that Shaw and other Fabian deserters thought the society had lost sight of in its journey "from fantasy to politics." Pierson suggests that the differences between Sidney Webb and the Fabian deserters indicate Webb's distance from the deeper ethical sources of socialism; I consider his reformism merely an attempt to translate those ethical impulses into a program designed to be socially effective rather than personally cathartic. Other influential accounts of Webb include Margaret Cole, ed., *The Webbs and their Work* (London, 1949); idem, *The Story of Fabian Socialism* (London, 1961); and especially E. J. Hobsbawm's biting critique in "Fabians and Fabianism, 1884–1914," Ph.D. diss., Cambridge University, 1950; and "The Fabians Reconsidered," in *Labouring Men*, 250–71. Hobsbawm's critical perspective informs the analysis of G. R. Searle, *The Quest for National Efficiency: A Study in British Politics and Political Thought, 1899–1914* (Berkeley, 1971).

6. Beatrice Webb's diary is available in several forms, including a microfilm of the entire diary. Her own edited version is available in two volumes, *My Apprenticeship* (1926; rpt. London, 1950), and *Our Partnership*, ed. Barbara Drake and Margaret Cole (London, 1945), which may be supplemented by her *American Diary, 1898*, ed. David A. Shannon (Madison, 1963). Norman and Jeanne MacKenzie are editing another version, The Diary of Beatrice Webb, vol. 1, *"Glitter Around and Darkness Within," 1873–1892* (Cambridge, Mass., 1982); and vol. 2, *"All the Good Things in Life," 1892–1905* (Cambridge, Mass., 1983). Studies of Beatrice Webb include Margaret Cole, *Beatrice Webb* (London, 1946); Kitty Muggeridge and Ruth Adam, *Beatrice Webb: A Life* (London, 1967); and Shirley Robin Letwin, *The Pursuit of Certainty: David Hume, Jeremy Bentham, John Stuart Mill, Beatrice Webb* (Cambridge, 1965). For accounts of her life and what led her from a Tory upbringing to Fabian socialism, cf. the interview with Beatrice Webb in *The Young Woman* 29 (1895): 145–51, a copy of which is in the Passfield Papers; and the detailed report of her lecture "The Faith I Hold," which was delivered on Oct. 11, 1907, in *Fabian News* 18 (1907): 81–82, also in the Passfield papers. The most illuminating account of the Webbs' courtship is available in *The Letters of Beatrice and Sidney Webb*, vol. 1, *Apprenticeships, 1873–1892*, ed. Norman and Jeanne MacKenzie (Cambridge, 1978). The quotations are from Beatrice's diary, Jan., 1890, in *Letters of B. and S. Webb*, 1: 128–29; her letter to Sidney, ?7 Dec., 1890, *Letters of B. and S. Webb*, 1: 238–40; and her diary, May 20, 1891, Ibid., 1: 270, and June 20, 1891, Ibid., 1: 274.

7. *The New Statesman*, April 12, 1913, 4. For information on the sales of *Fabian Essays in Socialism*, see Pease, *History of the Fabian Society*, 88; on the distribution of Fabian Tracts, see Pease's note to Harold Laski, *The State in the New Social Order*, Fabian Tract # 200. See also Edward S. Hyams, *The New Statesman: A History of the First Forty Years* (London, 1963). Historians have generally, and properly, played down the Webbs' role in the rise of the Labour party. See for example Ross McKibbin, *The Evolution of the Labour Party* (Oxford, 1974); and

John A. Hall, "The Crisis of the Edwardian Intelligentsia, 1900–1920," Ph.D. diss., University of London, 1976.

8. B. Webb, *My Apprenticeship*, 130.

9. See especially Crunden, *Ministers of Reform*, ix–xii, 274–78, on the generation of reformers who shifted their interests from religion to politics during the late nineteenth and early twentieth centuries.

10. Sombart's *Warum gibt es inden Vereinigten Staaten keinen Sozialismus?* (Tübingen, 1906) focused on the fluidity of the American class structure, which he attributed to the open frontier, the productivity of the American economy, and the high living standard enjoyed by American workers. Later commentators have also stressed these features of the American experience. Selig Perlman, in *A History of Trade Unionism in the United States* (New York, 1922), added to the emphasis on mobility an analysis of the importance of ethnic and religious cleavages and the strength of individualism in the American ethos. Leon Samson, *Toward a United Front* (New York, 1935), concentrated on ideology and offered "Americanism" as a "surrogate socialism" making radical change unnecessary. Daniel Bell, *Marxian Socialism in the United States*, 2nd ed. (Princeton, 1967), and Ira Kipnis, *The American Socialist Movement, 1897–1912* (New York, 1952), presented diametrically opposed analyses that focused on American socialists' alleged strategic mistakes as the cause of their failure: Bell argued that the rigid orthodoxy of American socialists crippled their efforts, whereas Kipnis insisted that the triumph of right-wing socialists like Victor Berger doomed the American Socialist party by vitiating its strength as a viable alternative to two-party politics. G. D. H. Cole, in *A History of Socialist Thought*, vol. 3, *The Second International, 1889–1914* (London, 1956), pointed to the role of political democracy in turning American labor away from political militancy and also stressed the role of ethnic and racial differences in the division between skilled and unskilled workers in the United States. Recent analyses developing variations on the theme of mobility include Seymour Martin Lipset and Reinhard Bendix, *Social Mobility in Industrial Society* (Berkeley, 1960); and Stephan Thernstrom, *Poverty and Progress: Social Mobility in a Nineteenth-Century City* (Cambridge, Mass., 1964). James Weinstein, *The Decline of Socialism in America, 1912–1925* (New York, 1967), emphasizes the party's tactical mistakes and the role of repression in the demise of the Socialist party after World War I. Milton Cantor, in *The Divided Left: American Radicalism, 1900–1975* (New York, 1978), invokes Gramsci's notion of hegemony as a kind of deus ex machina to explain away Sombart's question. Another attempt to escape what she calls the "ghost of Werner Sombart" is Aileen Kraditor's provocative *The Radical Persuasion, 1890–1917* (Baton Rouge, 1981). While her criticisms of many of the answers to Sombart's question are persuasive, her own analysis of the "cultural forms" and "private-sphere institutions" that rendered workers "impervious to radical propaganda" undercuts her contention that we should discard the basic problem of American exceptionalism, a problem that arises inevitably whenever historians try to place American social and political development in comparative perspective. A useful compendium of essays, excerpts, and spirited commentaries on this issue is John H. M. Laslett and Seymour Martin Lipset, eds., *Failure of a Dream? Essays in the History of American Socialism* (Garden City, N.Y., 1974).

11. I have chosen not to concentrate on such figures as Eugene Debs, Victor Berger, or Morris Hillquit for some of the same reasons I am not concentrating on Keir Hardie: they were important as organizers, and as symbols for American labor, but they contributed little to the development of socialist or social democratic theory. Of American socialist thinkers, only William English Walling developed a creative version of socialist theory, but his remarkable attempt to blend James, Dewey, and Nietzsche attracted little attention among his contemporaries. See Walling's *Socialism As It Is* (New York, 1912); *The Larger Aspects of Socialism* (New York, 1913); and *Progressivism—and After* (New York, 1914). A recent study that demonstrates Debs's symbolic significance as a martyr for socialism, and illustrates his insignificance

as a thinker, is Nick Salvatore, *Eugene Debs: Citizen and Socialist* (Urbana, 1982). For some of the reasons why workers and management ultimately proved more interested in wages and production than in socialism or the independence of laborers in the labor process, cf. the oddly complementary analyses of three very different studies: Daniel Rodgers, *The Work Ethic in Industrial America*, esp. 30–64; Herbert Gutman, *Work, Culture, and Society in Industrializing America* (New York, 1976), and Harry Braverman, *Labor and Monopoly Capital: The Degradation of Work in the Twentieth Century* (New York, 1974).

12. The periodization is suggested by Charles H. Hopkins, *Rise of the Social Gospel*. The other standard treatments of the social gospel are Henry F. May, *Protestant Churches and Industrial America* (New York, 1949); and William R. Hutchison, *The Modernist Impulse in American Protestantism* (New York, 1976). These may be supplemented by the "quasi-new left" approach of Peter J. Frederick, *Knights of the Golden Rule: The Intellectual as Christian Social Reformer in the 1890s* (Lexington, Ky., 1976). On the American ethical societies, see Howard B. Radest, *Toward Common Ground: Ethical Societies in America* (New York, 1969).

13. The standard biography of Ely is Benjamin G. Rader, *The Academic Mind and Reform: The Influence of Richard T. Ely in American Life* (Lexington, Ky., 1966), a sensitive and thoughtful study. Ely's own *Ground Under Our Feet: An Autobiography* (New York, 1938) contains useful information, but it is burdened by attempts at self-justification and the feelings of bitterness Ely carried with him into old age. The Richard T. Ely papers, the richest source on his career and his ideas, are in the State Historical Society of Wisconsin. The entire collection is now available on microfilm.

14. There is no adequate biography of Rauschenbusch. Dores Robinson Sharpe, *Walter Rauschenbusch* (New York, 1942) is a treasure chest of information and the best account of Rauschenbusch's life. Sharpe was Rauschenbusch's longtime personal secretary and a close friend; his account is not a critical biography but, in his words, an "act of love." More scholarly but limited in the depth of its analysis is Vernon P. Bodein, *The Social Gospel of Walter Rauschenbusch*, Yale Studies in Religious Education, vol. 15 (New Haven, 1944). See also the discussions of Rauschenbusch in Hopkins, 215–32; Hutchison, 164–74; and Frederick, 141–61. Rauschenbusch's personal papers are in the American Baptist Historical Society, Colgate-Rochester Divinity School, Rochester, N.Y.

15. On Ely's early years and his experiences in Germany, see his *Ground Under Our Feet*, 13–63, and esp. 40–42, 146. On German education and the rise of American social science, see Jürgen Herbst, *The German Historical School in American Scholarship: A Study in the Transfer of Culture* (Ithaca, 1965); and Fritz K. Ringer, "The German Academic Community," in Oleson and Voss, eds., *Organization of Knowledge in Modern America*, 409–29.

16. See Sharpe, *Rauschenbusch*, 24–58. On the broader transformation of American religious thought, see Flower and Murphy, *Philosophy in America*, 2: 746.

17. Rauschenbusch, Address to the Central YMCA, Cleveland, printed in the *Association Monthly*, Jan., 1913.

18. Ely's career at Johns Hopkins is discussed in Rader, *Ely*, 16–105. From 1881 to 1892, Ely published over fifty journal articles and seven monographs. Among his students were John Commons, E. A. Ross, Albion Small, Edward Bemis, Frederic Howe, and Woodrow Wilson. Ely's role in Wisconsin reform was emphasized by Charles McCarthy, *The Wisconsin Idea* (New York, 1912); and Frederic C. Howe, *Wisconsin: An Experiment in Democracy* (New York, 1912). More recent discussions of the relation between the University of Wisconsin and the state's progressive movement include David P. Thelen, *The New Citizenship: Origins of Progressivism in Wisconsin, 1885–1900* (Columbia, Mo., 1972); and J. David Hoeveler, Jr., "The University and the Social Gospel: The Intellectual Origins of the 'Wisconsin Idea,'" *Wisconsin Magazine of History* 59 (1976): 289–98. Webb's letters to Ely, Feb. 1 and 21, 1894, are in *Letters of B. and S. Webb*, 2: 13–14.

19. Rauschenbusch's letter to Ely concerning his trip to England, March 19, 1891, is in the Ely papers. See also his address "Dogmatic and Practical Socialism," delivered at the Rochester Labor Lyceum, Feb. 24, 1901, Rauschenbusch papers. Excerpts from this address are included in Sharpe, *Rauschenbusch*, 203–16, although many illuminating passages are inexplicably left out. For that reason I will cite Rauschenbusch's own ms. when referring to "Dogmatic and Practical Socialism."

20. Rauschenbusch, "Dogmatic and Practical Socialism," 32. See also Carl N. Degler, *Out of Our Past*, 2nd ed. (New York, 1970), 372.

21. See Rader, *Ely*, 161; Frederick, *Knights of the Golden Rule*, 156–57; and Ray Stannard Baker, "The Spiritual Unrest: A Vision of the New Christianity," *American Magazine*, Dec., 1909, 178.

22. Rauschenbusch reflected on his expectations in 1906 in an address reported in the *Rochester Democrat and Chronicle*, Jan. 25, 1913, and in a letter to George W. Coleman, June 17, 1908, Rauschenbusch papers. For a list of reviews of *Christianity and the Social Crisis*, see Hutchison, *The Modernist Impulse in American Protestantism*, Appendix B. For evidence of Ely's insecurity, see his letter to E. R. A. Seligman, Nov. 3, 1883, in the Seligman papers, Butler Library, Columbia University.

23. While Ely was at John Hopkins, J. Franklin Jameson noted in his diary that Ely "is certainly on the make," attempting "to bring everything he can under political economy, including all social and political science." See Rader, *Ely*, 108. On Ely's role in the professionalization of American social science, see Haskell, *The Emergence of Professional Social Science*; and cf. the contrasting analysis in Furner, *Advocacy and Objectivity*. Whereas Haskell contends that the American Economic Association was from the beginning concerned primarily with the occupational needs of academics, Furner argues that its focus shifted from "advocacy" to "objectivity." The initial reformist stance of the AEA is apparent from the prospectus sent out in 1885 stating the objectives and platform of the organization. Ely's own attitude toward the organization's purpose is muddied by his efforts to work both sides of the street depending on whose sympathies he was trying to enlist, as illustrated by his letters to E. R. A. Seligman on June 23, 1885, and Oct. 22, 1890, in the Seligman papers, Butler Library, Columbia University. The tension between reform and respectability in the new organization, and the ambivalent attitudes of the younger generation of "militants," including Ely, is examined in Dorothy Ross's essay "The Development of the Social Sciences," in Oleson and Voss, eds., *Organization of Knowledge in Modern America*, 107–38. Ely elaborated his "very ambitious plans" for the University of Wisconsin in a letter to Albert Shaw, Jan. 25, 1892, quoted in Ely, *Ground Under Our Feet*, 180–81.

24. Rauschenbusch, *Christianizing the Social Order* (New York, 1912), 9. Rauschenbusch's "instructions in case of my death," March, 1918, quoted in Sharpe, *Rauschenbusch*, 448–49. The dominant theme in Rauschenbusch's letters from 1915 until his death is World War I. For particularly poignant statements on the cost of his pacifism, see his letters to A. A. Boyden, Dec. 25, 1915; to Rep. Thomas B. Dunn, April 25, 1916; and to W. H. P. Faunce, Feb. 11, 1917, all in the Rauschenbusch papers.

25. Rauschenbusch's letter to Nathaniel Smith, Sept., 1896, quoted in Sharpe, *Rauschenbusch*, 106–7. See also his essay in *The Congregationalist and Advance*, July 11, 1918; his "Prayer in Time of War," in *The Independent*, Oct. 5, 1914; and cf. May, *Protestant Churches*, 150–51. On Great Britain, see Peter D'A. Jones, *The Christian Socialist Revival, 1877–1914* (Princeton, 1968); and Pierson, *British Socialists*, 138–47.

26. On the religious war in France in the late nineteenth century, a good overview is Jean-Marie Mayeur, *Les Débuts de la IIIᵉ République*, 135–61. Adrien Dansette, *Histoire religieuse de la France contemporaine*, 2nd ed. (Paris, 1965) is more comprehensive. On French socialist movements, see Madeleine Réberioux, *Le Socialisme français: de 1875 à 1918, Histoire générale*

du socialisme, ed. Jacques Droz, vol. 2 (Paris, 1974); and Georges Lefranc, *Le Mouvement socialiste sous la IIIᵉ République, 1875–1940*, 2nd ed. (Paris, 1977). On Guesde, cf. Claude Willard, *Le Mouvement socialiste en France, 1893–1905: les guesdists* (Paris, 1965) and Leslie Derfler, "Reformism and Jules Guesde, 1891–1904," *International Review of Social History* 11 (1967): 66–80. These studies may be supplemented by Aaron Noland, *The Founding of the French Socialist Party* (Cambridge, Mass., 1956); Robert Wohl, *French Communism in the Making, 1914–1924* (Stanford, 1966), 1–43; and Thomas Moodie, "The Reorientation of French Socialism, 1888–1890," *International Review of Social History* 20 (1975): 347–69.

27. Jaurès's recollection of his early political orientation appeared in *La Petite République*, April 15, 1894; it is quoted in the most comprehensive of the many biographies of Jaurès, Harvey Goldberg, *The Life of Jean Jaurès* (Madison, 1962). The most recent biography is Jean Rabaut, *Jean Jaurès*, 2nd ed. (Paris, 1981), an appreciative account written by the longtime secretary of the Society of Jaurès Studies. An organization dedicated to the "life, thought, action, and work of Jaurès," the society publishes the quarterly *Bulletin de la société d'études jaurèsiennes*. Studies concentrating on Jaurès's ideas are Maurice Boitel, *Les Idées liberales dans le socialisme de Jean Jaurès* (Paris, 1921); Félicien Challaye, *Jaurès* (Paris, n.d.); and André Robinet, *Jaurès et l'unité de l'être* (Paris, 1964). Also still valuable are the spirited analysis by Jaurès's contemporary Charles Rappoport, *Jean Jaurès, l'homme, le penseur, le socialiste* (Paris, 1915); and the moving portrait by his most celebrated disciple, Léon Blum, *Jean Jaurès* (Paris, 1933). The most important source of Jaurès's published writings is his *Oeuvres*, 9 vols., ed. Max Bonnafous (Paris, 1931–1939), but this includes no more than a small fraction of his work; his essays, editorials, and speeches are scattered in a wide variety of periodicals and in the debates of the Chamber of Deputies and the Senate. There is no comprehensive bibliography of Jaurès's writings or of the secondary literature, but a good place to begin is Goldberg, *Jaurès*, 569–80; which may be supplemented by the recent collection *Jaurès et la classe ouvrière*, ed. Madeleine Rébérioux (Paris, 1981), 229–37. A particularly useful list of Jaurès's important speeches in the Chamber of Deputies from 1886 to 1914 appears in Boitel, *Les Idées liberales*, 191–200. Only a few unpublished mss. and letters by Jaurès appear to have survived; for a guide to their location in scattered collections, see Goldberg, *Jaurès*, 569–70, and the notes on continuing discoveries in the *Bulletin d'études jaurèsiennes*.

28. Jaurès's Latin thesis was translated into French and published first in the *Revue socialiste* in 1892, then in book form as *Les Origines du socialisme allemand* (Paris, 1927). It has been republished with a preface by Lucien Goldmann (Paris, 1960); the quotation is from p. 150 of this edition. *De la réalité de la monde sensible* is vol. 8 of Jaurès's *Oeuvres*, ed. Bonnafous. Typical of the dismissive treatment of Jaurès's theses is the non sequitur in Zeldin's *Politics and Anger*, 395: "As a philosopher he was not the advocate of any particular doctrine: he sought to reconcile logic and common sense, to produce a synthesis of realism and idealism." That synthesis was precisely the "particular doctrine" Jaurès advocated, a synthesis that provided a coherent, radically empiricist foundation for the pragmatic and open-ended democratic socialism he championed. Because historians tend to view social democracy as a simple adaptation to political circumstances, they tend not to examine the philosophical ideas of social democratic thinkers. Particularly in the case of Jaurès, who took theoretical issues seriously indeed, such a perspective can be misleading.

29. A great deal of ink has been spilled on the sources of Jaurès's socialism, most of it devoted to proving that *either* Herr's ideas *or* the Carmaux miners' strike dislodged Jaurès from his liberal republicanism. The argument for Herr's influence has a long lineage. Maurice Boitel first emphasized it in *Les Idées liberales*, 8–10. Léon Blum confirmed Herr's decisive role, which was examined in detail in Charles Andler, *Vie de Lucien Herr* (Paris, 1932). The most recent champion of this argument is Georges Lefranc, *Jaurès et le socialisme des intellectuels* (Paris, 1968). The most persistent critic of this interpretation has been Madeleine Rébérioux, who

stresses the importance of Jaurès's participation in the strikes in Carmaux. See her review of Lefranc in the *Bulletin d'études jaurèsiennes* 39 (Oct.–Dec., 1970): 3–5; her exchange with Lefranc in 41 (April–June, 1971): 16–21; and her notes on Jaurès's road to socialism in 58 (July–Sept. 1975): 2–5. As if to accentuate the importance of this apparently minor point, Lefranc has dedicated the revised edition of his comprehensive *Le Mouvement socialiste* to the memory of Lucien Herr, "who 'converted' Jean Jaurès and Léon Blum to socialism." The intensity of such disputes, which might otherwise seem incomprehensible, underscores the centrality of Jaurès in the search for a usable past by French socialists of competing persuasions. For a sensible account of the complementary roles played by Herr and Carmaux in Jaurès's development, see Goldberg, *Jaurès*, 77–152. On the struggles that awakened Jaurès to the problems of the working class, see Rolande Trempé, *Les Mineurs de Carmaux, 1848–1914*, 2 vols. (Paris, 1971); and Joan Wallach Scott, *The Glassworkers of Carmaux: French Craftsmen and Political Action in a Nineteenth-Century City* (Cambridge, Mass., 1974).

30. Jaurès's speech, "Idéalisme et matérialisme dans la conception de l'histoire," originally published in 1895, is reprinted in *Oeuvres*, 6: 225–41. On the characterization of Jaurès as a social democrat, an interpretation many French socialists resist, Robert Wohl has written "Jaurèssianism must be counted an original French form of socialism, which combined flexibility in means with a commitment to the goal of revolution . . . it deserved more truly than any other working-class ideology in Europe the label of Social Democracy. What distinguished the French movement from other European labor movements was the division of the party from the unions, the continual and institutionalized contact between working class leaders and the bourgeoisie, and the tendency of both Right and Left to be swallowed up in the Jaurèssian version of the European center." Wohl, *French Communism in the Making*, 435–36. See also Alain Bergounioux and Bernard Manin, *La Social-démocratie ou le compromis* (Paris, 1979), 65–72, for a similar argument.

31. On Jaurès's failed effort to teach at the Sorbonne, see Michel Launay, "Jaurès, la Sorbonne, et l'affaire Dreyfus," *Revue Science Humaine*, Jan.–March, 1964, 113–18. Jaurès's contributions to the thirteen-volume *Histoire socialiste* (Paris, 1901–1908) were later reissued as *Histoire socialiste de la Révolution française*, 8 vols., ed. Albert Mathiez (Paris, 1922–1924). Georges Lefebvre paid tribute to Jaurès's skills as a historian and proclaimed himself a follower of no other "master." See Albert Soboul, "Georges Lefebvre, historien de la Révolution Française, 1874–1959," *Annales historiques de la Révolution française* 159 (1960): 3.

32. The statement adopted at Toulouse by the SFIO is reprinted in Georges Lefranc, *Le Mouvement socialiste*, 2: Appendix 3.

33. Jaurès, *Discours prononcé aux obsèques de Francis de Pressensé* (1914), quoted in Goldberg, *Jaurès*, 474. For Jaurès's ideas concerning a democratic citizens' army, see *L'Armée nouvelle* (1911), vol. 4 of his *Oeuvres*. In this remarkable book, Jaurès accurately predicted that war with Germany, if it came, would take the form of a rapid German offensive designed to pierce the French front line of defense—a fair approximation of the Schlieffen Plan that nearly succeeded in 1914. To defeat such a strategy, Jaurès advocated universal military training to create an insurmountable reserve militia that could be rapidly mobilized, a force available to a republic but impossible for an empire, such as Germany, which he thought would be unable to rely on its citizens.

34. For examples of the attacks on Jaurès by the nationalist press, see Charles Maurras in *L'Action française*, July 18 and 23, 1914; and Charles Péguy in *Cahiers de la quinzaine*, Feb. 13, 1913. Jaurès's speech in Brussels was reprinted in *L'Humanité*, July 30, 1914. On Jaurès's death, see Jean Rabaut, *Jaurès et son assassin* (Paris, 1967). Lefranc surveys the various schools of speculation concerning "What would Jaurès have done had he not been assassinated?" in *Le Mouvement socialiste*, 1: 193–95. Jacques Droz has argued that Jaurès's death, ironically, rallied the left to the *Union sacrée*, by inspiring misdirected sentiments of revenge. As Gustave Hervé

wrote in *La Gazette Sociale*, Aug. 1, 1914, "they have assassinated Jaurès, we will not assassinate France." See Droz, *Les Relations franco-allemandes intellectuelles de 1871 à 1914* (Paris, n.d.).

35. Judging from the outpouring of work in recent years, one might even speak of a "Bernstein renaissance," to borrow a phrase discussed at the conference dedicated to Bernstein in 1977. The proceedings of this conference have been published as *Bernstein und der demokratische Sozialismus*, ed. Horst Heimann and Thomas Meyer (Bonn, 1978). Until the late 1960s, the standard sources on Bernstein were Peter Gay, *The Dilemma of Democratic Socialism: Eduard Bernstein's Challenge to Marx* (New York, 1952); and Pierre Angel, *Eduard Bernstein et l'évolution du socialisme allemand* (Paris, 1961). These have now been superseded by a number of studies, including especially Thomas Meyer, *Bernsteins konstructiver Sozialismus: Eduard Bernsteins Beitrag zur Theorie des Sozialismus* (Bonn, 1974), a sophisticated analysis of Bernstein's ideas that includes a comprehensive bibliography. The Eduard Bernstein papers are in the International Institute of Social History (IISH), Amsterdam, which contains unmatched resources for the study of European socialism and the labor movement. Other studies of Bernstein and revisionism include Hans-Josef Steinberg, *Sozialismus und deutsche Sozialdemokratie: Zur Ideologie der Partei vor dem I. Weltkrieg* (Hannover, 1967); Bo Gustafsson, *Marxismus und Revisionismus: Eduard Bernsteins Kritik des Marxismus und ihre ideengeschichtlichen Voraussetzungen*, trans. Holger Heide (Frankfurt a.M., 1971); Peter Strutynski, *Die Auseinandersetzungen zwischen Marxisten und Revisionisten in der deutschen Arbeiterbewegung um die Jahrhundertwende* (Cologne, 1976); Detlef Lehnert, *Reform und Revolution in den Strategiediskussionen der klassischen Sozialdemokratie* (Bonn, 1977); Helmut Hirsch, *Der "Fabier" Eduard Bernstein: Zur Entwicklungsgeschichte des evolutionären Sozialismus* (Bonn, 1977); Herbert Frei, *Fabianismus und Bernstein'scher Revisionismus, 1884–1900* (Bern, 1979); and Sven Papcke, *Der Revisionismusstreit und die politische Theorie der Reform* (Stuttgart, 1979). The best introduction to Bernstein's ideas in English is Kolakowski, *Main Currents of Marxism*, vol. 2, *The Golden Age*, 98–114.

36. The most thorough accounts of Bernstein's life as opposed to his ideas are Gay, *The Dilemma of Democratic Socialism*; and Bernstein's memoirs, *My Years of Exile*.

37. For a clear example of Bernstein's strident opposition to the reformism of some British and French socialists during these years, see the response he wrote on behalf of the International Working Men's Congress in 1889, "A Reply to the Manifesto of the Social Democratic Federation," Archives of the Second International, IISH.

38. On the relation between socialist parties and trade unions, see Polanyi, *The Great Transformation*, 176; Albert S. Lindemann, *A History of European Socialism* (New Haven, 1983), 138–39; and Cole, *The Second International*, 273–74. Two recent accounts of the development of the SPD are Gary P. Steenson, *"Not One Man! Not One Penny!" German Social Democracy, 1863–1914* (Pittsburgh, 1981); and W. L. Guttsman, *The German Social Democratic Party, 1875–1933* (London, 1981), which contains a splendid bibliography.

39. This interpretation of Willhelmine Germany derives primarily from the work of Eckhart Kehr and his followers. See especially the essays in Kehr's *Economic Interest, Militarism, and Foreign Policy*. The most thorough elaboration of this argument is Hans-Ulrich Wehler, *Das deutsche Kaiserreich, 1871–1918*. For recent discussions of the work of Kehr and Wehler, and the complementary studies done by Hans-Jürgen Puhle and Jürgen Kocka, see Georg Iggers, *New Directions in European Historiography* (Middletown, Conn., 1975), 80–122; Jürgen Kocka, "Theory and Social History: Recent Developments in West Germany," *Social Research* 47 (1980): 426–57; and Kenneth D. Barkin, "From Uniformity to Pluralism: German Historical Writing Since World War I," *German Life and Letters* 34 (1981): 234–46. There are signs of a reaction against this prevailing view, including for example Volker Hentschel, *Wirtschaft und Wirtschaftspolitik im wilhelminischen Deutschland: Organisierter Kapitalismus und Interventionsstaat?* (Stuttgart, 1978); and the broader samplings of recent work in Evans, ed., *Society*

and *Politics in Wilhelmine Germany,* and John C. G. Röhl and Nicholaus Sombart, eds., *Kaiser Wilhelm II: New Interpretations* (New York, 1982).

40. Studies of the SPD and workers' culture are multiplying rapidly. A comprehensive bibliography is Hans-Josef Steinberg, *Die deutsche sozialistische Arbeiterbewegung bis 1914: Eine bibliographische Einführung* (New York, 1979). An influential study of the party leadership's commitment to "revolutionary waiting" is Dieter Groh, *Negative Integration und revolutionärer Attentismus: Die deutsche Sozialdemokratie am Vorabend des Ersten Weltkrieges* (Frankfurt a.M., 1973). The source of the concept of "negative integration" is Guenther Roth, *The Social Democrats in Imperial Germany: A Study in Working Class Isolation and National Integration* (Totawa, N.J., 1963). Useful overviews with differing emphases are Guttmann, *German Social Democratic Party;* and Steenson, *"Not One Man! Not One Penny!"* East German scholars have placed greater emphasis on the bureaucratization of the leadership of the SPD; for a discussion of this perspective, see Guttsman, 7–8. Gordon A. Craig concisely summarizes the effects of the combination of repression and negative integration in shaping the tragic fate of the SPD in Weimar in *Germany 1866–1945,* 266–72. Recent studies emphasizing the social and political diversity of the German working class include Mary Nolan, *Social Democracy and Society: Working-class Radicalism in Düsseldorf, 1890–1920* (New York, 1981); and the essays by Stephen Hickey, Alex Hall, and Dick Geary in Evans, ed., *Society and Politics in Wilhelmine Germany,* 215–86.

41. *Rheinische Zeitung,* May 19, 1842, quoted in Avineri, *Marx,* 137.

42. On Bernstein's contacts in England, see *My Years of Exile,* 150–249. On Bernstein's letters to Kautsky, which are contained in the Kautsky papers, IISH, see Hans-Josef Steinberg, "Die Herausbildung des Revisionismus von Eduard Bernstein im Lichte des Briefwechsels Bernstein-Kautsky," in Heimann and Meyer, eds., *Bernstein,* 37–46. The "keyword" in these letters, according to Steinberg, is "Empirie," which Bernstein considered the most attractive feature of the Webbs' approach to socialism.

43. See Bernstein's "Nachwort" to his edition of the Webbs' *Geschichte des britischen Trade Unionismus,* trans. Regina Bernstein (Stuttgart, 1895), 445–55. That year also marked the appearance of Bernstein's study of the English revolution, *Sozialismus und Demokratie in der grossen englischen Revolution* (Stuttgart, 1895), in which he linked the origins of socialist thinking in the Levellers and the Diggers to their love of liberty. For Engels's letters to Bebel on Bernstein's "Fabian craze," see Engels to Bebel, August 14 and 20, 1892, Marx and Engels, *Werke,* 38 (East Berlin, 1967): 426, 433; and cf. the discussion in Roger Fletcher, "Bernstein in Britain: Revisionism and Foreign Affairs," *The International History Review* 1 (1979): 352–53.

44. Bernstein to Kautsky, Oct. 21, 1895, Kautsky papers, IISH. On Kautsky's initial encouragement and later criticism of Bernstein's revisionism, see also Steinberg's comments in Heimann and Meyer, eds., *Bernstein,* 430–32. The *Voraussetzungen* was published in English, with a preface by Bernstein, as *Evolutionary Socialism,* trans. Edith Harvey (1909; rpt. New York, 1961). Unfortunately, more was lost in the translation than the title's awkwardness: the chapter on Hegel, the subject of considerable controversy for reasons to be examined later in this chapter, was also deleted.

45. On Bernstein's own efforts to minimize the importance of the Fabians in his development, see Meyer, *Bernsteins konstructiver Sozialismus,* 19. For various indications of the general consensus concerning the role of his exposure to Fabian ideas and English conditions in shaping Bernstein's revisionism, cf. Hirsch, *Der "Fabier" Eduard Bernstein,* 17–46; Gustafsson, *Marxismus und Revisionismus,* 127–80, 399–401; Frei, *Fabianismus und Bernstein'scher Revisionismus,* 67–117; Pease, *The History of the Fabian Society,* 239; McBriar, *Fabian Socialism,* 71; and Fletcher, "Bernstein in Britain," 350–61. The report of Bernstein's lecture appeared in *Fabian News,* Feb., 1897, 48; and see also Hirsch, *Der "Fabier" Eduard Bernstein,* 123, on this encounter. Bernstein's letter to Bebel, Oct. 20, 1898, is in the Bernstein papers.

46. On the political climate in Germany in the 1890s, see Kehr, "Anglophobia and *Weltpolitik*," in *Economic Interest*, 22–49; and Craig, *Germany 1866–1945*, 264–70. Bernstein's fate at Hannover and Dresden is discussed in Steinberg, *Sozialismus und deutsche Sozialdemokratie*, 119; Guttsman, *German Social Democratic Party*, 295–97; and Steenson, *"Not One Man! Not One Penny!"* 203. The Dresden resolution is quoted in Guttsman, 296.

47. Jaurès, *Les Origines du socialisme allemand*, 150–51.

48. In the Rauschenbusch papers, box 21, there are twenty-three pages of notes on Bernstein's *Voraussetzungen*; the similarities between Bernstein's analysis and Rauschenbusch's argument in "Dogmatic and Practical Socialism" are more than coincidental. In a file marked "Miscellaneous Notes" in box 102, Rauschenbusch indicated that he elaborated on the 1901 address in lectures delivered in Aug. and Sept., 1902. Bernstein's letter to the *Fabian News*, dated Oct. 4, 1902, is condensed in *Fabian News*, Nov., 1902, 43. On the series "Socialism Restated," see Passfield papers, Sec. IX, 1 (ii), ff. 53–56. Jaurès's "Socialism and Liberty" appeared in the *Revue de Paris*, Dec. 1, 1898, 481–515. An essay about Sidney Webb and the Fabians by Augustin Filon was published in the *Revue*, July 1, 1895; Webb's own essay, "Le Fabian Society et le mouvement socialiste en Angleterre," was published March 1, 1896, 112–37. Cf. Fabian Tract # 29, *What to Read on Social and Economic Subjects*, 1901; and Fabian Tract # 129, *More Books to Read on Social and Economic Subjects*, 1906. The list of subscriptions appears in the First Annual Report of the Fabian Common Room, March, 1916, Passfield papers.

49. It is apparent, for example, that the ties between British and American reform-minded intellectuals were closer than those between the Americans and the French or the Germans, as Melvyn Stokes has recently pointed out in "American Progressives and the European Left," *Journal of American Studies* 17 (1983): 5–28. Stokes notes that Americans active in the progressive reform movement, including Ely and Rauschenbusch, felt closer affinities with British progressives and social democrats such as the Webbs than with continental social democrats. Both Ely (in *French and German Socialism in Modern Times* [New York, 1883], 256–57) and Rauschenbusch (in a letter to J. E. Franklin, June 16, 1913, in the Rauschenbusch papers) emphasized the relative insignificance of Christian socialists in German reform activities compared to their prominence in Great Britain and the United States, and both linked their "rather tame" character, to use Rauschenbusch's term, to the polarization of German politics and the rigid Marxism of the SPD. Stokes concludes that it is "impossible to sustain the view put forward by George Mowry (in his essay "Social Democracy, 1910–1918," in C. Vann Woodward, ed., *The Comparative Approach to American History*, 271–84) and Arthur Ekirch (in *Progressivism in America: A Study of the Era from Theodore Roosevelt to Woodrow Wilson* [New York, 1974]) that American progressivism and European social democracy were essentially one movement. Social democracy was [1] too Marxist, [2] too doctrinaire, [3] and too class based to appeal to Americans who preferred [4] a pragmatic approach to reform and [5] did not recognize the existence of a hard-and-fast class division in their own society. The progressives were drawn to reformers cast in the same undogmatic mold as themselves. This limited their contact with the continental European left" (27). While that statement is doubtless correct if one looks at the majority of American progressives and takes Marxists such as Kautsky and Guesde as representatives of continental social democracy, it is also true that Ely and Rauschenbusch were more sympathetic to continental socialism than were other American progressives (as Stokes recognizes), and that Jaurès and Bernstein were critical of, and distinguished themselves from, the mainstreams of their parties for precisely the five reasons Stokes isolates: They considered Guesde and Kautsky (1) too Marxist, (2) too doctrinaire, (3) too limited in their focus on class politics, (4) unwilling to follow a pragmatic approach to reform, and (5) blind to the breakdown of hard-and-fast class divisions. In sum, while the main thrust of the American and British reform movements differed considerably from that of the French and German reform

movements, the radical wing of American progressivism—e.g., Ely and Rauschenbusch—and the moderate wing of continental socialism—e.g., Jaurès and Bernstein—both tried to shift their reform movements toward a common goal. Because of their different national political climates, they had to push reformers in quite different directions in order to guide them toward social democratic ends.

50. Bernstein's letter to Kautsky, Nov. 9, 1898, is in the Kautsky papers, IISH. See also Thomas Meyer, "Wissenschaft und Sozialismus bei Marx, in der Konzeption Eduard Bernsteins und in der Gegenwart," in Heimann and Meyer, eds., *Bernstein*, 254–72.

51. Jaurès's lectures given in 1882–1883 are quoted in Goldberg, *Jaurès*, 23–24. See also Robinet, *Jaurès*, 21–40; and Rappoport, *Jean Jaurès*, 98–104, for discussions of Jaurès's conception of experience.

52. Jaurès, *De la réalité du monde sensible*, *Oeuvres*, 8: 38–43, 183–93.

53. Ibid., 118.

54. Bernstein, "Zur Wurdingung F. A. Langes," *Die Neue Zeit* 10 (1892): 68–78, 101–9; and "Das realistische und ideologische Moment im Sozialismus," *Die Neue Zeit* 16 (1898): 264. Bernstein's debt to Lange and his relations with the neo-Kantians are discussed perceptively in Meyer, *Bernsteins konstruktiver Sozialismus*, 111–22; and Steinberg, *Sozialismus und deutsche Sozialdemocratie*, 89–90. Steinberg points out that Bernstein was hardly uncritical of Lange at this stage of his thinking; his more appreciative attitude emerged slowly through the 1890s as he formulated his revisionism. Roger Fletcher has argued in "Cobden as Educator: The Free-Trade Internationalism of Eduard Bernstein, 1899–1914," *American Historical Review* 88 (1983): 572–76, that Bernstein's debts to neo-Kantianism have been overestimated. While the limits of Bernstein's philosophical engagement—and ability—should be acknowledged, I see no reason to discount the importance of Lange in order to stress the influence of British thought on Bernstein. Influence is seldom an either/or sort of question, and it seems clear that Bernstein's thinking was influenced both by the neo-Kantians, especially Lange, and by British Fabians and ethical socialists. For a careful examination of the relation between revisionism and neo-Kantianism, see Willey, *Back to Kant*, 83–101, 174–78.

55. For Bebel's and Lily Braun's comments on Bernstein, see Gay, *Democratic Socialism*, 150, 147. Vorländer discussed the limits of Bernstein's neo-Kantianism in *Kant und Marx: Ein Beitrag zur Philosophie des Sozialismus* (Tübingen, 1911), 179–81.

56. Beatrice and Sidney Webb, *English Local Government. English Poor Law History*, Part 2, vol. 1 (London, 1927), vii.

57. Ely, *The Social Aspects of Christianity* (New York, 1889), 148. Cf. chap. 4 of Rauschenbusch's *Christianity and the Social Crisis*, ed. Robert D. Cross (1907; New York, 1964), 143–210, entitled "Why Has Christianity Never Undertaken the Work of Social Reconstruction?" in which Rauschenbusch stressed the importance of reorienting the Christian church toward its social responsibilities by providing knowledge of existing social problems and awakening the church to the necessity of social reform.

58. See Rauschenbusch's letter to Nathaniel Schmidt, Sept., 1896, quoted in Sharpe, *Rauschenbusch*, 106–7; Rauschenbusch, "The New Evangelism," in William R. Hutchison, ed., *American Protestant Thought: The Liberal Era* (New York, 1968), 109; and Ely, *Ground Under Our Feet*, 146.

59. Ely, *Social Aspects of Christianity*, 121; *An Introduction to Political Economy* (New York, 1893), 37–38; and see also Hopkins, *Rise of the Social Gospel*, 106.

60. Rauschenbusch, *The Social Principles of Jesus* (New York, 1916), 152.

61. Jaurès, *Les Origines du socialisme allemand*, 45; and "Socialism and Life," in *Studies in Socialism*, ed. and trans. Mildred Minturn (New York, 1906), 10. See also Boitel, *Les Idées libérales*, 21–23, on Jaurès's use of Kant.

62. Bernstein, "Nach zwei Fronten. Eine Antwort an Kadi Lan und Sadi Gunter," *Die Neue*

Zeit 17 (1899): 846–47. See also, on the "creative character" of individual volition, "Das realistische und das ideologische Moment im Sozialismus" (1889), in *Zur Geschichte und Theorie des Sozialismus* (Berlin, 1901), 262–85; *Wie ist wissenschaftlicher Sozialismus möglich?* (Berlin, 1901), 18–19; and "The Revival of the Will in German Literature," *Nation*, Jan. 9, 1909, 576–77.

63. B. Webb, *Our Partnership*, 16; and entry in diary dated March 13, 1910, *Our Partnership*, 448–49.

64. Jaurès quoted by Jean Rabaut in his notes to Jaurès's lecture "Idéalisme et materialisme dans la conception de l'histoire" (1894), reprinted in Jaurès, *L'Esprit du socialisme*, ed. Rabaut (Geneva, 1964), 180.

65. Bernstein, *Wie ist wissenschaftlicher Sozialismus möglich?* 19.

66. B. Webb, *Our Partnership*, 295. In this passage she also remarks that it might be best to live "as if" one were "in communion with a super human force which makes for righteousness." While that reference may have been to the ideas of Hans Vaihinger, I do not think either the Webbs or the other theorists of social democracy accepted the extreme voluntarism of Vaihinger's "fictionalism" because of their firm commitment to empiricism. While Vaihinger's and James's philosophies exhibit certain similarities, I believe that James's pragmatism had a firmer basis in social validation, as I argued in Chapter Three, and for that reason I distinguish pragmatism from the philosophy of "as if." James explicitly repudiated charges that he endorsed a position similar to Vaihinger's counsel of accepting "fictions," "ideas which are known to be false, but which are employed because of their utility." See Hans Vaihinger, *The Philosophy of "As If,"* trans. C. K. Ogden (London, 1924), xlii. For a different assessment of the relation between Vaihinger and James, see David M. Kennedy and Paul A. Robinson, eds., *Social Thought in America and Europe: Readings in Comparative Intellectual History* (Boston, 1970), 197–200.

67. B. Webb, diary entry dated Jan. 25, 1901, *Our Partnership*, 210–11. For similar statements on this distinction, see Sidney Webb to Beatrice Potter, June 29, 1890, in *Letters of B. and S. Webb*, 1: 158; and Sidney Webb to Bertrand Russell, Oct. 16, 1904, in *Letters of B. and S. Webb*, 2: 208–9. See also the discussion of the Webbs' value orientation in Pierson, *British Socialists*, 97.

68. Bernstein, *Wie ist wissenschaftlicher Sozialismus möglich?* 32. See also the discussion of this point in Christian Gneuss, "Die historischen und ideologischen Voraussetzungen für die Herausbildung des Revisionismus bei Eduard Bernstein," in Heimann and Meyer, eds., *Bernstein*, 82–83; and Frithjof Spreer, "Bernstein, Max Weber und das Verhältnis von Wissenschaft und Politik in der Gegenwartsdiskussion," in Heimann and Meyer, eds., *Bernstein*, 284–85.

69. Rauschenbusch, *Christianizing the Social Order*, 110; "Dogmatic and Practical Socialism," 35–36; and "The Value and Use of History," 12–13, Rauschenbusch papers. See also Jaurès, *La Question religieuse et le socialisme*, ed. Michel Launay (Paris, 1959), 44.

70. *The New Statesman*, April 12, 1913, 4.

71. S. Webb, "Historic," *Fabian Essays in Socialism*, ed. George Bernard Shaw, 2nd ed. (1920; rpt. London, 1931), 45.

72. Bernstein to Kautsky, Dec. 16, 1927, Bernstein papers. As the discussions at the Bernstein Congress in 1977 make clear, Bernstein's treatment of the dialectic continues to be hotly debated. See Heimann and Meyer, eds., *Bernstein*, 80–81, 452, 486, 494.

73. Bernstein, *Evolutionary Socialism*, 13–18.

74. Rosa Luxemburg, *Reform or Revolution?* (1900; New York, 1973), 12.

75. Jaurès, "Idéalisme et materialisme dans la conception de l'histoire," *L'Esprit du socialisme*, 11–12.

76. Jaurès, "Bernstein et l'évolution de la méthode socialiste," *Oeuvres*, 6: 117–40. Cf. the

discussion of Jaurès's critique of revisionism in Goldberg, *Jaurès*, 265–69; and Angel, *Bernstein*, 269–73.

77. Jaurès to Bernstein, Jan. 27, 1901, Bernstein papers.

78. Jaurès, "Question de méthode:'le manifeste communiste' de Marx et Engels," in *L'Esprit du socialisme*, 27–54.

79. Ely, *Socialism and Social Reform* (New York, 1894), 175 f. Dorothy Ross has argued that Ely's view of the role of economic factors in historical change altered in his later writings, but the passage she cites as evidence does not clearly establish that claim. In *Studies in the Evolution of an Industrial Society* (New York, 1903), Ely wrote, "When we have said all that we can about the power of the individual will, we will find that there are great social forces which compel us to act along certain lines." As I have suggested, that recognition of both economic conditions and individual volition characterized Ely's (and the other social democrats') theory of voluntary action from the outset. They emphasized different parts of the equation on different occasions, but they consistently argued that material factors and free choices, taken together, shape history. Cf. Dorothy Ross, "Socialism and American Liberalism: Academic Social Thought in the 1880s."

80. Ely, *Social Aspects of Christianity*, 118 ff.

81. Rauschenbusch, *Christianizing the Social Order*, 41–42; *Christianity and the Social Crisis*, 91; *A Theology for the Social Gospel* (New York, 1917), 141–45.

82. Rauschenbusch, "Dogmatic and Practical Socialism," 3–7. Jaurès made a similar argument about the perils of passively waiting for revolution in *La Petite République*, Sept. 12, 1903, when criticizing Kautsky's strategy.

83. See Anthony Giddens, *Capitalism and Modern Social Theory: An Analysis of the Writings of Marx, Durkheim, and Max Weber* (Cambridge, 1971), 189–90. In *The Social and Political Thought of Karl Marx*, 143–44, Shlomo Avineri writes, "Revolutionary praxis has thus a dialectical aspect. Objectively, it is the organization of the conditions leading toward ultimate human emancipation. Subjectively it is the self-change the proletariat achieves by its self-discovery through organization. . . . The mechanistic and determinist view, which characterized orthodox Marxism under the impact of Engels's later writings, suggested the necessary breaking out of the revolution because of the internal contradictions of capitalist development and not its subjective elements, is open to all of Marx's criticism in his *Theses on Feuerbach*. Such a view ultimately sees in man and in human will only an object of external circumstances and, *mutatis mutandis*, of political manipulation. . . . For Marx . . . the revolution needs a conscious urge and motor in the form of revolutionary praxis. . . . [Thus] the dilemma of determinism versus voluntarism is transcended by the dialectical nature of this revolutionary consciousness."

84. B. Webb, *My Apprenticeship*, 293.

85. Ely, *Socialism and Social Reform*, 4; *Social Law of Service* (New York, 1896), 167; and "The Past and Present of Political Economy," in *Johns Hopkins University Studies in Historical and Political Economy*, 2nd series, ed. Herbert B. Adams (Baltimore, 1884), 35–36.

86. Rauschenbusch, *The Social Principles of Jesus*, 13–14; "The Corporate Life of Humanity," a lecture delivered at the Rochester Theological Seminary, Oct. 19, 1896, Rauschenbusch papers; and cf. William G. McLoughlin, *Revivals, Awakenings, and Reform: An Essay on Religion and Social Change in America, 1607–1977* (Chicago, 1978), 171–72.

87. Jaurès's speech quoted in J. Hampden Jackson, *Jean Jaurès: His Life and Work* (London, 1943), 34–35.

88. Jaurès, *Histoire socialiste*, 1: 8.

89. Jaurès, *Oeuvres*, 3: 264. Significantly, those who have argued that Jaurès's historical writings are compatible with Marx's emphasize Marx's early writings, to which Jaurès did not have access, and point out that Jaurès's criticism of historical materialism applied more to those like Engels and Kautsky who vulgarized Marxism than to Marx himself. For three

complementary analyses along these lines, see the essays by Ernest Labrousse, Madeleine Réberioux, and Gian Mario Bravo, in the *Bulletin d'études jaurèsiennes* 41 (April–June, 1971): 2–8; 69–70 (April–June, July–September, 1978): 3–10; and 72 (Jan.–March, 1979): 3–17. For a different interpretation, which stresses Jaurès's evolutionary pantheism as a background for his historical studies, see Kolakowski, *Main Currents of Marxism*, vol. 2, *The Golden Age*, 122–25.

90. Jaurès, "Question de méthode," *L'Esprit du socialisme*, 51–52.

91. Jaurès, *Studies in Socialism*, 19–20.

92. Jaurès, "Moonlight," *La Dépêche de Toulouse*, Oct. 15, 1890, reprinted in *Studies in Socialism*, 184–92.

93. Cf. S. Webb, "Historic," *Fabian Essays in Socialism*, 30–31; McBriar, *Fabian Socialism*, 61–63; Gay, *Democratic Socialism*, 136–37; Cole, *The Second International*, 277–78; and Rauschenbusch, *Christianity and the Social Crisis*, 91.

94. In the *Second International*, 379, G. D. H. Cole wrote, "Jaurès, up to a point, used the phraseology of Marxism, which was the *lingua franca* of the parties of the Second International, and he accepted a substantial part of Marx's economic doctrine. But he was never really a Marxist. He always stressed both the ethical elements in socialism and its roots in a democracy which he conceived as a completion of existing democratic tendencies and not in terms of any sort of class dictatorship." Lucio Colletti disparaged Bernstein for a similar ethical preoccupation in *From Rousseau to Lenin: Studies in Ideology and Society*, trans. John Merrington and Judith White (New York, 1972), 233: "On what basis do we say that the reality of capitalism is upside down? According to Bernstein, on the basis of the *moral ideal*. The idea of 'justice,' Kant's ethics, tell me that the world should be corrected and reformed. Value and surplus are mere words. Socialism is the product of good wishes. Change the minds of men! Abandon scientific socialism for utopian socialism. Reality is not important. 'Facts' are of no account." For a discussion of Marx's antiethical perspective that illustrates the gap separating Bernstein and Jaurès from Marx, see Eugen Kamenka, *Marxism and Ethics*.

95. Bernstein discussed Kant's ethics in *Wie ist wissenschaftlicher Sozialismus möglich?* 18–19; the quotations are from his preface to the French edition of that work, translated by Edouard Schneider as *Socialisme et science* (Paris, 1902), 4–7; cf. Jaurès, *Les Origines du socialisme allemand*; S. Webb, *Socialism in England* (Baltimore, 1889), 12; and cf. Webb's lecture "The Ethics of Existence," delivered in 1880 or 1881, in the Passfield papers, which contains a critique of the utilitarians' hedonistic psychology. B Webb's diary entry, May 18, 1883, is in the Passfield papers. See also the emphasis on the ethical appeal of socialism for the Webbs in Wolfe, *From Radicalism to Socialism*, 194–214.

96. Ely, *Social Aspects of Christianity*, 60–63. See also *The Social Law of Service*, 75–102; and Rauschenbusch, *A Theology for the Social Gospel*, 14–15, for comparable treatments of ethics as responsible, benevolent social action.

97. Rauschenbusch, "Dogmatic and Practical Socialism," 36. Cf. this passage from the conclusion of Bernstein's *Evolutionary Socialism*, 223: "The contempt of the ideal, the magnifying of material factors until they become omnipotent forces for evolution, is a self deception."

98. See for example Bernstein, *Evolutionary Socialism*, 14.

99. *Die Neue Zeit* 11 (1892–1893): 10. See also Angel, *Bernstein*, 107, on Bernstein's initial reactions to the Fabians; Gay, *Democratic Socialism*, 244, for the "peasants do not sink" fragment; and Meyer, "Wissenschaft und Sozialismus bei Marx, in der Konzeption Eduard Bernsteins und in der Gegenwart," in Heimann and Meyer, eds., *Bernstein*, 256.

100. Bernstein, "Entwicklungsgang eines Sozialisten," in *Die Volkswirtschaftslehre der Gegenwart in Selbstdarstellungen*, 1 (Leipzig, 1924): 23. A passage from an essay Bernstein wrote for *The Progressive Review*, May, 1897, 145, "Karl Marx and Social Reform," illustrates the accuracy of his recollection. Those who claim to be orthodox followers of Marx, he wrote,

"will still be poor Marxists if they refuse to acknowledge changes in the economic evolution which contradict former assumptions, and decline to act accordingly."

101. Bernstein, *Evolutionary Socialism*, xi–xv.

102. The Fabians did not construct a coherent economic theory. Here as elsewhere they displayed a talent for imaginative synthesis, drawing ideas from Marx, Mill, Henry George, and the German historical school. On the pivotal role of Philip Wicksteed in the Fabians' critique of Marxist economic theory, see Eric Hobsbawm, "Dr. Marx and the Victorian Critics," in *Labouring Men*, 247–48. The best discussion of the diverse sources of Fabian economic ideas is McBriar, *Fabian Socialism*, 29–38. On the influence of Henry George on the Fabians, see E. P. Lawrence, *Henry George in the British Isles* (East Lansing, Mich., 1957). On pp. 75–76, Lawrence points out the impact of George's ideas during the early stages of the Fabian movement, but he notes on pp. 170–72 that the Fabians "adopted a patronizing attitude toward George and the single tax" because "the single tax . . . was not socialism." See also Henry Pelling, *America and the British Left*, 56–58. Pelling argues that George's influence diminished after 1886. Webb discussed George's contributions sympathetically in "Henry George and Socialism," *The Church Reformer*, Jan., 1889, 11–13; and March, 1889, 60–61. See Shaw, "Economic," *Fabian Essays in Socialism*, esp. 24–25; and cf. McBriar, *Fabian Socialism*, 11, 44, 47.

103. See especially Gustafsson, *Marxismus und Revisionismus*, 168–80; on p. 180, Gustafsson concludes that revisionist economics was simply "Fabianism suited to the German Social Democratic public and German conditions," a judgment I consider overstated. See also Hirsch, *Der "Fabier" Eduard Bernstein*, esp. 17–27, on Bernstein's relation to the Webbs. Hirsch also reprints useful documents tracing the connections between revisionism and Fabianism, including the 1897 lecture "What Marx Really Taught," translated into German from the report in *Fabian News*, Feb., 1897, 48. Gay stresses the similarities between revisionism and Fabianism in *Democratic Socialism*, but while his characterization of the two as "brothers if not twins" (97) suggests their family resemblance as versions of social democracy, it overlooks their quite different intellectual parentage. The best brief discussion of this question is Hirsch, "Die Bezüglich der Fabian Society transparenten Kommunikationsstrukturen als Teilaspekte der internationalen Voraussetzungen der Herausbildung des Revisionismus von Eduard Bernstein," in Heimann and Meyer, eds., *Bernstein*, 47–58.

104. B. Webb, "The Economic Theory of Karl Marx," four mss. marked A, B, C, D, in the Passfield papers, is dated 1886 in Mary A. Hamilton, *Beatrice and Sidney Webb* (New York, 1933). S. Webb, "On Economic Method," a lecture given in 1885 or 1886, is in the Passfield papers. See also Webb's "Rent, Interest, and Wages: Being a Criticism of Karl Marx and a Statement of Economic Theory," 1886, a detailed review of *Capital*, also in the Passfield papers. Shaw recalled that Webb read through the first volume of *Capital* within an hour, but even for Webb, a notoriously quick study whom Bernstein described as a "walking encyclopedia" and "manifestly the most powerful brain among the Fabians," that claim strains credulity. See Margaret Cole, *The Webbs and Their Work*, 6; Bernstein, *My Years of Exile*, 242; and Wolfe, *From Radicalism to Socialism*, 204–8, on Webb's economics and his critique of Marx.

105. S. Webb, "On Economic Method," 26; "Rent, Interest, and Wages," 3; "The Economic Basis of Socialism and its political Programme," Dec., 1887, incomplete ms., with conclusion missing, in the Passfield papers; and Fabian Tract #15, *English Progress Toward Social Democracy*, 1890, 1. Webb's activities in the 1880s in The London Working Men's College, which can be followed by examining the lecture notes in Sec. VI of the Passfield papers, are ignored in J. A. Hall's portrait of Webb as an elitist uninterested in the working class and concerned only with social engineering: "The Roles and Influence of Political Intellectuals: Tawney vs. Sidney Webb," *British Journal of Sociology* 28 (1977): 351–62.

106. S. Webb to Bernstein, Oct. 15, 1895, Bernstein papers. See also Bernstein's ms. "Die

Gewerkschaftsbewegung des Auslands, E.78.a. England," in the Bernstein papers, for his comments on the Webbs' economic analysis; and cf. S. Webb to Lujo Brentano, April 13, 1894, in *Letters of B. and S. Webb*, 2: 16, on the shortcomings of *The History of English Trade Unionism* and their plans for a more theoretical volume.

107. See Ely to Sidgwick, June 2, 1887, informing Sidgwick of his selection as one of the first honorary members of the American Economic Association, Sidgwick papers; and Ely, "The Past and the Present of Political Economy," 42. See also Furner, *Advocacy and Objectivity*, 59–60. On the role of the German historical school in shaping Ely's ideas, and the ideas of American social scientists of his generation, see Herbst, *German Historical School*.

108. Ely, *The Labor Movement in America*, 3rd ed. (New York, 1890), 99–101; and *Introduction to Political Economy*, esp. 323–26. See also Rader, *Ely*, 28–53, on Ely's "new economics." Like the Fabians, Ely recognized the importance of Henry George's contribution to social reform, but he disagreed "decidedly" with George's overly simplified version of economic analysis and his single tax panacea. See *The Labor Movement in America*, 125–26, 183–84. Rauschenbusch stressed the importance of Henry George in first attracting him to socialism; see his letter to G. H. Roller, March 12, 1915. As he wrote to C. J. Bullock, Feb. 4, 1915, he no longer took "the singleness seriously . . . the main thing is to draw on the unearned increment." Both letters are in the Rauschenbusch papers.

109. Jaurès, "Bernstein and the Evolution of Socialist Method," a lecture delivered before a group of socialist students in Feb., 1900, is reprinted in his *Oeuvres*, 6: 121–24. Jaurès's attitude toward Marxist economics is a much discussed question, particularly in the *Bulletin d'études jaurèsiennes*. For a sensible assessment of Jaurès's remarks on Bernstein, and his general attitude toward Marx, see Goldberg, *Jaurès*, 266–68, 288–89. While Jaurès never questioned the centrality of the class struggle, and to that extent remained true to Marx's fundamental principle, his scattered remarks about such topics as the labor theory of value and the immiseration of the proletariat through capitalist development do not display the same degree of engagement or sophistication of analysis as do the writings of Bernstein, Webb, or Ely.

110. Bernstein, "Arbeitswert oder Nutzwert?" *Die Neue Zeit* 17 (1899): 548–54. Bernstein's essays on the "problems of socialism" were reprinted, in slightly abridged form, as vol. 2 of *Zur Geschichte und Theorie des Sozialismus*. Bernstein's specific arguments and those of various Fabians are examined in Gustafsson, *Marxismus und Revisionismus*, 173–78, and summarized by Roger Fletcher, "Bernstein in Britain," 360–61, as

> firstly, the contention that Marx's theory of value was an abstraction (Wicksteed); secondly, that Jevons's marginal utility abstractions were of equal merit with Marx's labour-theory abstractions (Shaw prior to his final change of viewpoint); thirdly, that the theories of Marx and of the theorists of utility were both correct (Wallas); fourthly, that Marx's analysis of the reduction of abstract labour to simple labour was unsatisfactory (Wallas); fifthly, that Marx's theory of surplus value did not differ in principle from that of his predecessors, that is, from the Ricardian socialists (the Webbs); and finally, that surplus value might be explained as absolute rent just as easily as it could be explained as unpaid labour (Rodbertus, Dühring, the Fabians).

111. Bernstein, *Evolutionary Socialism*, 34–35.

112. B. Webb, "The Economic Theory of Karl Marx," 28–29, 37–40; and cf. S. Webb, "Rent, Interest, and Wages," 8–12. On Bernstein's quest for the perennially elusive unified value theory in economics, see Gerhard Himmelmann, "Die Rolle der Werttheorie in Bernsteins Konzept der politischen Ökonomie des Sozialismus," in Heimann and Meyer, eds., *Bernstein*, 300–19; and the discussion of Bernstein's economics on 506–29, which makes clear that one of the principal impediments in assessing the accuracy of Bernstein's view of Marx's economics is the continuing disagreement about the meaning of what Marx himself wrote. Another useful guide through the thicket of controversy surrounding Marx's theory of value is Kolakowski's discussion of the

disagreements between Hilferding and Böhm-Bawerk in *Main Currents of Marxism*, vol. 2, *The Golden Age*, 290–97. Kolakowski points out the different purposes of political economists interested in explaining the movement of *prices* and Marxists interested in tracing the origin of *value*, and concludes sensibly that the "controversy between Marxists and critics of the theory of value is thus insoluble, as the latter expect from a general economic theory something that Marx's doctrine is unable to provide." As a theory attempting to explain the origins of profit in unremunerated labor, Marx's theory of value does not pretend to account for the shifting of prices in commodity exchange. Kolakowski also notes that Jaurès accepted Marx's theory of value, at least in part, because he understood that it was a piece of "social metaphysics," a theoretical account of the exploitation of the working class by capitalists, not a theory of prices (138–39).

113. See Colletti, *From Rousseau to Lenin*, 101–2, for a recent response to Bernstein's analysis that relies on the idea of relative deprivation and emphasizes exploitation rather than impoverishment as the more important element in capitalist expropriation.

114. B. Webb, diary entry, March, 1895, in *Our Partnership*, 70 f. Collini advances a similar explanation of the rise of moderate socialism in Britain in *Liberalism and Sociology*, 32 f.

115. Jaurès, "The Question of Method," in *Studies in Socialism*, 160–62, 167–68.

116. Bernstein, *Evolutionary Socialism*, 93. For a provocative defense of this argument, and an answer to Bernstein's critics, particularly Lenin, see Kolakowski, *Main Currents of Marxism*, vol. 2, *The Golden Age*, 112–14.

117. S. Webb, "Historic," and William Clarke, "Industrial," in *Fabian Essays in Socialism*, 28–95; Bernstein, *Wirtschaftswesen und Wertschaftswerden* (Berlin, 1920), 36; *Evolutionary Socialism*, chap. 2, 28–94; and Rauschenbusch, "Dogmatic and Practical Socialism," 12–16. See also R. Laurence Moore, *European Socialists and the American Promised Land* (New York, 1970), 84–87, 94–95, on the effect of trusts and cartels on socialist attitudes toward capitalism; James B. Gilbert, *Designing the Industrial State: The Intellectual Pursuit of Collectivism in America, 1880–1940* (Chicago, 1972), 40–54, for the career of this argument in America; and Colletti's perceptive analysis of Bernstein's argument in *From Rousseau to Lenin*, 97–103.

118. Bernstein, *Evolutionary Socialism*, 42–48. Bernstein's treatment of the concentration of capital has been widely discussed by socialists eager to turn later developments against his arguments. For a guide to these critical analyses, particularly Kautsky's *Bernstein and the Social Democratic Program* and Hilferding's *Finance Capital*, see Angel, *Bernstein*, 218–28, 236–41; and Colletti, *From Rousseau to Lenin*, 99–100.

119. Bernstein, *Evolutionary Socialism*, 49.

120. Ely, "Social Studies: I—The Nature of the Railway Problem," *Harper's New Monthly Magazine*, July, 1886, 251; Ely, *The Social Law of Service*, 139; Fabian Tract # 4, *What Socialism Is*, 1886; and cf. S. Webb's essay "What Socialism Means: A Call to the Unconverted," *The Practical Socialist*, June, 1886, 91: "Socialism is founded upon . . . the emphatic assertion of two leading principles: We recognize first, as the central truth of modern society, the interdependence of all. . . . No individual can henceforth claim as his own, the product to which he is in reality giving only certain final touches. We claim, in the second place, to be but applying the doctrines of the economists in insisting on the ethical right of the joint workers, and the workers alone, to the whole produce of their labour." See also B. and S. Webb, *Industrial Democracy*, 2nd ed. (London, 1920), 850; and the splendid discussion of interdependence in Haskell, *The Emergence of Professional Social Science*, 24–47.

121. Rauschenbusch, *Christianizing the Social Order*, 368; *Christianity and the Social Crisis*, 382.

Chapter 7. Social Democratic Politics

1. Jaurès, "Truth or Fiction," in *Studies in Socialism*, 176–83. This account, whose veracity is obviously challenged by its title, first appeared in *La Petite République*, Oct. 26, 1901.

2. See also Bernstein, "Karl Marx and Social Reform," *The Progressive Review*, May, 1897, 145, in which Bernstein argued that Marx should be understood as a "revolutionary evolution-ist"; and Rauschenbusch's "Declaration of Principles" for a proposed Christian Socialist Society, published in *For the Right*, April, 1890, in which he described the revolutionary nature of the society's socialist aim and the evolutionary nature of the process that would bring society to that goal.

3. Bernstein, *Evolutionary Socialism*, 210.

4. S. Webb, "Historic," *Fabian Essays in Socialism*, 29; and cf. "What Socialism Means," 91.

5. B. and S. Webb, *A Constitution for the Socialist Commonwealth of Great Britain* (London, 1920), xviii.

6. Fabian Manifesto # 1, 1887, is in the Passfield papers.

7. On this point see Ely, *Socialism and Social Reform*, 330.

8. Bernstein, "Die Zusammenbruchstheorie und die Kolonialpolitik," *Die Neue Zeit* 16 (1897–1898): 555–56; reprinted in *Zur Geschichte und Theorie des Sozialismus*, 234. See also *Evolutionary Socialism*, 145, 202–4; and the interview with Bernstein in the *Jewish Chronicle*, Nov. 24, 1899, 21.

9. Bernstein, "Blanquismus und Sozialdemokratie," Bernstein papers, is discussed by Meyer in Heimann and Meyer, eds., *Bernstein*, 429–30. See also Bernstein's preface to *Science et socialisme*, 7, where he argued, "For me communism is more a means than an end. It is, from my point of view, up to the future to decide what forms and also what degree of communism will be, in each historical period, necessary to assure the greatest sum of material and moral well being." Interestingly, Bernstein offered these remarks as a response to Jaurès's comments in *Etudes socialistes* on the dangers of opportunism implicit in Bernstein's revisionism; cf. also Jaurès's review in *La Petite République*, April 9, 1896, in which he argued that democracy makes possible the achievement of revolutionary changes without revolution. Rauschenbusch made a similar argument in "The Development of Democracy," an address delivered before the Suffrage School of Monroe County, N.Y., Feb. 17, 1914, in the Rauschenbusch papers.

10. Ely, *French and German Socialism*, 261; "Recent American Socialism," 6, 73; and *The Labor Movement in America*, ix–xi, 63–64. Those who accuse Ely of "recanting" in his later trial at the University of Wisconsin tend to overlook the moderation of his earlier socialism and the intensity of his criticism of the idea of revolution.

11. S. Webb, "Historic," *Fabian Essays in Socialism*, 31–35. In testimony before the Royal Commission on Labour in 1892, Webb described "collectivism" as "the economic obverse of democracy." Asked to elaborate, he answered:

> It appears to me that if you allow the tramway conductor to vote he will not forever be satisfied with exercising that vote over such matters as the appointment of the Ambassador to Paris, or even the position of the franchise. He will realize that the forces that keep him at work for sixteen hours a day for three shillings a day are not the forces of hostile kings, of nobles, or priests; but whatever forces they are he will, it seems to me, seek so far as possible to control them by his vote. That is to say, he will more and more seek to convert his political democracy into what one may roughly term industrial democracy, so that he may obtain some kind of control as a voter over the conditions under which he lives.

See the Royal Commission on Labour, *Minutes of Evidence, Fourth Report*, Nov. 15, 1892, 268, quoted in Gilbert, *The Evolution of National Insurance in Great Britain*, 25–26. Webb made a similar argument regarding democracy and socialism in a letter to Ely, Feb. 21, 1894, in *Letters of B. and S. Webb*, 2: 13–14; and cf. p. 203 above.

12. Rauschenbusch, *Christianizing the Social Order*, 408–11; cf. 59.

13. Rauschenbusch, *Christianity and the Social Crisis*, 410–11; *A Theology for the Social Gospel*, 223–27.

14. Jaurès, "The Question of Method," in *Studies in Socialism*, 146–47.

15. The statement of purpose adopted by the SFIO at Toulouse in 1908 is reprinted in Lefranc, *Le Mouvement socialiste*, 2: 401–2.

16. These various declarations of principles, legislative programs, manifestos, and philosophies can be compared by examining two excellent collections: Ely's *Socialism and Social Reform*, and *Modern Socialism*, ed. R. C. K. Ensor (London, 1904). Ensor was an active member of the Fabian Society, and his collection provides a useful compendium of moderate socialist programs.

17. The Erfurt program is reprinted in Ely's *Socialism and Social Reform*, 357–63. See also Bernstein, *Evolutionary Socialism*, 167. Bernstein modified his position somewhat in later years. In 1909 he wrote an alternative program which reflects his revisionist analysis of Marxist economics in its treatment of social democratic reform 'strategy. See "Leitsätze für den theoretischen Teil eines sozialdemokratischen Parteiprogramms," appendix to *Der Revisionismus in der Sozialdemokratie* (Amsterdam, 1909), 42–48.

18. See Goldberg, *Jaurès*, 308. The Tours program of the *Parti socialist français* is reprinted in Ensor's *Modern Socialism*, 338–49. See also the correspondence between Rauschenbusch and W. D. P. Bliss in the Rauschenbusch papers.

19. Rauschenbusch, *Christianizing the Social Order*, 3.

20. S. and B. Webb, *Industrial Democracy*, 766–84. See also their *Constitution*, 321–23; and McBriar, *Fabian Socialism*, 107–8. See also Rodgers, *The Work Ethic in Industrial America*, 156 ff.; and Cole, *The Second International*, 3–9. Bernstein accurately described the Webbs' *Industrial Democracy* in *Evolutionary Socialism* as "the most thorough work" on the subject of trade unions in their role as "indispensable organs of the democracy" (140). Jaurès's commitment to the labor movement dated from his involvement in the Carmaux glass workers' strike of 1895, and his dedication to the struggle for workers' rights intensified throughout the rest of his life. See Rabaut, *Jaurès*, 81–123; and Goldberg, *Jaurès*, 137–52. Ely argued for unionization and reform in *The Labor Movement in America*; see esp. 295–332. Rauschenbusch expressed his support of the eight-hour day, unionization, employment bureaus, industrial safety regulations, and workmen's compensation insurance in "Dogmatic and Practical Socialism," 27–31; and in *Christianizing the Social Order*, 347–48, 387–88, 414–15. For recent literature on the welfare state, see n. 89 to Chapter Five above.

21. See for example S. Webb, "What Socialism Means," 89; and two speeches by Jaurès in the French Chamber of Deputies, Dec. 1, 1898, and Jan. 21 and 24, 1909, both printed in the *Journal officiel* of the Chamber.

22. To cite only one illustration of the breadth of the welfare state's appeal, in the first decade of the twentieth century Sidney Webb was advocating "a National Minimum below which the individual, whether he likes it or not, cannot, in the interests of the well being of the whole, ever be allowed to fall"; while Winston Churchill at the same time wanted "to draw a line below which we will not allow persons to live and labour." See Webb, *The Necessary Basis of Society*, Fabian Tract # 159, July, 1911, 8; Churchill, *Liberalism and the Social Problem* (London, 1909), 80.

23. The SPD resolution from the 1883 congress in Copenhagen is quoted in Guttsman, *German Social Democratic Party*, 65. For Bernstein's ambivalent attitude toward the welfare state, see *Evolutionary Socialism*, 152–53, 192; Rauschenbusch and Ely agreed that such measures were useful but would fail to satisfy the working class; their views are discussed in Stokes, "American Progressives and the European Left," 20. See also Ely, *French*

and German Socialism, 216–21; and Rauschenbusch, "Dogmatic and Practical Socialism," 27–31.

24. Rauschenbusch, *Christianizing the Social Order*, 430. On the importance of Germany and Britain as models for Rauschenbusch's and Ely's ideas about the welfare state, see *Christianity and the Social Crisis*, 237; *Christianizing the Social Order*, 346, 416; and Ely, *Socialism and Social Reform*, 331–32. The German experience with social insurance decisively influenced those intellectuals, including Ely, who were responsible for "the Wisconsin idea" which inspired so much of American progressive reform. On this point see Charles McCarthy, *The Wisconsin Idea*; Rader, *Ely*, 90–91, 172–75; and Herbst, *German Historical School*, 176–77. Jaurès explained his support of workers' old-age pensions, a position that earned him the scorn of much of the French left, in *L'Armée nouvelle*, 2nd ed., with a preface by Lucien Lévy-Bruhl (Paris, 1915), 432–35.

25. Bernstein, *Evolutionary Socialism*, 108; Fritz Vilmar, "Beiträge Eduard Bernsteins zu einer Theorie der Wirtschaftsdemokratie," in Heimann and Meyer, eds., *Bernstein*, 333–45; and Gay, *Democratic Socialism*, 49–50. See also Bernstein's revisionist response to the Erfurt program, "Leitsätze," esp. 42–44.

26. S. Webb quoted in David Thomson, *England in the Nineteenth Century, 1815–1914* (1950; rpt. London, 1977), 180. Webb elaborated this argument in "The Economic Heresies of the London County Council," reprinted by the Fabian Society from *London*, Aug. 16, 1894, Fabian archive, Nuffield College Library, Oxford. Jaurès formulated an almost identical argument in *La Petite République*, Feb. 24, 1903.

27. Ely, *Socialism and Social Reform*, 215–32, 262–76. Rauschenbusch, *Christianizing the Social Order*, 435–39, 9, 289–90, 347 n.; 425 n.; and *Christianity and the Social Crisis*, 386–89. See also Rader, *The Academic Mind and Reform*, 90–96; and Stokes, "American Progressives and the European Left," 25–27.

28. Ely, *Socialism and Social Reform*, 291: "To interfere at every turn with private management renders illusory the benefits of private ownership of the instruments of production. Moreover, in this attempted minute control, society is likely to be worsted. The special skill is necessarily on the side of those who are to be controlled, because this special skill is acquired by experience in the management of these private industries. The result is that the public authorities wage an unequal contest against private persons, who, in addition, are thereby rendered hostile to the state—a most unfortunate condition of affairs." Ely thus articulated the now standard critique of regulation offered seventy years later by Theodore J. Lowi in *The End of Liberalism: Ideology, Policy, and the Crisis of Public Authority* (New York, 1969); and Grant McConnell, *Private Power and American Democracy* (New York, 1967).

29. Rauschenbusch, *Christianizing the Social Order*, 435–7. Rauschenbusch cited as the source for this argument Ely's discussion of railroad regulation in *Socialism and Social Reform*, 270.

30. *The Manifesto of the Fabian Parliamentary Leagues* was printed in *The Practical Socialist*, April, 1887. The Fabians' idea of permeation has been the subject of considerable controversy. The most complete discussion is in McBriar, *Fabian Socialism*, 95–97, 245–48; for a less sympathetic treatment, cf. Paul Thompson, *Socialists, Liberals, and Labour: The Struggle for London, 1885–1914* (Toronto, 1967), 138–42, 296–97. Thompson concludes that the policy kept the Fabians from exerting much influence at all in London politics. Wolfe, *From Liberalism to Socialism*, 258–62, 309–12, provides a balanced overview of the strengths and weaknesses of permeation.

31. S. Webb, Fabian Tract # 11, *The Workers' Political Program* (1891); and Fabian Tract # 108, *Twentieth Century Politics: A Policy of National Efficiency* (1901). Recent studies confirming the accuracy of Webb's reading of the evolution of the Liberal party include Peter F. Clarke, *Lancashire and the New Liberalism* (Cambridge, 1971); H. V. Emy, *Liberals, Radicals,*

and Social Politics, 1892–1914 (Cambridge, 1973); and Pugh, *The Making of Modern British Politics*. See also the review essay by Michael Freeden in *The Journal of Modern History* 48 (1976): 547–52.

32. "To Your Tents, Oh Israel!" was written by S. Webb and Shaw. It first appeared in *Fortnightly Review*, Nov., 1893, and was published in 1894 by the Fabian Society as Tract #49, bearing the title *A Plan of Campaign for Labour*. For the article's impact on the Liberal party, see B. Webb, *Our Partnership*, 110; and McBriar, *Fabian Socialism*, 245–53. On the return to permeation and the Fabians' involvement with the Liberal Imperialists, see Norman and Jeanne MacKenzie, *The Fabians* (New York, 1977), 231–2; McBriar, *Fabian Socialism*, 253–9; H. C. G. Matthew, *The Liberal Imperialists: The Ideas and Politics of a Post-Gladstonian Elite* (Oxford, 1973); and Bernard Semmel, *Imperialism and Social Reform* (Cambridge, Mass., 1960).

33. S. Webb, introduction to the 1919 ed. of *Fabian Essays in Socialism*, xxx. On the Webbs' inability to read the public mood concerning politicians' prospects, cf. Hobsbawm, "The Fabians Reconsidered," *Labouring Men*, 252–53; and Wolfe, *From Liberalism to Socialism*, 310–11.

34. The most persuasive discussion of the consistency of Jaurès's allegiance to the paradoxical dual ideals of unity on the left and unity of all republicans is Elise Feller-Benoit, "Jaurès et l'Unité socialiste de 1898 à 1905," *Bulletin d'études jaurèsiennes* 20 (Jan.–March, 1966): 1–16.

35. See Chapter Nine below, especially pp. 355–56.

36. Jaurès's role in the Millerand controversy is discussed in Goldberg, *Jaurès*, 249–56, 261–5. Cf. the differing assessments in Rébérioux, *La République radicale?* 75–82; and Lefranc, *Le Mouvement socialiste*, 1: 105–17. On the leading figure in this controversy, see Leslie Derfler, ed., *Alexandre Millerand: The Socialist Years* (Hawthorne, N.Y., 1977).

37. For different interpretations of Jaurès's analysis of revisionism, both of which emphasize the distance separating Jaurès from Bernstein, see Rébérioux, "Le 'Socialisme des Intellectuels' et Jaurès," *Bulletin des études jaurèsiennes* 39 (Oct.–Dec., 1970): 35; and Rabaut, *Jaurès*, 125–28.

38. Bernstein quoted in Guttsman, *German Social Democratic Party*, 110. Bernstein explained why he thought the SPD should claim the vice-presidency in "Was folgt aus dem Ergebnis der Reichstagswahlen," *Sozialistische Monatshefte* 2 (1903): 478–86. On Bernstein's attitude toward socialist-liberal alliance, see Lehnert, *Reform und Revolution*, 194–203; Fletcher, "Bernstein in Britain," 364–66; Fletcher, "The Free Trade Internationalism of Eduard Bernstein," 572–74; and Meyer, "Wissenschaft und Sozialismus bei Marx, in der Konzeption Eduard Bernsteins und in der Gegenwart," in Heimann and Meyer, eds., *Bernstein*, 268–72.

39. See especially Kocka, *White Collar Workers*, 251–67; and the discussion in Iggers, *New Directions in European Historiography*, 116–17. For a provocative contrast, which demonstrates how the legacy of corporatism could function in support of working-class aims when democracy was not undercut by autocratic interference, see Daniel Levine, "Conservatism and Tradition in Danish Social Welfare Legislation, 1890–1933: A Comparative View," *Comparative Studies in Society and History* 20 (1978): 54–69.

40. Auer quoted in Steinberg, *Sozialismus und deutsche Sozialdemokratie*, 123. For details on the Dresden debate, see Gay, *Democratic Socialism*, 224–26, 265–66; and Strutynski, *Deutsche Arbeiterbewegung*, 186–201.

41. Jaurès's speech of Aug. 9, 1904, was published in *Le Journal des débats, 6ᵉ congrès socialiste international* (1904); it is discussed in detail in Goldberg, *Jaurès*, 325–28; and Rabaut, *Jaurès*, 166–68. As Goldberg points out (538 n. 95), Jaurès's ideas concerning the necessity of adopting different tactics for different socialist movements echoed Engels's own; it is also noteworthy that Bernstein expressed an almost identical opinion in *Evolutionary Socialism*, 161: "At a given moment, therefore, one can probably set up general political principles of social democracy with a claim that they apply to all countries, but no programme of action applicable for all countries is possible."

42. *L'Humanité*, Sept. 5, 7, 9, 12, 14, and 16, 1914. Interestingly, Gordon A. Craig's analysis of the birth of the Reich in *Germany 1866–1945*, 44–58, strongly resembles the argument Jaurès advanced in this series of articles.

43. A detailed report of the Amsterdam Congress of the Second International by William Sanders was included in *Fabian News*, Sept., 1904, 33–34. The Fabians had applauded Millerand's participation in the Waldeck-Rousseau ministry as a splendid example of permeation at work; they could not fathom the reasons for objecting to ministerialism. See *Fabian News*, Aug., 1899, 21.

44. Rauschenbusch, *Christianizing the Social Order*, 399. See also "The Ministry and the Social Crisis," a lecture delivered at the Yale Divinity School in Jan., 1911, Rauschenbusch papers.

45. Ely, *French and German Socialism*, 214–15; *Socialism and Social Reform*, v.

46. Rauschenbusch, "The Socialist Movement and the World-Wide Unrest," *Rochester Times*, Dec. 16, 1911; *Christianity and the Social Crisis*, 409; "The New Evangelism," *The Independent*, May 12, 1904, reprinted in Rauschenbusch, *A Gospel for the Social Awakening*, ed. Benjamin E. Mays (New York, 1950), 125–53. Rauschenbusch explained his reasons for refusing to join the Socialist Party, although he frequently proclaimed himself a socialist, in letters to F. E. Volck, June 17, 1913; and to A. G. Breckinridge, Jan. 15, 1914; both are in the Rauschenbusch papers. See also Stokes, "American Progressives and the European Left," 16, 19, on this point.

47. The most detailed account of this incident is in Rader, *Ely*, 130–58. The proceedings of the hearing are in the Ely papers. Mary Furner, in *Advocacy and Objectivity*, 147–62, calls Ely's case a "microcosm" of the struggle waged in the late nineteenth century between contrasting modes of scholarship, an example of the progression "from advocacy to objectivity." Rader similarly concludes that Ely's willingness to deny the charges of socialism leveled against him indicates the triumph of professional ambition over political principle. By contrast, David Thelen, in *The New Citizenship*, 67, contends that Ely's trial gave greater visibility to his social democratic ideas, prompted most prominent journalists and political activists to come to his defense, and generally contributed to the ferment of reform in Wisconsin in the closing years of the nineteenth century. Finally, Dorothy Ross, in her splendid essay "Socialism and American Liberalism," uses Ely to illustrate the process by which American academic economists were deflected from their egalitarian and fraternal impulses by the constraints of American society and their "insecurity of class identity."

48. Ely, *Socialism and Social Reform*, 30–31. The Fabians appear to have coined the word "municipalization," which other social democrats also used to express their preference for local self-government and municipal socialism. See in particular Sidney Webb's contribution to *Fabian Essays in Socialism*, xxiii. The Fabians were not always worried about the dangers of state socialism, because they had confidence in the vitality of local democratic institutions. See for example Fabian Tract # 70, *Report on Fabian Policy and Resolution Presented by the Fabian Society to the International Socialist Workers and Trade Union Congress, London, 1896* (July, 1896), 5, where Britain's strong tradition of local government is contrasted to the centralization of political authority in Germany. See also McBriar, *Fabian Socialism*, 108–9, and Cole, *The Second International*, 118–19, on the Webbs' commitment to decentralization and municipal socialism.

49. Robert Michels, *Political Parties: A Sociological Study of the Oligarchical Tendencies of Modern Democracy*, trans. Eden and Cedar Paul (1915; rpt. New York, 1962), 364–65. See also Hughes, *Consciousness and Society*, 249–73, on Michels, Vilfredo Pareto, and Gaetano Mosca; and Soffer, *Ethics and Society in England*, 217–52, on William McDougall, Wilfred Trotter, and the rise of social psychology in England.

50. Bernstein to Kautsky, Feb. 20, 1898, Kautsky papers; *Evolutionary Socialism*, 161–62;

Wie ist wissenschaftlicher Sozialismus möglich? 42. See also the discussion of this issue in Meyer, "Wissenschaft und Sozialismus," in Heimann and Meyer, eds., *Bernstein*, 266–71; and his comments in the general discussion of Bernstein's revisionism on 441–43.

51. Jaurès's articles from *La Revue socialiste* are reprinted in vol. 3 of his *Oeuvres*. For his discussion of bureaucracy in capitalism and socialism, see 322–25. See also Jaurès's essays in *L'Humanité*, June 7 and Sept. 22, 1905; his speech at Trocadéro, reprinted in *L'Humanité*, Dec. 18, 1906; and *L'Armée nouvelle*, 410.

52. Ely, "Pullman: A Social Study," *Harper's New Monthly Magazine*, Feb., 1885, 453–59; *The Labor Movement in America*, 320–21; and "Fundamental Beliefs in My Social Philosophy," *Forum*, Oct., 1894, 183. See also Theron F. Schlabach, "An Aristocrat on Trial: The Case of Richard T. Ely," *Wisconsin Magazine of History* 47 (1963–1964): 146–57. The pervasiveness of the apparently contradictory impulses toward social cooperation and social efficiency in American progressivism is emphasized by Daniel T. Rodgers, "In Search of Progressivism," *Reviews in American History* 10 (1982): 113–32.

53. S. Webb to Beatrice Potter, June 16, 1890, in *Letters of B. and S. Webb*, 1: 152.

54. Webb's lectures on "The Machinery of Democracy" were delivered between Oct. 2 and Dec. 11, 1896, and reported in *Fabian News*, Nov., 1896, through Jan., 1897.

55. S. Webb to G. B. Shaw, April 26, 1898, Passfield papers; B. Webb, *American Diary, 1898*, 100–1. For a sampling of criticism of the Webbs' elitism, see Eric Hobsbawm, "The Fabians Reconsidered," in *Labouring Men*, 264–66; G. R. Searle, *The Quest for National Efficiency* 62–63; and Donald Read, *Edwardian England, 1901–1915: Society and Politics* (London, 1972), 95.

56. B. Webb's diary, Sept. 16, 1896, Passfield papers.

57. B. and S. Webb, *Industrial Democracy*, 843–48.

58. The Minority Report of the Poor Law Commission, signed by Beatrice Webb, George Lansbury, Russell Wakefield, and Francis Chandler, was published in 1909 by the Fabian Society under the title *Break Up the Poor Law and Abolish the Workhouse*. Much of the report was written by Sidney Webb. Of the many analyses of the Minority Report and the controversy surrounding health insurance, I have found the following especially useful: Bruce, *The Coming of the Welfare State*; Gilbert, *The Evolution of National Insurance in Great Britain*; Searle, *The Quest for National Efficiency*; and Pierson, *British Socialists*, 315–21.

59. B. Webb to M. Playne, May 5, 1904, Passfield papers; diary entry from Oct. 16, 1908, in *Our Partnership*, 417, from Jan., 1911, 468. On Speenhamland and the original Poor Law, see Polanyi, *The Great Transformation*, 77–129.

60. Churchill quoted in Pierson, *British Socialists*, 320.

61. The series "What is Socialism?" appeared from April 12 through July 19, 1913. The quotations are from the fourth essay, "Participation in Power and the Consciousness of Consent," *The New Statesman*, May 3, 1913, 107–8.

62. B. and S. Webb, *Constitution*, 198, 86, 89, 99–100. On the Labour party and the Fabians, see Ross McKibbin, *The Evolution of the Labour Party*; and Pierson, *British Socialists*, 331–44.

63. A letter written by the German liberal Lujo Brentano to Beatrice Webb in 1892 suggests the difference between the German and Anglo-American perspectives on this problem, a difference examined systematically by Max Weber, whose sobering assessment of the relation between authority and popular government will be discussed in Chapter Nine. Brentano, who was writing the preface to the German edition of Beatrice Webb's study of the British cooperative movement, disagreed strongly with her optimism concerning the potential of highly trained civil servants to act as agents of progressive change. The German experience with such officials, particularly under Bismarck's state socialism, Brentano argued, was "most deplorable." The worst of these autocrats were more unscrupulous than the most notorious capitalists, because "ambition is the stronger motive power than love of gain." Precisely the sort of

democratic and cooperative institutions so prevalent in Britain were missing in Germany, and Brentano concluded that if Beatrice would study German economics and social policy as carefully as she had studied the British experience with capitalism, she "would come to prefer the latter, tempered by trade unionism and cooperation, to the stupid absence of liberty of the reign of the civil servant." As I have noted, the Webbs became increasingly sensitive to this problem in their later writings, but they never abandoned their faith that it could be solved by careful adherence to the priority of the public will over the prerogatives of administrators. Germany's very different experience with the exercise of government authority prevented Brentano from sharing their faith. Lujo Bretano to B. Webb, Oct. 16, 1892, Passfield papers. For comments on the difference between the German experience and their own, cf. Fabian Tract # 70, *Report on Fabian Policy*; and Ely, *Ground Under Our Feet*, 258–63.

64. Jaurès quoted in Louis Soulé, *La Vie de Jaurès* (Paris, 1921), 55–56; Bernstein, *Evolutionary Socialism*, 166; B. and S. Webb, "Participation in Power and the Consciousness of Consent," 108.

65. Ely, *Evolution of an Industrial Society*, 420–22; Rauschenbusch, *Christianizing the Social Order*, 356. See also Jaurès's speech in the Chamber of Deputies, Nov. 18, 1909, *Journal officiel*, 2762–63, in which he related international patterns of taxation to the growth of capitalism and liberalism and criticized the abstract conception of liberty in French republicanism; and Bernstein, *Evolutionary Socialism*, 153–54.

66. Jaurès, *Les Origines du socialisme allemand*, 62; *La Petite République*, June 30, 1893; speech in the Chamber of Deputies, March 21, 1896, *Journal officiel*, 581; S. Webb, Fabian Tract # 15, *English Progress Toward Social Democracy*, 13–14; B. and S. Webb, *Industrial Democracy*, 847; Rauschenbusch, *Christianizing the Social Order*, 350; and cf. *Christianity and the Social Crisis*, 263.

67. Ely, *Socialism and Social Reform*; Jaurès quoted in *Le Signal de Genève*, March 1, 1902, a speech reprinted in the *Bulletin d'études jaurèsiennes* 16 (Jan.–March, 1965): 4–5; *L'Humanité*, Nov. 9, 1906; Rauschenbusch, *Christianizing the Social Order*, 421, 372–73; and see also S. Webb, Fabian Tract # 69, *The Difficulties of Individualism*, June, 1896.

68. Ely, *Evolution of an Industrial Society*, 420–22; S. Webb, "Anarchism," Passfield papers; and see the discussion of the influence of philosophical idealism on Webb's socialism in Wolfe, *From Radicalism to Socialism*, 274–78. In a letter to Margery Davidson, Dec. 12, 1888, in *Letters of B. and S. Webb*, 1: 118–23, Sidney Webb encapsulated his "theory of life" as the attempt always to act as if he were part of a committee. "This theoretically combined action involves rules, deliberation, discussion, concert, the disregard of one's own impulses, and in fact is Collectivism or Communism." Jaurès, "Socialisme et liberté," *La Revue de Paris*, Dec. 1, 1898, 482; "Organisation socialiste," *La Revue socialiste*, April, 1895, 408; speech in the Chamber of Deputies, Nov. 13, 1906, *Journal officiel*, 2503.

69. Rauschenbusch, *Christianity and the Social Crisis*, 388–93, 381–86; Ely, "Recent American Socialism," *Johns Hopkins University Studies in Historical and Political Science*, 3rd series, ed. Herbert B. Adams (Baltimore, 1885), 71; *The Labor Movement in America*, 311; *Property and Contract in their Relation to the Distribution of Wealth*, (New York, 1914); and *Ground Under Our Feet*, 270–71; and Rauschenbusch, *Christianizing the Social Order*, 358.

70. B. and S. Webb, *Constitution*, 343; S. Webb, "Historic," *Fabian Essays in Socialism*, 55–56.

71. Jaurès, *Studies in Socialism*, 7–9, 12–13, 22–23.

72. Ely, *Introduction to Political Economy*, 241. This argument recapitulated in part his presentation of socialist ideas in *Socialism and Social Reform*. In that book he wrote that "modern socialism does not propose to abolish private property. Quite the contrary . . . [it] proposes to extend the institution of private property in such manner as to secure to each individual in society property in an annual income" (16–17).

73. Bernstein, *Evolutionary Socialism*, 169; Rauschenbusch, *Christianity and the Social Crisis*, 247, 406–8; and see also Ely, *French and German Socialism*, 218 ff. In *Fabian Essays in Socialism*, 198, Hubert Bland wrote, "It must not be forgotten that although Socialism involves State control, State control does not imply Socialism, at least in any modern meaning of the term. It is not so much to the thing the State does, as to the end for which it does it that we must look before we can decide whether it is a Socialist State or not. Socialism is the common holding of the means of production and exchange, and *the holding of them for the equal benefit of all*."

74. Jaurès, *Oeuvres*, 3: 306.

75. B. and S. Webb, *Industrial Democracy*, 598–99.

76. Ely, *Socialism and Social Reform*, 233–34; *Social Aspects of Christianity*, 124; cf. Rader, *Ely*, 102–3; Ross, "Socialism and American Liberalism," 41–42. For the differing perspectives of Green and Sidgwick on this issue, see above, pp. 129–30, 184.

77. Rauschenbusch, *Christianity and the Social Crisis*, 247–50; *Christianizing the Social Order*, 363–64.

78. Ibid., 353. For the discussion of James, see above, pp. 135–36.

79. Rauschenbusch, *A Theology for the Social Gospel*, 223 ff.

80. Ely, *Socialism and Social Reform*, 7, 179; and cf. *French and German Socialism*, 28; and Rader, *Ely*, 98 ff.

81. Bernstein, *Zur Geschichte und Theorie des Sozialismus*, 382–83. See also the incisive discussion of this issue, and the reasons behind Bernstein's strategic retreat in his later work from the position expressed in the quoted passages, in Meyer, "Wissenschaft und Sozialismus," Heimann and Meyer, eds., *Bernstein*, 268–72; and cf. Carl Schorske, *German Social Democracy, 1905–1917: The Development of the Great Schism* (Cambridge, Mass., 1955), 18. Colletti, *From Rousseau to Lenin*, 108, disputes the adequacy of the theoretical underpinnings Bernstein tried to provide for his idea of a coalition across classes. For a more sympathetic discussion, see Cole, *The Second International*, 278; and on the Fabians, McBriar, *Fabian Socialism*, 6–7, 100–1. This debate is placed in the context of later challenges by Soviet and Eastern European scholars in Bergounioux and Manin, *La Social-démocratie ou le compromis*, 56–60.

82. Jaurès, *Studies in Socialism*, 103; "Socialisme et liberté," 481–82. The tendency of French scholars to emphasize Jaurès's more militant statements on behalf of the working class, statements suggesting he had little faith in the bourgeoisie, appear to me to reflect more the tensions in contemporary French politics than Jaurès's own sentiments. For an example of this inclination, see *Jaurès et la classe ouvrière*, especially the introduction by Madeleine Rébérioux. I do not dispute Jaurès's allegiance to the cause of the French working class nor his hostility to capitalism, but I believe his political vision was broader than that of some of his followers.

83. B. and S. Webb, *Industrial Democracy*, 818–19, 823–25; *The Consumers Co-operative Movement* (London, 1921), 448–62.

84. The guild socialism championed by G. D. H. Cole served as the principal target of the Webbs' analysis. In *The Second International*, 213–18, Cole critically analyzes the Webbs' treatment of guild socialism and concludes that "they never worked out any clear plans of administrative control." That judgment is reasonable, but the guild socialists were no more successful in devising a solution for this conflict. Securing a balance of power between the interests of producers and consumers has continued to be a difficult problem in socialist theory. For a more thorough exposition of Cole's guild socialism, see his *Guild Socialism Restated* (London, 1919). Elsewhere Cole has even more explictly indicated the similarities between his position and the Webbs'. In an essay entitled "Beatrice Webb as an Economist" published in *The Webbs and Their Work*, he reflected on his relationship with the Webbs and assessed the tension between expertise and democracy in their thinking:

> In my cocksureness, I [at first] very thoroughly misunderstood Beatrice Webb, regarding her and Sidney as the quintessential representatives of bureaucratic collectivism,

and brushing aside the large concessions made in *Industrial Democracy* and their other writings to the claims of the producers. I was not, I think, *wholly* wrong; for the Webbs, both in their dislike of disorder and untidy thinking and in their opposition to Syndicalism, were disposed in those days to lean over towards bureaucracy. But it took me a long time to discover that, at all events in Beatrice Webb, this leaning over involved an effort, because her natural sympathies were on the side of voluntary organisation, of producers as well as of consumers, and she was very much alive to the need for variety and diversity of experiment in social structure. Gradually, I came to understand better her fundamental point of view, and to appreciate how much closer my own was to it than I had for a long period believed (280).

85. Bernstein, *Evolutionary Socialism*, 117–18.

86. B. and S. Webb, *Industrial Democracy*, 597–98.

87. Ely, *Socialism and Social Reform*, 224; Bernstein, *Evolutionary Socialism*, 115–16.

88. Jaurès's articles originally appeared in *La Revue socialiste* from March to May, 1896; they are reprinted in vol. 3 of his *Oeuvres*; the quotations are from 346–48. Even Goldberg, who generally gives Jaurès the benefit of the doubt, concedes at the end of a discussion of these articles in *Jaurès*, 134–36, that "it would be tendentious to deny that they raised more questions than they answered." Another careful treatment of Jaurès's ideas on this subject, which concentrates on a speech given in Aug., 1895, entitled "Esquisse provisoire de l'organisation socialiste" (reprinted in *Oeuvres*, 1: *Etudes socialistes*, 338–72), is Madeleine Réberioux, "Jaurès et l'avenir," *Bulletin d'études jaurèsiennes* 78 (July–Sept., 1980): 3–12. See also Boitel, *Les Idées liberales de Jaurès*, 170–72, for a sampling of Jaurès's comments on cooperatives, planning commissions, and their integration in a socialist state.

89. Ely, *Socialism and Social Reform*, 351; *The Social Law of Service*, 127–28, 140; and *Social Aspects of Christianity*, 129–30.

90. On Wisconsin progressivism, see McCarthy, *The Wisconsin Idea*; Thelen, *The New Citizenship*; and J. David Hoeveler, Jr., "The University and the Social Gospel"; all of whom emphasize the importance of Ely.

91. While I will have more to say about the literature of progressivism in Chapter Nine, I am referring here primarily to the work of David Thelen, *The New Citizenship*; Richard L. McCormick, *From Realignment to Reform: Political Change in New York State, 1893–1910* (Ithaca, 1981); idem, "The Party Period and Public Policy: An Exploratory Hypothesis," *Journal of American History* 66 (1979): 279–98; idem, "The Discovery that Business Corrupts Politics: A Reappraisal of the Origins of Progressivism," *American Historical Review* 86 (1981): 247–74; and John D. Buenker's essay in *Progressivism*. In their recognition of the gap separating the intentions of reform-minded intellectuals from the steps taken by politicians more interested in preserving power than effecting change, these studies represent an advance on the provocative but less carefully nuanced work of Samuel P. Hays and Robert H. Wiebe. Cf. in particular Hays, "The Politics of Reform in Municipal Government in the Progressive Era," "The Social Analysis of American Political History," and "Political Parties and the Community-Society Continuum," all reprinted in his *American Political History as Social Analysis* (Knoxville, 1980); and Wiebe, *The Search for Order, 1877–1920* (New York, 1967).

92. Ely's advocacy of compulsory labor arbitration indicated his enthusiasm for administrative solutions. Despite opposition from many labor unions as well as from conservative business groups, the idea of arbitration intrigued many reformers because it placed authority in the hands of presumably disinterested experts and removed the issue from labor and management. See Ely, "Arbitration," *North American Review* 143 (1886): 317–28; and on the larger question of arbitration in American law, see Keller, *Affairs of State*, 399–401. Ely eventually became quite critical of Wisconsin progressivism, breaking with Robert M. La Follette, significantly, because he came to believe that La Follette was too confident that the people could govern themselves fairly and efficiently. See Rader, *Ely*, 190–91.

93. S. Webb, "Historic," *Fabian Essays in Socialism*, 52–53.

94. B. and S. Webb, *Industrial Democracy*, 822–23. See also B. Webb's diary entry dated Jan. 25, 1901, discussed above on p. 229; and B. and S. Webb, *Constitution*, 352.

95. Bernstein, *Evolutionary Socialism*, 143–50; Bernstein to Kautsky, Dec. 16, 1927, Bernstein papers.

96. On the question of Fabian influence, see McBriar, *Fabian Socialism*, 187–345; Hobsbawm, "The Fabians Reconsidered," *Labouring Men*, 250 ff.; Gilbert, *National Insurance*, 15, 45–46; Searle, *The Quest for Efficiency*, 250–56; and Thompson, *Socialists, Liberals, and Labour*, 138–42.

97. Cf. Schorske, *German Social Democracy*, 322–30; Gay, *Democratic Socialism*, xi; Kocka, *White Collar Workers*, 53; and the comments by Heimann, Steinberg, Meyer, and Vilmar in Heimann and Meyer, eds., *Bernstein*, 438–44, 454–56. In *Germany 1866–1945*, 269, Gordon A. Craig writes:

> In the last decade of the nineteenth century trade-unionism was the strongest of those forces that were changing the Social Democratic party, for all practical purposes, into a reformist democratic movement. The ability of union leaders to make agreements with representatives of industry and commerce, like the participation by representatives of labor in communal health, housing, and unemployment boards, and the collaboration between Socialist deputies and representatives of middle-class parties in town councils and provincial assemblies, was palpable evidence that neither the working class nor the political class that represented it was a force bent on the destruction of the existing political system. There were any number of examples to prove the opposite, like the effective coalition between the socialist and liberal parties in the Badenese Landtag. It was a tragedy for Germany—and the word, all things considered, is not too strong—that the ruling forces in Germany in the 1890s failed, or refused, to recognize this fact, preferring to portray the threat of socialism as Bismarck had done.

The resistance of the SPD to revisionism was the consequence of that refusal, and its rejection of reformism the other side of that tragedy.

98. Rauschenbusch, *Christianizing the Social Order*, 328, 272.

99. Rauschenbusch, *Christianity and the Social Crisis*, 408, 253; see also 70–71; and "Dogmatic and Practical Socialism," 35.

100. Jaurès, in *La Dépêche de Toulouse*, Jan. 1, 1891, quoted in Goldberg, *Jaurès*, 79. Jaurès expressed his thoughts about religion and capitalism in a long essay left substantially unpublished until it appeared as *La Question religieuse et le socialisme*. On Jaurès's attitude toward religion, see also Lucien Goldmann, "La Question religieuse et le socialisme," *Bulletin d'études jaurèsiennes* 1 (June, 1960): 7–12.

101. Rauschenbusch, *Christianity and the Social Crisis*, 420–21; and cf. this passage from "The Contribution of Socialism to the New Social Feeling," an undated lecture in the Rauschenbusch papers: "I am exceedingly conservative in my expectations about the future of socialism. I should regard it as miraculous if the movement realized all that it now hopes to realize. . . . But I feel very sure that for a long time to come the demand of the wisest and most patriotic men in our country will be for more, and still more, steps in the direction of socialism" (20–21). Critics contrasting Rauschenbusch's position to the more self-consciously "realistic" stance of later neo-orthodox Protestant thinkers such as Reinhold Niebuhr often overlook this dimension of Rauschenbusch's thought. See for example Donald B. Meyer, *The Protestant Search for Political Realism: 1919–1941* (Berkeley, 1960).

102. *Le Matin*, April 8, 1907; *De la réalité du monde sensible*, 92.

103. Jaurès, "Léon Tolstoi," *La Revue socialiste*, March, 1911, 209.

Chapter 8. From Liberalism to Progressivism

1. Walter Lippmann, *Drift and Mastery* (New York, 1914), 152–53, 196.

2. On the use of the term "progressive" in Britain, see Emy, *Liberals, Radicals, and Social Politics*, 105–6; and Clarke, *Lancashire and the New Liberalism*, 397–98. On the founding of *The Progressive Review*, see Clarke, *Liberals and Social Democrats* (Cambridge, 1978), 57–58. On the "progressive" position in German politics and the formation of the *Fortschrittliche Volkspartei* in 1910, see Thomas Nipperdey, *Die Organisation der deutschen Parteien vor 1918* (Düsseldorf, 1961), 187 ff.; S. T. Robson, "Left-wing Liberalism in Germany, 1900–1919," Ph.D. diss., Oxford University, 1966, chap. 3; James Sheehan, *German Liberalism in the Nineteenth Century*, 258–71; Leonard Krieger, *The German Idea of Freedom*, 458–67; and Carl Schorske, *German Social Democracy, 1905–1917*, 151–55. Daniel T. Rodgers discusses the origins of the word "progressivism" in America in his essay "In Search of Progressivism," 127 n. 1. The association of Croly and Lippmann with Roosevelt's campaign is discussed in Charles Forcey, *The Crossroads of Liberalism: Croly, Weyl, Lippmann, and the Progressive Era, 1900–1925* (New York, 1961), 121–217; Ronald Steel, *Walter Lippmann and the American Century* (Boston, 1980), 58–66; and David W. Levy, *Herbert Croly of "The New Republic"* (Princeton, 1985), 136–41, 151–61. The changing vocabulary of *The New Republic* is examined in Richard Crockett, "American Liberalism and the Atlantic World, 1916–1917," *American Studies* 11 (1977): 123–43. The metamorphosis of the term *progressist* is recounted in Zeldin, *Politics and Anger*, 19; see also Jean-Thomas Nordmann, *Histoire des radicaux, 1820–1973* (Paris, 1974), 110.

3. Léon Bourgeois, *Solidarité*, 7th ed. (1896; Paris, 1912), 6; *La Solidarité humaine* (Paris, 1914), 10.

4. Despite his central role in the political and intellectual history of the Third Republic, there is no adequate biography of Bourgeois. Maurice Hamburger, *Léon Bourgeois* (Paris, 1932), is standard, but it is largely uncritical. It may be supplemented by Paul Loppin, *Léon Bourgeois* (Paris, 1964), an equally appreciative, somewhat more personal memoir. On Bourgeois's role in the Carmaux strike, cf. Michelle Perrot, *Les Ouvriers en grève, 1871–1890* (Paris, 1974), 702; and Roland Trempé, *Les Mineurs de Carmaux, 1848–1914*, 2: 645–46, 672–74. Both Perrot and Trempé emphasize the workers' "profound respect" for Bourgeois's efforts as a mediator. The new generation of republicans is discussed in Mayeur, *Le Débuts de la IIIᵉ République*, 210–11; and in Nordmann, *Histoire des radicaux*, 106–7.

5. The best account of the Bourgeois ministry is in Kayser, *Les Grandes Batailles du radicalisme*, 223–43. See also Mayeur, *Le Débuts de la IIIᵉ République*, 213–17; and Hamburger, *Bourgeois*, 79–212, which reprints many of the exchanges between Bourgeois and his opponents. Bourgeois's speech of April 30, 1896, was printed in the *Journal officiel* of the Chamber of Deputies, 1896, 2: 761–64; it was published later that year as a pamphlet by the Ligue pour la Défense du Suffrage Universel. On the politics of ministerial power, see the instructive discussion in Zeldin, *Politics and Anger*, 223–37. The most thorough treatment of Jaurès's support of the Bourgeois ministry is in Goldberg, *Jaurès*, 153–67.

6. Bourgeois, *Solidarité*, 7th ed., 14–15.

7. The best discussion of the diffusion of solidarist ideas is a series of articles by J. E. S. Hayward: "Educational Pressure Groups and the Indoctrination of the Radical Ideology of Solidarism, 1895–1914," *International Review of Social History* 8 (1963): 1–17; "The Official Social Philosophy of the French Third Republic: Léon Bourgeois and Solidarism," *International Review of Social History* 6 (1961): 19–48; and "Solidarity: The Social History of an Idea in Nineteenth-Century France," *International Review of Social History* 4 (1959): 261–84. Reports of the proceedings at various conferences devoted to solidarity include the account of the *Congrès international de l'education sociale* (1900) and the *Procès verbal sommaire* (1902), published by the Ministère du Commerce et de l'Industrie; *L'Ecole des Hautes Etudes sociales,*

1900–1910; and Bourgeois et al., *Essai d'une philosophie de la solidarité* (Paris, 1902). Although Durkheim shared many of Bourgeois's political inclinations, the foundation and aim of his sociology differ too decisively from the ideas discussed in this study for him to be included here. He considered pragmatism too unsystematic, too much a "form of irrationalism," and his own attempt to make a science of sociology ran counter to the efforts of the thinkers I am examining. For a brilliant analysis of Durkheim's ideas that reveals their fundamentally different, counterpragmatic thrust, see Steven Lukes, *Emile Durkheim: His Life and Work. A Historical and Critical Study* (New York, 1973), esp. 399, 404, 412–34, 448–49, 486–96. In 1916, Dewey revealingly criticized the "Durkheim school of collective mind" because "it reduces the role of mind to that of beholding and recording the operations of man." Durkheim's aim, in short, was insufficiently instrumentalist, and his method too positivistic, to satisfy Dewey. See "The Need for Social Psychology," *MW*, 10: 53–63. A recent study that examines in some detail the ideas of Durkheim and several others associated with solidarist theory, especially Célestin Bouglé and Léon Duguit, is Logue, *From Philosophy to Sociology*. Although Logue discusses Bourgeois only briefly, his analysis provides an account of the development of French thought that emphasizes Fouillée's pivotal role and is thus in certain respects complementary to my own. His book replaces the overly schematic treatment in John A. Scott, *Republican Ideas and the Liberal Tradition in France, 1870–1914*.

8. On the crisis of 1899, see Kayser, *Les Grandes Batailles du radicalisme*, 284–87; Nordmann, *Histoire des radicaux*, 115–19; and Goldberg, *Jaurès*, 249–56. Jaurès's comment concerning Bourgeois appeared in *La Petite République*, June 23, 1899. Critical assessments of the achievements of the Radical ministries of René Waldeck-Rousseau (1899–1902) and Emile Combes (1902–1905) are available in Madeleine Rebérioux, *La République radicale?*, 42–116; and Zeldin, *Politics and Anger*, 276–334. On the ill-fated career of another champion of the income tax and international accommodation, Joseph Caillaux, see Rudolph Binion, *Defeated Leaders: The Political Fate of Caillaux, Jouvenel, and Tardieu* (New York, 1960) 17–116.

9. The most thorough account of Bourgeois's involvement in foreign affairs and his role in the creation of the League of Nations is Hamburger, *Bourgeois*, 213–59. On the Hague conferences, see F. S. L. Lyons, *Internationalism in Europe, 1815–1914* (Leyden, 1963).

10. *The Progressive Review*, Dec., 1896, 283–85.

11. For biographical information on Hobhouse, see the work by his friend John A. Hobson and his student Morris Ginsberg, *L. T. Hobhouse: His Life and Work* (London, 1931). Stefan Collini, *Liberalism and Sociology: L. T. Hobhouse and Political Argument in England, 1880–1914* (Cambridge, 1979), provides a solid analysis, and I have followed his account of Hobhouse closely. Peter F. Clarke, *Liberals and Social Democrats*, is a brilliant and sensitive group portrait of Hobhouse, Hobson, Graham Wallas, J. L. and Barbara Hammond, and a supporting cast including various other Fabians and progressives. On Hobhouse's early years and his Oxford experiences, see Hobson and Ginsberg, 18–36; Collini, 51–61; and Clarke, 10–11, 22–27. Hobhouse's letter to Mary Howard is quoted in Hobson and Ginsberg, 27.

12. Hobhouse quoted in Hobson and Ginsberg, *L. T. Hobhouse*, 26. For his intellectual autobiography, see the introduction to his essay "The Philosophy of Development" (1924), reprinted in Hobhouse, *Sociology and Philosophy: A Centenary Collection of Essays and Articles*, ed. Sydney Caine and Morris Ginsberg (Cambridge, Mass., 1966), 296.

13. S. to B. Webb, May 21, 1892, in *The Letters of B. and S. Webb*, 1: 413; B. Webb, *Our Partnership*, 92. See also the discussion of Hobhouse's *The Labour Movement* (London, 1897) in Clarke, *Liberals and Social Democrats*, 45–46; and esp. in Collini, *Liberalism and Sociology*, 61–71.

14. Peter Weiler, in "The New Liberalism of L. T. Hobhouse," *Victorian Studies* 16 (1972): 141–61, pointed out accurately that "almost nothing" had been written about Hobhouse. That is no longer true. In addition to the studies by Collini and Clarke cited above, examinations of

Hobhouse's ideas include C. M. Griffin, "L. T. Hobhouse and the Idea of Harmony," *Journal of the History of Ideas* 35 (1974): 647–61; George Mariz, "L. T. Hobhouse as a Theoretical Sociologist," *Albion* 6 (1974): 307–19; and Michael Freeden, *The New Liberalism: An Ideology of Social Reform* (Oxford, 1978), which focuses primarily on Hobson and Hobhouse. These interpreters disagree whether Hobhouse should be categorized as an empiricist or an idealist, whether his ideas rested on a metaphysical conception of progress or a careful study of history, and whether he was more influenced by socialism or liberalism. It is a central argument of this study that such distinctions are misleading when applied to theorists such as Hobhouse, since he aimed to break down—or break out of—these categories by conceptualizing philosophy and politics in a radically different way.

15. Hobhouse to J. L. Hammond, Nov. 26, 1901, quoted in Collini, *Liberalism and Sociology*, 235; J. S. Mackenzie, review of Hobhouse, *The Theory of Knowledge*, in *Mind* n.s. 5 (1896): 396–410.

16. Hobhouse, *The Theory of Knowledge: A Contribution to Some Problems of Logic and Metaphysics* (London, 1896), 59, 45 n. 1, 558–76, 623.

17. Hobhouse, *Development and Purpose: An Essay towards a Philosophy of Evolution* (London, 1913), 368. Collini points out in *Liberalism and Sociology*, 241, that *Development and Purpose* reveals three aspects of Hobhouse's development: "First, the extent to which his theory rested upon a teleological conception of reality which was heavily Idealist in origin; secondly, the way in which this involved something of a rapprochement with religion; and thirdly, how it also accentuated the tendency of Hobhouse's theory generally to concentrate on the potential for harmony at the expense of analysing the actuality of conflict." For accounts that emphasize the empiricist dimensions of Hobhouse's epistemology, see Weiler, "The New Liberalism of L. T. Hobhouse," 142–43; and Mariz, "L. T. Hobhouse as a Theoretical Sociologist," 309–13. Dewey's annotations in his copy of Hobhouse's *Theory of Knowledge*, which he acquired in 1900, evidence his close reading and his favorable assessment of Hobhouse's arguments; it is in the Dewey papers. James also owned a "much marked" copy of Hobhouse's *Theory of Knowledge*, according to Perry, but its whereabouts is unknown. See "William James's Sources" in the James papers.

18. Hobhouse, "Faith and the Will to Believe," *Proceedings of the Aristotelian Society* 4 (1904): 91–109.

19. James to Hobhouse, Aug. 12, 1904, in *Letters of William James*, 2: 207–9. In a letter to J. C. F. Schiller, James was less charitable in discussing Hobhouse's essay. He pointed out that he considered Hobhouse's position quite close to his and Schiller's, but then he asked, "What is the virus, the insane root, the screw loose (or what?), that condemns these fellows to judicial blindness in their reading?" Hobhouse's "travesty" of the will to believe notwithstanding, James admitted that in "all its positive contentions" he found Hobhouse's article "very *simpatico*." Perry, *James*, 2: 504.

20. Hobhouse, "The Philosophy of Development," *Sociology and Philosophy*, 297–331.

21. C. P. Scott's letter to Arthur Sidgwick, Nov. 20, 1896, is quoted in Collini, *Liberalism and Sociology*, 80. On Hobhouse's activities as a political journalist in Manchester and London, see Collini, 79–95; and Clarke, *Liberals and Social Democrats*, 62–74, 77–82, 100–4, 109–18. He made his reputation as a sociologist with *Mind in Evolution* (London, 1901) and *Morals in Evolution: A Study in Comparative Ethics*, 7th ed., ed. Morris Ginsberg (1906; London, 1951), and it is these books, with their focus on stages of social development and their apparent affinities with the grand visions of Comte, Spencer, and Lester Ward, that cause sociologists to treat Hobhouse as a rather naive theorist of cosmic evolution, an ancestor whom they would just as soon forget. Works discussing Hobhouse in his role as the father of British sociology include Geoffrey Hawthorne, *Enlightenment and Despair: A History of Sociology* (Cambridge, 1976); Philip Abrams, *The Origins of British Sociology*; W. Warren Wagar, *Good Tidings: The Belief in*

Progress from Darwin to Marcuse (Bloomington, Ind., 1972); and Robert Nisbet, *History of the Idea of Progress* (New York, 1980). This interpretation is accurate as a description of part of Hobhouse's *oeuvre*, and especially suits *Development and Purpose*. But Hobhouse's conceptions of harmony and progress, as I will indicate in the next section of this chapter, resembled the ideas of Aristotle and Dewey more than those of Spencer and Comte. Whether Hobhouse conceived of progress as an inevitable consequence of the necessity of cosmic purpose to realize its ends, or whether he thought progress derived instead from the conscious efforts of individuals seeking to solve problems, is a more difficult question to answer than some of Hobhouse's sociological interpreters assume.

22. In *The History of European Liberalism* (Oxford, 1927), 155–56, Guido de Ruggiero characterized Hobhouse's *Liberalism* as the "best formulation of the new English liberalism of the twentieth century." In *The Marxists*, C. Wright Mills agreed, calling it "the best twentieth-century statement of liberal ideas I know." The book's impact and its legacy are discussed by Alan P. Grimes in his introduction to the most recent reprint of *Liberalism* (1911; rpt. New York, 1971), 1–8.

23. Collini discusses Hobhouse's prolific, but for the purposes of this analysis less important, production after the outbreak of World War I in *Liberalism and Sociology*, 147–234. Hobhouse expressed his enthusiasm for international arbitration in *Morals in Evolution*, 1: 278–79. His letter to Margaret Llewellyn Davies, written as he was preparing a revised edition of *Development and Purpose* in early 1927, is quoted in Hobson and Ginsberg, *L. T. Hobhouse*, 259. James's letter to his friend Tom Ward is discussed on p. 64 above.

24. Hobhouse's review appeared in the *Nation*, May 14, 1910, 246–47.

25. His friend Graham Wallas wrote in *The New Statesman*, April 25, 1931, that Hobhouse, "with his very human restlessness and fits of depression, was the kind of saint which modern civilisation most requires."

26. "The Progressive Movement Abroad, I: The United States," *The Progressive Review*, Jan., 1897, 359–61; Hobhouse, "The New Spirit in America," *The Contemporary Review* 100 (1911): 6.

27. This brief portrait of a complicated phenomenon relies primarily on Rodgers, "In Search of Progressivism"; McCormick, "The Discovery that Business Corrupts Politics"; Morton Keller, "Anglo-American Politics, 1900–1930, in Anglo-American Perspective: A Case Study in Comparative History," *Comparative Studies in Society and History* 22 (1980): 458–77; Buenker's contribution to *Progressivism*; and David M. Kennedy, "Progressivism: An Overview," *Historian* 37 (1975): 453–68. Viewing progressivism as a series of shifting coalitions helps to make sense of the differences between rival schools of interpretation. Varieties of the interpretation emphasizing social control, or efficiency, as the central impulse of progressivism include Hays, *American Political History as Social Analysis*; Gabriel Kolko, *The Triumph of Conservatism* (New York, 1963); Wiebe, *The Search for Order*; and James Weinstein, *The Corporate Ideal in the Liberal State, 1900–1918* (Boston, 1968). The antimonopoly wing of progressivism is mistaken for the entire movement in the influential analysis of Hartz, *The Liberal Tradition in America*. In a different but complementary brand of analytical synecdoche, the role of "status anxiety" in accounting for the participation of old American elites in American progressivism is emphasized in Richard Hofstadter, *The Age of Reform* (New York, 1955). This dimension of progressivism receives a different twist in the contributions of John C. Burnham and Robert Crunden to *Progressivism*. Thelen, *The New Citizenship*, and John D. Buenker, *Urban Liberalism and Progressive Reform* (New York, 1973) emphasize the importance of the idea of the common good as a motive in progressive reform. One further characteristic of progressivism that complicates its interpretation is the intermingling of these various reformist streams. Historians have gained greater clarity from the careful separation of different groups with different goals, but the progressives themselves did not draw such careful distinctions

between social reform and social control, or between opposition to monopoly and opposition to liquor. Any account of progressivism pretending to neatness thus distorts the cluttered reality it attempts to explain.

28. There is no collection of Croly's personal papers. Among the groups of letters scattered around American libraries, the most useful are those in the Learned Hand papers at the Harvard Law School and the Felix Frankfurter papers in the Library of Congress. There is a fascinating portrait of Croly's early years in the memorial by Edmund Wilson, which originally appeared in the issue of *The New Republic* dedicated to Croly after his death on May 17, 1930, in *The Shores of Light* (New York, 1952), 476–84. For a thorough account of Croly's family and his years at Harvard, see Levy, *Croly*, 3–71. Both of Croly's parents were celebrities of a sort. His father was a journalist who edited the most important Democratic party paper in New York, the *New York World*, from 1863 to 1872. He later founded and edited the *Real Estate Record and Builder's Guide*, to which he contributed a regular column on any topic of interest to him (i.e., almost anything), aptly entitled "Our Prophetic Department." Croly's mother, under the pseudonym "Jenny June," was a syndicated columnist who, in her commentaries on fashion and social topics, covered as broad a range as her husband did. In addition to his courses with Palmer and Royce, Croly also enrolled in a course with William James on logic and psychology. It might be too much to claim that James's influence was as decisive at this stage of Croly's intellectual development as it was to become later. After all, Croly also completed a course in forensics to help overcome his extraordinary shyness, and a course in economics to help him understand the idea of laissez-faire, and neither seems to have had any effect on him.

29. Croly, *Real Estate Record and Builder's Guide*, Aug. 30, 1890, 272; Alvin S. Johnson, *A Pioneer's Progress: An Autobiography* (New York, 1972), 241. The years between Croly's first sojourn at Harvard and his emergence as a major figure in 1909, when *The Promise of American Life* appeared, have previously puzzled historians. Although Levy's chapter on this period in *Croly* (72–95) is entitled "The Blank Years," he has unearthed a great deal of revealing information, and my discussion here—although not all of my interpretations—follows his account closely. Croly's father's strong presence, and his mother's almost total absence, in his writings from and about his early years, his painful liberation from his father's carefully instilled beliefs, his psychological collapse, his vocational crisis, and his overwhelming shyness throughout his life, all point tantalizingly toward the plausible, perhaps even predictable, psychological explanation of Croly's career that Levy resolutely refuses to offer in his biography.

30. Croly to Felix Frankfurter, June 29 and July 14, 1913, Frankfurter papers, Library of Congress. As if to accentuate how tortured this rationalization was, the two sentences of Croly's letter explaining his change of career plans to Frankfurter uncharacteristically contain a dozen crossed-out words and letters, most notably in the several appearances of the word "philosophy," which Croly's pen stumbled over repeatedly. It should also be noted that Croly had an ulterior motive: he was trying to persuade Frankfurter to remain in New York on the staff of *The New Republic*.

31. Croly's autobiographical fragment, a typescript with his handwritten comments, is in the Frankfurter papers, Library of Congress. The quoted passages are from 13–14.

32. On this theme, see the following essays by Croly, all of which appeared in the *Architectural Record*: "American Artists and their Public," Feb., 1901, 258; "The New World and the New Art," June, 1902, 149–51; "New York as the American Metropolis," March, 1903, 193–206; "Democracy and Fine Art," Sept., 1903, 225–32; and "The Architect in Recent American Fiction," Feb., 1905, 137–39. In *Croly*, 84–93, Levy argues persuasively that these articles, published under the pseudonym A. C. David, were actually written by Croly.

33. Croly to Frankfurter, July 14, 1913, Frankfurter papers; *Outlook*, Dec. 4, 1909, 788–89; and "At the Parting of the Ways," *Outlook*, April 16, 1910, 830–31; Croly to Learned Hand, Dec. 5, 1909; and Hand to Croly, Feb. 6, 1911, both in the Learned Hand papers, Harvard

University Law School. For comprehensive lists of reviews of *The Promise of American Life*, and of historians' estimates of its importance, see Levy, *Croly*, 132–36.

34. Perhaps the most influential attempt to underplay Croly's influence on Roosevelt is Eric Goldman, *Rendezvous with Destiny: A History of Modern American Reform* (New York, 1952), 159–61; for a similar account, which suggests that Croly "promised to American life little that Roosevelt had not already offered," see John Morton Blum, *The Republican Roosevelt* (Cambridge, Mass., 1954), 122. This view threatens to become orthodox, since it also appears in the splendid dual biography by John Milton Cooper, Jr., *The Warrior and the Priest: Woodrow Wilson and Theodore Roosevelt* (Cambridge, Mass., 1983), 145–49. For a conflicting interpretation, see 136–41 of *Croly*, in which Levy demonstrates conclusively what some have doubted—viz., that TR actually read the *Promise*—and offers a persuasive account of Croly and Roosevelt's similar purposes and reciprocal influence.

35. Croly to Learned Hand, Nov. 28? 1912, Hand papers.

36. Croly, *The Promise of American Life*, ed. John William Ward, The American Heritage Series (1909; Indianapolis, 1965), 453–54. David W. Noble, first in "Herbert Croly and American Progressive Thought," *Western Political Quarterly* 7 (1954): 537–53, and then in *The Paradox of Progressive Thought* (Minneapolis, 1958), emphasized the importance of Hegel in shaping Croly's idea of the nation state. Charles Forcey, in *The Crossroads of Liberalism*, emphasized James's influence on Croly. Eric Goldman, in *Rendezvous with Destiny*, asserted that Croly decided while he was still at Harvard that Comte "was a pompous fool"; Arthur Schlesinger, Jr., adopted a similar position in his introduction to the edition of the *Promise* published in 1965 by Harvard University Press. Levy challenges these interpretations in *Croly*, 119, arguing that "the origins of *The Promise of American Life* are to be found in the social, political, and economic thought of Auguste Comte as that thought was applied to American conditions by David Goodman Croly." While he sensibly acknowledges the importance of other sources, such as James, Royce, Santayana, and Charles Eliot Norton, Levy seems to me too intent on establishing the primacy of David Croly's influence to pay sufficient attention to those ideas in the *Promise* that are inconsistent with positivism. Croly rejected any notion of scientific laws and a rigid scheme of historical progress, both of which were at the heart of Comte's philosophy but play no part in Croly's analysis. In "My Aim in *The Promise of American Life*: Why I Wrote My Latest Book," *World's Work*, June, 1910, Croly himself emphasized Robert Grant's novel *Unleavened Bread* (New York, 1900), which concerned the fate of a sensitive architect in an insensitive world. Given Croly's preoccupation with this theme in the articles cited in n. 32 above, I think his account merits more credence than Levy gives it. As Levy points out, Croly did admit in a letter he wrote in 1916 that "many of the leading trains of thought" in the *Promise* could be traced back to his father. But when Levy contends that this letter represents Croly's efforts to look "most carefully and searchingly" for the book's origins, and that it therefore reveals both "the transitory influence of Grant's *Unleavened Bread*" and "the true source of opinions," he seems to me guilty of special pleading. As in the case of Hobhouse's debts to Mill and Green, there seems to me no reason to deny the evidence that Croly's ideas were shaped by a variety of sources that were in no way consistent with one another. Croly's dedication of the book "to the memory of David Goodman Croly" was an act of understandable filial piety; it does not mean that the *Promise* should be read as David Croly's last book rather than Herbert Croly's first. Like most intellectuals of his generation, Croly's loyalties were divided, and the *Promise* illustrates the depth of that division.

37. Croly to Theodore Roosevelt, Nov. 5, 1914, Theodore Roosevelt papers, Library of Congress.

38. Croly, *Progressive Democracy* (New York, 1914), 378.

39. Ibid., 25, 178; and cf. James, "Pragmatism's Conception of Truth," *Pragmatism*, 95–113. It is instructive that those historians who disagree about the most important influence on the

Promise are unanimous in emphasizing the role of James and Dewey in *Progressive Democracy*. Cf. Noble, *The Paradox of Progressive Thought*, 66–77; Forcey, *The Crossroads of Liberalism*, 155–60; and Levy, *Croly*, 176–82.

40. Croly, *Progressive Democracy*, 358, 424–25; and cf. 35–37, 154.

41. On the founding of *The New Republic*, see Johnson, *Pioneer's Progress*, 233, for his recollection of the tale as Croly told it to him; and cf. the accounts in Forcey, *The Crossroads of Liberalism*, 169–74; W. A. Swanberg, *Whitney Father, Whitney Heiress* (New York, 1980), 339–43; and Levy, *Croly*, 185–89.

42. Croly to Learned Hand, Jan. 5, 1914, Hand papers. On Lippmann, the most valuable source is the Walter Lippmann papers in the Sterling Library, Yale University, which contains not only correspondence and diaries but also a complete bibliography of writings by and about Lippmann. Of the many studies of Lippmann and his career, the most valuable are the fine portrait by Steel, *Walter Lippmann and the American Century*; and Forcey, *Crossroads of Liberalism*. Summaries of Lippmann's books are presented in Benjamin F. Wright, *Five Public Philosophies of Walter Lippmann* (Austin, 1973); his ideas are analyzed perceptively in David A. Hollinger, "Science and Anarchy: Walter Lippmann's *Drift and Mastery*," *American Quarterly* 39 (1977): 463–75; and in a series of essays by Heinz Eulau, "Mover and Shaker: Walter Lippmann as a Young Man," *Antioch Review* 11 (1951): 291–312; "Man Against Himself: Walter Lippmann's Years of Doubt," *American Quarterly* 4 (1952): 291–304; "Wilsonian Idealist: Walter Lippmann Goes to War," *Antioch Review* 14 (1954): 87–108; and "From *Public Opinion* to *Public Philosophy*: Walter Lippmann's Classic Reexamined," *American Journal of Economics and Sociology* 15 (1956): 439–51. Lippmann's essay on James, "An Open Mind: William James," appeared in *Everybody's*, Dec., 1910. On Lippmann's childhood and his experiences at Harvard, see Steel, *Lippmann*, 3–22.

43. Lippmann's rapid ascent was due in part to his ability to ingratiate himself with older men who thought they saw in him a younger version of themselves. His correspondence with Lincoln Steffens is typical. Seeking a position with Steffens, he vowed, "There is no kind of work that appeals to me as much as yours does," and when it was all over, he gushed, "Whenever I understand a man, and like him, instead of hating him or ignoring him, it'll be your work. You've got into my blood, I think, and there'll be a little less bile in the world as a result." It is only the recurrence of this pattern that makes one skeptical about Lippmann's sincerity. See Lippman to Steffens, May 18, 1910, and April 17, 1911, Steffens papers, Butler Library, Columbia University. Lippmann's essay "Schenectady the Unwise" appeared in the *Call* on June 9, 1912; his letter to Wallas, July 31, 1912, is in the Lippmann papers.

44. Lippmann to Wallas, July 31 and Oct. 30, 1912, Lippmann papers; *A Preface to Politics* (1913; Ann Arbor, 1962), 29. On the cultural ferment of the prewar years, see Henry F. May, *The End of American Innocence: The First Years of Our Own Time, 1912–1917* (1959; rpt. New York, 1979); Arthur Frank Wertheim, *The New York Little Renaissance: Iconoclasm, Modernism, and Nationalism in American Culture, 1908–1917* (New York, 1976); and Leslie Fishbein, *Rebels in Bohemia: The Radicals of "The Masses," 1911–1917* (Chapel Hill, N.C., 1982).

45. Randolph Bourne to Dorothy Teall, June 14, 1915, Bourne papers, Butler Library, Columbia University. Bourne did not remain an admirer of Lippmann. See Paul Bourke, "Culture and the Status of Politics, 1910–1917: Studies in the Social Criticism of Herbert Croly, Walter Lippmann, Randolph Bourne, and Van Wyck Brooks," Ph.D. diss., University of Wisconsin, 1967; idem, "The Social Critics and the End of American Innocence," *Journal of American Studies* 3 (1969): 57–72; and idem, "The Status of Politics, 1909–1919: *The New Republic*, Randolph Bourne and Van Wyck Brooks," *Journal of American Studies* 8 (1974): 171–202; Lippmann, *Drift and Mastery*, 206–8.

46. Lippmann, *Drift and Mastery*, 274–75. See also Hollinger, "Science and Anarchy"; idem,

"The Problem of Pragmatism in American History," *Journal of American History* 67 (1980): 88–107; and for an instructive discussion of the significance of intersubjectivity and the ideal of a scientific community in these years, Thomas L. Haskell, "Professionalism *versus* Capitalism: R. H. Tawney, Emile Durkheim, and C. S. Peirce on the Disinterestedness of Professional Communities," in Haskell, ed., *The Authority of Experts: Studies in History and Theory* (Bloomington, Ind., 1984), 180–225.

47. Lippmann, *Drift and Mastery*, 295, 329, xii–xiii.

48. Harold Laski to Oliver Wendell Holmes, Jr., April 23, 1919, in *Holmes/Laski Letters*, ed. Mark DeWolfe Howe, abridged by Alger Hiss (New York, 1963), 148. Croly expressed his desire to make *The New Republic* "something like *The New Statesman*" in his letter to Randolph Bourne, June 3, 1914, Bourne papers. The quotation from the circular appears in Levy, *Croly*, 201; for an account of Croly's speech, see 216–17.

49. Croly to Learned Hand, March 7, 1914, Hand papers: "I am very much depressed at the idea of abandoning the quiet contemplative life of the last eight years. It has been thoughtful and it has been satisfying. I am much better fitted for it than I am for editing a weekly paper." Cf. Lippmann to Wallas, Oct. 22, 1914, Lippmann papers: "The preliminary work on the paper has been tremendously hard. I begin to see somewhat more clearly why administrators have not time to think, and why people who think often can't administer."

50. Lippmann, *Public Opinion* (1922; rpt. New York, 1965), 229; idem, "George Santayana—A Sketch," *The International*, Aug., 1911.

51. The critical literature on Weber is immense, and I can mention only a small fraction of it here. The most comprehensive bibliography is Constans Seyfarth and Gert Schmidt, *Max Weber Bibliographie: Eine Dokumentation der Sekundärliteratur* (Stuttgart, 1977). A recent survey of this literature in English is Guenther Roth's introduction to the revised edition of Reinhard Bendix, *Max Weber: An Intellectual Portrait* (1960; Berkeley, 1977), xiii–xxxvii. I am grateful for the assistance of Ingrid Wenzel-Stengel and Christiane Worth, who guided me through the voluminous files of the Weber archive in the Bavarian Academy of Sciences in Munich. Weber's own writings are currently being collected, under the direction of Horst Baier, in the mammoth *Max Weber Gesamtausgabe*, which is projected to include twenty-three volumes of Weber's published writings, eight volumes of his letters, and two volumes of his lecture notes. This edition will provide general access for the first time to Weber's correspondence, thanks to the Herculean labors of Manfred Schön, who is transcribing Weber's almost completely illegible scrawl. This will no doubt contribute to the even more rapid growth of Weber studies, which already threaten to extend beyond the reach of any single investigator. A detailed prospectus of the edition is available from the publisher, J. C. B. Mohr of Tübingen. The range of critical perspectives on Weber is nowhere better illustrated than in the transactions of the Fifteenth German Sociological Congress, held on the centenary of Weber's birth in 1964, which have been published in English as *Max Weber and Sociology Today*, ed. Otto Stammer, trans. Kathleen Morris (New York, 1971). The structure of that conference neatly reflected the principal scholarly disagreements surrounding Weber: papers were delivered by Talcott Parsons, the leading proponent of the view that Weber championed an objective, value-free sociology; by Raymond Aron, who examined Weber's commitment to power politics; and by Herbert Marcuse, who viewed Weber's treatment of bureaucratization and rationalization as an inadequate response to Marx's critique of bourgeois culture. The torrent of criticism greeting their papers, also included in this volume, suggests both the terms and the intensity of scholarly disagreements about Weber. A solid, brief introduction to Weber in English is "The Man and His Work" in *From Max Weber: Essays in Sociology*, ed. and trans. Hans Gerth and C. Wright Mills (1946; rpt. New York, 1976), 3–74. Bendix, *Max Weber*, provides competent summaries of all of Weber's writings. More detailed studies in English include, on Weber's methodology, Hans Henrik Bruun, *Science, Values, and Politics in Max Weber's Methodology* (Copenhagen, 1972); W. G. Runciman, *A*

Critique of Max Weber's Philosophy of Social Science (Cambridge, 1972); and Thomas Burger, *Max Weber's Theory of Concept Formation: History, Laws, and Ideal Types* (Durham, N.C., 1976), which places Weber in league with the neo-Kantian Heinrich Rickert. On Weber's politics, see J. P. Mayer, *Max Weber and German Politics*, 2nd ed. (London, 1964), which offers a spirited indictment of Weber; David Beetham, *Max Weber and the Theory of Modern Politics* (London, 1974), and Anthony Giddens, *Politics and Sociology in the Thought of Max Weber* (London, 1972), which are useful correctives to Mayer's excesses; and Wolfgang Mommsen, *The Age of Bureaucracy: Perspectives on the Political Sociology of Max Weber* (New York, 1974), which provides a more persuasive supplement to his earlier *Max Weber und die deutsche Politik, 1890–1920* (Tübingen, 1959) than does Karl Loewenstein, *Max Weber's Political Ideas in the Perspective of Our Time*, trans. Richard and Clara Winston (Amherst, 1966). Two recent studies that splendidly recover the multidimensional quality of Weber's *oeuvre* are Jeffrey C. Alexander, *Theoretical Logic in Sociology*, vol. 3: *The Classical Attempt at Synthesis: Max Weber* (Berkeley, 1983); and the essays by Wolfgang Schluchter in Schluchter and Guenther Roth, *Max Weber's Vision of History: Ethics and Methods* (Berkeley, 1979).

52. On this dispute see Fritz Ringer, *The Decline of the German Mandarins*; idem, "The German Academic Community," in Oleson and Voss, *Organization of Knowledge in Modern America*, 409–29; Fritz Stern, *The Politics of Cultural Despair*; and Walter Struve, *Elites Against Democracy: Leadership Ideals in Bourgeois Political Thought in Germany, 1890–1933* (Princeton, 1973).

53. Weber's letter about his response to Dilthey's *Einleitung in die Geisteswissenschaften* is quoted in Mayer, *Max Weber and German Politics*, 26. The standard biography of Weber is the study by his wife, Marianne Weber, *Max Weber: A Biography*, ed. and trans. Harry Zohn (1926; New York, 1975); the passages concerning Channing are quoted on p. 86. Marianne Weber's biography, despite its thoroughness, is not without its faults. It may be supplemented by Eduard Baumgarten, *Max Weber, Werk und Person* (Tübingen, 1964); and Arthur Mitzman, *The Iron Cage: An Historical Interpretation of Max Weber* (1969; New York, 1971), 309.

54. Weber quoted in Marianne Weber, *Weber*, 165, 187–88.

55. Weber's speech quoted in Beetham, *Weber*, 43–44.

56. Weber, "Der Nationalstaat und die Volkswirtschaftspolitik," in his *Gesammelte Politische Schriften* (hereafter cited as *GPS*), ed. Johannes Winckelmann (Tübingen, 1958), 1–25. See the discussions of this issue in Beetham, *Weber*, 36–44; and Mommsen, *Max Weber und die deutsche Politik*, 76–77.

57. Cf. the treatments of these events in Marianne Weber, *Weber*, 226–64; and Mitzman, *Iron Cage*, 148–63. Weber himself analyzed his breakdown in a manuscript that, according to Karl Jaspers and Eduard Baumgarten, was a masterpiece of detailed self-understanding. Unfortunately, Weber's followers feared the manuscript would be used by the Nazis to discredit him, and Marianne destroyed it in 1945. See Mitzman, 285.

58. Weber, *Roscher and Knies: The Logical Problems of Historical Economics*, ed. and trans. Guy Oakes (New York, 1975), 160–61, 176, and esp. 264–66. On the circumstances surrounding the writing of these essays, see Marianne Weber, *Weber*, 311–15. Oakes provides an insightful discussion of these issues in the conclusion to his introduction to this volume, 32–39. For the view that Weber was "not concerned with the problem" of knowledge, see Parsons, "Value Freedom and Objectivity," in Stammer, ed., *Max Weber and Sociology Today*, 39. This position has recently been defended by Roth in his introduction to Bendix, *Weber*, xiii–xiv, where he claims that Weber was "not interested" in an "epistemological buttressing . . . since he merely wanted to construct baseline concepts this side of epistemology and philosophy of science from which to get on with his empirical inquiries." While this view can be sustained at a certain level (see n. 62 below), it is clear that Weber intended in *Roscher and Knies* to accomplish precisely what Parsons and Roth contend he never tried to do. Indeed, as Thomas

Burger has pointed out exhaustively, if rather polemically, in *Max Weber's Theory of Concept Formation*, Weber took for granted a neo-Kantian epistemology that renders impossible the sort of sociology Parsons' followers want to construct. It may be argued that Weber's sociology suffers from its reliance on the neo-Kantianism he shared with Heinrich Rickert, and both Marxists and structuralists have assailed Weber on those grounds. See for example Jürgen Habermas's contribution to the discussion of Parsons' paper in Stammer, 59–60; and for a structuralist critique, see David Goddard, "Max Weber and the Objectivity of Social Science," *History and Theory* 12 (1973): 1–22. But asserting that Weber's failure to examine the conditions of knowledge reveals a positivistic inclination qualifying him as a forerunner of modern empirical sociology, which more properly traces its roots to Durkheim, seems to me historically inaccurate. For illuminating accounts of Weber's modified neo-Kantianism, see also Giddens, *Capitalism and Modern Social Theory*, 133–38; and J. E. T. Eldridge's introduction to Max Weber, *The Interpretation of Social Reality* (New York, 1971), 11–19.

59. Weber, "'Objectivity' in Social Science," in *The Methodology of the Social Sciences*, ed. and trans. Edward A. Shils and Henry A. Finch (Glencoe, Ill., 1949), 66, and see also 68–69.

60. Weber, *The Protestant Ethic and the Spirit of Capitalism*, trans. Talcott Parsons (New York, 1958), 183. A recent review of the literature surrounding this controversial study is Gordon Marshall, *In Search of the Spirit of Capitalism: An Essay on Max Weber's Protestant Ethic Thesis* (New York, 1982).

61. Weber, "Critical Studies in the Logic of the Cultural Sciences," *Methodology*, 124–25. Weber first developed this analysis in *Roscher and Knies*; see 192–93.

62. It is unfortunate that Weber never returned to epistemology after these forays; he might have left a legacy more useful to his followers than the destruction of the prevailing approaches of early twentieth-century social science. But Weber was an economist and historian by choice and a philosopher only by necessity. He complained, at the beginning of a lengthy methodological excursion, that such efforts are no more the precondition of successful scholarship than the study of anatomy is necessary for successful walking; indeed, in both cases such efforts may impede progress. Only if methodological work better equips the historian to "escape from the danger of being imposed on by a philosophically embellished dilettantism" can its pursuit be justified. Only substantive findings are valuable in any science, and "purely epistemological and methodological reflections have never played the crucial role in such developments." Philosophical disputes arise, and must be settled, only when a prevailing "'viewpoint'" becomes problematical, because "a revision of the logical forms in which the 'enterprise' has heretofore operated" then becomes necessary. Weber conceded that such a condition prevailed "unambiguously" in historical studies due to the inadequacy of the positivist and idealist approaches. He believed, however, that since he had said all that had to be said about the methods appropriate to the science of interpretation, it was time to get on with his substantive work. But being satisfied with the adequacy of a certain theory of knowledge after careful consideration of the problems involved, as Weber was with his modified neo-Kantianism, is quite different from being unconcerned with the issue of epistemology. For the pragmatic justification of metatheoretical inquiries quoted above, see "The Logic of the Cultural Sciences," *Methodology*, 115–16.

63. The case against Weber's nationalism was made most strongly by J. P. Mayer, *Max Weber and German Politics*, and most persuasively by Mommsen, *Max Weber und die deutsche Politik*. In the wake or Beetham's incisive analysis in *Max Weber and the Theory of Modern Politics* and Giddens' argument in *Politics and Sociology in the Thought of Max Weber*, Mommsen has moderated his stance considerably. Perhaps the best brief discussion of Weber's view of international politics is Mommsen's chapter on "The Champion of Nationalist Power Politics and Imperialism," in *The Age of Bureaucracy*, 22–46.

64. Weber quoted in J. P. Mayer, *Max Weber and German Politics*, 33. See also T. S. Simey,

"Max Weber: Man of Affairs or Theoretical Sociologist?" *Sociological Review* 14 (1966): 303–27; and Steven Seidman, *Liberalism and the Origins of European Social Theory* (Berkeley, 1983), 236, 350–51 n. 1.

65. Weber's speech to the meeting of the Verein für Sozialpolitik in Vienna in 1909, in his *Gesammelte Aufsätze zur Soziologie und Sozialpolitik* (Tübingen, 1924), 414.

66. Weber's remark is quoted in Marianne Weber, *Weber*, 698. On Weber and Nietzsche, see E. Fleischmann, "De Weber à Nietzsche," *Archives Européennes de Sociologie* 5 (1964): 190–238; and Robert Eden, *Political Leadership and Nihilism: A Study of Weber and Nietzsche* (Gainesville, Fla., 1984).

67. Dewey, *The Ethics of Democracy, EW*, 1: 232; cf. the discussion of this passage on p. 97 above.

68. Bourgeois, *Solidarité*, 3, 17–22; his address on "La Justice sociale," and the ensuing discussion, both of which are in *Solidarité*, 159–89. See also *La Solidarité sociale*, 11, and the discussion of these ideas in Hamburger, *Bourgeois*, 46–48. On Fouillée, see *La Morale*, 6–10, and cf. above, p. 96.

69. Croly, *Progressive Democracy*, 196–97, 186–87. See also 60–62, 134, of Croly's manuscript "The Breach in Civilization", written during the mid-1920s but never published. One copy of the proofs of the first seven chapters of this book is in the Frankfurter papers; another copy is in the Houghton Library, Harvard University.

70. Hobhouse, *Theory of Knowledge*, 59. Cf. *Liberalism*, 19, 41. For Hobhouse's analysis of voluntarism, which shows his debt to James and Dewey, see his essay "Are Psychological Categories Irreducible?" in *Sociology and Philosophy*, 285–93. Much of the confusion in discussions of Hobhouse derives from the inability to identify his polemical intent and the failure to keep separate—and to realize the consistency of—his attacks on empiricists and his quite different attacks on idealists. For a fine discussion of this point, see Collini, *Liberalism and Sociology*, 226–27.

71. Weber presented this complicated argument, which I have treated in a rather schematic fashion, in its clearest form in "'Objectivity' in Social Science," in *Methodology*, 72–85; see esp. 80–82.

72. Weber, *Economy and Society*, ed. Guenther Roth and Claus Wittich, trans. Ephraim Fischoll et al. (1968; rpt. Berkeley, 1978) 1: 4, 9–10. See also the discussion in Bendix, *Weber*, 267–68, 473–78, 489; Goddard, "Max Weber and the Objectivity of Social Science," 10–18; and Lelan McLemore, "Max Weber's Defense of Historical Inquiry," *History and Theory* 23 (1984): 277–95.

73. Weber, "The Meaning of 'Ethical Neutrality,'" in *Methodology*, 40.

74. Dilthey's remarks on Weber, from the Berlin *Nachlass*, are quoted in Ermarth, *Dilthey*, 167. For Weber's remarks on Dilthey, see *Roscher and Knies*, 11, 119, 150–52, 251 n. 47; and the comments by Oakes on 28–32 of his introduction to that volume, which I consider somewhat misleading for the reasons offered in the text. The importance for Weber of Rickert's criticism of Dilthey can be understood by comparing Burger, *Max Weber's Theory of Concept Formation*, 3–56, and Ermarth, *Dilthey*, 192–95. There is another reason why the similarities between Dilthey's hermeneutics and Weber's "understanding sociology" have been overlooked. During the twentieth century, Weber has come to be identified, particularly in the United States, with a variety of empirical sociology that pretends to scientific status and has little patience with *Verstehen* as a tool. Although Weber's writings indicate his desire to chart a middle course for his methodology, his caveats have sometimes been ignored by sociologists more interested in constructing social laws than interpreting social action. Just as Dilthey's critics have tried to pull him away from his position between positivism and idealism, so have a number of Weber's followers tried to find in his writings an imprimatur for their version of empirical sociology. Weber was certainly interested in sociology as *Wissenschaft*, but he remained conscious of

subjective meanings as integral to both the objects of analysis and the experience of the investigator. My reading of Weber's sociology as hermeneutical as well as scientific has been influenced primarily by Karl Löwith, "Max Weber und Karl Marx," part of which has been translated by Salvator Attanasio as "Weber's Interpretation of the Bourgeois Capitalistic World in Terms of the Guiding Principle of 'Rationalization,'" in *Max Weber*, ed. Dennis Wrong (Englewood Cliffs, N.J., 1970), 101–22; Marianne Weber, *Weber*, 306–15; Habermas's comments on Parsons in Stammer, ed., *Max Weber and Sociology Today*, 59–66; and Giddens, *Capitalism and Modern Social Theory*, 133–48. Arnold Bergstraesser essayed a comparison of Weber and Dilthey in "Wilhelm Dilthey and Max Weber: An Empirical Approach to Historical Synthesis," *Ethics* 57 (1947): 92–110, but he provided more exposition than comparison of their ideas, and to my knowledge a more detailed comparison has not yet appeared. Alfred Schutz emphasized the differences between Weber and Dilthey in *The Phenomenology of the Social World* (Evanston, 1967), 240, but I think Schutz's own work relies on, and at least implicitly demonstrates, the possibilty of reconciling their ideas.

75. Weber, "The Meaning of 'Ethical Neutrality,'" *Methodology*, 33; and cf. *Roscher and Knies*, 108, 176.

76. Cf. the excerpts from Weber's GPS in Appendix II of *Economy and Society*, 2: 1381–1462, with Part Two of *Economy and Society*. Guenther Roth testifies, perhaps inadvertently, to the overlap between Weber's personal politics and his political sociology in his notes to Weber's political writings. See esp. *Economy and Society*, 2: 1462 n. 1.

77. For elaborations of this interpretation of Weber, see Löwith, "Weber's Interpretation of the Bourgeois Capitalistic World," in Wrong, ed., *Weber*; Mommsen, *The Age of Bureaucracy*, 7–8, 18–20, 109–10; Schluchter, "Value Neutrality and the Ethic of Responsibility," in *Max Weber's Vision of History*, 65–112; and Marianne Weber, *Weber*, 317. For Bernstein's laments, see Thomas Meyer, "Wissenschaft und Sozialismus bei Marx, in der Konzeption Eduard Bernsteins und in der Gegenwart," in Heimann and Meyer, eds., *Bernstein*, 257–59; and the rather more critical appraisal of Bernstein's confusion and Weber's relative clarity on this issue in Frithjof Spreer, "Bernstein, Max Weber und das Verhältnis von Wissenschaft und Politik in der Gegenwartsdiskussion," in Heimann and Meyer, eds., *Bernstein*, 285.

78. Hobhouse, "Sociology," *Encyclopedia of Religion and Ethics* 11 (London, 1920), in *Sociology and Philosophy*, 23–57. As Collini points out in *Liberalism and Sociology*, 228–29, Hobhouse differed from Weber not in his approach to value freedom but in his own value judgments, particularly in his idea of progress, which will be discussed below.

79. Croly, *Progressive Democracy*, 194–95; and cf. 173. See also Croly, "The Breach in Civilization," 63–64, 148–49, Frankfurter papers.

80. Bourgeois, *Solidarité*, 58; Lippmann, *Drift and Mastery*, xxi. For an analysis of the role this vision of history played in the thinking of American progressive intellectuals, see Noble, *The Paradox of Progressive Thought*.

81. Lippmann, *A Preface to Politics*, 182–83; Dewey, "Progress," *The International Journal of Ethics* 26 (1916): 311–22, MW, 10: 234–43. See also Lippmann, *Drift and Mastery*, 309–10, and Croly, *Progressive Democracy*, 178, where Marxists' attempts to be "scientific" about history, economics, and politics are dismissed for similar reasons.

82. Hobhouse, *Liberalism*, 88–89, 72–73. See also "Sociology and Ethics," *Independent Review* 12 (1907): 330–31, where Hobhouse contended, "There is an onward movement discernible among the many changes that are valueless or worse, and this we may identify with the growth of mind of which the development of thought is one expression."

83. Hobhouse, "The Philosophy of Development" (1924), in *Sociology and Philosophy*, 297–331. Hobhouse became increasingly enamored of the idea of history as purpose, particularly after World War I destroyed whatever empirical evidence of progress toward cooperation he had seen in his own lifetime. As this ideal began to seem further and further from reality, in

fact, he substituted an idealist vision of progress, inspired by Green's metaphysics, for the more pragmatic perspective of his earlier work. Cf. for example these passages: In *Social Evolution and Political Theory* (New York, 1911), he wrote, "The theory of continuous automatic inevitable progress is impossible." In *Development and Purpose*, 365, he gave progress a different twist: "A purpose runs through the world-whole, there is a Mind of which the world-purpose is the object." This progression in Hobhouse's thought is discussed at length in Collini, *Liberalism and Sociology*, and also in Clarke, *Liberals and Social Democrats*. Collini ultimately uses Hobhouse's belief in progress as a warrant for dismissing him as a serious thinker (e.g., 129, 235). Clarke, on the other hand (e.g., 146–47), directly challenges Harold Laski's treatment of Hobhouse as a rather naive believer in natural progress. Laski's critique in *The Decline of Liberalism* (1940), Clarke argues, indicates that Laski "could not have read what Hobhouse actually wrote in his prime," because Hobhouse explicitly denied that progress can be automatic or that cultures develop except through deliberate, conscious decisions and voluntary action. It should be apparent that my own interpretation stands closer to Clarke's than to Collini's. Although Collini notes the passages in which Hobhouse responded to critics misinterpreting his idea of progress, and although he understands that Hobhouse did not consider such progress inevitable, Collini seems to me to pay insufficient attention to the roots of Hobhouse's notion of progress in his pragmatic theory of knowledge as problem solving. I would not dispute, however, the fuzziness of much of Hobhouse's writing in the post-World War I years. Another useful analysis of Hobhouse's ideas about progress is Mariz, "L. T. Hobhouse as a Theoretical Sociologist," 314–17.

84. Weber, "'Objectivity' in Social Science," *Methodology*, 68–70. The literature on the relation between Weber and Marx is vast. For brief surveys, cf. Roth's introduction to Bendix, *Weber*, xxxii–xxxiii, nn. 32–34; and more recently, Alexander, *Theoretical Logic* 3: 161–62 n. 152.

85. Weber, "Die Verhältnisse der Landarbeiter im ostelbischen Deutschland," in Verein für Sozialpolitik, *Schriften* 55 (1892): 797–98, quoted in Alexander, *Theoretical Logic*, 3: 15.

86. Weber, "The Social Psychology of the World Religions," *From Max Weber*, 280.

87. Weber, *Economy and Society*, 1: 24–26. Recent contributions to this controversy include Ann Swidler, "The Concept of Rationality in the Work of Max Weber," *Sociological Inquiry* 43 (1973): 35–42; Stephen Kalberg, "Max Weber's Types of Rationality: Cornerstones for the Analysis of Rationalization Processes in History," *American Journal of Sociology* 85 (1980): 1145–79; Alexander, *Theoretical Logic*, 3: 24–29, 134–35; and of special importance, Donald L. Levine, "Rationality and Freedom: Weber and Beyond," *Sociological Inquiry* 51 (1981): 5–26; and Schluchter, "The Paradox of Rationalization: On the Relation of Ethics and World," in *Max Weber's Vision of History*, 11–64.

88. See especially, in addition to *The Protestant Ethic and the Spirit of Capitalism*, Weber's essays "The Social Psychology of the World Religions," and "Religious Rejections of the World and Their Directions," in *From Max Weber*, 267–301, 323–59. The most important recent contributions to the understanding of Weber's theory of rationalization in relation to religious history are Friedrich Tenbruck, "The Problem of Thematic Unity in the Work of Max Weber," *British Journal of Sociology* 31 (1980): 316–51; Schluchter, "The Paradox of Rationalization," esp. 32–45; and Stephen Kalberg, "The Search for Thematic Orientations in a Fragmented Oeuvre: The Discussion of Max Weber in Recent German Sociological Literature," *Sociology* 13 (1979): 127–39.

89. Weber, "'Objectivity' in Social Science," *Methodology*, 81.

90. Marianne Weber, *Weber*, 325. See also Löwith, "Weber's Interpretation of the Bourgeois Capitalistic World," in Wrong, ed., *Weber*, 105–6, 119–20.

91. Lippmann, *Drift and Mastery*, 266–69. James's influence on Lippmann is apparent in this passage, but Graham Wallas's role should also be noted. Cf. these remarks in Wallas's *The Great*

Society: A Psychological Analysis (London, 1914), the book he prefaced with a letter urging Lippmann to write "that sequel to your *Preface to Politics* for which all your friends are looking": "We are forced now to recognize that a society whose intellectual direction consists only of unrelated specialisms must drift, and that we dare not drift any longer. . . . We must let our minds play freely over all the conditions of life till we can either *justify* our civilization or change it" (15). See also Martin J. Wiener, *Between Two Worlds: The Political Thought of Graham Wallas* (Oxford, 1971), 169–71, on the relation between Wallas's ideas and Lippmann's.

92. The exact date of Weber's lecture "Politik als Beruf" ("Politics as a Vocation") has long been a puzzle. For the most recent attempt to solve it, see Schluchter, "Excursus: The Question of the Dating of 'Science as a Vocation' and 'Politics as a Vocation,'" in *Max Weber's Vision of History*, 113–16. For the context of Weber's speech, see Allan Mitchell, *Revolution in Bavaria, 1918–1919: The Eisner Regime and the Soviet Republic* (Princeton, 1965). See Marianne Weber, *Weber*, 626–31, for Weber's comment on Eisner's coup and the letter from G. W. Klein to Weber on Nov. 6 and 7, 1918. Cf. also 622–23 for a letter from one of Weber's old friends to his mother dated Oct. 2, 1918, suggesting that a number of social democrats believed the selection of Prince Max of Baden as Chancellor had been a mistake: the nation would have done better to choose "the other Max of Baden," Max Weber. Weber's discussion of Eisner's demagoguery is in *Economy and Society*, 1: 242.

93. Weber's "Politics as a Vocation," which was published in revised form in the spring of 1919, is in *From Max Weber*, 77–128, but there are a number of problems with the translation, which I have altered at several points. The most serious problem is the rendering of what Weber termed *"die Gesinnungsethik"* as "the ethic of ultimate ends," which, in its suggestion of the importance of results, seems to me almost precisely the opposite of Weber's meaning, and has led to a good deal of confusion among Weber's critics. In using the phrase "ethic of conviction" I am following the lead of Bruun in *Science, Value and Politics* and of Schluchter in *Max Weber's Vision of History*. For the passages cited, see Weber, *GPS*, 493, 537, 540, 545.

94. Lippmann, *A Preface to Politics*, 152.

95. Bourgeois, *Solidarité*, 36–38.

96. Weber, "'Objectivity' in Social Science," *Methodology*, 57.

97. Lippmann, *A Preface to Politics*, 152, 170.

98. Croly, *Progressive Democracy*, 194–95. See also Noble, *The Paradox of Progressive Thought*, 125; and Herbst, *German Historical School*, 198–99.

99. Lippmann, "The Footnote," *The New Republic*, July 17, 1915, 284–85, in Lippmann, *Early Writings*, ed. Arthur Schlesinger, Jr. (New York, 1970), 307–10. See also "Taking a Chance," *The New Republic*, Aug. 7, 1915, 24, in *Early Writings*, 96–99, on H. G. Wells and William James.

100. Weber, "The Meaning of 'Ethical Neutrality,'" *Methodology*, 15–18. See also Marianne Weber, *Weber*, 89–90, 156–57, 322, on this conflict.

101. Bourgeois, *Solidarité*, 33–35, 39, 193; and see also his essay "L'Education social," in *L'Education et la démocratie française* (Paris, 1897), 275–78; and his *Discours au Chambre du 16 novembre, 1897* (Amiens, 1897), 15–16.

102. Hobhouse, *Democracy and Reaction*, ed. Peter F. Clarke (1904; rpt. Brighton, 1972), 125 n. These ideas were not held solely by followers of Green, of course. Hobhouse was fond of quoting a definition of man proposed by the British positivist J. H. Bridges: "Of each man's life one part has been personal, the other social: one part consists in actions for the common good, the other part in actions of pure self-indulgence, and even of active hostility to the common welfare. . . . Humanity consists . . . only of those parts of each man's life, which are impersonal, which are social, which have converged to the common good" (J. H. Bridges, *Essays and Addresses*, 86–88). Hobhouse quoted the passage in *Morals in Evolution: A Study in Comparative Ethics*, 593; and in *The Metaphysical Theory of the State* (1918; rpt. London, 1951), 115. See

also Collini, *Liberalism and Sociology*, 183–84, 216. On 206–7, and again on 226–27, Collini quotes a long passage from Hobhouse's remarks in a discussion of the Sociological Society on "the relation of ethics to sociology," published in *Sociological Papers*, 2: 188, concerning the integral connection between ethics and progress in Hobhouse's view of sociology. Cf. the similar discussion of these ideas in Hobhouse, "The Ethical Basis of Collectivism," *International Journal of Ethics* 8 (1898): 137–56. The centrality of these ethical ideas, and their clear debt to Green—which Collini points out—make it difficult to accept without qualification Freeden's claim in *The New Liberalism* that Hobhouse's generation owed less to Green than to earlier liberals. In Hobhouse's ethically charged evolutionary progressivism, the egoism, hedonism, and utilitarianism of early nineteenth-century liberal philosophy all came under direct fire.

103. On Dewey's ethics in relation to the rest of his philosophy, and some of the problems involved in his attempt to integrate Sidgwick's and Green's contrasting ethical ideas, see above, pp. 130–32.

104. Weber has attracted criticism from several different angles on this issue. Partisans of natural law such as Leo Strauss and Eric Voegelin have characterized him as a dangerous relativist, an argument Arnold Brecht discusses insightfully in *Political Theory*, 262–66. Marxists, on the other hand, have treated Weber as an apologist for irresponsible "decisionist self-assertion," a position taken by Jürgen Habermas in Stammer, ed., *Max Weber and Sociology Today*, 59–66. Weber expressed his ambivalence about the decline of religion in a letter to Ferdinand Tönnies, Feb. 19, 1909:

> When I studied modern Catholic literature in Rome a few years ago, I became convinced how hopeless it is to think that there are any scientific results this church cannot digest. . . . I could not honestly participate in such anti-clericalism [as that based on "metaphysical 'naturalism'"]. It is true that I am absolutely unmusical in matters religious and that I have neither the need nor the ability to erect any religious edifices within me—that is simply impossible for me, and I reject it. But after examining myself carefully I must say that I am neither anti-religious nor irreligious. In this regard too I consider myself a cripple, a stunted man whose fate it is to admit honestly that he must put up with this state of affairs (so as not to fall for some romantic swindle). . . . For you a theologian of liberal persuasion (whether Catholic or Protestant) is necessarily most abhorrent as the typical representative of a half way position; for me he is in human terms infinitely more valuable and interesting . . . than the intellectual (and basically cheap) pharisaism of naturalism, which is intolerably fashionable and in which there is much less life than in the religious position (again depending on the case, of course).

Weber's letter translated from Baumgarten, ed., *Max Weber: Werk und Person*, 670, by Schluchter, "Value-Neutrality and the Ethic of Responsibility," *Max Weber's Vision of History*, 82–83 n. 44.

105. Weber, "Politik als Beruf," *GPS*, 536, 547; cf. *From Max Weber*, 117, 127.

106. Disagreements about Weber's ethics have been sharp. For three recent accounts, cf. Mommsen, "Rezension," *Historische Zeitschrift* 215 (1972): 434 ff., and *Max Weber und die deutsche Politik, 1890–1920*, rev. ed. (Tübingen, 1974), 472; Schluchter, "The Paradox of Rationalization: On the Relation of Ethics and World," in *Max Weber's Vision of History*, 50–59; and Alexander, *Theoretical Logic in Sociology* 3: 212–13 especially. Whereas Mommsen considers the tension between Weber's ethics of conviction and responsibility necessary and unresolved, Schluchter believes that because such an interpretation "does not provide any solution" to the problems of ethics, it is necessary "to argue in Weber's own terms against him" in order to reconcile the competing ethics. Schluchter offers such a resolution by conceiving of the ethic of responsibility not in terms of adjustment to the world but in terms of the infusion of convictions into the notion of responsibility. Alexander dismisses that argument as a somewhat misleading attempt to find a solution that is not present in Weber's own writings. Without disputing

the difficulty of this problem, I disagree with Mommsen, Schluchter, and Alexander about the need to go beyond Weber's writings to find a solution; it is necessary instead to realize, as Weber did, that no such solution is available. That position may seem unsatisfactory to those similarly unsatisfied by Sidgwick's ethics, but holding these competing values in tension may be less inadequate than any other alternative. Weber, like Sidgwick, understood that ethics cannot provide any final answers for the dilemmas we encounter in experience.

107. Criticism of these thinkers' "moralism" continues to proliferate. Cf. the following recent examples. On Hobhouse, see Collini, *Liberalism and Sociology*, 235–44; and Weiler, "The New Liberalism of L. T. Hobhouse," 157–59. On Bourgeois, see Zeldin, *Politics and Anger*, 291–306; and Logue, *From Philosophy to Sociology*, 204; on Croly and Lippmann, see R. Jeffrey Lustig, *Corporate Liberalism: The Origins of Modern American Political Theory* (Berkeley, 1982), 209–26. On Dewey, see Crunden's essay in Buenker et al., *Progressivism*, 71–103; and his elaboration of this argument for the entire phenomenon of American progressivism in *Ministers of Reform*. I am not challenging these interpreters' emphasis on the moralism of progressive thinkers, but I see that moralism in a rather different light: while it is often treated as a quaint vestige of an earlier religious sensibility or a peculiar species of self delusion, it seems to me an integral part of these progressives' radically empiricist world view. Without the ethical ideas that seem so vulnerable or unnecessary to many historians, there would have been no progressivism—at least in the sense in which these theorists understood it.

108. Hobhouse, *Social Evolution and Political Theory*, 199–200. See also Weber's letter to Edgar Jaffé, Sept. 13, 1907, expressing his reasons for rejecting an article submitted to the *Archiv für Sozialwissenschaft und Sozialpolitik*, in Marianne Weber, *Weber*, 379–80:

> *Where* is there the slightest indication of the *substance* of those new relativistic *and yet ideal (nota bene!)* values that are to serve as the basis of the critique of the "old," "dubious" values! One will look for them in vain, and for good reason: any attempt to outline them would expose them to criticism and show that the problem has not been solved but only put off. An idealistic ethic that demands "sacrifices" and does not eliminate *responsibility* can never produce any other results. But it will not do to criticize an ethic on any *other* basis than that of one's *own* ideals; otherwise one gets into the area of the shabbiest "calculation of costs," and, as I have said before, the ideal will then inevitably be the normal health snob [*Gesundheitsprotz*] and medically supervised philistine of macrobiotics."

Chapter 9. Progressive Politics

1. For an influential statement of the opposite claim that progressives offered cultural solutions for political problems, and vice versa, see Christopher Lasch, *The New Radicalism in America, 1889–1963: The Intellectual as a Social Type* (New York, 1965).

2. Bourgeois, *Lettre au Congrès Radical et Radical-Socialiste de Nantes, octobre, 1909* (Paris, 1909), 15.

3. Dewey to William Torrey Harris, Jan. 17, 1884, Harris papers, University of Southern California Library; Dewey, *The Ethics of Democracy, EW*, 1: 240–43.

4. Dewey, *The Study of Ethics, EW*, 4: 357. See also Dewey, "Moral Philosophy," first published in *Johnson's Universal Cyclopaedia*, ed. Charles Kendall Adams (New York, 1894), 880–85, *EW*, 4: 132–51, where Dewey offers a similar analysis of Aristotle's ethics: "Aristotle distinctly separates the practical and social virtues from the contemplative virtues, making the latter higher in type, and thus prepares the way for the later isolation of the individual, and the divorce of ethics from politics" (138).

5. Dewey and Tufts, *Ethics, MW*, 5: 423–33, 383–85; and cf. Hobhouse, *Morals in Evolution*, 1: 367–68. Italics added by Dewey and Tufts.

6. Dewey, *Reconstruction in Philosophy*, *MW*, 12: 192. See also Croly, *The Promise of American Life*, 415; and Lippmann, *A Preface to Politics*, 52–53, on this point. In *A Preface to Politics*, Lippmann criticized the Fabians for concentrating on specific reforms of the political process and overlooking the "profound regeneration of society" that must accompany such reforms (57–59).

7. Hobhouse, *The Labour Movement*, 4–5; *Liberalism*, 73; and *The Labour Movement*, 2nd ed., 18. See also the discussion of this issue in Collini, *Liberalism and Sociology*, 67–68, 142; and Emy, *Liberals, Radicals, and Social Politics*, xxi, 2.

8. Weber, "Politik als Beruf," *GPS*, 542; cf. *From Max Weber*, 123.

9. For a few examples of analyses that emphasize the gap between the initial impulses and the eventual results of progressive reform, see the following: On France, Nordmann, *Histoire des radicaux, 1820–1973*, 134–37; Rebérioux, *La République radicale? 1898–1914*, 42–82; and Zeldin, *Politics and Anger*, 307–18, 334–36, 350–60. On Great Britain, see Bruce, *The Coming of the Welfare State*, 13–14; Gilbert, *The Evolution of National Insurance*, 13; Emy, *Liberals, Radicals, and Social Politics*, 161–62, 175; and Pugh, *Modern British Politics*, 112–29. On the United States, see Buenker's essay in Buenker, et al., *Progressivism*, 31–69; McCormick, "The Discovery that Business Corrupts Politics," and *From Realignment to Reform*; Hays, "The Politics of Reform in Municipal Government in the Progressive Era," and "Political Parties and the Community-Society Continuum," in *American Political History as Social Analysis*, 205–32, 293–325; and Wiebe, *The Search for Order*, 111–223. In Germany, of course, there was little question of progressives translating their ideas into policies. As Miquel wrote matter-of-factly after Königgrätz, "The time of ideals is past. Today politicians must ask not so much as formerly what is desirable but rather what is possible." Miquel quoted in Craig, *Germany 1866–1945*, 255 n. 8.

10. Croly, *The Promise of American Life*, 315–16; see also 416–17. Weber, "Speech for the General Information of Austrian Officers in Vienna," trans. D. Hÿtch, in Weber, *The Interpretation of Social Reality*, 212–15. See also Lippmann, "Unrest," *The New Republic*, Nov. 12, 1919, 315, in *Early Writings*, 283; and Dewey, "The New Social Science," *The New Republic*, April 6, 1918, 292–94, in *MW*, 11: 87–92, for similar appraisals of the desirability of reform rather than revolution.

11. On the principle of progressive taxation as an expression of social responsibility, see Croly, *The Promise of American Life*, 219–20, 382–84; Lippmann, *Drift and Mastery*, 108–9; and Hobhouse, *The Labour Movement*, 45–46, 78. This measure also attracted social democrats' support. See for example S. Webb's notes for a lecture delivered to the Fabian Society on Nov. 9, 1915, Passfield papers; and his essay "National Finance and a Levy on Capital: What the Labour Party Intends," Fabian Tract # 188, March, 1919. For the broader efforts on behalf of the income tax, see Wolfe, *From Radicalism to Socialism*, 201–2; Keller, *Affairs of State*, 326; and Rodgers, "In Search of Progressivism," 120–21.

12. For the speeches of Jaurès and Bourgeois, see the Chamber of Deputies, *Journal officiel*, 1896, 1: 573–82, 650–52. Jaurès's speech was also reprinted in *La Petite République*, March 24, 1896. The celebration of the measure's passage by the Chamber was in the March 28, 1896, issue.

13. See Bourgeois, "La Cooperation et l'idéal social," in *L'Education de la démocratie française*, 266–68; *Solidarité*, 71; and *Les Applications de la solidarité sociale*, 13–15. See also the discussion of this issue in Hamburger, *Bourgeois*, 137–58; Hayward, "The Official Philosophy of the French Third Republic," 35–36; and Goldberg, *Jaurès*, 154–55, 161–65. For Jaurès's speech, see the Chamber of Deputies, *Journal officiel*, 1914, 1: 2944–48.

14. Dewey, *The Ethics of Democracy*, *EW*, 1: 239. Hobhouse, *Democracy and Reaction*, 221–22. Cf. Dewey and Tufts, *Ethics*, *MW*, 5: 426: "One of the chief moral problems of the present day is, then, that of making governmental machinery such a prompt and flexible organ for expressing the *common* interest and purpose as will do away with that distrust of government

which properly must endure so long as 'government' is something imposed from above and exercised from without." On this point also see Bourgeois, *Solidarité*, 93–94, where he contrasts the significance of government in the French Republic to its quite different status in the Germany dominated by Bismarck.

15. Lippmann, *Drift and Mastery*, 254; Bourgeois, "La Solidarité et la liberté," *Solidarité*, 95–96. Hobhouse, "Old-Age Pensions: The Principle," *Manchester Guardian*, Feb. 29, 1908; *Liberalism*, 91–96; Croly, *The Promise of American Life*, 398. See also Lippmann, "Integrated America," *The New Republic*, Feb. 19, 1916, 62–67. In *La Solidarité humaine*, 22–23, Bourgeois stressed the need for welfare services on an international scale in order to prevent any single nation from being placed at a competitive disadvantage economically vis-à-vis less generous neighbors; he made a similar argument in *Les Applications de la solidarité social*, 7–8. Bertrand de Jouvenal, in his *Cours d'histoire des idées politiques à partir du XIXᵉ siècle* (Paris, 1967), 285, argues that most of the welfare legislation in France during the late 1890s and the pre-war years was inspired by the philosophy of solidarity, even though it took shape according to a characteristically convoluted process in which competing interest groups played crucial roles. On Hobhouse and the national minimum, cf. Clarke, *Liberals and Social Democrats*, 45–6, Collini, *Liberalism and Sociology*, 107–13, 138–41; and Freeden, *The New Liberalism*, 194–245. American progressivism attracted not only supporters of government action such as Croly, Lippmann, and Dewey, it also enlisted descendents of Jefferson who hoped the state would refrain from welfare legislation. Historians who have looked at one group and ignored the other have presented oddly mismatched portraits of progressivism. A classic version of the Jeffersonian interpretation is Hartz, *The Liberal Tradition in America*, 228–55. Completely ignoring Croly, Lippmann, and Dewey, Hartz asserted that there were no American progressives similar to Bourgeois or Hobhouse, an argument that is completely without foundation. Indeed, Hartz's neglect of the part of the American liberal tradition represented by these progressives skewed his entire account of American politics, a problem that I intend to explore in a later study. For contrasting illustrations of the close connection between progressives of the Croly ilk and European reformers, see Rodgers, "In Search of Progressivism," 125–26; Kenneth O. Morgan, "The Future at Work: Anglo-American Progressivism, 1870–1917," in H. C. Allen and Roger Thompson, eds., *Contrast and Connection: Bicentennial Essays in Anglo-American History* (London, 1976), 245–71; and Benjamin R. Beede, "Foreign Influences on American Progressivism," *The Historian* 5 (1983): 529–49; and see n. 27 to Chapter Eight above.

16. Weber, "Parliament and Government in a Reconstructed Germany," reprinted from Weber's *GPS* as Appendix II of *Economy and Society*, 2: 1391–92. On Weber's view of the German welfare state, also see Mommsen, "Political Sociology," in Wrong, ed., *Max Weber*, 191–92.

17. Hobhouse, *Labour Movement*, 94; cf. *Liberalism*, 81.

18. Croly, *Progressive Democracy*, 282, 390–91; see also 383–85, and cf. the similar argument in Lippmann, *Drift and Mastery*, 91–100. On Croly's attitude toward fascism, see John P. Diggins, *Mussolini and Fascism: The View from America* (Princeton, 1972), 228–34.

19. Dewey, "Outlines of Ethics," *EW*, 3: 318–19. Cf. Hobhouse, *Liberalism*, 83–84.

20. In an editorial entitled "A Government Plea for Health Insurance," which appeared in *The New Republic*, May 29, 1916, 55, the editors predicted the situation facing those historians who now try to sort out all the starry-eyed idealists and hard-headed realists who called themselves progressives during these years:

> When historians of the future come to examine the origins of the movement for social advance that gives the present its distinction, they doubtless will be impressed by the antithetical impulses that generated our enthusiasm for reform. They will find the passion of the humanitarian yoked with the zeal of the scientist; the sentimentalist and the rationalist fighting side by side against the established order. Rebellion born of pity

joins hands with rebellion born of exact knowledge and clear analysis. It matters little that one sees the enemy as injustice and suffering, the other as stupidity and waste. Pseudo-science may bring down on its head the imprecations of the humanitarian; scientists may curse the "insane fringe" of the army of sentiment. But the two forces work together.

In fact, the situation seems even more complicated than prophesied, since historians now see standing beside these different sorts of reformers the efficiency experts and prophets of scientific management who wanted to tack the label "social advance" on the dramatically different future they envisioned. Two examples illustrate the tendency to confuse thinkers such as James, Dewey, and Croly with "reformers" of a very different stripe such as Frederick Taylor. Lustig, in *Corporate Liberalism*, attempts to build from the solid foundation of studies by Theodore Lowi and Grant McConnell a case against pragmatism, but he fails to distinguish between the quite different ideas of Lester Ward and William James, for example, or between Arthur Bentley and John Dewey, or between Frederick Taylor and Herbert Croly. Lustig thus unwittingly presents as a bitter critique of their ideas what is actually a paraphrase of the arguments James, Dewey, and Croly themselves offered against their contemporaries who emphasized the scientific method without reference to the purposes it served (262–64). James B. Gilbert, *Work Without Salvation: America's Intellectuals and Industrial Alienation, 1880–1910* (Baltimore, 1977), while a far more careful study than Lustig's polemic, likewise tends to muddy the differences between James's pragmatism and the social engineering of post-World War I industrial psychologists. His own evidence indicates that the decisive shift occurred in the 1920s; for that reason his analysis of "collectivists" and "corporatists" seems inapplicable to the very different ethos of pragmatic and progressive theorists such as James and Dewey. For a splendid response to arguments tracing the fact of the welfare state's inadequacies to the efforts of progressive theorists, see the brief discussion in Peter Clarke's prologue to *Liberals and Social Democrats*, 1–8.

21. Bourgeois, "La Cooperation et l'idéal social," a speech delivered June 14, 1896, published in *L'Education et la démocratie française*, 270–78; Hobhouse, *Liberalism*, 87; *Democracy and Reaction*, 118; and Croly, *The Promise of American Life*, 209.

22. Weber, "Speech for the General Information of Austrian Officers in Vienna," in *The Interpretation of Social Reality*, 206–11; *Economy and Society*, 2: 926; and "Parliament and Government in a Reconstructed Germany," *Economy and Society*, 2: 1399.

23. Weber, "Parliament and Government in a Reconstructed Germany," *Economy and Society*, 2: 1401; "Speech for the General Information of Austrian Officers in Vienna," 203–4. See also Beetham, *Max Weber*, 71, 84–89, 223–24; and Marianne Weber, *Weber*, 631.

24. Hobhouse, *Liberalism*, 88–90; Lippmann quoted in Steel, *Walter Lippmann and the American Century*, 69–79.

25. Hobhouse, *Liberalism*, 54; *Democracy and Reaction*, 217. See also Croly, *The Promise of American Life*, 105–17, 333–81; Lippmann, *Drift and Mastery*, 27–65; Dewey, Lecture Notes on Political Philosophy, 1892, 112, 170–71, Dewey papers. An enlightening comparative analysis of the strange career of the regulatory agency is Morton Keller, "The Pluralist State: American Economic Regulation in Comparative Perspective, 1900–1930," in McCraw, ed., *Regulation in Perspective*, 56–94. For contrasting views of the origins of regulation in the late nineteenth century, cf. Keller, *Affairs of State*, 409–38, who stresses the complex and ambiguous nature of these reforms; and Trachtenberg, *The Incorporation of America*, 162–73, who sees regulation as a carefully calculated way of insulating elites from popular pressures by using "experts immune from the vagaries of electoral politics" (164). For Croly's views on a specific agency, see Douglas W. Jaenicke, "Herbert Croly, Progressive Ideology, and the FTC Act," *Political Science Quarterly* 93 (1978): 471–93.

26. Lippmann, *Drift and Mastery*, 182–90; "The Puzzle of Hughes," *The New Republic*,

Sept. 30, 1916, 213. On this issue, see also the fine essay by James A. Neuchterlein, "The Dream of Scientific Liberalism: *The New Republic* and American Progressive Thought, 1914–1920," *The Review of Politics* 42 (1980): 167–90.

27. The variety of interpretations of progressivism is discussed in n. 27 to Chapter Eight above.

28. For the literature on this issue, see n. 47 to Chapter Five above. The most persuasive attempt yet to link progressive reforms to the process of realignment is McCormick, *From Realignment to Reform*. It has been argued that the reorganization of American politics is responsible for the disillusionment of the American public with voting. That would be plausible except that the realignment of voters, and the decline in voting, predate the reforms that such an interpretation holds responsible for the public's lack of interest. For that reason McCormick's analysis appears preferable, and I have followed his lead here.

29. The most detailed accounts of Croly's and Lippmann's tortuous relations with Roosevelt and Wilson are in the biographies by Levy, *The Life and Thought of Herbert Croly*; and Steel, *Walter Lippmann and the American Century*.

30. Lippmann, "Unrest," *The New Republic*, Nov. 12, 1919, 315, in *Early Writings*, 274.

31. Weber's speech, in his *Gesammelte Aufsätze*, 407–12, and the letter he wrote later to Robert Michels, are discussed in Beetham, *Max Weber*, 166–68. On the squabbles between the SPD and left-liberal parties, see Sheehan, *German Liberalism*, 219–71; Guttsman, *German Social Democratic Party*, 100–29; Friedrich C. Sell, *Die Tragödie des deutschen Liberalismus* (Stuttgart, 1953), 330–53; and Ludwig Elm, *Zwischen Fortschritt und Reaktion: Geschichte der Parteien der liberalen Bourgeoisie in Deutschland, 1893–1918* (Berlin, 1968). Recent challenges to these pessimistic assessments of the viability of alliance between socialists and progressives include Beverly Heckart, *From Bassermann to Bebel: The Grand Bloc's Quest for Reform in the Kaiserreich, 1900–1914* (New Haven, 1974); and Richard J. Evans, "Liberalism and Society: The Feminist Movement and Social Change," in Evans, ed., *Society and Politics in Wilhelmine Germany*, 186–89, 206.

32. Weber, "Capitalism and Rural Society in Germany," *From Max Weber*, 363–85; *Gesammelte Aufsätze*, 403; *GPS*, 233. See also Beetham, *Max Weber*, 152–64; and Roth's epilogue in *Max Weber's Vision of History*, 200–1.

33. Marianne Weber, *Weber*, 639–45, provides details of Weber's postwar activities and the confusion that might have cost him a chance at a political career. See also Weber, "Parliament and Government in a Reconstructed Germany," *Economy and Society*, 2: 1428, 1458; and Baumgarten, ed., *Max Weber: Werk und Person*, 530. A number of commentators have argued that Weber moved closer to the SPD after the war. Beetham challenges that interpretation, arguing sensibly that Weber moved to the left less dramatically than the left moved toward him in the wake of the abortive Spartacist revolution. His misgivings about the bureaucratization inherent in socialism remained. See Beetham, *Max Weber*, 173–76, for a thorough discussion of this controversial issue.

34. Bourgeois's May 25, 1896, speech is quoted in Kayser, *Les Grandes Batailles du radicalisme*, 243. His later speech appeared as *Discours prononcé à la séance de la Chambre des Députés du 12 mars, 1898* (Paris, 1898). The Minutes of the Congresses of the Parti Républicain Radical et Radical-Socialiste from 1901 to 1914, with the exception of 1905, are in the Library of the Fondation Nationale des sciences politiques, Paris.

35. Bourgeois's letter to the Lille Congress of 1906 is in the Minutes of the Party Congresses, Library of the Fondation Nationale des sciences politiques, Paris. His 1909 letter was published after the congress as *Lettre au Congrès Radical et Radical-Socialiste de Nantes, octobre, 1909*. On the realignment of parties and the instability of the Radical Republic, see Hoffman, "Paradoxes of the French Political Community," *In Search of France*, 1–117; Nordmann, *Histoire des radicaux*, 145–88; Zeldin, *Politics and Anger*, 241–423; Anderson, *France, 1870–*

1914, 88–99; and Rebérioux *La République radicale? 1898–1914*, 42–116. An extremely valuable contemporary account is the study by the solidarist Ferdinand Buisson, *La Politique radicale: études sur les doctrines du parti radical et radical-socialiste* (Paris, 1908), which includes a history of radical parties, various platforms and policy statements, and an introduction by Bourgeois that provides the best brief presentation of his philosophy of solidarity. On Buisson, who was also a theorist of some significance, see Logue, *From Philosophy to Sociology*, 81–94.

36. Bourgeois to Poincaré, Aug. 2, 1912, Poincaré papers, Salle des manuscrits, Bibliothèque Nationale, Paris. For another discussion of this issue, see Hayward, "The Official Philosophy of the French Third Republic," 21 n. 1.

37. Discussions of Hobhouse's aversion to a political career include Hobson and Ginsberg, *L. T. Hobhouse*, 89, where his son's comment is quoted; and Collini, *Liberalism and Sociology*, 90–95. For Hobhouse's history of late nineteenth-century British political thinking, see *Liberalism*, 112–14. His optimistic assessment of the consensus on progressivism appeared in his essay "The Contending Forces," *English Review* 4 (1910): 369; it is discussed in Clarke, *Liberals and Social Democrats*, 117.

38. For the argument that the transformation of the Liberal party occurred prior to WWI, see Clarke, *Lancashire and the New Liberalism*; and Emy, *Liberals, Radicals, and Social Politics, 1892–1914*. Pugh generally accepts their interpretation, but adds information that complicates their portraits of prewar liberalism, in *The Making of Modern British Politics*. For an alternative interpretation, see D. A. Hamer, *Liberal Politics in the Age of Gladstone and Rosebery*, whose argument differs from those of Clarke and Emy at least in part due to its different focus; and Martin Petter, "The Progressive Alliance," *History* 58 (1973): 45–59, who emphasizes the constraints imposed on liberalism by its heritage of individualism and laissez-faire.

39. See Hobhouse, *Liberalism*, 110; and his letter to C. P. Scott, Nov. 7, 1924, quoted in Collini, *Liberalism and Sociology*, 247. Norman Stone argues, in *Europe Transformed, 1878–1919*, 141, that the "self-consciously progressive" governments of the prewar years were "strangely barren of achievement," an assessment that seems to me unbalanced.

40. "The Nationalism of the British Labor Party," *The New Republic*, Aug. 17, 1918, 63–65; "Why a Labor Party?" *The New Republic*, April 29, 1919, 397–400; and Croly, "The Obstacle to Peace," *The New Republic*, April 26, 1919, 406. See also Croly, "Why Liberalism Fails," an unpublished and undated essay written after WWI, in the Frankfurter papers, and "The Breach in Civilization," 65.

41. An adequate treatment of these thinkers' attitude toward foreign policy would require more extensive analysis than is possible here. On this issue, see Hamburger, *Bourgeois*, 239–60; Collini, *Liberalism and Sociology*, 245–53; Clarke, *Liberals and Social Democrats*, 164–204; Steel, *Walter Lippmann and the American Century*, 88–170; Levy, *Croly*, 218–62; Dykhuizen, *Dewey*, 153–67, 182–85; and John A. Thompson, "American Progressive Publicists and the First World War, 1914–1917," *Journal of American History* 58 (1971): 364–83.

42. Dewey, "Conscience and Compulsion," *The New Republic*, July 14, 1917, 297–98, *MW*, 10: 260–64; see also "Force and Coercion," *International Journal of Ethics* 26 (1916): 359–67, *MW*, 10: 244–51; "The Future of Pacifism," *The New Republic*, July 28, 1917, 358–60, *MW*, 10: 265–70; and Dykhuizen, *Dewey*, 162–67.

43. Hobhouse to C. P. Scott, May 20, 1919, quoted in Clarke, *Liberals and Social Democrats*, 204; Dewey, "Shall We Join the League?" *The New Republic*, March 7, 1923, in *Characters and Events: Popular Essays in Social and Political Philosophy*, ed. Joseph Ratner, 2 vols. (New York, 1929), 2: 625–26; Lippmann to Ray Stannard Baker, May 19, 1919, Lippmann papers; "Peace at any Price," *The New Republic*, May 24, 1919, 100–2. Croly's editorial on the war, "Pacifism vs. Passivism," appeared in *The New Republic*, Dec. 12, 1914, 6–7.

44. Croly, "Pacifism vs. Passivism"; Dewey, "The Discrediting of Idealism," *The New Republic*, Oct. 8, 1919, 285–87, *MW*, 11: 180–85. Dewey's most relentless critic was Randolph Bourne; on their dispute cf. Robert B. Westbrook, "The Open-Door World of John Dewey: Democratic Theory and the Politics of War," paper presented at the annual convention of the Pacific Coast branch of the American Historical Association, Aug., 1978; and Paul Bourke, "The Social Critics and the End of American Innocence." See too the well-balanced discussion in David M. Kennedy, *Over Here: The First World War and American Society* (New York, 1980), 45–92.

45. For the effects of the war on Croly, see Levy, *Croly*, 263–76. On Hobhouse and the other British progressives in the 1920s, see Clarke, *Liberals and Social Democrats*, 205–42. A brilliant analysis of postwar disillusionment is Robert Wohl, *The Generation of 1914* (Cambridge, Mass., 1979); see esp. 230–31.

46. Dewey, *Democracy and Education, MW*, 9: 92–94. Dewey to Horace Kallen, July 1, 1916, Horace M. Kallen papers, American Jewish Archives, Hebrew Union College, Cincinnati; copy in Center for Dewey Studies, Carbondale, Ill.

47. Dewey's notes to his lectures on politics, 1892, are in the Dewey papers; "My Pedagogic Creed," *School Journal* 54 (1897): 77–80, *EW*, 5: 93–94. See also "From Absolutism to Experimentalism," 22–23, for an equally strong statement of the centrality of education in philosophy and social reform.

48. Dewey, *The School and Society, MW*, 1: 7–8, 37–38, 49–50.

49. Dewey, *The School and Society, MW*, 1: 69–71, 93; *Democracy and Education, MW*, 9: 82. Holmes to Frederick Pollock, May 15, 1931, *Holmes-Pollock Letters: The Correspondence of Mr. Justice Holmes and Sir Frederick Pollock, 1874–1932*, ed. Mark DeWolfe Howe (Cambridge, Mass., 1941), 2: 287. On the strange career of progressive education in America, see Lawrence Cremin, *The Transformation of the School: Progressivism in American Education, 1876–1957* (New York, 1961).

50. Lippmann, *A Preface to Politics*, 229; *Drift and Mastery*, 161–69; "Schenectady the Unwise," *Call*, June 9, 1912, quoted in Steel, *Walter Lippmann and the American Century*, 42.

51. Croly, *The Promise of American Life*, 400; *Progressive Democracy*, 408, 423–24; see also 208–14; and Levy, *Croly*, 168–69, 178–84.

52. Bourgeois, "La Solidarité et la liberté" (1900), and "Les Risques sociaux et l'assurance sociale" (1901), in *Solidarité*, 97–102, and 249–50. See also *Les Applications de la solidarité sociale*, 4–8.

53. Croly, *Progressive Democracy*, 412–18. Examples of the argument that progressive education led smoothly into education as social control include Lasch, *The New Radicalism in America*, 14; Paul Bourke, "Culture and the Status of Politics," 68–69, 81, 85; and Jean B. Quandt, *From the Small Town to the Great Community: The Social Thought of Progressive Intellectuals* (New Brunswick, N.J., 1970), esp. 81–82, 127, 212 nn. 3 and 4.

54. Croly, "A Great School of Political Science," *The World's Work*, May, 1910, 128–30; Dewey and Tufts, *Ethics, MW*, 5: 201. For an early attempt to reveal the circularity of Croly's reliance on education, see Royal Meeker's review of *The Promise of American Life* in *Political Science Quarterly* 25 (1910): 667–68.

55. See McBriar, *Fabian Socialism*, 219–22; and Scott, *Republican Ideas and the Liberal Tradition in France*, 181 n. 56. On the more general question of solidarity and education, see J. E. S. Hayward, "Educational Pressure Groups."

56. Ely, *Socialism and Social Reform*, 348–49. Cynical interpreters of American history might argue that the nation followed Ely's formula with precision, although reversing the balance he had in mind. On the question of professionalization, see Haskell, *The Emergence of Professional Social Science*; Furner, *Advocacy and Objectivity*; Bledstein, *The Culture of*

Professionalism; Herbst, *German Historical School*; Oleson and Voss, eds., *Organization of Knowledge in Modern America*; and Haskell, ed., *The Authority of Experts*.

57. Croly, "A School of Social Research," *The New Republic*, June 8, 1918, 167–71. On the founding of the New School, see Alvin Johnson, *Pioneer's Progress*, 271–88; and James Harvey Robinson, "The New School," *School and Society* 11 (1920): 129–32. For Croly's involvement, see Levy, *Croly*, 269–71; on Dewey's role, see Dykhuizen, *Dewey*, 171. On the quite different purpose of the Ecole Libre des Sciences Politiques, see the brief discussion in Zeldin, *Intellect and Pride*, 343–44.

58. *The National Civic Federation Review* is quoted in Luther V. Hendricks, "James Harvey Robinson and the New School for Social Research," *Journal of Higher Education* 20 (1949): 10–11. See also Johnson, *Pioneer's Progress*, on the school's later years. During World War II, the New School recovered a measure of its original radical élan by hosting a number of European emigrés, but it soon discovered—as have other universities saddled with reputations for radicalism—that such inclinations have an adverse effect on an institution's financial health.

59. Weber, *Economy and Society*, 2: 1090, 998–1003. For contrasting interpretations of the effect on German intellectual and political life of the distinction drawn between *Kultur* and *Zivilisation*, see Ringer, *The Decline of the German Mandarins*, and Struve, *Elites Against Democracy*.

60. Weber, "Science as a Vocation," *From Max Weber*, 147, 152.

61. Weber stated the contradiction in especially clear form in *Economy and Society*, 2: 948–52.

62. Bourgeois discussed his vision of the state's limited role in *Solidarité*, 244–47.

63. Hobhouse, *Democracy and Reaction*, 186–87, 242–43; Hobhouse quoted in C. R. Ashbee's journal, Jan., 1900, cited in Collini, *Liberalism and Sociology*, 68; Hobhouse, "The Career of Fabianism," *Nation*, March 20, 1907, 182–83 (attributed to Hobhouse by Peter Clarke, *Liberals and Social Democrats*, 310). On the Minority Report, articles attributed to Hobhouse by Peter Clarke (311) appeared in the *Manchester Guardian*, Feb. 18 and 20, 1909; and cf. *Liberalism*, 72, 89–90, 118–19. On this point, see also Freeden, *The New Liberalism*, 186–90; Searle, *The Quest for National Efficiency*, 102–4; Clarke, *Liberals and Social Democrats*, 67, 71, 119–22; and Collini, *Liberalism and Sociology*, 74–78, 140.

64. Lippmann, *A Preface to Politics*, 201; *Drift and Mastery*, 318–24.

65. Croly, *Progressive Democracy*, 271–72, 281–82. Cf. *The Promise of American Life*, 336–37.

66. Lippmann, *Drift and Mastery*, 273–88; Dewey, "Psychology and Philosophical Method" (1889), *MW*, 1: 128. For similar formulations of this argument, see "Intelligence and Morals," *MW*, 4: 38–42; and *Democracy and Education, MW*, 9: 87–94. On Lippmann, see Hollinger, "Science and Anarchy."

67. Croly, *Progressive Democracy*, 351–61, 364–77. For other examples of this approach to regulation, see Lippmann, "An Ineffective Remedy," *The New Republic*, Nov. 25, 1916, 83–84, in *Early Writings*, 220–23; and "Can the Strike Be Abandoned?" *The New Republic*, Jan. 21, 1920, 224–27, in *Early Writings*, 224–32. The literature on the failure of regulatory agencies to regulate is extensive. See especially Lowi, *The End of Liberalism*; and McConnell, *Private Power and American Democracy*. Marver Bernstein, in *Regulating Business by Independent Commission* (Princeton, 1955), recounts the typical "life-cycle" of regulatory agencies as they arise in response to public unrest, gradually become targets of criticism for overzealousness, and finally settle into a pattern in which protection of the interests to be regulated is their primary concern. See also McCraw, ed., *Regulation in Perspective*.

68. Weber, *Economy and Society*, 2: 994.

69. Weber, "Der Nationalstaat und die Volkswirtschaftspolitik," *GPS*, 1–25; for Brentano's correspondence with the Webbs on this issue, see p. 479 n. 63 above. Weber claimed in a debate

with *Verein* members in 1905 that the independence of the labor movement from the state was essential to the development of a politically alert working class. See Beetham, *Max Weber,* 207–9.

70. Weber, *Economy and Society,* 2: 992. See also Bendix, *Weber,* 449–57.

71. Weber, "Science as a Vocation," *From Max Weber,* 139.

72. As an illustration of the depth of the disagreement on this issue, consider the fact that two of the most insightful of Weber's interpreters, David Beetham and Wolfgang Mommsen, have both noted Herbert Marcuse's argument that in modern capitalism "formal rationality" is equated with "substantive rationality." But whereas Beetham argues that Weber's own political sociology is vulnerable to that criticism, Mommsen considers Weber's analysis its source. In *The Age of Bureaucracy,* xv, Mommsen contends that Weber "largely anticipated" Marcuse's critique in his own account of capitalism, an argument I find useful if ahistorical. Cf. Beetham, *Max Weber,* 274–75. For a recent discussion of the other participants in this lively debate, including Guenther Roth, Johannes Winkelmann, Jürgen Kocka, Karl Loewenstein, and Eduard Baumgarten, see Schluchter, "Value-Neutrality and the Ethic of Responsibility," 102 n. 105.

73. Weber, "Zur Lage der bürgerlichen Demokratie in Russland," *GPS,* 30–65. The concluding section of this essay is included in Runciman, ed., *Max Weber: Selections in Translation;* the quoted passages appear on 281–82. See also Weber, "The Meaning of Ethical Neutrality," *Methodology,* 23: "I, for my part, will not try to dissuade the nation from the view that actions are to be judged not merely by their instrumental value but by their intrinsic value as well."

74. Weber, *Economy and Society,* 1: 268–71.

75. Marianne Weber, *Weber,* 653.

76. In "Parliament and Government in a Reconstructed Germany," Weber wrote:

> The political danger of mass democracy for the polity lies first of all in the possibility that emotional elements will predominate in politics. The "mass" as such (irrespective of the social strata which it comprises in any given case) thinks only in short-run terms. For it is, as every experience teaches, always exposed to direct, purely emotional and irrational influence. (It has this in common, incidentally, with the modern "self-governing" monarchy, which produces the same phenomena.) A cool and clear mind— and successful politics, especially democratic politics depends, after all, on that—prevails in responsible decision-making the more, (1) the smaller the number of decision-makers is, and (2) the clearer the responsibilities are to each of them and to those whom they lead. . . . In Germany, too, the difficult first postwar years will be a severe test for the discipline of the masses.

(Appendix II, *Economy and Society,* 2: 1459–60).

77. Weber quoted in Mommsen, *The Age of Bureaucracy,* 87. The phrase "open-yet-authoritarian elite" comes from Struve, *Elites Against Democracy.* Although my treatment of Weber departs from Struve's, I have found his analysis of German politics instructive. Cf. the discussion of German politics in the nineteenth century, and the anemia of German liberalism, on pp. 166–68 above.

78. Weber, "Speech for Austrian Officers in Vienna," in *The Interpretation of Social Reality,* 197. See also Weber, *Economy and Society,* 1: 284–88, 2: 948–52; and cf. Beetham, *Max Weber,* 70, 78, 101–6; and Alexander, *Theoretical Logic in Sociology,* 3: 107–12.

79. Weber, "Politik als Beruf," *GPS,* 532; cf. "Politics as a Vocation," *From Max Weber,* 113–14; Weber, "Der Reichspräsident," *GPS,* 488–89. See also the incisive discussions of this question in Beetham, *Max Weber,* 215–49; and Roslyn Wallach Bologh, "Max Weber and the Dilemma of Rationality," in *Max Weber's Political Sociology: A Pessimistic Vision of a Rationalized World,* ed. Ronald M. Glassman and Vatro Murvar (Westport, 1984), 175–86.

80. Weber to Michels, April 8, 1908, quoted in Struve, *Elites Against Democracy,* 124.

81. Croly, *Progressive Democracy,* 279; cf. 356–57.

82. Lippmann to Wallas, Aug. 31 and Nov. 4, 1920, Lippmann papers.

83. Croly, "Behaviorism in Religion," *The New Republic*, Feb. 22, 1922, 368. In addition to "The Breach in Civilization," see Croly's unpublished essays "Christianity and Modern Life" and "Religion in Life," also in the Frankfurter papers. Levy discusses Croly's final flurry of interest in mysticism in *Croly*, 289–99.

84. Laski to Lippmann, Jan. 29, 1919, Lippmann papers. Cf. Laski's letter of June 11, 1919: "Please keep in mind that for me you and Herbert are the two political thinkers in America who are doing work of absolutely first class importance."

85. Lippmann, *Public Opinion*, 195. Lippmann's analysis made a deep impression on another radical whose democratic impulses had proved somewhat unsteady, Sidney Webb. In a letter to Lippmann dated July 21, 1922, in the Lippmann papers, Webb wrote, "We are delighted with your *Public Opinion* . . . your analysis of the position is excellent and most convincing." Yet Webb differed from Lippmann on a question of basic importance. Getting solid information into the hands of the public, Webb maintained, "seems an insoluble problem so long as the great instruments of production are in private hands for the purpose of making profit—and with them, necessarily so much of the government power. Thus, in my view, we can only progress by advancing step by step into collectivism—which we have got to prove to be practicable."

86. Croly's autobiographical fragment is in the Frankfurter papers; the quotation is from the introductory paragraph on p. 1.

87. Hobhouse, *The Elements of Social Justice* (London, 1922), 188.

88. Dewey's review of *Public Opinion* originally appeared in *The New Republic*, May 3, 1922, 286–88; it is reprinted in *MW*, 13: 337–44.

89. See above, pp. 43–44, 141–44.

90. Dewey, "Individuality, Equality, and Superiority," *The New Republic*, Dec. 13, 1922, 61–63; reprinted in *MW*, 13: 295–300.

91. Dewey, *The Public and Its Problems* (New York, 1927), 215–16.

92. Ibid., 207.

Chapter 10. The Prospect of Justice

1. *The Progressive Review*, Oct., 1896, 3–9.

2. Green, *Lectures on the Philosophy of Kant, Works*, 2: 312, 314.

3. See above, pp. 181–82.

4. Dewey's 1892 lectures on political philosophy are in the Dewey papers, Morris Library, Southern Illinois University; see 58–60, 81–82, 90–91. See also his lecture, "Christianity and Democracy," also delivered in 1892, discussed above on pp. 43–44.

5. Dewey and Tufts, *Ethics, MW*, 5: 392, 397–99, 430–33.

6. Hobhouse, *Liberalism*, 21; see also 16–29, 97–99.

7. Hobhouse, "The Historical Evolution of Property," originally appeared in a collection of essays entitled *Property: Its Duties and Rights Historically, Philosophically, and Religiously Regarded* (London, 1914); it was reprinted in *Sociology and Philosophy*, 83–106. The distinction between property for use and property for power appears to have originated in Aristotle; its echoes are still reverberating. For a recent example, see Walzer, *Spheres of Justice*, which illustrates that specifying the appropriate "sphere" in which the power of money should be allowed to matter remains as important as it is elusive. For discussions of Hobhouse's view of property, cf. Collini, *Liberalism and Sociology*, 130–44; and Clarke, *Liberals and Social Democrats*, 153.

8. Bourgeois, *Solidarité*, 95–96, 140–42, 226; *Lettre au Congrès Radical et Radical-Socialiste de Nantes*, 15. See also *La Solidarité humaine*, 14; *Les Applications de la solidarité sociale*, 15; and *Discours au Chambre du 16 novembre, 1897*, 9–10, 16–17.

9. Weber, *Economy and Society*, 2: 729–31.

10. The phrase is from Wolfgang Mommsen, *The Age of Bureaucracy*, chap. 5, 95–115. On Weber's commitment to autonomy, see Marianne Weber, *Weber*, 88, 120; Giddens, *Politics and Sociology in the Thought of Max Weber*, 55–56; Beetham, *Max Weber*, 54–55; Maurice Merleau-Ponty, "The Crisis of the Understanding," in *The Primacy of Perception* ed. James M. Edie (Evanston, 1964), 208; Alexander, *Theoretical Logic in Sociology*, 3: 123–24; and Seidman, *Liberalism and the Origins of European Social Theory*, 213–34. I am also indebted to Mark Hulliung for clarification of this issue.

11. Lippmann to Marie Howe, Feb. 16, 1915, Lippmann papers. For the social democrats' discussion of property rights, see above, pp. 280–82.

12. On the ideas of Fouillée and the other philosophers of the *via media* on the question of property, see above, pp. 182–83.

13. Lippmann, *A Preface to Politics*, 152–53, 127. David Hollinger has argued that Lippmann's *Drift and Mastery* illustrates how members of his generation tried simultaneously to "search for order" and "revolt against formalism." As Hollinger argues, Lippmann's ideas demonstrate that those two familiar descriptions of progressivism are not as incompatible as they seem; it is merely necessary to understand what such progressive theorists as Lippmann had in mind when they called for "order" and criticized "formalism." See Hollinger, "Science and Anarchy."

14. Croly, *Progressive Democracy*, 425, 409, 418; see also 198–99.

15. Hobhouse, *Morals in Evolution*, 1: 367–68. The passage is quoted in Dewey and Tufts, *Ethics, MW*, 5: 384–85. Hobhouse offered a similar argument in *Liberalism*, 78; Dewey presented his own version of this analysis earlier in "The Ethics of Democracy," in *EW*, 1: 244; and later in *Reconstruction in Philosophy, MW*, 12: 136.

16. Dewey, *Democracy and Education, MW*, 9: 88–93.

17. Croly, *Progressive Democracy*, 211, 27.

18. Croly, *The Promise of American Life*, 454.

19. Hobhouse, *Liberalism*, 69; "The Prospects of Liberalism," *Contemporary Review* 93 (1907): 353. On the tension in utilitarianism between natural and artificial identity of interests, see Halévy, *The Growth of Philosophic Radicalism*, 15–17, 370–72.

20. Bourgeois, *Solidarité*, 186; *Lettre au Congrès Radical et Radical-Socialiste de Nantes*, 15.

21. Hobhouse, "Sociology" (1920), in *Sociology and Philosophy*, 50–55. For Sidgwick's critique of Green, see pp. 129–30 above. For contrasting assessments of Hobhouse's ideas about freedom and harmony, see Clarke, *Liberals and Social Democrats*, 145–54; and Collini, *Liberalism and Sociology*, 232–34, both of which seem to me more convincing than the account in Freeden, *The New Liberalism*, 105–9.

22. Weber, "Zur Gründung einer national-sozialen Partei," a speech given to the Verein für Sozialpolitik, Nov. 23, 1896, in *GPS*, 28–29; "Politik als Beruf," *GPS*, 546; cf. "Politics as a Vocation," *From Max Weber*, 126; "Zur Lage der bürgerlichen Demokratie in Russland," *GPS*, 40. See also Ilse Dronberger, *The Political Thought of Max Weber: In Quest of Statesmanship* (New York, 1971), 129, 147 n. 50.

23. Cf. Weber, *The Protestant Ethic and the Spirit of Capitalism*, 85–86, 112–14; Giddens, *Politics and Sociology in the Thought of Max Weber*, 30–33; Bourgeois quoted in Nordmann, *Histoire des radicaux*, 134; and Hobhouse, *Liberalism*, 118–19.

24. On this topic, see especially Quandt, *From the Small Town to the Great Community*; Wilson, *In Quest of Community*; and Hays, "Political Parties and the Community-Society Continuum," in *American Political History as Social Analysis*, 293–325. Even Weber expressed a measure of faith in intermediate-level voluntary organizations, such as the Freistudentische Bund in Bavaria, before whom he delivered both his "Science as a Vocation" and his "Politics as a

Vocation" speeches. But he was less optimistic about their significance than were the other progressives. On this question see Marianne Weber, *Weber*, 628.

25. Weber, *Economy and Society*, 2: 1156; see also Löwith, "Weber's Interpretation of the Bourgeois-Capitalistic World," in Wrong, ed., *Weber*, 119–22, 107–8.

26. Croly, *Progressive Democracy*, 402; Dewey, *Democracy and Education, MW*, 9: 91.

27. Croly, *Progressive Democracy*, 404.

28. Weber, "Science as a Vocation," *From Max Weber*, 143. For Weber's historical sociology of law, see vol. 2 of *Economy and Society*, esp. 866–75. For a recent discussion of the critical literature on this issue, see Alexander, *Theoretical Logic in Sociology*, 3: 202–4 n. 89. Alexander follows Habermas in treating Weber as a proponent of the technical rationality he describes in *Economy and Society*. I think that argument confuses Weber's own values with the results of his research. While I find Habermas's critique of capitalist values useful and in many ways persuasive, I share Mommsen's view that such a critique follows Weber's lead more than challenges him. Cf. Habermas, *Toward a Rational Society*, trans. Jeremy J. Shapiro (Boston, 1970), 81–90; *Theory and Practice*, trans. John Viertel (Boston, 1973), 82–86; and Mommsen, *The Age of Bureaucracy*, 95–115.

29. Weber, *The Protestant Ethic and the Spirit of Capitalism*, 180–83. For the origins of Weber's image of the iron cage, see Edward Tiryakian, "The Sociological Import of a Metaphor: Tracking the Source of Max Weber's 'Iron Cage,'" *Sociological Inquiry* 51 (1981): 27–36.

30. Croly, *Progressive Democracy*, 405; *The Promise of American Life*, 452–53.

31. Dewey, Address of the president before the American Psychological Association, New Haven, 1899, *Psychological Review* 7 (1900), *MW*, 1: 130–50.

32. Weber, "Politics as a Vocation," *From Max Weber*, 128; cf. "Politik als Beruf," *GPS*, 548.

33. Weber, "Economic Policy and the National Interest in Germany," in W. G. Runciman, ed., *Weber, Selections*, trans. Eric Matthews (Cambridge, 1978), 267.

34. Dewey, "Nature in Experience," *On Experience, Nature, and Freedom*, 255.

35. Reinhold Niebuhr, "The Twilight of Liberalism," *The New Republic*, June 14, 1919, 218. Niebuhr elaborated his argument for the necessity of illusions and the inadequacy of social democratic and progressive ideas in *Moral Man and Immoral Society: A Study in Ethics and Politics* (New York, 1932), 220–32, in which he focused particularly on Bernstein and Jaurès.

36. James to Lutoslawski, March 20, 1900, Beinecke Library, Yale University.

37. Bourgeois's introduction to Buisson, *La Politique radicale*, iv–vii.

38. James, *The Principles of Psychology*, 2: 579.

Selected Bibliography

Principal Manuscript Collections Consulted

Eduard Bernstein papers, International Institute for Social History, Amsterdam.

Randolph Bourne papers, Butler Library, Columbia University, New York.

John Dewey papers, Center for Dewey Studies, Carbondale, Illinois; and Morris Library, Southern Illinois University, Carbondale, Illinois.

Richard T. Ely papers, Wisconsin State Historical Society, Madison, Wisconsin.

Fabian Society archive, Nuffield College Library, Oxford University, Oxford.

Alfred Fouillée letters, Bibliothèque Nationale, Paris.

Felix Frankfurter papers, Library of Congress, Washington D.C.

T. H. Green papers, Balliol College Library, Oxford University, Oxford.

Learned Hand papers, Law School Library, Harvard University, Cambridge.

William James papers, Beinecke Library, Yale University, New Haven; and Houghton Library, Harvard University, Cambridge.

Karl Kautsky papers, International Institute for Social History, Amsterdam.

Walter Lippmann papers, Sterling Library, Yale University, New Haven.

Passfield papers, British Library of Political and Economic Science, London School of Economics, London.

Walter Rauschenbusch papers, American Baptist Historical Society, Colgate-Rochester Divinity School, Rochester, New York.

E. R. A. Seligman papers, Butler Library, Columbia University, New York.

Henry Sidgwick papers, Wren Library, Trinity College, Cambridge University, Cambridge.

Max Weber archive, Bavarian Academy of Sciences, Munich.

Because the following bibliography is designed primarily to help readers identify sources cited frequently in the notes, it is arranged in a single alphabetical list. More comprehensive references, and critical discussions of the sources, will be found in the notes. Most sources mentioned only once in the notes are omitted here. Articles are included when the use of short titles in the notes might make their identification difficult. I have included original dates of publication when that information might prove useful.

Abrams, Philip. *The Origins of British Sociology, 1834–1914*. Chicago: University of Chicago Press, 1968.

Alexander, Jeffrey C. *Theoretical Logic in Sociology*. Volume 3. *The Classical Attempt at Synthesis: Max Weber*. Berkeley: University of California Press, 1983.

Allen, Gay Wilson. *William James*. New York: Viking Press, 1967.

Anderson, R. D. *France, 1870–1914: Politics and Society*. London: Routledge & Kegan Paul, 1977.

Angel, Pierre. *Eduard Bernstein et l'evolution du socialisme allemand*. Paris: Marcel Didier, 1961.

Ayer, A.J. *The Origins of Pragmatism: Studies in the Philosophy of Charles Sanders Peirce and William James*. San Francisco: Freeman, Cooper & Co., 1968.

Azéma, Jean-Pierre, and Winock, Michel. *La IIIᵉ République: "naissance et mort."* 2nd ed. Paris: Calmann-Lévy, 1976.

Barzun, Jacques. *A Stroll with William James*. New York: Harper & Row, 1983.

Baumgarten, Eduard. *Max Weber, Werk und Person*. Tübingen: J. C. B. Mohr, 1964.

Beer, Samuel H. *British Politics in the Collectivist Age*. New York: Knopf, 1965.

Beetham, David. *Max Weber and the Theory of Modern Politics*. London: George Allen & Unwin, 1974.

Bendix, Reinhard. *Max Weber: An Intellectual Portrait*. 1960. 2nd ed., with an Introduction by Guenther Roth. Berkeley: University of California Press, 1977.

Bergounioux, Alain, and Manin, Bernard. *La Social-démocratie ou le compromis*. Paris: P.U.F., 1979.

Bernstein, Eduard. "Entwicklungsgang eines Sozialisten." In *Die Volkswirtschaftslehre der Gegenwart in Selbstdarstellungen*, vol. 1. Leipzig: Meiner, 1924.

———. *Evolutionary Socialism*. Translated by Edith C. Harvey. 1909. Reprint New York: Schocken Books, 1961.

———. *Zur Geschichte und Theorie des Sozialismus*. Berlin: Edelheim, 1901.

———. "Leitsätze für den theoretischen Teil eines sozialdemokratischen Parteiprogramms." Appendix to *Der Revisionismus in der Sozialdemocratie*. Amsterdam: Martin Cohen, 1909.

———. *My Years in Exile: Reminiscences of a Socialist*. Translated by Bernard Miall. 1921. Reprint New York: Schocken Books, 1961.

———. *Socialisme et science*. Translated by Edouard Schneider. Paris: Giard & Brière, 1902.

———. *Sozialismus und Demokratie in der grossen englischen Revolution*. Stuttgart: Dietz, 1895.

———. *Die Voraussetzungen des Sozialismus und die Aufgaben der Sozialdemokratie*. Stuttgart: Dietz, 1899.

———. *Wie ist wissenschaftlicher Sozialismus möglich?* Berlin: Sozialistische Monatshefte, 1901.

———. *Wirtschaftswesen und Wertschaftswerden*. Berlin: Vörwarts, 1920.

Bernstein, Richard J. *Praxis and Action: Contemporary Philosophies of Human Activity*. Philadelphia: University of Pennsylvania Press, 1971.

———. *The Restructuring of Social and Political Theory*. New York: Harcourt Brace Jovanovich, 1976.

Blum, Léon. *Jean Jaurès*. Paris: Librairie populaire, 1933.

Bodein, Vernon P. *The Social Gospel of Walter Rauschenbusch*. Yale Studies in Religious Education, vol. 15. New Haven: Yale University Press, 1944.

Boitel, Maurice. *Les Idées liberales dans le socialisme de Jean Jaurès*. Paris: L'Emancipatrice, 1921.

Bourgeois, Léon. *Discours au Chambre du 16 novembre, 1897*. Amiens: P. Duchatel, 1897.

——. *Discours prononcé à la séance de la Chambre des Députés du 12 mars, 1898*. Paris: Alcan-Lévy, 1898.

——. *L'Education et la démocratie française*. Paris: Cornély, 1897.

——. *Essai d'une philosophie de la solidarité*. Paris: Alcan, 1902.

——. *Lettre au Congrès Radical et Radical-Socialiste de Nantes, octobre, 1909*. Paris: D'Hardricourt, 1909.

——. *Solidarité*. 1896. 7th ed. Paris: Colin, 1912.

——. *La Solidarité humaine*. Paris: M. Lepêcheux, 1914.

Bourke, Paul. "Culture and the Status of Politics, 1910–1917: Studies in the Social Criticism of Herbert Croly, Walter Lippmann, Randolph Bourne, and Van Wyck Brooks." Ph.D. diss., University of Wisconsin, 1967.

——. "The Social Critics and the End of American Innocence, 1907–1921." *Journal of American Studies* 3 (1969): 57–72.

——. "The Status of Politics, 1909–1919: *The New Republic*, Randolph Bourne, and Van Wyck Brooks." *Journal of American Studies* 8 (1974): 171–202.

Boydston, Jo Ann, and Poulos, Kathleen. *Checklist of Writings about John Dewey, 1887–1977*. 2nd ed. Carbondale: Southern Illinois University Press, 1978.

Braunthal, Julius. *History of the International, 1864–1914*. Translated by Henry Collins and Kenneth Mitchell. London: Thomas Nelson & Sons, 1966.

Brecht, Arnold. *Political Theory: The Foundations of Twentieth-Century Political Thought*. Princeton: Princeton University Press, 1959.

Broad, C. D. *Ethics and the History of Philosophy*. New York: The Humanities Press, 1952.

——. *Five Types of Ethical Theory*. New York: Harcourt, Brace & Co., 1930.

Bruce, Maurice. *The Coming of the Welfare State*. London: B. T. Batsford, 1961.

Bruun, Hans Henrik. *Science, Values, and Politics in Max Weber's Methodology*. Copenhagen: Munksgaard, 1972.

Buenker, John D. *Urban Liberalism and Progressive Reform*. New York: Scribner's, 1973.

——; Burnham, John C.; and Crunden, Robert M. *Progressivism*. Cambridge: Schenkman, 1977.

Buisson, Ferdinand. *La Politique radicale: études sur les doctrines du parti radical et radical-socialiste*. Paris: Giard et Brière, 1908.

Bullert, Gary. *The Politics of John Dewey*. Buffalo: Prometheus Books, 1983.

Bulhof, Ilse N. *Wilhelm Dilthey: A Hermeneutic Approach to the Study of History and Culture*. Martinus Nijhoff Philosophy Library, vol. 2. The Hague: Martinus Nijhoff, 1980.

Burger, Thomas. *Max Weber's Theory of Concept Formation: History, Laws, and Ideal Types*. Durham: Duke University Press, 1976.

Cacoullos, Ann R. *Thomas Hill Green: Philosopher of Rights*. New York: Twayne, 1974.

Cahn, Stephen M., ed. *New Studies in the Philosophy of John Dewey*. Hanover: University Press of New England, 1977.

Challaye, Félicien. *Jaurès*. Paris: Editions Mellottée, n.d.

Clark, Terry N. *Prophets and Patrons: The French University and the Emergence of the Social Sciences*. Cambridge: Harvard University Press, 1973.

Clarke, Peter F. *Lancashire and the New Liberalism*. Cambridge: Cambridge University Press, 1971.

——. *Liberals and Social Democrats*. Cambridge: Cambridge University Press, 1978.

Cole, G. D. H. *A History of Socialist Thought*. Volume 3. *The Second International, 1889–1914*. London: Macmillan & Co., 1956.

Cole, Margaret. *Beatrice Webb*. London: Longmans, Green & Co., 1946.

——. *The Story of Fabian Socialism*. London: Heinemann, 1961.

————, ed. *The Webbs and their Work*. London: Frederick Muller, 1949.

Colletti, Lucio. *From Rousseau to Lenin: Studies in Ideology and Society*. Translated by John Merrington and Judith White. New York. Monthly Review Press, 1972.

Collini, Stefan. *Liberalism and Sociology: L. T. Hobhouse and Political Argument in England, 1880–1914*. Cambridge: Cambridge University Press, 1979.

————; Winch, Donald; and Burrow, John. *That Noble Science of Politics: A Study in Nineteenth-Century Intellectual History*. Cambridge: Cambridge University Press, 1983.

Corti, W. Robert, ed. *The Philosophy of William James*. Winterthur: Archiv für genetische Philosophie, 1975.

Coughlan, Neil. *Young John Dewey: An Essay in American Intellectual History*. Chicago: University of Chicago Press, 1973.

Craig, Gordon A. *Germany 1866–1945*. Oxford: Oxford University Press, 1978.

Croly, Herbert. *Progressive Democracy*. New York: Macmillan Co., 1914.

————. *The Promise of American Life*. 1909. Edited by John William Ward. The American Heritage Series. Indianapolis: Bobbs-Merrill, 1965.

Crunden, Robert M. *Ministers of Reform: The Progressives' Achievement in American Civilization, 1889–1920*. New York: Basic Books, 1982.

Degler, Carl N. *The Age of the Economic Revolution, 1876–1900*. Glenview, Ill.: Scott, Foresman, & Co., 1967.

————. *Out of Our Past: The Forces That Shaped Modern America*. 2nd ed. New York: Harper & Row, 1970.

Dewey, John. *Characters and Events: Popular Essays in Social and Political Philosophy*. Edited by Joseph Ratner. 2 vols. New York: Henry Holt & Co., 1929.

————. "The Development of American Pragmatism." In *Studies in the History of Ideas*. 2 vols. New York: Columbia University Press, 1925. 2: 353–77.

————. *The Early Works, 1882–1898*. Edited by Jo Ann Boydston et al. 5 vols. Carbondale: Southern Illinois University Press, 1967–1972.

————. *Experience and Nature*. Chicago: The Open Court, 1925.

————. "From Absolutism to Experimentalism." In *Contemporary American Philosophy*. Edited by George P. Adams and William P. Montague. 2 vols. New York: Macmillan Co., 1930. 2: 13–27.

————. *Liberalism and Social Action*. The Page-Barbour Lectures. New York: G. P. Putnam's Sons, 1935.

————. *The Middle Works, 1899–1924*. Edited by Jo Ann Boydston et al. 14 vols. to date. Carbondale: Southern Illinois University Press, 1976–1983.

————. *On Experience, Nature, and Freedom*. Edited by Richard J. Bernstein. Indianapolis: Bobbs-Merrill, 1960.

————. *The Public and Its Problems*. New York: Henry Holt & Co., 1927.

————. *The Quest for Certainty*. Gifford Lectures. 1929. Reprint New York: Capricorn Books, 1960.

Dilthey, Wilhelm. *Briefwechsel zwischen Wilhelm Dilthey und dem Grafen Paul Yorck von Wartenburg, 1877–1897*. Edited by Sigrid von der Schulenburg. Halle a.d.S.: Niemeyer, 1923.

————. *Descriptive Psychology and Historical Understanding*. Translated by Richard M. Zaner. The Hague: Martinus Nijhoff, 1977.

————. *Gesammelte Schriften*. Edited by Bernard Groethuysen et al. 18 vols. Stuttgart: B. G. Tuebner; Göttingen: Vandenhoeck & Ruprecht, 1914–1977.

————. *Der junge Dilthey: Ein Lebensbild in Briefen und Tagebüchern, 1852–1870*. 2nd ed. Edited by Clara Misch. Stuttgart: B. G. Tuebner; Göttingen: Vandenhoeck & Ruprecht, 1960.

——. *Pattern and Meaning in History: Thoughts on History and Society.* Edited and translated by H. P. Rickman. New York: Harper Torchbooks, 1961.

——. *Selected Writings.* Edited and translated by H. P. Rickman. Cambridge: Cambridge University Press, 1976.

Dronberger, Ilse. *The Political Thought of Max Weber: In Quest of Statesmanship.* New York: Appleton-Century-Crofts, 1971.

Dykhuizen, George. *The Life and Mind of John Dewey.* Carbondale: Southern Illinois University Press, 1973.

Eden, Robert. *Political Leadership and Nihilism: A Study of Weber and Nietzsche.* Gainesville: University Presses of Florida, 1984.

Elm, Ludwig. *Zwischen Fortschritt und Reaktion: Geschichte der Parteien der liberalen Bourgeoisie in Deutschland, 1893–1918.* Berlin: Akademie–Verlag, 1968.

Ely, Richard, T. *French and German Socialism in Modern Times.* New York: Harper & Brothers, 1883.

——. *Ground Under Our Feet: An Autobiography.* New York: Macmillan Co., 1938.

——. *An Introduction to Political Economy.* New York: Hunt & Eaton, 1893.

——. *The Labor Movement in America.* 3rd ed. New York: Thomas Y. Crowell & Co., 1890.

——. "The Past and the Present of Political Economy." *Johns Hopkins University Studies in Historical and Political Science.* 2nd series. Edited by Herbert B. Adams. Baltimore: Johns Hopkins University Press, 1884.

——. *Property and Contract in their Relation to the Distribution of Wealth.* New York: Macmillan Co., 1914.

——. "Recent American Socialism." *Johns Hopkins University Studies in Historical and Political Science.* 3rd series. Edited by Herbert B. Adams. Baltimore: John Murphy & Co., 1885.

——. *The Social Aspects of Christianity.* New York: Thomas Y. Crowell & Co., 1889.

——. *The Social Law of Service.* New York: Eaton & Mains, 1896.

——. *Socialism and Social Reform.* New York: Thomas Y. Crowell & Co., 1894.

——. *Studies in the Evolution of an Industrial Society.* New York: Macmillan Co., 1903.

Emy, H. V. *Liberals, Radicals, and Social Politics, 1892–1914.* Cambridge: Cambridge University Press, 1973.

Ensor, R. C. K., ed. *Modern Socialism.* London: Harper & Brothers, 1904.

Ermarth, Michael. "The Transformation of Hermeneutics: 19th-Century Ancients and 20th-Century Moderns." *The Monist* 64 (1981): 176–94.

——. *Wilhelm Dilthey: The Critique of Historical Reason.* Chicago: University of Chicago Press, 1978.

Evans, Richard J., ed. *Society and Politics in Wilhelmine Germany.* London: Croom Helm, 1978.

Everett, John Rutherford. *Religion in Economics: A Study of John Bates Clark, Richard T. Ely, Simon N. Patten.* New York: King's Crown Press, 1946.

Feinstein, Howard M. *Becoming William James.* Ithaca: Cornell University Press, 1984.

Fine, Sidney. *Laissez Faire and the General-Welfare State: A Study of Conflict in American Thought, 1865–1901.* 1956. Reprint Ann Arbor: University of Michigan Press, 1969.

Fletcher, Roger. "Bernstein in Britain: Revisionism and Foreign Affairs." *The International History Review* 1 (1979): 349–75.

——. "Cobden as Educator: The Free-Trade Internationalism of Eduard Bernstein, 1899–1914." *American Historical Review* 88 (1983): 561–78.

Flora, Peter, and Heidenheimer, Arnold J., eds. *The Development of Welfare States in Europe and America, 1850–1950.* New Brunswick, N.J.: Transaction Books, 1981.

Flower, Elizabeth, and Murphy, Murray G. *A History of Philosophy in America.* 2 vols. New York: Putnam, 1977.

Forcey, Charles. *The Crossroads of Liberalism: Croly, Weyl, Lippmann, and the Progressive Era, 1900–1925.* New York: Oxford University Press, 1961.

Fouillée, Alfred. *L'Avenir de la métaphysique fondée sur l'expérience.* Paris: Alcan, 1889.

———. *Critique des systèmes de morale contemporains.* 1887. 5th ed. Paris: Alcan, 1906.

———. *La Démocratie politique et sociale en France.* Paris: Alcan, 1910.

———. *Education from a National Standpoint.* Edited and translated by W. J. Greenstreet. New York: D. Appleton & Co., 1892.

———. *Esquisse psychologique des peuples européens.* Paris: Alcan, 1905.

———. *Les Etudes classiques et la démocratie.* Paris: Colin, 1898.

———. *L'Evolutionisme des idées-forces.* Paris: Alcan, 1890.

———. *La France au point de vue moral.* 1900. 5th ed. Paris: Alcan, 1911.

———. *Histoire générale de la philosophie.* 1875. 11th ed. Paris: Delagrave, 1910.

———. *L'Idée moderne du droit en Allemagne, en Angleterre et en France.* Paris: Hachette, 1878.

———. *La Liberté et le déterminisme.* 1872. 8th ed. Paris: Alcan, 1911.

———. *Morale des idées-forces.* Paris: Alcan, 1908.

———. *Le Moralisme de Kant et l'amoralisme contemporain.* Paris: Alcan, 1905.

———. *Le Mouvement idéaliste et la réaction contre la science positive.* Paris: Alcan, 1896.

———. *Nietzsche et l'immoralisme.* Paris: Alcan, 1902.

———. *La Pensée et les nouvelles écoles anti-intellectualistes.* Paris: Alcan, 1911.

———. "Le Progrès sociale en France." *Revue des Deux Mondes* 15 (1899): 816–17.

———. *La Propriété sociale et la démocratie.* Paris: Hachette, 1884.

———. *La Psychologie des idées-forces.* 2 vols. Paris: Alcan, 1893.

———. *La Science sociale contemporaine.* 1880. 2nd ed. Paris: Hachette, 1885.

———. *Le Socialisme et la sociologie réformiste.* Paris: Alcan, 1910.

Frederick, Peter J. *Knights of the Golden Rule: The Intellectual as Christian Social Reformer in the 1890s.* Lexington: University Press of Kentucky, 1976.

Freeden, Michael. *The New Liberalism: An Ideology of Social Reform.* Oxford: Oxford University Press, 1978.

Frei, Herbert. *Fabianismus und Bernstein'scher Revisionismus, 1884–1900.* Bern: Peter Lang, 1979.

Furner, Mary O. *Advocacy and Objectivity: A Crisis in the Professionalization of American Social Science, 1865–1905.* Lexington: University Press of Kentucky, 1975.

Ganne de Beaucoudrey, Elisabeth. *La Psychologie et la métaphysique des idées-forces chez Alfred Fouillée.* Paris: Lipschutz, 1936.

Gay, Peter. *The Dilemma of Democratic Socialism: Eduard Bernstein's Challenge to Marx.* New York: Columbia University Press, 1952.

Giddens, Anthony. *Capitalism and Modern Social Theory: An Analysis of the Writings of Marx, Durkheim, and Max Weber.* Cambridge: Cambridge Univesity Press, 1971.

———. *Politics and Sociology in the Thought of Max Weber.* London: Macmillan & Co., 1972.

Gilbert, Bentley B. *The Evolution of National Insurance in Great Britain: The Origins of the Welfare State.* London: Michael Joseph, 1966.

Gilbert, James B. *Designing the Industrial State: The Intellectual Pursuit of Collectivism in America, 1880–1940.* Chicago: Quadrangle Books, 1972.

———. *Work Without Salvation: America's Intellectuals and Industrial Alienation, 1880–1910.* Baltimore: Johns Hopkins University Press, 1977.

Glassman, Ronald M., and Murvar, Vatro, eds. *Max Weber's Political Sociology: A Pessimistic Vision of a Rationalized World.* Westport, Conn.: Greenwood Press, 1984.

Goldberg, Harvey. *The Life of Jean Jaurès.* Madison: University of Wisconsin Press, 1962.

Goldman, Eric. *Rendezvous with Destiny: A History of Modern American Reform.* New York: Knopf, 1952.

Gouinlock, James. *John Dewey's Philosophy of Value.* New York: Humanities Press, 1972.

Green, Thomas Hill. *The Political Theory of T. H. Green.* Edited by John Rodman. New York: Appleton-Century-Crofts, 1964.

———. *Prolegomena to Ethics.* Edited by A. C. Bradley. 1883. Reprint New York: Thomas Y. Crowell & Co., 1969.

———. *Works.* Edited by R. L. Nettleship. 3 vols. London: Longmans, Green & Co., 1885–1889.

Greengarten, I. M. *Thomas Hill Green and the Development of Liberal-Democratic Thought.* Toronto: University of Toronto Press, 1981.

Griffin, C. M. "L. T. Hobhouse and the Idea of Harmony." *Journal of the History of Ideas* 35 (1974): 647–61.

Groh, Dieter. *Negative Integration und revolutionärer Attentismus: Die deutsche Sozialdemokratie am Vorabend des Ersten Weltkrieges.* Frankfurt a.M.: Propyläen, 1973.

Gustafsson, Bo. *Marxismus und Revisionismus: Eduard Bernsteins Kritik des Marxismus und ihre ideengeschichtlichen Voraussetzungen.* Translated by Holger Heide. Frankfurt a.M.: Europäische Verlanganstalt, 1972.

Guttsman, W. L. *The German Social Democratic Party, 1875–1933.* London: George Allen & Unwin, 1981.

Guyau, Augustin. *La Philosophie et la sociologie d'Alfred Fouillée.* Paris: Alcan, 1913.

Halévy, Elie. *The Growth of Philosophic Radicalism.* Translated by Mary Morris. London: Faber & Faber, 1934.

Hamburger, Maurice. *Léon Bourgeois.* Paris: Marcel Rivière, 1932.

Hartz, Louis. *The Liberal Tradition in America.* New York: Harcourt, Brace & World, 1955.

Haskell, Thomas L. *The Emergence of Professional Social Science: The American Social Science Association and the Nineteenth-Century Crisis of Authority.* Urbana: University of Illinois Press, 1977.

———, ed. *The Authority of Experts: Studies in History and Theory.* Bloomington: Indiana University Press, 1984.

Havard, William C. *Henry Sidgwick and Later Utilitarian Political Philosophy.* Gainesville: University of Florida Press, 1959.

Hawthorne, Geoffrey. *Enlightenment and Despair: A History of Sociology.* Cambridge: Cambridge University Press, 1976.

Hay, J. R. *The Development of the British Welfare State, 1880–1975.* London: Arnold, 1978.

———. *The Origins of Liberal Welfare Reforms, 1906–1914.* London: Macmillan & Co., 1975.

Hays, Samuel P. *American Political History as Social Analysis.* Knoxville: University of Tennessee Press, 1980.

———. *The Response to Industrialism, 1885–1914.* The Chicago History of American Civilization. Edited by Daniel Boorstin. Chicago: University of Chicago Press, 1957.

Hayward, J. E. S. "Educational Pressure Groups and the Indoctrination of the Radical Ideology of Solidarism, 1895–1914." *International Review of Social History* 8 (1963): 1–17.

———. "The Idea of Solidarity in French Social and Political Thought in the Nineteenth and Early Twentieth Centuries." Ph.D. diss., University of London, 1958.

———. "The Official Social Philosophy of the French Third Republic: Léon Bourgeois and Solidarism." *International Review of Social History* 6 (1961): 19–48.

———. "'Solidarity' and the Reformist Sociology of Alfred Fouillée." *American Journal of Economics and Sociology* 22 (1963): 205–22, 305–12.

———. "Solidarity: The Social History of an Idea in Nineteenth-Century France." *International Review of Social History* 4 (1959): 261–84.

Heckart, Beverly. *From Bassermann to Bebel: The Grand Bloc's Quest for Reform in the Kaiserreich, 1900–1914.* New Haven: Yale University Press, 1974.

Heimann, Horst, and Meyer, Thomas, eds. *Bernstein und der demokratische Sozialismus.* Bonn: Dietz, 1978.

Herbst, Jürgen. *The German Historical School in American Scholarship: A Study in the Transfer of Culture.* Ithaca: Cornell University Press, 1965.

Hermann, Ulrich. *Bibliographie Wilhelm Dilthey: Quellen und Literatur.* Berlin: Julius Beltz, 1969.

Hirsch, Helmut. *Der "Fabier" Eduard Bernstein: Zur Entwicklungsgeschichte des evolutionären Sozialismus.* Bonn: Dietz, 1977.

Hobhouse, Leonard T. *Democracy and Reaction.* Edited by Peter F. Clarke. 1904. Reprint Brighton: The Harvester Press, 1972.

——. *Development and Purpose: An Essay towards a Philosophy of Evolution.* London: Macmillan & Co., 1913.

——. *The Elements of Social Justice.* London: George Allen & Unwin, 1922.

——. "The Ethical Basis of Collectivism." *International Journal of Ethics* 8 (1898): 137–56.

——. "Faith and the Will to Believe." *Proceedings of the Aristotelian Society* 4 (1904): 91–109.

——. *The Labour Movement.* London: Macmillan & Co., 1897.

——. *Liberalism.* 1911. Edited by Alan P. Grimes. Reprint New York: Oxford University Press, 1971.

——. *The Metaphysical Theory of the State.* 1918. Reprint London: George Allen & Unwin, 1951.

——. *Mind in Evolution.* London: Macmillan & Co., 1901.

——. *Morals in Evolution: A Study in Comparative Ethics.* 1906. 7th ed. Edited by Morris Ginsberg. London: Chapman & Hall, 1951.

——. *Social Evolution and Political Theory.* New York: Columbia University Press, 1911.

——. *Sociology and Philosophy: A Centenary Collection of Essays and Articles.* Edited by Sidney Caine and Morris Ginsberg. Cambridge: Harvard University Press, 1966.

——. *The Theory of Knowledge: A Contribution to Some Problems of Logic and Metaphysics.* London: Methuen & Co., 1896.

Hobsbawm, E. J. "Fabians and Fabianism, 1884–1914." Ph.D. diss., Cambridge University, 1950.

——. *Labouring Men: Studies in the History of Labour.* 1964. Reprint London: Weidenfeld & Nicholson, 1976.

Hobson, John A., and Ginsberg, Morris. *L. T. Hobhouse: His Life and Work.* London: George Allen & Unwin, 1931.

Hodges, H. A. *The Philosophy of Wilhelm Dilthey.* London: Routledge & Kegan Paul, 1952.

——. *Wilhelm Dilthey: An Introduction.* New York: Howard Fertig, 1969.

Hoeveler, J. David, Jr. "The University and the Social Gospel: The Intellectual Origins of the 'Wisconsin Idea.'" *Wisconsin Magazine of History* 59 (1976): 289–98.

Hoffmann, Stanley. "Paradoxes of the French Political Community." In *In Search of France.* Edited by Stanley Hoffmann et al. Cambridge: Harvard University Press, 1963.

Hofstadter, Richard. *The Age of Reform.* New York: Vintage Books, 1955.

——. *Anti-Intellectualism in American Life.* New York: Vintage Books, 1962.

——. *Social Darwinism in American Thought.* 2nd ed. Boston: Beacon Press, 1955.

Holborn, Hajo. *A History of Modern Germany.* Volume 3. *1840–1945.* Princeton: Princeton University Press, 1969.

——. "Wilhelm Dilthey and the Critique of Historical Reason." *Journal of the History of Ideas* 11 (1950) 93–118.

Hollinger, David A. "The Problem of Pragmatism in American History." *Journal of American History* 67 (1980): 88–107.

——. "Science and Anarchy: Walter Lippmann's *Drift and Mastery.*" *American Quarterly* 39 (1977): 463–75.

——. "The Voice of Intellectual History in the Conversation of Mankind: A Note on Rorty's *Philosophy and the Mirror of Nature.*" *Newsletter of the Intellectual History Group* 4 (1982): 23–28.

——. "William James and the Culture of Inquiry." *Michigan Quarterly Review* 20 (1981): 264–83.

Hook, Sidney. *John Dewey: An Intellectual Portrait.* New York: John Day Co., 1939.

Hopkins, Charles Howard. *The Rise of the Social Gospel in American Protestantism, 1865–1915.* New Haven: Yale University Press, 1940.

Howe, Daniel Walker, ed. *Victorian America.* Philadelphia: University of Pennsylvania Press, 1976.

Howe, Frederic C. *Wisconsin: An Experiment in Democracy.* New York: Scribner's, 1912.

Hughes, H. Stuart. *Consciousness and Society: The Reorientation of European Social Thought, 1890–1930.* 1958. Reprint New York: Vintage Books, 1961.

Hutchison, William R. *The Modernist Impulse in American Protestantism.* New York: Oxford University Press, 1976.

——, ed. *American Protestant Thought: The Liberal Era.* New York: Harper & Row, 1968.

Iggers, Georg. *New Directions in European Historiography.* Middletown: Wesleyan University Press, 1975.

Ineichen, Hans. *Erkenntnistheorie und geschichtlich-gesellschaftliche Welt: Diltheys Logik der Geisteswissenschaften.* Frankfurt a.M.: Vittorio Klostermann, 1975.

Jackson, J. Hampden. *Jean Jaurès: His Life and Work.* London: George Allen & Unwin, 1943.

James, D. G. *Henry Sidgwick: Science and Faith in Victorian England.* Oxford: Oxford University Press, 1970.

James, William. *Collected Essays and Reviews.* Edited by Ralph Barton Perry. New York: Longmans, Green & Co., 1920.

——. *Essays in Philosophy. The Works of William James.* Edited by Frederick H. Burkhardt et al. Cambridge: Harvard University Press, 1978.

——. *Essays in Radical Empiricism.* 1912. *The Works of William James.* Edited by Frederick H. Burkhardt et al. Cambridge: Harvard University Press, 1976.

——. *The Letters of William James.* Edited by Henry James. 2 vols. 1920. Reprint New York: Kraus Reprint Co., 1969.

——. *The Meaning of Truth.* 1909. *The Works of William James.* Edited by Frederick H. Burkhardt et al. Cambridge: Harvard University Press, 1975.

——. *Memories and Studies.* New York: Longmans, Green & Co., 1911.

——. *A Pluralistic Universe.* 1909. *The Works of William James.* Edited by Frederick H. Burkhardt et al. Cambridge: Harvard University Press, 1977.

——. *Pragmatism.* 1907. *The Works of William James.* Edited by Frederick H. Burkhardt et al. Cambridge: Harvard University Press, 1975.

——. *The Principles of Psychology.* 2 vols. New York: Henry Holt & Co., 1890.

——. *Psychology. The Briefer Course.* New York: Henry Holt & Co., 1892.

——. *Some Problems of Philosophy.* 1911. *The Works of William James.* Edited by Frederick H. Burkhardt et al. Cambridge: Harvard University Press, 1979.

——. *Talks to Teachers on Psychology; and to Students on Some of Life's Ideals.* New York: Henry Holt & Co., 1901.

——. *The Varieties of Religious Experience.* 1902. 2nd ed. The Modern Library. New York: Random House, 1929.

——. *The Will to Believe.* 1897. *The Works of William James.* Edited by Frederick H. Burkhardt et al. Cambridge: Harvard University Press, 1979.

Jaurès, Jean. *L'Armée nouvelle.* 2nd ed. Edited by Lucien Lévy-Bruhl. Paris: Editions de la librairie de *L'Humanité*, 1915.

———. *L'Esprit du socialisme.* Edited by Jean Rabaut. Geneva: Editions Gonthier, 1964.

———. *Histoire socialiste de la Révolution française.* Edited by Albert Mathiez. 8 vols. Paris: Editions de la librairie de *L'Humanité,* 1922–1924.

———. *Oeuvres.* Edited by Max Bonnafous. 9 vols. Paris: Rieder, 1931–1939.

———. *Les Origines du socialisme allemand.* Edited by Lucien Goldmann. 1892. Paris: François Maspero, 1960.

———. *La Question religieuse et le socialisme.* Edited by Michel Launay. Paris: Les Editions de Minuit, 1959.

———. *Studies in Socialism.* Edited and translated by Mildred Minturn. New York: G. P. Putnam's Sons, 1906.

Jensen, Bernard Eric. "The Recent Trend in the Interpretation of Dilthey." *Philosophy of the Social Sciences* 8 (1978): 419–38.

Johach, Helmut. *Handelnder Mensch und objektiver Geist: Zur Theorie der Geistes- und Sozial-wissenschaften bei Wilhelm Dilthey.* Meisenheim: Hain, 1974.

Kalberg, Stephen. "Max Weber's Types of Rationality: Cornerstones for the Analysis of Rationalization Processes in History." *American Journal of Sociology* 85 (1980): 1145–79.

———. "The Search for Thematic Orientations in a Fragmented Oeuvre: The Discussion of Max Weber in Recent German Sociological Literature." *Sociology* 13 (1979): 127–39.

Kayser, Jacques. *Les Grandes Batailles du radicalisme: des origines aux portes du pouvoir, 1820–1901.* Paris: Marcel Rivière, 1961.

Kehr, Eckhart. *Battleship Building and Party Politics in Germany, 1848–1901.* 1930. Translated by Pauline R. and Eugene N. Anderson. Chicago: University of Chicago Press, 1973.

———. *Economic Interest, Militarism, and Foreign Policy.* 1965. Edited by Gordon A. Craig and translated by Grete Heinz. Berkeley: University of California Press, 1977.

Keller, Morton. *Affairs of State: Public Life in Late Nineteenth Century America.* Cambridge: Harvard University Press, 1977.

———. "Anglo-American Politics, 1900–1930, in Anglo-American Perspective: A Case Study in Comparative History." *Comparative Studies in Society and History* 22 (1980): 458–77.

Kelley, Robert. *The Transatlantic Persuasion: The Liberal Democratic Mind in the Age of Gladstone.* New York: Knopf, 1969.

Kennedy, David M. "Progressivism: An Overview." *Historian* 37 (1975): 453–68.

———. *Over Here: The First World War and American Society.* New York: Oxford University Press, 1980.

Kern, Stephen. *The Culture of Time and Space, 1880–1918.* Cambridge: Harvard University Press, 1983.

Kocka, Jürgen. "Theory and Social History: Recent Developments in West Germany." *Social Research* 47 (1980): 426–57.

———. *White Collar Workers in America, 1890–1940: A Social-Political History in International Perspective.* Translated by Maura Kealey. Sage Studies in 20th Century History, vol. 10. London: Sage Publications, 1980.

Kolakowski, Leszek. "Historical Understanding and the Intelligibility of History." Translated by Henry Beitscher. *Triquarterly* 22 (1971): 103–17.

———. *Main Currents of Marxism.* Translated by P. S. Falla. 3 vols. Oxford: Oxford University Press, 1978.

Kolko, Gabriel. *The Triumph of Conservatism.* New York: Free Press, 1963.

Kraditor, Aileen. *The Radical Persuasion, 1890–1917.* Baton Rouge: Louisiana State University Press, 1981.

Krausser, Peter. "Dilthey's Revolution in the Theory of the Structure of Scientific Inquiry and Rational Behavior." *Review of Metaphysics* 22 (1968): 262–80.

——. *Kritik der endlichen Vernunft: Diltheys Revolution der allgemeinen Wissenschafts- und Handlungstheorie.* Stuttgart: Kohlhammer, 1969.

Krieger, Leonard. *The German Idea of Freedom: History of a Political Tradition.* Chicago: University of Chicago Press, 1957.

Kuklick, Bruce. *Churchmen and Philosophers: From Jonathan Edwards to John Dewey.* New Haven: Yale University Press, 1985.

——. *The Rise of American Philosophy: Cambridge, Massachusetts, 1860–1930.* New Haven: Yale University Press, 1977.

Landauer, Carl. *European Socialism: A History of Ideas and Movements from the Industrial Revolution to Hitler's Seizure of Power.* 2 vols. Berkeley: University of California Press, 1959.

Lasch, Christopher. *The New Radicalism in America, 1889–1963: The Intellectual as a Social Type.* New York: Vintage Books, 1965.

Lefranc, Georges. *Jaurès et le socialisme des intellectuels.* Paris: Aubier, 1968.

——. *Le Mouvement socialiste sous la IIIᵉRépublique, 1875–1940.* 2nd ed. Paris: Payot, 1977.

Lehnert, Detlef. *Reform und Revolution in den Strategiediskussionen der klassischen Sozialdemokratie.* Bonn: Neue Gesellschaft, 1977.

Letwin, Shirley Robin. *The Pursuit of Certainty: David Hume, Jeremy Bentham, John Stuart Mill, Beatrice Webb.* Cambridge: Cambridge University Press, 1965.

Levinson, Henry S. *The Religious Investigations of William James.* Chapel Hill: University of North Carolina Press, 1981.

Levy, David W. *Herbert Croly of "The New Republic."* Princeton: Princeton University Press, 1985.

Lindemann, Albert S. *A History of European Socialism.* New Haven: Yale University Press, 1983.

Linschoten, Johannes. *On the Way Toward a Phenomenological Psychology: The Psychology of William James.* Edited by Amedeo Giorgi. Pittsburgh: Duquesne University Press, 1968.

Lippmann, Walter. *Drift and Mastery.* New York: Mitchell Kennerley, 1914.

——. *Early Writings.* Edited by Arthur Schlesinger, Jr. New York: Liveright, 1970.

——. *A Preface to Politics.* 1913. Reprint Ann Arbor: University of Michigan Press, 1962.

——. *Public Opinion.* 1922. Reprint New York: Free Press, 1965.

Loewenstein, Karl. *Max Weber's Political Ideas in the Perspective of Our Time.* Translated by Richard and Clara Winston. Amherst: University of Massachusetts Press, 1966.

Logue, William. *From Philosophy to Sociology: The Evolution of French Liberalism, 1870–1914.* De Kalb: Northern Illinois University Press, 1983.

Loppin, Paul. *Léon Bourgeois.* Paris: Pierre Béarn, 1964.

Lowi, Theodore J. *The End of Liberalism: Ideology, Policy, and the Crisis of Public Authority.* New York: Norton, 1969.

Löwith, Karl. *From Hegel to Nietzsche: The Revolution in Nineteenth-Century Thought.* Translated by David Green. New York: Holt, Rinehart & Winston, 1964.

McBriar, A. M. *Fabian Socialism and English Politics, 1884–1918.* Cambridge: Cambridge University Press, 1966.

McCarthy, Charles. *The Wisconsin Idea.* New York: Macmillan Co., 1912.

McConnell, Grant. *Private Power and American Democracy.* New York: Knopf, 1967.

McCormick, Richard L. "The Discovery that Business Corrupts Politics: A Reappraisal of the Origins of Progressivism." *American Historical Review* 86 (1981): 247–74.

——. "Ethno-cultural Interpretations of Nineteenth-Century American Voting Behavior." *Political Science Quarterly* 89 (1974): 351–77.

——. *From Realignment to Reform: Political Change in New York State, 1893–1910.* Ithaca: Cornell University Press, 1981.

———. "The Party Period and Public Policy: An Exploratory Hypothesis." *Journal of American History* 66 (1979): 279–98.

McCraw, Thomas K., ed. *Regulation in Perspective: Historical Essays.* Cambridge: Harvard University Press, 1981.

MacKenzie, Norman and Jeanne. *The Fabians.* New York: Simon & Schuster, 1977.

McKibbin, Ross. *The Evolution of the Labour Party.* Oxford: Oxford Univeristy Press, 1974.

Makkreel, Rudolf A. *Dilthey: Philosopher of the Human Studies.* Princeton: Princeton University Press, 1975.

Mandelbaum, Maurice. *History, Man, and Reason: A Study in Nineteenth-Century Thought.* Baltimore: Johns Hopkins University Press, 1971.

Mann, Arthur. "British Social Thought and American Reformers of the Progressive Era." *Mississippi Valley Historical Review* 42 (1956): 672–92.

Marcell, David W. *Progress and Pragmatism: James, Dewey, Beard, and the American Idea of Progress.* Westport, Conn.: Greenwood Press, 1974.

Mariz, George. "L. T. Hobhouse as a Theoretical Sociologist." *Albion* 6 (1974): 307–19.

Marshall, Gordon. *In Search of the Spirit of Capitalism: An Essay on Max Weber's Protestant Ethic Thesis.* New York: Columbia University Press, 1982.

Masur, Gerhard. *Prophets of Yesterday: Studies in European Culture, 1895–1919.* New York: Macmillan Co., 1961.

Matson, Floyd W. *The Broken Image: Man, Science, and Society.* Garden City, N.J.: Anchor Books, 1966.

Matthew, H. C. G. *The Liberal Imperialists: The Ideas and Politics of a Post-Gladstonian Elite.* Oxford: Oxford University Press, 1973.

Matthiessen, F. O. *The James Family: A Group Biography.* New York: Knopf, 1947.

May, Henry F. *The End of American Innocence: The First Years of Our Own Time, 1912–1917.* 1959. Reprint New York: Oxford University Press, 1979.

———. *Protestant Churches and Industrial America.* New York: Harper & Brothers, 1949.

Mayer, J. P. *Max Weber and German Politics.* 2nd ed. London: Faber & Faber, 1964.

Mayeur, Jean-Marie. *Les Débuts de la IIIᵉ République: 1871–1898.* Nouvelle Histoire de la France contemporaine, vol. 10. Paris: Editions du Seuil, 1973.

Meyer, Thomas. *Bernsteins konstructiver Sozialismus: Eduard Bernsteins Beitrag zur Theorie des Sozialismus.* Bonn: Dietz, 1974.

Mill, John Stuart. *Autobiography.* 1873. Reprint New York: Columbia University Press, 1960.

Milne, A. J. M. *The Social Philosophy of English Idealism.* London: George Allen & Unwin, 1962.

Misch, Georg. *Lebensphilosophie und Phänomenologie: Eine Auseinandersetzung der Diltheyschen Richtung mit Heidegger und Husserl.* 2nd ed. Stuttgart: B. G. Tuebner, 1967.

Mitzman, Arthur. *The Iron Cage: An Historical Interpretation of Max Weber.* 1969. Reprint New York: Grosset & Dunlap, 1971.

Mommsen, Wolfgang J. *The Age of Bureaucracy: Perspectives on the Political Sociology of Max Weber.* New York: Harper & Row, 1974.

———. *Max Weber und die deutsche Politik, 1890–1920.* 1959. Revised ed. Tübingen: J. C. B. Mohr, 1974.

———, ed. *The Emergence of the Welfare State in Britain and Germany, 1850–1950.* London: Croom Helm, 1981.

Moore, Edward Carter. *American Pragmatism: Peirce, James, and Dewey.* New York: Columbia University Press, 1961.

Moore, R. Laurence. *European Socialists and the American Promised Land.* New York: Oxford University Press, 1970.

———. *In Search of White Crows: Spiritualism, Parapsychology, and American Culture.* New York: Oxford University Press, 1977.

Morgan, Kenneth O. "The Future at Work: Anglo-American Progressivism, 1870–1917." In *Contrast and Connection: Bicentennial Essays in Anglo-American History.* Edited by H. C. Allen and Roger Thompson. London: Betts, 1976.

Muggeridge, Kitty, and Adam, Ruth. *Beatrice Webb: A Life.* London: Secker & Warburg, 1967.

Mueller-Vollmer, Kurt. *Towards a Phenomenological Theory of Literature: A Study of Wilhelm Dilthey's Poetik.* The Hague: Mouton, 1963.

Murphy, Murray G. "Kant's Children: The Cambridge Pragmatists." *Transactions of the Charles S. Peirce Society* 4 (1968): 3–33.

Nettleship, R. L. *Memoir of Thomas Hill Green.* London: Longmans, Green & Co., 1906.

Nipperdey, Thomas. *Die Organisation der deutschen Parteien vor 1918.* Düsseldorf: Droste Verlag, 1961.

Noble, David W. "Herbert Croly and American Progressive Thought." *Western Political Quarterly* 7 (1954): 537–53.

———. *The Paradox of Progressive Thought.* Minneapolis: University of Minnesota Press, 1958.

Nolan, Mary. *Social Democracy and Society: Working-class Radicalism in Düsseldorf, 1890–1920.* New York: Cambridge University Press, 1981.

Nordmann, Jean-Thomas. *Histoire des radicaux, 1820–1973.* Paris: Editions de la table ronde, 1974.

Oleson, Alexandra, and Voss, John, eds. *The Organization of Knowledge in Modern America, 1860–1920.* Baltimore: Johns Hopkins University Press, 1979.

Owen, John E. *L. T. Hobhouse: Sociologist.* Columbus: Ohio State University Press, 1974.

Papcke, Sven. *Der Revisionismusstreit und die politische Theorie der Reform.* Stuttgart: Kohlhammer, 1979.

Patterson, James T. *America's Struggle Against Poverty, 1900–1980.* Cambridge: Harvard University Press, 1981.

Pease, Edward. *History of the Fabian Society.* London: The Fabian Society and George Allen & Unwin, 1916.

Pelling, Henry. *America and the British Left: From Bright to Bevan.* London: Adam and Charles Black, 1956.

———. *Origins of the Labour Party.* 2nd ed. Oxford: Oxford University Press, 1965.

Perrot, Michelle. *Les Ouvriers en grève, 1871–1890.* Paris: Mouton, 1974.

Perry, Ralph Barton. *The Thought and Character of William James.* 2 vols. Boston: Little, Brown & Co., 1935.

Pierson, Stanley. *British Socialists: The Journey from Fantasy to Politics.* Cambridge: Harvard University Press, 1979.

———. *Marxism and the Origins of British Socialism.* Ithaca: Cornell University Press, 1973.

Plantinga, Theodore. *Historical Understanding and the Thought of Wilhelm Dilthey.* Toronto: University of Toronto Press, 1980.

Polanyi, Karl. *The Great Transformation: The Political and Economic Origins of Our Time.* 2nd ed. Boston: Beacon Press, 1957.

Pucelle, Jean. *La Nature et l'esprit dans la philosophie de T. H. Green: la renaissance de l'idéalisme en Angleterre au XIXe siècle.* 2 vols. Louvain and Paris: Nauwelaerts, 1965.

Pugh, Martin. *The Making of Modern British Politics, 1867–1939.* Oxford: Basil Blackwell, 1982.

Quandt, Jean B. *From the Small Town to the Great Community: The Social Thought of Progressive Intellectuals.* New Brunswick, N.J.: Rutgers University Press, 1970.

Rabaut, Jean. *Jaurès et son assassin.* Paris: Editions du Centurion, 1967.

———. *Jean Jaurès.* 2nd ed. Paris: Perrin, 1981.

Rader, Benjamin G. *The Academic Mind and Reform: The Influence of Richard T. Ely in American Life.* Lexington: The University Press of Kentucky, 1966.

Rappoport, Charles. *Jean Jaurès, l'homme, le penseur, le socialiste.* Paris: L'Emancipatrice, 1915.

Rauschenbusch, Walter. *Christianity and the Social Crisis.* 1907. Edited by Robert D. Cross. New York: Harper Torchbooks, 1964.

———. *Christianizing the Social Order.* New York: Macmillan Co., 1912.

———. "Dogmatic and Practical Socialism." Address delivered at Rochester Labor Lyceum, February 24, 1901. Rauschenbusch papers. American Baptist Historical Society, Colgate–Rochester Divinity School, Rochester, N.Y.

———. *A Gospel for the Social Awakening.* Edited by Benjamin E. Mays. New York: Association Press, 1950.

———. *The Righteousness of the Kingdom.* Edited by Max L. Stackhouse. New York: Abingdon Press, 1968.

———. *The Social Principles of Jesus.* New York: Association Press, 1916.

———. *A Theology for the Social Gospel.* New York: Macmillan Co., 1917.

Rawls, John. *A Theory of Justice.* Cambridge: Harvard University Press, 1971.

Réberioux, Madeleine. *La République radicale? 1898–1914.* Nouvelle Histoire de la France contemporaine, vol. 11. Paris: Editions du Seuil, 1975.

———. *Le Socialisme français: de 1815 à 1918. Histoire générale du socialisme.* Edited by Jacques Droz. vol. 2. Paris: P.U.F., 1974.

———, ed. *Jaurès et la classe ouvrière.* Paris: Editions ouvrières, 1981.

Richter, Melvin. *The Politics of Conscience: T. H. Green and His Age.* Cambridge: Harvard University Press, 1964.

Rickman, H. P. *Wilhelm Dilthey: Pioneer of the Human Studies.* Berkeley: University of California Press, 1979.

Rimlinger, Gaston. *Welfare Policy and Industrialization in Europe, America, and Russia.* New York: Wiley, 1971.

Ringer, Fritz K. *The Decline of the German Mandarins: The German Academic Community, 1890–1933.* Cambridge: Harvard University Press, 1969.

Ritter, Gerhard A. *Die deutschen Parteien vor 1918.* Cologne: Kiepenheuer & Witsch, 1973.

Robinet, André. *Jaurès et l'unité de l'être.* Paris: Seghers, 1964.

Rodgers, Daniel T. "In Search of Progressivism." *Reviews in American History* 10 (1982): 113–32.

———. *The Work Ethic in Industrial America, 1850–1920.* Chicago: University of Chicago Press, 1978.

Rodi, Frithjof. *Morphologie und Hermeneutik: Zur Methode von Diltheys Ästhetik.* Stuttgart, Kohlhammer, 1969.

Romein, Jan. *The Watershed of Two Eras: Europe in 1900.* Translated by Arnold Pomerans. Middletown: Wesleyan University Press, 1978.

Rorty, Richard. *Consequences of Pragmatism.* Minneapolis: University of Minnesota Press, 1982.

———. *Philosophy and the Mirror of Nature.* Princeton: Princeton University Press, 1979.

Ross, Dorothy. "Socialism and American Liberalism: Academic Social Thought in the 1880s." *Perspectives in American History* 11 (1977–1978): 5–79.

Roth, Guenther. *The Social Democrats in Imperial Germany: A Study in Working Class Isolation and National Integration.* Totawa, N.J.: Bedminster Press, 1963.

Roth, John K. *Freedom and the Moral Life: The Ethics of William James.* Philadelphia: Westminster Press, 1969.

Ruggiero, Guido de. *The History of European Liberalism.* Oxford: Oxford University Press, 1927.

Runciman, W. G. *A Critique of Max Weber's Philosophy of Social Science.* Cambridge: Cambridge University Press, 1972.

Sauerland, Karol. *Diltheys Erlebnisbegriff.* Berlin: de Gruyter, 1972.

Schluchter, Wolfgang, and Roth, Guenther. *Max Weber's Vision of History: Ethics and Methods.* Berkeley: University of California Press, 1979.

Schneewind, Jerome B. *Sidgwick's Ethics and Victorian Moral Philosophy.* Oxford: Oxford University Press, 1977.

Schorske, Carl E. *German Social Democracy, 1905–1917: The Development of the Great Schism.* Cambridge: Harvard University Press, 1955.

Schwehn, Mark R. "The Makers of Modern Consciousness in America: The Works and Careers of Henry Adams and William James." Ph.D. diss., Stanford University, 1977.

——, ed. *A William James Renaissance: Four Essays by Young Scholars. Harvard Library Bulletin* 30 (1982): 367–479.

Scott, Joan Wallach. *The Glassworkers of Carmaux: French Craftsmen and Political Action in a Nineteenth-Century City.* Cambridge: Harvard University Press, 1974.

Scott, John A. *Republican Ideas and the Liberal Tradition in France, 1870–1914.* New York: Columbia University Press, 1951.

Searle, G. R. *The Quest for National Efficiency: A Study in British Politics and Political Thought, 1899–1914.* Berkeley: University of California Press, 1971.

Seeber, Gustav. *Zwischen Bebel und Bismarck: Zur Geschichte des Linksliberalismus in Deutschland, 1871–1893.* East Berlin: Akademie Verlag, 1965.

Seidman, Steven. *Liberalism and the Origins of European Social Theory.* Berkeley: University of California Press, 1983.

Sell, Friedrich C. *Die Tragödie des deutschen Liberalismus.* Stuttgart: Deutsche Verlags-Anstalt, 1953.

Semmel, Bernard. *Imperialism and Social Reform.* Cambridge: Harvard University Press, 1960.

Seyfarth, Constans, and Schmidt, Gert, eds. *Max Weber Bibliographie: Eine Dokumentation der Sekundärliteratur.* Stuttgart: Enke, 1977.

Sharpe, Dores Robinson. *Walter Rauschenbusch.* New York: Macmillan Co., 1942.

Shaw, George Bernard, ed. *Fabian Essays in Socialism.* 2nd ed. 1920. Reprint London: The Fabian Society, 1931.

Sheehan, James J. *German Liberalism in the Nineteenth Century.* Chicago: University of Chicago Press, 1978.

——. *Lujo Brentano: A Study of Liberalism and Social Reform in Germany.* Chicago: University of Chicago Press, 1966.

Sidgwick, Arthur, and Sidgwick, Eleanor Mildred. *Henry Sidgwick: A Memoir.* London: Macmillan & Co., 1906.

Sidgwick, Henry. *The Development of European Polity.* London: Macmillan & Co., 1903.

——. *The Elements of Politics.* London: Macmillan & Co., 1891.

——. *Lectures on the Ethics of T. H. Green, Mr. Herbert Spencer, and J. Martineau.* London: Macmillan & Co., 1891.

——. *The Methods of Ethics.* 1874. 7th ed. London: Macmillan & Co., 1907.

——. *Miscellaneous Essays and Addresses.* London: Macmillan & Co., 1904.

——. *Philosophy, Its Scope and Relations: An Introductory Course of Lectures.* Edited by James Ward. London: Macmillan & Co., 1902.

——. *Practical Ethics.* London: Swan Sonnenschein, 1898.

——. *The Principles of Political Economy.* London: Macmillan & Co., 1883.

Smith, John E. *Purpose and Thought: The Meaning of Pragmatism.* New Haven: Yale University Press, 1978.

Soffer, Reba. *Ethics and Society in England: The Revolution in the Social Sciences, 1870–1914.* Berkeley: University of California Press, 1978.

Soltau, Roger. *French Political Thought in the Nineteenth Century.* New Haven: Yale University Press, 1931.

Somjee, A. H. *The Political Theory of John Dewey.* New York: Teachers College Press, 1968.

Soulé, Louis. *La Vie de Jaurès.* Paris: Floréal, 1921.

Spiller, Gustav, ed. *The Ethical Movement in Great Britain: A Documentary History.* London: Farleigh Press, 1934.

Stammer, Otto, ed. *Max Weber and Sociology Today.* Translated by Kathleen Morris. New York: Harper & Row, 1971.

Steel, Ronald. *Walter Lippmann and the American Century.* Boston: Atlantic-Little Brown, 1980.

Steenson, Gary P. *"Not One Man! Not One Penny!" German Social Democracy, 1863–1914.* Pittsburgh: University of Pittsburgh Press, 1981.

Steinberg, Hans-Josef. *Die deutsche sozialistische Arbeiterbewegung bis 1914: Eine bibliographische Einführung.* New York: Campus, 1979.

——. *Sozialismus und deutsche Sozialdemokratie: Zur Ideologie der Partei vor dem I. Weltkrieg.* Hannover: Verlag für Literatur und Zeitgeschehen, 1967.

Stern, Fritz. *The Politics of Cultural Despair: A Study in the Rise of the German Ideology.* Berkeley: University of California Press, 1961.

Stokes, Melvyn. "American Progressives and the European Left." *Journal of American Studies* 17 (1983): 5–28.

Stone, Norman. *Europe Transformed, 1878–1919.* Cambridge: Harvard University Press, 1984.

Strout, Cushing. "William James and the Twice-Born Sick Soul." *Daedalus* 97 (1968): 1062–82.

Strutynski, Peter. *Die Auseinandersetzungen zwischen Marxisten und Revisionisten in der deutschen Arbeiterbewegung um die Jahrhundertwende.* Cologne: Pahl-Rugenstein, 1976.

Struve, Walter. *Elites Against Democracy: Leadership Ideals in Bourgeois Political Thought in Germany, 1890–1933.* Princeton: Princeton University Press, 1973.

Sullivan, William M. *Reconstructing Public Philosophy.* Berkeley: University of California Press, 1982.

Tannenbaum, Edward R. *1900: The Generation Before the Great War.* Garden City, N.Y.: Anchor Books, 1976.

Tenbruck, Friedrich. "The Problem of Thematic Unity in the Work of Max Weber." *British Journal of Sociology* 31 (1980): 316–51.

Thayer, H. S. *Meaning and Action: A Critical History of Pragmatism.* Indianapolis: Bobbs-Merrill, 1968.

Thelen, David P. *The New Citizenship: Origins of Progressivism in Wisconsin, 1885–1900.* Columbia: University of Missouri Press, 1972.

Thompson, Paul. *Socialists, Liberals and Labour: The Struggle for London, 1885–1914.* Toronto: University of Toronto Press, 1967.

Trachtenberg, Alan. *The Incorporation of America: Culture and Society in the Gilded Age.* New York: Hill & Wang, 1982.

Trempé, Roland. *Les Mineurs de Carmaux, 1848–1914.* 2 vols. Paris: Editions ouvrières, 1971.

Tuchman, Barbara W. *The Proud Tower: A Portrait of the World Before the War, 1890–1914.* New York: Macmillan Co., 1966.

Ulam, Adam B. *Philosophical Foundations of English Socialism.* Cambridge: Cambridge University Press, 1951.

Wagar, W. Warren. *Good Tidings: The Belief in Progress from Darwin to Marcuse.* Bloomington: Indiana University Press, 1972.

Wallas, Graham. *The Great Society: A Psychological Analysis*. London: Macmillan & Co., 1914.

Walzer, Michael. *Spheres of Justice: A Defense of Pluralism and Equality*. New York: Basic Books, 1983.

Webb, Beatrice. *American Diary, 1898*. Edited by David A. Shannon. Madison: University of Wisconsin Press, 1963.

———. *The Diary of Beatrice Webb*. Edited by Norman and Jeanne MacKenzie. 2 vols. Cambridge: Harvard University Press, 1982–1983.

———. *My Apprenticeship*. 1926. Reprint London: Longmans, Green & Co., 1950.

———. *Our Partnership*. Edited by Barbara Drake and Margaret Cole. London: Longmans, Green & Co., 1945.

———, et al. *Break Up the Poor Law and Abolish the Workhouse*. Minority Report of the Poor Law Commission. London: Fabian Society, 1909.

Webb, Sidney. *Socialism in England*. Baltimore: Johns Hopkins University Press, 1889.

———. "What Socialism Means: A Call to the Unconverted." *The Practical Socialist*, June, 1886.

Webb, Beatrice, and Webb, Sidney. *A Constitution for the Socialist Commonwealth of Great Britain*. London: Longmans, Green & Co., 1920.

———. *The Consumers Co-operative Movement*. London: Longmans, Green & Co., 1921.

———. *English Local Government. English Poor Law History*. London: Longmans, Green & Co., 1927.

———. *Industrial Democracy*. 2nd ed. London: Longmans, Green & Co., 1920.

———. *The Letters of Beatrice and Sidney Webb*. Edited by Norman and Jeanne MacKenzie. Cambridge: Cambridge University Press, 1978.

———. "What is Socialism?" *The New Statesman*, April 12–July 19, 1913.

Weber, Marianne. *Max Weber: A Biography*. Edited and translated by Harry Zohn. 1926. New York: John Wiley & Sons, 1975.

Weber, Max. *Economy and Society*. Edited by Guenther Roth and Claus Wittich. Translated by Ephraim Fischoll et al. 2 vols. 1968. Reprint Berkeley: University of California Press, 1978.

———. *From Max Weber*. Edited and translated by Hans Gerth and C. Wright Mills. 1946. Reprint New York: Oxford University Press, 1976.

———. *Gesammelte Aufsätze zur Soziologie und Sozialpolitik*. Tübingen: J. C. B. Mohr, 1924.

———. *Gesammelte Politische Schriften*. Edited by Johannes Winckelmann. Tübingen: J. C. B. Mohr, 1958.

———. *The Interpretation of Social Reality*. Edited by J. E. T. Eldridge. New York: Scribner's, 1971.

———. *The Methodology of the Social Sciences*. Edited and translated by Edward A. Shils and Henry A. Finch. Glencoe, Ill.: Free Press, 1949.

———. *The Protestant Ethic and the Spirit of Capitalism*. Translated by Talcott Parsons. New York: Scribner's, 1958.

———. *Roscher and Knies: The Logical Problem of Historical Economics*. Edited and translated by Guy Oakes. New York: Free Press, 1975.

———. *Selections*. Edited by W. G. Runciman. Translated by Eric Matthews. Cambridge: Cambridge University Press, 1978.

Wehler, Hans-Ulrich. *Das deutsche Kaiserreich, 1871–1918*. Göttingen: Vandenhoeck & Ruprecht, 1973.

Weiler, Peter. "The New Liberalism of L. T. Hobhouse." *Victorian Studies* 16 (1972): 141–61.

Weinstein, James. *The Corporate Ideal in the Liberal State, 1900–1918*. Boston: Beacon Press, 1968.

———. *The Decline of Socialism in America, 1912–1925*. New York: Monthly Review Press, 1967.

Weiss, John H. "Origins of the French Welfare State: Poor Relief in the Third Republic." *French Historical Studies* 13 (1983): 47–77.

Wellborn, Charles. *Twentieth Century Pilgrimage: Walter Lippmann and the Public Philosophy.* Baton Rouge: Louisiana State University Press, 1969.

White, Morton G. *The Origin of Dewey's Instrumentalism.* New York: Columbia University Press, 1943.

———. *Pragmatism and the American Mind: Essays and Reviews in Philosophy and Intellectual History.* New York: Oxford University Press, 1973.

———. *Science and Sentiment in America: Philosophical Thought from Jonathan Edwards to John Dewey.* New York: Oxford University Press, 1972.

———. *Social Thought in America: The Revolt Against Formalism.* 1949. 3rd ed. New York: Oxford University Press, 1976.

Wiebe, Robert. *The Search for Order, 1877–1920.* New York: Hill & Wang, 1967.

Wiener, Martin J. *Between Two Worlds: The Political Thought of Graham Wallas.* Oxford: Oxford University Press, 1971.

———. *English Culture and the Decline of the Industrial Spirit, 1850–1980.* Cambridge: Cambridge University Press, 1981.

Wiener, Philip P. *Evolution and the Founders of Pragmatism.* 1949. 2nd ed. Philadelphia: University of Pennsylvania Press, 1972.

Wild, John. *The Radical Empiricism of William James.* Garden City, N.Y.: Doubleday & Co., 1969.

Willey, Thomas E. *Back to Kant: The Revival of Kantianism in German Social and Historical Thought, 1860–1914.* Detroit: Wayne State University Press, 1978.

Wilshire, Bruce. *William James and Phenomenology: A Study of "The Principles of Psychology."* Bloomington: Indiana University Press, 1968.

Wilson, R. Jackson. *In Quest of Community: Social Philosophy in the United States, 1860–1920.* New York: Wiley, 1968.

Wohl, Robert. *French Communism in the Making, 1914–1924.* Stanford: Stanford University Press, 1966.

———. *The Generation of 1914.* Cambridge: Harvard University Press, 1979.

Wolfe, Willard. *From Radicalism to Socialism: Men and Ideas in the Formation of British Socialist Doctrines, 1881–1889.* New Haven: Yale University Press, 1975.

Wolin, Sheldon A. *Politics and Vision: Continuity and Innovation in Western Political Thought.* Boston: Little, Brown & Co., 1960.

Woodward, C. Vann, ed. *The Comparative Approach to American History.* New York: Basic Books, 1968.

Wright, Benjamin F. *Five Public Philosophies of Walter Lippmann.* Austin: University of Texas Press, 1973.

Wright, Gordon. *France in Modern Times: From the Enlightenment to the Present.* 2nd ed. Chicago: Rand McNally, 1974.

Wrong, Dennis, ed. *Max Weber.* Englewood Cliffs, N.J.: Prentice-Hall, 1970.

Zeldin, Theodore. *France 1848–1945: Intellect and Pride.* Oxford: Oxford University Press, 1980.

———. *France 1848–1945: Politics and Anger.* Oxford: Oxford University Press, 1979.

———. *France 1848–1945: Taste and Corruption.* Oxford: Oxford University Press, 1980.

Zöckler, Christofer. *Dilthey und die Hermeneutik: Diltheys Begründung der Hermeneutik als "Praxiswissenschaft" und die Geschichte ihrer Rezeption.* Stuttgart: J. B. Metzler, 1975.

Index